Frank Sinatra

Frank Sinatra

A Complete Recording History of
Techniques, Songs, Composers, Lyricists,
Arrangers, Sessions and First-Issue Albums,
1939–1984

RICHARD W. ACKELSON

McFarland & Company, Inc., Publishers
Jefferson, North Carolina, and London

The present work is a reprint of the library bound edition of Frank Sinatra: A Complete Recording History of Techniques, Songs, Composers, Lyricists, Arrangers, Sessions and First-Issue Albums, 1939–1984, *first published in 1992 by McFarland.*

LIBRARY OF CONGRESS CATALOGUING-IN-PUBLICATION DATA

Ackelson, Richard W., 1942–
    Frank Sinatra : a complete recording history of techniques, songs, composers, lyricists, arrangers, sessions and first-issue albums, 1939–1984 / by Richard W. Ackelson.
        p.   cm.
    Includes index.

    ISBN 978-0-7864-6701-3
    softcover : 50# alkaline paper ∞

    1. Sinatra, Frank, 1915– — Discography. I. Title.
ML156.7.S56A25 2012
016.78242'163'092 — dc20   91-52629

BRITISH LIBRARY CATALOGUING DATA ARE AVAILABLE

On the cover: Frank Sinatra (Photofest); front cover design by David K. Landis (Shake It Loose Graphics)

Manufactured in the United States of America

McFarland & Company, Inc., Publishers
  Box 611, Jefferson, North Carolina 28640
    www.mcfarlandpub.com

To the artists who make the records —
songwriters, singers, arrangers, musicians —
and to Frank Sinatra

Contents

Acknowledgments

The author is indebted to several books and many people for their aid in the preparation of this manuscript.

The following published materials helped me to keep my facts straight, especially in the order of events, dates and the spelling of names:

"Me and My Music"
Frank Sinatra
article, *Life* magazine
April 23, 1965

Sinatra: An Unauthorized Biography
Earl Wilson
Macmillan
New York, 1976

Sinatra: An American Classic
John Rockwell
Random House/Rolling Stone Press
New York, 1984

Frank Sinatra, My Father
Nancy Sinatra
Doubleday
Garden City NY, 1985

Frank Sinatra: A Celebration
Derek Jewell
Little, Brown
Boston, 1985

And a special thanks to the dozens of kind people who guided my way: the owners of used record stores around the country; librarians and archivists; the keepers of record catalogs at music stores; Sinatra fans and collectors; the publishers of trade journals; staff at radio stations; and the authors of endless reference books on the world of music.

Love and thanks also to my wife, Marianne, who was invaluable in her assistance with computer databases, the conversion of data into text, and text editing and proofreading.

Introduction

Frank Sinatra has performed in many realms of show business. As a singer, he has appeared in roadhouses, nightclubs, theaters, concert halls, and giant outdoor arenas; he has also sung for radio, television and the movies. As an actor, Sinatra has appeared in over fifty films and a number of television shows. He has served as orchestral conductor, songwriter, painter, producer of records, television shows, and movies, record company owner, film director and impresario of presidential galas.

But this book concerns itself with the very core of Frank Sinatra's achievement, his work as a recording artist. That recording career of more than 45 years ended on May 18, 1984. Sinatra has continued to perform live — right up to the present — but it is most unlikely that he will ever record again.

The decade-bridging period of 1989/1990 encompassed the fiftieth anniversary of Frank Sinatra's career as a recording artist. The exact date depends on whether you measure the anniversary from the date of:

His first studio-recorded demonstration disk,
Our Love (2/3/39);
His earliest — uncredited — commercial track,
From the Bottom of My Heart (7/13/39);
The early uncredited record that — four years later — was a big hit,
All or Nothing at All (8/31/39);
Or his entry into big-time recording with Tommy Dorsey,
The Sky Fell Down (2/1/40).

Some writers even measure the start of this unique recording career from later in 1940, when Sinatra first became a credited soloist, but no matter which date you consider the "official" start, the 50-year mark has been reached. During that half-century, Frank Sinatra provided the content of literally thousands of singles and albums; these comprise one to four separate recordings of nearly a thousand different songs.

This book concerns itself with those songs — their composition, arrangement and recording — along with the evolution of Sinatra's vocal technique and its role in the expression of American song through half a century. It is not my intention to deal extensively with Frank Sinatra's personal life in this book. That has been done before in dozens of volumes, ranging in tone from worshipful to scandal-mongering. Certainly there is no need for repetition. The first chapter does cover Sinatra's professional biography, but only as a framework supporting the rest of the book, material which illuminates his recording career.

As far as I know, this is the first time a work about Sinatra has concentrated on the *songs,* the music, the very aspect of his life which appears to have been paramount to the man himself.

My immediate inspiration to do this book came from studying an interview in which a 72-year-old Sinatra bemoaned the fact that, for many people, his stardom has overshadowed his art, the songs. A further stimulus came from the approach of that fiftieth anniversary as a recording artist. But my deepest motivation went back much further.

When I was 14, I went to work in a record store in Longview, Washington, about 35 miles from Mount Saint Helens. The volcano was just a pretty little snow-capped mountain in the background of my daily life. No volcanic fireworks then. The explosion for me that year was my first contact with Sinatra's music.

As a new employee in a sizable record store, I was getting familiar with all the different kinds of records we had to sell. My own taste in pop music, up to 1956, leaned toward the novelty tunes and early rock and roll which dominated the radio. I had liked Bill Haley and the Comets, and a young singer with the funny name of Elvis Presley was beginning to grow on me. Because I'd been introduced to Gershwin's orchestral works, I was also starting to explore the world of symphonic music. But I didn't think much of "show tunes" or standard love songs. They were out of date.

One day, going through the many racks of 45 rpm singles in the store, I spotted the name Gershwin on a record label. It was *The Gal*

That Got Away, and the lyrics were by Ira Gershwin. I knew he'd written the words to many of his brother's great songs, so I was intrigued. Alone in the store at the end of the day, I put the record on a phonograph which played through big speakers around the ceiling. I noticed that the arranger was Nelson Riddle and the singer was Frank Sinatra. I'd heard of Sinatra, of course. He was a movie star who used to sing with a band. But my only interest was the Gershwin lyric.

The throbbing horns and strings of Nelson Riddle's arrangement filled the store. And then the melody, the words, and that unique voice. When the record ended, I played it again. During the next few days, I replayed the disc whenever I had a few minutes. I was hooked. The whole world of American song would become one of my most persistent interests and pleasures. And the singing of Sinatra would remain central to that world.

What follows are eight chapters, each focusing on a different aspect of the music and its recording. Within these chapters are a number of catalogs and indexes, plus a Master Song List which provides—for the first time in one reference—the key data covering Sinatra's full studio recording career, plus commercially-available examples of radio, TV and movie performances, special wartime Victory Discs, and "bootleg" records.

Preparing for this project, I've listened to nearly all of these recordings—mostly in chronological order—and have freshly experienced the creative, technical, and historical developments which led from the beginning in 1939 up to the 1953 recording of *The Gal That Got Away*, and beyond that to the extraordinary work which emerged between 1953 and 1984. It is my hope that this volume will give the reader some new points of view when looking at the Sinatra epoch in American music and the many talented artists who contributed to it.

Chapter 1: The Man

Since the beginnings of recorded sound, there have been singers reaching out through time and space. They have sung opera, romantic ballads, novelty tunes, dance music, jazz songs, the blues, art songs and the current fads of pop music. Some were fine artists, while some longed for simple commercial hits. Many have achieved broad popular success, a few made intense contact with a special small audience, and a handful became mass phenomena. Only Frank Sinatra fits all of these descriptions.

For better than fifty years, Sinatra has been renowned as a singer and actor. He has commanded newspaper space as a lady's man, a family man, a business man and as a pugnacious supercelebrity.

This book will concentrate on the heart of Sinatra's career, his work as a master of recorded song, a voice spanning the decades on platters of shellacked hard-rubber, vinylite discs, optical soundtracks, magnetic tape, and—most recently—on laser-read digital compact discs.

The first chapter will deal with the background and experience which shaped Sinatra's studio work, plus changing times and technologies in the music business. Aspects of his personal life will be included when it is necessary as a context for the story of his work as a recording artist.

Frank Sinatra was 23 when he cut his first studio recording, but he had been dreaming about the possibility since childhood. At gatherings of the Italian community in Hoboken, New Jersey, Sinatra's extended family was engaged with the music of their native land. There was appreciation of music in his close family as well, with impromptu singing and playing during celebrations; little Frank often took part. When he was 15, his Uncle Dom gave him a ukelele to strum as he sang

1

to adults on the sidewalks of Hoboken and to other kids at beach parties.

Recordings of Italian singers, including the beloved Enrico Caruso, had been part of community life since well before Sinatra's birth. Local radio stations broadcast a variety of instrumental and vocal music, performed live. The emphasis on emotion and story-telling in the traditions of Italian *bel canto* singing were comingled in the young Sinatra's experience with American idioms, both Europe-derived and native.

Coast-to-coast radio networks began in 1927 (NBC) and 1928 (CBS). This brought more opportunity for Sinatra to hear Al Jolson and Rudy Vallee. Newer singing stars included Russ Columbo and Bing Crosby, just at the time they were beginning to emerge from the shadow of big bands.

Sinatra was brought up in fairly comfortable circumstances, but it was a tough neighborhood, with Italians near the bottom of the social heap. He took some beatings on the streets of Hoboken. He was a small kid. But he was a battler. Having nearly died at birth and con-tending with the loneliness of being an only child in a large-family Catholic culture, he had learned to sustain himself. Inside this child of a striving family, dreams of success sparked and smoldered. He listened to the radio and to recordings of his favorite singers. He imag-ined himself in their place.

Sinatra tried out his singing voice and found it good. The kids at school reacted favorably to his early efforts, especially the girls. Though his family had other professional plans for their boy, Frank clearly en-visioned singing as his road to fame and fortune. But he was a serious child and knew he needed to work at his dream. Though he loved to sing, it was not a natural, flowing process for him. He began a con-scious program of swimming and running to improve breath control, and began making the rounds of local clubs in 1932. He listened, he planned, he sang, he learned.

His professional singing career began in 1933. Frank Sinatra was 17 years old, going on 18, and a high-school dropout since 15. He first heard a live performance of his chief idol, Bing Crosby, in 1933 at a Jersey City theater, making the pilgrimage with his girl, Nancy Barbato. It is reported that this event provided a key inspiration, a major *I can do that, too* kind of jolt. His parents resisted the idea, but Sinatra was insistent. Shortly after that energizing Crosby show, his mom gave him $65 for a secondhand portable sound system. This equipment, along with a borrowed family car and sheet music arrangements collected from Tin Pan Alley publishing houses, gave him an edge over other hopefuls in the local area, and for the next five years he hustled to find work at clubs and dance halls for a few bucks, singing in amateur shows and on local radio broadcasts. Those who knew him during that period say the kid was a pusher, but polite, and well prepared to follow through on any opportunity that came his way. He was learning the basics of his craft on stage and on the radio. As for the "art" of singing, Sinatra began to hang out on 52nd Street during this same period, taking informal but intense lessons as he grooved on the great performers in the clubs there.

His mother became increasingly supportive of her son's career hopes, lending her energy, political savvy and persuasive abilities to the task of getting him singing engagements at Hoboken social lodges and wangling him into a group called the Three Flashes, later the Hoboken Four. They rehearsed as a foursome, played local clubs, and made some "basement" recordings that were not released. Then the quartet won on the prominent Major Bowes Amateur Hour in 1935, performed in a Bowes film short, and toured the country with the Bowes team. It was a taste of life on the road; Sinatra decided it was a dead end. He left the group to concentrate on getting New Jersey radio air time. Radio was a more promising brand of exposure than the Jersey club scene, which was active but self-contained, usually leading nowhere. He got air time, all right, but virtually no money.

Now back in the New York vicinity, he resumed his "studies" on 52nd Street, learned about the handling of lyric poetry from Mabel Mercer, phrasing and drama from Billie Holiday, the possibilities of musical color and style from the likes of Sarah Vaughan, Fats Waller, and Count Basie.

In August of 1937, at age 21, Sinatra got a job as emcee, waiter and singer at a Route 9W roadhouse called The Rustic Cabin, outside Alpine, New Jersey. This spot offered him two important advantages in addition to the modest pay; the chance to sing regularly with the same band, plus weekly radio remote broadcasts over roadhouse's "wire." He stayed at The Rustic Cabin for almost two years, until June of 1939.

What took him away from The Rustic Cabin — the sort of job that dead-ended for many a young singer — was the kind of chance Sinatra had persistently dreamed of and planned for, an alchemy mixing the gold of Fate with the base-metal of all his hard work and preparation.

Harry James was starting his own first band, the Music Makers, after two years as a trumpet player for the hot Benny Goodman orchestra. James needed a vocalist. He'd received Sinatra's publicity stills and heard him sing on WNEW's "Dance Parade" broadcast during a Rustic Cabin remote. James liked the handling of lyrics and the unusual voice. He went to the roadhouse the following night and offered a job with his fledgling band. Sinatra took it and the next day he played the Paramount Theater for the first time. Soon the band went on the road. Girls started hanging around the bandstand. James later reported that he was impressed by Frank's obvious love for singing, and by the girls' reaction to him as he sang. This augmented his personal taste for the way his new vocalist expressed the meaning of a song's words.

The band went into the studio on July 13, 1939, and recorded two selections, *From the Bottom of My Heart* and *Melancholy Mood,* for Brunswick Records, a label which had presented the great Bing Crosby. Sinatra was the featured but uncredited vocalist on both tracks. He had made a demo disc of *Our Love* back in February of that year, on the eve of his wedding to Nancy Barbato, but this was his first commercially released record. Finally he was a recorded singer, like the ones he'd admired as a kid and dreamed of becoming. But he was an unknown, nationally, and the James band was new in a crowded field. It was no surprise the record didn't hit. But one of the most fabulous recording careers in history had begun.

There was just that one record on Brunswick (nowadays a collector's item), but the following month Harry James's group was back in the studio for Columbia Records. Between August and November of 1939, Sinatra performed on eight tracks, including the now-classic recording of *All or Nothing at All.* None sold particularly well. The James band was floundering. Highly successful Tommy Dorsey was looking for another vocalist. When Sinatra got the chance to go with Dorsey, Harry James had the kindness to let his contracted singer move to the big time.

Still uncredited, but now anticipating records that would have a large audience, Sinatra first recorded with the Tommy Dorsey orchestra on February 1, 1940. Through the months that followed, he began to be featured more and more prominently, and was finally given name-credit on the record labels. Sinatra's vocal development during this period will be covered more thoroughly in Chapter 2. For now, suffice it to say that the RCA Victor years with Dorsey were pivotal for him, not only in terms of money and public acknowledgment, but also in terms of learning his art and his craft.

There were 83 songs released on RCA by the Dorsey band which had vocals including — and usually featuring — the growing art of Frank Sinatra. A number were substantial hits, 18 making the *Billboard* Top-10 charts, *I'll Never Smile Again* hitting the number one spot and remaining on the chart for 15 weeks. The Sinatra name was growing in tandem with his skills; the trade journals, *Billboard* and *Downbeat,* named him Outstanding Male Vocalist in 1941; in the case of *Downbeat,* this meant displacing his idol, Bing Crosby, who had held the title four successive years. Dorsey later said he had trouble believing what he saw each time the skinny young guy got up in front of the band, a reaction from young women that was unprecedented in his experience.

Toward the end of this period, in January of 1942, Dorsey allowed Sinatra to make his first four recordings as a soloist — without the Dorsey band — on the lower-prestige RCA subsidiary label, Bluebird Records. They were not substantial hits, but the experience of singing as the key soloist was a thrill that required repetition for the 26-year-old.

The die was cast. On July 2, 1942, amidst struggle and speculation over the handling of his contract, Sinatra cut his last record with the Tommy Dorsey orchestra. He would appear live with the group for a few months, then depart for a solo career.

He was packing a lot of experience by this time: on the road in clubs, theaters and dance halls; on the radio; in the studio; with all kinds of musical arrangement and instrumental and vocal accompaniment. He got his first solo radio show ("Reflections") that year, and had even appeared in a movie with the Dorsey orchestra. His name was well-known in the music business and he had a substantial number of fans. But was this a good time to go it alone? World War II was raging abroad, touching all aspects of American life. The music scene was in flux. As he made his last concert appearance with Dorsey in October of 1942, Sinatra had to be wondering if he could make it outside the nest. Leaving such a position was a rare phenomenon among swing band singers of that time, and only Bing Crosby had negotiated the move with real success.

Fatefully, a major musicians' strike occurred just before Sinatra was to sign with Columbia Records. The American Federated Musicians went on strike against recording companies in August 1942. Almost a year passed between his last Dorsey/RCA recording session (7/2/42) and his first for Columbia (6/22/43), and the strike didn't end until November of 1944. This could have been a disaster of bad timing. Actually, it worked the other way. Columbia had planned to rerecord *All or Nothing at All*. The strike spoiled that idea, but they managed to dig up the 1939 "master" of that song as recorded with Harry James. Shortly after release, the record shot up to #2 on the *Billboard* survey and remained in the Top–10 for 18 weeks. RCA rereleased one of the later Dorsey recordings from 1942 and another from 1941. Both did very well; *In the Blue of Evening* was in the Top–10 for 17 weeks, reaching the number one spot, and the still-earlier *It's Always You* reached number six during a seven-week stay. To multiply the effect of these reissues, in June of 1943 Sinatra went into the studio without instrumentalists and recorded with just a vocal backing—from the Bobby Tucker Singers—imaginatively arranged by Axel Stordahl and Alec Wilder. Of the nine songs recorded this way, five spent weeks in the Top–10 between July 1943 and February 1944. Only a few other vocalists (such as Bing) were making these *a cappella* recordings, so that Sinatra was nearly alone with brand-new records—for radio and jukebox—during the early months of the long strike. Later, singers also honored the strike.

Adding to this great success on records, Sinatra joined Lucky Strike's "Your Hit Parade" on radio in 1943, as well as "The Broadway Bandbox" show. He also appeared in two 1943 movie releases, singing five songs and co-starring in one of them, *Higher and Higher*.

After first losing momentum without the constant popular exposure of singing with Dorsey, and during the relative hiatus of the musicians' recording strike, Sinatra's career resumed speed and kept accelerating. But until he began to appear on the stage of the great Paramount Theater, no one knew how far his star had risen.

His first solo appearance at the Paramount—December 30, 1942—as a special-added-attraction with Benny Goodman's orchestra—

drew nearly 5,000 teenagers, mostly female. The shrieking and swooning that ensued when Sinatra came on stage caught everyone, including the nervous singer, unprepared. It was the beginning of Sinatra-mania, a surge as intense as the later waves that carried Elvis Presley and the Beatles. Before Frank Sinatra's time, famous operatic tenors had thrilled the masses, Vallee and Columbo had charmed big fandoms, as had Crosby for a wide age-range of enthusiastic fans, but the fever which burned for the 28-year-old Sinatra surpassed anything before it in popular music. This reached its ultimate publicity peak with the "Columbus Day Riot" in 1944, when 30,000 young girls jammed the streets around Times Square, frenzied and worshipful, waiting for a seat in the 3,600-to-5,000-capacity Paramount Theater. When many thousands learned they wouldn't make it inside, store windows were smashed, and hundreds of police came to subdue the mob.

During this period, Sinatra was working intensely, his lifetime peak volume of live performance: 100 songs a day, what with several solo shows at the Paramount, rehearsals, radio broadcasts and benefits.

The musicians' strike ended, and Sinatra plunged into his Columbia recording years with a vengeance, releasing over 250 recordings before his Columbia contract ended in 1953; the majority of these sold well, with 22 placing in the *Billboard* Top–15 charts.

And still more singing: several continuing Sinatra radio shows; 11 major-studio motion pictures; a number of recording sessions for the "Victory Discs" distributed to overseas servicemen fighting in World War II; plus many live performances in theaters and nightclubs.

Altogether, an unbelievable time for the skinny kid from Hoboken. He was *Modern Screen*'s "Most Popular Screen Star" of 1946. When long-play albums began selling in 1946, Sinatra had the first LP to reach number one. He debuted on the encroaching TV medium in 1950's "The Frank Sinatra Show." It all seemed destined to go on forever, without pause. But it didn't.

The world of popular music was changing. Since the '20s, there had been specialty recordings of such regional music as black blues and white hillbilly; by the late '40s, variations on such music were working into the mainstream, transmogrifying into rhythm and blues, country, pseudo-folk, novelty tunes, and the earliest forms of rock and roll. The big bands were ghosts of their former selves. In the mid-'50s radio scene, Broadway and pop standards were heard less often than novelty tunes and white-soul shouters, which in turn were giving way to a proliferating rock and roll. Sinatra's sales had already begun to diminish as the 1940s ended, due to such competition as Frankie Laine, Johnny Ray and Eddie Fisher. Many of the new Top-40 artists moved easily into novelty songs, along with the likes of Doris Day and Patty Page, but it rubbed against Sinatra's grain. Columbia wanted to boost his profitability by requiring him to go with the flow and sing songs he didn't respect. His contract demanded compliance. Sinatra had some success with contemporary hits. *The Huckle Buck, Chattanooga Shoe Shine Boy* and *Castle Rock* all made it into the Top-30 charts but, in general, his sales and mood were way down. The nadir, perhaps, was recording the *Mamma Will Bark* duet with busty actress Dagmar to the accompaniment of dog-barking by Donald Bain. His relationship with Columbia's new Artists-and-Repertoire man, Mitch Miller, was ragged. Miller's strategy was to push novelty tunes, seemingly as a means to resist folk, rock, and soul. During his next-to-last Columbia session, Sinatra recorded *Bim Bam Baby* and *Tennessee Newsboy*. The only song at the very last session was, ironically, *Why Try to Change Me Now?*

His marriage to Nancy was coming apart. A love affair with Ava Gardner brought confusion and pain; Sinatra even cancelled work in order to be with her. Then came divorce. His two 1951 movies were flopping. He had nothing on *Billboard*'s Top-30 from October 1951 until February 1954. His radio and TV shows were drawing smaller audiences. Club dates and concerts also sold poorly; he suffered a complete loss of voice during a show at the Copacabana. Then, all at once — or so it seemed to the news reading public — he had no recording contract, no movie contract, no TV show, no agent. Frank Sinatra bore all the marks of a has-been.

Chroniclers of the Sinatra legend usually focus on his Oscar-winning performance in *From Here to Eternity* as the key to his giant comeback. I concede there's truth to this, but often ignored is the hard work, artistic integrity, and happy circumstance that played equally important roles in the resuscitation of the singer's failing career.

He went on the road with small combos and bands, singing great tunes to a set of fresh, swinging arrangements by George Siravo. Journalists attending these nightclub appearances commented on how well he was singing, the deepening pitch of his voice, the wider range of emotional textures. Gradually, the image of the crooning teen idol was being altered.

He married Ava, but they fought and ultimately divorced. There was pain, but also a sort of resolution to disrupting emotion.

Then Sinatra got a new contract with the young, vigorous Capitol Records. Very quickly, the recordings made in this new atmosphere began to revive his image as a singer. The dramatic performance in *From Here to Eternity* — and the resulting Academy Award — certainly made it clear to the public that Frank Sinatra was alive and gifted, but if the Capitol career had not been building, to backstop that movie celebrity, how long would the post–Oscar plaudits have lasted?

At Capitol Records, the air was alive with ambition, innovation and marketing strategy. This record company was out to challenge Columbia, Decca, and the other major labels. An important aspect of competition in this period was the microgroove vinyl record, both the new 7-inch, 45-revolutions-per-minute "single" with one (sometimes two) songs on each side, and the newly deployed 10-inch, 33.3 rpm "album" with four songs per side. Producers at Capitol were especially aware of the marketing and artistic possibilities of the 10-inch album, a lightweight, "unbreakable," eight-song format. (For more on this subject, see the 1940s and 1950s sections of Chapter 8.)

Sinatra's time at Capitol began with singles. His first session, on May 3, 1953, was arranged and conducted by his long-time friend and colleague Axel Stordahl. None of the three songs recorded in that session made a significant mark in the business. Sinatra's version of *I'm Walking Behind You* was eclipsed by Eddie Fisher's. Producer Voyle Gilmore felt the Sinatra/Stordahl combination could not take real advantage of the singer's maturing talents. There were several exciting arrangers in Capitol's stable, and Gilmore wanted Sinatra to work with Bill May and Nelson Riddle. Billy May was approached for Sinatra's second Capitol session, with Riddle held in reserve. Gilmore thought May's swinging and humorous approach would be great for the new Sinatra, but May was too busy to accept the assignment — it would be four and a half years before they collaborated — so he gave his blessing for Riddle to write in his style. Nelson Riddle prepared for a four-song session at the end of April 1953. He did the two arrangements requested by Gilmore with the "Billy May sound" *(South of the*

Border and *I Love You),* and then two more that were classic examples of his own emerging style, *I've Got the World on a String* and *Don't Worry 'Bout Me.* The latter two records demarked the two sides of the singer's work with Riddle, one up-tempo, one reflective ballad.

More singles followed. Then, in November of that same year, Sinatra entered the studio with Riddle to record his first full album for the long-playing format. Nelson Riddle had taken eight of the finer George Siravo nightclub band arrangements, which Sinatra had been using on the road, and rewritten them for a full recording-studio orchestra. Two days of recording produced the **Songs for Young Lovers** album, released in time to capitalize on the public attention given to Sinatra's performance in *From Here to Eternity* and the Oscar he would win for the role. Between the new-sounding single records on the radio, the hit movie and this fine new LP release, Sinatra's career transport was entirely back in gear and accelerating rapidly.

More movies (including several straight dramatic parts), singles and albums followed without delay. The singles kept his name as a singer before the young audience. The albums captured a growing musical market among adults. For the rest of the decade, Sinatra's stature and fame grew steadily. In 1957, Gordon Jenkins began his series of Sinatra albums, and Billy May joined the rotation of con-ductor/arrangers later that same year; Riddle remained the dominant figure during the Capitol years. Sinatra expressed the value of this ar-ranger triumvirate by praising May's driving energy, Riddle's depth, and Jenkins's beautiful simplicity.

While regular Capitol single and album releases appeared, Co-lumbia Records issued a series of albums comprising collected singles, and RCA Victor also got into the act with compilation albums. But it was the Capitol albums that made history. They created a new kind of musical experience, more like attending a musical show than just listening to a series of songs. But whereas a show had several per-formers and a variety of tones in a group setting, the LP was a single performer intimately connecting with a romantic couple or a person alone. One mood could be sustained effectively. The shows Sinatra presented ranged from the happily swinging to the devastatingly lonely to the lushly romantic, and in each case the communication was personal and strong.

To complete this discussion of the Capitol years, I will summarize with some highlights of the period. Details of Sinatra's collaborations and achievements at Capitol are covered in parts of Chapters 6, 7 and 8. His top Capitol singles can be found at the end of Chapter 3.

Right after Sinatra signed with Capitol, he conducted music for *Tone Poems of Color,* the very first album recorded at the new Capitol Records Tower. Delivering singles was his next assignment. In the early '50s, some top singles were still in the "pop" realm (Sinatra's first big hit at Capitol was *Young at Heart,* which reached number two and remained on the *Billboard* charts for over five months), but hit singles tended to be a teenage dance medium. That was rock and roll by the mid-'50s, so albums had to be Sinatra's route. And along with saloon song and ballad albums, a swinging option was needed for younger listeners, those growing up with the records of the rhythm and blues belters and soul shouters who were shifting taste away from sweet ballads. The epitome of this swinging sound was the *Songs for Swingin' Lovers!* album, which was in such hot demand that it was finished recording on a Friday and shipped to stores on Monday. Sinatra was hot again, for a second generation. His popularity reached a new plateau with the album *Frank Sinatra Sings for Only the Lonely,* which entered the charts in September of 1958 and held there for 120 weeks. *Come Dance with Me!* stayed in the hot hundred albums for 140 weeks starting in early 1959. He was also big in movies and live shows, particularly at the Sands in Las Vegas and the Fontainebleau in Miami Beach. Life was a ring-a-ding thing.

Sinatra's record producers at Capitol were Voyle Gilmore (from 1953 to 1958) and Dave Cavanaugh (1958–1961). These men oversaw the logistics of sessions, took care of business matters and set the mood and venues for making records. The singer was happy with that side of his days in the Tower off Hollywood Boulevard, so unlike his production woes at Columbia. But relations with Capitol were deteriorating by the end of the fifties. While down on his luck, Sinatra had signed a less than top contract with the company. He had less than he wanted to say about the choice of material, production techniques and marketing. Perhaps, as the '60s began, the company would want to get more into the modern technological approach to record-making, would want to move into contemporary songs. Also, Sinatra felt there was too much repetition in what he was doing, riding on past success to the detriment of other possibilities. While still fulfilling the last of his Capitol contract commitments, Frank Sinatra formed his own record company and started to make new music.

The shift to his own label, Reprise Records, was made when Sinatra was at the height of his powers, both in terms of commercial influence and artistic range. His voice was now deeper and more subtle than ever, and he began to experiment with an even wider range of music. At Reprise, he and the other admired singers and musicians he signed to his label could buck the trends, do their thing. The company still had a regular output of single records, as in the latter years at Capitol, but LPs and the adult audience were their marketing focus. Between 1957 and 1966, Sinatra had not one Top–10 single, but he had 27 Top–10 albums. He was the king of album sales, with virtually every LP making it into the Top–100, with several LPs simultaneously riding the *Cash Box* and *Billboard* charts, and **September of My Years** winning Grammys for Album of the Year and Best Solo Vocal Performance. Though rock continued to dominate pop singles, Sinatra regularly placed singles in the Top–100. Radio stations around the nation began the practice of playing long sessions of his recordings in "Sinatra-thons." This recording activity was accompanied by a life that continued to be very full of other things: an engagement to dancer Juliet Prowse; his outrageous shows with "Clan" buddies at the Sands in Vegas; concert appearances on the road, including a world tour for various children's charities; serving as producer for President Kennedy's 1960 inaugural gala; and numerous star-turns in movies (where *The Manchurian Candidate* was one of his best) and on television (where he welcomed Elvis Presley home from the army).

Free from the demands and restraints of his Capitol contract, Sinatra engaged in the most artistically experimental period of his entire singing career. A big element was the increase in jazz-based recordings, working with a plethora of prominent jazz musicians, several new arrangers, and bands like the Count Basie and Duke Ellington organizations. He did an album of Dorsey material for which he managed to sing as Tommy played. There were albums saturated with stringed instruments, concept albums with national themes, one with a symphonic approach, replications of Broadway shows, an LP of "moon" songs, sets incorporating more contemporary songs, albums devoted to single composers and styles, live performance albums, and **Watertown,** a domestic drama set to song. And all this was on top of his more traditional albums of peppy swingers and late-night heartbreakers. (See the '60s through the '80s in Chapter 8 for details.)

Nelson Riddle was tied to Capitol for some time after Sinatra left, and they could not work together again until 1963. Billy May and Gordon Jenkins had no such contract restrictions, and they both continued to collaborate with the singer on his Reprise albums, but Sinatra also took advantage of his new freedom and control to work with a wide range of other arrangers and conductors, talents such as Johnny Mandel, Don Costa, Neal Hefti, Quincy Jones and nearly two dozen others. Through time, Don Costa came to be a dominant factor in Sinatra's later career, as a producer as well as an arranger/conductor. Sonny Burke, Jimmy Bowen and several other producers served during Reprise sessions, and Felix Slatkin was a frequent concertmaster.

Another important factor, during Sinatra's Reprise years, was the way his authority made it possible to resist the growing industry preference for overdubbing, multiple tracks and no live audience at studio recording sessions. (For more on this, see Chapter 7.)

Not only was the world receiving a strong flow of new Sinatra albums on Reprise, it was getting a barrage of recompilations and old singles released in album form from RCA Victor, Columbia and Capitol, as well as radio and TV recordings, unofficial movie soundtracks and outright bootleg issues of unreleased master tapes. (For the full scope of the Reprise LPs, see Chapter 8.) Capitol was particularly vigorous in its release of Sinatra discs, anxious to compete forcefully with the singer's own product. Commentators sometimes expressed the view that this glut would damage Sinatra's career. It only seemed to strengthen it, as he continued to prevail as an industry force during the height of the rock era.

The early 1960s were a continuing high time for Sinatra and friends. This was the heyday of "The Summit" performances and pals partying around Las Vegas. But darker times were ahead. Sinatra had been social friends with John Fitzgerald Kennedy, and it struck him especially hard when the President was murdered on November 22, 1963. Then his 19-year-old son, Frank Sinatra, Jr., was kidnapped only 16 days later. Fortunately, his son made it back alive.

Still, there were good times and fine records. His third marriage, with a young Mia Farrow, took place in July of 1966. It was a relatively short union; perhaps the 30-year spread of age and experience was just too great. In 1967, he had a big year at the Grammys, taking the awards for single Record of the Year, Album of the Year, and Top

Male Vocalist. Then came a terrible blow when Sinatra's father, Martin, died as the end of the grand decade neared.

The start of the new decade brought a convergence of problems to Frank Sinatra. He had felt the need to reassert himself in the hit single field during the mid–1960s, and had successfully done so with the help of arranger Ernie Freeman, producer Jimmy Bowen and others. Now he worked to similar ends with Don Costa, contemporizing his repertoire and his recordings (see the Costa profile in Chapter 6), but he found himself more and more unhappy with the lack of appropriate songs available to him. He was also growing tired, had health problems, and was suffering a significant reduction of his vocal powers. In addition, he was increasingly fed up with the effect of his battles with journalists and the regular resurfacing of press stories linking him with organized crime. There was a lack of movie scripts he liked, and songwriting stalwarts who could provide him with new material in an earlier mode—like his friend Jimmy Van Heusen— were finally drying up. All of this combined, through 1970, to produce serious thoughts of retirement.

In 1967 he had one of his biggest hits in *Something Stupid,* a duet recorded with his daughter, Nancy. Having decided to retire, Sinatra acted to close out things by recording again with Nancy Sinatra, a fairly successful recording artist in her own right. They got together with Don Costa and a studio orchestra, in what was expected to be his final recording session, on November 2, 1970, the two songs with Nancy later released on an Italian LP from Reprise, one also a single in the U.S.A.

But the retirement didn't take. It proved to be more in the way of a rest-stop along the career road. Some have argued that Sinatra should have stayed retired, that his voice was never the same again after that break. Certainly this is true. But the voice had been naturally changing each year, and noticeably so every five years, and each change was balanced with new insight and depth of feeling.

The same thing proved true following the retirement, and Frank Sinatra produced some of his finest recordings in that period, although admittedly they came with more struggle. There were fewer and shorter recording sessions, more "masters" destroyed and tracks not released, a whole album concept with Nelson Riddle scrapped after two days of recording. But overall some extraordinary records were born.

As the voice continued to deepen and roughen, Sinatra picked songs, arrangements, styles and tempos to exploit the deep notes and raspy tones. Sophistication and emotional breadth substituted for effortless beauty of vocal production. Technique outwitted diminishing breath control.

Sinatra tried his vocal wings before a live crowd in October of 1972. He first returned to the recording studio on April 29, 1973, after a two and a half year break. Attempting three brand-new songs for a coming-out-of-retirement album, Sinatra was so dissatisfied with the results that he had the master recordings destroyed. Then came some vocal coaching by opera star and friend, Robert Merrill, and a regimen of voice and body exercise. By altering features of his breathing and opening the throat more, plus warming up and loosening his overall physical being, a Frank Sinatra nearing 60 got ready to record.

On June 4, 1973, he occupied a recording studio in Hollywood, with orchestra arranged and conducted by Gordon Jenkins, and completed three recordings. The next day he finished two more. By August 20 they had everything they needed for an album. It was released later that year as ***Ol' Blue Eyes Is Back***. The album was heralded by a successful TV special of the same name. The LP entered the top-seller charts in October and stayed there for six months, reaching number seven on the *Cash Box* chart and number 13 in the *Billboard* rankings. An ironically titled single release from the album, *Let Me Try Again,* even made it into the Top–100 singles for two months. The year was capped off by the Songwriters of America when they voted to name him Entertainer of the Century.

Sinatra was off and running again. During the next eight years, while being heaped with awards, honorary degrees and publicity, Sinatra built up to an intense live performance schedule, as if trying to get everything possible done while there was still time and voice to work with. He toured Japan and Australia, then the United States, Canada, Europe, Israel and Egypt. He did several broadcast and cable TV specials, produced and directed the 1981 inaugural gala for President Reagan, and performed dramatic leading roles in a few movies.

There were special concert collaborations: on Broadway, he performed with Ella Fitzgerald and the Basie band; at the London Palladium, it was Sarah Vaughan and Basie; Luciano Pavarotti and George Shearing joined him in the Radio City Music Hall. There were solo concerts at New York's Carnegie Hall, London's Royal Albert Hall and — in Rio de Janeiro — Sinatra established a record for the largest live paid audience ever assembled for a solo performer.

Somehow, during all this (he was twice a grandfather, lost his mother in 1976 to a plane crash and became a husband to fourth wife, Barbara) Sinatra delivered five more new albums. *Some Nice Things I've Missed* dealt exclusively with contemporary songs, including the work of such composer/lyricists as Neil Diamond, Floyd Huddleston, David Gates, Stevie Wonder and Jim Croce. A live album, *Sinatra — The Main Event,* was drawn from the live TV special of the same name, as well as other East Coast concert appearances.

Then, in 1980, came what many consider to be Sinatra's last great LP, the three-disc monument to his career titled *Trilogy/Past, Present, Future.* (For the details of this work, see Chapter 8.) The *Trilogy* album spent months on both the *Billboard* and *Cash Box* charts, won six Grammy nominations, and stimulated another round of honors such as the Johnny Mercer Award from the Songwriters Hall of Fame. The "Present" disc from the album included Sinatra's last Top–40 single release, the theme from the film *New York, New York.*

Nearly two years later, Sinatra followed up this triumph with a contemporary album, *She Shot Me Down.* Seven of the nine songs were brand-new, four of them composed with Sinatra in mind. Parts of the LP were great, and it sold quite well, but his voice was showing the strain of all the years of hard living and the recent onslaught of live performances. After one Hollywood session in April of 1981, it took five sporadic New York studio visits between July 20 and September 10 to complete the project, each session producing only one, two or three master tapes.

Now the end was near. Six sessions between December 1981 and March 1983 produced only three songs released on singles and seven tracks never officially released. The live performances continued, many for charity, but it seemed the final curtain had been rung down on recording.

But a little over a year later, on April 13, 1984, Frank Sinatra reentered the studio to begin his *L.A. Is My Lady* album. He was rested, refreshed, the master's throat and voice in condition for what will almost certainly remain his final album. Inspired by a red-hot Quincy Jones — the LP's producer and conductor — and energized by a great all-star jazz band winging around the instrumentation of seven largely untested arrangers, Sinatra delivered his final recorded performances in a manner which did him proud. On his next birthday, he would be 69 years old. There would be more live tours and concerts — a prominent one in the late 1980s with Sammy Davis and Liza Minnelli and a 75th birthday world tour in 1991 — but the studio recording days were over.

During the 45-year period that Sinatra recorded these songs, he generated a wide range of response from the media, among historians, fans, critics and reporters. Scholarly texts on American music often refer to him as the greatest male popular vocalist to date. Sensational news stories have branded him as a rude, egotistical thug. His records, films and public broadcasts have provoked a full gamut of appraisal. But one thing has been consistent, the world's awareness of Sinatra, as both man and artist. He has remained in the public consciousness for most of his recording years and beyond. That awareness is demonstrated by a small sampling of honors not fully detailed in this career summary:

Longest-span between Top–40 singles; 40 years, from *I'll Never Smile Again* (July 1941) to *New York, New York* (July 1981).

Sixty singles in the *Billboard/Cash Box* Top–30s.

Most number one albums and Top–10 singles by solo act during the rock era.

Domination of the top album charts during the late '50s and early '60s.

One of the most written-about entertainers in history.

An unprecedented maintenance of fans from the 1940s to the present, with ever-expanding national and international fan clubs.

Downbeat magazine's Top Male Vocalist in two decades, 1941 and 1954.

He topped a 1956 *Metronome* magazine poll of 109 jazz performers who were asked to name their choice for the "musician's musician."

Playboy Jazz Poll's Top Male Vocalist every year from 1957 to 1969.

He won the 1959 Grammys for ***Come Dance with Me!*** (Album of the Year) and for Best Solo Vocal Performance.

Film Exhibitors of America's Top Box-Office Star of 1960.

In 1965, Sinatra won the Emmy for Outstanding Musical Program ("Sinatra: A Man and His Music"), which also won a coveted Peabody Award.

Named as Entertainer of the Century in October 1973 by the Songwriters of America.

On January 26, 1980, Sinatra set the record for the largest live audience ever for a single performer—175,000 at his one-man concert at the Maracana Stadium in Rio de Janeiro—which held for a decade until Paul McCartney broke the record at the same facility in 1990.

One of only nine winners in the long history of the ASCAP Pied Piper Lifetime Achievement Award; the most recent was Peggy Lee in May 1990.

A sold-out performance at Mexico City's 30,000-seat Sports Palace in June of 1991, concluding his 75th birthday world tour; seat prices ranged from $25 to $85.

This continuing presence was accomplished by an ongoing evolution of personality and vocal technique, through interaction with musicians, songwriters, arrangers, and fans. Along the way he has lived many lives, including that of the ambitious low-income Italian kid, the eager and dreamy idol-worshiping teen, the working singer, the young married man with children, the first mass-craze teen idol, the movie star, the intense student of opera, jazz and song, the rich man, the has-been, the comeback king, the lover, the brokenhearted loser, the growing professional and collaborator, the mature artist with freedom, the aging vocalist, the legend.

A man of high-highs and low-lows, of extremes in compassion and hostility, Frank Sinatra has brought this wide emotional range to every facet of his art.

Chapter 2: The Singer

During the past several months, I've listened to most of the records covered by this book, playing many of them several times. As often as it was practical, I listened to the songs in the order they were recorded. This process took me deeper and deeper into the subtle interplay of words, music, instrumental arrangement, emotional tone, singer's attitude — the totality of recording a song. Here is what I heard.

In the beginning, there was a very young man singing new songs — popular songs of the day — with a swing band. The voice was delicate and sweet, pitched somewhere between tenor and light-baritone. Even then, the timbre of that voice was unique. Something about the formation of chest, larynx, throat and nasal chambers produced an unfamiliar sound. Most noteworthy popular singers have a distinctive voice, but they can be mimicked; Frank Sinatra's voice was inimitable, and became even more so with each passing decade.

Voice

The voice came from nature, but Sinatra augmented it with extensive training and study. He swam underwater laps and ran around the school track in order to enhance his breath control. From his mid-teens into his twenties, he sang and sang and sang, eager to explore the different aspects of vocal production. Although he never took a formal course of study in either music or voice, he later had short training sessions and advice from teachers involved with both opera and the Broadway stage. Sinatra learned how to open the throat and let his voice flow into the resonating cavities of the head. His was an attractive, unique, basically self-trained voice. But a voice is never more than a starting point for a singer.

Style and Technique

As a youngster, Sinatra enjoyed the radio broadcasts and record-ings of many singers, encompassing both the Metropolitan Opera and Tin Pan Alley. He studied the work of popular favorites, from Al Jolson and Rudy Vallee to Russ Columbo and Bing Crosby. He was an especially great fan of Crosby, who was the king of vocalists as Sinatra began his career. Unlike other aspirants to the throne, young Sinatra was determined not to copy Bing's style. Or anyone elses.

He succeeded in avoiding imitation right from the outset of his recording career. By that time, in 1939 and 1940, he'd been sing-ing professionally for six years. He was 23, with lots of public perfor-mance behind him. His own nascent style was in place on that first record.

It's worth a moment's digression to discuss the aspect of singing known as style. What is often meant by the term is the "song stylist," the performer who has created and/or modified a style so distinctive and uniform that every song they record bears certain hallmarks, whether the song is fast or slow, happy or sad.

In that sense of the term, Frank Sinatra didn't have a clear style. He performed each song with an attitude appropriate to its content. As a band singer, his expressive range was confined to the limits of romantic dance music. Once he went solo, Sinatra's dramatic expres-sion deepened but was still confined to youth's narrowness. From that point, it broadened with each decade of life and experience. By the closing years of his recording career, he was selecting from a tremen-dous emotional range of songs and applying a variety of approaches to each category. (More on this in Chapters 3 and 8.)

So Frank Sinatra was not a "song stylist." In another sense, how-ever, Sinatra's singing possessed a great deal of style. This style was formed by the existence of the microphone, by some basic choices in vocal production, and by the evolution of expressive techniques which were variously applied to each performance of each song.

Style and technique. With Sinatra, these concepts are interlocked and have to be discussed together. Let's consider the issues chrono-logically.

From the beginning, Sinatra was a microphone singer. While Jolson belted on the stage, producing a large volume of brilliant sound — as did twentieth century opera singers — the star vocalists which came after Rudy Vallee all used the microphone. The earliest carbon microphone was invented in 1876 and was part of the telephone. By the 1920s, a form of mike had been developed for use on the bandstand and, shortly after that, for radio stations. This changed popular singing forever. Mechanical amplification made possible a softer, more conversational and intimate kind of singing, which became exemplified by Bing Crosby. It was called "crooning." Crosby was an extreme opposite to the brilliant, loud, vowel-laden singers of the stage. He was so laid back and casual that only his melifluous voice made his crooning seem like singing rather than poetic talking.

In differentiating himself from Crosby, Sinatra pushed away from the extreme of crooning back toward the melodic warmth and richness of traditional Italian singing. This required a more conscious, technical performance. That was very different than Bing — which was good, since Sinatra wanted to be distinct from his idol — but he didn't want to be too different, so this "working at singing" had to be hidden. The songs should appear to flow naturally, without effort or artifice.

The first fundamental was the manipulation of the microphone. With the mike, obviously, one didn't have to sing loudly to be heard. Crosby had used that new reality to replace forced volume with conversational expression, subtle textures and implied feelings. But Sinatra gradually learned to go well beyond that point, to use the mike as a tool, an instrument to play upon. Move very close to the mike and you could almost whisper, move well away and you added resonance, a reverberation on extended vowel sounds; also, you could hide the sound of inhaling air. When the hand-held microphone came along, even more could be done with it. Pull it away briefly when you wanted to hide the hissing of C's, S's and X's, the pop of B's and P's. Bring it close to catch a sudden drop in volume, or to initiate a change in tempo. Change the mike's position during a note to "bend" the sound of the note. Also, the ratio of band-to-singer loudness could be altered by a shift of the microphone.

Sinatra took advantage of the mike to sing as if he were talking and telling a story, but he also wanted the definite color of music. One way to musically approximate speech is by what Italian musical terminology calls *legato*. This means "bound" or tied together. A musically legato line doesn't show the gaps, the pauses created by breathing and the stylistic breaks of poetry. Here the enhanced Sinatra breath control came into play. He could sing up to eight bars of music without a breath, up to six bars at high volume. That much of a melody and lyric could be "tied together" by the continuous exhalation of air. Beyond that, there were tricks to extend the effect of the legato line, the seemingly unbroken flow. Some of these techniques Sinatra picked up early, others he learned from Tommy Dorsey and other musicians in the early 1940s, and he added to his arsenal of techniques right up until the end of his recording career.

There is an experiential reasoning — a logic — behind Frank Sinatra's development of style and technique. Perhaps much of it was intuitive, although some was certainly conscious. That logic proceeded in six simple steps. One: the mike allowed singing to be an intimate communication of a story. Two: the *legato,* "bound together" flow of words and music enhanced the story with a quality of naturalness and spontaneity. Three: in storytelling with a song, the words were as important as the music, so they must be enunciated clearly for easy understanding. Four: beyond clearly pronouncing the words, they must be interpreted for meaning and phrased in music accordingly. Five: both words and music must be explored for emotional content. Six: in order to attract attention to that content, the performance must be given a compelling energy.

That is the sequence of logic which produced the attitudes and techniques which form the singing style of Frank Sinatra. We've already considered the role of the microphone. Now let me cover each of the other logic-steps with examples of specific techniques used to implement it.

• *Legato Line:* Watching Tommy Dorsey play the trombone, Sinatra observed him sneaking little breaths through the corners of his mouth, keeping the horn full of air and sliding from note to note. He adapted this idea to his singing, and soon created the illusion that he was singing through several phrases without a breath.

Sinatra would find places in the song where a pause was natural to the meaning of the words — or to the drama of the melody — then breathe in that place with the mike withdrawn.

He would call attention to the lack of a breath-stop by tying phrases together with their common sounds. Here are three hypothetical examples: "so we dance through the lovelleeeeee/eeeeevening starlight night"; "believed in love on that sorry daaaayyy/yyyyouuuwwwalked away"; and "here beside the wallllllll/lllllike a statue's pose."

It was also possible to take quick, unnoticed breaths at places in the song where no one would expect a pause for breath. Some commentators have even claimed that Sinatra could, in certain circumstances, breathe in through his nose and sing out through his mouth at the same time.

He would often sing just a fraction behind the beat, unlike most pop singers. This had the effect of his voice being "pulled along" by that beat, which extended an impression of the legato line. It also created a tension, followed by relief and resolution as he caught up to the beat at the end of a phrase. These techniques and others weave a song into a seamless fabric.

• *Enunciation:* Sinatra placed great emphasis on proper and precise enunciation. He trained himself away from a Jersey accent by reading aloud and studying national media pronunciation. The key was enunciating all the consonants clearly, especially the final T's and D's which are so often neglected by pop singers.

With opening and closing consonants pronounced fully and clearly, the vowel sounds between would be framed and "presented," and since the notes of a song ride on the vowel sounds, this created a beauty of rich vowels set among precise consonants ("WheeeRe Shaaall Weee Goooo wheN iT StaartS Tooo eeenD").

This emphatic pronunciation of consonants led to some deliberate exaggeration for effect; snappy T's, extended FFFF's, hissed S's, drum-beat D's, and droning L's, for example. These exaggerations could aid effects ranging from comedy ("lovin' with lots offfFFFiddle-De-De") to tragedy ("drinking for my pain, and it leads to jaillllllllllll/iiiillllll get hopeless"), or could simply force one's attention to a dramatically important phrase ("aaaaaaaaaaaannnnD if I can't Have you now, I'm gonna lose you anyhow").

Above all, the care in enunciating assured that the words of the story would be correctly understood at the moment they were sung.

• *Word Meaning and Phrasing:* Sinatra would write out a song's lyrics in longhand, so he could see the words dissociated from the music. Memorizing them in this fashion allowed him to plumb their content as poetry and emotion, and taught him how to phrase for meaning as well as musical tone. Having so absorbed this meaning, Sinatra could "believe" the words, and become a master at projecting that belief onto the audience. Even the most clichéd phrase could be uttered without seeming silly.

A side benefit of this word absorption was the discovery of hidden rhythms in words and groups of words. Singing such a rhythm pointedly could bring the listener's attention to what might otherwise be missed. A related practice found words sounding like what they were describing. This could be emphasized by added notes and syllables, until a phrase about dancing sounded just like a waltz.

• *Emotional Content:* One of the fundamental techniques Sinatra used to underscore emotions was to create strong variations in such vocal textures as tone, vibrato, volume, pace, repetition, distinct breathing or no breathing, and by pushing the extremes of his vocal range.

When he was a young crooner of love ballads, a long passage of tender feeling would be interrupted by a more "knowing" and insinuating slur of tone and word. This invariably provoked shrieks from the bobby-soxers in the audience.

He observed how Ziggy Elman varied the speed of his vibrato while playing trumpet for the Dorsey band, using different vibrato-speeds within the same song or even the same note. Sinatra found he could replicate these effects with his voice to stress an assortment of emotions. A very slow vibrato brought out a young man's throbbing passion; when pushed to the opposite extreme, a fast, shrill vibrato was like sobbing or an old man's tremulous cry.

Sudden changes in volume could be used to dramatize the appropriate feelings. This was effective with shouts (she WON'T talk that trash") as well as whispers ("IN TIME YOU SAID goodbye AND THAT WAS ALL").

Changes of pace—tempo—within a song, a phrase, or even a word, became a powerful emotional device as Sinatra's recording career proceeded through the years from Tommy Dorsey onward. There was the trombone-like "sliding" bend in the middle of a word ("and it floated wherHhuuueere you lay"), the gradual speed-up of a phrase capped by a touch of vibrato ("Never . . . . . thought . . . I'd cry-y-y-y"), and the slow downshift of gears within a song ("hope was . . just . . . a . . . . breath . . . . . away, a . . . griev-ing . . . . mo-ment's . . . . . death . . . . . . a-way"). Sinatra's sensitive ear for rhythm and timing made these devices work.

Repetition of words was an infrequent device for Sinatra, but when he did use it, the effect was a happy one. In the song *Mood Indigo*, as cut for the album *In the Wee Small Hours,* Sinatra turns the phrase "no, no, no" into a string of seventeen "No's." Emphatic! He wraps up *Don'tcha Go 'Way Mad* on **Sinatra & Swingin' Brass** with a run of ten "Baby's."

Usually, Sinatra's aim is to make his breathing inaudible, yet there are calculated exceptions. Since he usually avoids evident breath-stops, when they are consciously applied, they make a strong punctuation, calling closer attention to whatever follows. Here are two examples of the special use of breathing; one is to color a phrase by throwing an extra push of breath into a note ("so when that moooOOOOOoonnnn appears"), and the other is singing a long, un-broken phrase to its end, then calling on reserves of breath control to lunge into a new phrase where a pause for air would be expected ("to put the glow back in my lifePLEEEEASE sun, dry away these tears"). Such techniques seem natural because they reflect the drama of par-ticular moments in a song.

A final kind of textural variation is accomplished by Sinatra push-ing the upper and lower limits of his vocal range. His highest notes, available to the singer in the first half of his recording career, were used both as shouts of triumph and as a sound of desperation. The lowest notes, in the latter half of that career, could bring an aura of darkness and mystery.

• *Energy:* Techniques which Sinatra employs to impart energy and interest to a song are the hardest to define. I will end this discus-sion of style and technique with five typical examples.

Singing behind the beat creates a feeling of tension in the listener, and thus holds their focus on the song. A related technique is to attack a note just a hair under pitch, then trombone-slide up into the proper pitch for the held note, adding a little vibrato at the end. This not only creates tension but makes you appreciate the note more by making you wait for it a little bit.

Singing a phrase which ends with a long-held note, Sinatra will sometimes abbreviate that last note in order to make time for him to bob and weave and lag on the earlier part of the phrase.

A major area of song-energizing lies in Sinatra's interaction with his instrumental arrangements. This will be covered more in Chapter 6, but let me give two instances here. During rehearsals, he would pick up on special riffs that individual musicians were devising; when recording later, he would imitate the sound of that player in his vocal. Reacting to the band as a unit, Sinatra sometimes added words to the lyric so that his vocal line exactly matched the instrumental line.

Emotional Storehouse

All the style and technique in the world won't put believable emotion into a song if those feelings are not present in the singer to begin with. Frank Sinatra has lived a highly dramatic life in the glare of the spotlight. (Some features of this life were referenced in Chapter 1 and others have been widely discussed in the media.) That lifetime has provided a full range of emotion on which the singer can draw.

Sinatra's basic temperament was as volatile as his experience was full of extremes. He has had a lion's share of triumph, joy and satisfaction; there has always been a balancing portion of uncertainty, loss, grief and pain. Close friends report that Sinatra faces most things without kidding himself or sparing others. Out of this welter of emotion and judgment came an art that managed to illuminate many varieties of passion, humor, grief, sophistication, honesty and a rare joy. Through the decades, his work has displayed an artist who—while always sexual—is alternately tender and aggressive, cocky and pleading, wounded and vital, domineering and vulnerable. But never drab. And never remote or hidden.

Song Choice

Often the songs performed by Sinatra have been initially selected by others; bandleaders, record companies with their Artists and Repertoire men, arrangers, song compilers for radio programs, producers of records or movies or television, and sometimes by friends. When recording for Dorsey, the bandleader had the final say. During the declining years of his Columbia contract, a number of tunes were forced on the singer. But for most of his career, Sinatra has had the power of veto, and frequently he picked songs to suit his personal taste from the ocean of tunes presented by songwriters, publishers and producers.

Some pieces were chosen because they'd been tailored to exploit the current popular trends. Some had inspired Sinatra's arrangers.

Others were written by gifted pals. Still others promoted various causes. But mostly the songs were recorded because they inspired Frank Sinatra, because he thought they were fine songs. This is evidenced by the fierce determination with which he has fought to maintain his choice of material in the face of both commercial opposition and the tides of change in music.

Recording a song one time was usually enough. Either it was a limited piece and had been drained of possibilities, or the single recording was so fine it was pointless to try again. But sometimes the nature of a song — or its meaning to Sinatra — offered new ways to express the changes in music and in his own growth. A second, third, or even fourth recording could open up those new arenas. In some cases, multiple recordings were made to take advantage of new technology, or to bring royalties from a fan-favorite to his own label.

The songs covered by the book constitute an amazing range of material. The details of that variety, and the many sources from which the songs were drawn, are the subject of Chapter 3.

Performance and Collaboration

The development of Sinatra's performing style in the studio was influenced by the interplay of his personality, his experience, various professional collaborations, and a changing technical environment. Over the decades — as he gained and maintained control over his recording sessions — Sinatra settled on an environment that was congenial to his best work. Singing live for concert, radio, movie and television audiences sparked attitudes and techniques which Sinatra also brought to recording. The nature of his fame and his relationships also fed the mixture.

After recording for Harry James and Tommy Dorsey in the standard studio environments of that era, the solo Sinatra at Columbia Records began to have more choice in the interplay of arranger, orchestra, backing group or chorus, duet partners, and session audiences. His performing energy began to shift a little from the imagined record listener to the musicians and audience at the session.

During the 1940s, when Sinatra recorded great standards (such as *Begin the Beguine*), there was a little tentativeness, a respectful distance from the music; less warmth, less personality, less taking charge of the song than when he recorded new tunes. This seemed to be an expression of his youthful admiration for famous songwriters. In the 1950s, he moved right in and took possession of some of the same songs, expressing his love for them in the opposite manner.

As the '50s progressed, the Top–40 was infused with more and more popularized regional music, early rock, and novelties. In 1955, the hot sound of *Rock Around the Clock* was succeeded in the number one spot by *The Yellow Rose of Texas*. That same year, Sinatra had four singles and a number two album on the charts, and he dominated the album charts for nearly a decade. To maintain this popularity in the rock era, he had to reinvent the feeling of his music, which came from one and two generations earlier. New feeling — fresh and strong — came from recording sessions that were intimate mini-nightclub gigs, played with a coterie of top musicians (many with jazz roots), intense new arrangements and a small audience of friends and musical peers. Recording "live," without multiple tracks, echo, or prerecording backing, Sinatra worked a past era into new life. While his studio contemporaries found "hit" gimmicks and repeated them, Sinatra continuously fed his style with new ideas and energies. He avoided using a concept more than once, so each stylistic fillip was memorable, special, and recognizably his alone. Many of these ideas were inspired by instrumentalists and came from the great orchestration commissioned especially for Sinatra (more on this in Chapter 6). As the 1960s came, his interaction with Las Vegas audiences added more improvisational punch to his recording work. He experimented with bands and arrangers and material. His voice had deepened a good deal by the 1970s, and he spiced songs with sounds that had been out of his lower range previously. Still later there was less breath control, a small range of pitch, the voice grew rougher — hesitant in upper registers and sometimes raspy in the lower. He used it all, radiating the experience of his years in increasingly jazz-like versions of old and new songs. As the recording sessions grew fewer and farther between, they became even more a special event, with loving pals in attendance to drink in the last drops of music.

Although Sinatra took advantage of modern technology, he never gave up singing live, interacting with an interpretive arranger and a gang of creative musicians, singing to a roomful of known friends, as well as to those imagined friends listening to phonographs and radios in the future.

All the factors discussed in this chapter—whether considered separately or in concert—add up to less than the sum of Sinatra's singing. But what do you add to make a full total? Something I'm unable to define; love of craft . . . intuitive inspiration . . . genius? These are issues beyond words and reasoning, different for every listener who serves as audience and makes a personal link with singer and song. For me, one thing is constant for each Sinatra record; underneath the worldly toughness, the sophisticated art, the tone of command, there remains a haunting echo of a high sweet young voice singing words that are—somehow—truly believed.

Chapter 3: The Songs

More than 300,000 songs were copyrighted between 1900 and 1950. The number published each year has continued to grow since the 1950s, so the count for the century will probably pass a million songs by the year A.D. 2000. That's a lot to choose from if you're a singer, producer, arranger, or record company A & R man.

Many singers perform only one or two types of songs, which somewhat narrows the field of choice. Sinatra has done almost every category of song during his long career: love songs, saloon, jazz, and art songs; Christmas carols; show tunes; city anthems and novelty numbers; early rock; the blues and rhythmic-blues; translated foreign works; operatic arias; movie scores; two Beatles songs and other soft-rock pieces; even a few country and western ditties.

Though Sinatra didn't begin recording until 1939 — and continued until 1984 with breaks during 1943–44, 1973–74, and 1981–84 — his song choice was dominantly from the 1930s and 1940s. Over half of the recordings in this compilation are of songs written during those years; 697 out of 1,251.

Here is the breakdown of recordings by song publication date:

pre–1900s	23
1900–1919	21
1920–1929	87
1930–1939	279
1940–1949	418
1950–1959	193
1960–1969	162
1970–1979	55
1980–1984	13

The concentration on songs from the years between 1930 and 1949 seems natural enough for the young Sinatra. He was 15 years old in 1930 and very focused on the popular music around him as he worked to become a singer. Songs from the first decade of his recording career would also be naturals for him to interpret. What is remarkable is the fact that he continued to perform these same songs — live and on record — right up to the end of his recording career in 1984. His final album of new recordings contains one song from 1918, four from the 1930s, three from the 1950s and three from the 1980s. Of course, this music loyalty didn't usually extend to lightweight compositions of that twenty-year period. The repeat recordings were devoted to great work. Examples would include: *Memories of You, I've Got a Crush on You, April in Paris, The Song Is You, Night and Day, Stormy Weather, I've Got You Under My Skin, Fools Rush In, Everything Happens to Me, That Old Black Magic, One for My Baby* and *Some Enchanted Evening*.

Popular music has been dominated by one beat style at a time, from minstrel rhythm to ragtime to jazz to swing to rock. During the rock era — which took over pop music starting in the 1950s — for Sinatra to have continued performing such songs from past decades is quite remarkable. For him to have reached his best-selling peak doing it between 1954 and 1969 is amazing. Even when he recorded songs written in the period 1960–1984, he often recorded them several years after they were written and sometimes sang them in the manner of the '40s or '50s.

The earliest-written pieces recorded by Frank Sinatra were mostly spirituals and Christmas songs. The exceptions to that rule (for songs written before 1900) were an aria by Mozart, a Russian folk song, Braham's "lullaby," and *America the Beautiful.*

From the first two decades of the twentieth century, Sinatra recorded songs from the musical stage, plus tunes by persevering black musicians, European composers, and music with folk roots in the USA.

Drawing from the 1920s, the emphasis was on Tin Pan Alley (men such as Ray Henderson and Walter Donaldson), dance band numbers (Isham Jones), and the dynamic Broadway stage productions that were coming into their own (Irving Berlin, George Gershwin and Cole Porter). Love songs predominated, but blues, novelties, big production numbers and hot up-tempo pieces also found a place.

Every kind of song was included in the selection Sinatra recorded from the crop of the '30s, but the great majority were dreams of love-to-be, celebrations of love found, and laments for love lost. The dominant source for these songs was the musical theater, now thriving with the simultaneous presence of Harold Arlen, Irving Berlin, George Gershwin, Jerome Kern, Cole Porter and Richard Rogers. Movie musicals had been growing in quality since the advent of the talkies, and composers like Harry Warren, Walter Donaldson and Jimmy McHugh were collaborating with fine lyricists on original film songs. Tunes popularized by dance bands—live and on the radio—were yet another strong source of material.

Movie scores and dance/radio tunes gained ascendancy over Broadway in the 1940s as the source of songs recorded by Sinatra. He sang with the Tommy Dorsey orchestra at the beginning of the decade, and that brought him into contact with music by great songwriting teams such as Jimmy Van Heusen/Johnny Burke and Matt Dennis/Tom Adair. Another big factor was Sinatra's own entry into motion pictures, his first starring role coming in 1943. The team of Jimmy McHugh and Harold Adamson produced eight movie songs for him in the early '40s; his pals Jule Styne and Sammy Cahn delivered 25. Later in the decade, Sinatra film songs came from the Nacio Herb Brown/Edward Heyman team and from Roger Edens/Betty Comden and Adolph Green. And though Broadway was reduced as a song source, it was still there with its new plot-oriented shows like *Pal Joey, Oklahoma, Annie Get Your Gun, Carousel, Finian's Rainbow, Kiss Me Kate* and *South Pacific*. On top of all that was the ongoing "pop" output from Tin Pan Alley writers. Nearly every variety of song was included in Sinatra's recording of 1940s tunes—even the art-song sensibility of three pieces by Alec Wilder—but a high percentage were romantic ballads, performed lushly for Columbia Records when they were new, rerecorded with more punch and swing in later years.

The 1950s brought a shift in the world of American songwriters. As the decade progressed, the pop charts and radio time were more and more taken over by the work of young writers of original rock and rhythm and novelty tunes, as well as the numerous adapters of black R & B and other regional music. Resisting this change in the style and craft of songs, Sinatra began to develop his own "rear-guard" of tune-smiths to maintain the earlier traditions. He had performed the music of Jimmy Van Heusen and Johnny Burke (one of Crosby's favorite teams) since his time with Dorsey. He had done many Jule Styne/ Sammy Cahn songs, beginning in the early '40s. And he had continued with the work of both teams in the early '50s. In the middle of the decade, Sinatra persuaded Van Heusen and Cahn — now without their previous partners — to form a new team for the TV production of *Our Town* and a few movie title songs. The pair fused. Their great success as prolific songwriters kept Sinatra supplied with his kind of music for ten more years, a number of songs being custom-written for his albums, many as title tracks to enunciate an album's theme. Apart from encouraging song production for himself, Sinatra remained loyal to Broadway creators; '50s shows like Loesser's *Guys and Dolls,* Rodgers and Hammerstein's *The King and I,* and Porter's *Can-Can* gave him a number of songs to interpret for recordings. Sinatra collaborated on a few songs himself, and sampled some of the emerging "standard" songwriters of the time. He tried a little rock. He had even done some contemporary novelty tunes he despised — at the insistence of Mitch Miller — near the end of his days with Columbia Records.

By the dawn of the 1960s, American rock and roll was thoroughly ensconsed. The British rock invasion hit a few years later. Sinatra recorded a couple of Beatles songs and a few soft rock and contemporary pop numbers, but his major emphasis remained on the style of earlier times. He recorded 17 more Jimmy Van Heusen/Sammy Cahn songs written in the '60s, but by the middle of the decade the team was nearly finished. Through their association with composer Lew Spence, Sinatra also became attracted to the lyrics of Alan Bergman and Marilyn Keith, a team who married in the latter part of the decade; their songs with Spence were recorded for some of Sinatra's later Capitol albums, and their lyrics to melodies by French composer Michel Legrand gave the singer several admired tunes to work with from the late '60s. Other European songs, translated into English, formed part of Sinatra's output of '60s songs; this work retained links to the '30s–'40s sound he loved. These foreign composers included Antonio Carlos Jobim, Riz Ortolani, Jacques Brel, Bert Kaempfert, and the coupling of Jacques Reveaux and Claude Francois. The consequence of these international songs for Sinatra was impressive: two great albums focused on the Jobim *bossa nova* sound; Paul Anka's translation from the French gave Sinatra a new signature tune in *My Way;* a song by Bert Kaempfert became *Strangers in the Night,* one of Sinatra's biggest single records ever. And from back home, the singer recorded pieces by newly prominent American composers like John Denver, Kris Kristofferson, Jimmy Webb, John Hartford (all with country roots), Henry Mancini, Burt Bacharach (new pop), Teddy Randazzo, Neil Diamond and Paul Simon (ballad rock). At the end of the decade came two works written expressly for Frank Sinatra. Poet and songwriter Rod McKuen produced the material for a reflective theme album called *A Man Alone.* Bob Gaudio — who, with Bob Crewe, had written a string of hits for Frankie Vali and the Four Seasons — produced a true narrative concept album called *Watertown,* writing all the songs in collaboration with Jake Holmes.

Sinatra's first attempt at retirement came in the early 1970s. When he reentered the recording studio, Sinatra temporarily left behind the standards of the past. As for current Broadway songs, Stephen Sondheim was one of the few chosen. His postretirement album, *Ol' Blues Eyes Is Back,* was dominated by optimistic tunes from Joe Raposo, prominent as songwriter for the great children's TV show "Sesame Street." Beyond that LP, Sinatra's song selection continued the foreign-source and contemporary-domestic trends he started in the '60s; new to that mixture were David Gates, Jim Croce, Stevie Wonder, Billy Joel and Peter Allen. A handful of movie songs filled out the decade's choices, especially Kander and Ebb's theme from *New York, New York,* Sinatra's last Top-40 single. The singer's giant *Trilogy* album was recorded at the end of the '70s; it comprised three discs. The first disc, "The Past," contained songs mostly from the '20s and '30s. "The Present" contained '60s and '70s numbers. "The Future" was a cantata composed by longtime friend and arranger Gordon Jenkins; it consisted of orchestral passages and songs exploring Sinatra's life and art. This three-part album served as a summing up of career.

Finally, a few songs from the 1980s were recorded for Sinatra's late singles and last two LPs. These looked to past traditions more than the present: one by Sammy Cahn with a new collaborator; two by Jule Styne with a new lyricist; two by longtime favored composer Alec Wilder; great melodies by Don Costa, Stephen Sondheim, Michel Legrand. Then came the final retirement from recording.

To present some highly successful examples from this plethora of songs, I will include two lists of recordings singled out for recognition.

Ever since the early days of commercial song recording, the sale of a million records has been a status symbol. Enrico Caruso's 1903 recording of the *Vesti La Giubba* aria from *Pagliacci* was the first to achieve the million mark. In the years since, the volume of million-sellers has grown steadily. By the time Sinatra's record career flowered in the early 1940s, several songs were qualifying each year; during the rock era, there were long annual lists of songs reaching sales of a million. In this market environment, a record didn't have to reach the Top–10 to sell a million and the number one spot did not guarantee a million sales.

Reflecting the top chart position attained (either the *Billboard* or *Cash Box* list, whichever was highest), and showing the total number of weeks on that chart, here are Sinatra's dozen songs that sold a million or more copies in single-record format:

Sales Year	Song Title	Recording Session	Top-Chart/Weeks
1942	There Are Such Things	July 1, 1942	#1/24
1943	All or Nothing at All	Aug. 31, 1939	#2/18
1944	White Christmas	Nov. 13, 1944	#7/9
1954	Young at Heart	Dec. 9, 1953	#2/22
1955	Learnin' the Blues	Mar. 23, 1955	#2/20
1955	Love and Marriage	Aug. 15, 1955	#5/17
1957	All the Way (side A)	Aug. 13, 1957	#15/30
1957	Chicago (side B)	Aug. 13, 1957	#84/5
1966	Strangers in the Night	Apr. 11, 1966	#1/15
1967	Something Stupid	Feb. 1, 1967	#1/14
1969	My Way	Dec. 30, 1968	#27/8
1980	New York, New York	Sept. 19, 1979	#21/12

In the field of million-selling singles, Frank Sinatra's even dozen songs doesn't stack up to his two successors as teen mass-idols, Elvis Presley and the Beatles. This is especially true when you consider how short their careers were compared to his. The key factor is Sinatra's concentration on albums for the last thirty years of his recording life. If you use a standard industry formula — equating a million-selling LP with six two-sided singles — then the numbers change, with Elvis coming in over the 70-million mark, the Fab Four gaining sales in the CD format and now approaching 70 million, and Sinatra topping 100 million.

For a broader look at popular songs recorded by Sinatra, here is the full list of his singles chart entries. The *Billboard* charts included only the Top-10 when begun in 1940, switched to Top-15 in 1947, then to Top-30 in 1948, to Top-20 in 1953, back to Top-30 in 1954, to Top-25 in June 1955 and finally to the Top-100 in December 1955, where it has remained to the present. *Cash Box* magazine started their listings (in 1962) with the Top-100 singles and has remained the same. Most songs appeared on both charts after 1962, but a few were listed on just one or the other. Here are Sinatra's single best-sellers over four decades:

The 1940s

I'll Never Smile Again
Imagination
Trade Wind
Our Love Affair
We Three (My Echo, My Shadow and Me)
Star Dust [Nov. 11, 1940, recording]
Oh! Look at Me Now!
Do I Worry?
Dolores
Everything Happens to Me
Let's Get Away from It All
This Love of Mine
Two in Love
Just as Though You Were Here
Take Me
Daybreak
There Are Such Things
It Started All Over Again
All or Nothing at All
In the Blue of Evening
It's Always You
You'll Never Know
Close to You
Sunday, Monday or Always

People Will Say We're in Love
I Couldn't Sleep a Wink Last Night
White Christmas
I Dream of You (More Than You Dream I Do)
Saturday Night (Is the Loneliest Night of the Week)
Dream
Nancy (With the Laughing Face)
Oh, What It Seemed to Be
Day by Day
They Say It's Wonderful
Five Minutes More
The Coffee Song
White Christmas [2nd appearance on chart of same record]
Mam'selle
Nature Boy
Sunflower
The Huckle Buck
Some Enchanted Evening
Bali Ha'i
Don't Cry Joe
Old Master Painter

The 1950s

Chattanoogie Shoe Shine Boy
Goodnight, Irene
Castle Rock
Young at Heart
Don't Worry 'bout Me
Three Coins in the Fountain
Learnin' the Blues
Same Old Saturday Night
Love and Marriage
The Tender Trap
Flowers Mean Forgiveness
You'll Get Yours
How Little We Know
Five Hundred Guys
You're Sensational

Wait for Me
Hey! Jealous Lover
Can I Steal a Little Love?
Your Love for Me
Crazy Love
So Long My Love
All the Way [side A]
Chicago [side B]
Witchcraft
How Are Ya Fixed for Love?
Mr. Success
French Foreign Legion
High Hopes
Talk to Me

The 1960s

River Stay 'way from My Door
Nice 'n' Easy
Ol' MacDonald
The Moon Was Yellow
The Second Time Around
Granada
I'll Be Seeing You
Pocketful of Miracles
Star Dust [Nov. 20, 1961, recording]
Everybody's Twistin'
Me and My Shadow
Call Me Irresponsible
Come Blow Your Horn
Stay with Me
Softly, As I Leave You
Somewhere in Your Heart
Anytime at All
Tell Her (You Love Her Each

Day)
Forget Domani
It Was a Very Good Year
Strangers in the Night
Summer Wind
That's Life
Something Stupid
The World We Knew (Over and Over)
This Town
I Can't Believe I'm Losing You
My Way of Life
Cycles
Rain in My Heart
My Way
Love's Been Good to Me
Goin' Out of My Head
Forget to Remember

The 1970s

I Would Be in Love (Anyway)
Let Me Try Again
Bad, Bad Leroy Brown

You Turned My World Around
Anytime
I Believe I'm Gonna Love You

The 1980s

New York, New York [title song
      from movie]

L.A. Is My Lady
Mack the Knife

This chapter has two catalogs. The first — a Master Song List — organizes the 1,251 recordings alphabetically by title. The second catalog more simply lists the songs in terms of their Publication Dates. The following introduction will provide information required for the fullest use of the Master Song List.

Introduction to the *Master Song List*

In this chapter, we have considered the wide variety of songs recorded by Frank Sinatra. Several favorite songs were recorded more than once. Dozens of arrangers and hundreds of songwriters were encompassed by the singer's career. The identity of these songs and people — plus the facts concerning the single or multiple recordings — is the subject of the book's major catalog.

The Master Song List is organized alphabetically. In the case of titles beginning with "the," "a," and "an," these articles are ignored in alphabetizing. Each song has several lines of information. A few points follow which will aid your understanding of these data.

The first entry line begins with a key number. This number can be used to cross-reference entries with the other Catalogs in the book. The composer and lyricist indexes also reference these key numbers.

Next is the song title; special notes exist for song titles followed by the * symbol. These notes are listed at the end of the song's entry. If a given song has an ancillary title, that is listed following the main title. Such subtitles appear several ways. An ancillary title enclosed by parentheses (xxx) designates an official subordinate title, copyrighted at publication; if the subordinate title comes before the main title, that is shown by a dash mark, as with *Anytime (I'll Be There—)*, and if subordinate titles come both before and after the main title, those portions are separated by dash marks and ellipses, as with *Ballerina (Dance—* ... *—Dance)*. If an ancillary title is enclosed by square brackets—[xxx]—that is a subtitle I have added to differentiate the song from others with the same main title. An ancillary title is enclosed by double carets «xxx» designates an official alternate title; this could be merely a second title, or an original non-English title, or a translation to English from another language.

When a recording was made with featured singers, the others are named. In cases when more than three others sang with Sinatra, the item is marked "cast ensemble." Backup groups or choruses are not listed.

If a song was recorded more than once, there is a reference to whether it was the "1st recording," "2nd recording," et cetera.

The entry for "Publication Date" is the year of the song's completion; this is the earliest of the dates representing copyright, publication, or the first Sinatra recording session, if that came before formal publication of the work. Dates from A.D. 580 through A.D. 1800 are approximations based on other researchers' estimates. Dates from 1841 onward are exact. When two or more conflicting dates were given by various sources, the earliest date was used.

The "Music" line gives the melody's composer(s), plus any special notes that may apply; for example, the name of a classical composer if the song's melody was directly lifted or derived from a concert source. If a date follows the composer's name, it indicates the melody was originally written during a different year than the song's publication date. When two or more names are separated by the ampersand (&), an equal creative role is implied. When a diagonal (/) separates names, those following the mark had a subordinate role, or created an earlier piece from which the song melody was developed. If the composer is not known, that is labeled as "traditional." In cases where one person or team collaborated on the whole song, this is listed under "Music & Words."

The "Words" line gives the song's lyricist(s), plus any special notes that may apply; for example, the words may be a translation from another language, or special words may have been added to the original lyric. If a date follows the writer's name, it indicates the lyric was originally written during a different year than the song's publication date. When two or more names are separated by the ampersand (&), an equal creative role is implied. When a diagonal (/) separates names, those following the mark had a subordinate role, or created an earlier lyric in either the same or a different language. If the lyric writer is not known, that is labeled as "traditional." In cases where one person or team collaborated on the whole song, this is listed under "Music & Words."

The "Recorded" line gives the date on which the particular recording was made. This is numerically listed in month/day/year order; the single letter following the date indicates the sequence of recording within that session (a = 1st, b = 2nd, etc.). This volume disregards which "take" of a song was released. In the case of recordings made from radio broadcasts, movie soundtracks, and television broadcasts, the session date is replaced by year and source references. When the source is a special wartime Victory Disc recording session — or when a V-Disc was made from a radio broadcast or dress rehearsal — that specific date and source are listed.

The "Arranger(s)" line lists the people who wrote the orchestration for a particular recording of a song.

The "Conductor/Band" line gives the name of the principal orchestra conductor during the recording process — and most often during rehearsals, as well — plus the nature of the group of musicians involved. The formal, ongoing bands are listed with capital letters (Billy May & his Orchestra), while the groups brought together specifically for a recording session or media broadcast are listed in lower-case letters (television orchestra).

The "Key Release" names the album on which the recording first appeared, or the one most readily available on LP at the present time. In the few cases where an LP source is not known, reference is made to the number of the original release as a 45 or 78 rpm single record. When a nonofficial movie soundtrack is the only known release of a film song, both the title of the movie and the name of the "bootleg" LP are given.

The final line of each Master Song List entry consists of useful cross-references to the three Album Lists at the end of Chapter 8. In the case of singles, there is only a cross-reference to Album List #1.

Master Song List

Special titles listed after the main song title include:
«alternate titles»   (subordinate titles)   [differentiating titles]
Recording Session 9/18/50-a = Sept. 18, 1950 — first tune of session.

#1   Accidents Will Happen
Publication Date: 1950
Music: Jimmy Van Heusen
Words: Johnny Burke
Recorded: 9/18/50-a
Arranger: Axel Stordahl
Conductor/Band: A. Stordahl/studio
    orchestra
Key Release: **Sinatra Rarities — The
    Columbia Years** (Volume 1)
see Album Lists: alphabetic by title;
    1986 — 1st LP; Columbia/50th

#2   Adelaide
Publication Date: 1950
Music & Words: Frank Loesser
Recorded: 1955 — 1st soundtrack (il-
    legally taken from film sound)
Arranger: Nelson Riddle
Conductor/Band: Jay Blackton/
    MGM Orchestra
Key Release: *"Guys and Dolls"* [LP:
    Score from *Guys and Dolls*]
see Album Lists: alphabetic under
    "soundtrack"; mid-1960s; boot-
    leg Mv. #18

**#3   Adeste Fidelis «O Come, All
    Ye Faithful»**   *1st recording*
Publication Date: 1841
Music: John Reading, from an
    18th-century Portuguese hymn
Words: Frederick Oakeley, from
    Latin words by John Francis
    Wade
Recorded: 8/8/46-a

Arranger: Axel Stordahl
Conductor/Band: A. Stordahl/studio
    orchestra
Key Release: **Christmas Dreaming**
see Album Lists: alphabetic by title;
    1957 — 3rd LP; Columbia/25th

**#4   Adeste Fidelis «O Come, All
    Ye Faithful»**   *2nd recording*
Publication Date: 1841
Music: John Reading, from an
    18th-century Portuguese hymn
Words: Frederick Oakeley, from
    Latin words by John Francis
    Wade
Recorded: 7/10/57-d
Arranger: Gordon Jenkins
Conductor/Band: G. Jenkins/studio
    orchestra
Key Release: **A Jolly Christmas from
    Frank Sinatra**
see Album Lists: alphabetic by title;
    1957 — 6th LP; Capitol/14th

#5   After I Say I'm Sorry
Publication Date: 1926
Music & Words: Walter Donaldson
    & Abe Lyman
Recorded: 1943 radio — Lucky
    Strike's "Your Hit Parade"
Arranger: Axel Stordahl
Conductor/Band: A. Stordahl/radio
    orchestra
Key Release: **Frank Sinatra**
see Album Lists: alphabetic under
    "radio"; early 1960s; Cameron/4th

#6 After You've Gone
Publication Date: 1918
Music & Words: Turner Layton &
  Harry Creamer
Recorded: 4/17/84-c
Arranger: Frank Foster
Conductor/Band: Quincy Jones & a
  special all-star jazz band
Key Release: **L.A. Is My Lady**
see Album Lists: alphabetic by title;
  1984 — 1st LP; Qwest/1st

#7 Ain't She Sweet?
Publication Date: 1927
Music: Milton Ager
Words: Jack Yellin
Recorded: 4/10/62-c
Arranger: Neal Hefti
Conductor/Band: N. Hefti/studio
  orchestra
Key Release: **Sinatra and Swingin'
  Brass**
see Album Lists: alphabetic by title;
  1962 — 4th LP; Reprise/5th

#8 Ain'tcha Ever Comin' Back?
Publication Date: 1947
Music: Axel Stordahl & Paul
  Weston
Words: Irving Taylor
Recorded: 3/11/47-b
Arranger: Axel Stordahl
Conductor/Band: A. Stordahl/studio
  orchestra
Key Release: **Put Your Dreams
  Away**
see Album Lists: alphabetic by title;
  1958 — 3rd LP; Columbia/26th

#9 All Alone
Publication Date: 1924
Music & Words: Irving Berlin
Recorded: 1/15/62-b
Arranger: Gordon Jenkins
Conductor/Band: G. Jenkins/studio
  orchestra
Key Release: **All Alone**

see Album Lists: alphabetic by title;
  1962 — 7th LP; Reprise/8th

#10 All I Need Is the Girl
Publication Date: 1959
Music: Jule Styne
Words: Stephen Sondheim
Recorded: 12/11/67-a
Arranger: Billy May
Conductor/Band: Duke Ellington &
  his Band
Key Release: **Francis A. & Edward
  K.**
see Album Lists: alphabetic by title;
  1968 — 2nd LP; Reprise/33rd

#11 All My Tomorrows *1st
  recording*
Publication Date: 1958
Music: Jimmy Van Heusen
Words: Sammy Cahn
Recorded: 12/29/58-c
Arranger: Nelson Riddle
Conductor/Band: N. Riddle/studio
  orchestra
Key Release: **All the Way**
see Album Lists: alphabetic by title;
  1961 — 2nd LP; Capitol/29th

#12 All My Tomorrows *2nd
  recording*
Publication Date: 1958
Music: Jimmy Van Heusen
Words: Sammy Cahn
Recorded: 2/13/69-d
Arranger: Don Costa
Conductor/Band: D. Costa/studio
  orchestra
Key Release: **My Way**
see Album Lists: alphabetic by title;
  1969 — 1st LP; Reprise/38th

#13 All of Me *1st recording*
Publication Date: 1931
Music: Gerald Marks
Words: Seymour Simons
Recorded: 7/8/44-b (exclusively for

Victory-Disc effort)
Arranger: Axel Stordahl
Conductor/Band: A. Stordahl/assembled V-Disc orchestra
Key Release: Sinatra for the Collector: Vol. 2—The V-Disc Years (Canadian release only; album of wartime Victory Discs)
see Album Lists: alphabetic under "v/disc"; early 1970s; My Way/2nd

#14   All of Me   *2nd recording*
Publication Date: 1931
Music: Gerald Marks
Words: Seymour Simons
Recorded: 11/7/46-b
Arranger: George Siravo
Conductor/Band: G. Siravo/studio orchestra
Key Release: 78rpm single #DB-2330 (English release only)
see Album List #1: 1947 Columbia (3) single record—listed by number

#15   All of Me   *3rd recording*
Publication Date: 1931
Music: Gerald Marks
Words: Seymour Simons
Recorded: 10/19/47-c
Arranger: George Siravo
Conductor/Band: G. Siravo/studio orchestra
Key Release: Frankie
see Album Lists: alphabetic by title; 1955—8th LP; Columbia/20th

#16   All of Me   *4th recording*
Publication Date: 1931
Music: Gerald Marks
Words: Seymour Simons
Recorded: 4/19/54-a
Arranger: Nelson Riddle: full-orch. arrng. from G. Siravo band arrng.
Conductor/Band: N. Riddle/studio

orchestra
Key Release: Swing Easy! (original 10″ LP)
see Album Lists: alphabetic by title; 1954—5th LP; Capitol/4th

#17   All of You
Publication Date: 1954
Music & Words: Cole Porter
Recorded: 9/17/79-a
Arranger: Billy May
Conductor/Band: B. May/studio orchestra
Key Release: Trilogy: The Past [Collectibles of the Early Years]
see Album Lists: alphabetic by title; 1980—1st LP; Reprise/52nd

#18   All or Nothing at All   *1st recording*
Publication Date: 1939
Music: Arthur Altman
Words: Jack Lawrence
Recorded: 8/31/39-b
Arranger: Andy Gibson
Conductor/Band: Harry James & his Orchestra
Key Release: The Frank Sinatra Story in Music (2 discs)
see Album Lists: alphabetic by title; 1959—2nd LP; Columbia/27th

#19   All or Nothing at All   *2nd recording*
Publication Date: 1939
Music: Arthur Altman
Words: Jack Lawrence
Recorded: 11/22/61-c
Arranger: Don Costa
Conductor/Band: D. Costa/studio orchestra
Key Release: Sinatra & Strings
see Album Lists: alphabetic by title; 1962—1st LP; Reprise/4th

20   All or Nothing at All   *3rd recording*

Publication Date: 1939
Music: Arthur Altman
Words: Jack Lawrence
Recorded: 5/16/66-b
Arranger: Nelson Riddle
Conductor/Band: N. Riddle/studio
orchestra
Key Release: **Strangers in the Night**
see Album Lists: alphabetic by title;
1966 — 1st LP; Reprise/27th

#21 All or Nothing at All *4th
recording*
Publication Date: 1939
Music: Arthur Altman
Words: Jack Lawrence
Recorded: 2/16/77-b
Arranger: Joe Beck
Conductor/Band: J. Beck/studio
orchestra
Key Release: **The Unissued Sinatra**
(illegal; from Reprise Masters)
see Album Lists: alphabetic under
"bootleg"; early 1980s; bootleg
Alb. #4

#22 All the Things You Are
Publication Date: 1939
Music: Jerome Kern
Words: Oscar Hammerstein II
Recorded: 1/29/45-c
Arranger: Axel Stordahl
Conductor/Band: A. Stordahl/studio
orchestra
Key Release: **Reflections**
see Album Lists: alphabetic by title;
1961 — 4th LP; Columbia/31st

#23 All the Way *1st recording*
Publication Date: 1957
Music: Jimmy Van Heusen
Words: Sammy Cahn & Lillian
Small
Recorded: 8/13/57-c
Arranger: Nelson Riddle
Conductor/Band: N. Riddle/studio
orchestra

Key Release: **All the Way**
see Album Lists: alphabetic by title;
1961 — 2nd LP; Capitol/29th

#24 All the Way *2nd recording*
Publication Date: 1957
Music: Jimmy Van Heusen
Words: Sammy Cahn & Lillian
Small
Recorded: 4/29/63-e
Arranger: Nelson Riddle
Conductor/Band: N. Riddle/studio
orchestra
Key Release: **Sinatra's Sinatra**
see Album Lists: alphabetic by title;
1963 — 7th LP; Reprise/15th

#25 All This and Heaven Too
Publication Date: 1939
Music: Jimmy Van Heusen
Words: Eddie DeLange
Recorded: 5/23/40-b
Arranger: Dorsey "house" arrng:
T. Dorsey, S. Oliver, F. Stulce,
P. Weston
Conductor/Band: Tommy Dorsey &
his Orchestra
Key Release: **The Dorsey/Sinatra
Sessions** (Volume 2)
see Album Lists: alphabetic by title;
1972 — 2nd LP; RCA Victor/18th

#26 All Through the Day
Publication Date: 1945
Music: Jerome Kern
Words: Oscar Hammerstein II
Recorded: 2/3/46-a
Arranger: Axel Stordahl
Conductor/Band: A. Stordahl/studio
orchestra
Key Release: **The Voice: 1943–1952**
(6 discs)
see Album Lists: alphabetic by title;
1987 — 1st LP; Columbia/51st

**#27 Almost Like Being in
Love** *1st recording*

Publication Date: 1947
Music: Frederick Loewe
Words: Alan Jay Lerner
Recorded: 3/31/47-b
Arranger: Axel Stordahl
Conductor/Band: A. Stordahl/studio orchestra
Key Release: Frankie
see Album Lists: alphabetic by title; 1955—8th LP; Columbia/20th

#28   Almost Like Being in Love   *2nd recording*
Publication Date: 1947
Music: Frederick Loewe
Words: Alan Jay Lerner
Recorded: 3/22/61-b
Arranger: Billy May
Conductor/Band: B. May/studio orchestra
Key Release: Come Swing with Me!
see Album Lists: alphabetic by title; 1961—5th LP; Capitol/30th

#29   Always   *1st recording*
Publication Date: 1925
Music & Words: Irving Berlin
Recorded: 1/9/47-a
Arranger: Axel Stordahl
Conductor/Band: A. Stordahl/studio orchestra
Key Release: Come Back to Sorrento
see Album Lists: alphabetic by title; 1960—5th LP; Columbia/30th

#30   Always   *2nd recording*
Publication Date: 1925
Music & Words: Irving Berlin
Recorded: 8/23/60-c
Arranger: Nelson Riddle
Conductor/Band: N. Riddle/studio orchestra
Key Release: Sinatra's Swingin' Session!!!
see Album Lists: alphabetic by title; 1961—1st LP; Capitol/28th

#31   America the Beautiful
1st recording
Publication Date: 1895
Music: Samuel Ward—1882
Words: Katherine Lee Bates
Recorded: 8/27/45-a
Arranger: Axel Stordahl
Conductor/Band: A. Stordahl/studio orchestra
Key Release: 78rpm single #36886
see Album List #1: 1945 Columbia (4) single record—listed by number

#32   America the Beautiful
2nd recording
Publication Date: 1895
Music: Samuel Ward—1882
Words: Katherine Lee Bates
Recorded: 2/20/63-c
Arranger: Nelson Riddle
Conductor/Band: N. Riddle/studio orchestra
Key Release: 45rpm single #P20,157—side B
see Album List #1: 1966 Reprise (5) single record—listed by number

#33   American Beauty Rose
1st recording
Publication Date: 1950
Music: Arthur Altman
Words: Hal David & Redd Evans
Recorded: 3/10/50-a
Arranger: Mitch Miller
Conductor/Band: M. Miller/studio orchestra
Key Release: Love Is a Kick
see Album Lists: alphabetic by title; 1960—3rd LP; Columbia/28th

#34   American Beauty Rose
2nd recording
Publication Date: 1950
Music: Arthur Altman
Words: Hal David & Redd Evans
Recorded: 3/21/61-b

Arranger: Heinie Beau
Conductor/Band: Billy May/studio
   orchestra
Key Release: **Come Swing with Me!**
see Album Lists: alphabetic by title;
   1961 — 5th LP; Capitol/30th

#35   Among My Souvenirs
Publication Date: 1927
Music: Horatio Nicholls
Words: Edgar Leslie
Recorded: 7/30/46-a
Arranger: Axel Stordahl
Conductor/Band: A. Stordahl/studio
   orchestra
Key Release: **Come Back to Sorrento**
see Album Lists: alphabetic by title;
   1960 — 5th LP; Columbia/30th

#36   And Then You Kissed Me
Publication Date: 1944
Music: Jule Styne
Words: Sammy Cahn
Recorded: 5/24/44-b; Sinatra's
   "Vimms Vitamins Show"
Arranger: Axel Stordahl
Conductor/Band: A. Stordahl/radio
   orchestra
Key Release: **Sinatra for the Collec-
tor: Vol. 2 — The V-Disc Years**
   (Canadian release only; album
   of wartime Victory Discs)
see Album Lists: alphabetic under
   "v/disc"; early 1970s; My
   Way/2nd

#37   Angel Eyes   *1st recording*
Publication Date: 1946
Music: Matt Dennis
Words: Earl K. Brent
Recorded: 5/29/58-c
Arranger: Nelson Riddle
Conductor/Band: Felix Slatkin/studio
   orchestra
Key Release: **Frank Sinatra Sings
for Only the Lonely**
see Album Lists: alphabetic by title;

1958 — 5th LP; Capitol/19th

#38   Angel Eyes   *2nd recording*
Publication Date: 1946
Music: Matt Dennis
Words: Earl K. Brent
Recorded: 2/1/66-n
Arranger: Quincy Jones
Conductor/Band: Count Basie & his
   Band
Key Release: **Sinatra at the Sands**
   (Live Recording — 2 discs)
see Album Lists: alphabetic by title;
   1966 — 3rd LP; Reprise/29th

#39   Angel Eyes   *3rd recording*
Publication Date: 1946
Music: Matt Dennis
Words: Earl K. Brent
Recorded: 10/4/74-g
Arranger: Nelson Riddle
Conductor/Band: Bill Miller/Woody
   Herman's Young Thundering
   Herd band
Key Release: **Sinatra — The Main
Event** (Live Recording)
see Album Lists: alphabetic by title;
   1974 — 2nd LP; Reprise/48th

#40   Anything
Publication Date: 1929
Music: Frank Signorelli
Words: Eddie DeLange/Phil
   Napoleon
Recorded: 9/9/40-b
Arranger: Dorsey "house" arrng:
   T. Dorsey, S. Oliver, F. Stulce,
   P. Weston
Conductor/Band: Tommy Dorsey &
   his Orchestra
Key Release: **The Dorsey/Sinatra
Sessions** (Volume 3)
see Album Lists: alphabetic by title;
   1972 — 3rd LP; RCA Victor/19th

#41   Anything Goes
Publication Date: 1934

Music & Words: Cole Porter
Recorded: 1/16/56-c
Arranger: Nelson Riddle
Conductor/Band: N. Riddle/studio
orchestra
Key Release: **Songs for Swingin'
Lovers!**
see Album Lists: alphabetic by title;
1956—1st LP; Capitol/7th

#42   Anytime (I'll Be There—)
Publication Date: 1975
Music & Words: Paul Anka
Recorded: 3/3/75-a
Arranger: Don Costa
Conductor/Band: Bill Miller/studio
orchestra
Key Release: **I Sing the Songs**
(Italian release only)
see Album Lists: alphabetic by title;
1982—5th LP; Reprise/60th

#43   Anytime—Anywhere
Publication Date: 1953
Music: Lenny Adelson
Words: Imogene Carpenter
Recorded: 5/2/53-a
Arranger: Nelson Riddle
Conductor/Band: N. Riddle/studio
orchestra
Key Release: **Look to Your Heart**
see Album Lists: alphabetic by title;
1959—4th LP; Capitol/22nd

#44   Anytime at All
Publication Date: 1964
Music & Words: Baker Knight
Recorded: 11/11/64-b
Arranger: Ernie Freeman
Conductor/Band: E. Freeman/studio
orchestra
Key Release: **Sinatra '65**
see Album Lists: alphabetic by title;
1965—2nd LP; Reprise/24th

#45   April in Paris   *1st recording*
Publication Date: 1932

Music: Vernon Duke
Words: E. Y. ("Yip") Harburg
Recorded: 10/9/50-b
Arranger: Axel Stordahl
Conductor/Band: A. Stordahl/studio
orchestra
Key Release: **The Frank Sinatra
Story in Music** (2 discs)
see Album Lists: alphabetic by title;
1959—2nd LP; Columbia/27th

#46   April in Paris   *2nd recording*
Publication Date: 1932
Music: Vernon Duke
Words: E. Y. ("Yip") Harburg
Recorded: 10/3/57-c
Arranger: Billy May
Conductor/Band: Billy May & his
Orchestra
Key Release: **Come Fly with Me**
see Album Lists: alphabetic by title;
1958—2nd LP; Capitol/17th

#47   April Played the Fiddle
Publication Date: 1940
Music: James V. Monaco
Words: Johnny Burke
Recorded: 4/10/40-a
Arranger: Dorsey "house" arrng: T.
Dorsey, S. Oliver, F. Stulce, P.
Weston
Conductor/Band: Tommy Dorsey &
his Orchestra
Key Release: **The Dorsey/Sinatra
Sessions** (Volume 1)
see Album Lists: alphabetic by title;
1972—1st LP; RCA Victor/17th

**#48   Are You Lonesome
Tonight?**
Publication Date: 1926
Music: Lou Handman
Words: Roy Turk
Recorded: 1/17/62-c
Arranger: Gordon Jenkins
Conductor/Band: G. Jenkins/studio

orchestra
Key Release: **All Alone**
see Album Lists: alphabetic by title;
1962 — 7th LP; Reprise/8th

#49   Aren't You Glad You're You?

Publication Date: 1945
Music: Jimmy Van Heusen
Words: Johnny Burke
Recorded: 10/3/45-a; "The Frank Sinatra Old Gold Show"
Arranger: Axel Stordahl
Conductor/Band: A. Stordahl/radio orchestra
Key Release: **Sinatra for the Collector: Vol. 1 — The V-Disc Years** (Canadian release only; album of wartime Victory Discs)
see Album Lists: alphabetic under "v/disc"; early 1970s; My Way/1st

#50   Around the World

Publication Date: 1956
Music: Victor Young
Words: Harold Adamson
Recorded: 10/8/57-c
Arranger: Billy May
Conductor/Band: Billy May & his Orchestra
Key Release: **Come Fly with Me**
see Album Lists: alphabetic by title;
1958 — 2nd LP; Capitol/17th

#51   As Long as There's Music

Publication Date: 1944
Music: Jule Styne
Words: Sammy Cahn
Recorded: 1944 soundtrack (illegally taken from film sound)
Arranger: Axel Stordahl
Conductor/Band: Constantin Bakaleinikoff/RKO Orchestra
Key Release: **"Step Lively"** [LP: Complete *Step Lively* Film Soundtrack]

see Album Lists: alphabetic under "soundtrack"; mid–1960s; bootleg Mv. #5

#52   As Time Goes By

Publication Date: 1931
Music & Words: Herman Hupfeld
Recorded: 9/12/61-d
Arranger: Axel Stordahl
Conductor/Band: A. Stordahl/studio orchestra
Key Release: **Point of No Return**
see Album Lists: alphabetic by title;
1962 — 2nd LP; Capitol/31st

#53   As You Desire Me

Publication Date: 1932
Music & Words: Allie Wrubel
Recorded: 11/20/61-a
Arranger: Don Costa
Conductor/Band: D. Costa/studio orchestra
Key Release: **Sinatra & Strings** (1972 Japanese version only)
see Album Lists: alphabetic by title;
1962 — 1st LP; Reprise/4th

#54   At Long Last Love   *1st recording*

Publication Date: 1938
Music: Cole Porter
Words: Cole Porter/Robert Katscher
Recorded: 11/20/56-a
Arranger: Nelson Riddle
Conductor/Band: N. Riddle/studio orchestra
Key Release: **A Swingin' Affair!**
see Album Lists: alphabetic by title;
1957 — 2nd LP; Capitol/12th

#55   At Long Last Love   *2nd recording*

Publication Date: 1938
Music: Cole Porter
Words: Cole Porter/Robert Katscher

Recorded: 4/11/62-a
Arranger: Neal Hefti
Conductor/Band: N. Hefti/studio
orchestra
Key Release: **Sinatra and Swingin'
Brass**
see Album Lists: alphabetic by title;
1962—4th LP; Reprise/5th

#56   At Sundown
Publication Date: 1927
Music & Words: Walter Donaldson
Recorded: 1957 soundtrack (illegally
taken from film sound)
Arranger: Nelson Riddle
Conductor/Band: Walter Scharf/
Paramount Orchestra
Key Release: **"The Joker Is Wild"**
[LP: Score from *The Joker Is
Wild*]
see Album Lists: alphabetic under
"soundtrack"; mid–1960s;
bootleg Mv. #21

#57   Autumn in New York   *1st
recording*
Publication Date: 1934
Music & Words: Vernon Duke
Recorded: 12/4/47-b
Arranger: Axel Stordahl
Conductor/Band: A. Stordahl/studio
orchestra
Key Release: **That Old Feeling**
see Album Lists: alphabetic by title;
1956—2nd LP; Columbia/23rd

#58   Autumn in New York   *2nd
recording*
Publication Date: 1934
Music & Words: Vernon Duke
Recorded: 10/3/57-a
Arranger: Billy May
Conductor/Band: Billy May & his
Orchestra
Key Release: **Come Fly with Me**
see Album Lists: alphabetic by title;
1958—2nd LP; Capitol/17th

#59   Autumn in New York   *3rd
recording*
Publication Date: 1934
Music & Words: Vernon Duke
Recorded: 10/12/74-d
Arranger: Billy May
Conductor/Band: Bill Miller/Woody
Herman's Young Thundering
Herd band
Key Release: **Sinatra — The Main
Event** (Live Recording)
see Album Lists: alphabetic by title;
1974—2nd LP; Reprise/48th

**#60   Autumn Leaves «Les
Feuille Mortes»**
Publication Date: 1950
Music: Joseph Kosma—1947
Words: Johnny Mercer/Jacques
Prevert—1947
Recorded: 4/10/57-d
Arranger: Gordon Jenkins
Conductor/Band: G. Jenkins/studio
orchestra
Key Release: **Where Are You?**
see Album Lists: alphabetic by title;
1957—4th LP; Capitol/13th

#61   Available
Publication Date: 1964
Music: E. Wynn & H. Marks
Words: Sammy Cahn
Recorded: 7/17/64-d
Arranger: Ernie Freeman
Conductor/Band: E. Freeman/studio
orchestra
Key Release: **Softly, As I Leave You**
see Album Lists: alphabetic by title;
1964—8th LP; Reprise/21st

#62   Azure'te «Paris Blues»
Publication Date: 1950
Music: W. B. Davis
Words: Jack Wolf
Recorded: 6/3/52-c
Arranger: Axel Stordahl

Conductor/Band: A. Stordahl/studio
orchestra
*Key Release: The Essential Frank
Sinatra* (Volume 3)
see Album Lists: alphabetic by title;
1967 — 4th LP; Columbia/36th

#63   Baby, Won't You Please Come Home?
Publication Date: 1919
Music & Words: Clarence Williams
& Charles Warfield
Recorded: 4/29/57-d
Arranger: Gordon Jenkins
Conductor/Band: G. Jenkins/studio
orchestra
Key Release: Where Are You?
see Album Lists: alphabetic by title;
1957 — 4th LP; Capitol/13th

#64   Bad, Bad Leroy Brown
1st recording
Publication Date: 1972
Music & Words: Jim Croce
Recorded: 12/10/73-a
Arranger: Don Costa
Conductor/Band: D. Costa/studio
orchestra
*Key Release: Some Nice Things I've
Missed*
see Album Lists: alphabetic by title;
1974 — 1st LP; Reprise/47th

#65   Bad, Bad Leroy Brown
2nd recording
Publication Date: 1972
Music & Words: Jim Croce
Recorded: 10/13/74-f
Arranger: Don Costa
Conductor/Band: Bill Miller/Woody
Herman's Young Thundering
Herd band
*Key Release: Sinatra — The Main
Event* (Live Recording)
see Album Lists: alphabetic by title;
1974 — 2nd LP; Reprise/48th

#66   Bali Ha'i
Publication Date: 1949
Music: Richard Rodgers
Words: Oscar Hammerstein II
Recorded: 2/28/49-b
Arranger: Axel Stordahl
Conductor/Band: A. Stordahl/studio
orchestra
Key Release: The Broadway Kick
see Album Lists: alphabetic by title;
1960 — 4th LP; Columbia/29th

#67   Ballerina (Dance — ... — Dance)
Publication Date: 1947
Music: Carl Sigman
Words: Bob Russell
Recorded: 1947 radio — Lucky
Strike's "Your Hit Parade"
Arranger: Axel Stordahl
Conductor/Band: A. Stordahl/radio
orchestra
Key Release: Frank Sinatra
see Album Lists: alphabetic under
"radio"; early 1960s;
Cameron/4th

#68   Bang Bang (My Baby Shot Me Down)
Publication Date: 1966
Music & Words: Sonny Bono
Recorded: 4/8/81-a
Arranger: Gordon Jenkins
Conductor/Band: G. Jenkins/studio
orchestra
Key Release: She Shot Me Down
see Album Lists: alphabetic by title;
1981 — 1st LP; Reprise/55th

#69   Barbara
Publication Date: 1977
Music & Words: Paul Anka
Recorded: 3/14/77-c
Arranger: Nelson Riddle
Conductor/Band: N. Riddle/studio
orchestra
Key Release: Frank's Girls (illegal;

from Reprise masters)
see Album Lists: alphabetic under
"bootleg"; early 1980s; bootleg
Alb. #5

**#70   Baubles, Bangles and
Beads**   *1st recording*
Publication Date: 1953
Music: George Forrest & Robert
Wright; from A. Borodin
Words: Robert Wright & George
Forrest
Recorded: 12/22/58-b
Arranger: Billy May
Conductor/Band: Billy May & his
Orchestra
Key Release: **Come Dance with Me!**
see Album Lists: alphabetic by Title;
1959—1st LP; Capitol/20th

**#71   Baubles, Bangles and
Beads**   *2nd recording—duet with
Antonio Carlos Jobim*
Publication Date: 1953
Music: George Forrest & Robert
Wright; from A. Borodin
Words: Robert Wright & George
Forrest
Recorded: 1/30/67-a
Arranger: Claus Ogerman
Conductor/Band: C. Ogerman/studio
orchestra
Key Release: **Francis Albert Sinatra
& Antonio Carlos Jobim**
see Album Lists: alphabetic by title;
1967—1st LP; Reprise/31st

#72   Be Careful, It's My Heart
1st recording
Publication Date: 1942
Music & Words: Irving Berlin
Recorded: 6/9/42-b
Arranger: Axel Stordahl
Conductor/Band: Tommy Dorsey &
his Orchestra
Key Release: **The Dorsey/Sinatra
Sessions** (Volume 6)

see Album Lists: alphabetic by title;
1972—6th LP; RCA Victor/
22nd

#73   Be Careful, It's My Heart
2nd recording
Publication Date: 1942
Music & Words: Irving Berlin
Recorded: 12/20/60-b
Arranger: Johnny Mandel
Conductor/Band: J. Mandel/studio
orchestra
Key Release: **Ring-a-Ding Ding!**
see Album Lists: alphabetic by title;
1961—3rd LP; Reprise/1st

#74   The Beautiful Strangers
Publication Date: 1969
Music & Words: Rod McKuen
Recorded: 3/20/69-a
Arranger: Don Costa
Conductor/Band: D. Costa/studio
orchestra
Key Release: **A Man Alone**
see Album Lists: alphabetic by title;
1969—3rd LP; Reprise/39th

#75   Before the Music Ends
finale of "The Future" Cantata
Publication Date: 1979
Music & Words: Gordon Jenkins
Recorded: 12/18/79-a
Arranger: Gordon Jenkins
Conductor/Band: G. Jenkins and the
L.A. Philharmonic Symphony
Orchestra
Key Release: **Trilogy: The Future
[Reflections on the Future in 3
Tenses]**
see Album Lists: alphabetic by title;
1980—3rd LP; Reprise/54th

#76   Begin the Beguine
Publication Date: 1935
Music & Words: Cole Porter
Recorded: 2/24/46-c
Arranger: Axel Stordahl

Conductor/Band: A. Stordahl/studio
orchestra
*Key Release: The Frank Sinatra
Story in Music* (2 discs)
see Album Lists: alphabetic by title;
1959 — 2nd LP; Columbia/27th

#77   Bein' Green
Publication Date: 1970
Music & Words: Joe Raposo
Recorded: 10/26/70-b
Arranger: Don Costa
Conductor/Band: D. Costa/studio
orchestra
Key Release: Sinatra & Company
see Album Lists: alphabetic by title;
1971 — 2nd LP; Reprise/42nd

#78   The Bells of Christmas
«Greensleeves»   *sung with
Nancy, Frank Jr. and Tina Sinatra*
Publication Date: 1580
Music: Traditional; England in the
1500s
Words: Traditional; England —
adapted by Sammy Cahn
Recorded: 8/12/68-b
Arranger: Nelson Riddle
Conductor/Band: N. Riddle/studio
orchestra
*Key Release: The Sinatra Family
Wish You a Merry Christmas*
see Album Lists: alphabetic by title;
1968 — 4th LP; Reprise/35th

#79   The Best I Ever Had
Publication Date: 1976
Music: Angelique Vesta
Words: Jack Daniels
Recorded: 6/21/76-a
Arranger: Billy May
Conductor/Band: B. May/studio
orchestra
Key Release: The Singles (Italian
release only)
see Album Lists: alphabetic by title;
1982 — 6th LP; Reprise/61st

#80   The Best Is Yet to Come
Publication Date: 1959
Music: Cy Coleman
Words: Carolyn Leigh
Recorded: 6/9/64-a
Arranger: Quincy Jones
Conductor/Band: Count Basie & his
Band
*Key Release: It Might as Well Be
Swing*
see Album Lists: alphabetic by title;
1964 — 5th LP; Reprise/19th

#81   The Best of Everything
Publication Date: 1984
Music: John Kander
Words: Fred Ebb
Recorded: 4/13/84-c
Arranger: Joe Parnello
Conductor/Band: Quincy Jones & a
special all-star jazz band
Key Release: L.A. Is My Lady
see Album Lists: alphabetic by title;
1984 — 1st LP; Qwest/1st

**#82   Between the Devil and the
Deep Blue Sea**
Publication Date: 1931
Music: Harold Arlen
Words: Ted Koehler
Recorded: 1943 radio — Lucky
Strike's "Your Hit Parade"
Arranger: Axel Stordahl
Conductor/Band: A. Stordahl/radio
orchestra
Key Release: Frank Sinatra
see Album Lists: alphabetic under
"radio"; early 1960's;
Cameron/4th

**#83   Bewitched (Bothered and
Bewildered)**   *1st recording*
Publication Date: 1940
Music: Richard Rodgers
Words: Lorenz Hart
Recorded: 8/13/57-b
Arranger: Nelson Riddle

Conductor/Band: Morris Stoloff/
studio orchestra
Key Release: "Pal Joey" (Official
Soundtrack LP)
see Album Lists: alphabetic by title;
1957 — 8th LP; Capitol/15th

**#84   Bewitched (Bothered and
Bewildered)**
2nd recording
Publication Date: 1940
Music: Richard Rodgers
Words: Lorenz Hart
Recorded: 2/20/63-b
Arranger: Nelson Riddle
Conductor/Band: N. Riddle/studio
orchestra
*Key Release: **The Concert Sinatra***
see Album Lists: alphabetic by title;
1963 — 2nd LP; Reprise/10th

#85   Bim Bam Baby
Publication Date: 1952
Music & Words: Sammy Mysels
Recorded: 6/3/52-e
Arranger: Axel Stordahl
Conductor/Band: A. Stordahl/studio
orchestra
*Key Release: **Love Is a Kick***
see Album Lists: alphabetic by title;
1960 — 3rd LP; Columbia/28th

#86   The Birth of the Blues
Publication Date: 1926
Music: Ray Henderson
Words: B. G. (Buddy) DeSylva &
Lew Brown
Recorded: 6/3/52-b
Arranger: Heinie Beau
Conductor/Band: Axel Stordahl/
studio orchestra
*Key Release: **The Frank Sinatra
Story in Music*** (2 discs)
see Album Lists: alphabetic by title;
1959 — 2nd LP; Columbia/27th

#87   Black Eyes «derived from
"Otchi Tchorniya"»

Publication Date: 1884
Music & Words: Traditional;
Russia in the 1800s
Recorded: 1947 soundtrack (illegally
taken from film sound)
Arranger: Axel Stordahl
Conductor/Band: Johnny Green/
MGM Orchestra
*Key Release: "It Happened in
Brooklyn"* [LP: Score from *It
Happened in Brooklyn]*
see Album Lists: alphabetic under
"soundtrack"; mid–1960s; boot-
leg Mv. #9

#88   Blame It on My Youth
Publication Date: 1934
Music: Oscar Levant
Words: Edward Heyman
Recorded: 4/4/56-b
Arranger: Nelson Riddle
Conductor/Band: N. Riddle with or-
chestra & the Hollywood String
Quartet
*Key Release: **Close to You***
see Album Lists: alphabetic by title;
1957 — 1st LP; Capitol/11th

#89   Blue Hawaii
Publication Date: 1937
Music & Words: Ralph Rainger &
Leo Robin
Recorded: 8/10/57-a
Arranger: Billy May
Conductor/Band: Billy May & his
Orchestra
*Key Release: **Come Fly with Me***
see Album Lists: alphabetic by title;
1958 — 2nd LP; Capitol/17th

#90   Blue Moon
Publication Date: 1934
Music: Richard Rodgers — 1932, as
"Prayer" & 1933, as "The Bad in
Every Man"
Words: Lorenz Hart
Recorded: 9/1/60-c

Arranger: Nelson Riddle
Conductor/Band: N. Riddle/studio
  orchestra
Key Release: **Sinatra's Swingin'
  Session!!!**
see Album Lists: alphabetic by title;
  1961—1st LP; Capitol/28th

#91   Blue Skies   *1st recording*
Publication Date: 1927
Music & Words: Irving Berlin
Recorded: 7/15/41-a
Arranger: Harry Rodgers
Conductor/Band: Tommy Dorsey &
  his Orchestra
Key Release: **The Dorsey/Sinatra
  Sessions** (Volume 5)
see Album Lists: alphabetic by title;
  1972—5th LP; RCA Victor/21st

#92   Blue Skies   *2nd recording*
Publication Date: 1927
Music & Words: Irving Berlin
Recorded: 7/30/46-d
Arranger: Axel Stordahl
Conductor/Band: A. Stordahl/studio
  orchestra
Key Release: **That Old Feeling**
see Album Lists: alphabetic by title;
  1956—2nd LP; Columbia/23rd

#93   Blues in the Night
Publication Date: 1941
Music: Harold Arlen
Words: Johnny Mercer
Recorded: 6/24/58-a
Arranger: Nelson Riddle
Conductor/Band: N. Riddle/studio
  orchestra
Key Release: **Frank Sinatra Sings
  for Only the Lonely**
see Album Lists: alphabetic by title;
  1958—5th LP; Capitol/19th

#94   Body and Soul
Publication Date: 1930
Music: Johnny Green & Frank
  Eyton

Words: Edward Heyman & Robert
  Sour
Recorded: 11/9/47-a
Arranger: Axel Stordahl
Conductor/Band: A. Stordahl/studio
  orchestra
Key Release: **Reflections**
see Album Lists: alphabetic by title;
  1961—4th LP; Columbia/31st

#95   Bonita
Publication Date: 1959
Music & Words: Antonio Carlos
  Jobim
Recorded: 2/11/69-d
Arranger: Eumir Deodato
Conductor/Band: Morris Stoloff/
  studio orchestra
Key Release: **Portrait of Sinatra [40
  Songs in the Life of a Man]**
  (English release only—2 discs)
see Album Lists: alphabetic by title;
  1979—1st LP; Reprise/51st

#96   Bop! Goes My Heart
Publication Date: 1949
Music: Jule Styne
Words: Walter Bishop
Recorded: 12/15/48-c
Arranger: Phil Moore
Conductor/Band: P. Moore/studio
  orchestra
Key Release: **Sinatra Rarities — The
  Columbia Years** (Volume 1)
see Album Lists: alphabetic by title;
  1986—1st LP; Columbia/50th

#97   Born Free
Publication Date: 1966
Music: John Barry
Words: Don Black
Recorded: 7/24/67-a
Arranger: Gordon Jenkins
Conductor/Band: G. Jenkins/studio
  orchestra
Key Release: **Frank Sinatra &
  Frank and Nancy**

see Album Lists: alphabetic by title;
1967 — 5th LP; Reprise/32nd

#98   Boys and Girls Like You and Me*
Publication Date: 1943
Music: Richard Rodgers
Words: Oscar Hammerstein II
Recorded: 1949 — 1st soundtrack (il-legally taken from film sound)
Arranger: Axel Stordahl
Conductor/Band: Adolph Deutsch/ MGM Orchestra
Key Release: "Take Me Out to the Ball Game" [LP: Five Films]
see Album Lists: alphabetic under "soundtrack'" mid–1960s; bootleg MV. #12
*This song was deleted from the final soundtrack of the 1949 MGM film *Take Me Out to the Ball Game.*

#99   Brazil «Aquarela do Brasil»
Publication Date: 1943
Music: Ary Barroso — 1939
Words: S. K. Russell/Ary Barroso — 1939
Recorded: 10/8/57-e
Arranger: Billy May
Conductor/Band: Billy May & his Orchestra
Key Release: Come Fly with Me
see Album Lists: alphabetic by title;
1958 — 2nd LP; Capitol/17th

#100   The Brooklyn Bridge
Publication Date: 1946
Music: Jule Styne
Words: Sammy Cahn
Recorded: 10/31/46-b
Arranger: Axel Stordahl
Conductor/Band: A. Stordahl/studio orchestra
Key Release: Frank Sinatra in Hollywood, 1943–1949

see Album Lists: alphabetic by title;
1968 — 1st LP; Columbia/38th

#101   But Beautiful
Publication Date: 1947
Music: Jimmy Van Heusen
Words: Johnny Burke
Recorded: 8/17/47-a
Arranger: Axel Stordahl
Conductor/Band: A. Stordahl/studio orchestra
Key Release: Reflections
see Album Lists: alphabetic by title;
1961 — 4th LP; Columbia/31st

#102   But None Like You
Publication Date: 1947
Music: Charlie Spivak
Words: Sonny Burke
Recorded: 12/26/47-a
Arranger: Axel Stordahl
Conductor/Band: A. Stordahl/studio orchestra
Key Release: 78rpm single #38129
see Album List #1: 1948 Columbia (4) single record — listed by number

#103   But Not for Me
Publication Date: 1930
Music: George Gershwin
Words: Ira Gershwin
Recorded: 9/18/79-b
Arranger: Billy May
Conductor/Band: B. May/studio orchestra
Key Release: Trilogy: The Past [Collectibles of the Early Years]
see Album Lists: alphabetic by title;
1980 — 1st LP; Reprise/52nd

#104   By the Time I Get to Phoenix
Publication Date: 1967
Music & Words: Jim Webb
Recorded: 11/12/68-c
Arranger: Don Costa

Conductor/Band: Bill Miller/studio
orchestra
Key Release: **Cycles**
see Album Lists: alphabetic by title;
1968 — 6th LP; Reprise/37th

#105   Bye Bye Baby
Publication Date: 1949
Music: Jule Styne
Words: Leo Robin
Recorded: 7/10/49-b
Arranger: Hugo Winterhalter
Conductor/Band: H. Winterhalter/
studio orchestra
Key Release: **Love Is a Kick**
see Album Lists: alphabetic by title;
1960 — 3rd LP; Columbia/28th

#106   California
Publication Date: 1963
Music: Jimmy Van Heusen
Words: Sammy Cahn
Recorded: 2/20/63-a
Arranger: Nelson Riddle
Conductor/Band: N. Riddle/studio
orchestra
Key Release: 45rpm single
#P20,157 — side A
see Album List #1: 1966 Reprise (5)
single — listed by number

#107   Call Me
Publication Date: 1965
Music & Words: Tony Hatch
Recorded: 5/16/66-c
Arranger: Nelson Riddle
Conductor/Band: N. Riddle/studio
orchestra
Key Release: **Strangers in the Night**
see Album Lists: alphabetic by title;
1966 — 1st LP; Reprise/27th

#108   Call Me Irresponsible
Publication Date: 1962
Music: Jimmy Van Heusen
Words: Sammy Cahn
Recorded: 1/21/63-b

Arranger: Nelson Riddle
Conductor/Band: N. Riddle/studio
orchestra
Key Release: **Sinatra's Sinatra**
see Album Lists: alphabetic by title;
1963 — 7th LP; Reprise/15th

#109   The Call of the Canyon
Publication Date: 1940
Music & Words: Billy Hill
Recorded: 7/17/40-a
Arranger: Dorsey "house" arrng:
T. Dorsey, S. Oliver, F. Stulce,
P. Weston
Conductor/Band: Tommy Dorsey &
his Orchestra
Key Release: **The Dorsey/Sinatra
Sessions** (Volume 2)
see Album Lists: alphabetic by title;
1972 — 2nd LP; RCA Victor/
18th

#110   Can I Steal a Little Love?
Publication Date: 1956
Music & Words: Phil Tuminello
Recorded: 12/3/56-b
Arranger: Nelson Riddle
Conductor/Band: N. Riddle/studio
orchestra
Key Release: **Forever Frank**
see Album Lists: alphabetic by title;
1966 — 4th LP; Capitol/36th

#111   Can't We Be Friends?   *1st
recording*
Publication Date: 1929
Music: Kay Swift
Words: James Warburg
Recorded: 2/8/55-b
Arranger: Nelson Riddle
Conductor/Band: N. Riddle/studio
orchestra
Key Release: **In the Wee Small
Hours** (12" LP version)
see Album Lists: alphabetic by title;
1955 — 7th LP; Capitol/5th

#112 Can't We Be Friends?
2nd recording — duet with Ella Fitzgerald
Publication Date: 1929
Music: Kay Swift
Words: James Warburg (plus new lyrics by Sammy Cahn)
Recorded: 1959 television special
Arranger: Nelson Riddle
Conductor/Band: N. Riddle/television orchestra
Key Release: **Frank Sinatra — Through the Years: 1944–1966**
see Album Lists: alphabetic under "television"; mid–1960s; Ajazz/1st

#113 Can't You Just See Yourself?
Publication Date: 1947
Music: Jule Styne
Words: Sammy Cahn
Recorded: 10/19/47-a
Arranger: Dick Jones
Conductor/Band: D. Jones/studio orchestra
Key Release: **The Broadway Kick**
see Album Lists: alphabetic by title; 1960/4th LP; Columbia/29th

#114 Castle Rock
Publication Date: 1951
Music: Al Sears
Words: Ervin Drake & Jimmy Shirl
Recorded: 7/9/51-a
Arranger: Ray Conniff
Conductor/Band: Harry James & his Orchestra
Key Release: **The Frank Sinatra Story in Music** (2 discs)
see Album Lists: alphabetic by title; 1959 — 2nd LP; Columbia/27th

#115 Catana
Publication Date: 1947
Music & Words: Alfred Newman

Recorded: 12/26/47-b
Arranger: Axel Stordahl
Conductor/Band: A. Stordahl/studio orchestra
Key Release: **MM-1** (illegal; from Columbia masters)
see Album Lists: alphabetic under "bootleg"; early 1970s; bootleg Alb. #1

#116 C'est Magnifique
Publication Date: 1953
Music & Words: Cole Porter
Recorded: 2/19/60-b
Arranger: Nelson Riddle
Conductor/Band: N. Riddle/studio orchestra
Key Release: **"Can-Can"** (Official Soundtrack LP)
see Album Lists: alphabetic by title; 1960 — 1st LP; Capitol/24th

#117 Change Partners
Publication Date: 1938
Music & Words: Irving Berlin
Recorded: 1/30/67-d
Arranger: Claus Ogerman
Conductor/Band: C. Ogerman/studio orchestra
Key Release: **Francis Albert Sinatra & Antonio Carlos Jobim**
see Album Lists: alphabetic by title; 1967 — 1st LP; Reprise/31st

#118 The Charm of You
Publication Date: 1944
Music: Jule Styne
Words: Sammy Cahn
Recorded: 12/3/44-e
Arranger: Axel Stordahl
Conductor/Band: A. Stordahl/studio orchestra
Key Release: **Frank Sinatra in Hollywood, 1943–1949**
see Album Lists: alphabetic by title; 1968 — 1st LP; Columbia/38th

#119   Charmaine
Publication Date: 1926
Music: Erno Rapee
Words: Lew Pollack
Recorded: 1/15/62-c
Arranger: Gordon Jenkins
Conductor/Band: G. Jenkins/studio
  orchestra
Key Release: **All Alone**
see Album Lists: alphabetic by title;
  1962 — 7th LP; Reprise/8th

#120   Chattanoogie Shoe Shine Boy
Publication Date: 1950
Music and Words: Jack Stapp &
  Henry Stone
Recorded: 1/12/50-c
Arranger: Axel Stordahl
Conductor/Band: A. Stordahl/studio
  orchestra
Key Release: 78rpm single #38708,
  side B
see Album Lists: 1950 Columbia (4)
single — listed by number

#121   Cheek to Cheek
Publication Date: 1935
Music and Words: Irving Berlin
Recorded: 12/22/58-e
Arranger: Billy May
Conductor/Band: Billy May & his
  Orchestra
Key Release: **Come Dance with Me!**
see Album Lists: alphabetic by title;
  1959 — 1st LP; Capitol/20th

#122   Cherry Pies Ought to Be You   *duet with Rosemary Clooney*
Publication Date: 1950
Music and Words: Cole Porter
Recorded: 12/11/50-b
Arranger: Axel Stordahl
Conductor/Band: A. Stordahl/studio
  orchestra
Key Release: 45rpm single #4-39141
see Album List #1: 1951 Columbia (5)

single — listed by number

#123   Chicago (That Toddling Town)
Publication Date: 1922
Music & Words: Fred Fisher
Recorded: 8/13/57-e
Arranger: Nelson Riddle
Conductor/Band: N. Riddle/studio
  orchestra
Key Release: **Sinatra Sings . . . of Love and Things**
see Album Lists: alphabetic by title;
  1962 — 3rd LP; Capitol/32nd

#124   Christmas Dreaming (A Little Late This Year)
Publication Date: 1947
Music & Words: Lester Lee & Irving Gordon
Recorded: 6/26/47-b
Arranger: Axel Stordahl
Conductor/Band: A. Stordahl/studio
  orchestra
Key Release: **Christmas Dreaming**
see Album Lists: alphabetic by title;
  1957 — 3rd LP; Columbia/25th

#125   The Christmas Song
Publication Date: 1946
Music & Words: Mel Torme &
  Robert Wells
Recorded: 7/17/57-b
Arranger: Gordon Jenkins
Conductor/Band: G. Jenkins/studio
  orchestra
Key Release: **A Jolly Christmas from Frank Sinatra**
see Album Lists: alphabetic by title;
  1957 — 6th LP; Capitol/14th

#126   The Christmas Waltz   *1st recording*
Publication Date: 1954
Music: Jule Styne
Words: Sammy Cahn
Recorded: 8/23/54-c

Arranger: Nelson Riddle
Conductor/Band: N. Riddle/studio
orchestra
Key Release: 45rpm single #2954,
side B
see Album Lists: 1954 Capitol (5)
single—listed by number

#127   The Christmas Waltz
2nd recording
Publication Date: 1954
Music: Jule Styne
Words: Sammy Cahn
Recorded: 7/16/57-d
Arranger: Gordon Jenkins
Conductor/Band: G. Jenkins/studio
orchestra
Key Release: **A Jolly Christmas from
Frank Sinatra**
see Album Lists: alphabetic by title;
1957—6th LP; Capitol/14th

#128   The Christmas Waltz   *3rd
recording*
Publication Date: 1954
Music: Jule Styne
Words: Sammy Cahn
Recorded: 8/12/68-d
Arranger: Nelson Riddle
Conductor/Band: N. Riddle/studio
orchestra
Key Release: **The Sinatra Family
Wish You a Merry Christmas**
see Album Lists: alphabetic by title;
1968—4th LP; Reprise/35th

**#129   Ciribiribin (They're So in
Love)**
Publication Date: 1938
Music: Alberto Pestalozza—1898/
Harry James
Words: Jack Lawrence & Harry
James/Rudolf Thaler—1898
Recorded: 11/8/39-a
Arranger: Andy Gibson
Conductor/Band: Harry James & his
Orchestra

Key Release: **The Frank Sinatra
Story in Music** (2 discs)
see Album Lists: alphabetic by title;
1959—2nd LP; Columbia/27th

**#130   Civilization «Bongo,
Bongo, Bongo»**
Publication Date: 1947
Music: Carl Sigman
Words: Bob Hilliard & Carl
Sigman
Recorded: 1947 radio—Lucky
Strike's "Your Hit Parade"
Arranger: Axel Stordahl
Conductor/Band: A. Stordahl/radio
orchestra
Key Release: **The Original . . .
Frank Sinatra**
see Album Lists: alphabetic under
"radio"; early 1960s;
Cameron/2nd

**#131   Close to You [I Will
Always Stay]**   *1st recording*
Publication Date: 1943
Music: Al Hoffman
Words: Jerry Livingston & Nor-
man Lampi
Recorded: 6/7/43-a
Arranger: Axel Stordahl
Conductor/Band: Bobby Tucker
Singers only; during musician's
strike
Key Release: **The Essential Frank
Sinatra** (Volume 1)
see Album Lists: alphabetic by title;
1967—2nd LP; Columbia/34th

**#132   Close to You [I Will
Always Stay]**   *2nd recording*
Publication Date: 1943
Music: Al Hoffman
Words: Jerry Livingston & Nor-
man Lampi
Recorded: 10/1/56-c
Arranger: Nelson Riddle
Conductor/Band: N. Riddle with

orchestra & the Hollywood
String Quartet
Key Release: Close to You
see Album Lists: alphabetic by title;
1957 — 1st LP; Capitol/11th

#133   Close to You (They Long to Be —)
Publication Date: 1963
Music: Burt Bacharach
Words: Hal David
Recorded: 10/29/70-b
Arranger: Don Costa
Conductor/Band: D. Costa/studio
orchestra
Key Release: Sinatra & Company
see Album Lists: alphabetic by title;
1971 — 2nd LP; Reprise/42nd

#134   The Coffee Song   *1st recording*
Publication Date: 1946
Music: Dick Miles
Words: Bob Hilliard
Recorded: 7/24/46-d
Arranger: Axel Stordahl
Conductor/Band: A. Stordahl/studio
orchestra
Key Release: Frank Sinatra's Great-est Hits: The Early Years (Vol-ume 1)
see Album Lists: alphabetic by title;
1964 — 3rd LP; Columbia/32nd

#135   The Coffee Song   *2nd recording*
Publication Date: 1946
Music: Dick Miles
Words: Bob Hilliard
Recorded: 12/20/60-a
Arranger: Johnny Mandel
Conductor/Band: J. Mandel/studio
orchestra
Key Release: Ring-a-Ding Ding!
see Album Lists: alphabetic by title;
1961 — 3rd LP; Reprise/1st

#136   Come Back to Me
Publication Date: 1965
Music: Burton Lane
Words: Alan Jay Lerner
Recorded: 12/11/67-d
Arranger: Billy May
Conductor/Band: Duke Ellington &
his Band
Key Release: Francis A. & Edward K.
see Album Lists: alphabetic by title;
1968 — 2nd LP; Reprise/33rd

#137   Come Back to Sorrento «Torne a Surriento»
Publication Date: 1904
Music: Ernesto De Curtis & G. B.
De Curtis
Words: Ernesto De Curtis &
Claude Aveling
Recorded: 10/9/50-a
Arranger: Axel Stordahl
Conductor/Band: A. Stordahl/studio
orchestra
Key Release: Come Back to Sorrento
see Album Lists: alphabetic by title;
1960 — 5th LP; Columbia/30th

#138   Come Blow Your Horn
Publication Date: 1963
Music: Jimmy Van Heusen
Words: Sammy Cahn
Recorded: 1/21/63-a
Arranger: Nelson Riddle
Conductor/Band: N. Riddle/studio
orchestra
Key Release: Softly, As I Leave You
see Album Lists: alphabetic by title;
1964 — 8th LP; Reprise/21st

#139   Come Dance with Me
Publication Date: 1958
Music: Jimmy Van Heusen
Words: Sammy Cahn
Recorded: 12/23/58-c
Arranger: Billy May

Conductor/Band: Billy May & his
Orchestra
Key Release: **Come Dance with Me!**
see Album Lists: alphabetic by title;
1959 — 1st LP; Capitol/20th

#140   Come Fly with Me   *1st recording*
Publication Date: 1957
Music: Jimmy Van Heusen
Words: Sammy Cahn
Recorded: 10/8/57-b
Arranger: Billy May
Conductor/Band: Billy May & his
Orchestra
Key Release: **Come Fly with Me**
see Album Lists: alphabetic by title;
1958 — 2nd LP; Capitol/17th

#141   Come Fly with Me   *2nd recording*
Publication Date: 1957
Music: Jimmy Van Heusen
Words: Sammy Cahn
Recorded: 10/11/65-a
Arranger: Billy May
Conductor/Band: Sonny Burke/
studio orchestra
Key Release: **Frank Sinatra: A Man and His Music** (2 discs)
see Album Lists: alphabetic by title;
1965 — 5th LP; Reprise/26th

#142   Come Fly with Me   *3rd recording*
Publication Date: 1957
Music: Jimmy Van Heusen
Words: Sammy Cahn
Recorded: 2/1/66-p
Arranger: Quincy Jones
Conductor/Band: Count Basie & his
Band
Key Release: **Sinatra at the Sands**
(Live Recording — 2 discs)
see Album Lists: alphabetic by title;
1966 — 3rd LP; Reprise/29th

#143   Come Out, Come Out, Wherever You Are
Publication Date: 1944
Music: Jule Styne
Words: Sammy Cahn
Recorded: 5/16/44-b; Sinatra's
"Vimms Vitamins Show" re-
hearsal
Arranger: Axel Stordahl
Conductor/Band: A. Stordahl/radio
orchestra
Key Release: **Frank Sinatra on V-Disc, Volume 1** (English release
only; album of wartime Victory
Discs)
see Album Lists: alphabetic under
"v/disc"; early 1970s; Apex/1st

#144   Come Rain or Come Shine   *1st recording*
Publication Date: 1946
Music: Harold Arlen
Words: Johnny Mercer
Recorded: 6/5/46-a
Arranger: Axel Stordahl
Conductor/Band: A. Stordahl/radio
orchestra
Key Release: **Frank Sinatra on V-Disc** (Japanese release only;
album of wartime Victory
Discs)
see Album Lists: alphabetic under
"v/disc"; early 1970s; Dan/1st

#145   Come Rain or Come Shine   *2nd recording*
Publication Date: 1946
Music: Harold Arlen
Words: Johnny Mercer
Recorded: 11/22/61-a
Arranger: Don Costa
Conductor/Band: D. Costa/studio
orchestra
Key Release: **Sinatra & Strings**
see Album Lists: alphabetic by title;
1962 — 1st LP; Reprise/4th

#146   Come Up to My Place
duet with Betty Garrett
Publication Date: 1944
Music: Leonard Bernstein
Words: Betty Comden & Adolph
Green
Recorded: 1949 — 2nd soundtrack (il-
legally taken from film sound)
Arranger: Conrad Salinger
Conductor/Band: Lenny Hayton/
MGM Orchestra
Key Release: "On the Town" [LP:
"On the Town" & Others]
see Album Lists: alphabetic under
"soundtrack"; mid-1960s; boot-
leg Mv. #13

#147   Come Waltz with Me
Publication Date: 1960
Music: Rube Bloom
Words: Ted Koehler
Recorded: 1/17/62-d
Arranger: Gordon Jenkins
Conductor/Band: G. Jenkins/studio
orchestra
Key Release: All Alone (1972 Japa-
nese version only)
see Album Lists: alphabetic by title;
1962–7th LP; Reprise/8th

#148   Comin' In on a Wing and
a Prayer
Publication Date: 1943
Music: Jimmy McHugh
Words: Harold Adamson
Recorded: 1943 radio — "Songs by
Sinatra"
Arranger: Axel Stordahl
Conductor/Band: A. Stordahl/radio
orchestra
*Key Release: My Best Songs — My
Best Years* (Volume 4)
see Album Lists: alphabetic under
"radio"; early 1970s; Pentagon/
4th

#149   Comme Ci, Comme Ca
«Clopin, Clopant»
Publication Date: 1948
Music: Bruno Coquatrix—1947
Words: Joan Whitney & Alex
Kramer/Pierre Dudan—1947
Recorded: 12/19/48-a
Arranger: Axel Stordahl
Conductor/Band: A. Stordahl/studio
orchestra
*Key Release: The Essential Frank
Sinatra* (Volume 2)
see Album Lists: alphabetic by title;
1967 — 3rd LP; Columbia/35th

#150   The Continental «You
Kiss While You're Dancing»
1st recording
Publication Date: 1934
Music: Con Conrad
Words: Herb Magidson
Recorded: 4/24/50-d
Arranger: George Siravo
Conductor/Band: G. Siravo/studio
orchestra
Key Release: Love Is a Kick
see Album Lists: alphabetic by title;
1960 — 3rd LP; Columbia/28th

#151   The Continental «You
Kiss While You're Dancing»
2nd recording
Publication Date: 1934
Music: Con Conrad
Words: Herb Magidson
Recorded: 1/27/64-e
Arranger: Nelson Riddle
Conductor/Band: N. Riddle/studio
orchestra
*Key Release: Frank Sinatra Sings
"Days of Wine and Roses,"
"Moon River," and Other
Academy Award Winners*
see Album Lists: alphabetic by title;
1964 — 1st LP; Reprise/17th

#152   A Cottage for Sale
Publication Date: 1930
Music: Willard Robison
Words: Larry Conley
Recorded: 3/26/59-c
Arranger: Gordon Jenkins
Conductor/Band: G. Jenkins/studio
   orchestra
Key Release: No One Cares
see Album Lists: alphabetic by title;
   1959 — 5th LP; Capitol/23rd

#153   Could'ja
Publication Date: 1946
Music: Carl Fischer
Words: Bill Carey
Recorded: 5/28/46-d
Arranger: Axel Stordahl
Conductor/Band: A. Stordahl/studio
   orchestra
*Key Release: Sinatra Rarities — The
   Columbia Years* (Volume 1)
see Album Lists: alphabetic by title;
   1986 — 1st LP; Columbia/50th

#154   Count on Me (You
   Can—)   *sung with cast ensemble*
Publication Date: 1949
Music: Roger Edens
Words: Betty Comden & Adolph
   Green
Recorded: 1949 — 2nd soundtrack (il-
   legally taken from film sound)
Arranger: Conrad Salinger
Conductor/Band: Lenny
   Hayton/MGM Orchestra
Key Release: "On the Town" [LP:
   "On the Town" & Others]
see Album Lists: alphabetic under
   "soundtrack"; mid-1960s;
   bootleg Mv. #13

#155   The Cradle Song
   «Lullaby»
Publication Date: 1868
Music: Johannes Brahms
Words: Natalia MacFarren (trans-

lation from anonymous lyric)
Recorded: 12/3/44-b
Arranger: Axel Stordahl
Conductor/Band: A. Stordahl/studio
   orchestra
Key Release: Reflections
see Album Lists: alphabetic by title;
   1961 — 4th LP; Columbia/31st

#156   Crazy Love
Publication Date: 1956
Music: Phil Tuminello
Words: Sammy Cahn
Recorded: 3/14/57-b
Arranger: Nelson Riddle
Conductor/Band: N. Riddle/studio
   orchestra
*Key Release: This Is Sinatra,
   Volume Two*
see Album Lists: alphabetic by title;
   1958 — 4th LP; Capitol/18th

#157   The Curse of an Aching
   Heart
Publication Date: 1913
Music: Al Pientadosi
Words: Henry Fink
Recorded: 5/18/61-a
Arranger: Billy May
Conductor/Band: Billy May & his
   Orchestra
Key Release: Sinatra Swings
   (original title: "Swing Along
   with Me")
see Album Lists: alphabetic by title;
   1961 — 6th LP; Reprise/2nd

#158   Cycles
Publication Date: 1968
Music & Words: Gayle Caldwell
Recorded: 7/24/68-b
Arranger: Don Costa
Conductor/Band: D. Costa/studio
   orchestra
Key Release: Cycles
see Album Lists: alphabetic by title;
   1968 — 6th LP; Reprise/37th

159   Dancing in the Dark
Publication Date: 1931
Music: Arthur Schwartz
Words: Howard Dietz
Recorded: 12/22/58-c
Arranger: Billy May
Conductor/Band: Billy May & his
   Orchestra
*Key Release: **Come Dance with Me!***
see Album Lists: alphabetic by title;
   1959 — 1st LP; Capitol/20th

#160   Dancing on the Ceiling
Publication Date: 1930
Music: Richard Rodgers
Words: Lorenz Hart
Recorded: 2/8/55-a
Arranger: Nelson Riddle
Conductor/Band: N. Riddle/studio
   orchestra
*Key Release: **In the Wee Small
   Hours*** (12″ LP version)
see Album Lists: alphabetic by title;
   1955 — 7th LP; Capitol/5th

#161   Day by Day   *1st recording*
Publication Date: 1945
Music: Axel Stordahl & Paul
   Weston
Words: Sammy Cahn
Recorded: 8/22/45-b
Arranger: Axel Stordahl
Conductor/Band: A. Stordahl/studio
   orchestra
*Key Release: **Come Back to Sorrento***
see Album Lists: alphabetic by title;
   1960 — 5th LP; Columbia/30th

#162   Day by Day   *2nd recording*
Publication Date: 1945
Music: Axel Stordahl & Paul
   Weston
Words: Sammy Cahn
Recorded: 3/20/61-b
Arranger: Billy May
Conductor/Band: B. May/studio
   orchestra

*Key Release: **Come Swing with Me!***
see Album Lists: alphabetic by title;
   1961 — 5th LP; Capitol/30th

#163   Day In — Day Out   *1st
   recording*
Publication Date: 1939
Music: Rube Bloom
Words: Johnny Mercer
Recorded: 3/1/54-a
Arranger: Nelson Riddle
Conductor/Band: N. Riddle/studio
   orchestra
*Key Release: **The Rare Sinatra: Vol-
   ume 1*** (Australian release only)
see Album Lists: alphabetic by title;
   1978 — 1st LP; Capitol/65th

#164   Day In — Day Out   *2nd
   recording*
Publication Date: 1939
Music: Rube Bloom
Words: Johnny Mercer
Recorded: 12/22/58-a
Arranger: Billy May
Conductor/Band: Billy May & his
   Orchestra
*Key Release: **Come Dance with Me!***
see Album Lists: alphabetic by title;
   1959 — 1st LP; Capitol/20th

**#165   A Day in the Life of a
   Fool «Manha de Carnaval»**
Publication Date: 1966
Music: Luis Bonfa — 1959
Words: Carl Sigman/Antonio
   Maria & Francois Lienas — 1959
Recorded: 2/20/69-a
Arranger: Don Costa
Conductor/Band: D. Costa/studio
   orchestra
*Key Release: **My Way***
see Album Lists: alphabetic by title;
   1969 — 1st LP; Reprise/38th

#166   Daybreak   *1st recording*
Publication Date: 1942

Music: Ferde Grofe; from Grofe's
own 1926 "Mississippi Suite"
Words: Harold Adamson
Recorded: 7/1/42-b
Arranger: Axel Stordahl
Conductor/Band: Tommy Dorsey &
his Orchestra
*Key Release: The Dorsey/Sinatra
Sessions* (Volume 6)
see Album Lists: alphabetic by title;
1972 — 6th LP; RCA
Victor/22nd

#167   Daybreak   *2nd recording*
Publication Date: 1942
Music: Ferde Grofe; from Grofe's
own 1926 "Mississippi Suite"
Words: Harold Adamson
Recorded: 5/2/61-c
Arranger: Sy Oliver
Conductor/Band: S. Oliver/studio
orchestra
*Key Release: I Remember
Tommy...*
see Album Lists: alphabetic by title;
1961 — 7th LP; Reprise/3rd

#168   Days of Wine and Roses
Publication Date: 1962
Music: Henry Mancini
Words: Johnny Mercer
Recorded: 1/28/64-d
Arranger: Nelson Riddle
Conductor/Band: N. Riddle/studio
orchestra
*Key Release: Frank Sinatra Sings
"Days of Wine and Roses,"
"Moon River," and other
Academy Award Winners*
see Album Lists: alphabetic by title;
1964 — 1st LP; Reprise/17th

#169   Dear Heart
Publication Date: 1964
Music: Henry Mancini
Words: Jay Livingston & Ray
Evans

Recorded: 10/3/64-c
Arranger: Nelson Riddle
Conductor/Band: N. Riddle/studio
orchestra
Key Release: Softly, As I Leave You
see Album Lists: alphabetic by title;
1964 — 8th LP; Reprise/21st

#170   Dear Little Boy of Mine
Publication Date: 1918
Music: Ernest R. Ball
Words: J. Keirn Brennan
Recorded: 6/28/50-b
Arranger: Mitch Miller
Conductor/Band: M. Miller/studio
orchestra
Key Release: Reflections
see Album Lists: alphabetic by title;
1961 — 4th LP; Columbia/31st

#171   Deep in a Dream
Publication Date: 1938
Music: Jimmy Van Heusen
Words: Eddie DeLange
Recorded: 3/4/55-c
Arranger: Nelson Riddle
Conductor/Band: N. Riddle/studio
orchestra
*Key Release: In the Wee Small
Hours* (12" LP version)
see Album Lists: alphabetic by title;
1955 — 7th LP; Capitol/5th

#172   Deep Night
Publication Date: 1929
Music: Charles Henderson
Words: Rudy Vallee
Recorded: 7/9/51-c
Arranger: Ray Conniff
Conductor/Band: Harry James & his
Orchestra
Key Release: Love Is a Kick
see Album Lists: alphabetic by title;
1960 — 3rd LP; Columbia/28th

#173   Desafinado «Off Key»
duet with Antonio Carlos Jobim

Publication Date: 1962
Music: Antonio Carlos Jobim —
1959
Words: Jon Hendricks & Jessie
Cavanaugh/Newton Men-
donca — 1959
Recorded: 2/12/69-b
Arranger: Eumir Deodato
Conductor/Band: Morris Stoloff/
studio orchestra
Key Release: **The Unissued Sinatra**
(illegal; from Reprise masters)
see Album Lists: alphabetic under
"bootleg"; early 1980s; bootleg
Alb. #4

#174   Devil May Care
Publication Date: 1940
Music: Harry Warren
Words: Johnny Burke
Recorded: 3/29/40-c
Arranger: Dorsey "house" arrng:
T. Dorsey, S. Oliver, F. Stulce,
P. Weston
Conductor/Band: Tommy Dorsey &
his Orchestra
Key Release: **The Dorsey/Sinatra
Sessions** (Volume 1)
see Album Lists: alphabetic by title;
1972 — 1st LP; RCA Victor/17th

#175   Didn't We?
Publication Date: 1967
Music & Words: James Webb
Recorded: 2/13/69-e
Arranger: Don Costa
Conductor/Band: D. Costa/studio
orchestra
Key Release: **My Way**
see Album Lists: alphabetic by title;
1969 — 1st LP; Reprise/38th

#176   Dig Down Deep
Publication Date: 1942
Music: Gerald Marks
Words: Walter Hirsch & Sano
Marco; lyric promoting war

bonds
Recorded: 6/17/42-b
Arranger: Dorsey "house" arrng:
T. Dorsey, S. Oliver, F. Stulce,
P. Weston
Conductor/Band: Tommy Dorsey &
his Orchestra
Key Release: **The Dorsey/Sinatra
Sessions** (Volume 6)
see Album Lists: alphabetic by title;
1972 — 6th LP; RCA Victor/
22nd

#177   Dindi
Publication Date: 1965
Music: Antonio Carlos Jobim
Words: Ray Gilbert & Aloysio
(Louis) Oliveira
Recorded: 1/30/67-c
Arranger: Claus Ogerman
Conductor/Band: C. Ogerman/studio
orchestra
Key Release: **Francis Albert Sinatra
& Antonio Carlos Jobim**
see Album Lists: alphabetic by title;
1967 — 1st LP; Reprise/31st

#178   Do I Worry?
Publication Date: 1941
Music & Words: Bobby Worth &
Stanley Cowan
Recorded: 2/7/41-a
Arranger: Dorsey "house" arrng:
T. Dorsey, S. Oliver, F. Stulce,
P. Weston
Conductor/Band: Tommy Dorsey &
his Orchestra
Key Release: **The Dorsey/Sinatra
Sessions** (Volume 4)
see Album Lists: alphabetic by title;
1972 — 4th LP; RCA Victor/20th

#179   Do You Know Why?
Publication Date: 1940
Music: Jimmy Van Heusen
Words: Johnny Burke
Recorded: 10/16/40-a

Arranger: Dorsey "house" arrng:
T. Dorsey, S. Oliver, F. Stulce,
P. Weston
Conductor/Band: Tommy Dorsey &
his Orchestra
*Key Release: The Dorsey/Sinatra
Sessions* (Volume 3)
see Album Lists: alphabetic by title;
1972 — 3rd LP; RCA Victor/19th

#180   Dolores
Publication Date: 1941
Music: Louis Alter
Words: Frank Loesser
Recorded: 1/20/41-b
Arranger: Sy Oliver
Conductor/Band: Tommy Dorsey &
his Orchestra
*Key Release: The Dorsey/Sinatra
Sessions* (Volume 4)
see Album Lists: alphabetic by title;
1972 — 4th LP; RCA Victor/20th

#181   Don'cha Go 'Way Mad
Publication Date: 1950
Music: Jimmy Mundy — 1941/Il-
linois Jacquet
Words: Al Stillman
Recorded: 4/11/62-d
Arranger: Neal Hefti
Conductor/Band: N. Hefti/studio
orchestra
*Key Release: Sinatra and Swingin'
Brass*
see Album Lists: alphabetic by title;
1962 — 4th LP; Reprise/5th

#182   Don't Be a Do-Badder
sung with Bing Crosby, Dean Mar-
tin and Sammy Davis Jr.
Publication Date: 1964
Music: Jimmy Van Heusen
Words: Sammy Cahn
Recorded: 4/10/64-c
Arranger: Nelson Riddle
Conductor/Band: N. Riddle/studio
orchestra

*Key Release: "Robin and the 7
Hoods"* (Official Soundtrack LP)
see Album Lists: alphabetic by title;
1964 — 6th LP; Reprise/20th

#183   Don't Be That Way
Publication Date: 1937
Music: Edgar Sampson/Benny
Goodman
Words: Mitchell Parish
Recorded: 5/19/61-a
Arranger: Billy May
Conductor/Band: Billy May & his
Orchestra
Key Release: Sinatra Swings (origi-
nal title: "Swing Along with
Me")
see Album Lists: alphabetic by title;
1961 — 6th LP; Reprise/2nd

#184   Don't Change Your Mind About Me
Publication Date: 1954
Music: Lenny Adelson
Words: Imogene Carpenter
Recorded: 9/23/54-a
Arranger: Nelson Riddle
Conductor/Band: N. Riddle/studio
orchestra
Key Release: 45rpm single #3050
see Album List #1: 1954 Capitol (5)
single record — listed by num-
ber

#185   Don't Cry Joe (Let Her Go, Let Her Go, Let Her Go)
1st recording
Publication Date: 1949
Music & Words: Joe Marsala
Recorded: 7/10/49-c
Arranger: Hugo Winterhalter
Conductor/Band: H. Winterhalter/
studio orchestra
Key Release: That Old Feeling
see Album Lists: alphabetic by title;
1956 — 2nd LP; Columbia/23rd

186   Don't Cry Joe (Let Her Go, Let Her Go, Let Her Go)
2nd recording
Publication Date: 1949
Music & Words: Joe Marsala
Recorded: 5/23/61-a
Arranger: Billy May
Conductor/Band: Billy May & his Orchestra
Key Release: **Sinatra Swings** (original title: "Swing Along with Me")
see Album Lists: alphabetic by title; 1961 — 6th LP; Reprise/2nd

#187   Don't Ever Be Afraid to Go Home
Publication Date: 1952
Music: Carl Sigman
Words: Bob Hilliard
Recorded: 2/6/52-c
Arranger: Axel Stordahl
Conductor/Band: A. Stordahl/studio orchestra
Key Release: 45rpm single #4-39687
see Album List #1: 1952 Columbia (5) single record — listed by number

#188   Don't Ever Go Away «Por Causa de Voce»
Publication Date: 1964
Music: Antonio Carlos Jobim
Words: Ray Gilbert & O. Duran
Recorded: 2/11/69-b
Arranger: Eumir Deodato
Conductor/Band: Morris Stoloff/studio orchestra
Key Release: **Sinatra & Company**
see Album Lists: alphabetic by title; 1971 — 2nd LP; Reprise/42nd

#189   Don't Forget Tonight, Tomorrow   *1st recording*
Publication Date: 1945
Music & Words: Jay Milton & Ukie Sherin

Recorded: 5/16/45-b
Arranger: Axel Stordahl
Conductor/Band: A. Stordahl/studio orchestra
Key Release: 78rpm single #36854, side B
see Album List #1: 1945 Columbia (4) single record — listed by number

#190   Don't Forget Tonight, Tomorrow   *2nd recording*
Publication Date: 1945
Music & Words: Jay Milton & Ukie Sherin
Recorded: 1945 radio — "The Frank Sinatra Old Gold Show"
Arranger: Axel Stordahl
Conductor/Band: A. Stordahl/radio orchestra
Key Release: **My Best Songs — My Best Years** (Volume 4)
see Album Lists: alphabetic under "radio"; early 1970s; Pentagon/4th

#191   Don't Like Goodbyes
Publication Date: 1955
Music: Harold Arlen
Words: Truman Capote
Recorded: 3/8/56-a
Arranger: Nelson Riddle
Conductor/Band: N. Riddle with orchestra & the Hollywood String Quartet
Key Release: **Close to You**
see Album Lists: alphabetic by title; 1957 — 1st LP; Capitol/11th

#192   Don't Make a Beggar of Me
Publication Date: 1953
Music & Words: Al Sherman
Recorded: 4/2/53-c
Arranger: Axel Stordahl
Conductor/Band: A. Stordahl/studio orchestra

Key Release: **Forever Frank**
see Album Lists: alphabetic by title;
1966 — 4th LP; Capitol/36th

#193   Don't Sleep in the Subway

Publication Date: 1967
Music & Words: Tony Hatch &
Jackie Trent
Recorded: 7/24/67-d
Arranger: Ernie Freeman
Conductor/Band: E. Freeman/studio
orchestra
Key Release: **Frank Sinatra &**
Frank and Nancy
see Album Lists: alphabetic by title;
1967 — 5th LP; Reprise/32nd

#194   Don't Take Your Love
from Me   *1st recording*

Publication Date: 1941
Music & Words: Henry Nemo
Recorded: 3/20/61-d
Arranger: Heinie Beau
Conductor/Band: Billy May/studio
orchestra
Key Release: **Come Swing with Me!**
see Album Lists: alphabetic by title;
1961 — 5th LP; Capitol/30th

#195   Don't Take Your Love
from Me   *2nd recording*

Publication Date: 1941
Music & Words: Henry ·Nemo
Recorded: 11/21/61-d
Arranger: Don Costa
Conductor/Band: D. Costa/studio
orchestra
Key Release: **Sinatra & Strings**
(1972 Japanese version only)
see Album Lists: alphabetic by title;
1962 — 1st LP; Reprise/4th

#196   Don't Wait Too Long

Publication Date: 1949
Music & Words: Sunny Skylar
Recorded: 4/13/65-a

Arranger: Gordon Jenkins
Conductor/Band: G. Jenkins/studio
orchestra
Key Release: **September of My Years**
see Album Lists: alphabetic by title;
1965 — 1st LP; Reprise/23rd

#197   Don't Worry 'Bout Me
1st recording

Publication Date: 1939
Music: Rube Bloom
Words: Ted Koehler
Recorded: 4/30/53-b
Arranger: Nelson Riddle
Conductor/Band: N. Riddle/studio
orchestra
Key Release: **This Is Sinatra** (Volume 1)
see Album Lists: alphabetic by title;
1956 — 6th LP; Capitol/10th

#198   Don't Worry 'Bout Me
2nd recording

Publication Date: 1939
Music: Rube Bloom
Words: Ted Koehler
Recorded: 2/1/66-i
Arranger: Quincy Jones
Conductor/Band: Count Basie & his
Band
Key Release: **Sinatra at the Sands**
(Live Recording — 2 discs)
see Album Lists: alphabetic by title;
1966 — 3rd LP; Reprise/29th

#199   Downtown

Publication Date: 1964
Music & Words: Tony Hatch
Recorded: 5/16/66-e
Arranger: Nelson Riddle
Conductor/Band: N. Riddle/studio
orchestra
Key Release: **Strangers in the Night**
see Album Lists: alphabetic by title;
1966 — 1st LP; Reprise/27th

#200   Dream   *1st recording*
Publication Date: 1945

Music & Words: Johnny Mercer
Recorded: 3/6/45-c
Arranger: Axel Stordahl
Conductor/Band: A. Stordahl/studio
orchestra
Key Release: **Put Your Dreams
Away**
see Album Lists: alphabetic by title;
1958 — 3rd LP; Columbia/26th

#201   Dream   *2nd recording*
Publication Date: 1945
Music & Words: Johnny Mercer
Recorded: 3/3/60-a
Arranger: Nelson Riddle
Conductor/Band: N. Riddle/studio
orchestra
Key Release: **Nice 'n' Easy**
see Album Lists: alphabetic by title;
1960 — 2nd LP; Capitol/25th

#202   Dream Away
Publication Date: 1973
Music: John Williams
Words: Paul Williams
Recorded: 8/20/73-b
Arranger: Don Costa
Conductor/Band: Gordon Jenkins/
studio orchestra
Key Release: **Ol' Blue Eyes Is Back**
see Album Lists: alphabetic by title;
1973 — 2nd LP; Reprise/45th

#203   Drinking Again
Publication Date: 1966
Music: Doris Tauber
Words: Johnny Mercer
Recorded: 2/1/67-c
Arranger: Claus Ogerman
Conductor/Band: C. Ogerman/studio
orchestra
Key Release: **Frank Sinatra &
Frank and Nancy**
see Album Lists: alphabetic by title;
1967 — 5th LP; Reprise/32nd

**#204   Drinking Water «Aqua de
Beber»**   *duet with Antonio Carlos
Jobim*
Publication Date: 1963
Music: Antonio Carlos Jobim
Words: Norman Gimbel/Vincius
De Moraes
Recorded: 2/12/69-c
Arranger: Eumir Deodato
Conductor/Band: Morris Stoloff/
studio orchestra
Key Release: **Sinatra & Company**
see Album Lists: alphabetic by title;
1971-2nd LP; Reprise/42nd

#205   Dry Your Eyes
Publication Date: 1976
Music: Neil Diamond
Words: Jaime Robbie Robertson
Recorded: 9/27/76-a
Arranger: Don Costa
Conductor/Band: Bill Miller/studio
orchestra
Key Release: **The Singles** (Italian
release only)
see Album Lists: alphabetic by title;
1982 — 6th LP; Reprise/61st

**#206   The Dum Dot Song «I
Put the Penny in the Gum
Slot»**
Publication Date: 1946
Music & Words: Julian Kay
Recorded: 11/7/46-a
Arranger: Axel Stordahl
Conductor/Band: A. Stordahl/studio
orchestra
Key Release: 78rpm single #37966
see Album List #1: 1947 Columbia
(4) single record — listed by
number

**#207   East of the Sun (And
West of the Moon)**   *1st recording*
Publication Date: 1934
Music & Words: Brooks Bowman
Recorded: 4/23/40-b

Arranger: Sy Oliver
Conductor/Band: Tommy Dorsey &
his Orchestra
Key Release: **The Dorsey/Sinatra
Sessions** (Volume 2)
see Album Lists: alphabetic by Title;
1972 — 2nd LP; RCA Victor/18th

**#208   East of the Sun (And West
of the Moon)**   *2nd recording*
Publication Date: 1934
Music & Words: Brooks Bowman
Recorded: 5/3/61-e
Arranger: Sy Oliver
Conductor/Band: S. Oliver/studio
orchestra
Key Release: **I Remember Tommy . . .**
see Album Lists: alphabetic by title;
1961 — 7th LP; Reprise/3rd

**#209   Easy to Love (You'd Be
So—)**
Publication Date: 1936
Music & Words: Cole Porter
Recorded: 12/19/60-f
Arranger: Johnny Mandel
Conductor/Band: J. Mandel/studio
orchestra
Key Release: **Ring-a-Ding Ding!**
see Album Lists: alphabetic by title;
1961 — 3rd LP; Reprise/1st

#210   Ebb Tide
Publication Date: 1953
Music: Robert Maxwell
Words: Carl Sigman
Recorded: 5/29/58-b
Arranger: Nelson Riddle
Conductor/Band: Felix Slatkin/studio
orchestra
Key Release: **Frank Sinatra Sings
for Only the Lonely**
see Album Lists: alphabetic by title;
1958 — 5th LP; Capitol/19th

#211   Elizabeth
Publication Date: 1969
Music & Words: Bob Gaudio &

Jake Holmes
Recorded: 7/15/69-b
Arranger: Charles Calello
Conductor/Band: C. Calello/studio
orchestra
Key Release: **Watertown [a love
story]**
see Album Lists: alphabetic by title;
1970 — 1st LP; Reprise/40th

#212   Embraceable You   *1st
recording*
Publication Date: 1930
Music: George Gershwin
Words: Ira Gershwin
Recorded: 12/19/44-a
Arranger: Axel Stordahl
Conductor/Band: A. Stordahl/studio
orchestra
Key Release: **Come Back to Sorrento**
see Album Lists: alphabetic by title;
1960 — 5th LP; Columbia/30th

#213   Embraceable You   *2nd
recording*
Publication Date: 1930
Music: George Gershwin
Words: Ira Gershwin
Recorded: 3/3/60-c
Arranger: Nelson Riddle
Conductor/Band: N. Riddle/studio
orchestra
Key Release: **Nice 'n' Easy**
see Album Lists: alphabetic by title;
1960 — 2nd LP; Capitol/25th

#214   Emily   *1st recording*
Publication Date: 1964
Music: Johnny Mandel
Words: Johnny Mercer
Recorded: 10/3/64-b
Arranger: Nelson Riddle
Conductor/Band: N. Riddle/studio
orchestra
Key Release: **Softly, As I Leave You**
see Album Lists: alphabetic by title;
1964 — 8th LP; Reprise/21st

#215   Emily   *2nd recording*
Publication Date: 1964
Music: Johnny Mandel
Words: Johnny Mercer
Recorded: 3/9/77-c
Arranger: Nelson Riddle
Conductor/Band: N. Riddle/studio
  orchestra
Key Release: Frank's Girls (illegal;
  from Reprise masters)
see Album Lists: alphabetic under
  "bootleg"; early 1980s; bootleg
  Alb. #5

#216   Empty Is
Publication Date: 1969
Music & Words: Rod McKuen
Recorded: 3/19/69-b
Arranger: Don Costa
Conductor/Band: D. Costa/studio
  orchestra
Key Release: A Man Alone
see Album Lists: alphabetic by title;
  1969 — 3rd LP; Reprise/39th

#217   Empty Tables   *1st recording*
Publication Date: 1973
Music: Jimmy Van Heusen
Words: Johnny Mercer
Recorded: 6/22/73-a
Arranger: Gordon Jenkins
Conductor/Band: G. Jenkins/studio
  orchestra
Key Release: I Sing the Songs
  (Italian release only)
see Album Lists: alphabetic by title;
  1982 — 5th LP; Reprise/60th

218   Empty Tables   *2nd recording*
Publication Date: 1973
Music: Jimmy Van Heusen
Words: Johnny Mercer
Recorded: 2/5/76-b
Arranger: Don Costa
Conductor/Band: Bill Miller/studio
  orchestra
Key Release: Portrait of Sinatra [40

Songs in the Life of a Man]
  (English release only — 2 discs)
see Album Lists: alphabetic by title;
  1979 — 1st LP; Reprise/51st

#219   The End of a Love Affair
Publication Date: 1950
Music & Words: Edward C.
  Redding
Recorded: 4/5/56-a
Arranger: Nelson Riddle
Conductor/Band: N. Riddle with or-
  chestra & the Hollywood String
  Quartet
Key Release: Close to You
see Album Lists: alphabetic by title;
  1957 — 1st LP — Capitol/11th

#220   Ever Homeward
Publication Date: 1947
Music: Jule Styne; from K.
  Lubomirski
Words: Sammy Cahn (Polish and
  English)
Recorded: 12/8/47-c
Arranger: Axel Stordahl
Conductor/Band: A. Stordahl/studio
  orchestra
*Key Release: Frank Sinatra in
  Hollywood, 1943–1949*
see Album Lists: alphabetic by title;
  1968 — 1st LP; Columbia/38th

#221   Evergreen
Publication Date: 1976
Music: Barbra Streisand
Words: Paul Williams
Recorded: 11/12/76-b
Arranger: Nelson Riddle
Conductor/Band: N. Riddle/studio
  orchestra
Key Release: Late Sinatra Goodies
  (illegal; from Reprise masters)
see Album Lists: alphabetic under
  "bootleg"; mid–1980s; bootleg
  Alb. #6

#222   Every Day of My Life
Publication Date: 1939
Music: Harry James & Morty Berk
Words: Billy Hays & Morty Berk
Recorded: 11/8/39-b
Arranger: Andy Gibson
Conductor/Band: Harry James & his
  Orchestra
Key Release: 78rpm single #35531
see Album List #1: 1943 Columbia
  (2) single record—listed by
  number

#223   Every Man Should Marry
Publication Date: 1948
Music: Abner Silver
Words: Benny Davis
Recorded: 7/21/49-b
Arranger: Morris Stoloff
Conductor/Band: M. Stoloff/studio
  orchestra
Key Release: 78rpm single #38572
see Album List #1: 1949 Columbia
  (4) single record—listed by
  number

**#224   Everybody Has the Right
  to Be Wrong**
Publication Date: 1965
Music: Jimmy Van Heusen
Words: Sammy Cahn
Recorded: 8/23/65-a
Arranger: Torry Zito
Conductor/Band: T. Zito/studio
  orchestra
Key Release: **My Kind of Broadway**
see Album Lists: alphabetic by title;
  1965—4th LP; Reprise/25th

**#225   Everybody Loves Some-
  body** *1st recording*
Publication Date: 1947
Music: Ken Lane
Words: Irving Taylor
Recorded: 12/4/47-c
Arranger: Axel Stordahl
Conductor/Band: A. Stordahl/studio
  orchestra

Key Release: **The Essential Frank
  Sinatra (Volume 2)**
see Album Lists: alphabetic by title;
  1967—3rd LP; Columbia/35th

**#226 Everybody Loves Some-
  body** *2nd recording*
Publication Date: 1947
Music: Ken Lane
Words: Irving Taylor
Recorded: 11/25/57-b
Arranger: Nelson Riddle
Conductor/Band: N. Riddle/studio
  orchestra
Key Release: **This Is Sinatra, Vol-
  ume Two**
see Album Lists: alphabetic by title;
  1958—4th LP; Capitol/18th

**#227   Everybody Ought to Be
  in Love**
Publication Date: 1977
Music & Words: Paul Anka
Recorded: 2/16/77-c
Arranger: Charles Calello
Conductor/Band: C. Calello/studio
  orchestra
Key Release: **The Singles** (Italian
  release only)
see Album Lists: alphabetic by title;
  1982—6th LP; Reprise/61st

#228   Everybody's Twistin'
Publication Date: 1961
Music: Rube Bloom
Words: Ted Koehler
Recorded: 2/27/62-a
Arranger: Neal Hefti
Conductor/Band: N. Hefti/studio
  orchestra
Key Release: **The Voice: Volume 1**
  (Italian release only)
see Album Lists: alphabetic by title;
  1982—1st LP; Reprise/56th

**#229   Everything Happens to
  Me** *1st recording*
Publication Date: 1941

Music: Matt Dennis
Words: Tom Adair
Recorded: 2/7/41-b
Arranger: Dorsey "house" arrng:
    T. Dorsey, S. Oliver, F. Stulce,
    P. Weston
Conductor/Band: Tommy Dorsey &
    his Orchestra
*Key Release: The Dorsey/Sinatra
    Sessions* (Volume 4)
see Album Lists: alphabetic by title;
    1972 — 4th LP; RCA Victor/20th

**#230   Everything Happens to
    Me** *2nd recording*
Publication Date: 1941
Music: Matt Dennis
Words: Tom Adair
Recorded: 4/4/56-c
Arranger: Nelson Riddle
Conductor/Band: N. Riddle with or-
    chestra & the Hollywood String
    Quartet
Key Release: Close to You
see Album Lists: alphabetic by title;
    1957 — 1st LP; Capitol/11th

**#231   Everything Happens to
    Me** *3rd recording*
Publication Date: 1941
Music: Matt Dennis
Words: Tom Adair
Recorded: 4/8/81-b
Arranger: Nelson Riddle
Conductor/Band: Vinnie Falcone/
    studio orchestra
Key Release: Late Sinatra Goodies
    (illegal; from Reprise masters)
see Album Lists: alphabetic under
    "bootleg"; mid-1980s; bootleg
    Alb. #6

#232   Exactly Like You
Publication Date: 1930
Music: Jimmy McHugh
Words: Dorothy Fields
Recorded: 1944 radio — Sinatra's

"Vimms Vitamins Show"
Arranger: Axel Stordahl
Conductor/Band: A. Stordahl/radio
    orchestra
*Key Release: Frank Sinatra —
    Through the Years: 1944–1966*
see Album Lists: alphabetic under
    "television"; mid-1960s; Ajazz/1st

#233   The Fable of the Rose
Publication Date: 1940
Music: Josef Myrow
Words: Bickley Reichner
Recorded: 3/12/40-a
Arranger: Axel Stordahl
Conductor/Band: Tommy Dorsey &
    his Orchestra
*Key Release: The Dorsey/Sinatra
    Sessions* (Volume 1)
see Album Lists: alphabetic by title;
    1972 — 1st LP; RCA Victor/17th

#234   Fairy Tale
Publication Date: 1955
Music: Jerry Livingston
Words: Dak Stanford
Recorded: 7/29/55-b
Arranger: Nelson Riddle
Conductor/Band: N. Riddle/studio
    orchestra
Key Release: Look to Your Heart
see Album Lists: alphabetic by title;
    1959 — 4th LP; Capitol/22nd

#235   Faithful
Publication Date: 1950
Music: Andy Ackers
Words: Sunny Skylar
Recorded: 1/16/51-a
Arranger: Axel Stordahl
Conductor/Band: A. Stordahl/studio
    orchestra
Key Release: 45rpm single #39213
see Album List #1: 1951 Columbia (5)
    single record — listed by number

**#236   Falling in Love with
    Love** *1st recording*

Publication Date: 1938
Music: Richard Rodgers
Words: Lorenz Hart
Recorded: 8/8/46-d
Arranger: Axel Stordahl
Conductor/Band: A. Stordahl/studio
orchestra
Key Release: **Frankie**
see Album Lists: alphabetic by title;
1955 — 8th LP; Columbia/20th

**#237   Falling in Love with
Love**   *2nd recording*
Publication Date: 1938
Music: Richard Rodgers
Words: Lorenz Hart
Recorded: 5/19/61-c
Arranger: Billy May
Conductor/Band: Billy May & his
Orchestra
Key Release: **Sinatra Swings** (origi-
nal title: "Swing Along with
Me")
see Album Lists: alphabetic by title;
1961 — 6th LP; Reprise/2nd

**#238   Farewell, Farewell to
Love**
Publication Date: 1951
Music: Jack Wolf
Words: George Siravo
Recorded: 7/9/51-b
Arranger: Ray Conniff
Conductor/Band: Harry James & his
Orchestra
Key Release: **Love Is a Kick**
see Album Lists: alphabetic by title;
1960 — 3rd LP; Columbia/28th

#239   A Fella with an Umbrella
Publication Date: 1947
Music & Words: Irving Berlin
Recorded: 3/16/48-b
Arranger: Axel Stordahl
Conductor/Band: A. Stordahl/studio
orchestra
Key Release: 78rpm single #38192

see Album List #1: 1948 Columbia
(4) single record — listed by
number

#240   A Fellow Needs a Girl
Publication Date: 1947
Music: Richard Rodgers
Words: Oscar Hammerstein II
Recorded: 8/17/47-b
Arranger: Axel Stordahl
Conductor/Band: A. Stordahl/studio
orchestra
Key Release: **That Old Feeling**
see Album Lists: alphabetic by title;
1956 — 2nd LP; Columbia/
23rd

#241   A Fine Romance
Publication Date: 1936
Music: Jerome Kern
Words: Dorothy Fields
Recorded: 12/19/60-g
Arranger: Johnny Mandel
Conductor/Band: J. Mandel/studio
orchestra
Key Release: **Ring-a-Ding Ding!**
see Album Lists: alphabetic by title;
1961 — 3rd LP; Reprise/1st

#242   The First Noel
Publication Date: 1600s
Music & Words: traditional; France
in the 1600s
Recorded: 7/16/57-b
Arranger: Gordon Jenkins
Conductor/Band: G. Jenkins/studio
orchestra
Key Release: **A Jolly Christmas from
Frank Sinatra**
see Album Lists: alphabetic by title;
1957 — 6th LP; Capitol/14th

#243   Five Hundred Guys
Publication Date: 1956
Music: Donald Canton
Words: Ira Kosloff
Recorded: 4/9/56-b
Arranger: Nelson Riddle

Conductor/Band: N. Riddle/studio orchestra
Key Release: **Forever Frank**
see Album Lists: alphabetic by title; 1966 — 4th LP; Capitol/36th

#244 Five Minutes More *1st recording*
Publication Date: 1946
Music: Jule Styne
Words: Sammy Cahn
Recorded: 5/28/46-e
Arranger: Axel Stordahl
Conductor/Band: A. Stordahl/studio orchestra
Key Release: **Love Is a Kick**
see Album Lists: alphabetic by title; 1960 — 3rd LP; Columbia/28th

#245 Five Minutes More *2nd recording*
Publication Date: 1946
Music: Jule Styne
Words: Sammy Cahn
Recorded: 3/22/61-a
Arranger: Billy May
Conductor/Band: B. May/studio orchestra
Key Release: **Come Swing with Me!**
see Album Lists: alphabetic by title; 1961 — 5th LP; Capitol/30th

#246 Flowers Mean Forgiveness
Publication Date: 1956
Music & Words: Al Frisch & Edward R. White & Mack Wolfson
Recorded: 1/12/56-c
Arranger: Nelson Riddle
Conductor/Band: N. Riddle/studio orchestra
Key Release: **Forever Frank**
see Album Lists: alphabetic by title; 1966 — 4th LP; Capitol/36th

#247 Fly Me to the Moon «In Other Words» *1st recording*
Publication Date: 1954
Music & Words: Bart Howard

Recorded: 6/9/64-d
Arranger: Quincy Jones
Conductor/Band: Count Basie & his Band
Key Release: **It Might as Well Be Swing**
see Album Lists: alphabetic by title; 1964 — 5th LP; Reprise/19th

#248 Fly Me to the Moon «In Other Words» *2nd recording*
Publication Date: 1954
Music & Words: Bart Howard
Recorded: 2/1/66-l
Arranger: Quincy Jones
Conductor/Band: Count Basie & his Band
Key Release: **Sinatra at the Sands** (Live Recording — 2 discs)
see Album Lists: alphabetic by title; 1966 — 3rd LP; Reprise/29th

#249 A Foggy Day *1st recording*
Publication Date: 1937
Music: George Gershwin
Words: Ira Gershwin
Recorded: 11/5/53-a
Arranger: Nelson Riddle: full-orch. arrng. from G. Siravo band arrng.
Conductor/Band: N. Riddle/studio orchestra
Key Release: **Songs for Young Lovers** (original 10" LP)
see Album Lists: alphabetic by title; 1954 — 1st LP; Capitol/2nd

#250 A Foggy Day *2nd recording*
Publication Date: 1937
Music: George Gershwin
Words: Ira Gershwin
Recorded: 12/19/60-d
Arranger: Johnny Mandel
Conductor/Band: J. Mandel/studio orchestra
Key Release: **Ring-a-Ding Ding!**

see Album Lists: alphabetic by title; 1961-3rd LP; Reprise/1st

#251   Follow Me
Publication Date: 1960
Music: Frederick Loewe
Words: Alan Jay Lerner
Recorded: 12/12/67-b
Arranger: Billy May
Conductor/Band: Duke Ellington & his Band
Key Release: Francis A. & Edward K.
see Album Lists: alphabetic by title; 1968 — 2nd LP; Reprise/33rd

#252   Fools Rush In (Where Angels Fear to Tread)   *1st recording*
Publication Date: 1940
Music: Rube Bloom
Words: Johnny Mercer
Recorded: 3/29/40-b
Arranger: Dorsey "house" arrng: T. Dorsey, S. Oliver, F. Stulce, P. Weston
Conductor/Band: Tommy Dorsey & his Orchestra
Key Release: The Dorsey/Sinatra Sessions (Volume 1)
see Album Lists: alphabetic by title; 1972 — 1st LP; RCA Victor/17th

#253   Fools Rush In (Where Angels Fear to Tread)   *2nd recording*
Publication Date: 1940
Music: Rube Bloom
Words: Johnny Mercer
Recorded: 10/31/47-c
Arranger: Axel Stordahl
Conductor/Band: A. Stordahl/studio orchestra
Key Release: The Voice
see Album Lists: alphabetic by title; 1955 — 9th LP; Columbia/21st

#254   Fools Rush In (Where Angels Fear to Tread)   *3rd recording*
Publication Date: 1940
Music: Rube Bloom
Words: Johnny Mercer
Recorded: 3/1/60-b
Arranger: Nelson Riddle
Conductor/Band: N. Riddle/studio orchestra
Key Release: Nice 'n' Easy
see Album Lists: alphabetic by title; 1960 — 2nd LP; Capitol/25th

#255   For a While
Publication Date: 1969
Music & Words: Bob Gaudio & Jake Holmes
Recorded: 7/17/69-a
Arranger: Charles Calello
Conductor/Band: C. Calello/studio orchestra
Key Release: Watertown [a love story]
see Album Lists: alphabetic by title; 1970 — 1st LP; Reprise/40th

#256   For Every Man There's a Woman
Publication Date: 1947
Music: Harold Arlen
Words: Leo Robin
Recorded: 12/28/47-d
Arranger: Axel Stordahl
Conductor/Band: A. Stordahl/studio orchestra
Key Release: That Old Feeling
see Album Lists: alphabetic by title; 1956 — 2nd LP; Columbia/23rd

#257   For Once in My Life
Publication Date: 1965
Music: Orlando Murden
Words: Ronald Miller
Recorded: 2/24/69-b
Arranger: Don Costa

Conductor/Band: D. Costa/studio
orchestra
*Key Release: **My Way***
see Album Lists: alphabetic by title;
1969 — 1st LP; Reprise/38th

#258   For the Good Times   *duet*
with Eileen Farrell
Publication Date: 1968
Music & Words: Kris Kristofferson
Recorded: 8/21/79-a
Arranger: Don Costa
Conductor/Band: D. Costa/studio
orchestra
*Key Release: **Trilogy: The Present
[Some Very Good Years]***
see Album Lists: alphabetic by title;
1980 — 2nd LP; Reprise/53rd

#259   Forget Domani
Publication Date: 1965
Music: Riziero Ortolani
Words: Norman Newell
Recorded: 5/6/65-a
Arranger: Ernie Freeman
Conductor/Band: E. Freeman/studio
orchestra
*Key Release: **Frank Sinatra's Great-
est Hits*** (Volume 1)
see Album Lists: alphabetic by title;
1968 — 3rd LP; Reprise/34th

#260   Forget to Remember
Publication Date: 1969
Music & Words: Teddy Randazzo
& Victoria Pike
Recorded: 8/18/69-a
Arranger: Don Costa
Conductor/Band: D. Costa/studio
orchestra
*Key Release: **The Voice: Volume 3***
(Italian release only)
see Album Lists: alphabetic by title;
1982 — 3rd LP; Reprise/58th

#261   Free for All
Publication Date: 1939
Music & Words: Bobby Shorter

Recorded: 6/27/41-d
Arranger: Dorsey "house" arrng:
T. Dorsey, S. Oliver, F. Stulce,
P. Weston
Conductor/Band: Tommy Dorsey &
his Orchestra
*Key Release: **The Dorsey/Sinatra
Sessions*** (Volume 5)
see Album Lists: alphabetic by title;
1972 — 5th LP; RCA Victor/21st

#262   French Foreign Legion
Publication Date: 1958
Music: Guy Wood
Words: Aaron Schroeder
Recorded: 12/29/58-d
Arranger: Nelson Riddle
Conductor/Band: N. Riddle/studio
orchestra
*Key Release: **All the Way***
see Album Lists: alphabetic by title;
1961 — 2nd LP; Capitol/29th

#263   A Friend of Yours
Publication Date: 1944
Music: Jimmy Van Heusen
Words: Johnny Burke
Recorded: 3/6/45-d
Arranger: Axel Stordahl
Conductor/Band: A. Stordahl/studio
orchestra
*Key Release: **The Essential Frank
Sinatra*** (Volume 1)
see Album Lists: alphabetic by title;
1967 — 2nd LP; Columbia/34th

**#264   From Both Sides, Now
«Clouds»**
Publication Date: 1967
Music & Words: Joni Mitchell
Recorded: 11/14/68-c
Arranger: Don Costa
Conductor/Band: Bill Miller/studio
orchestra
*Key Release: **Cycles***
see Album Lists: alphabetic by title;
1968 — 6th LP; Reprise/37th

#265   From Here to Eternity
Publication Date: 1953
Music: Fred Karger
Words: Robert Wells
Recorded: 5/2/53-c
Arranger: Nelson Riddle
Conductor/Band: N. Riddle/studio
   orchestra
Key Release: This Is Sinatra!
   (Volume 1)
see Album Lists: alphabetic by title;
   1956 — 6th LP; Capitol/10th

**#266   From Promise to Prom-
ise**   *poetry recited to music*
Publication Date: 1969
Music: Rod McKuen (nonvocal
   melody)
Words: Rod McKuen
Recorded: 3/21/69-d
Arranger: Don Costa
Conductor/Band: D. Costa/studio
   orchestra
Key Release: A Man Alone
see Album Lists: alphabetic by title;
   1969 — 3rd LP; Reprise/39th

**#267   From the Bottom of My
Heart**
Publication Date: 1939
Music: Harry James & Morty Berk
Words: Billy Hays & Andy Gibson
Recorded: 7/13/39-a
Arranger: Andy Gibson
Conductor/Band: Harry James & his
   Orchestra
Key Release: 78rpm single #8443,
   side A (first commercial release)
see Album List #1: 1939 Brunswick
   (1) single record — listed by
   number

**#268   From the Bottom to the
Top**
Publication Date: 1955
Music & Words: Gee Wilson
Recorded: 3/7/55-d

Arranger: Dave Cavanaugh
Conductor/Band: Dave Cavanaugh
   & his Band
Key Release: Forever Frank
see Album Lists: alphabetic by title;
   1966 — 4th LP; Capitol/36th

#269   From This Day Forward
Publication Date: 1945
Music & Words: Mort Greene
Recorded: 2/24/46-a
Arranger: Axel Stordahl
Conductor/Band: A. Stordahl/studio
   orchestra
Key Release: 78rpm single #36987
see Album List #1: 1946 Columbia
   (4) single record — listed by
   number

#270   From This Moment On
Publication Date: 1948
Music & Words: Cole Porter
Recorded: 11/28/56-b
Arranger: Nelson Riddle
Conductor/Band: N. Riddle/studio
   orchestra
Key Release: A Swingin' Affair!
see Album Lists: alphabetic by title;
   1957 — 2nd LP; Capitol/12th

#271   Fugue for Tinhorns   *sung
   with Bing Crosby & Dean Martin*
Publication Date: 1950
Music & Words: Frank Loesser
Recorded: 6/29/63-a
Arranger: Bill Loose
Conductor/Band: Morris Stoloff/
   studio orchestra
Key Release: Reprise Musical
   Repertory Theatre: *"Guys and
   Dolls"*
see Album Lists: alphabetic by title;
   1963 — 4th LP; Reprise/12th

**#272   Full Moon and Empty
Arms**
Publication Date: 1945

Music: Ted Mossman; from S. Rachmaninoff
Words: Buddy Kaye
Recorded: 11/19/45-a
Arranger: Axel Stordahl
Conductor/Band: A. Stordahl/studio orchestra
Key Release: **That Old Feeling**
see Album Lists: alphabetic by title; 1956 — 2nd LP; Columbia/23rd

#273   The Future: Future *from "The Future" cantata*
Publication Date: 1979
Music & Words: Gordon Jenkins
Recorded: 12/17/79-a
Arranger: Gordon Jenkins
Conductor/Band: G. Jenkins and the L.A. Philharmonic Symphony Orchestra
Key Release: **Trilogy: The Future [Reflections on the Future in 3 Tenses]**
see Album Lists: alphabetic by title; 1980 — 3rd LP; Reprise/54th

#274   The Future: I've Been There *from "The Future" cantata*
Publication Date: 1979
Music & Words: Gordon Jenkins
Recorded: 12/17/79-b
Arranger: Gordon Jenkins
Conductor/Band: G. Jenkins and the L.A. Philharmonic Symphony Orchestra
Key Release: **Trilogy: The Future [Reflections on the Future in 3 Tenses]**
see Album Lists: alphabetic by title; 1980 — 3rd LP; Reprise/54th

#275   The Future: Song Without Words *from "The Future" cantata*
Publication Date: 1979
Music & Words: Gordon Jenkins
Recorded: 12/17/79-c

Arranger: Gordon Jenkins
Conductor/Band: G. Jenkins and the L.A. Philharmonic Symphony Orchestra
Key Release: **Trilogy: The Future [Reflections on the Future in 3 Tenses]**
see Album Lists: alphabetic by title; 1980 — 3rd LP; Reprise/54th

#276   The Gal (Man) That Got Away *1st recording*
Publication Date: 1954
Music: Harold Arlen
Words: Ira Gershwin
Recorded: 5/13/54-a
Arranger: Nelson Riddle
Conductor/Band: N. Riddle/studio orchestra
Key Release: **This Is Sinatra!** (Volume 1)
see Album Lists: alphabetic by title; 1956 — 6th LP; Capitol/10th

#277   The Gal (Man) That Got Away/It Never Entered My Mind *2nd recording of "Gal"; 3rd recording of "Never"*
Publication Dates: 1954/1940
Music: Harold Arlen/Richard Rodgers
Words: Ira Gershwin/Lorenz Hart
Recorded: 4/8/81-c
Arranger: Nelson Riddle
Conductor/Band: Vinnie Falcone/ studio orchestra
Key Release: **She Shot Me Down**
see Album Lists: alphabetic by title; 1981 — 1st LP; Reprise/55th

#278   A Garden in the Rain
Publication Date: 1928
Music: Carroll Gibbons
Words: James Dyrenforth
Recorded: 6/12/62-d
Arranger: Robert Farnon

Conductor/Band: R. Farnon/studio
orchestra
*Key Release: Sinatra Sings Great
Songs from Great Britain*
(English release only)
see Album Lists: alphabetic by title;
1962 — 5th LP; Reprise/6th

#279   Gentle on My Mind
Publication Date: 1967
Music & Words: John Hartford
Recorded: 11/12/68-b
Arranger: Don Costa
Conductor/Band: Bill Miller/studio
orchestra
Key Release: Cycles
see Album Lists: alphabetic by title;
1968 — 6th LP; Reprise/37th

#280   Get Happy
Publication Date: 1930
Music: Harold Arlen
Words: Ted Koehler
Recorded: 4/19/54-c
Arranger: Nelson Riddle: full-orch.
arrng. from G. Siravo band
arrng.
Conductor/Band: N. Riddle/studio
orchestra
Key Release: Swing Easy! (original
10" LP)
see Album Lists: alphabetic by title;
1954 — 5th LP; Capitol/4th

**#281   Get Me to the Church on
Time**
Publication Date: 1956
Music: Frederick Loewe
Words: Alan Jay Lerner
Recorded: 2/1/66-m
Arranger: Quincy Jones
Conductor/Band: Count Basie & his
Band
Key Release: Sinatra at the Sands
(Live Recording — 2 discs)
see Album Lists: alphabetic by title;
1966 — 3rd LP; Reprise/29th

**#282   A Ghost of a Chance (I
Don't Stand —)**   *1st recording*
Publication Date: 1932
Music: Victor Young
Words: Ned Washington & Bing
Crosby
Recorded: 12/7/45-a
Arranger: Axel Stordahl
Conductor/Band: A. Stordahl/studio
orchestra
Key Release: The Voice
see Album Lists: alphabetic by title;
1955 — 9th LP; Columbia/21st

**#283   A Ghost of a Chance (I
Don't Stand —)**   *2nd recording*
Publication Date: 1932
Music: Victor Young
Words: Ned Washington & Bing
Crosby
Recorded: 3/24/59-a
Arranger: Gordon Jenkins
Conductor/Band: G. Jenkins/studio
orchestra
Key Release: No One Cares
see Album Lists: alphabetic by title;
1959 — 5th LP; Capitol/23rd

#284   The Girl from Ipanema
«Garota de Ipanema»   *duet
with Antonio Carlos Jobim*
Publication Date: 1963
Music: Antonio Carlos Jobim
Words: Norman Gimbel/Vincius
De Moraes
Recorded: 1/31/67-c
Arranger: Claus Ogerman
Conductor/Band: C. Ogerman/studio
orchestra
*Key Release: Francis Albert Sinatra
& Antonio Carlos Jobim*
see Album Lists: alphabetic by title;
1967 — 1st LP; Reprise/31st

#285   The Girl (Boy) Next Door
1st recording
Publication Date: 1944

Music: Hugh Martin
Words: Ralph Blane
Recorded: 11/6/53-d
Arranger: Nelson Riddle: full-orch.
    arrng. from G. Siravo band
    arrng.
Conductor/Band: N. Riddle/studio
    orchestra
Key Release: **Songs for Young Lovers**
    (original 10" LP)
see Album Lists: alphabetic by title;
    1954 — 1st LP; Capitol/2nd

#286   The Girl (Boy) Next Door
  2nd recording
Publication Date: 1944
Music: Hugh Martin
Words: Ralph Blane
Recorded: 1/16/62-c
Arranger: Gordon Jenkins
Conductor/Band: G. Jenkins/studio
    orchestra
Key Release: **All Alone**
see Album Lists: alphabetic by title;
    1962 — 7th LP; Reprise/8th

#287   The Girl That I Marry
Publication Date: 1944
Music & Words: Irving Berlin
Recorded: 3/10/46-c
Arranger: Axel Stordahl
Conductor/Band: A. Stordahl/studio
    orchestra
Key Release: **Put Your Dreams
    Away**
*see Album Lists: alphabetic by title;
    1958 — 3rd LP; Columbia/26th*

#288   Give Her Love
Publication Date: 1966
Music & Words: Jim Harbert
Recorded: 11/17/66-a
Arranger: Ernie Freeman
Conductor/Band: E. Freeman/studio
    orchestra
Key Release: **That's Life**
see Album Lists: alphabetic by title;
    1966 — 5th LP; Reprise/30th

#289   Glad to Be Unhappy
Publication Date: 1936
Music: Richard Rodgers
Words: Lorenz Hart
Recorded: 2/8/55-c
Arranger: Nelson Riddle
Conductor/Band: N. Riddle/studio
    orchestra
Key Release: **In the Wee Small
    Hours** (12" LP version)
see Album Lists: alphabetic by title;
    1955 — 7th LP; Capitol/5th

#290   Go Tell It on the Moun-
  tain   *duet with Bing Crosby*
Publication Date: 1800s
Music & Words: traditional; black
    America in the 1800s
Recorded: 6/19/64-a
Arranger: Jack Halloran
Conductor/Band: J. Halloran/studio
    orchestra
Key Release: **Twelve Songs of
    Christmas**
see Album Lists: alphabetic by title;
    1964 — 9th LP; Reprise/22nd

#291   God's Country
Publication Date: 1950
Music: Beasley Smith
Words: Haven Gillespie
Recorded: 1/12/50-a
Arranger: Axel Stordahl
Conductor/Band: A. Stordahl/studio
    orchestra
Key Release: 78rpm single #38708,
    side A
see Album List #1: 1950 Columbia
    (4) single record — listed by
    number

#292   Goin' Out of My Head
Publication Date: 1964
Music & Words: Teddy Randazzo
    & Bobby Weinstein
Recorded: 8/18/69-b
Arranger: Don Costa

Conductor/Band: D. Costa/studio
orchestra
Key Release: **Frank Sinatra's Greatest Hits!** (Volume 2)
see Album Lists: alphabetic by title;
1971—3rd LP; Reprise/43rd

#293   Golden Earrings
Publication Date: 1946
Music: Victor Young
Words: Jay Livingston & Ray
Evans
Recorded: 1946 radio—"The Frank
Sinatra Old Gold Show"
Arranger: Axel Stordahl
Conductor/Band: A. Stordahl/radio
orchestra
Key Release: **My Best Songs — My Best Years** (Volume 1)
see Album Lists: alphabetic under
"radio"; early 1970s; Pentagon/
1st

#294   Golden Moment
Publication Date: 1965
Music: Kenny Jacobson
Words: Rhoda Roberts
Recorded: 8/23/65-c
Arranger: Nelson Riddle
Conductor/Band: Torry Zito/studio
orchestra
Key Release: **My Kind of Broadway**
see Album Lists: alphabetic by title;
1965—4th LP; Reprise/25th

#295   "Gone with the Wind"
Publication Date: 1937
Music: Allie Wrubel
Words: Herb Magidson
Recorded: 6/24/58-c
Arranger: Nelson Riddle
Conductor/Band: N. Riddle/studio
orchestra
Key Release: **Frank Sinatra Sings for Only the Lonely**
see Album Lists: alphabetic by title;
1958—5th LP; Capitol/19th

#296   The Good Life
Publication Date: 1962
Music: Sascha Distel
Words: Jack Reardon
Recorded: 6/10/64-b
Arranger: Quincy Jones
Conductor/Band: Count Basie & his
Band
Key Release: **It Might as Well Be Swing**
see Album Lists: alphabetic by title;
1964—5th LP; Reprise/19th

#297   A Good Man Is Hard to Find   *1st recording—duet with Shelley Winters*
Publication Date: 1918
Music & Words: Eddie Green
Recorded: 1943 radio—"Songs by
Sinatra"
Arranger: Axel Stordahl
Conductor/Band: A. Stordahl/radio
orchestra
Key Release: **My Best Songs — My Best Years** (Volume 4)
see Album Lists: alphabetic under
"radio"; early 1970s; Pentagon/
4th

#298   A Good Man Is Hard to Find   *2nd recording—duet with Shelley Winters*
Publication Date: 1918
Music & Words: Eddie Green
Recorded: 10/16/51-a
Arranger: Joseph Gershenson
Conductor/Band: J. Gershenson/studio orchestra
Key Release: **MM-1** (illegal; from
Columbia masters)
see Album Lists: alphabetic under
"bootleg"; early 1970s; bootleg
Alb. #1

#299   Good Thing Going (Going, Gone)
Publication Date: 1981

Music & Words: Stephen Sondheim
Recorded: 8/19/81-a
Arranger: Don Costa
Conductor/Band: D. Costa/studio
  orchestra
Key Release: **She Shot Me Down**
see Album Lists: alphabetic by title;
  1981 — 1st LP; Reprise/55th

#300   Goodbye (She Quietly Says —)
Publication Date: 1969
Music & Words: Bob Gaudio &
  Jake Holmes
Recorded: 7/14/69-c
Arrangers: Joseph Scott & Bob
  Gaudio
Conductor/Band: Joseph Scott/studio
  orchestra
Key Release: **Watertown [a love story]**
see Album Lists: alphabetic by title;
  1970 — 1st LP; Reprise/40th

#301   Goodbye [You Take the High Road]
Publication Date: 1935
Music & Words: Gordon Jenkins
Recorded: 6/25/58-a
Arranger: Nelson Riddle
Conductor/Band: N. Riddle/studio
  orchestra
Key Release: **Frank Sinatra Sings for Only the Lonely**
see Album Lists: alphabetic by title;
  1958 — 5th LP; Capitol/19th

#302   Goodnight, Irene
Publication Date: 1950
Music: Huddie Ledbetter — 1936
Words: John Lomax/Huddie Led-
  better — 1936
Recorded: 6/28/50-a
Arranger: Mitch Miller
Conductor/Band: M. Miller/studio
  orchestra
Key Release: **Reflections**

see Album Lists: alphabetic by title;
  1961 — 4th LP; Columbia/31st

#303   Goody Goody
Publication Date: 1936
Music & Words: Matty Malneck &
  Johnny Mercer
Recorded: 4/11/62-c
Arranger: Neal Hefti
Conductor/Band: N. Hefti/studio
  orchestra
Key Release: **Sinatra and Swingin' Brass**
see Album Lists: alphabetic by title;
  1962 — 4th LP; Reprise/5th

#304   Granada*
Publication Date: 1932
Music: Augustin Lara
Words: Dorothy Dodd/Augustin
  Lara
Recorded: 5/23/61-d
Arranger: Billy May
Conductor/Band: Billy May & his
  Orchestra
Key Release: **Sinatra Swings**
  (original title: "Swing Along
  with Me")
see Album Lists: alphabetic by title;
  1961 — 6th LP; Reprise/2nd
* *The unedited recording of this song
  only appears on the monaural version
  of the LP Sinatra Swings* (Re-
  prise F-1002); *an edited version
  of the track appears on the
  stereo release of that album.*

#305   Grass
Publication Date: 1973
Music & Words: I. Moulding
Recorded: 3/3/75-d
Arranger: Don Costa
Conductor/Band: Bill Miller/studio
  orchestra
Key Release: **Late Sinatra Goodies**
  (illegal; from Reprise masters)
see Album Lists: alphabetic under

"bootleg"; mid-1980s; bootleg
Alb. #6

**#306 Guess I'll Hang My Tears
Out to Dry** *1st recording*
Publication Date: 1944
Music: Jule Styne
Words: Sammy Cahn
Recorded: 7/30/46-e
Arranger: Axel Stordahl
Conductor/Band: A. Stordahl/studio
orchestra
Key Release: **The Essential Frank
Sinatra** (Volume 2)
see Album Lists: alphabetic by title;
1967 — 3rd LP; Columbia/35th

**#307 Guess I'll Hang My Tears
Out to Dry** *2nd recording*
Publication Date: 1944
Music: Jule Styne
Words: Sammy Cahn
Recorded: 5/29/58-e
Arranger: Nelson Riddle
Conductor/Band: Felix Slatkin/studio
orchestra
Key Release: **Frank Sinatra Sings
for Only the Lonely**
see Album Lists: alphabetic by title;
1958 — 5th LP; Capitol/19th

#308 Guys and Dolls *1st record-
ing — duet with Dean Martin*
Publication Date: 1950
Music & Words: Frank Loesser
Recorded: 7/10/63-b
Arranger: Bill Loose
Conductor/Band: Morris Stoloff/
studio orchestra
Key Release: **Reprise Musical Rep-
ertory Theatre: "Guys and Dolls"**
see Album Lists: alphabetic by title;
1963 — 4th LP; Reprise/12th

#309 Guys and Dolls *2nd
recording — song reprised in a duet
with Dean Martin*

Publication Date: 1950
Music & Words: Frank Loesser
Recorded: 7/24/63-d
Arranger: Bill Loose
Conductor/Band: Morris Stoloff/
studio orchestra
Key Release: **Reprise Musical Rep-
ertory Theatre: "Guys and Dolls"**
see Album Lists: alphabetic by title;
1963 — 4th LP; Reprise/12th

#310 The Gypsy
Publication Date: 1945
Music & Words: Billy Reid
Recorded: 6/13/62-b
Arranger: Robert Farnon
Conductor/Band: R. Farnon/studio
orchestra
Key Release: **Sinatra Sings Great
Songs from Great Britain**
(English release only)
see Album Lists: alphabetic by title;
1962 — 5th LP; Reprise/6th

#311 Hair of Gold, Eyes of Blue
Publication Date: 1948
Music & Words: Sunny Skylar
Recorded: 1948 radio — Lucky
Strike's "Your Hit Parade"
Arranger: Axel Stordahl
Conductor/Band: A. Stordahl/radio
orchestra
Key Release: **The First Times . . .
Frank Sinatra**
see Album Lists: alphabetic under
"radio"; early 1960s; Cameron/
1st

**#312 Half as Lovely (Twice as
True)**
Publication Date: 1953
Music: Lew Spence
Words: Sammy Gallop
Recorded: 5/13/54-b
Arranger: Nelson Riddle
Conductor/Band: N. Riddle/studio
orchestra

Key Release: **This Is Sinatra, Volume Two**
see Album Lists: alphabetic by title; 1958 — 4th LP; Capitol/18th

#313   Hallelujah, I Love Her So
Publication Date: 1956
Music & Words: Ray Charles
Recorded: 2/24/69-d
Arranger: Don Costa
Conductor/Band: D. Costa/studio orchestra
Key Release: **My Way**
see Album Lists: alphabetic by title; 1969 — 1st LP; Reprise/38th

#314   Hark! The Herald Angels Sing
Publication Date: 1855
Music: Felix Mendelssohn — 1840
Words: Charles Wesley
Recorded: 7/10/57-c
Arranger: Gordon Jenkins
Conductor/Band: G. Jenkins/studio orchestra
Key Release: **A Jolly Christmas from Frank Sinatra**
see Album Lists: alphabetic by title; 1957 — 6th LP; Capitol/14th

#315   The Hat My Father Wore
Publication Date: 1949
Music: Roger Edens
Words: Betty Comden & Adolph Green
Recorded: 1949 — 1st soundtrack (illegally taken from film sound)
Arranger: Conrad Salinger
Conductor/Band: Adolph Deutsch/ MGM Orchestra
Key Release: **"Take Me Out to the Ball Game"** [LP: Five Films]
see Album Lists: alphabetic under "soundtrack"; mid–1960s; bootleg Mv. #12

#316   Haunted Heart
Publication Date: 1948
Music: Arthur Schwartz
Words: Howard Dietz
Recorded: 1948 radio — Lucky Strike's "Your Hit Parade"
Arranger: Axel Stordahl
Conductor/Band: A. Stordahl/radio orchestra
Key Release: **The Original . . . Frank Sinatra**
see Album Lists: alphabetic under "radio"; early 1960s; Cameron/2nd

#317   Have You Met Miss Jones? *1st recording*
Publication Date: 1938
Music: Richard Rodgers
Words: Lorenz Hart
Recorded: 12/20/60-c
Arranger: Johnny Mandel
Conductor/Band: J. Mandel/studio orchestra
Key Release: **Love Songs** (illegal; from Reprise masters)
see Album Lists: alphabetic under "bootleg"; early 1970s; bootleg Alb. #3

#318   Have You Met Miss Jones? *2nd recording*
Publication Date: 1938
Music: Richard Rodgers
Words: Lorenz Hart
Recorded: 5/18/61-d
Arranger: Billy May
Conductor/Band: Billy May & his Orchestra
Key Release: **Sinatra Swings** (original title: "Swing Along with Me")
see Album Lists: alphabetic by title; 1961 — 6th LP; Reprise/2nd

#319   Have Yourself a Merry Little Christmas *1st recording*

Publication Date: 1944
Music: Hugh Martin
Words: Ralph Blane
Recorded: 6/26/47-a
Arranger: Axel Stordahl
Conductor/Band: A. Stordahl/studio
orchestra
Key Release: **Christmas Dreaming**
see Album Lists: alphabetic by title;
1957 — 3rd LP; Columbia/25th

**#320   Have Yourself a Merry
Little Christmas**   *2nd recording*
Publication Date: 1944
Music: Hugh Martin
Words: Ralph Blane
Recorded: 7/16/57-c
Arranger: Gordon Jenkins
Conductor/Band: G. Jenkins/studio
orchestra
Key Release: **A Jolly Christmas from
Frank Sinatra**
see Album Lists: alphabetic by title;
1957 — 6th LP; Capitol/14th

**#321   Have Yourself a Merry
Little Christmas**   *3rd recording*
Publication Date: 1944
Music: Hugh Martin
Words: Ralph Blane
Recorded: 10/13/63-a
Arranger: Gil Frau
Conductor/Band: Gus Levene/studio
orchestra
Key Release: **Have Yourself a Merry
Little Christmas**
see Album Lists: alphabetic by title;
1963 — 8th LP; Reprise/16th

#322   Head on My Pillow
Publication Date: 1940
Music: Pierre Norman Connor
Words: Jack Palmer
Recorded: 4/23/40-c
Arranger: Dorsey "house" arrng:
T. Dorsey, S. Oliver, F. Stulce,
P. Weston

Conductor/Band: Tommy Dorsey &
his Orchestra
Key Release: **The Dorsey/Sinatra
Sessions** (Volume 2)
see Album Lists: alphabetic by title;
1972 — 2nd LP; RCA Victor/
18th

**#323   Hear My Song, Violetta
«Hor Mein Lied, Violetta»**
Publication Date: 1938
Music: Othmar Klose & Rudolf
Luckesch — 1936
Words: Buddy Bernier & Bob
Emmerich
Recorded: 3/29/40-a
Arranger: Dorsey "house" arrng:
T. Dorsey, S. Oliver, F. Stulce,
P. Weston
Conductor/Band: Tommy Dorsey &
his Orchestra
Key Release: **The Dorsey/Sinatra
Sessions** (Volume 1)
see Album Lists: alphabetic by title;
1972 — 1st LP; RCA Victor/17th

#324   Hello, Dolly!
Publication Date: 1963
Music: Jerry Herman/Mack
David — 1948 (see song #0995)
Words: Jerry Herman
Recorded: 6/10/64-a
Arranger: Quincy Jones
Conductor/Band: Count Basie & his
Band
Key Release: **It Might as Well Be
Swing**
see Album Lists: alphabetic by title;
1964 — 5th LP; Reprise/19th

#325   Hello, Young Lovers   *1st
recording*
Publication Date: 1951
Music: Richard Rodgers
Words: Oscar Hammerstein II
Recorded: 3/2/51-a
Arranger: Axel Stordahl

Conductor/Band: A. Stordahl/studio
orchestra
*Key Release: **Frankie***
see Album Lists: alphabetic by title;
1955 — 8th LP; Columbia/20th

#326   Hello, Young Lovers
2nd recording
Publication Date: 1951
Music: Richard Rodgers
Words: Oscar Hammerstein II
Recorded: 4/13/65-d
Arranger: Gordon Jenkins
Conductor/Band: G. Jenkins/studio
orchestra
*Key Release: **September of My Years***
see Album Lists: alphabetic by title;
1965 — 1st LP; Reprise/23rd

#327 Help Yourself to My Heart
Publication Date: 1947
Music: Jimmy McHugh
Words: Buddy Kaye
Recorded: 12/28/47-e
Arranger: Axel Stordahl
Conductor/Band: A. Stordahl/studio
orchestra
*Key Release: **Rare Songs of Sinatra***
(illegal; from Columbia masters)
see Album Lists: alphabetic under
"bootleg"; early 1970s; bootleg
Alb. #2

**#328   Here Comes the Night
«These Are the Things I
Love»**
Publication Date: 1939
Music: F. Mason
Words: K. Stegal
Recorded: 8/31/39-a
Arranger: Andy Gibson
Conductor/Band: Harry James & his
Orchestra
*Key Release: **The Essential Frank
Sinatra*** (Volume 1)
see Album Lists: alphabetic by title;
1967 — 2nd LP; Columbia/34th

#329   Here's That Rainy Day
Publication Date: 1953
Music: Jimmy Van Heusen
Words: Johnny Burke
Recorded: 3/25/59-a
Arranger: Gordon Jenkins
Conductor/Band: G. Jenkins/studio
orchestra
*Key Release: **No One Cares***
see Album Lists: alphabetic by title;
1959 — 5th LP; Capitol/23rd

#330   Here's to the Band
Publication Date: 1981
Music: Artie Schroeck
Words: Artie Schroeck & Sharman
Howe & Alfred Nittoli
Recorded: 1/25/83-a
Arranger: Joe Parnello
Conductor/Band: J. Parnello/studio
orchestra
Key Release: 45rpm single
#7-29677, side A
see Album List #1: 1983 Reprise (5)
single record — listed by num-
ber

#331   Here's to the Losers
Publication Date: 1962
Music: Jack Segal
Words: Robert Wells
Recorded: 7/31/63-c
Arranger: Marty Paich
Conductor/Band: M. Paich/studio
orchestra
*Key Release: **Softly, As I Leave You***
see Album Lists: alphabetic by title;
1964 — 8th LP; Reprise/21st

#332   Hey! Jealous Lover
Publication Date: 1956
Music & Words: Bee Walker &
Sammy Cahn & Kay Twomey
Recorded: 4/9/56-c
Arranger: Nelson Riddle
Conductor/Band: N. Riddle/studio
orchestra

*Key Release: **This Is Sinatra,
Volume Two***
see Album Lists: alphabetic by title;
1958 — 4th LP; Capitol/18th

#333   Hey Look, No Crying*
Publication Date: 1980
Music: Jule Styne
Words: Susan Birkenhead
Recorded: 9/10/81-b
Arranger: Gordon Jenkins
Conductor/Band: G. Jenkins/studio
orchestra
*Key Release: **She Shot Me Down***
see Album Lists: alphabetic by title;
1981 — 1st LP; Reprise/55th
* *The unedited version of this recording
was not released. An edited version
appears on the LP **She Shot Me
Down** (Reprise FS-2305).*

#334   Hidden Persuasion
Publication Date: 1960
Music & Words: Churchill
Wainright
Recorded: 8/31/60-c
Arranger: Nelson Riddle
Conductor/Band: N. Riddle/studio
orchestra
*Key Release: **Sinatra Sings ... of
Love and Things***
see Album Lists: alphabetic by title;
1962 — 3rd LP; Capitol/32nd

#335   High Hopes
Publication Date: 1959
Music: Jimmy Van Heusen
Words: Sammy Cahn
Recorded: 5/8/59-a
Arranger: Nelson Riddle
Conductor/Band: N. Riddle/studio
orchestra
*Key Release: **All the Way***
see Album Lists: alphabetic by title;
1961 — 2nd LP; Capitol/29th

#336   Home on the Range
Publication Date: 1904

Music & Words: William Goodwin
(authorship disputed; claims
from 1873)
Recorded: 3/10/46-f
Arranger: Axel Stordahl
Conductor/Band: A. Stordahl/studio
orchestra
*Key Release: **MM-1** (illegal; from
Columbia masters)
see Album Lists: alphabetic under
"bootleg"; early 1970s; bootleg
Alb. #1

**#337   Homesick, That's All   *1st
recording***
Publication Date: 1945
Music & Words: Gordon Jenkins
Recorded: 3/6/45-b
Arranger: Axel Stordahl
Conductor/Band: A. Stordahl/studio
orchestra
Key Release: 78rpm single #36820
see Album List #1: 1945 Columbia
(4) single record — listed by
number

#338   Homesick, That's All
2nd recording
Publication Date: 1945
Music & Words: Gordon Jenkins
Recorded: 1945 radio — "The Frank
Sinatra Old Gold Show"
Arranger: Axel Stordahl
Conductor/Band: A. Stordahl/radio
orchestra
*Key Release: **My Best Songs — My
Best Years** (Volume 5)
see Album Lists: alphabetic under
"radio"; early 1970s; Pentagon/
5th

**#339   Hot Time in the Town of
Berlin (There'll Be a —)**
Publication Date: 1943
Music: Joe Bushkin
Words: John DeVries

Recorded: 10/17/43-c; "Broadway Bandbox" rehearsal
Arranger: Axel Stordahl
Conductor/Band: A. Stordahl/radio orchestra
Key Release: **Frank Sinatra on V-Disc, Volume 1** (English release only; album of wartime Victory Discs)
see Album Lists: alphabetic under "v/disc"; early 1970s; Apex/1st

#340   The House I Live In (That's America to Me)   *1st recording*
Publication Date: 1942
Music & Words: Earl Robinson & Lewis Allan
Recorded: 8/22/45-a
Arranger: Axel Stordahl
Conductor/Band: A. Stordahl/studio orchestra
Key Release: **The Frank Sinatra Story in Music** (2 discs)
see Album Lists: alphabetic by title; 1959 — 2nd LP; Columbia/27th

#341   The House I Live In (That's America to Me)   *2nd recording*
Publication Date: 1942
Music & Words: Earl Robinson & Lewis Allan
Recorded: 1/2/64-b
Arranger: Nelson Riddle
Conductor/Band: N. Riddle/studio orchestra
Key Release: **America, I Hear You Singing**
see Album Lists: alphabetic by title; 1964 — 2nd LP; Reprise/18th

#342   The House I Live In (That's America to Me)   *3rd recording*
Publication Date: 1942
Music & Words: Earl Robinson &

Lewis Allan
Recorded: 10/2/74-i
Arranger: Nelson Riddle
Conductor/Band: Bill Miller/Woody Herman's Young Thundering Herd band
Key Release: **Sinatra — The Main Event** (Live Recording)
see Album Lists: alphabetic by title; 1974 — 2nd LP; Reprise/48th

#343   How About You?   *1st recording*
Publication Date: 1941
Music: Burton Lane
Words: Ralph Freed
Recorded: 12/22/41-a
Arranger: Dorsey "house" arrng: T. Dorsey, S. Oliver, F. Stulce, P. Weston
Conductor/Band: Tommy Dorsey & his Orchestra
Key Release: **The Dorsey/Sinatra Sessions** (Volume 5)
see Album Lists: alphabetic by title; 1972 — 5th LP; RCA Victor/21st

#344   How About You?   *2nd recording*
Publication Date: 1941
Music: Burton Lane
Words: Ralph Freed
Recorded: 1/10/56-b
Arranger: Nelson Riddle
Conductor/Band: N. Riddle/studio orchestra
Key Release: **Songs for Swingin' Lovers!**
see Album Lists: alphabetic by title; 1956 — 1st LP; Capitol/7th

#345   How Are Ya Fixed for Love?   *duet with Keely Smith*
Publication Date: 1958
Music: Jimmy Van Heusen
Words: Sammy Cahn
Recorded: 3/3/58-b

Arranger: Billy May
Conductor/Band: Billy May & his
    Orchestra
Key Release: 45rpm single #3952/E,
    side B
see Album List #1: 1958 Capitol (5)
    single record—listed by number

#346   How Could You Do a Thing Like That to Me?

Publication Date: 1954
Music: Tyree Glenn
Words: Allan Roberts
Recorded: 3/7/55-b
Arranger: Nelson Riddle
Conductor/Band: N. Riddle/studio
    orchestra
Key Release: Swing Easy (later 12″
    version of LP)
see Album Lists: alphabetic by title;
    1960—6th LP; Capitol/26th

#347   How Cute Can You Be?

Publication Date: 1945
Music: Carl Fischer
Words: Billy Carey
Recorded: 2/3/46-d
Arranger: Axel Stordahl
Conductor/Band: A. Stordahl/studio
    orchestra
Key Release: Frankie
see Album Lists: alphabetic by title;
    1955—8th LP; Columbia/20th

#348   How Deep Is the Ocean?

1st recording
Publication Date: 1932
Music & Words: Irving Berlin
Recorded: 3/10/46-e
Arranger: Axel Stordahl
Conductor/Band: A. Stordahl/studio
    orchestra
*Key Release: The Frank Sinatra
    Story in Music* (2 discs)
see Album Lists: alphabetic by title;
    1959—2nd LP; Columbia/27th

#349   How Deep Is the Ocean?

2nd recording
Publication Date: 1932
Music & Words: Irving Berlin
Recorded: 3/3/60-e
Arranger: Nelson Riddle
Conductor/Band: N. Riddle/studio
    orchestra
Key Release: Nice 'n' Easy
see Album Lists: alphabetic by title;
    1960—2nd LP; Capitol/25th

#350   How Do You Do Without Me?

Publication Date: 1941
Music: Joe Bushkin
Words: John DeVries
Recorded: 9/18/41-b
Arranger: Dorsey "house" arrng:
    T. Dorsey, S. Oliver, F. Stulce,
    P. Weston
Conductor/Band: Tommy Dorsey &
    his Orchestra
*Key Release: The Dorsey/Sinatra
    Sessions* (Volume 5)
see Album Lists: alphabetic by title;
    1972—5th LP; RCA Victor/21st

#351   How Do You Keep the Music Playing?

Publication Date: 1982
Music: Michel Legrand
Words: Alan & Marilyn Bergman
Recorded: 4/13/84-b
Arranger: Joe Parnello
Conductor/Band: Quincy Jones & a
    special all-star jazz band
Key Release: L.A. Is My Lady
see Album Lists: alphabetic by title;
    1984—1st LP; Qwest/1st

#352   How Insensitive «Insensatez» *duet with Antonio Carlos Jobim*

Publication Date: 1964
Music: Antonio Carlos Jobim—
    1963

Words: Norman Gimbel/Vincius
De Moraes — 1963
Recorded: 2/1/67-b
Arranger: Claus Ogerman
Conductor/Band: C. Ogerman/studio
orchestra
*Key Release: Francis Albert Sinatra
& Antonio Carlos Jobim*
see Album Lists: alphabetic by title;
1967 — 1st LP; Reprise/31st

**#353 How Little We Know
(How Little It Matters —)** *1st
recording*
Publication Date: 1956
Music: Philip Springer
Words: Carolyn Leigh
Recorded: 4/5/56-e
Arranger: Nelson Riddle
Conductor/Band: N. Riddle/studio
orchestra
*Key Release: This Is Sinatra,
Volume Two*
see Album Lists: alphabetic by title;
1958 — 4th LP; Capitol/18th

**#354 How Little We Know
(How Little It Matters —)**
2nd recording
Publication Date: 1956
Music: Philip Springer
Words: Carolyn Leigh
Recorded: 4/30/63-b
Arranger: Nelson Riddle
Conductor/Band: N. Riddle / studio
orchestra
Key Release: Sinatra's Sinatra
see Album Lists: alphabetic by title;
1963 — 7th LP; Reprise/15th

#355 How Old Am I?
Publication Date: 1965
Music & Words: Gordon Jenkins
Recorded: 4/22/65-e
Arranger: Gordon Jenkins
Conductor/Band: G. Jenkins/studio
orchestra

Key Release: September of My Years
see Album Lists: alphabetic by title;
1965 — 1st LP; Reprise/23rd

**#356 How Soon? (Will I Be
Seeing You)**
Publication Date: 1944
Music & Words: Jack Owens &
Carroll Lucas
Recorded: 1944 radio — Lucky
Strike's "Your Hit Parade"
Arranger: Axel Stordahl
Conductor/Band: A. Stordahl/radio
orchestra
*Key Release: The Original . . .
Frank Sinatra*
see Album Lists: alphabetic under
"radio"; early 1960s; Cameron/
2nd

#357 The Huckle-Buck
Publication Date: 1948
Music: Andy Gibson
Words: Roy Alfred
Recorded: 4/10/49-a
Arranger: Axel Stordahl
Conductor/Band: A. Stordahl/studio
orchestra
*Key Release: The Essential Frank
Sinatra* (Volume 3)
see Album Lists: alphabetic by title;
1967 — 4th LP; Columbia/36th

**#358 The Hurt Doesn't Go
Away**
Publication Date: 1973
Music & Words: Joe Raposo
Recorded: 6/5/73-b
Arranger: Gordon Jenkins
Conductor/Band: G. Jenkins/studio
orchestra
Key Release: I Sing the Songs (Ital-
ian release only)
see Album Lists: alphabetic by title;
1982 — 5th LP; Reprise/60th

#359 Hush-a-Bye Island
Publication Date: 1946

Music: Jimmy McHugh
Words: Harold Adamson
Recorded: 8/22/46-a
Arranger: Axel Stordahl
Conductor/Band: A. Stordahl/studio
orchestra
Key Release: 78rpm single #37193,
side B
see Album List #1: 1946 Columbia
(4) single record—listed by
number

#360   I Am Loved
Publication Date: 1950
Music & Words: Cole Porter
Recorded: 11/16/50-b
Arranger: Axel Stordahl
Conductor/Band: A. Stordahl/studio
orchestra
Key Release: **Adventures of the
Heart**
see Album Lists: alphabetic by title;
1956—3rd LP; Columbia/24th

#361   I Begged Her
Publication Date: 1944
Music: Jule Styne
Words: Sammy Cahn
Recorded: 12/1/44-b
Arranger: Axel Stordahl
Conductor/Band: A. Stordahl/studio
orchestra
Key Release: **Frank Sinatra in
Hollywood, 1943–1949**
see Album Lists: alphabetic by title;
1968—1st LP; Columbia   38th

**#362   I Believe [in Wishing
Wells]**   *1st recording*
Publication Date: 1946
Music: Jule Styne
Words: Sammy Cahn
Recorded: 10/31/46-c
Arranger: Axel Stordahl
Conductor/Band: A. Stordahl/studio
orchestra
Key Release: **Frank Sinatra in**

Hollywood, 1943–1949
see Album Lists: alphabetic by title;
1968—1st LP; Columbia/38th

**#363   I Believe [in Wishing
Wells]**   *2nd recording*
Publication Date: 1946
Music: Jule Styne
Words: Sammy Cahn
Recorded: 11/25/57-a
Arranger: Nelson Riddle
Conductor/Band: N. Riddle/studio
orchestra
Key Release: **This Is Sinatra,
Volume Two**
see Album Lists: alphabetic by title;
1958—4th LP; Capitol/18th

**#364   I Believe I'm Gonna Love
You**
Publication Date: 1974
Music & Words: Gloria Sklerov &
Harry Lloyd
Recorded: 3/3/75-c
Arranger: Al Capps
Conductor/Band: Bill Miller/studio
orchestra
Key Release: **Portrait of Sinatra [40
Songs in the Life of a Man]**
(English release only—2 discs)
see Album Lists: alphabetic by title;
1979—1st LP; Reprise/51st

#365   I Believe in You
Publication Date: 1961
Music & Words: Frank Loesser
Recorded: 6/9/64-c
Arranger: Quincy Jones
Conductor/Band: Count Basie & his
Band
Key Release: **It Might as Well Be
Swing**
see Album Lists: alphabetic by title;
1964—5th LP; Reprise/19th

**#366   I Can Read Between the
Lines**
Publication Date: 1953

Music: Ray Getzov
Words: Sid Frank
Recorded: 5/2/53-d
Arranger: Nelson Riddle
Conductor/Band: N. Riddle/studio orchestra
Key Release: **Songs for Young Lovers** (later 12" version of LP)
see Album Lists: alphabetic by title; 1960 — 7th LP; Capitol/27th

#367   I Can't Believe I'm Losing You
Publication Date: 1963
Music: Don Costa
Words: Phil Zeller
Recorded: 4/8/64-c
Arranger: Don Costa
Conductor/Band: D. Costa/studio orchestra
Key Release: **Softly, As I Leave You**
see Album Lists: alphabetic by title; 1964 — 8th LP; Reprise/21st

#368   I Can't Believe That You're in Love with Me
Publication Date: 1927
Music: Jimmy McHugh
Words: Clarence Gaskill
Recorded: 8/23/60-b
Arranger: Nelson Riddle
Conductor/Band: N. Riddle/studio orchestra
Key Release: **Sinatra's Swingin' Session!!!**
see Album Lists: alphabetic by title; 1961 — 1st LP; Capitol/28th

#369   I Can't Get Started (with You)
Publication Date: 1935
Music: Vernon Duke
Words: Ira Gershwin
Recorded: 3/26/59-a
Arranger: Gordon Jenkins
Conductor/Band: G. Jenkins/studio orchestra

Key Release: **No One Cares**
see Album Lists: alphabetic by title; 1959 — 5th LP; Capitol/23rd

#370   I Can't Stop Loving You
Publication Date: 1958
Music & Words: Don Gibson
Recorded: 6/12/64-a
Arranger: Quincy Jones
Conductor/Band: Count Basie & his Band
Key Release: **It Might as Well Be Swing**
see Album Lists: alphabetic by title; 1964 — 5th LP; Reprise/19th

#371   I Concentrate on You   *1st recording*
Publication Date: 1940
Music & Words: Cole Porter
Recorded: 1/9/47-b
Arranger: Axel Stordahl
Conductor/Band: A. Stordahl/studio orchestra
Key Release: **The Frank Sinatra Story in Music** (2 discs)
see Album Lists: alphabetic by title; 1959 — 2nd LP; Columbia/27th

#372   I Concentrate on You
2nd recording
Publication Date: 1940
Music & Words: Cole Porter
Recorded: 8/22/60-b
Arranger: Nelson Riddle
Conductor/Band: N. Riddle/studio orchestra
Key Release: **Sinatra's Swingin' Session!!!**
see Album Lists: alphabetic by title; 1961 — 1st LP; Capitol/28th

#373   I Concentrate on You
3rd recording — duet with Antonio Carlos Jobim
Publication Date: 1940
Music & Words: Cole Porter

Recorded: 1/30/67-b
Arranger: Claus Ogerman
Conductor/Band: C. Ogerman/studio
  orchestra
Key Release: **Francis Albert Sinatra
  & Antonio Carlos Jobim**
see Album Lists: alphabetic by title;
  1967 — 1st LP; Reprise/31st

#374 I Could Have Danced All Night
Publication Date: 1956
Music: Frederick Loewe
Words: Alan Jay Lerner
Recorded: 12/23/58-b
Arranger: Billy May
Conductor/Band: Billy May & his
  Orchestra
Key Release: **Come Dance with Me!**
see Album Lists: alphabetic by title;
  1959 — 1st LP; Capitol/20th

#375 I Could Have Told You
Publication Date: 1953
Music: Jimmy Van Heusen
Words: Carl Sigman & Arthur
  Williams
Recorded: 12/9/53-c
Arranger: Nelson Riddle
Conductor/Band: N. Riddle/studio
  orchestra
Key Release: **Look to Your Heart**
see Album Lists: alphabetic by title;
  1959 — 4th LP; Capitol/22nd

#376 I Could Make You Care
Publication Date: 1940
Music: Saul Chaplin
Words: Sammy Cahn
Recorded: 7/17/40-c
Arranger: Dorsey "house" arrng:
  T. Dorsey, S. Oliver, F. Stulce,
  P. Weston
Conductor/Band: Tommy Dorsey &
  his Orchestra
Key Release: **The Dorsey/Sinatra
  Sessions** (Volume 3)

see Album Lists: alphabetic by title;
  1972 — 3rd LP; RCA Victor/19th

#377 I Could Write a Book
1st recording
Publication Date: 1940
Music: Richard Rodgers
Words: Lorenz Hart
Recorded: 1/7/52-a
Arranger: Axel Stordahl
Conductor/Band: A. Stordahl/studio
  orchestra
Key Release: **Adventures of the
  Heart**
see Album Lists: alphabetic by title;
  1956 — 3rd LP; Columbia/24th

#378 I Could Write a Book
2nd recording
Publication Date: 1940
Music: Richard Rodgers
Words: Lorenz Hart
Recorded: 8/13/57-a
Arranger: Nelson Riddle
Conductor/Band: Morris Stoloff/
  studio orchestra
Key Release: **"Pal Joey"** (Official
  Soundtrack LP)
see Album Lists: alphabetic by title;
  1957 — 8th LP; Capitol/15th

#379 I Couldn't Care Less
Publication Date: 1958
Music: Jimmy Van Heusen
Words: Sammy Cahn
Recorded: 10/1/58-a
Arranger: Nelson Riddle
Conductor/Band: N. Riddle/studio
  orchestra
Key Release: **The Rare Sinatra:
  Volume 1** (Australian release
  only)
see Album Lists: alphabetic by title;
  1978 — 1st LP; Capitol/65th

#380 I Couldn't Sleep a Wink Last Night *1st recording*

Publication Date: 1943
Music: Jimmy McHugh
Words: Harold Adamson
Recorded: 11/3/43-a
Arranger: Axel Stordahl
Conductor/Band: Bobby Tucker
   Singers only; during musicians'
   strike
Key Release: **Frank Sinatra in
   Hollywood, 1943–1949**
see Album Lists: alphabetic by title;
   1968 — 1st LP; Columbia/38th

**#381   I Couldn't Sleep a Wink
   Last Night** *2nd recording*
Publication Date: 1943
Music: Jimmy McHugh
Words: Harold Adamson
Recorded: 10/1/56-a
Arranger: Nelson Riddle
Conductor/Band: N. Riddle with or-
   chestra & the Hollywood String
   Quartet
Key Release: **Close to You**
see Album Lists: alphabetic by title;
   1957 — 1st LP; Capitol/11th

#382   I Cover the Waterfront*
Publication Date: 1931
Music: Johnny Green
Words: Edward Heyman
Recorded: 4/29/57-a
Arranger: Gordon Jenkins
Conductor/Band: G. Jenkins/studio
   orchestra
Key Release: **Where Are You?**
see Album Lists: alphabetic by title;
   1957 — 4th LP; Capitol/13th
*This song only appears on the
   monaural version of the LP
   Where Are You? (Capitol
   W-855); it was eliminated from
   the stereo version of the album.

**#383   I Cried for You (Now It's
   Your Turn to Cry Over Me)**
Publication Date: 1923

Music: Gus Arnheim & Abe
   Lyman
Words: Arthur Freed
Recorded: 1957 soundtrack (illegally
   taken from film sound)
Arranger: Nelson Riddle
Conductor/Band: Walter Scharf/
   Paramount Orchestra
Key Release: **"The Joker Is Wild"**
   (LP: Score from *The Joker Is
   Wild*)
see Album Lists: alphabetic under
   "soundtrack"; mid–1960s; boot-
   leg Mv. #21

**#384   I Didn't Know What
   Time It Was**
Publication Date: 1939
Music: Richard Rodgers
Words: Lorenz Hart
Recorded: 9/25/57-a
Arranger: Nelson Riddle
Conductor/Band: Morris Stoloff/
   studio orchestra
Key Release: **"Pal Joey"** (Official
   Soundtrack LP)
see Album Lists: alphabetic by title;
   1957 — 8th LP; Capitol/15th

**#385   I Don't Know Why (I
   Just Do)**
Publication Date: 1931
Music: Fred Ahlert
Words: Roy Turk
Recorded: 7/30/45-d
Arranger: Axel Stordahl
Conductor/Band: A. Stordahl/studio
   orchestra
Key Release: **The Voice**
see Album Lists: alphabetic by title;
   1955 — 9th LP; Columbia/21st

**#386   I Dream of You (More
   Than You Dream I Do)**
Publication Date: 1944
Music & Words: Edna Osser &
   Marjorie Goetschius

Recorded: 12/1/44-a
Arranger: Axel Stordahl
Conductor/Band: A. Stordahl/studio
  orchestra
Key Release: **Put Your Dreams
  Away**
see Album Lists: alphabetic by title;
  1958 – 3rd LP; Columbia/26th

#387   I Fall in Love Too Easily
Publication Date: 1944
Music: Jule Styne
Words: Sammy Cahn
Recorded: 12/1/44-d
Arranger: Axel Stordahl
Conductor/Band: A. Stordahl/studio
  orchestra
Key Release: **Frank Sinatra in
  Hollywood, 1943–1949**
see Album Lists: alphabetic by title;
  1968 – 1st LP; Columbia/38th

**#388   I Fall in Love with You
  Ev'ry Day**
Publication Date: 1946
Music & Words: Sam H. Stept
Recorded: 3/10/46-d
Arranger: Axel Stordahl
Conductor/Band: A. Stordahl/studio
  orchestra
Key Release: **Hello, Young Lovers** (2
  discs)
see Album Lists: alphabetic by title;
  1987 – 2nd LP; Columbia/52nd

#389   I Get a Kick Out of You
1st recording
Publication Date: 1934
Music & Words: Cole Porter
Recorded: 11/6/53-b
Arranger: Nelson Riddle; full-orch.
  arrng. from G. Siravo band
  arrng.
Conductor/Band: N. Riddle/studio
  orchestra
Key Release: **Songs for Young Lovers**
  (original 10″ LP)

see Album Lists: alphabetic by title;
  1954 – 1st LP; Capitol/2nd

#390   I Get a Kick Out of You
2nd recording
Publication Date: 1934
Music & Words: Cole Porter
Recorded: 4/10/62-b
Arranger: Neal Hefti
Conductor/Band: N. Hefti/studio
  orchestra
Key Release: **Sinatra and Swingin'
  Brass**
see Album Lists: alphabetic by title;
  1962 – 4th LP; Reprise/5th

#391   I Get a Kick Out of You
3rd recording
Publication Date: 1934
Music & Words: Cole Porter
Recorded: 10/13/74-b
Arranger: Neal Hefti
Conductor/Band: Bill Miller/Woody
  Herman's Young Thundering
  Herd band
Key Release: **Sinatra — The Main
  Event** (Live Recording)
see Album Lists: alphabetic by title;
  1974 – 2nd LP; Reprise/48th

**#392   I Get Along Without You
  Very Well**
Publication Date: 1939
Music & Words: Hoagy Carmichael
Recorded: 2/17/55-a
Arranger: Nelson Riddle
Conductor/Band: N. Riddle/studio
  orchestra
Key Release: **In the Wee Small
  Hours** (12″ LP version)
see Album Lists: alphabetic by title;
  1955 – 7th LP; Capitol/5th

**#393   I Got a Gal I Love (in
  North and South Dakota)**
Publication Date: 1946
Music: Jule Styne

Words: Sammy Cahn
Recorded: 10/31/46-d
Arranger: Axel Stordahl
Conductor/Band: A. Stordahl/studio
  orchestra
Key Release: 78rpm single #37231
see Album List #1: 1946 Columbia
  (4) single record — listed by
  number

#394   I Got It Bad (and That Ain't Good)
Publication Date: 1941
Music: Duke Ellington
Words: Paul Francis Webster
Recorded: 11/28/56-a
Arranger: Nelson Riddle
Conductor/Band: N. Riddle/studio
  orchestra
Key Release: **A Swingin' Affair!**
see Album Lists: alphabetic by title;
  1957 — 2nd LP; Capitol/12th

#395   I Got Plenty o' Nuttin'
Publication Date: 1935
Music: George Gershwin
Words: DuBose Heyward & Ira
  Gershwin
Recorded: 11/15/56-a
Arranger: Nelson Riddle
Conductor/Band: N. Riddle/studio
  orchestra
Key Release: **A Swingin' Affair!**
see Album Lists: alphabetic by title;
  1957 — 2nd LP; Capitol/12th

#396   I Gotta Right to Sing the Blues*
Publication Date: 1932
Music: Harold Arlen
Words: Ted Koehler
Recorded: 3/6/62-a
Arranger: Skip Martin
Conductor/Band: S. Martin/studio
  orchestra
Key Release: **Sinatra Sings . . . of Love and Things**

see Album Lists: alphabetic by title;
  1962 — 3rd LP; Capitol/32nd
*The last song Sinatra recorded
  for Capitol Records — the session
  took place on March 6, 1962 —
  wrapping up a decade of growth
  and success, having already
  shifted to his own label, Reprise
  Records, to gain artistic control.

#397   I Guess I'll Have to Change My Plan
Publication Date: 1929
Music: Arthur Schwartz
Words: Howard Dietz
Recorded: 11/20/56-b
Arranger: Nelson Riddle
Conductor/Band: N. Riddle/studio
  orchestra
Key Release: **A Swingin' Affair!**
see Album Lists: alphabetic by title;
  1957 — 2nd LP; Capitol/12th

#398   I Guess I'll Have to Dream the Rest   *1st recording*
Publication Date: 1941
Music: Harold Green
Words: Mickey Stoner & Martin
  Block
Recorded: 6/27/41-a
Arranger: Axel Stordahl
Conductor/Band: Tommy Dorsey &
  his Orchestra
Key Release: **The Dorsey/Sinatra Sessions** (Volume 5)
see Album Lists: alphabetic by title;
  1972 — 5th LP; RCA Victor/21st

#399   I Guess I'll Have to Dream the Rest   *2nd recording*
Publication Date: 1941
Music: Harold Green
Words: Mickey Stoner & Martin
  Block
Recorded: 10/9/50-c
Arranger: Axel Stordahl

Conductor/Band: A. Stordahl/studio
orchestra
Key Release: **Adventures of the
Heart**
see Album Lists: alphabetic by title;
1956 — 3rd LP; Columbia/24th

#400   I Had the Craziest Dream
Publication Date: 1942
Music: Harry Warren
Words: Mack Gordon
Recorded: 7/18/79-a
Arranger: Billy May
Conductor/Band: B. May/studio
orchestra
Key Release: **Trilogy: The Past
[Collectibles of the Early Years]**
see Album Lists: alphabetic by title;
1980 — 1st LP; Reprise/52nd

#401   I Hadn't Anyone Till You
Publication Date: 1938
Music & Words: Ray Noble
Recorded: 11/20/61-d
Arranger: Don Costa
Conductor/Band: D. Costa/studio
orchestra
Key Release: **Sinatra & Strings**
see Album Lists: alphabetic by title;
1962 — 1st LP; Reprise/4th

#402   I Have But One Heart
«O Marenariello»
Publication Date: 1945
Music: Johnny Farrow
Words: Marty Symes
Recorded: 11/30/45-a
Arranger: Axel Stordahl
Conductor/Band: A. Stordahl/studio
orchestra
Key Release: **Put Your Dreams
Away**
see Album Lists: alphabetic by title;
1958 — 3rd LP; Columbia/26th

#403   I Have Dreamed
Publication Date: 1951

Music: Richard Rodgers
Words: Oscar Hammerstein II
Recorded: 2/19/63-c
Arranger: Nelson Riddle
Conductor/Band: N. Riddle/studio
orchestra
Key Release: **The Concert Sinatra**
see Album Lists: alphabetic by title;
1963 — 2nd LP; Reprise/10th

**#404   I Haven't Time to Be a
Millionaire**
Publication Date: 1940
Music: James V. Monaco
Words: Johnny Burke
Recorded: 4/10/40-b
Arranger: Dorsey "house" arrng:
T. Dorsey, S. Oliver, F. Stulce,
P. Weston
Conductor/Band: Tommy Dorsey &
his Orchestra
Key Release: **The Dorsey/Sinatra
Sessions** (Volume 1)
see Album Lists: alphabetic by title;
1972 — 1st LP; RCA Victor/
17th

#405   I Hear a Rhapsody
Publication Date: 1940
Music & Words: George Fragos &
Jack Baker & Dick Gasparre
Recorded: 1/7/52-b
Arranger: Axel Stordahl
Conductor/Band: A. Stordahl/studio
orchestra
Key Release: **Come Back to Sorrento**
see Album Lists: alphabetic by title;
1960 — 5th LP; Columbia/30th

**#406   I Heard the Bells on
Christmas Day**
Publication Date: 1956
Music: Johnny Marks
Words: Johnny Marks; from
H. W. Longfellow
Recorded: 6/16/64-b
Arranger: Nelson Riddle

Conductor/Band: N. Riddle/studio orchestra
Key Release: Twelve Songs of Christmas
see Album Lists: alphabetic by title; 1964 — 9th LP; Reprise/22nd

#407   I Heard You Cried Last Night (and So Did I)
Publication Date: 1943
Music: Ted Grouya
Words: Jerrie Kruger
Recorded: 1943 radio — Lucky Strike's "Your Hit Parade"
Arranger: Axel Stordahl
Conductor/Band: A. Stordahl/radio orchestra
Key Release: The Original . . . Frank Sinatra
see Album Lists: alphabetic under "radio"; early 1960s; Cameron/2nd

#408   I Left My Heart in San Francisco
Publication Date: 1954
Music: George Cory
Words: Douglass Cross
Recorded: 8/27/62-b
Arranger: Nelson Riddle
Conductor/Band: Neil Hefti/studio orchestra
Key Release: The Voice: Volume 1 (Italian release only)
see Album Lists: alphabetic by title; 1982 — 1st LP; Reprise/56th

#409   I Like the Sunrise
Publication Date: 1947
Music: Duke Ellington; from Ellington's own 1947 "Liberian Suite"
Words: Duke Ellington & Mercer Ellington
Recorded: 12/12/67-c
Arranger: Billy May

Conductor/Band: Duke Ellington & his Band
Key Release: Francis A. & Edward K.
see Album Lists: alphabetic by title; 1968 — 2nd LP; Reprise/33rd

#410   I Like to Lead When I Dance
Publication Date: 1964
Music: Jimmy Van Heusen
Words: Sammy Cahn
Recorded: 4/8/64-b
Arranger: Nelson Riddle
Conductor/Band: N. Riddle/studio orchestra
Key Release: "Robin and the 7 Hoods" (Official Soundtrack LP)
see Album Lists: alphabetic by title; 1964 — 6th LP; Reprise/20th

#411   I Love My Wife
Publication Date: 1976
Music: Cy Coleman
Words: Michael Stewart
Recorded: 11/12/76-a
Arranger: Nelson Riddle
Conductor/Band: N. Riddle/studio orchestra
Key Release: The Singles (Italian release only)
see Album Lists: alphabetic by title; 1982 — 6th LP; Reprise/61st

#412   I Love Paris   *1st recording — duet with Maurice Chevalier*
Publication Date: 1953
Music & Words: Cole Porter
Recorded: 2/19/60-c
Arranger: Nelson Riddle
Conductor/Band: N. Riddle/studio orchestra
Key Release: "Can-Can" (Official Soundtrack LP)
see Album Lists: alphabetic by title; 1960 — 1st LP; Capitol/24th

#413 I Love Paris *2nd recording*
Publication Date: 1953
Music & Words: Cole Porter
Recorded: 4/12/60-c
Arranger: Nelson Riddle
Conductor/Band: N. Riddle/studio
orchestra
*Key Release: Sinatra Sings . . . of
Love and Things*
see Album Lists: alphabetic by title;
1962 — 3rd LP; Capitol/32nd

**#414 I Love You [Hums the
April Breeze]**
Publication Date: 1944
Music & Words: Cole Porter
Recorded: 4/10/62-d
Arranger: Neal Hefti
Conductor/Band: N. Hefti/studio
orchestra
*Key Release: Sinatra and Swingin'
Brass*
see Album Lists: alphabetic by title;
1962 — 4th LP; Reprise/5th

**#415 I Love You «Ich Liebe
Dich»**
Publication Date: 1944
Music: George Forrest & Robert
Wright; from E. Grieg
Words: Robert Wright & George
Forrest
Recorded: 7/30/46-b
Arranger: Axel Stordahl
Conductor/Band: A. Stordahl/studio
orchestra
Key Release: 78rpm single #38684
see Album List #1: 1949 Columbia
(4) single record — listed by
number

**#416 I Love You [Three
Words]**
Publication Date: 1923
Music: Harry Archer
Words: Harlan Thompson
Recorded: 4/30/53-c

Arranger: Nelson Riddle; writing in
the style of a Billy May arrng.
Conductor/Band: N. Riddle/studio
orchestra
Key Release: Swing Easy (later 12"
version of LP)
see Album Lists: alphabetic by title;
1960 — 6th LP; Capitol/26th

#417 I Loved Her
Publication Date: 1981
Music & Words: Gordon Jenkins
Recorded: 7/20/81-b
Arranger: Gordon Jenkins
Conductor/Band: G. Jenkins/studio
orchestra
Key Release: She Shot Me Down
see Album Lists: alphabetic by title;
1981 — 1st LP; Reprise/55th

#418 I Never Knew
Publication Date: 1925
Music: Ted Fiorito
Words: Gus Kahn
Recorded: 5/19/61-b
Arranger: Billy May
Conductor/Band: Billy May & his
Orchestra
Key Release: Sinatra Swings (origi-
nal title: "Swing Along with
Me")
see Album Lists: alphabetic by title;
1961 — 6th LP; Reprise/2nd

#419 I Only Have Eyes for You
1st recording
Publication Date: 1934
Music: Harry Warren
Words: Al Dubin
Recorded: 8/27/45-d
Arranger: Axel Stordahl
Conductor/Band: A. Stordahl/studio
orchestra
Key Release: Frankie
see Album Lists: alphabetic by title;
1955 — 8th LP; Columbia/20th

#420   I Only Have Eyes for You   *2nd recording*
Publication Date: 1934
Music: Harry Warren
Words: Al Dubin
Recorded: 10/3/62-b
Arranger: Neal Hefti
Conductor/Band: Count Basie & his Band
*Key Release: **Sinatra — Basie: An Historic Musical First***
see Album Lists: alphabetic by title; 1963 — 1st LP; Reprise/9th

#421   I Saw You First   *duet with Marcy McGuire*
Publication Date: 1943
Music: Jimmy McHugh
Words: Harold Adamson
Recorded: 1943 soundtrack (illegally taken from film sound)
Arranger: Axel Stordahl
Conductor/Band: Constantin Bakaleinikoff/RKO Orchestra
*Key Release: **"Higher and Higher"*** (LP: Four Sinatra Movies)
see Album Lists: alphabetic under "soundtrack"; mid-1960s; bootleg Mv. #4

#422   I See It Now
Publication Date: 1941
Music: Alec Wilder
Words: Bill Engvick
Recorded: 4/14/65-a
Arranger: Gordon Jenkins
Conductor/Band: G. Jenkins/studio orchestra
*Key Release: **September of My Years***
see Album Lists: alphabetic by title; 1965 — 1st LP; Reprise/23rd

#423   I See Your Face Before Me
Publication Date: 1937
Music: Arthur Schwartz
Words: Howard Dietz

Recorded: 2/16/55-c
Arranger: Nelson Riddle
Conductor/Band: N. Riddle/studio orchestra
*Key Release: **In the Wee Small Hours*** (12″ LP version)
see Album Lists: alphabetic by title; 1955 — 7th LP; Capitol/5th

#424   I Should Care
Publication Date: 1945
Music: Axel Stordahl & Paul Weston
Words: Sammy Cahn
Recorded: 3/6/45-a
Arranger: Axel Stordahl
Conductor/Band: A. Stordahl/studio orchestra
*Key Release: **The Essential Frank Sinatra*** (Volume 1)
see Album Lists: alphabetic by title; 1967 — 2nd LP; Columbia/34th

#425   I Sing (Write) the Songs
Publication Date: 1974
Music & Words: Bruce Johnston
Recorded: 2/5/76-a
Arranger: Don Costa
Conductor/Band: Bill Miller/studio orchestra
*Key Release: **I Sing the Songs*** (Italian release only)
see Album Lists: alphabetic by title; 1982 — 5th LP; Reprise/60th

#426   I Think of You   *1st recording*
Publication Date: 1941
Music: Don Marcotte; from S. Rachmaninoff
Words: Jack Elliott
Recorded: 9/18/41-a
Arranger: Dorsey "house" arrng: T. Dorsey, S. Oliver, F. Stulce, P. Weston
Conductor/Band: Tommy Dorsey & his Orchestra

Key Release: **The Dorsey/Sinatra Sessions** (Volume 5)
see Album Lists: alphabetic by title; 1972 — 5th LP; RCA Victor/21st

#427   I Think of You   *2nd recording*
Publication Date: 1941
Music: Don Marcotte; from S. Rachmaninoff
Words: Jack Elliott
Recorded: 5/1/57-b
Arranger: Gordon Jenkins
Conductor/Band: G. Jenkins/studio orchestra
Key Release: **Where Are You?**
see Album Lists: alphabetic by title; 1957 — 4th LP; Capitol/13th

#428   I Thought About You
Publication Date: 1939
Music: Jimmy Van Heusen
Words: Johnny Mercer
Recorded: 1/9/56-b
Arranger: Nelson Riddle
Conductor/Band: N. Riddle/studio orchestra
Key Release: **Songs for Swingin' Lovers!**
see Album Lists: alphabetic by title; 1956 — 1st LP; Capitol/7th

#429   I Tried
Publication Date: 1940
Music: Matt Dennis
Words: Carl Nutter & Lloyd Hand
Recorded: 1/20/41-a
Arranger: Dorsey "house" arrng: T. Dorsey, S. Oliver, F. Stulce, P. Weston
Conductor/Band: Tommy Dorsey & his Orchestra
Key Release: **The Dorsey/Sinatra Sessions** (Volume 4)
see Album Lists: alphabetic by title; 1972 — 4th LP; RCA Victor/20th

#430   I Wanna Be Around
Publication Date: 1959
Music & Words: Johnny Mercer & Sadie Vimmerstedt
Recorded: 6/9/64-b
Arranger: Quincy Jones
Conductor/Band: Count Basie & his Band
Key Release: **It Might as Well Be Swing**
see Album Lists: alphabetic by title; 1964 — 5th LP; Reprise/19th

#431   I Want to Thank Your Folks
Publication Date: 1946
Music & Words: Bennie Benjamin & George Weiss
Recorded: 12/15/46-b
Arranger: Axel Stordahl
Conductor/Band: A. Stordahl/studio orchestra
Key Release: 78rpm single #37251
see Album List #1: 1947 Columbia (4) single record — listed by number

#432   I Went Down to Virginia
Publication Date: 1947
Music: Dave Mann
Words: Sammy Mysels
Recorded: 11/25/47-a
Arranger: Axel Stordahl
Conductor/Band: A. Stordahl/studio orchestra
Key Release: **The Essential Frank Sinatra** (Volume 2)
see Album Lists: alphabetic by title; 1967 — 3rd LP; Columbia/35th

#433   I Whistle a Happy Tune
Publication Date: 1951
Music: Richard Rodgers
Words: Oscar Hammerstein II
Recorded: 3/27/51-a
Arranger: Axel Stordahl

Conductor/Band: A. Stordahl/studio
orchestra
Key Release: The Broadway Kick
see Album Lists: alphabetic by title;
1960 — 4th LP; Columbia/29th

#434   I Will Drink the Wine
Publication Date: 1970
Music & Words: Paul Ryan
Recorded: 10/26/70-a
Arranger: Don Costa
Conductor/Band: D. Costa/studio
orchestra
Key Release: Sinatra & Company
see Album Lists: alphabetic by title;
1971 — 2nd LP; Reprise/42nd

#435   I Will Wait for You
Publication Date: 1965
Music: Michel Legrand — 1964
Words: Norman Gimbel/Jacques
Demy — 1964
Recorded: 11/18/66-a
Arranger: Ernie Freeman
Conductor/Band: E. Freeman/studio
orchestra
Key Release: That's Life
see Album Lists: alphabetic by title;
1966 — 5th LP; Reprise/30th

**#436   I Wish I Didn't Love You
So**
Publication Date: 1947
Music & Words: Frank Loesser
Recorded: 1947 radio — Lucky
Strike's "Your Hit Parade"
Arranger: Axel Stordahl
Conductor/Band: A. Stordahl/radio
orchestra
*Key Release: The First Times . . .
Frank Sinatra*
see Album Lists: alphabetic under
"radio"; early 1960s; Cameron/
1st

**#437   I Wish I Were in Love
Again**
Publication Date: 1937

Music: Richard Rodgers
Words: Lorenz Hart
Recorded: 11/20/56-c
Arranger: Nelson Riddle
Conductor/Band: N. Riddle/studio
orchestra
Key Release: A Swingin' Affair!
see Album Lists: alphabetic by title;
1957 — 2nd LP; Capitol/12th

**#438   I Wish You Love «Que
Reste — il de Nos Amours»**
Publication Date: 1955
Music: Charles Trenet — 1946
Words: Lee Wilson/Charles
Trenet — 1946
Recorded: 6/10/64-c
Arranger: Quincy Jones
Conductor/Band: Count Basie & his
Band
*Key Release: It Might as Well Be
Swing*
see Album Lists: alphabetic by title;
1964 — 5th LP; Reprise/19th

#439   I Wished on the Moon
Publication Date: 1935
Music: Ralph Rainger
Words: Dorothy Parker
Recorded: 11/30/65-a
Arranger: Nelson Riddle
Conductor/Band: N. Riddle/studio
orchestra
Key Release: Moonlight Sinatra
see Album Lists: alphabetic by title;
1966 — 2nd LP; Reprise/28th

**#440   I Wonder Who's Kissing
Her Now**
Publication Date: 1909
Music: Harold Orlob & Joseph E.
Howard
Words: Frank R. Adams & Will
M. Hough
Recorded: 1943 radio — Lucky
Strike's "Your Hit Parade"
Arranger: Axel Stordahl

Conductor/Band: A. Stordahl/radio orchestra
Key Release: **The First Times . . . Frank Sinatra**
see Album Lists: alphabetic under "radio"; early 1960s; Cameron/ 1st

#441   I Won't Dance   *1st recording*
Publication Date: 1935
Music: Jerome Kern/Jimmy McHugh
Words: Otto Harbach & Oscar Hammerstein II/Dorothy Fields
Recorded: 11/15/56-b
Arranger: Nelson Riddle
Conductor/Band: N. Riddle/studio orchestra
Key Release: **A Swingin' Affair!**
see Album Lists: alphabetic by title; 1957 — 2nd LP; Capitol/12th

#442   I Won't Dance   *2nd recording*
Publication Date: 1935
Music: Jerome Kern/Jimmy McHugh
Words: Otto Harbach & Oscar Hammerstein II/Dorothy Fields
Recorded: 10/2/62-c
Arranger: Neal Hefti
Conductor/Band: Count Basie & his Band
Key Release: **Sinatra-Basie: An Historic Musical First**
see Album Lists: alphabetic by title; 1963 — 1st LP; Reprise/9th

#443   I Would Be in Love (Anyway)
Publication Date: 1969
Music & Words: Bob Gaudio & Jake Holmes
Recorded: 7/14/69-a
Arrangers: Joseph Scott & Bob Gaudio

Conductor/Band: Joseph Scott/studio orchestra
Key Release: **Watertown [a love story]**
see Album Lists: alphabetic by title; 1970 — 1st LP; Reprise/40th

#444   I'd Know You Anywhere
Publication Date: 1940
Music: Jimmy McHugh
Words: Johnny Mercer
Recorded: 9/17/40-c
Arranger: Dorsey "house" arrng: T. Dorsey, S. Oliver; F. Stulce, P. Weston
Conductor/Band: Tommy Dorsey & his Orchestra
Key Release: **The Dorsey/Sinatra Sessions** (Volume 3)
see Album Lists: alphabetic by title; 1972 — 3rd LP; RCA Victor/19th

#445   If
Publication Date: 1971
Music & Words: David Gates
Recorded: 5/7/74-b
Arranger: Gordon Jenkins
Conductor/Band: G. Jenkins/studio orchestra
Key Release: **Some Nice Things I've Missed**
see Album Lists: alphabetic by title; 1974 — 1st LP; Reprise/47th

#446   If I Could Be with You (One Hour Tonight)
Publication Date: 1926
Music & Words: Jimmy Johnson & Henry Creamer
Recorded: 1957 soundtrack (illegally taken from film sound)
Arranger: Nelson Riddle
Conductor/Band: Walter Scharf/ Paramount Orchestra
Key Release: **"The Joker Is Wild"** (LP: Score from *The Joker Is Wild*)

see Album Lists: alphabetic under "soundtrack"; mid–1960s; bootleg Mv. #21

#447   If I Ever Love Again
Publication Date: 1949
Music & Words: Russ Carlyle & Dick Reynolds
Recorded: 7/15/49-b
Arranger: Hugo Winterhalter
Conductor/Band: H. Winterhalter/ studio orchestra
Key Release: **The Essential Frank Sinatra** (Volume 3)
see Album Lists: alphabetic by title; 1967 – 4th LP; Columbia/36th

#448   If I Forget You
Publication Date: 1933
Music & Words: Irving Caesar
Recorded: 12/30/47-a
Arranger: Axel Stordahl
Conductor/Band: A. Stordahl/studio orchestra
Key Release: **Put Your Dreams Away**
see Album Lists: alphabetic by title; 1958 – 3rd LP; Columbia/26th

#449   If I Had Three Wishes
Publication Date: 1954
Music: Lew Spence
Words: Claude Baum
Recorded: 3/7/55-a
Arranger: Nelson Riddle
Conductor/Band: N. Riddle/studio orchestra
Key Release **Look to Your Heart**
see Album Lists: alphabetic by title; 1959 – 4th LP; Capitol/22nd

#450   If I Had You   *1st recording*
Publication Date: 1929
Music & Words: Ted Shapiro & Jimmy Campbell & Reg Connelly
Recorded: 8/11/47-b
Arranger: Axel Stordahl

Conductor/Band: A. Stordahl/studio orchestra
Key Release: **The Voice: 1943–1952** (6 discs)
see Album Lists: alphabetic by title; 1987 – 1st LP; Columbia/51st

#451   If I Had You   *2nd recording*
Publication Date: 1929
Music & Words: Ted Shapiro & Jimmy Campbell & Reg Connelly
Recorded: 11/26/56-d
Arranger: Nelson Riddle
Conductor/Band: N. Riddle/studio orchestra
Key Release: **A Swingin' Affair!**
see Album Lists: alphabetic by title; 1957 – 2nd LP; Capitol/12th

#452   If I Had You   *3rd recording*
Publication Date: 1929
Music & Words: Ted Shapiro & Jimmy Campbell & Reg Connelly
Recorded: 6/12/62-a
Arranger: Robert Farnon
Conductor/Band: R. Farnon/studio orchestra
Key Release: **Sinatra Sings Great Songs from Great Britain** (English release only)
see Album Lists: alphabetic by title; 1962 – 5th LP; Reprise/6th

#453   If I Loved You
Publication Date: 1945
Music: Richard Rodgers
Words: Oscar Hammerstein II
Recorded: 5/1/45-d
Arranger: Axel Stordahl
Conductor/Band: A. Stordahl/studio orchestra
Key Release: **The Frank Sinatra Story in Music** (2 discs)

see Album Lists: alphabetic by title; 1959 — 2nd LP; Columbia/27th

#454   If I Only Had a Match
Publication Date: 1947
Music & Words: Arthur Johnston & George W. Meyer & Lee Morris
Recorded: 11/25/47-b
Arranger: Axel Stordahl
Conductor/Band: A. Stordahl/studio orchestra
Key Release: The Essential Frank Sinatra (Volume 2)
see Album Lists: alphabetic by title; 1967 — 3rd LP; Columbia/35th

#455   If I Should Lose You
Publication Date: 1935
Music & Words: Ralph Rainger & Leo Robin
Recorded: 4/16/84-c
Arranger: Sam Nestico
Conductor/Band: Quincy Jones & a special all-star jazz band
Key Release: L.A. Is My Lady
see Album Lists: alphabetic by title; 1984 — 1st LP; Qwest/1st

#456   If I Steal a Kiss
Publication Date: 1947
Music: Nacio Herb Brown
Words: Edward Heyman
Recorded: 12/4/47-a
Arranger: Axel Stordahl
Conductor/Band: A. Stordahl/studio orchestra
Key Release: Frank Sinatra in Hollywood, 1943–1949
see Album Lists: alphabetic by title; 1968 — 1st LP; Columbia/38th

#457   If It's the Last Thing I Do
Publication Date: 1937
Music: Saul Chaplin
Words: Sammy Cahn

Recorded: 3/8/56-d
Arranger: Nelson Riddle
Conductor/Band: N. Riddle with orchestra & the Hollywood String Quartet
Key Release: Forever Frank
see Album Lists: alphabetic by title; 1966 — 4th LP; Capitol/36th

#458   If Only She'd Look My Way
Publication Date: 1950
Music: R. Melville
Words: Ivor Novello
Recorded: 9/21/50-b
Arranger: Axel Stordahl
Conductor/Band: A. Stordahl/studio orchestra
Key Release: Adventures of the Heart
see Album Lists: alphabetic by title; 1956 — 3rd LP; Columbia/24th

#459   If You Are But a Dream
1st recording
Publication Date: 1941
Music: Nat Bonx; from A. Rubinstein
Words: Moe Jaffe & Jack Fulton
Recorded: 11/14/44-a
Arranger: Axel Stordahl
Conductor/Band: A. Stordahl/studio orchestra
Key Release: The Frank Sinatra Story in Music (2 discs)
see Album Lists: alphabetic by title; 1959 — 2nd LP; Columbia/27th

#460   If You Are But a Dream
2nd recording
Publication Date: 1941
Music: Nax Bonx; from A. Rubinstein
Words: Moe Jaffe & Jack Fulton
Recorded: 12/11/57-b
Arranger: Nelson Riddle
Conductor/Band: N. Riddle/studio orchestra

Key Release: **This Is Sinatra, Volume Two**
see Album Lists: alphabetic by title; 1958 — 4th LP; Capitol/18th

#461   If You Could Read My Mind
Publication Date: 1969
Music & Words: Gordon Lightfoot
Recorded: 5/21/74-d
Arranger: Don Costa
Conductor/Band: D. Costa/studio orchestra
Key Release: **Late Sinatra Goodies** (illegal; from Reprise masters)
see Album Lists: alphabetic under "bootleg"; mid–1980s; bootleg Alb. #6

#462   If You Go Away «Ne Me Quitte Pas»
Publication Date: 1966
Music: Jacques Brel — 1956
Words: Rod McKuen/Jacques Brel — 1961
Recorded: 2/20/69-c
Arranger: Don Costa
Conductor/Band: D. Costa/studio orchestra
Key Release: **My Way**
see Album Lists: alphabetic by title; 1969 — 1st LP; Reprise/38th

#463   If You Knew Susie
parody; duet with Gene Kelly
Publication Date: 1925
Music: Joseph Meyer & B. G. (Buddy) DeSylva
Words: B. G. (Buddy) DeSylva & Joseph Meyer; parody by Sammy Cahn
Recorded: 1945 soundtrack (illegally taken from film sound)
Arranger: Axel Stordahl
Conductor/Band: George Stoll/ MGM Orchestra
Key Release: **"Anchors Aweigh"** (LP: Score from *Anchors Away*)
see Album Lists: alphabetic under "soundtrack"; mid–1960s; bootleg Mv. #7

#464   If You Never Come to Me
Publication Date: 1965
Music: Antonio Carlos Jobim
Words: Ray Gilbert & Aloysio (Louis) Oliveira
Recorded: 1/31/67-b
Arranger: Claus Ogerman
Conductor/Band: C. Ogerman/studio orchestra
Key Release: **Francis Albert Sinatra & Antonio Carlos Jobim**
see Album Lists: alphabetic by title; 1967 — 1st LP; Reprise/31st

#465   If You Please
Publication Date: 1943
Music: Jimmy Van Heusen
Words: Johnny Burke
Recorded: 6/22/43-b
Arranger: Axel Stordahl
Conductor/Band: Bobby Tucker Singers only; during musicians' strike
Key Release: **MM-1** (illegal; from Columbia masters)
see Album Lists: alphabetic under "bootleg"; early 1970s; bootleg Alb. #1

#466   If You Stub Your Toe on the Moon
Publication Date: 1949
Music: Jimmy Van Heusen
Words: Johnny Burke
Recorded: 1/4/49-a
Arranger: Phil Moore
Conductor/Band: P. Moore/studio orchestra
Key Release: **The Essential Frank Sinatra** (Volume 2)
see Album Lists: alphabetic by title; 1967 — 3rd LP; Columbia/35th

#467 I'll Be Around *1st recording*
Publication Date: 1943
Music & Words: Alec Wilder
Recorded: 11/21/43-c; "Songs by Sinatra" rehearsal
Arranger: Alec Wilder
Conductor/Band: Axel Stordahl/ radio orchestra
Key Release: **Frank Sinatra on V-Disc, Volume 1** (English release only; album of wartime Victory Discs)
see Album Lists: alphabetic under "v/disc"; early 1970s; Apex/1st

#468 I'll Be Around *2nd recording*
Publication Date: 1943
Music & Words: Alec Wilder
Recorded: 2/8/55-d
Arranger: Nelson Riddle
Conductor/Band: N. Riddle/studio orchestra
Key Release: **In the Wee Small Hours** (12" LP version)
see Album Lists: alphabetic by title; 1955 — 7th LP; Capitol/5th

#469 I'll Be Home for Christmas
Publication Date: 1943
Music & Words: Walter Kent & Buck Ram & Kim Gannon
Recorded: 7/17/57-d
Arranger: Gordon Jenkins
Conductor/Band: G. Jenkins/studio orchestra
Key Release: **A Jolly Christmas from Frank Sinatra**
see Album Lists: alphabetic by title; 1957 — 6th LP; Capitol/14th

#470 I'll Be Seeing You *1st recording*
Publication Date: 1938
Music: Sammy Fain

Words: Irving Kahal
Recorded: 2/26/40-c
Arranger: Dorsey "house" arrng: T. Dorsey, S. Oliver, F. Stulce, P. Weston
Conductor/Band: Tommy Dorsey & his Orchestra
Key Release: **The Dorsey/Sinatra Sessions** (Volume 1)
see Album Lists: alphabetic by title; 1972 — 1st LP; RCA Victor/17th

#471 I'll Be Seeing You *2nd recording*
Publication Date: 1938
Music: Sammy Fain
Words: Irving Kahal
Recorded: 5/1/61-a
Arranger: Sy Oliver
Conductor/Band: S. Oliver/studio orchestra
Key Release: **I Remember Tommy . . .**
see Album Lists: alphabetic by title; 1961 — 7th LP; Reprise/3rd

#472 I'll Be Seeing You *3rd recording*
Publication Date: 1938
Music: Sammy Fain
Words: Irving Kahal
Recorded: 9/11/61-a
Arranger: Axel Stordahl
Conductor/Band: A. Stordahl/studio orchestra
Key Release: **Point of No Return**
see Album Lists: alphabetic by title; 1962 — 2nd LP; Capitol/31st

#473 I'll Buy That Dream
Publication Date: 1942
Music: Allie Wrubel
Words: Herb Magidson
Recorded: 1942 radio — a broadcast with the Dorsey orchestra
Arranger: Dorsey "house" arrng: T. Dorsey, S. Oliver, F. Stulce, P. Weston

Conductor/Band: Tommy Dorsey & his Orchestra
Key Release: **Tommy Dorsey & His Orchestra, Featuring Frank Sinatra**
see Album Lists: alphabetic under "radio"; 1962—8th LP; Coronet/1st

#474   I'll Dance at Your Wedding
Publication Date: 1947
Music: Ben Oakland
Words: Herb Magidson
Recorded: 1947 radio—Lucky Strike's "Your Hit Parade"
Arranger: Axel Stordahl
Conductor/Band: A. Stordahl/radio orchestra
Key Release: **My Best Songs—My Best Years** (Volume 1)
see Album Lists: alphabetic under "radio"; early 1970s; Pentagon/1st

#475   I'll Follow My Secret Heart   *1st recording*
Publication Date: 1934
Music & Words: Noel Coward
Recorded: 7/8/44-j (exclusively for Victory-Disc effort)
Arranger: Axel Stordahl
Conductor/Band: A. Stordahl/assembled V-disc orchestra
Key Release: **Sinatra for the Collector: Vol. 2—The V-Disc Years** (Canadian release only; album of wartime Victory Discs)
see Album Lists: alphabetic under "v/disc"; early 1970s; My Way/2nd

#476   I'll Follow My Secret Heart   *2nd recording*
Publication Date: 1934
Music & Words: Noel Coward
Recorded: 6/12/62-c

Arranger: Robert Farnon
Conductor/Band: R. Farnon/studio orchestra
Key Release: **Sinatra Sings Great Songs from Great Britain** (English release only)
see Album Lists: alphabetic by title; 1962—5th LP; Reprise/6th

#477   I'll Get By (as Long as I Have You)
Publication Date: 1928
Music: Fred Ahlert
Words: Roy Turk
Recorded: 1943 radio—Lucky Strike's "Your Hit Parade"
Arranger: Axel Stordahl
Conductor/Band: A. Stordahl/radio orchestra
Key Release: **The First Times . . . Frank Sinatra**
see Album Lists: alphabetic under "radio"; early 1960s; Cameron/1st

#478   I'll Make Up for Everything
Publication Date: 1947
Music & Words: Sol Parker
Recorded: 10/22/47-a
Arranger: Axel Stordahl
Conductor/Band: A. Stordahl/studio orchestra
Key Release: 78rpm single #38089
see Album List #1: 1947 Columbia (4) single record—listed by number

#479   I'll Never Be the Same
Publication Date: 1932
Music: Matty Maineck & Frank Signorelli
Words: Gus Kahn
Recorded: 3/4/55-d
Arranger: Nelson Riddle
Conductor/Band: N. Riddle/studio orchestra

Key Release: **In the Wee Small Hours** (12″ LP version)
see Album Lists: alphabetic by title; 1955 — 7th LP; Capitol/5th

#480   I'll Never Let a Day Pass By
Publication Date: 1941
Music: Victor Schertzinger
Words: Frank Loesser
Recorded: 5/28/41-a
Arranger: Dorsey "house" arrng: T. Dorsey, S. Oliver, F. Stulce, P. Weston
Conductor/Band: Tommy Dorsey & his Orchestra
Key Release: **The Dorsey/Sinatra Sessions** (Volume 4)
see Album Lists: alphabetic by title; 1972 — 4th LP; RCA Victor/20th

#481   I'll Never Smile Again
1st recording
Publication Date: 1939
Music & Words: Ruth Lowe
Recorded: 5/23/40-a
Arranger: Fred Stulce
Conductor/Band: Tommy Dorsey & his Orchestra
Key Release: **The Dorsey/Sinatra Sessions** (Volume 2)
see Album Lists: alphabetic by title; 1972 — 2nd LP; RCA Victor/18th

#482   I'll Never Smile Again
2nd recording
Publication Date: 1939
Music & Words: Ruth Lowe
Recorded: 10/24/45-a; "The Frank Sinatra Old Gold Show" rehearsal
Arranger: Axel Stordahl
Conductor/Band: Tommy Dorsey & his Orchestra
Key Release: **Frank Sinatra on V-Disc** (Japanese release only; album of wartime Victory Discs)

see Album Lists: alphabetic under "v/disc"; early 1970s; Dan/1st

#483   I'll Never Smile Again
3rd recording
Publication Date: 1939
Music & Words: Ruth Lowe
Recorded: 5/14/59-d
Arranger: Gordon Jenkins
Conductor/Band: G. Jenkins/studio orchestra
Key Release: **No One Cares**
see Album Lists: alphabetic by title; 1959 — 5th LP; Capitol/23rd

#484   I'll Never Smile Again
4th recording
Publication Date: 1939
Music & Words: Ruth Lowe
Recorded: 10/11/65-b
Arranger: Fred Stulce
Conductor/Band: Sonny Burke/ studio orchestra
Key Release: **Frank Sinatra: A Man and His Music** (2 discs)
see Album Lists: alphabetic by title; 1965 — 5th LP; Reprise/26th

#485   I'll Only Miss Her When I Think of Her
Publication Date: 1965
Music: Jimmy Van Heusen
Words: Sammy Cahn
Recorded: 8/23/65-b
Arranger: Torry Zito
Conductor/Band: T. Zito/studio orchestra
Key Release: **My Kind of Broadway**
see Album Lists: alphabetic by title; 1965 — 4th LP; Reprise/25th

#486   I'll Remember April *1st recording*
Publication Date: 1941
Music: Gene DePaul
Words: Don Raye & Pat Johnston
Recorded: 1944 radio — Sinatra's "Vimms Vitamins Show"

Arranger: Axel Stordahl
Conductor/Band: A. Stordahl/radio
orchestra
Key Release: **Frank Sinatra—
Through the Years: 1944–1966**
see Album Lists: alphabetic under
"television"; mid–1960s; Ajazz/
1st

#487   I'll Remember April   *2nd
recording*
Publication Date: 1941
Music: Gene DePaul
Words: Don Raye & Pat Johnston
Recorded: 9/12/61-f
Arranger: Heinie Beau
Conductor/Band: Axel Stordahl/
studio orchestra
Key Release: **Point of No Return**
see Album Lists: alphabetic by title;
1962 — 2nd LP; Capitol/31st

#488   I'll See You Again
Publication Date: 1929
Music & Words: Noel Coward
Recorded: 9/11/61-b
Arranger: Axel Stordahl
Conductor/Band: A. Stordahl/studio
orchestra
Key Release: **Point of No Return**
see Album Lists: alphabetic by title;
1962 — 2nd LP; Capitol/31st

#489   I'll String Along with You
Publication Date: 1934
Music: Harry Warren
Words: Al Dubin
Recorded: 1943 radio — Lucky
Strike's "Your Hit Parade"
Arranger: Axel Stordahl
Conductor/Band: A. Stordahl/radio
orchestra
Key Release: **The Original . . .
Frank Sinatra**
see Album Lists: alphabetic under
"radio"; early 1960s; Cameron/
2nd

#490   I'll Take Tallulah   *sung
with Jo Stafford & Tommy Dorsey*
Publication Date: 1942
Music: Burton Lane
Words: E. Y. ("Yip") Harburg
Recorded: 2/19/42-c
Arranger: Sy Oliver
Conductor/Band: Tommy Dorsey &
his Orchestra
Key Release: **The Dorsey/Sinatra
Sessions** (Volume 6)
see Album Lists: alphabetic by title;
1972 — 6th LP; RCA Victor/
22nd

#491   Ill Wind
Publication Date: 1934
Music: Harold Arlen
Words: Ted Koehler
Recorded: 2/16/55-b
Arranger: Nelson Riddle
Conductor/Band: N. Riddle/studio
orchestra
Key Release: **In the Wee Small
Hours** (12" LP version)
see Album Lists: alphabetic by title;
1955 — 7th LP; Capitol/5th

#492   I'm a Fool to Want You
1st recording
Publication Date: 1951
Music: Jack Wolf & Joel Herron/
Frank Sinatra
Words: Frank Sinatra & Joel Her-
ron/Jack Wolf
Recorded: 3/27/51-b
Arranger: Axel Stordahl
Conductor/Band: A. Stordahl/studio
orchestra
Key Release: **The Essential Frank
Sinatra** (Volume 3)
see Album Lists: alphabetic by title;
1967 — 4th LP; Columbia/36th

#493   I'm a Fool to Want You
2nd recording
Publication Date: 1951

Music: Jack Wolf & Joel Herron/
Frank Sinatra
Words: Frank Sinatra & Joel Her-
ron/Jack Wolf
Recorded: 5/1/57-c
Arranger: Gordon Jenkins
Conductor/Band: G. Jenkins/studio
orchestra
Key Release: **Where Are You?**
see Album Lists: alphabetic by title;
1957 — 4th LP; Capitol/13th

#494   I'm Beginning to See the Light
Publication Date: 1944
Music: Duke Ellington & Harry
James/Johnny Hodges
Words: Don George
Recorded: 4/10/62-a
Arranger: Neal Hefti
Conductor/Band: N. Hefti/studio
orchestra
Key Release: **Sinatra and Swingin'
Brass**
see Album Lists: alphabetic by title;
1962 — 4th LP; Reprise/5th

#495   I'm Getting Sentimental Over You   *1st recording*
Publication Date: 1932
Music: George Bassman
Words: Ned Washington
Recorded: 5/1/61-b
Arranger: Sy Oliver
Conductor/Band: S. Oliver/studio
orchestra
Key Release: **I Remember Tommy. . .**
see Album Lists: alphabetic by title;
1961 — 7th LP; Reprise/3rd

#496   I'm Getting Sentimental Over You   *2nd recording — song reprised*
Publication Date: 1932
Music: George Bassman
Words: Ned Washington
Recorded: 5/1/61-c

Arranger: Sy Oliver
Conductor/Band: S. Oliver/studio
orchestra
Key Release: **I Remember Tommy. . .**
see Album Lists: alphabetic by title;
1961 — 7th LP; Reprise/3rd

#497   I'm Glad There Is You
Publication Date: 1941
Music & Words: Paul Madeira &
Jimmy Dorsey
Recorded: 11/9/47-b
Arranger: Axel Stordahl
Conductor/Band: A. Stordahl/studio
orchestra
Key Release: **The Frank Sinatra
Story in Music** (2 discs)
see Album Lists: alphabetic by title;
1959 — 2nd LP; Columbia/27th

#498   I'm Gonna Live Till I Die
Publication Date: 1950
Music: Al Hoffman
Words: Walter Kent & Mann
Curtis
Recorded: 12/13/54-b
Arranger: Dick Reynolds
Conductor/Band: Ray Anthony &
his Orchestra
Key Release: **Look to Your Heart**
see Album Lists: alphabetic by title;
1959 — 4th LP; Capitol/22nd

#499   I'm Gonna Make It All the Way
Publication Date: 1972
Music & Words: Floyd Huddleston
Recorded: 12/10/73-b
Arranger: Don Costa
Conductor/Band: D. Costa/studio
orchestra
Key Release: **Some Nice Things I've
Missed**
see Album Lists: alphabetic by title;
1974 — 1st LP; Reprise/47th

#500   I'm Gonna Sit Right Down and Write Myself a Letter   *1st recording*
Publication Date: 1935
Music: Fred Ahlert
Words: Joe Young
Recorded: 4/7/54-c
Arranger: Nelson Riddle: full-orch. arrng. from G. Siravo band arrng.
Conductor/Band: N. Riddle/studio orchestra
Key Release: **Swing Easy!** (original 10" LP)
see Album Lists: alphabetic by title; 1954 — 5th LP; Capitol/4th

#501   I'm Gonna Sit Right Down and Write Myself a Letter   *2nd recording*
Publication Date: 1935
Music: Fred Ahlert
Words: Joe Young
Recorded: 10/3/62-a
Arranger: Neal Hefti
Conductor/Band: Count Basie & his Band
Key Release: **Sinatra-Basie: An Historic Musical First**
see Album Lists: alphabetic by title; 1963 — 1st LP; Reprise/9th

#502   I'm in the Mood for Love   *1st recording*
Publication Date: 1935
Music: Jimmy McHugh
Words: Dorothy Fields
Recorded: 1943 radio — "Songs by Sinatra"
Arranger: Axel Stordahl
Conductor/Band: A. Stordahl/radio orchestra
Key Release: **My Best Songs — My Best Years** (Volume 1)
see Album Lists: alphabetic under "radio"; early 1970s; Pentagon/1st

#503   I'm in the Mood for Love   *2nd recording*
Publication Date: 1935
Music: Jimmy McHugh
Words: Dorothy Fields
Recorded: 1944 radio — Sinatra's "Vimms Vitamins Show"
Arranger: Axel Stordahl
Conductor/Band: A. Stordahl/radio orchestra
Key Release: **Frank Sinatra — Through the Years: 1944–1966**
see Album Lists: alphabetic under "television"; mid–1960s; Ajazz/1st

#504   I'm Not Afraid
Publication Date: 1970
Music: Jacques Brel — 1969
Words: Rod McKuen
Recorded: 10/28/70-a
Arranger: Lenny Hayton
Conductor/Band: L. Hayton/studio orchestra
Key Release: **Frank Sinatra's Greatest Hits!** (Volume 2)
see Album Lists: alphabetic by title; 1971 — 3rd LP; Reprise/43rd

#505   I'm Sorry I Made You Cry
Publication Date: 1916
Music & Words: N. J. Clesli
Recorded: 10/24/46-c
Arranger: Axel Stordahl
Conductor/Band: A. Stordahl/studio orchestra
Key Release: **Songs by Sinatra, Volume 1** (10" LP)
see Album Lists: alphabetic by title; 1950 — 1st LP; Columbia/5th

#506   I'm Walking Behind You
Publication Date: 1953
Music & Words: Billy Reid
Recorded: 4/2/53-b
Arranger: Axel Stordahl

Conductor/Band: A. Stordahl/studio
orchestra
Key Release: 45rpm single #2450/F
see Album List #1: 1953 Capitol (5)
single record—listed by number

#507   Imagination   *1st recording*
Publication Date: 1940
Music: Jimmy Van Heusen
Words: Johnny Burke
Recorded: 4/10/40-c
Arranger: Dorsey "house" arrng:
T. Dorsey, S. Oliver, F. Stulce,
P. Weston
Conductor/Band: Tommy Dorsey &
his Orchestra
Key Release: **The Dorsey/Sinatra
Sessions** (Volume 2)
see Album Lists: alphabetic by title;
1972—2nd LP; RCA Victor/18th

#508   Imagination   *2nd recording*
Publication Date: 1940
Music: Jimmy Van Heusen
Words: Johnny Burke
Recorded: 5/1/61-d
Arranger: Sy Oliver
Conductor/Band: S. Oliver/studio
orchestra
Key Release: **I Remember Tommy. . .**
see Album Lists: alphabetic by title;
1961—7th LP; Reprise/3rd

#509   The Impatient Years
Publication Date: 1955
Music: Jimmy Van Heusen
Words: Sammy Cahn
Recorded: 8/15/55-c
Arranger: Nelson Riddle
Conductor/Band: N. Riddle/studio
orchestra
Key Release: **Look to Your Heart**
see Album Lists: alphabetic by title;
1959—4th LP; Capitol/22nd

**#510   The Impossible Dream
«The Quest»**
Publication Date: 1965

Music: Mitch Leigh
Words: Joe Darion
Recorded: 11/18/66-d
Arranger: Ernie Freeman
Conductor/Band: E. Freeman/studio
orchestra
Key Release: **That's Life**
see Album Lists: alphabetic by title;
1966—5th LP; Reprise/30th

#511   In the Blue of Evening
1st recording
Publication Date: 1942
Music: Al D'Artega
Words: Tom Adair
Recorded: 6/17/42-a
Arranger: Axel Stordahl
Conductor/Band: Tommy Dorsey &
his Orchestra
Key Release: **The Dorsey/Sinatra
Sessions** (Volume 6)
see Album Lists: alphabetic by title;
1972—6th LP; RCA Victor/
22nd

#512   In the Blue of Evening
2nd recording
Publication Date: 1942
Music: Al D'Artega
Words: Tom Adair
Recorded: 3/21/61-f
Arranger: Sy Oliver
Conductor/Band: S. Oliver/studio
orchestra
Key Release: **Love Songs** (illegal;
from Reprise masters)
see Album Lists: alphabetic under
"bootleg"; early 1970s; bootleg
Alb. #3

**#513   In the Cool, Cool, Cool of
the Evening**
Publication Date: 1951
Music: Hoagy Carmichael
Words: Johnny Mercer
Recorded: 1/27/64-d
Arranger: Nelson Riddle

Conductor/Band: N. Riddle/studio
orchestra
Key Release: **Frank Sinatra Sings
"Days of Wine and Roses,"
"Moon River," and Other
Academy Award Winners**
see Album Lists: alphabetic by title;
1964 — 1st LP; Reprise/17th

#514   In the Still of the Night
Publication Date: 1937
Music & Words: Cole Porter
Recorded: 12/19/60-c
Arranger: Johnny Mandel
Conductor/Band: J. Mandel/studio
orchestra
Key Release: **Ring-a-Ding Ding!**
see Album Lists: alphabetic by title;
1961 — 3rd LP; Reprise/1st

#515   In the Wee Small Hours
of the Morning   1st recording
Publication Date: 1948
Music: Dave Mann
Words: Bob Hilliard/Jack Elliott
Recorded: 2/17/55-b
Arranger: Nelson Riddle
Conductor/Band: N. Riddle/studio
orchestra
Key Release: **In the Wee Small
Hours** (12" LP version)
see Album Lists: alphabetic by title;
1955 — 7th LP; Capitol/5th

#516   In the Wee Small Hours
of the Morning   2nd recording
Publication Date: 1948
Music: Dave Mann
Words: Bob Hilliard/Jack Elliott
Recorded: 4/29/63-a
Arranger: Nelson Riddle
Conductor/Band: N. Riddle/studio
orchestra
Key Release: **Sinatra's Sinatra**
see Album Lists: alphabetic by title;
1963 — 7th LP; Reprise/15th

#517   Indian Summer
Publication Date: 1939
Music: Victor Herbert — 1919
Words: Al Dubin
Recorded: 12/11/67-c
Arranger: Billy May
Conductor/Band: Duke Ellington &
his Band
Key Release: **Francis A. & Edward
K.**
see Album Lists: alphabetic by title;
1968 — 2nd LP; Reprise/33rd

#518   Indiscreet
Publication Date: 1958
Music: Jimmy Van Heusen
Words: Sammy Cahn
Recorded: 1/16/62-d
Arranger: Gordon Jenkins
Conductor/Band: G. Jenkins/studio
orchestra
Key Release: **All Alone**
see Album Lists: alphabetic by title;
1962 — 7th LP; Reprise/8th

#519   Isle of Capri*
Publication Date: 1935
Music: Will Grosz
Words: Jimmy Kennedy & Hugh
Williams
Recorded: 10/1/57-c
Arranger: Billy May
Conductor/Band: Billy May & his
Orchestra
Key Release: **Come Fly with Me**
see Album Lists: alphabetic by title;
1958 — 2nd LP; Capitol/17th
*This song only appears on the
monaural version of **Come Fly
with Me** (Capitol W-920); it was
eliminated from the stereo ver-
sion of the album.

#520   Isn't She Lovely?
Publication Date: 1976
Music & Words: Stevie Wonder
Recorded: 8/22/79-a

Arranger: Don Costa
Conductor/Band: D. Costa/studio orchestra
Key Release: **Late Sinatra Goodies** (illegal; from Reprise masters)
see Album Lists: alphabetic under "bootleg"; mid.1980s; bootleg Alb. #6

#521   It All Came True   *1st recording*
Publication Date: 1947
Music & Words: Sunny Skylar
Recorded: 7/23/47-a
Arranger: Axel Stordahl
Conductor/Band: A. Stordahl/studio orchestra
Key Release: 78rpm single #DB-2381 (English release only)
see Album List #1: 1947 Columbia (3) single record — listed by number

#522   It All Came True   *2nd recording*
Publication Date: 1947
Music & Words: Sunny Skylar
Recorded: 9/23/47-a
Arranger: Alvy West
Conductor/Band: A. West/studio orchestra
Key Release: **The Essential Frank Sinatra** (Volume 2)
see Album Lists: alphabetic by title; 1967 — 3rd LP; Columbia/35th

#523   It All Depends on You
1st recording
Publication Date: 1927
Music: Ray Henderson
Words: B. G. (Buddy) DeSylva & Lew Brown
Recorded: 7/10/49-a
Arranger: Hugo Winterhalter
Conductor/Band: H. Winterhalter/studio orchestra
Key Release: **Frankie**

see Album Lists: alphabetic by title; 1955 — 8th LP; Columbia/20th

#524   It All Depends on You
2nd recording
Publication Date: 1927
Music: Ray Henderson
Words: B. G. (Buddy) DeSylva & Lew Brown
Recorded: 9/30/58-a
Arranger: Billy May
Conductor/Band: Billy May & his Orchestra
Key Release: **The Rare Sinatra: Volume 1** (Australia release only)
see Album Lists: alphabetic by title; 1978 — 1st LP; Capitol/65th

#525   It All Depends on You
3rd recording
Publication Date: 1927
Music: Ray Henderson
Words: B. G. (Buddy) DeSylva & Lew Brown
Recorded: 8/23/60-d
Arranger: Nelson Riddle
Conductor/Band: N. Riddle/studio orchestra
Key Release: **Sinatra's Swingin' Session!!!**
see Album Lists: alphabetic by title; 1961 — 1st LP; Capitol/28th

#526   It Came Upon a Midnight Clear   *1st recording*
Publication Date: 1850
Music: Richard Storrs Willis — 1849
Words: Edmund Hamilton Sears
Recorded: 12/28/47-b
Arranger: Axel Stordahl
Conductor/Band: A. Stordahl/studio orchestra
Key Release: **Christmas Dreaming**
see Album Lists: alphabetic by title; 1957 — 3rd LP; Columbia/25th

#527   It Came Upon a Midnight Clear   *2nd recording*

Publication Date: 1850
Music: Richard Storrs Willis — 1849
Words: Edmund Hamilton Sears
Recorded: 7/10/57-a
Arranger: Gordon Jenkins
Conductor/Band: G. Jenkins/studio
orchestra
Key Release: A Jolly Christmas from
Frank Sinatra
see Album Lists: alphabetic by title;
1957 — 6th LP; Capitol/14th

#528   It Could Happen to You
Publication Date: 1944
Music: Jimmy Van Heusen
Words: Johnny Burke
Recorded: 4/5/56-b
Arranger: Nelson Riddle
Conductor/Band: N. Riddle with or-
chestra & the Hollywood String
Quartet
Key Release: **Close to You**
see Album Lists: alphabetic by title;
1957 — 1st LP; Capitol/11th

#529   It Gets Lonely Early
Publication Date: 1965
Music: Jimmy Van Heusen
Words: Sammy Cahn
Recorded: 4/22/65-d
Arranger: Gordon Jenkins
Conductor/Band: G. Jenkins/studio
orchestra
Key Release: **September of My Years**
see Album Lists: alphabetic by title;
1965 — 1st LP; Reprise/23rd

#530   It Had to Be You
Publication Date: 1924
Music: Isham Jones
Words: Gus Kahn
Recorded: 7/18/79-b
Arranger: Billy May
Conductor/Band: B. May/studio
orchestra
Key Release: **Trilogy: The Past**
[Collectibles of the Early Years]

see Album Lists: alphabetic by title;
1980 — 1st LP; Reprise/52nd

#531   It Happened in Monterey
Publication Date: 1930
Music: Mabel Wayne
Words: Billy Rose
Recorded: 1/12/56-a
Arranger: Nelson Riddle
Conductor/Band: N. Riddle/studio
orchestra
Key Release: **Songs for Swingin'**
Lovers!
see Album Lists: alphabetic by title;
1956 — 1st LP; Capitol/7th

#532   It Happens Every Spring
Publication Date: 1949
Music: Josef Myrow
Words: Mack Gordon
Recorded: 4/10/49-b
Arranger: Axel Stordahl
Conductor/Band: A. Stordahl/studio
orchestra
Key Release: **Sinatra Rarities — The**
Columbia Years (Volume 1)
see Album Lists: alphabetic by title;
1986 — 1st LP; Columbia/50th

#533   It Might as Well Be
Spring   *1st recording*
Publication Date: 1945
Music: Richard Rodgers
Words: Oscar Hammerstein II
Recorded: 11/21/61-a
Arranger: Don Costa
Conductor/Band: D. Costa/studio
orchestra
Key Release: **Sinatra & Strings**
see Album Lists: alphabetic by title;
1962 — 1st LP; Reprise/4th

#534   It Might as Well Be
Spring   *2nd recording*
Publication Date: 1945
Music: Richard Rodgers
Words: Oscar Hammerstein II

Recorded: 1/28/64-a
Arranger: Nelson Riddle
Conductor/Band: N. Riddle/studio
   orchestra
Key Release: **Frank Sinatra Sings
   "Days of Wine and Roses,"
   "Moon River," and Other
   Academy Award Winners**
see Album Lists: alphabetic by title;
   1964—1st LP; Reprise/17th

**#535   It Never Entered My
   Mind**   *1st recording*
Publication Date: 1940
Music: Richard Rodgers
Words: Lorenz Hart
Recorded: 11/5/47-b
Arranger: Axel Stordahl
Conductor/Band: A. Stordahl/studio
   orchestra
Key Release: **Put Your Dreams Away**
see Album Lists: alphabetic by title;
   1958—3rd LP; Columbia/26th

**#536   It Never Entered My
   Mind**   *2nd recording*
Publication Date: 1940
Music: Richard Rodgers
Words: Lorenz Hart
Recorded: 3/4/55-a
Arranger: Nelson Riddle
Conductor/Band: N. Riddle/studio
   orchestra
Key Release: **In the Wee Small
   Hours** (12" LP version)
see Album Lists: alphabetic by title;
   1955—7th LP; Capitol/5th

**#537   It Only Happens When I
   Dance with You**   *1st recording*
Publication Date: 1948
Music & Words: Irving Berlin
Recorded: 1948 radio—Lucky
   Strike's "Your Hit Parade"
Arranger: Axel Stordahl
Conductor/Band: A. Stordahl/radio
   orchestra

Key Release: **Frank Sinatra**
see Album Lists: alphabetic under
   "radio"; early 1960s; Cameron/
   4th

**#538   It Only Happens When I
   Dance with You**   *2nd recording*
Publication Date: 1948
Music & Words: Irving Berlin
Recorded: 3/16/48-a
Arranger: Axel Stordahl
Conductor/Band: A. Stordahl/studio
   orchestra
Key Release: **Sinatra Rarities — The
   Columbia Years** (Volume 1)
see Album Lists: alphabetic by title;
   1986—1st LP; Columbia/50th

#539   It Started All Over Again
   1st recording
Publication Date: 1942
Music: Carl Fischer
Words: Bill Carey
Recorded: 7/1/42-c
Arranger: Axel Stordahl
Conductor/Band: Tommy Dorsey &
   his Orchestra
Key Release: **The Dorsey/Sinatra
   Sessions** (Volume 6)
see Album Lists: alphabetic by title;
   1972—6th LP; RCA Victor/
   22nd

#540   It Started All Over Again
   2nd recording
Publication Date: 1942
Music: Carl Fischer
Words: Bill Carey
Recorded: 5/3/61-d
Arranger: Sy Oliver
Conductor/Band: S. Oliver/studio
   orchestra
Key Release: **I Remember Tommy...**
see Album Lists: alphabetic by title;
   1961—7th LP; Reprise/3rd

#541   It Was a Very Good Year
   1st recording

Publication Date: 1961
Music & Words: Ervin Drake
Recorded: 4/22/65-a
Arranger: Gordon Jenkins
Conductor/Band: G. Jenkins/studio
orchestra
Key Release: September of My Years
see Album Lists: alphabetic by title;
1965 — 1st LP; Reprise/23rd

#542   It Was a Very Good Year
2nd recording
Publication Date: 1961
Music & Words: Ervin Drake
Recorded: 2/1/66-h
Arranger: Quincy Jones
Conductor/Band: Count Basie & his
Band
Key Release: Sinatra at the Sands
(Live Recording — 2 discs)
see Album Lists: alphabetic by title;
1966 — 3rd LP; Reprise/29th

#543   It Worries Me
Publication Date: 1954
Music: J. Schultz & I. Reichel
Words: Carl Sigman
Recorded: 5/13/54-c
Arranger: Nelson Riddle
Conductor/Band: N. Riddle/studio
orchestra
Key Release: Songs for Young Lovers
(later 12" version of LP)
see Album Lists: alphabetic by title;
1960 — 7th LP; Capitol/27th

#544   It's a Blue World
Publication Date: 1940
Music & Words: George Forrest &
Robert Wright
Recorded: 9/12/61-e
Arranger: Heinie Beau
Conductor/Band: Axel Stordahl/
studio orchestra
Key Release: Point of No Return
see Album Lists: alphabetic by title;
1962 — 2nd LP; Capitol/31st

**#545   It's a Lonesome Old
Town***
Publication Date: 1930
Music & Words: Harry Tobias &
Charles Kisco
Recorded: 6/25/58-b
Arranger: Nelson Riddle
Conductor/Band: N. Riddle/studio
orchestra
*Key Release: Frank Sinatra Sings
for Only the Lonely*
see Album Lists: alphabetic by title;
1958 — 5th LP; Capitol/19th
*This song only appears on the
monaural version of the LP
*Frank Sinatra Sings for Only the
Lonely* (Capitol W-1053); it was
eliminated from the stereo ver-
sion of that album.

**#546   It's a Lovely Day Tomor-
row**
Publication Date: 1939
Music & Words: Irving Berlin
Recorded: 4/23/40-d
Arranger: Dorsey "house" arrng:
T. Dorsey, S. Oliver, F. Stulce,
P. Weston
Conductor/Band: Tommy Dorsey &
his Orchestra
*Key Release: The Dorsey/Sinatra
Sessions* (Volume 2)
see Album Lists: alphabetic by title;
1972 — 2nd LP; RCA Victor/18th

#547   It's a Wonderful World
Publication Date: 1940
Music: Jan Savitt & Johnny Wat-
son
Words: Harold Adamson
Recorded: 5/19/61-d
Arranger: Billy May
Conductor/Band: Billy May & his
Orchestra
Key Release: Sinatra Swings (origi-
nal title: "Swing Along with
Me")

see Album Lists: alphabetic by title;
1961 — 6th LP; Reprise/2nd

#548   It's All Right with Me
1st recording
Publication Date: 1953
Music & Words: Cole Porter
Recorded: 1959 television special
Arranger: Nelson Riddle
Conductor/Band: N. Riddle/television orchestra
Key Release: Frank Sinatra — Through the Years: 1944–1966
see Album Lists: alphabetic under "television"; mid–1960s; Ajazz/ 1st

#549   It's All Right with Me
2nd recording
Publication Date: 1953
Music & Words: Cole Porter
Recorded: 2/19/60-a
Arranger: Nelson Riddle
Conductor/Band: N. Riddle/studio orchestra
Key Release: "Can-Can" (Official Soundtrack LP)
see Album Lists: alphabetic by title;
1960 — 1st LP; Capitol/24th

#550   It's All Right with Me
3rd recording
Publication Date: 1953
Music & Words: Cole Porter
Recorded: 4/17/84-b
Arranger: Sam Nestico
Conductor/Band: Quincy Jones & a special all-star jazz band
Key Release: L.A. Is My Lady
see Album Lists: alphabetic by title;
1984 — 1st LP; Qwest/1st

#551   It's All Up to You   *1st recording — duet with Ella Fitzgerald*
Publication Date: 1946
Music: Jule Styne
Words: Sammy Cahn; charity

"Good Health" promotion lyric
Recorded: 1946 radio — "The Frank Sinatra Old Gold Show"
Arranger: Axel Stordahl
Conductor/Band: A. Stordahl/radio orchestra
Key Release: My Best Songs — My Best Years (Volume 4)
see Album Lists: alphabetic under "radio"; early 1970s; Pentagon/ 4th

#554   It's All Up to You   *2nd recording — duet with Dinah Shore*
Publication Date: 1946
Music: Jule Styne
Words: Sammy Cahn; charity
"Good Health" promotion lyric
Recorded: 11/7/46-c
Arranger: Axel Stordahl
Conductor/Band: A. Stordahl/studio orchestra
Key Release: 78rpm single #DO-3104 (Australian release only)
see Album List #1: 1948 Columbia (3) single record — listed by number

#553   It's Always You   *1st recording*
Publication Date: 1941
Music: Jimmy Van Heusen
Words: Johnny Burke
Recorded: 1/15/41-b
Arranger: Dorsey "house" arrng: T. Dorsey, S. Oliver, F. Stulce, P. Weston
Conductor/Band: Tommy Dorsey & his Orchestra
Key Release: The Dorsey/Sinatra Sessions (Volume 4)
see Album Lists: alphabetic by title;
1972 — 4th LP; RCA Victor/20th

#554   It's Always You   *2nd recording*
Publication Date: 1941

Music: Jimmy Van Heusen
Words: Johnny Burke
Recorded: 5/3/61-c
Arranger: Sy Oliver
Conductor/Band: S. Oliver/studio
  orchestra
Key Release: I Remember Tommy...
see Album Lists: alphabetic by title;
  1961 — 7th LP; Reprise/3rd

#555   It's Easy to Remember
Publication Date: 1935
Music: Richard Rodgers
Words: Lorenz Hart
Recorded: 10/1/56-b
Arranger: Nelson Riddle
Conductor/Band: N. Riddle with or-
  chestra & the Hollywood String
  Quartet
Key Release: Close to You
see Album Lists: alphabetic by title;
  1957 — 1st LP; Capitol/11th

**#556   It's Fate, Baby, It's
Fate**
  duet with Betty Garrett
Publication Date: 1949
Music: Roger Edens
Words: Betty Comden & Adolph
  Green
Recorded: 1949 — 1st soundtrack (il-
  legally taken from film sound)
Arranger: Conrad Salinger
Conductor/Band: Adolph Deutsch/
  MGM Orchestra
*Key Release: "Take Me Out to the
  Ball Game"* (LP: Five Films)
see Album Lists: alphabetic under
  "soundtrack"; mid-1960s; boot-
  leg Mv. #12

**#557   It's Funny to Everyone
But Me**
Publication Date: 1939
Music & Words: Jack Lawrence
Recorded: 8/17/39-b
Arranger: Andy Gibson

Conductor/Band: Harry James & his
  Orchestra
Key Release: 78rpm single #35209
see Album List #1: 1943 Columbia
  (2) single record — listed by
  number

#558   It's Nice to Go Trav'ling
Publication Date: 1957
Music: Jimmy Van Heusen
Words: Sammy Cahn
Recorded: 10/8/57-d
Arranger: Billy May
Conductor/Band: Billy May & his
  Orchestra
Key Release: Come Fly with Me
see Album Lists: alphabetic by title;
  1958 — 2nd LP; Capitol/17th

#559   It's Only a Paper Moon
  1st recording
Publication Date: 1932
Music: Harold Arlen
Words: E. Y. ("Yip") Harburg &
  Billy Rose
Recorded: 4/24/50-b
Arranger: George Siravo
Conductor/Band: G. Siravo/studio
  orchestra
Key Release: Adventures of the Heart
see Album Lists: alphabetic by title;
  1956 — 3rd LP; Columbia/24th

#560   It's Only a Paper Moon
  2nd recording
Publication Date: 1932
Music: Harold Arlen
Words: E. Y. ("Yip") Harburg &
  Billy Rose
Recorded: 8/31/60-a
Arranger: Nelson Riddle
Conductor/Band: N. Riddle/studio
  orchestra
*Key Release: Sinatra's Swingin'
  Session!!!*
see Album Lists: alphabetic by title;
  1961 — 1st LP; Capitol/28th

#561 It's Only Money *duet*
with Groucho Marx
Publication Date: 1950
Music: Jule Styne
Words: Sammy Cahn
Recorded: 1951—1st soundtrack (il-
legally taken from film sound)
Arranger: Leigh Harline
Conductor/Band: L. Harline/RKO
Orchestra
Key Release: "Double Dynamite"
(LP: "On the Town" and Others)
see Album Lists: alphabetic under
"soundtrack"; mid–1960s; boot-
leg Mv. #14

**#562 It's Over, It's Over, It's
Over**
Publication Date: 1960
Music: Matt Dennis
Words: Dak Stanford
Recorded: 4/12/60-d
Arranger: Nelson Riddle
Conductor/Band: N. Riddle/studio
orchestra
Key Release: All the Way
see Album Lists: alphabetic by title;
1961—2nd LP; Capitol/29th

#563 It's Sunday
Publication Date: 1980
Music: Jule Styne
Words: Susan Birkenhead
Recorded: 2/28/83-a
Arranger: Tony Mottola
Conductor/Band: T. Mottola, in solo
guitar accompaniment
Key Release: 45rpm single #7-29677,
side B
see Album List #1: 1983 Reprise (5)
single record—listed by number

#564 It's the Same Old Dream
1st recording
Publication Date: 1946
Music: Jule Styne
Words: Sammy Cahn

Recorded: 10/24/46-b
Arranger: Axel Stordahl
Conductor/Band: A. Stordahl/studio
orchestra
*Key Release: The Essential Frank
Sinatra* (Volume 2)
see Album Lists: alphabetic by title;
1967—3rd LP; Columbia/35th

#565 It's the Same Old Dream
2nd recording
Publication Date: 1946
Music: Jule Styne
Words: Sammy Cahn
Recorded: 11/25/57-c
Arranger: Nelson Riddle
Conductor/Band: N. Riddle/studio
orchestra
*Key Release: This Is Sinatra, Vol-
ume Two*
see Album Lists: alphabetic by title;
1958—4th LP; Capitol/18th

#566 I've Been to Town
Publication Date: 1969
Music & Words: Rod McKuen
Recorded: 3/19/69-a
Arranger: Don Costa
Conductor/Band: D. Costa/studio
orchestra
Key Release: A Man Alone
see Album Lists: alphabetic by title;
1969—3rd LP; Reprise/39th

#567 I've Found a New Baby
Publication Date: 1926
Music & Words: Spencer Williams
& Jack Palmer
Recorded: 1943 radio—"Songs by
Sinatra"
Arranger: Axel Stordahl
Conductor/Band: A. Stordahl/radio
orchestra
*Key Release: My Best Songs—My
Best Years* (Volume 1)
see Album Lists: alphabetic under

"radio"; early 1970s; Pentagon
1st

#568   I've Got a Crush on You
1st recording
Publication Date: 1930
Music: George Gershwin
Words: Ira Gershwin
Recorded: 11/5/47-c
Arranger: Axel Stordahl
Conductor/Band: A. Stordahl/studio
orchestra
*Key Release: The Frank Sinatra
Story in Music* (2 discs)
see Album Lists: alphabetic by title;
1959 — 2nd LP; Columbia/27th

#569   I've Got a Crush on You
2nd recording
Publication Date: 1930
Music: George Gershwin
Words: Ira Gershwin
Recorded: 3/3/60-b
Arranger: Nelson Riddle
Conductor/Band: N. Riddle/studio
orchestra
Key Release: Nice 'n' Easy
see Album Lists: alphabetic by title;
1960 — 2nd LP; Capitol/25th

570   I've Got a Crush on You
3rd recording
Publication Date: 1930
Music: George Gershwin
Words: Ira Gershwin
Recorded: 2/1/66-a
Arranger: Quincy Jones
Conductor/Band: Count Basie & his
Band
Key Release: Sinatra at the Sands
(Live Recording — 2 discs)
see Album Lists: alphabetic by title;
1966 — 3rd LP; Reprise/29th

#571   I've Got a Home in That Rock
Publication Date: 1800s

Music & Words: Traditional; black
America in the 1800s
Recorded: 5/16/45-c
Arranger: Axel Stordahl
Conductor/Band: A. Stordahl/studio
orchestra
Key Release: 78rpm single #37853,
side A
see Album List #1: 1947 Columbia
(4) single record — listed by
number

#572   I've Got My Love to Keep Me Warm
Publication Date: 1937
Music & Words: Irving Berlin
Recorded: 12/20/60-d
Arranger: Johnny Mandel
Conductor/Band: J. Mandel/studio
orchestra
Key Release: Ring-a-Ding Ding!
see Album Lists: alphabetic by title;
1961 — 3rd LP; Reprise/1st

#573   I've Got the World on a String
Publication Date: 1932
Music: Harold Arlen
Words: Ted Koehler
Recorded: 4/30/53-a
Arranger: Nelson Riddle
Conductor/Band: N. Riddle/studio
orchestra
Key Release: This Is Sinatra! (Volume 1)
see Album Lists: alphabetic by title;
1956 — 6th LP; Capitol/10th

#574   I've Got You Under My Skin   *1st recording*
Publication Date: 1936
Music & Words: Cole Porter
Recorded: 1/12/56-d
Arranger: Nelson Riddle
Conductor/Band: N. Riddle/studio
orchestra

Key Release: **Songs for Swingin'
Lovers!**
see Album Lists: alphabetic by title;
1956 — 1st LP; Capitol/7th

**#575 I've Got You Under My
Skin** *2nd recording*
Publication Date: 1936
Music & Words: Cole Porter
Recorded: 4/30/63-d
Arranger: Nelson Riddle
Conductor/Band: N. Riddle/studio
orchestra
Key Release: **Sinatra's Sinatra**
see Album Lists: alphabetic by title;
1963 — 7th LP; Reprise/15th

**#576 I've Got You Under My
Skin** *3rd recording*
Publication Date: 1936
Music & Words: Cole Porter
Recorded: 2/1/66-b
Arranger: Quincy Jones
Conductor/Band: Count Basie & his
Band
Key Release: **Sinatra at the Sands**
(Live Recording — 2 discs)
see Album Lists: alphabetic by title;
1966 — 3rd LP; Reprise/29th

**#577 I've Got You Under My
Skin** *4th recording*
Publication Date: 1936
Music & Words: Cole Porter
Recorded: 10/4/74-e
Arranger: Nelson Riddle
Conductor/Band: Bill Miller/Woody
Herman's Young Thundering
Herd band
Key Release: **Sinatra — The Main
Event** (Live Recording)
see Album Lists: alphabetic by title;
1974 — 2nd LP; Reprise/48th

#578 I've Had My Moments
Publication Date: 1934
Music: Walter Donaldson

Words: Gus Kahn
Recorded: 4/4/56-a
Arranger: Nelson Riddle
Conductor/Band: N. Riddle with or-
chestra & the Hollywood String
Quartet
Key Release: **Close to You**
see Album Lists: alphabetic by title;
1957 — 1st LP; Capitol/11th

**#579 I've Heard That Song
Before**
Publication Date: 1942
Music: Jule Styne
Words: Sammy Cahn
Recorded: 3/21/61-c
Arranger: Billy May
Conductor/Band: B. May/studio
orchestra
Key Release: **Come Swing with
Me!**
see Album Lists: alphabetic by title;
1961 — 5th LP; Capitol/30th

**#580 I've Never Been in Love
Before**
Publication Date: 1950
Music & Words: Frank Loesser
Recorded: 7/18/63-c
Arranger: Nelson Riddle
Conductor/Band: Morris Stoloff/
studio orchestra
Key Release: **Reprise Musical Reper-
tory Theatre: "Guys and Dolls"**
see Album Lists: alphabetic by title;
1963 — 4th LP; Reprise/12th

#581 Jeepers Creepers
Publication Date: 1938
Music: Harry Warren
Words: Johnny Mercer
Recorded: 4/19/54-b
Arranger: Nelson Riddle: full-orch.
arrng. from G. Siravo band
arrng.
Conductor/Band: N. Riddle/studio
orchestra

Key Release: **Swing Easy!** (original
10" LP)
see Album Lists: alphabetic by title;
1954 — 5th LP; Capitol/4th

#582   Jesus Is a Rock
Publication Date: 1800s
Music & Words: Traditional; black
America in the 1800s
Recorded: 5/16/45-d
Arranger: Axel Stordahl
Conductor/Band: A. Stordahl/studio
orchestra
Key Release: 78rpm single #37853,
side B
see Album List #1: 1947 Columbia
(4) single record — listed by
number

**#583   Jingle Bells «In a One-
Horse Open Sleigh»**   1st record-
ing
Publication Date: 1857
Music & Words: J. S. Pierpont
Recorded: 8/8/46-c
Arranger: Axel Stordahl
Conductor/Band: A. Stordahl/studio
orchestra
Key Release: **Christmas Dreaming**
see Album Lists: alphabetic by title;
1957 — 3rd LP; Columbia/25th

**#584   Jingle Bells «In a One-
Horse Open Sleigh»**   2nd re-
cording
Publication Date: 1857
Music & Words: J. S. Pierpont
Recorded: 7/16/57-a
Arranger: Gordon Jenkins
Conductor/Band: G. Jenkins/studio
orchestra
Key Release: **A Jolly Christmas from
Frank Sinatra**
see Album Lists: alphabetic by title;
1957 — 6th LP; Capitol/14th

#585   Just a Kiss Apart
Publication Date: 1949

Music: Jule Styne
Words: Leo Robin
Recorded: 7/21/49-a
Arranger: Morris Stoloff
Conductor/Band: M. Stoloff/studio
orchestra
Key Release: 78rpm single #38556
see Album List #1: 1949 Columbia
(4) single record — listed by
number

**#586   Just As Though You
Were Here**   1st recording
Publication Date: 1942
Music: John Benson Brooks
Words: Eddie DeLange
Recorded: 5/18/42-a
Arranger: Axel Stordahl
Conductor/Band: Tommy Dorsey &
his Orchestra
Key Release: **The Dorsey/Sinatra
Sessions** (Volume 6)
see Album Lists: alphabetic by title;
1972 — 6th LP; RCA Victor/22nd

**#587   Just As Though You
Were Here**   2nd recording
Publication Date: 1942
Music: John Benson Brooks
Words: Eddie DeLange
Recorded: 9/24/74-c
Arranger: Gordon Jenkins
Conductor/Band: G. Jenkins/studio
orchestra
Key Release: **Late Sinatra Goodies**
(illegal; from Reprise masters)
see Album Lists: alphabetic under
"bootleg"; mid–1980s; bootleg
Alb. #6

#588   Just for Now
Publication Date: 1947
Music & Words: John Redmond
Recorded: 10/26/47-c
Arranger: Axel Stordahl
Conductor/Band: A. Stordahl/studio
orchestra

Key Release: 78rpm single #38225
see Album List #1: 1948 Columbia
(4) single record — listed by
number

#589   Just Friends
Publication Date: 1931
Music: John Klenner
Words: Sam M. Lewis
Recorded: 3/26/59-d
Arranger: Gordon Jenkins
Conductor/Band: G. Jenkins/studio
orchestra
Key Release: No One Cares
see Album Lists: alphabetic by title;
1959 — 5th LP; Capitol/23rd

#590   Just in Time
Publication Date: 1956
Music: Jule Styne
Words: Betty Comden & Adolph
Green
Recorded: 12/9/58-c
Arranger: Billy May
Conductor/Band: Billy May & his
Orchestra
Key Release: Come Dance with Me!
see Album Lists: alphabetic by title;
1959 — 1st LP; Capitol/20th

#591   Just One of Those Things
Publication Date: 1935
Music & Words: Cole Porter
Recorded: 4/7/54-b
Arranger: Nelson Riddle: full-orch.
arrng. from G. Siravo band
arrng.
Conductor/Band: N. Riddle/studio
orchestra
Key Release: Swing Easy! (original
10"LP)
see Album Lists: alphabetic by title;
1954 — 5th LP; Capitol/4th

**#592   Just One Way to Say I
Love You**
Publication Date: 1949

Music & Words: Irving Berlin
Recorded: 5/6/49-b
Arranger: Axel Stordahl
Conductor/Band: A. Stordahl/studio
orchestra
Key Release: 78rpm single #38513,
side B
see Album List #1: 1949 Columbia
(4) single record — listed by
number

#593   Just the Way You Are
Publication Date: 1977
Music & Words: Billy Joel
Recorded: 8/22/79-b
Arranger: Don Costa
Conductor/Band: D. Costa/studio
orchestra
*Key Release: Trilogy: The Present
[Some Very Good Years]*
see Album Lists: alphabetic by title;
1980 — 2nd LP; Reprise/53rd

#594   Kiss Me Again
Publication Date: 1905
Music: Victor Herbert
Words: Henry Blossom
Recorded: 12/19/44-c
Arranger: Axel Stordahl
Conductor/Band: A. Stordahl/studio
orchestra
Key Release: 78rpm single #38287
see Album List #1: 1948 Columbia
(4) single record — listed by
number

#595   Kisses and Tears   *duet*
with Jane Russell
Publication Date: 1950
Music: Jule Styne
Words: Sammy Cahn
Recorded: 2/23/50-a
Arranger: Axel Stordahl
Conductor/Band: A. Stordahl/studio
orchestra
Key Release: Boys & Girls Together
(10" LP)

see Album Lists: alphabetic by title;
1955 — 5th LP; Columbia/16th

#596   L.A. Is My Lady
Publication Date: 1984
Music: Quincy Jones & Peggy Lipton Jones
Words: Alan & Marilyn Bergman
Recorded: 4/13/84-a
Arrangers: Quincy Jones & Dave Matthews & Jerry Hey & Torry Zito
Conductor/Band: Quincy Jones & a special all-star jazz band
Key Release: **L.A. Is My Lady**
see Album Lists: alphabetic by title;
1984 — 1st LP; Qwest/1st

#597   La Ci Darem La Mano
duet with Kathryn Grayson
Publication Date: 1787
Music: Wolfgang Amadeus Mozart
Words: Lorenzo DaPonte
Recorded: 1947 soundtrack (illegally taken from film sound)
Arranger: Ted Duncan
Conductor/Band: Johnny Green/ MGM Orchestra
Key Release: **"It Happened in Brooklyn"** (LP: Score from "It Happened in Brooklyn")
see Album Lists: alphabetic under "soundtrack"; mid–1960s; bootleg Mv. #9

#598   Lady Day   *1st recording*
Publication Date: 1969
Music & Words: Bob Gaudio & Jake Holmes
Recorded: 10/13/69-a
Arranger: Charles Calello
Conductor/Band: C. Calello/studio orchestra
Key Release: **Late Sinatra Goodies** (illegal; from Reprise masters)
see Album Lists: alphabetic under

"bootleg"; mid–1980s; bootleg Alb. #6

#599   Lady Day   *2nd recording*
Publication Date: 1969
Music & Words: Bob Gaudio & Jake Holmes
Recorded: 11/7/69-a
Arranger: Don Costa
Conductor/Band: D. Costa/studio orchestra
Key Release: **Sinatra & Company**
see Album Lists: alphabetic by title;
1971 — 2nd LP; Reprise/42nd

#600   The Lady from 29 Palms
Publication Date: 1947
Music & Words: Allie Wrubel
Recorded: 1947 radio — Lucky Strike's "Your Hit Parade"
Arranger: Axel Stordahl
Conductor/Band: A. Stordahl/radio orchestra
Key Release: **The Original . . . Frank Sinatra**
see Album Lists: alphabetic under "radio"; early 1960s; Cameron/ 2nd

#601   The Lady Is a Tramp
1st recording
Publication Date: 1937
Music: Richard Rodgers
Words: Lorenz Hart
Recorded: 11/26/56-a
Arranger: Nelson Riddle
Conductor/Band: N. Riddle/studio orchestra
Key Release: **"Pal Joey"** (Official Soundtrack LP)
see Album Lists: alphabetic by title;
1957 — 8th LP; Capitol/15th

#602   The Lady Is a Tramp
2nd recording
Publication Date: 1937
Music: Richard Rodgers

Words: Lorenz Hart
Recorded: 10/13/74-a
Arranger: Billy Byers
Conductor/Band: Bill Miller/Woody
  Herman's Young Thundering
  Herd band
Key Release: **Sinatra — The Main
  Event** (Live Recording)
see Album Lists: alphabetic by title;
  1974 — 2nd LP; Reprise/48th

**#603   The Lamplighter's Sere-
nade**
Publication Date: 1942
Music: Hoagy Carmichael
Words: Paul Francis Webster
Recorded: 1/19/42-b
Arranger: Axel Stordahl
Conductor/Band: A. Stordahl/studio
  orchestra
Key Release: **We Three**
see Album Lists: alphabetic by title;
  1957 — 7th LP; RCA Victor/12th

#604   The Last Call for Love
  (derived from 1863's "Taps")
Publication Date: 1942
Music: Burton Lane & E. Y.
  ("Yip") Harburg & Margery
  Cummings
Words: E. Y. ("Yip") Harburg &
  Margery Cummings
Recorded: 2/19/42-d
Arranger: Axel Stordahl
Conductor/Band: Tommy Dorsey &
  his Orchestra
Key Release: **The Dorsey/Sinatra
  Sessions** (Volume 6)
see Album Lists: alphabetic by title;
  1972 — 6th LP; RCA Victor/
  22nd

#605   The Last Dance   *1st re-
cording*
Publication Date: 1958
Music: Jimmy Van Heusen
Words: Sammy Cahn

Recorded: 12/23/58-d
Arranger: Heinie Beau
Conductor/Band: Billy May & his
  Orchestra
Key Release: **Come Dance with Me!**
see Album Lists: alphabetic by title;
  1959 — 1st LP; Capitol/20th

#606   The Last Dance   *2nd re-
cording*
Publication Date: 1958
Music: Jimmy Van Heusen
Words: Sammy Cahn
Recorded: 12/21/60-a
Arranger: Felix Slatkin
Conductor/Band: F. Slatkin/studio
  orchestra
Key Release: **Love Songs** (illegal;
  from Reprise masters)
see Album Lists: alphabetic under
  "bootleg"; early 1970s; bootleg
  Alb. #3

**#607   Last Night When We
  Were Young**   *1st recording*
Publication Date: 1936
Music: Harold Arlen
Words: E. Y. ("Yip") Harburg
Recorded: 3/1/54-b
Arranger: Nelson Riddle
Conductor/Band: N. Riddle/studio
  orchestra
Key Release: **In the Wee Small
  Hours** (12″ LP version)
see Album Lists: alphabetic by title;
  1955 — 7th LP; Capitol/5th

**#608   Last Night When We
  Were Young**   *2nd recording*
Publication Date: 1936
Music: Harold Arlen
Words: E. Y. ("Yip") Harburg
Recorded: 4/13/65-c
Arranger: Gordon Jenkins
Conductor/Band: G. Jenkins/studio
  orchestra
Key Release: **September of My Years**

see Album Lists: alphabetic by title; 1965 — 1st LP; Reprise/23rd

#609   Laura   *1st recording*
Publication Date: 1945
Music: David Raksin
Words: Johnny Mercer
Recorded: 10/22/47-c
Arranger: Axel Stordahl
Conductor/Band: A. Stordahl/studio orchestra
Key Release: **The Voice**
see Album Lists: alphabetic by title; 1955 — 9th LP; Columbia/21st

#610   Laura   *2nd recording*
Publication Date: 1945
Music: David Raksin
Words: Johnny Mercer
Recorded: 4/29/57-c
Arranger: Gordon Jenkins
Conductor/Band: G. Jenkins/studio orchestra
Key Release: **Where Are You?**
see Album Lists: alphabetic by title; 1957 — 4th LP; Capitol/13th

#611   Lean Baby*
Publication Date: 1951
Music: Billy May
Words: Roy Alfred
Recorded: 4/2/53-a
Arranger: Heinie Beau
Conductor/Band: Axel Stordahl/ studio orchestra
Key Release: **Swing Easy** (later 12″ version of LP)
see Album Lists: alphabetic by title; 1960 — 6th LP; Capitol/26th
*The first song Sinatra recorded for Capitol Records — the session took place on April 2, 1953 — and also the "B" side of his first single record for that label. It was the beginning of his comeback as a recording artist.

#612   Learnin' the Blues   *1st recording*
Publication Date: 1955
Music & Words: Dolores Vicki Silvers
Recorded: 3/23/55-a
Arranger: Nelson Riddle
Conductor/Band: N. Riddle/studio orchestra
Key Release: **This Is Sinatra!** (Volume 1)
see Album Lists: alphabetic by title; 1956 — 6th LP; Capitol/10th

#613   Learnin' the Blues   *2nd recording*
Publication Date: 1955
Music & Words: Dolores Vicki Silvers
Recorded: 10/2/62-d
Arranger: Neal Hefti
Conductor/Band: Count Basie & his Band
Key Release: **Sinatra-Basie: An Historic Musical First**
see Album Lists: alphabetic by title; 1963 — 1st LP; Reprise/9th

#614   Leaving on a Jet Plane
Publication Date: 1967
Music & Words: John Denver
Recorded: 10/29/70-a
Arranger: Don Costa
Conductor/Band: D. Costa/studio orchestra
Key Release: **Sinatra & Company**
see Album Lists: alphabetic by title; 1971 — 2nd LP; Reprise/42nd

#615   Let It Snow (Let It Snow, Let It Snow)
Publication Date: 1945
Music: Jule Styne
Words: Sammy Cahn
Recorded: 11/5/50-a
Arranger: Axel Stordahl

Conductor/Band: A. Stordahl/studio orchestra
Key Release: **Christmas Dreaming**
see Album Lists: alphabetic by title; 1957 — 3rd LP; Columbia/25th

#616   Let Me Love You To- night «No Te Importe Saber»
Publication Date: 1940
Music: Rene Touzet — 1939
Words: Mitchell Parish
Recorded: 1944 radio — Sinatra's "Vimms Vitamins Show"
Arranger: Axel Stordahl
Conductor/Band: A. Stordahl/radio orchestra
Key Release: **The First Times . . . Frank Sinatra**
see Album Lists: alphabetic under "radio"; early 1960s; Cameron/ 1st

#617   Let Me Try Again «Laisse Moi le Temps»   *1st re- cording*
Publication Date: 1973
Music: Francois Caravelli — 1972
Words: Paul Anka & Sammy Cahn/Michelle Jourdan — 1972
Recorded: 6/21/73-b
Arranger: Don Costa
Conductor/Band: Gordon Jenkins/ studio orchestra
Key Release: **Ol' Blue Eyes Is Back**
see Album Lists: alphabetic by title; 1973 — 2nd LP; Reprise/45th

#618   Let Me Try Again «Laisse Moi le Temps»   *2nd recording*
Publication Date: 1973
Music: Francois Caravelli — 1972
Words: Paul Anka & Sammy Cahn/Michelle Jourdan — 1972
Recorded: 10/13/74-c
Arranger: Don Costa
Conductor/Band: Bill Miller/Woody Herman's Young Thundering Herd band
Key Release: **Sinatra — The Main Event** (Live Recording)
see Album Lists: alphabetic by title; 1974 — 2nd LP; Reprise/48th

#619   Let Us Break Bread To- gether   *duet with Bing Crosby*
Publication Date: 1800s
Music & Words: Traditional; black America in the 1800s
Recorded: 2/4/64-a
Arranger: Roy Ringwald
Conductor/Band: R. Ringwald/ studio orchestra
Key Release: **America, I Hear You Singing**
see Album Lists: alphabetic by title; 1964 — 2nd LP; Reprise/18th

#620   Let's Do It (Let's Fall in Love)   *duet with Shirley Mac- Laine*
Publication Date: 1928
Music & Words: Cole Porter
Recorded: 2/20/60-a
Arranger: Nelson Riddle
Conductor/Band: N. Riddle/studio orchestra
Key Release: **"Can-Can"** (Official Soundtrack LP)
see Album Lists: alphabetic by title; 1960 — 1st LP; Capitol/24th

#621   Let's Face the Music and Dance   *1st recording*
Publication Date: 1936
Music & Words: Irving Berlin
Recorded: 12/19/60-e
Arranger: Johnny Mandel
Conductor/Band: J. Mandel/studio orchestra
Key Release: **Ring-a-Ding Ding!**
see Album Lists: alphabetic by title; 1961 — 3rd LP; Reprise/1st

**#622   Let's Face the Music and
Dance**   *2nd recording*
Publication Date: 1936
Music & Words: Irving Berlin
Recorded: 9/19/79-a
Arranger: Billy May
Conductor/Band: B. May/studio
orchestra
Key Release: **Trilogy: The Past
[Collectibles of the Early Years]**
see Album Lists: alphabetic by title;
1980 — 1st LP; Reprise/52nd

**#623   Let's Fall in Love [Why
Shouldn't We?]**
Publication Date: 1933
Music: Harold Arlen
Words: Ted Koehler
Recorded: 12/19/60-b
Arranger: Johnny Mandel
Conductor/Band: J. Mandel/studio
orchestra
Key Release: **Ring-a-Ding Ding!**
see Album Lists: alphabetic by title;
1961 — 3rd LP; Reprise/1st

**#624   Let's Get Away from It
All**   *1st recording — sung with Con-
nie Haines & Jo Stafford*
Publication Date: 1941
Music: Matt Dennis
Words: Tom Adair
Recorded: 2/17/41-a
Arranger: Sy Oliver
Conductor/Band: Tommy Dorsey &
his Orchestra
Key Release: **The Dorsey/Sinatra
Sessions** (Volume 4)
see Album Lists: alphabetic by title;
1972 — 4th LP; RCA Victor/20th

**#625   Let's Get Away from It
All**   *2nd recording*
Publication Date: 1941
Music: Matt Dennis
Words: Tom Adair
Recorded: 10/1/57-b

Arranger: Billy May
Conductor/Band: Billy May & his
Orchestra
Key Release: **Come Fly with Me**
see Album Lists: alphabetic by title;
1958 — 2nd LP; Capitol/17th

**#626   Let's Take an Old-Fash-
ioned Walk**
Publication Date: 1949
Music & Words: Irving Berlin
Recorded: 5/6/49-a
Arranger: Axel Stordahl
Conductor/Band: A. Stordahl/studio
orchestra
Key Release: 78rpm single #38513,
side A
see Album List #1: 1949 Columbia
(4) single record — listed by
number

#627   Life Is So Peculiar   *duet
with Helen Carroll*
Publication Date: 1950
Music: Jimmy Van Heusen
Words: Johnny Burke
Recorded: 8/2/50-a
Arranger: Percy Faith
Conductor/Band: P. Faith/studio
orchestra
Key Release: 78rpm single #38960
see Album List #1: 1950 Columbia
(4) single record — listed by
number

**#628   Light a Candle in the
Chapel**
Publication Date: 1942
Music: Harry Pease & Johnny
Johnson
Words: Duke Leonard & Ed Nel-
son
Recorded: 7/2/42-a
Arranger: Axel Stordahl
Conductor/Band: Tommy Dorsey &
his Orchestra

Key Release: **The Dorsey/Sinatra Sessions** (Volume 6)
see Album Lists: alphabetic by title; 1972—6th LP; RCA Victor/22nd

#629   Like a Sad Song (Sometimes I Feel—)
Publication Date: 1976
Music & Words: John Denver
Recorded: 9/27/76-b
Arranger: Claus Ogerman
Conductor/Band: C. Ogerman/studio orchestra
Key Release: **The Singles** (Italian release only)
see Album Lists: alphabetic by title; 1982—6th LP; Reprise/61st

#630   Like Someone in Love
Publication Date: 1944
Music: Jimmy Van Heusen
Words: Johnny Burke
Recorded: 11/6/53-a
Arranger: Nelson Riddle; full-orch. arrng. from G. Siravo band arrng.
Conductor/Band: N. Riddle/studio orchestra
Key Release: **Songs for Young Lovers** (original 10" LP)
see Album Lists: alphabetic by title; 1954—1st LP; Capitol/2nd

#631   Lilli Bolero (Laroo, Laroo—)
Publication Date: 1948
Music: Elizabeth Moore
Words: Sid Lippman
Recorded: 1948 radio—Lucky Strike's "Your Hit Parade"
Arranger: Axel Stordahl
Conductor/Band: A. Stordahl/radio orchestra
Key Release: **The First Times ... Frank Sinatra**
see Album Lists: alphabetic under "radio"; early 1960s; Cameron/ 1st

#632   Lily Belle   *1st recording*
Publication Date: 1945
Music & Words: Dave Franklin & Irving Taylor
Recorded: 1945 radio—Sinatra's "Max Factor Show"
Arranger: Axel Stordahl
Conductor/Band: A. Stordahl/radio orchestra
Key Release: **My Best Songs—My Best Years** (Volume 4)
see Album Lists: alphabetic under "radio"; early 1970s; Pentagon/ 4th

#633   Lily Belle   *2nd recording*
Publication Date: 1945
Music & Words: Dave Franklin & Irving Taylor
Recorded: 5/16/45-a
Arranger: Axel Stordahl
Conductor/Band: A. Stordahl/studio orchestra
Key Release: 78rpm single #36854, side A
see Album List #1: 1945 Columbia (4) single record—listed by number

#634   Linda
Publication Date: 1944
Music & Words: Ann Ronell & Jack Lawrence
Recorded: 3/14/77-a
Arranger: Nelson Riddle
Conductor/Band: N. Riddle/studio orchestra
Key Release: **Frank's Girls** (illegal; from Reprise masters)
see Album Lists: alphabetic under "bootleg"; early 1980s; bootleg Alb. #5

#635   The Little Drummer Boy
Publication Date: 1958

Music & Words: Harry Simeone &
Henry Onorati & Katherine
Davis
Recorded: 6/16/64-c
Arranger: Dick Reynolds
Conductor/Band: D. Reynolds/studio
orchestra
*Key Release: Twelve Songs of
Christmas*
see Album Lists: alphabetic by title;
1964 — 9th LP; Reprise/22nd

#636   Little Girl Blue
Publication Date: 1935
Music: Richard Rodgers
Words: Lorenz Hart
Recorded: 11/6/53-c
Arranger: Nelson Riddle; full-orch.
arrng. from G. Siravo band
arrng.
Conductor/Band: N. Riddle/studio
orchestra
Key Release: Songs for Young Lovers
(original 10″ LP)
see Album Lists: alphabetic by title;
1954 — 1st LP; Capitol/2nd

#637   Little Green Apples
Publication Date: 1968
Music & Words: Bobby Russell
Recorded: 11/12/68-a
Arranger: Don Costa
Conductor/Band: Bill Miller/studio
orchestra
Key Release: Cycles
see Album Lists: alphabetic by title;
1968 — 6th LP; Reprise/37th

#638   A Little Learnin' Is a
Dang'rous Thing   *duet with
Pearl Bailey*
Publication Date: 1947
Music: Sy Oliver
Words: Al Jacobs
Recorded: 12/8/47-a
Arranger: Axel Stordahl

Conductor/Band: A. Stordahl/studio
orchestra
Key Release: 45rpm extended-play
single #B-2542
see Album List #1: 1948 Columbia
(6) single record — listed by
number

#639   Little White Lies
Publication Date: 1930
Music & Words: Walter Donaldson
Recorded: 1943 radio — Lucky
Strike's "Your Hit Parade"
Arranger: Axel Stordahl
Conductor/Band: A. Stordahl/radio
orchestra
*Key Release: The Original . . .
Frank Sinatra*
see Album Lists: alphabetic under
"radio"; early 1960s; Cameron/
2nd

#640   London by Night   *1st re-
cording*
Publication Date: 1950
Music & Words: Carroll Coates
Recorded: 9/21/50-c
Arranger: Axel Stordahl
Conductor/Band: A. Stordahl/studio
orchestra
*Key Release: Sinatra Rarities — The
Columbia Years* (Volume 1)
see Album Lists: alphabetic by title;
1986 — 1st LP; Columbia/50th

#641   London by Night   *2nd re-
cording*
Publication Date: 1950
Music & Words: Carroll Coates
Recorded: 10/3/57-b
Arranger: Billy May
Conductor/Band: Billy May & his
Orchestra
Key Release: Come Fly with Me
see Album Lists: alphabetic by title;
1958 — 2nd LP; Capitol/17th

#642   London by Night   *3rd recording*
Publication Date: 1950
Music & Words: Carroll Coates
Recorded: 6/13/62-a
Arranger: Robert Farnon
Conductor/Band: R. Farnon/studio orchestra
Key Release: **Sinatra Sings Great Songs from Great Britain** (English release only)
see Album Lists: alphabetic by title; 1962 — 5th LP; Reprise/6th

#643   Lonely Town
Publication Date: 1944
Music: Leonard Bernstein
Words: Betty Comden & Adolph Green
Recorded: 4/29/57-b
Arranger: Gordon Jenkins
Conductor/Band: G. Jenkins/studio orchestra
Key Release: **Where Are You?**
see Album Lists: alphabetic by title; 1957 — 4th LP; Capitol/13th

#644   Lonesome Cities
Publication Date: 1969
Music & Words: Rod McKuen
Recorded: 3/19/69-d
Arranger: Don Costa
Conductor/Band: D. Costa/studio orchestra
Key Release: **A Man Alone**
see Album Lists: alphabetic by title; 1969 — 3rd LP; Reprise/39th

#645   Lonesome Man Blues
Publication Date: 1942
Music & Words: Sy Oliver
Recorded: 1951 — 2nd soundtrack (illegally taken from film sound)
Arranger: Joseph Gershenson
Conductor/Band: J. Gershenson/ Universal-International Orchestra

Key Release: **"Meet Danny Wilson"** (LP: Score from "Meet Danny Wilson")
see Album Lists: alphabetic under "soundtrack"; mid–1960s; bootleg Mv. #15

#646   The Lonesome Road
Publication Date: 1929
Music: Gene Austin
Words: Nathaniel Shilkret
Recorded: 11/26/56-c
Arranger: Nelson Riddle
Conductor/Band: N. Riddle/studio orchestra
Key Release: **A Swingin' Affair!**
see Album Lists: alphabetic by title; 1957 — 2nd LP; Capitol/12th

#647   Long Ago (and Far Away)
Publication Date: 1944
Music: Jerome Kern
Words: Ira Gershwin
Recorded: 1944 radio — Sinatra's "Vimms Vitamins Show"
Arranger: Axel Stordahl
Conductor/Band: A. Stordahl/radio orchestra
Key Release: **The First Times . . . Frank Sinatra**
see Album Lists: alphabetic under "radio"; early 1960s; Cameron/ 1st

#648   A Long Night
Publication Date: 1981
Music: Alec Wilder
Words: Loonis R. McGlohan
Recorded: 7/20/81-c
Arranger: Gordon Jenkins
Conductor/Band: G. Jenkins/studio orchestra
Key Release: **She Shot Me Down**
see Album Lists: alphabetic by title; 1981 — 1st LP; Reprise/55th

#649   The Look of Love [I've Seen—]
Publication Date: 1962
Music: Jimmy Van Heusen
Words: Sammy Cahn
Recorded: 8/27/62-a
Arranger: Nelson Riddle
Conductor/Band: Neil Hefti/studio orchestra
Key Release: Softly, As I Leave You
see Album Lists: alphabetic by title; 1964—8th LP; Reprise/21st

#650   Look to Your Heart
Publication Date: 1955
Music: Jimmy Van Heusen
Words: Sammy Cahn
Recorded: 8/15/55-a
Arranger: Nelson Riddle
Conductor/Band: N. Riddle/studio orchestra
Key Release: Look to Your Heart
see Album Lists: alphabetic by title; 1959—4th LP; Capitol/22nd

#651   Looking at the World Through Rose-Colored Glasses
Publication Date: 1926
Music & Words: Jimmy Steiger & Tommy Malie
Recorded: 10/3/62-f
Arranger: Neal Hefti
Conductor/Band: Count Basie & his Band
Key Release: Sinatra-Basie: An Historic Musical First
see Album Lists: alphabetic by title; 1963—1st LP; Reprise/9th

#652   Looking for Yesterday
Publication Date: 1940
Music: Jimmy Van Heusen
Words: Eddie DeLange
Recorded: 8/29/40-b
Arranger: Dorsey "house" arrng: T. Dorsey, S. Oliver, F. Stulce, P. Weston

Conductor/Band: Tommy Dorsey & his Orchestra
Key Release: The Dorsey/Sinatra Sessions (Volume 3)
see Album Lists: alphabetic by title; 1972—3rd LP; RCA Victor/19th

#653   Lost in the Stars   *1st recording*
Publication Date: 1938
Music: Kurt Weill
Words: Maxwell Anderson
Recorded: 8/8/46-b
Arranger: Axel Stordahl
Conductor/Band: A. Stordahl/studio orchestra
Key Release: Put Your Dreams Away
see Album Lists: alphabetic by title; 1958—3rd LP; Columbia/26th

#654   Lost in the Stars   *2nd recording*
Publication Date: 1938
Music: Kurt Weill
Words: Maxwell Anderson
Recorded: 2/18/63-a
Arranger: Nelson Riddle
Conductor/Band: N. Riddle/studio orchestra
Key Release: The Concert Sinatra
see Album Lists: alphabetic by title; 1963—2nd LP; Reprise/10th

#655   Love and Marriage   *1st recording*
Publication Date: 1955
Music: Jimmy Van Heusen
Words: Sammy Cahn
Recorded: 8/15/55-b
Arranger: Nelson Riddle
Conductor/Band: N. Riddle/studio orchestra
Key Release: This Is Sinatra! (Volume 1)
see Album Lists: alphabetic by title; 1956—6th LP; Capitol/10th

#656 Love and Marriage *2nd recording*
Publication Date: 1955
Music: Jimmy Van Heusen
Words: Sammy Cahn
Recorded: 10/21/65-b
Arranger: Nelson Riddle
Conductor/Band: N. Riddle/studio orchestra
Key Release: **Frank Sinatra: A Man and His Music** (2 discs)
see Album Lists: alphabetic by title; 1965 — 5th LP; Reprise/26th

#657 Love Is a Many-Splendored Thing
Publication Date: 1955
Music: Sammy Fain
Words: Paul Francis Webster
Recorded: 1/28/64-e
Arranger: Nelson Riddle
Conductor/Band: N. Riddle/studio orchestra
Key Release: **Frank Sinatra Sings "Days of Wine and Roses," "Moon River" and Other Academy Award Winners**
see Album Lists: alphabetic by title; 1964 — 1st LP; Reprise/17th

#658 Love Is Here to Stay *1st recording*
Publication Date: 1938
Music: George Gershwin
Words: Ira Gershwin
Recorded: 10/17/55-b
Arranger: Nelson Riddle
Conductor/Band: N. Riddle/studio orchestra
Key Release: **Songs for Swingin' Lovers!**
see Album Lists: alphabetic by title; 1956 — 1st LP; Capitol/7th

#659 Love Is Here to Stay *2nd recording*
Publication Date: 1938
Music: George Gershwin
Words: Ira Gershwin
Recorded: 1959 television special
Arranger: Nelson Riddle
Conductor/Band: N. Riddle/television orchestra
Key Release: **Frank Sinatra — Through the Years: 1944–1966**
see Album Lists: alphabetic under "television"; mid-1960s; Ajazz/ 1st

#660 Love Is Just Around the Corner
Publication Date: 1935
Music: Lewis E. Gensler
Words: Leo Robin
Recorded: 4/10/62-f
Arranger: Neal Hefti
Conductor/Band: N. Hefti/studio orchestra
Key Release: **Sinatra and Swingin' Brass**
see Album Lists: alphabetic by title; 1962 — 4th LP; Reprise/5th

#661 Love Isn't Just for the Young
Publication Date: 1962
Music: Ronald Miller
Words: C. Kane
Recorded: 7/31/63-d
Arranger: Marty Paich
Conductor/Band: M. Paich/studio orchestra
Key Release: **Softly, As I Leave You**
see Album Lists: alphabetic by title; 1964 — 8th LP; Reprise/21st

#662 Love Lies
Publication Date: 1940
Music & Words: Carl Sigman & Joseph Meyer & Ralph Freed
Recorded: 7/17/40-b
Arranger: Dorsey "house" arrng: T. Dorsey, S. Oliver, F. Stulce, P. Weston

Conductor/Band: Tommy Dorsey &
his Orchestra
Key Release: **The Dorsey/Sinatra
Sessions** (Volume 2)
see Album Lists: alphabetic by title;
1972 — 2nd LP; RCA Victor/18th

#663   Love Locked Out
Publication Date: 1933
Music: Ray Noble
Words: Max Kester
Recorded: 3/8/56-c
Arranger: Nelson Riddle
Conductor/Band: N. Riddle with or-
chestra & the Hollywood String
Quartet
Key Release: **Close to You**
see Album Lists: alphabetic by title;
1957 — 1st LP; Capitol/11th

**#664   Love Looks So Well on
You**
Publication Date: 1959
Music: Lew Spence
Words: Alan Bergman & Marilyn
Keith (Bergman)
Recorded: 5/8/59-b
Arranger: Nelson Riddle
Conductor/Band: N. Riddle/studio
orchestra
Key Release: **Sinatra Sings . . . of
Love and Things**
see Album Lists: alphabetic by title;
1962 — 3rd LP; Capitol/32nd

#665   Love Me
Publication Date: 1934
Music: Victor Young
Words: Ned Washington
Recorded: 3/27/51-c
Arranger: Axel Stordahl
Conductor/Band: A. Stordahl/studio
orchestra
Key Release: **Adventures of the
Heart**
see Album Lists: alphabetic by title;
1956 — 3rd LP; Columbia/24th

#666   Love Me As I Am
Publication Date: 1941
Music: Louis Alter
Words: Frank Loesser .
Recorded: 5/28/41-b
Arranger: Dorsey "house" arrng:
T. Dorsey, S. Oliver, F. Stulce,
P. Weston
Conductor/Band: Tommy Dorsey &
his Orchestra
Key Release: **The Dorsey/Sinatra
Sessions** (Volume 4)
see Album Lists: alphabetic by title;
1972 — 4th LP; RCA Victor/20th

#667   Love Me Tender (derived
from "Aura Lee")
Publication Date: 1956
Music: Vera Matson; from G.
Poulton — 1861
Words: Elvis Presley
Recorded: 8/21/79-c
Arranger: Don Costa
Conductor/Band: D. Costa/studio
orchestra
Key Release: **Trilogy: The Present
[Some Very Good Years]**
see Album Lists: alphabetic by title;
1980 — 2nd LP; Reprise/53rd

#668   Love Walked In
Publication Date: 1938
Music: George Gershwin
Words: Ira Gershwin
Recorded: 5/18/61-b
Arranger: Billy May
Conductor/Band: Billy May & his
Orchestra
Key Release: **Sinatra Swings** (origi-
nal title: "Swing Along with
Me")
see Album Lists: alphabetic by title;
1961 — 6th LP; Reprise/2nd

**#669   A Lovely Way to Spend
an Evening**
Publication Date: 1943

Music: Jimmy McHugh
Words: Harold Adamson
Recorded: 11/10/43-a
Arranger: Axel Stordahl
Conductor/Band: Bobby Tucker
   singers only; during musicians'
   strike
*Key Release: Frank Sinatra in
   Hollywood, 1943–1949*
see Album Lists: alphabetic by title;
   1968 — 1st LP; Columbia/38th

#670   Lover   *1st recording*
Publication Date: 1932
Music: Richard Rodgers
Words: Lorenz Hart
Recorded: 4/14/50-c
Arranger: George Siravo
Conductor/Band: G. Siravo/studio
   orchestra
Key Release: The Voice
see Album Lists: alphabetic by title;
   1955 — 9th LP; Columbia/21st

#671   Lover   *2nd recording*
Publication Date: 1932
Music: Richard Rodgers
Words: Lorenz Hart
Recorded: 3/22/61-c
Arranger: Heinie Beau
Conductor/Band: Billy May/studio
   orchestra
Key Release: Come Swing with Me!
see Album Lists: alphabetic by title;
   1961 — 5th LP; Capitol/30th

#672   A Lover Is Blue
Publication Date: 1939
Music: Jimmy Mundy — 1938/Joe
   Young
Words: Imogene Carpenter
Recorded: 1944 radio — Sinatra's
   "Vimms Vitamins Show"
Arranger: Axel Stordahl
Conductor/Band: A. Stordahl/radio
   orchestra

*Key Release: My Best Songs — My
   Best Years* (Volume 1)
see Album Lists: alphabetic under
   "radio"; early 1970s; Pentagon/
   1st

#673   Love's Been Good to Me
Publication Date: 1969
Music & Words: Rod McKuen
Recorded: 3/20/69-d
Arranger: Don Costa
Conductor/Band: D. Costa/studio
   orchestra
Key Release: A Man Alone
see Album Lists: alphabetic by title;
   1969 — 3rd LP; Reprise/39th

#674   Luck Be a Lady
Publication Date: 1950
Music & Words: Frank Loesser
Recorded: 7/24/63-c
Arranger: Billy May
Conductor/Band: Morris Stoloff/
   studio orchestra
*Key Release: Reprise Musical Reper-
   tory Theatre: "Guys and Dolls"*
see Album Lists: alphabetic by title;
   1963 — 4th LP; Reprise/12th

#675   Lulu's Back in Town
Publication Date: 1935
Music: Harry Warren
Words: Al Dubin
Recorded: 1944 radio — Sinatra's
   "Vimms Vitamins Show"
Arranger: Axel Stordahl
Conductor/Band: A. Stordahl/radio
   orchestra
*Key Release: My Best Songs — My
   Best Years* (Volume 5)
see Album Lists: alphabetic under
   "radio"; early 1970s; Pentagon/
   5th

#676   Luna Rossa «Blushing
   Moon»
Publication Date: 1952

Music: A. Vian—1951
Words: Kermit Goell/Vincenzo De
Crescenzo—1951
Recorded: 6/3/52-a
Arranger: Axel Stordahl
Conductor/Band: A. Stordahl/studio
orchestra
Key Release: Come Back to Sorrento
see Album Lists: alphabetic by title;
1960—5th LP; Columbia/30th

#677   MacArthur Park   *only the*
"release"; no verse or chorus
Publication Date: 1968
Music & Words: Jimmy Webb
Recorded: 8/20/79-c
Arranger: Don Costa
Conductor/Band: D. Costa/studio
orchestra
Key Release: Trilogy: The Present
[Some Very Good Years]
see Album Lists: alphabetic by title;
1980—2nd LP; Reprise/53rd

#678   Mack the Knife «Moritat»
Publication Date: 1955
Music: Kurt Weill—1928
Words: Marc Blitzstein/Bertolt
Brecht—1928
Recorded: 4/17/84-d
Arranger: Frank Foster
Conductor/Band: Quincy Jones & a
special all-star jazz band
Key Release: L.A. Is My Lady
see Album Lists: alphabetic by title;
1984—1st LP; Qwest/1st

#679   Mad About You
Publication Date: 1949
Music: Victor Young
Words: Ned Washington
Recorded: 9/15/49-b
Arranger: Jeff Alexander
Conductor/Band: J. Alexander/
studio orchestra
Key Release: Adventures of the
Heart

see Album Lists: alphabetic by title;
1956—3rd LP; Columbia/24th

#680   Makin' Whoopee
Publication Date: 1928
Music: Walter Donaldson
Words: Gus Kahn
Recorded: 1/16/56-a
Arranger: Nelson Riddle
Conductor/Band: N. Riddle/studio
orchestra
Key Release: Songs for Swingin'
Lovers!
see Album Lists: alphabetic by title;
1956—1st LP; Capitol/7th

#681   Mama Will Bark   *duet*
with "Dagmar"
Publication Date: 1951
Music & Words: Dick Manning
Recorded: 5/10/51-a
Arranger: Axel Stordahl
Conductor/Band: A. Stordahl/studio
orchestra
Key Release: 45rpm single #4-39425
see Album List #1: 1951 Columbia
(5) single record—listed by
number

#682   Mam'selle   *1st recording*
Publication Date: 1946
Music: Edmund Goulding
Words: Mack Gordon
Recorded: 3/11/47-a
Arranger: Axel Stordahl
Conductor/Band: A. Stordahl/studio
orchestra
Key Release: Put Your Dreams
Away
see Album Lists: alphabetic by title;
1958—3rd LP; Columbia/26th

#683   Mam'selle   *2nd recording*
Publication Date: 1946
Music: Edmund Goulding
Words: Mack Gordon
Recorded: 3/3/60-d

Arranger: Nelson Riddle
Conductor/Band: N. Riddle/studio
orchestra
Key Release: Nice 'n' Easy
see Album Lists: alphabetic by title;
1960 — 2nd LP; Capitol/25th

#684   A Man Alone   *1st recording*
Publication Date: 1969
Music & Words: Rod McKuen
Recorded: 3/20/69-b
Arranger: Don Costa
Conductor/Band: D. Costa/studio
orchestra
Key Release: A Man Alone
see Album Lists: alphabetic by title;
1969 — 3rd LP; Reprise/39th

#685   A Man Alone   *2nd record-*
ing (song reprised)
Publication Date: 1969
Music & Words: Rod McKuen
Recorded: 3/20/69-c
Arranger: Don Costa
Conductor/Band: D. Costa/studio
orchestra
Key Release: A Man Alone
see Album Lists: alphabetic by title;
1969 — 3rd LP; Reprise/39th

**#686   The Man in the Looking
Glass**
Publication Date: 1965
Music & Words: Bart Howard
Recorded: 4/22/65-b
Arranger: Gordon Jenkins
Conductor/Band: G. Jenkins/studio
orchestra
Key Release: September of My Years
see Album Lists: alphabetic by title;
1965/1st LP; Reprise/23rd

**#687   The Man with the
Golden Arm***
Publication Date: 1955
Music: Jimmy Van Heusen
Words: Sammy Cahn

Recorded: 1955 — 2nd soundtrack (illegally taken from film sound)
Arranger: Fred Steiner
Conductor/Band: Elmer Bernstein/
commissioned film orchestra
*Key Release: "The Man with the
Golden Arm"* (LP: "On the
Town" & Others)
see Album Lists: alphabetic under
"soundtrack"; mid–1960s; bootleg Mv. #19
*This song was deleted from the
final soundtrack for the dramatic 1955 Carlyle/United Artists film of the same name.

#688   Maybe You'll Be There
Publication Date: 1947
Music: Rube Bloom
Words: Sammy Gallop
Recorded: 5/1/57-d
Arranger: Gordon Jenkins
Conductor/Band: G. Jenkins/studio
orchestra
Key Release: Where Are You?
see Album Lists: alphabetic by title;
1957 — 4th LP; Capitol/13th

#689   Me and My Shadow   *duet
with Sammy Davis Jr.*
Publication Date: 1927
Music: Dave Dreyer/Al Jolson
Words: Billy Rose
Recorded: 10/22/62-a
Arranger: Billy May
Conductor/Band: Billy May & his
Orchestra
Key Release: The Voice: Volume 1
(Italian release only)
see Album Lists: alphabetic by title;
1982 — 1st LP; Reprise/56th

#690   Mean to Me
Publication Date: 1929
Music: Fred Ahlert
Words: Roy Turk
Recorded: 10/31/47-a

Arranger: Axel Stordahl
Conductor/Band: A. Stordahl/studio
  orchestra
Key Release: **That Old Feeling**
see Album Lists: alphabetic by title;
  1956—2nd LP; Columbia/23rd

#691   Meditation «Meditacao»
Publication Date: 1963
Music: Antonio Carlos Jobim
Words: Norman Gimbel/Newton
  Mendonca
Recorded: 1/31/67-d
Arranger: Claus Ogerman
Conductor/Band: C. Ogerman/studio
  orchestra
Key Release: **Francis Albert Sinatra
  & Antonio Carlos Jobim**
see Album Lists: alphabetic by title;
  1967—1st LP; Reprise/31st

#692   Melancholy Mood
Publication Date: 1939
Music: Walter Schumann
Words: Vick R. Knight, Sr.
Recorded: 7/13/39-b
Arranger: Andy Gibson
Conductor/Band: Harry James & his
  Orchestra
Key Release: 78rpm single #8443,
  side B (first commercial release)
see Album List #1: 1939 Brunswick
  (1) single record—listed by num-
  ber

**#693   Melody of Love «Melody
  d'Amour»**
Publication Date: 1954
Music: Hans Engelmann—1903
Words: Tom Glazer
Recorded: 12/13/54-a
Arranger: Dick Reynolds
Conductor/Band: Ray Anthony &
  his Orchestra
Key Release: **Forever Frank**
see Album Lists: alphabetic by title;
  1966—4th LP; Capitol/36th

#694   Memories of You   *1st re-
  cording*
Publication Date: 1930
Music & Words: Eubie Blake &
  Andy Razaf
Recorded: 1/9/56-d
Arranger: Nelson Riddle
Conductor/Band: N. Riddle/studio
  orchestra
Key Release: **The Rare Sinatra: Vol-
  ume 1** (Australian release only)
see Album Lists: alphabetic by title;
  1978—1st LP; Capitol/65th

#695   Memories of You   *2nd re-
  cording*
Publication Date: 1930
Music & Words: Eubie Blake &
  Andy Razaf
Recorded: 9/11/61-d
Arranger: Axel Stordahl
Conductor/Band: A. Stordahl/studio
  orchestra
Key Release: **Point of No Return**
see Album Lists: alphabetic by title;
  1962—2nd LP; Capitol/31st

#696   Michael and Peter
Publication Date: 1969
Music & Words: Bob Gaudio &
  Jake Holmes
Recorded: 7/15/69-c
Arranger: Charles Calello
Conductor/Band: C. Calello/studio
  orchestra
Key Release: **Watertown [a love
  story]**
see Album Lists: alphabetic by title;
  1970—1st LP; Reprise/40th

#697   Mighty Lak' a Rose
Publication Date: 1901
Music: Ethelbert Nevin
Words: Frank Stanton
Recorded: 1/29/45-d
Arranger: Axel Stordahl

Conductor/Band: A. Stordahl/studio orchestra
Key Release: **Reflections**
see Album Lists: alphabetic by title; 1961 — 4th LP; Columbia/31st

#698   A Million Dreams Ago
Publication Date: 1940
Music & Words: Lew Quadling & Dick Jurgens & Eddy Howard
Recorded: 9/12/61-b
Arranger: Axel Stordahl
Conductor/Band: A. Stordahl/studio orchestra
Key Release: **Point of No Return**
see Album Lists: alphabetic by title; 1962 — 2nd LP; Capitol/31st

#699   Mimi
Publication Date: 1932
Music: Richard Rodgers
Words: Lorenz Hart
Recorded: 1943 radio — Lucky Strike's "Your Hit Parade"
Arranger: Axel Stordahl
Conductor/Band: A. Stordahl/radio orchestra
Key Release: **Frank Sinatra**
see Album Lists: alphabetic under "radio"; early 1960s; Cameron/4th

#700   Mind If I Make Love to You
Publication Date: 1956
Music & Words: Cole Porter
Recorded: 4/20/56-c
Arranger: Nelson Riddle
Conductor/Band: Johnny Green/MGM Orchestra
Key Release: **"High Society"** (Official Soundtrack LP)
see Album Lists: alphabetic by title; 1956 — 5th LP; Capitol/9th

#701   Mr. Booze   *sung with Bing Crosby & Dean Martin & Sammy Davis Jr.*

Publication Date: 1964
Music: Jimmy Van Heusen
Words: Sammy Cahn
Recorded: 4/10/64-b
Arranger: Nelson Riddle
Conductor/Band: N. Riddle/studio orchestra
Key Release: **"Robin and the 7 Hoods"** (Official Soundtrack LP)
see Album Lists: alphabetic by title; 1964 — 6th LP; Reprise/20th

#702   Mr. Success
Publication Date: 1958
Music: Ed Greines & Hank Sanicola
Words: Frank Sinatra & Hank Sanicola
Recorded: 9/11/58-a
Arranger: Nelson Riddle
Conductor/Band: N. Riddle/studio orchestra
Key Release: **Sinatra Sings . . . of Love and Things**
see Album Lists: alphabetic by title; 1962 — 3rd LP; Capitol/32nd

#703   Mistletoe and Holly
Publication Date: 1957
Music: Hank Sanicola
Words: Frank Sinatra & Dak Stanford
Recorded: 7/17/57-a
Arranger: Gordon Jenkins
Conductor/Band: G. Jenkins/studio orchestra
Key Release: **A Jolly Christmas from Frank Sinatra**
see Album Lists: alphabetic by title; 1957 — 6th LP; Capitol/14th

#704   Misty
Publication Date: 1955
Music: Erroll Garner
Words: Johnny Burke
Recorded: 11/21/61-e
Arranger: Don Costa

Conductor/Band: D. Costa/studio
orchestra
Key Release: **Sinatra & Strings**
see Album Lists: alphabetic by title;
1962 — 1st LP; Reprise/4th

#705   Moment to Moment
Publication Date: 1965
Music: Henry Mancini
Words: Johnny Mercer
Recorded: 10/21/65-a
Arranger: Nelson Riddle
Conductor/Band: N. Riddle/studio
orchestra
Key Release: **The Voice, Volume 1**
(Italian release only)
see Album Lists: alphabetic by title;
1982 — 1st LP; Reprise/56th

#706   Moments in the Moonlight
Publication Date: 1939
Music: Al Kaufman & Richard
Himber
Words: Mack Gordon & Richard
Himber
Recorded: 2/26/40-b
Arranger: Dorsey "house" arrng:
T. Dorsey, S. Oliver, F. Stulce,
P. Weston
Conductor/Band: Tommy Dorsey &
his Orchestra
Key Release: **The Dorsey/Sinatra
Sessions** (Volume 1)
see Album Lists: alphabetic by title;
1972 — 1st LP; RCA Victor/17th

#707   Monday Morning Quarterback
Publication Date: 1981
Music: Don Costa
Words: Pamela Phillips
Recorded: 9/10/81-a
Arranger: Gordon Jenkins
Conductor/Band: G. Jenkins/studio
orchestra
Key Release: **She Shot Me Down**

see Album Lists: alphabetic by title;
1981 — 1st LP; Reprise/55th

#708   Monique
Publication Date: 1958
Music: Elmer Bernstein
Words: Sammy Cahn
Recorded: 5/29/58-a
Arranger: Felix Slatkin
Conductor/Band: F. Slatkin/studio
orchestra
Key Release: **Sinatra Sings . . . of
Love and Things**
see Album Lists: alphabetic by title;
1962 — 3rd LP; Capitol/32nd

#709   Montmart'   *duet with
Maurice Chevalier ends overture*
Publication Date: 1953
Music & Words: Cole Porter
Recorded: 2/20/60-b
Arranger: Nelson Riddle
Conductor/Band: N. Riddle/studio
orchestra
Key Release: **"Can-Can"** (Official
Soundtrack LP)
see Album Lists: alphabetic by title;
1960 — 1st LP; Capitol/24th

#710   Mood Indigo
Publication Date: 1931
Music: Duke Ellington
Words: Irving Mills & Albany
(Barney) Bigard
Recorded: 2/16/55-d
Arranger: Nelson Riddle
Conductor/Band: N. Riddle/studio
orchestra
Key Release: **In the Wee Small
Hours** (12"LP version)
see Album Lists: alphabetic by title;
1955 — 7th LP; Capitol/5th

**#711   Moody River [More
Deadly Than the Vainest
Knife]**
Publication Date: 1961

Music & Words: Gary D. Bruce
Recorded: 11/13/68-a
Arranger: Don Costa
Conductor/Band: Bill Miller/studio orchestra
Key Release: **Cycles**
see Album Lists: alphabetic by title; 1968 — 6th LP; Reprise/37th

#712   The Moon Got in My Eyes
Publication Date: 1937
Music: Arthur Johnston
Words: Johnny Burke
Recorded: 11/29/65-c
Arranger: Nelson Riddle
Conductor/Band: N. Riddle/studio orchestra
Key Release: **Moonlight Sinatra**
see Album Lists: alphabetic by title; 1966 — 2nd LP; Reprise/28th

#713   Moon Love
Publication Date: 1939
Music: Andre Kostelanetz; from P. Tchaikovsky
Words: Mack David & Mack Davis
Recorded: 11/29/65-b
Arranger: Nelson Riddle
Conductor/Band: N. Riddle/studio orchestra
Key Release: **Moonlight Sinatra**
see Album Lists: alphabetic by title; 1966 — 2nd LP; Reprise/28th

#714   Moon River
Publication Date: 1961
Music: Henry Mancini
Words: Johnny Mercer
Recorded: 1/28/64-c
Arranger: Nelson Riddle
Conductor/Band: N. Riddle/studio orchestra
Key Release: **Frank Sinatra Sings "Days of Wine and Roses," "Moon River," and Other Academy Award Winners**

see Album Lists: alphabetic by title; 1964 — 1st LP; Reprise/17th

#715   Moon Song (That Wasn't Meant for Me)
Publication Date: 1932
Music: Arthur Johnston
Words: Sam Coslow
Recorded: 11/29/65-a
Arranger: Nelson Riddle
Conductor/Band: N. Riddle/studio orchestra
Key Release: **Moonlight Sinatra**
see Album Lists: alphabetic by title; 1966 — 2nd LP; Reprise/28th

#716   The Moon Was Yellow
1st recording
Publication Date: 1934
Music: Fred Ahlert
Words: Edgar Leslie
Recorded: 8/27/45-c
Arranger: Axel Stordahl
Conductor/Band: A. Stordahl/studio orchestra
Key Release: **Frank Sinatra's Greatest Hits: The Early Years** (Vol. 2)
see Album Lists: alphabetic by title; 1964 — 4th LP; Columbia/33rd

#717   The Moon Was Yellow
2nd recording
Publication Date: 1934
Music: Fred Ahlert
Words: Edgar Leslie
Recorded: 12/29/58-a
Arranger: Nelson Riddle
Conductor/Band: N. Riddle/studio orchestra
Key Release: **Sinatra Sings . . . of Love and Things**
see Album Lists: alphabetic by title; 1962 — 3rd LP; Capitol/32nd

#718   The Moon Was Yellow
3rd recording

Publication Date: 1934
Music: Fred Ahlert
Words: Edgar Leslie
Recorded: 11/30/65-e
Arranger: Nelson Riddle
Conductor/Band: N. Riddle/studio
  orchestra
Key Release: Moonlight Sinatra
see Album Lists: alphabetic by title;
  1966 — 2nd LP; Reprise/28th

#719   Moonlight Becomes You
Publication Date: 1942
Music: Jimmy Van Heusen
Words: Johnny Burke
Recorded: 11/30/65-b
Arranger: Nelson Riddle
Conductor/Band: N. Riddle/studio
  orchestra
Key Release: Moonlight Sinatra
see Album Lists: alphabetic by title;
  1966 — 2nd LP; Reprise/28th

#720   Moonlight in Vermont
  1st recording
Publication Date: 1944
Music: Karl Suessdorf
Words: John Blackburn
Recorded: 10/3/57-d
Arranger: Billy May
Conductor/Band: Billy May & his
  Orchestra
Key Release: Come Fly with Me
see Album Lists: alphabetic by title;
  1958 — 2nd LP; Capitol/17th

#721   Moonlight in Vermont
  2nd recording
Publication Date: 1944
Music: Karl Suessdorf
Words: John Blackburn
Recorded: 1966 television special
Arranger: Billy May
Conductor/Band: B. May/television
  orchestra
*Key Release: Frank Sinatra —
  Through the Years: 1944–1966*

see Album Lists: alphabetic under
  "television"; mid–1960s; Ajazz/
  1st

#722   Moonlight Mood
Publication Date: 1942
Music: Pete DeRose
Words: Harold Adamson
Recorded: 11/30/65-c
Arranger: Nelson Riddle
Conductor/Band: N. Riddle/studio
  orchestra
Key Release: Moonlight Sinatra
see Album Lists: alphabetic by title;
  1966 — 2nd LP; Reprise/28th

#723   Moonlight on the Ganges
Publication Date: 1926
Music: Sherman Myers
Words: Chester Wallace
Recorded: 5/23/61-c
Arranger: Billy May
Conductor/Band: Billy May & his
  Orchestra
Key Release: Sinatra Swings (origi-
  nal title: "Swing Along with
  Me")
see Album Lists: alphabetic by title;
  1961 — 6th LP; Reprise/2nd

#724   Moonlight Serenade
Publication Date: 1939
Music: Glenn Miller
Words: Mitchell Parish
Recorded: 11/29/65-d
Arranger: Nelson Riddle
Conductor/Band: N. Riddle/studio
  orchestra
Key Release: Moonlight Sinatra
see Album Lists: alphabetic by title;
  1966 — 2nd LP; Reprise/28th

#725   More
Publication Date: 1962
Music: Riziero Ortolani & N.
  Oliviero
Words: Norman Newell/M.
  Ciorciolini

Recorded: 6/12/64-b
Arranger: Quincy Jones
Conductor/Band: Count Basie & his Band
Key Release: **It Might as Well Be Swing**
see Album Lists: alphabetic by title; 1964 — 5th LP; Reprise/19th

#726   More Than You Know
Publication Date: 1929
Music: Vincent Youmans
Words: Billy Rose & Edward Eliscu
Recorded: 9/17/79-c
Arranger: Billy May
Conductor/Band: B. May/studio orchestra
Key Release: **Trilogy: The Past [Collectibles of the Early Years]**
see Album Lists: alphabetic by title; 1980 — 1st LP; Reprise/52nd

#727   The Most Beautiful Girl in the World   *1st recording*
Publication Date: 1935
Music: Richard Rodgers
Words: Lorenz Hart
Recorded: 5/11/66-d
Arranger: Nelson Riddle
Conductor/Band: N. Riddle/studio orchestra
Key Release: **Strangers in the Night**
see Album Lists: alphabetic by title; 1966 — 1st LP; Reprise/27th

#728   The Most Beautiful Girl in the World   *2nd recording*
Publication Date: 1935
Music: Richard Rodgers
Words: Lorenz Hart
Recorded: 1966 television special
Arranger: Billy May
Conductor/Band: B. May/television orchestra
Key Release: **Frank Sinatra — Through the Years: 1944–1966**

see Album Lists: alphabetic under "television"; mid–1960s; Ajazz/ 1st

#729   Mrs. Robinson
Publication Date: 1967
Music & Words: Paul Simon
Recorded: 2/24/69-c
Arranger: Don Costa
Conductor/Band: D. Costa/studio orchestra
Key Release: **My Way**
see Album Lists: alphabetic by title; 1969 — 1st LP; Reprise/38th

#730   The Music Stopped   *1st recording*
Publication Date: 1943
Music: Jimmy McHugh
Words: Harold Adamson
Recorded: 11/3/43-b
Arranger: Axel Stordahl
Conductor/Band: Bobby Tucker Singers only; during musicians' strike
Key Release: **Frank Sinatra in Hollywood, 1943–1949**
see Album Lists: alphabetic by title; 1968 — 1st LP; Columbia/38th

#731   The Music Stopped   *2nd recording*
Publication Date: 1943
Music: Jimmy McHugh
Words: Harold Adamson
Recorded: 10/29/47-d
Arranger: Axel Stordahl
Conductor/Band: A. Stordahl/studio orchestra
Key Release: 78rpm single #38683
see Album List #1: 1949 Columbia (4) single record — listed by number

#732   My Baby Cares for Me
Publication Date: 1928
Music: Walter Donaldson

Words: Gus Kahn
Recorded: 5/11/66-a
Arranger: Nelson Riddle
Conductor/Band: N. Riddle/studio
orchestra
Key Release: Strangers in the Night
see Album Lists: alphabetic by title;
1966 — 1st LP; Reprise/27th

#733   My Blue Heaven   *1st recording*
Publication Date: 1927
Music: Walter Donaldson
Words: George Whiting
Recorded: 4/24/50-c
Arranger: George Siravo
Conductor/Band: G. Siravo/studio
orchestra
Key Release: Love Is a Kick
see Album Lists: alphabetic by title;
1960 — 3rd LP; Columbia/28th

#734   My Blue Heaven   *2nd recording*
Publication Date: 1927
Music: Walter Donaldson
Words: George Whiting
Recorded: 8/23/60-a
Arranger: Nelson Riddle
Conductor/Band: N. Riddle/studio
orchestra
*Key Release: Sinatra's Swingin'
Session!!!*
see Album Lists: alphabetic by title;
1961 — 1st LP; Capitol/28th

#735   My Buddy
Publication Date: 1922
Music: Walter Donaldson
Words: Gus Kahn
Recorded: 8/17/39-a
Arranger: Andy Gibson
Conductor/Band: Harry James & his
Orchestra
*Key Release: The Essential Frank
Sinatra* (Volume 1)
see Album Lists: alphabetic by title;

1967 — 2nd LP; Columbia/34th

#736   My Cousin Louella
Publication Date: 1947
Music & Words: Bernard (Bernie)
Bierman & Jack Manus
Recorded: 10/24/47-a
Arranger: Tony Mottola
Conductor/Band: T. Mottola/studio
orchestra
Key Release: 78rpm single #38045,
side A
see Album List #1: 1947 Columbia
(4) single record — listed by
number

#737   My Funny Valentine
Publication Date: 1937
Music: Richard Rodgers
Words: Lorenz Hart
Recorded: 11/5/53-b
Arranger: Nelson Riddle; full-orch.
arrng. from G. Siravo band
arrng.
Conductor/Band: N. Riddle/studio
orchestra
Key Release: Songs for Young Lovers
(original 10" LP)
see Album Lists: alphabetic by title;
1954 — 1st LP; Capitol/2nd

#738   My Happiness
Publication Date: 1933
Music: Borney Bergantine
Words: Betty Peterson
Recorded: 1943 radio — Lucky
Strike's "Your Hit Parade"
Arranger: Axel Stordahl
Conductor/Band: A. Stordahl/radio
orchestra
*Key Release: The First Times . . .
Frank Sinatra*
see Album Lists: alphabetic under
"radio"; early 1960s; Cameron/
1st

#739   My Heart Stood Still
Publication Date: 1927

Music: Richard Rodgers
Words: Lorenz Hart
Recorded: 2/18/63-b
Arranger: Nelson Riddle
Conductor/Band: N. Riddle/studio
orchestra
Key Release: The Concert Sinatra
see Album Lists: alphabetic by title;
1963 — 2nd LP; Reprise/10th

#740 My Heart Tells Me
Publication Date: 1943
Music: Harry Warren
Words: Mack Gordon
Recorded: 1943 radio — Lucky
Strike's "Your Hit Parade"
Arranger: Axel Stordahl
Conductor/Band: A. Stordahl/radio
orchestra
Key Release: Frank Sinatra
see Album Lists: alphabetic under
"radio"; early 1960s; Cameron/
4th

#741 My Kind of Girl
Publication Date: 1961
Music & Words: Leslie Bricusse
Recorded: 10/3/62-c
Arranger: Neal Hefti
Conductor/Band: Count Basie & his
Band
Key Release: Sinatra-Basie: An Historic Musical First
see Album Lists: alphabetic by title;
1963 — 1st LP; Reprise/9th

#742 My Kind of Town
[Chicago Is —] *1st recording*
Publication Date: 1964
Music: Jimmy Van Heusen
Words: Sammy Cahn
Recorded: 4/8/64-a
Arranger: Nelson Riddle
Conductor/Band: N. Riddle/studio
orchestra
*Key Release: "Robin and the 7
Hoods"* (Official Soundtrack LP)

see Album Lists: alphabetic by title;
1964 — 6th LP; Reprise/20th

#743 My Kind of Town
[Chicago Is —] *2nd recording*
Publication Date: 1964
Music: Jimmy Van Heusen
Words: Sammy Cahn
Recorded: 2/1/66-j
Arranger: Quincy Jones
Conductor/Band: Count Basie & his
Band
Key Release: Sinatra at the Sands
(Live Recording — 2 discs)
see Album Lists: alphabetic by title;
1966 — 3rd LP; Reprise/29th

#744 My Kind of Town
[Chicago Is —] *3rd recording*
Publication Date: 1964
Music: Jimmy Van Heusen
Words: Sammy Cahn
Recorded: 10/13/74-j
Arranger: Nelson Riddle
Conductor/Band: Bill Miller/Woody
Herman's Young Thundering
Herd band
*Key Release: Sinatra — The Main
Event* (Live Recording)
see Album Lists: alphabetic by title;
1974 — 2nd LP; Reprise/48th

#745 My Love for You
Publication Date: 1946
Music: Abner Silver
Words: Sid Wayne
Recorded: 1/9/47-c
Arranger: Axel Stordahl
Conductor/Band: A. Stordahl/studio
orchestra
Key Release: MM-1 (illegal; from
Columbia masters)
see Album Lists: alphabetic under
"bootleg"; early 1970s; bootleg
Alb. #1

#746 My Melancholy Baby
«Melancholy»

Publication Date: 1911
Music: Ernie Burnett
Words: George A. Norton & Maybelle E. Watson
Recorded: 1/29/45-a
Arranger: Axel Stordahl
Conductor/Band: A. Stordahl/studio orchestra
Key Release: **Come Back to Sorrento**
see Album Lists: alphabetic by title; 1960 — 5th LP; Columbia/30th

#747   My One and Only Love
Publication Date: 1953
Music: Guy Wood
Words: Robert Mellin
Recorded: 5/2/53-b
Arranger: Nelson Riddle
Conductor/Band: N. Riddle/studio orchestra
Key Release: **This Is Sinatra!** (Volume 1)
see Album Lists: alphabetic by title; 1956 — 6th LP; Capitol/10th

#748   My Romance   *duet with Dinah Shore*
Publication Date: 1935
Music: Richard Rodgers
Words: Lorenz Hart
Recorded: 4/25/47-b
Arranger: Axel Stordahl
Conductor/Band: A. Stordahl/studio orchestra
Key Release: **The Essential Frank Sinatra** (Volume 2)
see Album Lists: alphabetic by title; 1967 — 3rd LP; Columbia/35th

#749   My Shawl
Publication Date: 1934
Music: Xavier Cugat
Words: Stanley Adams
Recorded: 5/24/45-b
Arranger: Xavier Cugat
Conductor/Band: X. Cugat/studio orchestra

Key Release: **The Essential Frank Sinatra** (Volume 1)
see Album Lists: alphabetic by title; 1967 — 2nd LP; Columbia/34th

#750   My Shining Hour   *1st recording*
Publication Date: 1943
Music: Harold Arlen
Words: Johnny Mercer
Recorded: 1/12/44-a; Sinatra's "Vimms Vitamins Show"
Arranger: Axel Stordahl
Conductor/Band: A. Stordahl/radio orchestra
Key Release: **Frank Sinatra on V-Disc, Volume 1** (English release only; album of wartime Victory Discs)
see Album Lists: alphabetic under "v/disc"; early 1970s; Apex/1st

#751   My Shining Hour   *2nd recording*
Publication Date: 1943
Music: Harold Arlen
Words: Johnny Mercer
Recorded: 9/17/79-b
Arranger: Billy May
Conductor/Band: B. May/studio orchestra
Key Release: **Trilogy: The Past [Collectibles of the Early Years]**
see Album Lists: alphabetic by title; 1980 — 1st LP; Reprise/52nd

#752   My Sweet Lady
Publication Date: 1970
Music & Words: John Denver
Recorded: 10/26/70-c
Arranger: Don Costa
Conductor/Band: D. Costa/studio orchestra
Key Release: **Sinatra & Company**
see Album Lists: alphabetic by title; 1971 — 2nd LP; Reprise/42nd

**#753 My Way «Comme d'habi-
tude»** *1st recording*
Publication Date: 1968
Music: Jacques Revaux & Claude
Francois — 1967
Words: Paul Anka/Gilles Thi-
bault — 1967
Recorded: 12/30/68-a
Arranger: Don Costa
Conductor/Band: D. Costa/studio
orchestra
Key Release: **My Way**
see Album Lists: alphabetic by title;
1969 — 1st LP; Reprise/38th

**#754 My Way «Comme d'habi-
tude»** *2nd recording*
Publication Date: 1968
Music: Jacques Revaux & Claude
Francois — 1967
Words: Paul Anka/Gilles Thi-
bault — 1967
Recorded: 10/2/74-k
Arranger: Don Costa
Conductor/Band: Bill Miller/Woody
Herman's Young Thundering
Herd band
Key Release: **Sinatra — The Main
Event** (Live Recording)
see Album Lists: alphabetic by title;
1974 — 2nd LP; Reprise/48th

#755 My Way of Life
Publication Date: 1968
Music: Bert Kaempfert & Herbert
Rehbein
Words: Carl Sigman
Recorded: 7/24/68-a
Arranger: Don Costa
Conductor/Band: D. Costa/studio
orchestra
Key Release: **Cycles**
see Album Lists: alphabetic by title;
1968 — 6th LP; Reprise/37th

**#756 Nancy (with the Laugh-
ing Face)** *1st recording*

Publication Date: 1944
Music: Jimmy Van Heusen
Words: Phil Silvers
Recorded: 8/22/45-c
Arranger: Axel Stordahl
Conductor/Band: A. Stordahl/studio
orchestra
Key Release: **Frankie**
see Album Lists: alphabetic by title;
1955 — 8th LP; Columbia/20th

**#757 Nancy (with the Laugh-
ing Face)** *2nd recording*
Publication Date: 1944
Music: Jimmy Van Heusen
Words: Phil Silvers
Recorded: 4/29/63-b
Arranger: Nelson Riddle
Conductor/Band: N. Riddle/studio
orchestra
Key Release: **Sinatra's Sinatra**
see Album Lists: alphabetic by title;
1963 — 7th LP; Reprise/15th

**#758 Nancy (with the Laugh-
ing Face)** *3rd recording*
Publication Date: 1944
Music: Jimmy Van Heusen
Words: Phil Silvers
Recorded: 3/9/77-a
Arranger: Nelson Riddle
Conductor/Band: N. Riddle/studio
orchestra
Key Release: **Frank's Girls** (illegal;
from Reprise masters)
see Album Lists: alphabetic under
"bootleg"; early 1980s; bootleg
Alb. #5

#759 Nature Boy
Publication Date: 1948
Music & Words: Eden Ahbez
Recorded: 4/10/48-a
Arranger: Jeff Alexander
Conductor/Band: J. Alexander/
studio orchestra
Key Release: **Reflections**

see *Album Lists:* alphabetic by title;
1961—4th LP; Columbia/31st

#760   The Nearness of You   *1st recording*
Publication Date: 1937
Music: Hoagy Carmichael
Words: Ned Washington
Recorded: 8/11/47-c
Arranger: Axel Stordahl
Conductor/Band: A. Stordahl/studio orchestra
Key Release: **That Old Feeling**
see *Album Lists:* alphabetic by title;
1956—2nd LP; Columbia/23rd

#761   The Nearness of You   *2nd recording*
Publication Date: 1937
Music: Hoagy Carmichael
Words: Ned Washington
Recorded: 3/2/60-b
Arranger: Nelson Riddle
Conductor/Band: N. Riddle/studio orchestra
Key Release: **Sinatra Sings . . . of Love and Things**
see *Album Lists:* alphabetic by title;
1962—3rd LP; Capitol/32nd

#762   Neiani
Publication Date: 1941
Music & Words: Axel Stordahl & Sy Oliver
Recorded: 6/27/41-c
Arranger: Axel Stordahl
Conductor/Band: Tommy Dorsey & his Orchestra
Key Release: **The Dorsey/Sinatra Sessions** (Volume 5)
see *Album Lists:* alphabetic by title;
1972—5th LP; RCA Victor/21st

#763   Nevertheless (I'm in Love with You)   *1st recording*
Publication Date: 1931
Music: Harry Ruby

Words: Bert Kalmar
Recorded: 10/9/50-d
Arranger: George Siravo
Conductor/Band: G. Siravo/studio orchestra
Key Release: **Adventures of the Heart**
see *Album Lists:* alphabetic by title;
1956—3rd LP; Columbia/24th

#764   Nevertheless (I'm in Love with You)   *2nd recording*
Publication Date: 1931
Music: Harry Ruby
Words: Bert Kalmar
Recorded: 3/2/60-c
Arranger: Nelson Riddle
Conductor/Band: N. Riddle/studio orchestra
Key Release: **Nice 'n' Easy**
see *Album Lists:* alphabetic by title;
1960—2nd LP; Capitol/25th

#765   New York, New York (a Wonderful Town)   *sung with Gene Kelly & Jules Munshin*
Publication Date: 1944
Music: Leonard Bernstein
Words: Betty Comden & Adolph Green
Recorded: 1949—2nd soundtrack (illegally taken from film sound)
Arranger: Conrad Salinger
Conductor/Band: Lenny Hayton/ MGM Orchestra
Key Release: **"On the Town"** (LP: "On the Town" & Others)
see *Album Lists:* alphabetic under "soundtrack"; mid–1960s; bootleg Mv. #13

#766   New York, New York
theme from New York, New York
Publication Date: 1977
Music: John Kander
Words: Fred Ebb
Recorded: 9/19/79-b

Arranger: Don Costa
Conductor/Band: Vinnie Falcone/
studio orchestra
Key Release: **Trilogy: The Present
[Some Very Good Years]**
see Album Lists: alphabetic by title;
1980 — 2nd LP; Reprise/53rd

#767   Nice 'n' Easy
Publication Date: 1960
Music: Lew Spence
Words: Alan Bergman & Marilyn
Keith (Bergman)
Recorded: 4/12/60-a
Arranger: Nelson Riddle
Conductor/Band: N. Riddle/studio
orchestra
Key Release: **Nice 'n' Easy**
see Album Lists: alphabetic by title;
1960 — 2nd LP; Capitol/25th

**#768   Nice Work If You Can
Get It**   *1st recording*
Publication Date: 1937
Music: George Gershwin
Words: Ira Gershwin
Recorded: 11/20/56-d
Arranger: Nelson Riddle
Conductor/Band: N. Riddle/studio
orchestra
Key Release: **A Swingin' Affair!**
see Album Lists: alphabetic by title;
1957 — 2nd LP; Capitol/12th

**#769   Nice Work If You Can
Get It**   *2nd recording*
Publication Date: 1937
Music: George Gershwin
Words: Ira Gershwin
Recorded: 10/2/62-a
Arranger: Neal Hefti
Conductor/Band: Count Basie & his
Band
Key Release: **Sinatra-Basie: An His-
toric Musical First**
see Album Lists: alphabetic by title;
1963 — 1st LP; Reprise/9th

#770   Night *poetry recited to music*
Publication Date: 1969
Music: Rod McKuen (nonvocal
melody)
Words: Rod McKuen
Recorded: 3/21/69-b
Arranger: Don Costa
Conductor/Band: D. Costa/studio
orchestra
Key Release: **A Man Alone**
see Album Lists: alphabetic by title;
1969 — 3rd LP; Reprise/39th

#771   Night After Night
Publication Date: 1948
Music: Axel Stordahl & Paul
Weston
Words: Irving Taylor
Recorded: 3/3/49-b
Arranger: Axel Stordahl
Conductor/Band: A. Stordahl/studio
orchestra
Key Release: 78rpm single #38456
see Album List #1: 1949 Columbia
(4) single record — listed by
number

#772   Night and Day   *1st record-
ing*
Publication Date: 1932
Music & Words: Cole Porter
Recorded: 1/19/42-d
Arranger: Axel Stordahl
Conductor/Band: A. Stordahl/studio
orchestra
Key Release: **We Three**
see Album Lists: alphabetic by title;
1957 — 7th LP; RCA Victor/12th

#773   Night and Day   *2nd re-
cording*
Publication Date: 1932
Music & Words: Cole Porter
Recorded: 11/26/56-b
Arranger: Nelson Riddle
Conductor/Band: N. Riddle/studio
orchestra

Key Release: **A Swingin' Affair!**
see Album Lists: alphabetic by title;
1957 — 2nd LP; Capitol/12th

#774   Night and Day *3rd recording*
Publication Date: 1932
Music & Words: Cole Porter
Recorded: 11/22/61-b
Arranger: Don Costa
Conductor/Band: D. Costa/studio
orchestra
Key Release: **Sinatra & Strings**
see Album Lists: alphabetic by title;
1962 — 1st LP; Reprise/4th

#775   Night and Day *4th recording*
Publication Date: 1932
Music & Words: Cole Porter
Recorded: 2/16/77-a
Arranger: Joe Beck
Conductor/Band: J. Beck/studio
orchestra
Key Release: **The Singles** (Italian
release only)
see Album Lists: alphabetic by title;
1982 — 6th LP; Reprise/61st

**#776   The Night Is Young and
You're So Beautiful** *duet with
Dinah Shore*
Publication Date: 1936
Music: Dana Suesse
Words: Irving Kahal & Billy Rose
Recorded: 9/26/45-b; "The Frank
Sinatra Old Gold Show"
Arranger: Axel Stordahl
Conductor/Band: A. Stordahl/radio
orchestra
Key Release: **Sinatra for the Collector: Vol. 2 — The V-Disc Years**
(Canadian release only; album
of wartime Victory Discs)
see Album Lists: alphabetic under
"v/disc"; early 1970s; My Way/
2nd

**#777   The Night We Called It a
Day** *1st recording*
Publication Date: 1942
Music: Matt Dennis
Words: Tom Adair
Recorded: 1/19/42-a
Arranger: Axel Stordahl
Conductor/Band: A. Stordahl/studio
orchestra
Key Release: **We Three**
see Album Lists: alphabetic by title;
1957 — 7th LP; RCA Victor/12th

**#778   The Night We Called It a
Day** *2nd recording*
Publication Date: 1942
Music: Matt Dennis
Words: Tom Adair
Recorded: 4/10/57-c
Arranger: Gordon Jenkins
Conductor/Band: G. Jenkins/studio
orchestra
Key Release: **Where Are You?**
see Album Lists: alphabetic by title;
1957 — 4th LP; Capitol/13th

**#779   A Nightingale Sang in
Berkeley Square**
Publication Date: 1940
Music: Sherwin Manning
Words: Eric Maschwitz
Recorded: 6/13/62-d
Arranger: Robert Farnon
Conductor/Band: R. Farnon/studio
orchestra
Key Release: **Sinatra Sings Great
Songs from Great Britain**
(English release only)
see Album Lists: alphabetic by title;
1962 — 5th LP; Reprise/6th

#780   No One Ever Tells You
Publication Date: 1956
Music & Words: Carroll Coates &
Hub Atwood
Recorded: 4/9/56-d
Arranger: Nelson Riddle

Conductor/Band: N. Riddle/studio
  orchestra
Key Release: A Swingin' Affair!
see Album Lists: alphabetic by title;
  1957 — 2nd LP; Capitol/12th

#781   No Orchids for My Lady
Publication Date: 1948
Music: Jack Strachey
Words: Alan Stranks
Recorded: 12/19/48-b
Arranger: Axel Stordahl
Conductor/Band: A. Stordahl/studio
  orchestra
Key Release: 78rpm single #38393
see Album List #1: 1948 Columbia
  (4) single record — listed by
  number

#782   Noah
Publication Date: 1973
Music & Words: Joe Raposo
Recorded: 6/4/73-c
Arranger: Gordon Jenkins
Conductor/Band: G. Jenkins/studio
  orchestra
Key Release: Ol' Blue Eyes Is Back
see Album Lists: alphabetic by title;
  1973 — 2nd LP; Reprise/45th

#783   Nobody Wins
Publication Date: 1972
Music & Words: Kris Kristofferson
Recorded: 6/5/73-a
Arranger: Gordon Jenkins
Conductor/Band: G. Jenkins/studio
  orchestra
Key Release: Ol' Blue Eyes Is Back
see Album Lists: alphabetic by title;
  1973 — 2nd LP; Reprise/45th

**#784   None but the Lonely
  Heart** *1st recording*
Publication Date: 1939
Music: Edward Brandt; from P.
  Tchaikovsky
Words: Gus Kahn/Edward Brandt

Recorded: 10/26/47-a
Arranger: Axel Stordahl
Conductor/Band: A. Stordahl/studio
  orchestra
Key Release: Come Back to Sorrento
see Album Lists: alphabetic by title;
  1960 — 5th LP; Columbia/30th

**#785   None but the Lonely
  Heart** *2nd recording*
Publication Date: 1939
Music: Edward Brandt; from P.
  Tchaikovsky
Words: Gus Kahn/Edward Brandt
Recorded: 3/24/59-c
Arranger: Gordon Jenkins
Conductor/Band: G. Jenkins/studio
  orchestra
Key Release: No One Cares
see Album Lists: alphabetic by title;
  1959 — 5th LP; Capitol/23rd

#786   Not As a Stranger
Publication Date: 1955
Music: Jimmy Van Heusen
Words: Buddy Kaye
Recorded: 3/4/55-b
Arranger: Nelson Riddle
Conductor/Band: N. Riddle/studio
  orchestra
Key Release: Look to Your Heart
see Album Lists: alphabetic by title;
  1959 — 4th LP; Capitol/22nd

#787   Not So Long Ago
Publication Date: 1940
Music: Al Frisch
Words: Charles Tobias
Recorded: 11/11/40-a
Arranger: Dorsey "house" arrng:
  T. Dorsey, S. Oliver, F. Stulce,
  P. Weston
Conductor/Band: Tommy Dorsey &
  his Orchestra
*Key Release: The Dorsey/Sinatra
  Sessions* (Volume 3)
see Album Lists: alphabetic by title;

1972 — 3rd LP; RCA Victor/
19th

#788   Nothing but the Best
Publication Date: 1960
Music & Words: John W. Rotella
Recorded: 2/27/62-b
Arranger: Neal Hefti
Conductor/Band: N. Hefti/studio
orchestra
Key Release: **The Voice: Volume 1**
(Italian release only)
see Album Lists: alphabetic by title;
1982 — 1st LP; Reprise/56th

#789   Nothing in Common
duet with Keely Smith
Publication Date: 1958
Music: Jimmy Van Heusen
Words: Sammy Cahn
Recorded: 3/3/58-a
Arranger: Billy May
Conductor/Band: Billy May & his
Orchestra
Key Release: 45rpm single #3952/E,
side A
see Album List #1: 1958 Capitol (5)
single record — listed by number

#790   Now Is the Hour «"Haere
Ra"; Maori Farewell»   *1st re-
cording*
Publication Date: 1946
Music: Clement Scott — 1913/
Dorothy Stewart
Words: Dorothy Stewart/Maewa
Kaihan — 1913
Recorded: 1943 radio — Lucky
Strike's "Your Hit Parade"
Arranger: Axel Stordahl
Conductor/Band: A. Stordahl/radio
orchestra
Key Release: **Frank Sinatra**
see Album Lists: alphabetic under
"radio"; early 1960s; Cameron/
4th

#791   Now Is the Hour «"Haere
Ra"; Maori Farewell»   *2nd re-
cording*
Publication Date: 1946
Music: Clement Scott — 1913/
Dorothy Stewart
Words: Dorothy Stewart/Maewa
Kaihan — 1913
Recorded: 6/14/62-b
Arranger: Robert Farnon
Conductor/Band: R. Farnon/studio
orchestra
Key Release: **Sinatra Sings Great
Songs from Great Britain**
(English release only)
see Album Lists: alphabetic by title;
1962 — 5th LP; Reprise/6th

#792   O Little Town of Bethle-
hem   *1st recording*
Publication Date: 1868
Music: Lewis H. Redner/
J. Scott — 1820
Words: Phillips Brooks
Recorded: 12/28/47-a
Arranger: Axel Stordahl
Conductor/Band: A. Stordahl/studio
orchestra
Key Release: **Christmas Dreaming**
see Album Lists: alphabetic by title;
1957 — 3rd LP; Columbia/25th

#793   O Little Town of Bethle-
hem   *2nd recording*
Publication Date: 1868
Music: Lewis H. Redner/J.
Scott — 1820
Words: Phillips Brooks
Recorded: 7/10/57-b
Arranger: Gordon Jenkins
Conductor/Band: G. Jenkins/studio
orchestra
Key Release: **A Jolly Christmas from
Frank Sinatra**
see Album Lists: alphabetic by title;
1957 — 6th LP; Capitol/14th

**#794 O'Brien to Ryan to Gold-
berg** *sung with Gene Kelly &
Jules Munshin*
Publication Date: 1949
Music: Roger Edens
Words: Betty Comden & Adolph
Green
Recorded: 1949 — 1st soundtrack
(illegally taken from film
sound)
Arranger: Conrad Salinger
Conductor/Band: Adolph Deutsh/
MGM Orchestra
*Key Release: "Take Me Out to the
Ball Game"* [LP: Five Films]
see Album Lists: alphabetic under
"soundtrack"; mid 1960s; bootleg
Mv. #12

**#795 Oh, Babe, What Would
You Say?**
Publication Date: 1972
Music & Words: E. B. ("Hurri-
cane") Smith
Recorded: 3/12/75-a
Arranger: Don Costa
Conductor/Band: D. Costa/studio
orchestra
Key Release: Late Sinatra Goodies
(illegal; from Reprise masters)
see Album Lists: alphabetic under
"bootleg"; mid–1980s; bootleg
Alb. #6

**#796 Oh, How I Miss You
Tonight**
Publication Date: 1925
Music & Words: Benny Davis &
Joe A. Burke & Mark Fisher
Recorded: 1/17/62-b
Arranger: Gordon Jenkins
Conductor/Band: G. Jenkins/studio
orchestra
Key Release: All Alone
see Album Lists: alphabetic by title;
1962 — 7th LP; Reprise/8th

#797 Oh! Look at Me Now!
*1st recording — duet with Connie
Haines*
Publication Date: 1941
Music: Joe Bushkin
Words: John DeVries
Recorded: 1/6/41-a
Arranger: Sy Oliver
Conductor/Band: Tommy Dorsey &
his Orchestra
*Key Release: The Dorsey/Sinatra
Sessions* (Volume 4)
see Album Lists: alphabetic by title;
1972 — 4th LP; RCA Victor/20th

#798 Oh! Look at Me Now!
2nd recording
Publication Date: 1941
Music: Joe Bushkin
Words: John DeVries
Recorded: 11/28/56-c
Arranger: Nelson Riddle
Conductor/Band: N. Riddle/studio
orchestra
Key Release: A Swingin' Affair!
see Album Lists: alphabetic by title;
1957 — 2nd LP; Capitol/12th

**#799 Oh, What a Beautiful
Morning**
Publication Date: 1943
Music: Richard Rodgers
Words: Oscar Hammerstein II
Recorded: 8/5/43-b
Arranger: Alec Wilder
Conductor/Band: Bobby Tucker
Singers only; during musicians'
strike
Key Release: The Voice: 1943–1952
(6 discs)
see Album Lists: alphabetic by title;
1987 — 1st LP; Columbia/51st

**#800 Oh, What It Seemed to
Be** *1st recording*
Publication Date: 1945
Music & Words: Bennie Benjamin

& George Weiss & Frankie
Carle
Recorded: 1945 radio — "The Frank
Sinatra Old Gold Show"
Arranger: Axel Stordahl
Conductor/Band: A. Stordahl/radio
orchestra
Key Release: **My Best Songs — My
Best Years** (Volume 5)
see Album Lists: alphabetic under
"radio"; early 1970s;
Pentagon/5th

**#801   Oh, What It Seemed to
Be**   *2nd recording*
Publication Date: 1945
Music & Words: Bennie Benjamin
& George Weiss & Frankie
Carle
Recorded: 11/19/45-b
Arranger: Axel Stordahl
Conductor/Band: A. Stordahl/studio
orchestra
Key Release: **Frankie**
see Album Lists: alphabetic by title;
1955 — 8th LP; Columbia/20th

**#802   Oh, What It Seemed to
Be**   *3rd recording*
Publication Date: 1945
Music & Words: Bennie Benjamin
& George Weiss & Frankie
Carle
Recorded: 4/30/63-e
Arranger: Nelson Riddle
Conductor/Band: N. Riddle/studio
orchestra
Key Release: **Sinatra's Sinatra**
see Album Lists: alphabetic by title;
1963 — 7th LP; Reprise/15th

#803   Oh, You Crazy Moon
Publication Date: 1939
Music: Jimmy Van Heusen
Words: Johnny Burke
Recorded: 11/30/65-d
Arranger: Nelson Riddle

Conductor/Band: N. Riddle/studio
orchestra
Key Release: **Moonlight Sinatra**
see Album Lists: alphabetic by title;
1966 — 2nd LP; Reprise/28th

#804   Old Devil Moon   *1st re-
cording*
Publication Date: 1947
Music: Burton Lane
Words: E. Y. ("Yip") Harburg
Recorded: 1/16/56-b
Arranger: Nelson Riddle
Conductor/Band: N. Riddle/studio
orchestra
Key Release: **Songs for Swingin'
Lovers!**
see Album Lists: alphabetic by title;
1956 — 1st LP; Capitol/7th

#805   Old Devil Moon   *2nd re-
cording*
Publication Date: 1947
Music: Burton Lane
Words: E. Y. ("Yip") Harburg
Recorded: 7/18/63-a
Arranger: Nelson Riddle
Conductor/Band: Morris Stoloff/
studio orchestra
Key Release: **Reprise Musical Reper-
tory Theatre: "Finian's Rainbow"**
see Album Lists: alphabetic by title;
1963 — 3rd LP; Reprise/11th

**#806   An Old Fashioned Christ-
mas**
Publication Date: 1953
Music & Words: Johnny Marks
Recorded: 6/16/64-a
Arranger: Nelson Riddle
Conductor/Band: N. Riddle/studio
orchestra
Key Release: **Twelve Songs of
Christmas**
see Album Lists: alphabetic by title;
1964 — 9th LP; Reprise/22nd

#807 Ol' MacDonald *1st recording*
Publication Date: 1960
Music: Lew Spence
Words: Alan Bergman & Marilyn Keith (Bergman)
Recorded: 9/1/60-b
Arranger: Nelson Riddle
Conductor/Band: N. Riddle/studio orchestra
*Key Release: **All the Way***
see Album Lists: alphabetic by title; 1961 — 2nd LP; Capitol/29th

#808 Ol' MacDonald *2nd recording*
Publication Date: 1960
Music: Lew Spence
Words: Alan Bergman & Marilyn Keith (Bergman)
Recorded: 1960 television special
Arranger: Nelson Riddle
Conductor/Band: N. Riddle/television orchestra
*Key Release: **Frank Sinatra — Through the Years: 1944–1966***
see Album Lists: alphabetic under "television"; mid–1960s; Ajazz/1st

#809 Ol' Man River *1st recording*
Publication Date: 1927
Music: Jerome Kern
Words: Oscar Hammerstein II
Recorded: 12/3/44-c
Arranger: Axel Stordahl
Conductor/Band: A. Stordahl/studio orchestra
*Key Release: **The Frank Sinatra Story in Music*** (2 discs)
see Album Lists: alphabetic by title; 1959 — 2nd LP; Columbia/27th

#810 Ol' Man River *2nd recording*
Publication Date: 1927

Music: Jerome Kern
Words: Oscar Hammerstein II
Recorded: 2/18/63-c
Arranger: Nelson Riddle
Conductor/Band: N. Riddle/studio orchestra
*Key Release: **The Concert Sinatra***
see Album Lists: alphabetic by title; 1963 — 2nd LP; Reprise/10th

#811 The Old Master Painter
Publication Date: 1949
Music: Beasley Smith
Words: Haven Gillespie
Recorded: 10/30/49-a
Arranger: Axel Stordahl
Conductor/Band: A. Stordahl/studio orchestra
Key Release: 78rpm single #38650
see Album List #1: 1949 Columbia (4) single record — listed by number

#812 The Oldest Established (Permanent Floating Crap Game in New York) *sung with Bing Crosby & Dean Martin*
Publication Date: 1950
Music & Words: Frank Loesser
Recorded: 7/29/63-b
Arranger: Billy May
Conductor/Band: Morris Stoloff/studio orchestra
*Key Release: **Reprise Musical Repertory Theatre: "Guys and Dolls"***
see Album Lists: alphabetic by title; 1963 — 4th LP; Reprise/12th

#813 On a Clear Day (You Can See Forever)
Publication Date: 1965
Music: Burton Lane
Words: Alan Jay Lerner
Recorded: 5/16/66-d
Arranger: Nelson Riddle
Conductor/Band: N. Riddle/studio orchestra

*Key Release: **Strangers in the Night***
see Album Lists: alphabetic by title;
1966 — 1st LP; Reprise/27th

#814   On a Little Street in Singapore
Publication Date: 1938
Music: Peter DeRose
Words: Billy Hill
Recorded: 10/13/39-a
Arranger: Andy Gibson
Conductor/Band: Harry James & his Orchestra
Key Release: 78rpm single #35261
see Album List #1: 1943 Columbia
(2) single record — listed by number

#815   On Moonlight Bay   *sung with cast ensemble*
Publication Date: 1912
Music: Percy Wenrich
Words: Edward Madden
Recorded: 1942 soundtrack (illegally taken from film sound)
Arranger: Axel Stordahl
Conductor/Band: George Stoll/ MGM Orchestra
*Key Release: "**Ship Ahoy**"* (LP: Four Sinatra Movies)
see Album Lists: alphabetic under "soundtrack"; mid–1960s; bootleg Mv. #2

#816   On the Road to Mandalay
Publication Date: 1907
Music: Oley Speaks
Words: Rudyard Kipling
Recorded: 10/1/57-a
Arranger: Billy May
Conductor/Band: Billy May & his Orchestra
*Key Release: **Come Fly with Me***
see Album Lists: alphabetic by title;
1958 — 2nd LP; Capitol/17th

#817   On the Sunny Side of the Street
Publication Date: 1930
Music: Jimmy McHugh
Words: Dorothy Fields
Recorded: 3/20/61-a
Arranger: Heinie Beau
Conductor/Band: Billy May/studio orchestra
*Key Release: **Come Swing with Me!***
see Album Lists: alphabetic by title;
1961 — 5th LP; Capitol/30th

#818   On the Town   *sung with cast ensemble*
Publication Date: 1949
Music: Roger Edens
Words: Betty Comden & Adolph Green
Recorded: 1949 — 2nd soundtrack (illegally taken from film sound)
Arranger: Conrad Salinger
Conductor/Band: Lenny Hayton/ MGM Orchestra
*Key Release: "**On the Town**"* (LP: "On the Town" & Others)
see Album Lists: alphabetic under "soundtrack"; mid–1960s; bootleg Mv. #13

#819   Once I Loved
Publication Date: 1964
Music: Antonio Carlos Jobim
Words: Ray Gilbert & Vincius De Moraes
Recorded: 2/1/67-a
Arranger: Claus Ogerman
Conductor/Band: C. Ogerman/studio orchestra
*Key Release: **Francis Albert Sinatra & Antonio Carlos Jobim***
see Album Lists: alphabetic by title;
1967 — 1st LP; Reprise/31st

#820   Once in Love with Amy
Publication Date: 1948
Music & Words: Frank Loesser

Recorded: 12/15/48-a
Arranger: Mitchell Ayres
Conductor/Band: M. Ayres/studio
   orchestra
*Key Release: **That Old Feeling***
see Album Lists: alphabetic by title;
   1956 — 2nd LP; Columbia/23rd

#821   Once Upon a Time
Publication Date: 1962
Music: Charles Strouse
Words: Lee Adams
Recorded: 4/14/65-c
Arranger: Gordon Jenkins
Conductor/Band: G. Jenkins/studio
   orchestra
*Key Release: **September of My Years***
see Album Lists: alphabetic by title;
   1965 — 1st LP; Reprise/23rd

#822   One Finger Melody
Publication Date: 1950
Music & Words: Al Hoffman &
   Kermit Goell & Fred Spielman
Recorded: 9/18/50-b
Arranger: Axel Stordahl
Conductor/Band: A. Stordahl/studio
   orchestra
Key Release: 45rpm single #4-39014
see Album List #1: 1950 Columbia
   (5) single record — listed by
   number

#823   One for My Baby (and
One More for the Road)   *1st
recording*
Publication Date: 1943
Music: Harold Arlen
Words: Johnny Mercer
Recorded: 8/11/47-d
Arranger: Axel Stordahl
Conductor/Band: A. Stordahl/studio
   orchestra
*Key Release: **The Frank Sinatra
   Story in Music*** (2 discs)
see Album Lists: alphabetic by title;
   1959 — 2nd LP; Columbia/27th

#824   One for My Baby (and
One More for the Road)   *2nd
recording*
Publication Date: 1943
Music: Harold Arlen
Words: Johnny Mercer
Recorded: 6/25/58-c
Arranger: Nelson Riddle
Conductor/Band: N. Riddle/studio
   orchestra
*Key Release: **Frank Sinatra Sings
   for Only the Lonely***
see Album Lists: alphabetic by title;
   1958 — 5th LP; Capitol/19th

#825   One for My Baby (and
One More for the Road)   *3rd
recording*
Publication Date: 1943
Music: Harold Arlen
Words: Johnny Mercer
Recorded: 2/1/66-k
Arranger: Quincy Jones
Conductor/Band: Count Basie & his
   Band
*Key Release: **Sinatra at the Sands***
   (Live Recording — 2 discs)
see Album Lists: alphabetic by title;
   1966 — 3rd LP; Reprise/29th

#826   One Hundred Years from
Today   *1st recording*
Publication Date: 1933
Music: Victor Young
Words: Ned Washington & Joe
   Young
Recorded: 1943 radio — Lucky
   Strike's "Your Hit Parade"
Arranger: Axel Stordahl
Conductor/Band: A. Stordahl/radio
   orchestra
*Key Release: **The First Times . . .
   Frank Sinatra***
see Album Lists: alphabetic under
   "radio"; early 1960s; Cameron/
   1st

#827 One Hundred Years from Today *2nd recording*
Publication Date: 1933
Music: Victor Young
Words: Ned Washington & Joe Young
Recorded: 4/16/84-d
Arranger: Sam Nestico
Conductor/Band: Quincy Jones & a special all-star jazz band
Key Release: L.A. Is My Lady
see Album Lists: alphabetic by title; 1984 — 1st LP; Qwest/1st

#828 The One I Love (Belongs to Somebody Else) *1st recording*
Publication Date: 1924
Music: Isham Jones
Words: Gus Kahn
Recorded: 6/27/40-b
Arranger: Sy Oliver
Conductor/Band: Tommy Dorsey & his Orchestra
Key Release: The Dorsey/Sinatra Sessions (Volume 2)
see Album Lists: alphabetic by title; 1972 — 2nd LP; RCA Victor/18th

#829 The One I Love (Belongs to Somebody Else) *2nd recording*
Publication Date: 1924
Music: Isham Jones
Words: Gus Kahn
Recorded: 3/25/59-b
Arranger: Gordon Jenkins
Conductor/Band: G. Jenkins/studio orchestra
Key Release: The Rare Sinatra: Volume 1 (Australian release only)
see Album Lists: alphabetic by title; 1978 — 1st LP; Capitol/65th

#830 The One I Love (Belongs to Somebody Else) *3rd recording — duet with Sy Oliver*

Publication Date: 1924
Music: Isham Jones
Words: Gus Kahn
Recorded: 5/3/61-a
Arranger: Sy Oliver
Conductor/Band: S. Oliver/studio orchestra
Key Release: I Remember Tommy...
see Album Lists: alphabetic by title; 1961 — 7th LP; Reprise/3rd

#831 One Love
Publication Date: 1930
Music: Harold Arlen
Words: Ted Koehler
Recorded: 2/3/46-b
Arranger: Axel Stordahl
Conductor/Band: A. Stordahl/studio orchestra
Key Release: The Essential Frank Sinatra (Volume 1)
see Album Lists: alphabetic by title; 1967 — 2nd LP; Columbia/34th

#832 One Note Samba *duet with Antonio Carlos Jobim*
Publication Date: 1961
Music: Antonio Carlos Jobim & Newton Mendonca
Words: Jon Hendricks/Newton Mendonca & Antonio Carlos Jobim
Recorded: 2/11/69-a
Arranger: Eumir Deodato
Conductor/Band: Morris Stoloff/ studio orchestra
Key Release: Sinatra & Company
see Album Lists: alphabetic by title; 1971 — 2nd LP; Reprise/42nd

#833 The Only Couple on the Floor
Publication Date: 1974
Music & Words: John Durrill
Recorded: 3/3/75-b
Arranger: Don Costa

Conductor/Band: Bill Miller/studio orchestra
Key Release: I Sing the Songs (Italian release only)
see Album Lists: alphabetic by title; 1982 — 5th LP; Reprise/60th

#834   Only the Lonely
Publication Date: 1958
Music: Jimmy Van Heusen
Words: Sammy Cahn
Recorded: 5/29/58-f
Arranger: Nelson Riddle
Conductor/Band: Felix Slatkin/studio orchestra
Key Release: Frank Sinatra Sings for Only the Lonely
see Album Lists: alphabetic by title; 1958 — 5th LP; Capitol/19th

#835   Our Love*
Publication Date: 1939
Music: Larry Clinton; from P. Tchaikovsky
Words: Buddy Bernier & Bob Emmerich
Recorded: 2/3/39-a
Arranger: Frank Manne
Conductor/Band: Frank Manne & his Orchestra
Key Release: demonstration disc (included for historical purposes only)
see Album List #1: 1939 demonstration disc — no label or number
*Sinatra's first recording done in professional circumstances, made on February 3, 1939, the day before his marriage to Nancy Barbato. This demonstration disc was cut in-studio with Frank Manne's Orchestra. Prior to that, he had done homemade records with the Hoboken Four (1935–36).

#836   Our Love Affair
Publication Date: 1940

Music & Words: Roger Edens & Arthur Freed
Recorded: 8/29/40-a
Arranger: Dorsey "house" arrng: T. Dorsey, S. Oliver, F. Stulce, P. Weston
Conductor/Band: Tommy Dorsey & his Orchestra
Key Release: The Dorsey/Sinatra Sessions (Volume 3)
see Album Lists: alphabetic by title; 1972 — 3rd LP; RCA Victor/19th

#837   Our Town
Publication Date: 1955
Music: Jimmy Van Heusen
Words: Sammy Cahn
Recorded: 8/15/55-d
Arranger: Nelson Riddle
Conductor/Band: N. Riddle/studio orchestra
Key Release: Look to Your Heart
see Album Lists: alphabetic by title; 1959 — 4th LP; Capitol/22nd

#838   Out Beyond the Window
poetry recited to music
Publication Date: 1969
Music: Rod McKuen (nonvocal melody)
Words: Rod McKuen
Recorded: 3/21/69-a
Arranger: Don Costa
Conductor/Band: D. Costa/studio orchestra
Key Release: A Man Alone
see Album Lists: alphabetic by title; 1969 — 3rd LP; Reprise/39th

#839   Out of Nowhere   *parody*
Publication Date: 1931
Music: John Green
Words: Edward Heyman; parody lyric by Harry Harris
Recorded: 1957 soundtrack (illegally taken from film sound)
Arranger: Nelson Riddle

Conductor/Band: Walter Scharf/
Paramount Orchestra
Key Release: "The Joker Is Wild"
(LP: Score from "The Joker Is
Wild")
see Album Lists: alphabetic under
"soundtrack"; mid–1960s; boot-
leg Mv. #21

#840　Over the Rainbow
Publication Date: 1939
Music: Harold Arlen
Words: E. Y. ("Yip") Harburg
Recorded: 5/1/45-b
Arranger: Axel Stordahl
Conductor/Band: A. Stordahl/studio
orchestra
Key Release: The Voice
see Album Lists: alphabetic by title;
1955 — 9th LP; Columbia/21st

#841　P.S. I Love You
Publication Date: 1934
Music: Gordon Jenkins
Words: Johnny Mercer
Recorded: 3/8/56-b
Arranger: Nelson Riddle
Conductor/Band: N. Riddle with or-
chestra & the Hollywood String
Quartet
Key Release: Close to You
see Album Lists: alphabetic by title;
1957 — 1st LP; Capitol/11th

#842　Pale Moon
Publication Date: 1920
Music: Frederick Knight Logan
Words: Jesse G. M. Glick
Recorded: 8/19/41-d
Arranger: Dorsey "house" arrng:
T. Dorsey, S. Oliver, F. Stulce,
P. Weston
Conductor/Band: Tommy Dorsey &
his Orchestra
*Key Release: The Dorsey/Sinatra
Sessions* (Volume 5)
see Album Lists: alphabetic by title;

1972 — 5th LP; RCA Victor/21st

#843　Paper Doll
Publication Date: 1930
Music & Words: Johnny Black
Recorded: 3/22/61-d
Arranger: Billy May
Conductor/Band: B. May/studio
orchestra
Key Release: Come Swing with Me!
see Album Lists: alphabetic by title;
1961 — 5th LP; Capitol/30th

#844　Paradise
Publication Date: 1932
Music & Words: Nacio Herb
Brown & Gordon Clifford
Recorded: 12/7/45-d
Arranger: Axel Stordahl
Conductor/Band: A. Stordahl/studio
orchestra
Key Release: The Voice
see Album Lists: alphabetic by title;
1955 — 9th LP; Columbia/21st

#845　Pass Me By
Publication Date: 1964
Music: Cy Coleman
Words: Carolyn Leigh
Recorded: 10/3/64-a
Arranger: Billy May
Conductor/Band: B. May/studio
orchestra
Key Release: Softly, As I Leave You
see Album Lists: alphabetic by title;
1964 — 8th LP; Reprise/21st

#846　Peach Tree Street　*duet
with Rosemary Clooney*
Publication Date: 1950
Music & Words: S. Williamson
Recorded: 4/8/50-a
Arranger: George Siravo
Conductor/Band: G. Siravo/studio
orchestra
Key Release: 78rpm single #38853
see Album List #1: 1950 Columbia

(4) single record — listed by number

#847 Pennies from Heaven *1st recording*
Publication Date: 1936
Music: Arthur Johnston
Words: Johnny Burke
Recorded: 1/10/56-a
Arranger: Nelson Riddle
Conductor/Band: N. Riddle/studio orchestra
*Key Release: **Songs for Swingin' Lovers!***
see Album Lists: alphabetic by title; 1956 — 1st LP; Capitol/7th

#848 Pennies from Heaven *2nd recording*
Publication Date: 1936
Music: Arthur Johnston
Words: Johnny Burke
Recorded: 10/3/62-d
Arranger: Neal Hefti
Conductor/Band: Count Basie & his Band
*Key Release: **Sinatra-Basie: An Historic Musical First***
see Album Lists: alphabetic by title; 1963 — 1st LP; Reprise/9th

#849 People Will Say We're in Love
Publication Date: 1943
Music: Richard Rodgers
Words: Oscar Hammerstein II
Recorded: 8/5/43-a
Conductor/Band: Bobby Tucker Singers only; during musicians' strike
*Key Release: **Frank Sinatra's Greatest Hits: The Early Years** (Vol. 2)*
see Album Lists: alphabetic by title; 1964 — 4th LP; Columbia/33rd

#850 Pick Yourself Up
Publication Date: 1936
Music: Jerome Kern
Words: Dorothy Fields
Recorded: 4/11/62-f
Arranger: Neal Hefti
Conductor/Band: N. Hefti/studio orchestra
*Key Release: **Sinatra and Swingin' Brass***
see Album Lists: alphabetic by title; 1962 — 4th LP; Reprise/5th

#851 Pistol Packing Mama
Publication Date: 1943
Music & Words: Al Dexter
Recorded: 1943 radio — "Songs by Sinatra"
Arranger: Axel Stordahl
Conductor/Band: A. Stordahl/radio orchestra
*Key Release: **My Best Songs — My Best Years** (Volume 1)*
see Album Lists: alphabetic under "radio"; early 1970s; Pentagon/ 1st

#852 Please Be Kind
Publication Date: 1938
Music: Saul Chaplin
Words: Sammy Cahn
Recorded: 10/2/62-b
Arranger: Neal Hefti
Conductor/Band: Count Basie & his Band
*Key Release: **Sinatra-Basie: An Historic Musical First***
see Album Lists: alphabetic by title; 1963 — 1st LP; Reprise/9th

#853 Please Don't Talk About Me When I'm Gone
Publication Date: 1930
Music: Sam H. Stept
Words: Sidney Clare
Recorded: 5/18/61-c
Arranger: Billy May

Conductor/Band: Billy May & his
   Orchestra
Key Release: **Sinatra Swings**
   (original title: "Swing Along
   with Me")
see Album Lists: alphabetic by title;
   1961—6th LP; Reprise/2nd

#854   Pocketful of Miracles*
Publication Date: 1961
Music: Jimmy Van Heusen
Words: Sammy Cahn
Recorded: 11/22/61-d
Arranger: Nelson Riddle
Conductor/Band: N. Riddle/studio
   orchestra
Key Release: **Sinatra's Sinatra**
see Album Lists: alphabetic by title;
   1963—7th LP; Reprise/15th
*The hit single release of this song
   appears on the stereo version of
   the LP **Sinatra's Sinatra** (Reprise FS-1010); an alternate-take
   appears on the monaural version of that album.

**#855   Poinciana «Song of the
   Tree»**   *1st recording*
Publication Date: 1943
Music: Nat Simon—1936
Words: Buddy Bernier/Manuel
   Lliso—1936
Recorded: 10/15/46-b
Arranger: Axel Stordahl
Conductor/Band: A. Stordahl/studio
   orchestra
Key Release: 78rpm single #DB2357
   (English release only)
see Album List #1: 1947 Columbia
   (3) single record—listed by
   number

**#856   Poinciana «Song of the
   Tree»**   *2nd recording*
Publication Date: 1943
Music: Nat Simon—1936
Words: Buddy Bernier/Manuel

   Lliso—1936
Recorded: 10/29/47-b
Arranger: Axel Stordahl
Conductor/Band: A. Stordahl/studio
   orchestra
Key Release: **That Old Feeling**
see Album Lists: alphabetic by title;
   1956—2nd LP; Columbia/23rd

**#857   Polka Dots and Moon-
   beams**   *1st recording*
Publication Date: 1940
Music: Jimmy Van Heusen
Words: Johnny Burke
Recorded: 3/4/40-b
Arranger: Axel Stordahl
Conductor/Band: Tommy Dorsey &
   his Orchestra
Key Release: **The Dorsey/Sinatra
   Sessions** (Volume 1)
see Album Lists: alphabetic by title;
   1972—1st LP; RCA Victor/
   17th

**#858   Polka Dots and Moon-
   beams**   *2nd recording*
Publication Date: 1940
Music: Jimmy Van Heusen
Words: Johnny Burke
Recorded: 5/2/61-b
Arranger: Sy Oliver
Conductor/Band: S. Oliver/studio
   orchestra
Key Release: **I Remember Tommy...**
see Album Lists: alphabetic by title;
   1961-7th LP; Reprise/3rd

#859   Poor Butterfly
Publication Date: 1916
Music: Raymond Hubbell
Words: John Golden
Recorded: 12/12/67-d
Arranger: Billy May
Conductor/Band: Duke Ellington &
   his Band
Key Release: **Francis A. & Ed-
   ward K.**

see Album Lists: alphabetic by title; 1968 — 2nd LP; Reprise/33rd

#860   Poor You
Publication Date: 1942
Music: Burton Lane
Words: E. Y. ("Yip") Harburg
Recorded: 2/19/42-b
Arranger: Axel Stordahl
Conductor/Band: Tommy Dorsey & his Orchestra
Key Release: **The Dorsey/Sinatra Sessions** (Volume 6)
see Album Lists: alphabetic by title; 1972 — 6th LP; RCA Victor/ 22nd

#861   Prehistoric Man   *sung with cast ensemble*
Publication Date: 1949
Music: Roger Edens
Words: Betty Comden & Adolph Green
Recorded: 1949 — 2nd soundtrack (illegally taken from film sound)
Arranger: Conrad Salinger
Conductor/Band: Lenny Hayton/ MGM Orchestra
Key Release: **"On the Town"** (LP: "On the Town" & Others)
see Album Lists: alphabetic under "soundtrack"; mid–1960s; bootleg Mv. #13

#862   Pretty Colors
Publication Date: 1968
Music & Words: Al Gorgoni & Chip Taylor
Recorded: 11/13/68-b
Arranger: Don Costa
Conductor/Band: Bill Miller/studio orchestra
Key Release: **Cycles**
see Album Lists: alphabetic by title; 1968 — 6th LP; Reprise/37th

#863   Prisoner of Love
Publication Date: 1931

Music: Russ Columbo & Clarence Gaskill
Words: Leo Robin
Recorded: 11/21/61-b
Arranger: Don Costa
Conductor/Band: D. Costa/studio orchestra
Key Release: **Sinatra & Strings**
see Album Lists: alphabetic by title; 1962 — 1st LP; Reprise/4th

#864   Put Your Dreams Away
1st recording
Publication Date: 1942
Music: Paul Mann & Stephan Weiss
Words: Ruth Lowe
Recorded: 5/1/45-a
Arranger: Axel Stordahl
Conductor/Band: A. Stordahl/studio orchestra
Key Release: **Put Your Dreams Away**
see Album Lists: alphabetic by title; 1958 — 3rd LP; Columbia/26th

#865   Put Your Dreams Away
2nd recording
Publication Date: 1942
Music: Paul Mann & Stephan Weiss
Words: Ruth Lowe
Recorded: 12/11/57-c
Arranger: Nelson Riddle
Conductor/Band: N. Riddle/studio orchestra
Key Release: **This Is Sinatra, Volume Two**
see Album Lists: alphabetic by title; 1958 — 4th LP; Capitol/18th

#866   Put Your Dreams Away
3rd recording
Publication Date: 1942
Music: Paul Mann & Stephan Weiss
Words: Ruth Lowe

Recorded: 4/30/63-c
Arranger: Nelson Riddle
Conductor/Band: N. Riddle/studio
  orchestra
Key Release: Sinatra's Sinatra
see Album Lists: alphabetic by title;
  1963 — 7th LP; Reprise/15th

#867   Quiet Nights of Quiet Stars «Corcovado»
Publication Date: 1962
Music: Antonio Carlos Jobim
Words: Gene Lees/Antonio Carlos
  Jobim
Recorded: 1/31/67-a
Arranger: Claus Ogerman
Conductor/Band: C. Ogerman/studio
  orchestra
Key Release: Francis Albert Sinatra & Antonio Carlos Jobim
see Album Lists: alphabetic by title;
  1967 — 1st LP; Reprise/31st

#868   Rain (Falling from the Skies)
Publication Date: 1953
Music: G. Finlay
Words: Robert Mellin
Recorded: 12/9/53-a
Arranger: Nelson Riddle
Conductor/Band: N. Riddle/studio
  orchestra
Key Release: This Is Sinatra! (Volume 1)
see Album Lists: alphabetic by title;
  1956 — 6th LP; Capitol/10th

#869   Rain in My Heart
Publication Date: 1967
Music & Words: Teddy Randazzo
  & Victoria Pike
Recorded: 11/14/68-a
Arranger: Don Costa
Conductor/Band: Bill Miller/studio
  orchestra
Key Release: Cycles
see Album Lists: alphabetic by title;

  1968 — 6th LP; Reprise/37th

#870   Reaching for the Moon
Publication Date: 1931
Music & Words: Irving Berlin
Recorded: 11/29/65-e
Arranger: Nelson Riddle
Conductor/Band: N. Riddle/studio
  orchestra
Key Release: Moonlight Sinatra
see Album Lists: alphabetic by title;
  1966 — 2nd LP; Reprise/28th

#871   Remember   *1st recording*
Publication Date: 1925
Music & Words: Irving Berlin
Recorded: 1/16/62-a
Arranger: Gordon Jenkins
Conductor/Band: G. Jenkins/studio
  orchestra
Key Release: All Alone
see Album Lists: alphabetic by title;
  1962 — 7th LP; Reprise/8th

#872   Remember   *2nd recording*
Publication Date: 1925
Music & Words: Irving Berlin
Recorded: 7/17/78-b
Arranger: Don Costa
Conductor/Band: D. Costa/studio
  orchestra
Key Release: Late Sinatra Goodies
  (illegal; from Reprise masters)
see Album Lists: alphabetic under
  "bootleg"; mid–1980s; bootleg
  Alb. #6

#873   Remember Me in Your Dreams
Publication Date: 1950
Music: Arthur Altman
Words: Hal David
Recorded: 9/21/50-a
Arranger: Axel Stordahl
Conductor/Band: A. Stordahl/studio
  orchestra
Key Release: 45rpm single #4-39069

see Album List #1: 1950 Columbia (5) single record — listed by number

#874   The Right Girl for Me (She's —)
Publication Date: 1949
Music: Roger Edens
Words: Betty Comden & Adolph Green
Recorded: 3/3/49-a
Arranger: Axel Stordahl
Conductor/Band: A. Stordahl/studio orchestra
Key Release: Frank Sinatra in Hollywood, 1943–1949
see Album Lists: alphabetic by title; 1968 — 1st LP; Columbia/38th

#875   The Right Kind of Love
Publication Date: 1949
Music: Mabel Wayne
Words: Kermit Goell
Recorded: 1949 radio — Lucky Strike's "Your Hit Parade"
Arranger: Axel Stordahl
Conductor/Band: A. Stordahl/radio orchestra
Key Release: My Best Songs — My Best Years (Volume 4)
see Album Lists: alphabetic under "radio"; early 1970s; Pentagon/4th

#876   Ring-a-Ding Ding
Publication Date: 1960
Music: Jimmy Van Heusen
Words: Sammy Cahn
Recorded: 12/19/60-a
Arranger: Johnny Mandel
Conductor/Band: J. Mandel/studio orchestra
Key Release: Ring-a-Ding Ding!
see Album Lists: alphabetic by title; 1961 — 3rd LP; Reprise/1st

#877   River Stay 'Way from My Door
Publication Date: 1931
Music: Harry Woods
Words: Mort Dixon
Recorded: 4/12/60-b
Arranger: Nelson Riddle
Conductor/Band: N. Riddle/studio orchestra
Key Release: All the Way
see Album Lists: alphabetic by title; 1961 — 2nd LP; Capitol/29th

#878   Roses of Picardy
Publication Date: 1916
Music: Haydn Wood
Words: F. E. Weatherly
Recorded: 6/13/62-c
Arranger: Robert Farnon
Conductor/Band: R. Farnon/studio orchestra
Key Release: Sinatra Sings Great Songs from Great Britain (1972 Japanese version only; not on 1962 English release)
see Album Lists: alphabetic by title; 1962 — 5th LP; Reprise/6th

#879   Saddest Thing of All
Publication Date: 1974
Music: Michel Legrand
Words: Carl Sigman/E. Barclay
Recorded: 8/18/75-a
Arranger: Gordon Jenkins
Conductor/Band: G. Jenkins/studio orchestra
Key Release: I Sing the Songs (Italian release only)
see Album Lists: alphabetic by title; 1982 — 5th LP; Reprise/60th

#880   Same Old Saturday Night
Publication Date: 1955
Music: Frank Reardon
Words: Sammy Cahn
Recorded: 7/29/55-a
Arranger: Nelson Riddle

Conductor/Band: N. Riddle/studio
orchestra
Key Release: **Look to Your Heart**
see Album Lists: alphabetic by title;
1959 — 4th LP; Capitol/22nd

#881   Same Old Song and Dance
Publication Date: 1958
Music: Jimmy Van Heusen
Words: Sammy Cahn & Bobby
Worth
Recorded: 3/3/58-c
Arranger: Billy May
Conductor/Band: Billy May & his
Orchestra
Key Release: **Forever Frank**
see Album Lists: alphabetic by title;
1966 — 4th LP; Capitol/36th

#882   Sand and Sea
Publication Date: 1963
Music: Gilbert Becaud
Words: Hal David/R. Vidalin
Recorded: 11/18/66-c
Arranger: Ernie Freeman
Conductor/Band: E. Freeman/studio
orchestra
Key Release: **That's Life**
see Album Lists: alphabetic by title;
1966 — 5th LP; Reprise/30th

**#883   Santa Claus Is Comin' to
Town**
Publication Date: 1932
Music: J. Fred Coots
Words: Haven Gillespie
Recorded: 12/28/47-f
Arranger: Axel Stordahl
Conductor/Band: A. Stordahl/studio
orchestra
Key Release: **Christmas Dreaming**
see Album Lists: alphabetic by title;
1957 — 3rd LP; Columbia/25th

**#884   Satisfy Me One More
Time**
Publication Date: 1972

Music & Words: Floyd Huddleston
Recorded: 5/21/74-c
Arranger: Don Costa
Conductor/Band: D. Costa/studio
orchestra
Key Release: **Some Nice Things I've
Missed**
see Album Lists: alphabetic by title;
1974 — 1st LP; Reprise/47th

**#885   Saturday Night (Is the
Loneliest Night of the Week)**
1st recording
Publication Date: 1944
Music: Jule Styne
Words: Sammy Cahn
Recorded: 11/14/44-b
Arranger: Axel Stordahl
Conductor/Band: A. Stordahl/studio
orchestra
Key Release: **Love Is a Kick**
see Album Lists: alphabetic by title;
1960 — 3rd LP; Columbia/28th

**#886   Saturday Night (Is the
Loneliest Night of the Week)**
2nd recording
Publication Date: 1944
Music: Jule Styne
Words: Sammy Cahn
Recorded: 12/22/58-d
Arranger: Heinie Beau
Conductor/Band: Billy May & his
Orchestra
Key Release: **Come Dance with Me!**
see Album Lists: alphabetic by title;
1959 — 1st LP; Capitol/20th

#887   Say Hello
Publication Date: 1981
Music: Richard Evan Behrke
Words: Sammy Cahn
Recorded: 7/21/81-a
Arranger: Don Costa
Conductor/Band: D. Costa/studio
orchestra

Key Release: 45rpm single
#RPS49827
see Album List #1: 1981 Reprise (5)
single record—listed by number

#888   Say It (Over and Over Again)
Publication Date: 1940
Music: Jimmy McHugh
Words: Frank Loesser
Recorded: 3/4/40-a
Arranger: Dorsey "house" arrng:
T. Dorsey, S. Oliver, F. Stulce, P. Weston
Conductor/Band: Tommy Dorsey & his Orchestra
Key Release: The Dorsey/Sinatra Sessions (Volume 1)
see Album Lists: alphabetic by title;
1972—1st LP; RCA Victor/17th

#889   The Second Time Around
1st recording
Publication Date: 1960
Music: Jimmy Van Heusen
Words: Sammy Cahn
Recorded: 12/21/60-b
Arranger: Felix Slatkin
Conductor/Band: F. Slatkin/studio orchestra
Key Release: The Voice: Volume 1
(Italian release only)
see Album Lists: alphabetic by title;
1982—1st LP; Reprise/56th

#890   The Second Time Around
2nd recording
Publication Date: 1960
Music: Jimmy Van Heusen
Words: Sammy Cahn
Recorded: 4/29/63-d
Arranger: Nelson Riddle
Conductor/Band: N. Riddle/studio orchestra
Key Release: Sinatra's Sinatra
see Album Lists: alphabetic by title;
1963—7th LP; Reprise/15th

#891   Secret Love
Publication Date: 1953
Music: Sammy Fain
Words: Paul Francis Webster
Recorded: 1/28/64-b
Arranger: Nelson Riddle
Conductor/Band: N. Riddle/studio orchestra
Key Release: Frank Sinatra Sings "Days of Wine and Roses," "Moon River," and Other Academy Award Winners
see Album Lists: alphabetic by title;
1964—1st LP; Reprise/17th

#892   Send in the Clowns   *1st recording*
Publication Date: 1973
Music & Words: Stephen Sondheim
Recorded: 6/22/73-c
Arranger: Gordon Jenkins
Conductor/Band: G. Jenkins/studio orchestra
Key Release: Ol' Blue Eyes Is Back
see Album Lists: alphabetic by title;
1973—2nd LP; Reprise/45th

#893   Send in the Clowns   *2nd recording*
Publication Date: 1973
Music & Words: Stephen Sondheim
Recorded: 2/5/76-c
Arranger: Don Costa
Conductor/Band: Bill Miller/studio orchestra
Key Release: The Singles (Italian release only)
see Album Lists: alphabetic by title;
1982—6th LP; Reprise/61st

#894   Senorita (I Offer You the Moon—)   *duet with Kathryn Grayson*
Publication Date: 1947
Music: Nacio Herb Brown
Words: Edward Heyman
Recorded: 10/29/47c

Arranger: Axel Stordahl
Conductor/Band: A. Stordahl/studio
orchestra
*Key Release: Frank Sinatra in
Hollywood, 1943–1949*
see Album Lists: alphabetic by title;
1968 — 1st LP; Columbia/38th

#895   Sentimental Baby
Publication Date: 1960
Music: Lew Spence
Words: Alan Bergman & Marilyn
Keith (Bergman)
Recorded: 9/1/60-a
Arranger: Nelson Riddle
Conductor/Band: N. Riddle/studio
orchestra
*Key Release: Sinatra Sings . . . of
Love and Things*
see Album Lists: alphabetic by title;
1962 — 3rd LP; Capitol/32nd

#896   Sentimental Journey
Publication Date: 1944
Music & Words: Bud Green & Les
Brown & Ben Homer
Recorded: 3/20/61-c
Arranger: Heinie Beau
Conductor/Band: Billy May/studio
orchestra
Key Release: Come Swing with Me!
see Album Lists: alphabetic by title;
1961 — 5th LP; Capitol/30th

#897   September in the Rain
Publication Date: 1937
Music: Harry Warren
Words: Al Dubin
Recorded: 8/31/60-b
Arranger: Nelson Riddle
Conductor/Band: N. Riddle/studio
orchestra
*Key Release: Sinatra's Swingin'
Session!!!*
see Album Lists: alphabetic by title;
1961 — 1st LP; Capitol/28th

**#898   The September of My
Years**   *1st recording*
Publication Date: 1965
Music: Jimmy Van Heusen
Words: Sammy Cahn
Recorded: 5/27/65-a
Arranger: Gordon Jenkins
Conductor/Band: G. Jenkins/studio
orchestra
Key Release: September of My Years
see Album Lists: alphabetic by title;
1965 — 1st LP; Reprise/23rd

**#899   The September of My
Years**   *2nd recording*
Publication Date: 1965
Music: Jimmy Van Heusen
Words: Sammy Cahn
Recorded: 2/1/66-c
Arranger: Quincy Jones
Conductor/Band: Count Basie & his
Band
Key Release: Sinatra at the Sands
(Live Recording — 2 discs)
see Album Lists: alphabetic by title;
1966 — 3rd LP; Reprise/29th

#900   September Song   *1st re-
cording*
Publication Date: 1938
Music: Kurt Weill
Words: Maxwell Anderson
Recorded: 7/30/46-c
Arranger: Axel Stordahl
Conductor/Band: A. Stordahl/studio
orchestra
Key Release: Come Back to Sorrento
see Album Lists: alphabetic by title;
1960 — 5th LP; Columbia/30th

#901   September Song   *2nd re-
cording*
Publication Date: 1938
Music: Kurt Weill
Words: Maxwell Anderson
Recorded: 9/11/61-c
Arranger: Axel Stordahl

Conductor/Band: A. Stordahl/studio orchestra
Key Release: **Point of No Return**
see Album Lists: alphabetic by title; 1962 — 2nd LP; Capitol/31st

#902   September Song   *3rd recording*
Publication Date: 1938
Music: Kurt Weill
Words: Maxwell Anderson
Recorded: 4/13/65-b
Arranger: Gordon Jenkins
Conductor/Band: G. Jenkins/studio orchestra
Key Release: **September of My Years**
see Album Lists: alphabetic by title; 1965 — 1st LP; Reprise/23rd

#903   Serenade in Blue
Publication Date: 1942
Music: Harry Warren
Words: Mack Gordon
Recorded: 4/11/62-b
Arranger: Neal Hefti
Conductor/Band: N. Hefti/studio orchestra
Key Release: **Sinatra and Swingin' Brass**
see Album Lists: alphabetic by title; 1962 — 4th LP; Reprise/5th

#904   Serenade of the Bells
Publication Date: 1947
Music & Words: Kay Twomey & Al Urbano & Al Goodhart
Recorded: 1947 radio — Lucky Strike's "Your Hit Parade"
Arranger: Axel Stordahl
Conductor/Band: A. Stordahl/radio orchestra
Key Release: **Frank Sinatra**
see Album Lists: alphabetic under "radio"; early 1960s; Cameron/4th

#905   The Shadow of Your Smile
Publication Date: 1965
Music: Johnny Mandel
Words: Paul Francis Webster
Recorded: 2/1/66-f
Arranger: Quincy Jones
Conductor/Band: Count Basie & his Band
Key Release: **Sinatra at the Sands** (Live Recording — 2 discs)
see Album Lists: alphabetic by title; 1966 — 3rd LP; Reprise/29th

#906   Shadows on the Sand
Publication Date: 1940
Music: George W. Meyer
Words: Stanley Adams
Recorded: 9/17/40-a
Arranger: Dorsey "house" arrng:
   T. Dorsey, S. Oliver, F. Stulce, P. Weston
Conductor/Band: Tommy Dorsey & his Orchestra
Key Release: **The Dorsey/Sinatra Sessions** (Volume 3)
see Album Lists: alphabetic by title; 1972 — 3rd LP; RCA Victor/19th

#907   Shake Down the Stars
Publication Date: 1940
Music: Jimmy Van Heusen
Words: Eddie DeLange
Recorded: 2/26/40-a
Arranger: Dorsey "house" arrng:
   T. Dorsey, S. Oliver, F. Stulce, P. Weston
Conductor/Band: Tommy Dorsey & his Orchestra
Key Release: **The Dorsey/Sinatra Sessions** (Volume 1)
see Album Lists: alphabetic by title; 1972 — 1st LP; RCA Victor/17th

#908   She Says
Publication Date: 1969

Music & Words: Bob Gaudio &
   Jake Holmes
Recorded: 7/16/69-a
Arrangers: Bob Gaudio & Joseph
   Scott
Conductor/Band: Joseph Scott/studio
   orchestra
Key Release: **Watertown [a love
   story]**
see Album Lists: alphabetic by title;
   1970 — 1st LP; Reprise/40th

#909   Sheila
Publication Date: 1949
Music & Words: G. Easterling
Recorded: 1/12/50-b
Arranger: Axel Stordahl
Conductor/Band: A. Stordahl/studio
   orchestra
Key Release: 45rpm single #4-40565
see Album List #1: 1952 Columbia
   (5) single record — listed by
   number

#910   She's Funny That Way
   1st recording
Publication Date: 1928
Music: Richard A. Whiting
Words: Neil Moret
Recorded: 12/19/44-d
Arranger: Axel Stordahl
Conductor/Band: A. Stordahl/studio
   orchestra
Key Release: **The Voice**
see Album Lists: alphabetic by title;
   1955 — 9th LP; Columbia/21st

#911   She's Funny That Way
   2nd recording
Publication Date: 1928
Music: Richard A. Whiting
Words: Neil Moret
Recorded: 3/2/60-a
Arranger: Nelson Riddle
Conductor/Band: N. Riddle/studio
   orchestra
Key Release: **Nice 'n' Easy**

see Album Lists: alphabetic by title;
   1960 — 2nd LP; Capitol/25th

#912   Should I?   *1st recording*
Publication Date: 1930
Music: Nacio Herb Brown
Words: Arthur Freed
Recorded: 2/27/46-a; "The Frank
   Sinatra Old Gold Show"
Arranger: Axel Stordahl
Conductor/Band: A. Stordahl/radio
   orchestra
Key Release: **Frank Sinatra on V-
   Disc** (Japanese release only; al-
   bum of wartime Victory Discs)
see Album Lists: alphabetic under
   "v/disc"; early 1970s; Dan/1st

#913   Should I?   *2nd recording*
Publication Date: 1930
Music: Nacio Herb Brown
Words: Arthur Freed
Recorded: 4/14/50-a
Arranger: George Siravo
Conductor/Band: G. Siravo/studio
   orchestra
Key Release: **Love Is a Kick**
see Album Lists: alphabetic by title;
   1960 — 3rd LP; Columbia/28th

#914   Should I?   *3rd recording*
Publication Date: 1930
Music: Nacio Herb Brown
Words: Arthur Freed
Recorded: 8/22/60-e
Arranger: Nelson Riddle
Conductor/Band: N. Riddle/studio
   orchestra
Key Release: **Sinatra's Swingin'
   Session!!!**
see Album Lists: alphabetic by title;
   1961 — 1st LP; Capitol/28th

#915   Siesta
Publication Date: 1947
Music: Nacio Herb Brown
Words: Earl K. Brent

Recorded: 1948 soundtrack (illegally taken from film sound)
Arranger: Leo Arnaud
Conductor/Band: George Stoll/ MGM Orchestra
Key Release: "The Kissing Bandit" (LP: Five Films)
see Album Lists: alphabetic under "soundtrack"; mid–1960s; bootleg Mv. #11

#916   Silent Night «Stille Nacht, Heilige Nacht»   *1st recording*
Publication Date: 1818
Music: Franz Gruber
Words: Joseph Mohr (from anonymous source)
Recorded: 8/27/45-b
Arranger: Axel Stordahl
Conductor/Band: A. Stordahl/studio orchestra
Key Release: Christmas Dreaming
see Album Lists: alphabetic by title; 1957 – 3rd LP; Columbia/25th

#917   Silent Night «Stille Nacht, Heilige Nacht»   *2nd recording*
Publication Date: 1818
Music: Franz Gruber
Words: Joseph Mohr (from anonymous source)
Recorded: 7/17/57-c
Arranger: Gordon Jenkins
Conductor/Band: G. Jenkins/studio orchestra
Key Release: A Jolly Christmas from Frank Sinatra
see Album Lists: alphabetic by title; 1957 – 6th LP; Capitol/14th

#918   The Single Man
Publication Date: 1969
Music & Words: Rod McKuen
Recorded: 3/19/69-c
Arranger: Don Costa

Conductor/Band: D. Costa/studio orchestra
Key Release: A Man Alone
see Album Lists: alphabetic by title; 1969 – 3rd LP; Reprise/39th

#919   A Sinner Kissed an Angel
Publication Date: 1941
Music: Ray Joseph
Words: Mack David
Recorded: 9/18/41-c
Arranger: Dorsey "house" arrng: T. Dorsey, S. Oliver, F. Stulce, P. Weston
Conductor/Band: Tommy Dorsey & his Orchestra
Key Release: The Dorsey/Sinatra Sessions (Volume 5)
see Album Lists: alphabetic by title; 1972 – 5th LP; RCA Victor/21st

#920   The Sky Fell Down
Publication Date: 1940
Music: Louis Alter
Words: Edward Heyman
Recorded: 2/1/40-a
Arranger: Axel Stordahl
Conductor/Band: Tommy Dorsey & his Orchestra
Key Release: The Dorsey/Sinatra Sessions (Volume 1)
see Album Lists: alphabetic by title; 1972 – 1st LP; RCA Victor/17th

#921   Sleep Warm
Publication Date: 1958
Music: Lew Spence
Words: Alan Bergman & Marilyn Keith (Bergman)
Recorded: 9/11/58-b
Arranger: Nelson Riddle
Conductor/Band: N. Riddle/studio orchestra
Key Release: All the Way
see Album Lists: alphabetic by title; 1961 – 2nd LP; Capitol/29th

#922   Snooty Little Cutie
(You're a—)   *duet with Connie Haines*
Publication Date: 1942
Music & Words: Bobby Troup
Recorded: 2/19/42-a
Arranger: Sy Oliver
Conductor/Band: Tommy Dorsey & his Orchestra
Key Release: **The Dorsey/Sinatra Sessions** (Volume 5)
see Album Lists: alphabetic by title; 1972—5th LP; RCA Victor/21st

#923   So Far
Publication Date: 1947
Music: Richard Rodgers
Words: Oscar Hammerstein II
Recorded: 8/17/47-c
Arranger: Axel Stordahl
Conductor/Band: A. Stordahl/studio orchestra
Key Release: **Sinatra Rarities — The Columbia Years** (Volume 1)
see Album Lists: alphabetic by title; 1986—1st LP; Columbia/50th

#924   So in Love   *duet with Keely Smith*
Publication Date: 1948
Music & Words: Cole Porter
Recorded: 7/24/63-a
Arranger: Nelson Riddle
Conductor/Band: Morris Stoloff/ studio orchestra
Key Release: **Reprise Musical Repertory Theatre: "Kiss Me Kate"**
see Album Lists: alphabetic by title; 1963 — 5th LP; Reprise/13th

#925   So Long, My Love
Publication Date: 1956
Music: Lew Spence
Words: Sammy Cahn
Recorded: 3/14/57-a
Arranger: Nelson Riddle
Conductor/Band: N. Riddle/studio

orchestra
Key Release: **This Is Sinatra, Volume Two**
see Album Lists: alphabetic by title; 1958 — 4th LP; Capitol/18th

#926   Softly, As I Leave You
«Piano»
Publication Date: 1962
Music: A. DeVita — 1960
Words: Hal Shaper/Gino Calabrese — 1960
Recorded: 7/17/64-a
Arranger: Ernie Freeman
Conductor/Band: E. Freeman/studio orchestra
Key Release: **Softly, As I Leave You**
see Album Lists: alphabetic by title; 1964 — 8th LP; Reprise/21st

#927   Soliloquy   *1st recording*
Publication Date: 1945
Music: Richard Rodgers
Words: Oscar Hammerstein II
Recorded: 4/7/46-a
Arranger: Axel Stordahl
Conductor/Band: A. Stordahl/studio orchestra
Key Release: **The Frank Sinatra Story in Music** (2 discs)
see Album Lists: alphabetic by title; 1959 — 2nd LP; Columbia/27th

#928   Soliloquy   *2nd recording*
Publication Date: 1945
Music: Richard Rodgers
Words: Oscar Hammerstein II
Recorded: 2/21/63-a
Arranger: Nelson Riddle
Conductor/Band: N. Riddle/studio orchestra
Key Release: **The Concert Sinatra**
see Album Lists: alphabetic by title; 1963 — 2nd LP; Reprise/10th

#929   Some Enchanted Evening
1st recording

Publication Date: 1949
Music: Richard Rodgers
Words: Oscar Hammerstein II
Recorded: 2/28/49-a
Arranger: Axel Stordahl
Conductor/Band: A. Stordahl/studio orchestra
Key Release: **The Broadway Kick**
see Album Lists: alphabetic by title; 1960 — 4th LP; Columbia/29th

#930   Some Enchanted Evening
2nd recording
Publication Date: 1949
Music: Richard Rodgers
Words: Oscar Hammerstein II
Recorded: 7/31/63-a
Arranger: Nelson Riddle
Conductor/Band: Morris Stoloff/ studio orchestra
Key Release: **Reprise Musical Repertory Theatre: "South Pacific"**
see Album Lists: alphabetic by title; 1963 — 6th LP; Reprise/14th

#931   Some Enchanted Evening
3rd recording — song reprised in a duet with Rosemary Clooney
Publication Date: 1949
Music: Richard Rodgers
Words: Oscar Hammerstein II
Recorded: 7/24/63-b
Arranger: Nelson Riddle
Conductor/Band: Morris Stoloff/ studio orchestra
Key Release: **Reprise Musical Repertory Theatre: "South Pacific"**
see Album Lists: alphabetic by title; 1963 — 6th LP; Reprise/14th

#932   Some Enchanted Evening
4th recording
Publication Date: 1949
Music: Richard Rodgers
Words: Oscar Hammerstein II
Recorded: 7/24/67-e
Arranger: H. B. Barnum

Conductor/Band: H. B. Barnum/ studio orchestra
Key Release: **Frank Sinatra & Frank and Nancy**
see Album Lists: alphabetic by title; 1967 — 5th LP; Reprise/32nd

#933   Some Other Time
Publication Date: 1944
Music: Jule Styne
Words: Sammy Cahn
Recorded: 5/16/44-a; Sinatra's "Vimms Vitamins Show" rehearsal
Arranger: Axel Stordahl
Conductor/Band: A. Stordahl/radio orchestra
Key Release: **Frank Sinatra on V-Disc, Volume 1** (English release only; album of wartime Victory Discs)
see Album Lists: alphabetic under "v/disc"; early 1970s; Apex/1st

#934   Some Traveling Music
poetry recited to music
Publication Date: 1969
Music: Rod McKuen (nonvocal melody)
Words: Rod McKuen
Recorded: 3/21/69-c
Arranger: Don Costa
Conductor/Band: D. Costa/studio orchestra
Key Release: **A Man Alone**
see Album Lists: alphabetic by title; 1969 — 3rd LP; Reprise/39th

#935   Somebody Loves Me
Publication Date: 1924
Music: George Gershwin
Words: B. G. (Buddy) DeSylva & Ira Gershwin
Recorded: 1944 radio — Sinatra's "Vimms Vitamins Show"
Arranger: Axel Stordahl

Conductor/Band: A. Stordahl/radio orchestra
Key Release: My Best Songs — My Best Years (Volume 5)
see Album Lists: alphabetic under "radio"; early 1970s; Pentagon/5th

#936   Someone to Light Up My Life
Publication Date: 1963
Music: Antonio Carlos Jobim
Words: Gene Lees/Vincius De Moraes
Recorded: 2/12/69-a
Arranger: Eumir Deodato
Conductor/Band: Morris Stoloff/studio orchestra
Key Release: Sinatra & Company
see Album Lists: alphabetic by title; 1971 — 2nd LP; Reprise/42nd

#937   Someone to Watch Over Me   *1st recording*
Publication Date: 1926
Music: George Gershwin
Words: Ira Gershwin
Recorded: 7/30/45-a
Arranger: Axel Stordahl
Conductor/Band: A. Stordahl/studio orchestra
Key Release: Come Back to Sorrento
see Album Lists: alphabetic by title; 1960 — 5th LP; Columbia/30th

#938   Someone to Watch Over Me   *2nd recording*
Publication Date: 1926
Music: George Gershwin
Words: Ira Gershwin
Recorded: 9/23/54-b
Arranger: Nelson Riddle
Conductor/Band: N. Riddle/studio orchestra
Key Release: Songs for Young Lovers (later 12" version of LP)
see Album Lists: alphabetic by title;

1960 — 7th LP; Capitol/27th

#939   Something   *1st recording*
Publication Date: 1969
Music & Words: George Harrison
Recorded: 10/28/70-b
Arranger: Lenny Hayton
Conductor/Band: L. Hayton/studio orchestra
Key Release: Frank Sinatra's Greatest Hits! (Volume 2)
see Album Lists: alphabetic by title; 1971 — 3rd LP; Reprise/43rd

#940   Something   *2nd recording*
Publication Date: 1969
Music & Words: George Harrison
Recorded: 12/3/79-a
Arranger: Nelson Riddle
Conductor/Band: Vinnie Falcone/studio orchestra
Key Release: Trilogy: The Present [Some Very Good Years]
see Album Lists: alphabetic by title; 1980 — 2nd LP; Reprise/53rd

#941   Something Old, Something New
Publication Date: 1946
Music & Words: Ramez Idriss & George Tibbles
Recorded: 2/24/46-d
Arranger: Axel Stordahl
Conductor/Band: A. Stordahl/studio orchestra
Key Release: The Essential Frank Sinatra (Volume 1)
see Album Lists: alphabetic by title; 1967 — 2nd LP; Columbia/34th

#942   Something Stupid   *duet with Nancy Sinatra*
Publication Date: 1967
Music & Words: Carson C. Parks
Recorded: 2/1/67-d
Arranger: Billy Strange

Conductor/Band: B. Strange/studio orchestra
Key Release: **Frank Sinatra & Frank and Nancy**
see Album Lists: alphabetic by title; 1967 — 5th LP; Reprise/32nd

#943   Something Wonderful Happens in Summer
Publication Date: 1956
Music: Joe Bushkin
Words: John DeVries
Recorded: 5/20/57-b
Arranger: Nelson Riddle
Conductor/Band: N. Riddle/studio orchestra
Key Release: **This Is Sinatra, Volume Two**
see Album Lists: alphabetic by title; 1958 — 4th LP; Capitol/18th

#944   Something's Gotta Give
Publication Date: 1954
Music & Words: Johnny Mercer
Recorded: 12/9/58-b
Arranger: Billy May
Conductor/Band: Billy May & his Orchestra
Key Release: **Come Dance with Me!**
see Album Lists: alphabetic by title; 1959 — 1st LP; Capitol/20th

#945   Somewhere a Voice Is Calling
Publication Date: 1911
Music: Arthur F. Tate
Words: Eileen Newton
Recorded: 3/9/42-a
Arranger: Sy Oliver
Conductor/Band: Tommy Dorsey & his Orchestra
Key Release: **The Dorsey/Sinatra Sessions** (Volume 6)
see Album Lists: alphabetic by title; 1972 — 6th LP; RCA Victor/22nd

#946   Somewhere Along the Way
Publication Date: 1952
Music: Kurt Adams
Words: Sammy Gallop
Recorded: 9/12/61-a
Arranger: Axel Stordahl
Conductor/Band: A. Stordahl/studio orchestra
Key Release: **Point of No Return**
see Album Lists: alphabetic by title; 1962 — 2nd LP; Capitol/31st

#947   Somewhere in the Night
Publication Date: 1946
Music: Josef Myrow
Words: Mack Gordon
Recorded: 5/28/46-c
Arranger: Axel Stordahl
Conductor/Band: A. Stordahl/studio orchestra
Key Release: 78rpm single #37054
see Album List #1: 1946 Columbia (4) single record — listed by number

#948   Somewhere in Your Heart
Publication Date: 1964
Music & Words: Clarence Wey Kehner & Russell Faith
Recorded: 11/11/64-a
Arranger: Ernie Freeman
Conductor/Band: E. Freeman/studio orchestra
Key Release: **Sinatra '65**
see Album Lists: alphabetic by title; 1965 — 2nd LP; Reprise/24th

#949   Somewhere My Love «Lara's Theme»
Publication Date: 1966
Music: Maurice Jarre
Words: Paul Francis Webster
Recorded: 11/17/66-c
Arranger: Ernie Freeman

Conductor/Band: E. Freeman/studio
orchestra
Key Release: **That's Life**
see Album Lists: alphabetic by title;
1966 — 5th LP; Reprise/30th

#950   The Song Is Ended
Publication Date: 1927
Music & Words: Irving Berlin
Recorded: 1/15/62-a
Arranger: Gordon Jenkins
Conductor/Band: G. Jenkins/studio
orchestra
Key Release: **All Alone**
see Album Lists: alphabetic by title;
1962 — 7th LP; Reprise/8th

#951   The Song Is You   *1st re-
cording*
Publication Date: 1932
Music: Jerome Kern
Words: Oscar Hammerstein II
Recorded: 1/19/42-c
Arranger: Axel Stordahl
Conductor/Band: A. Stordahl/studio
orchestra
Key Release: **We Three**
see Album Lists: alphabetic by title;
1957 — 7th LP; RCA Victor/12th

#952   The Song Is You   *2nd re-
cording*
Publication Date: 1932
Music: Jerome Kern
Words: Oscar Hammerstein II
Recorded: 10/26/47-b
Arranger: Axel Stordahl
Conductor/Band: A. Stordahl/studio
orchestra
Key Release: **Put Your Dreams
Away**
see Album Lists: alphabetic by title;
1958 — 3rd LP; Columbia/26th

#953   The Song Is You   *3rd recording*
Publication Date: 1932

Music: Jerome Kern
Words: Oscar Hammerstein II
Recorded: 12/9/58-a
Arranger: Billy May
Conductor/Band: Billy May & his
Orchestra
Key Release: **Come Dance with Me!**
see Album Lists: alphabetic by title;
1959 — 1st LP; Capitol/20th

#954   The Song Is You   *4th re-
cording*
Publication Date: 1932
Music: Jerome Kern
Words: Oscar Hammerstein II
Recorded: 9/18/79-a
Arranger: Billy May
Conductor/Band: B. May/studio
orchestra
Key Release: **Trilogy: The Past
[Collectibles of the Early Years]**
see Album Lists: alphabetic by title;
1980 — 1st LP; Reprise/52nd

#955   Song of the Sabia
Publication Date: 1960
Music & Words: Antonio Carlos
Jobim
Recorded: 2/13/69-a
Arranger: Eumir Deodato
Conductor/Band: Morris Stoloff/
studio orchestra
Key Release: **Portrait of Sinatra [40
Songs in the Life of a Man]**
(English release only — 2 discs)
see Album Lists: alphabetic by title;
1979 — 1st LP; Reprise/51st

#956   Song Sung Blue
Publication Date: 1972
Music & Words: Neil Diamond
Recorded: 8/22/79-c
Arranger: Don Costa
Conductor/Band: D. Costa/studio
orchestra
Key Release: **Trilogy: The Present
[Some Very Good Years]**

see Album Lists: alphabetic by title;
1980 — 2nd LP; Reprise/53rd

**#957   The Song's Gotta Come
from the Heart**   *duet with
Jimmy Durante*
Publication Date: 1947
Music: Jule Styne
Words: Sammy Cahn
Recorded: 1947 soundtrack (illegally
taken from film sound)
Arranger: Axel Stordahl
Conductor/Band: Johnny Green/
MGM Orchestra
Key Release: **"It Happened in
Brooklyn"** (LP: Score from "It
Happened in Brooklyn")
see Album Lists: alphabetic under
"soundtrack"; mid–1960s; boot-
leg Mv. #9

#958   Sorry
Publication Date: 1949
Music: Richard A. Whiting
Words: Buddy Pepper
Recorded: 11/8/49-a
Arranger: Axel Stordahl
Conductor/Band: A. Stordahl/studio
orchestra
Key Release: **Adventures of the
Heart**
see Album Lists: alphabetic by title;
1956 — 3rd LP; Columbia/24th

#959   South of the Border
Publication Date: 1939
Music & Words: Michael Carr &
Jimmy Kennedy
Recorded: 4/30/53-d
Arranger: Nelson Riddle; writing in
the style of a Billy May arrng.
Conductor/Band: N. Riddle/studio
orchestra
Key Release: **This Is Sinatra!** (Vol-
ume 1)
see Album Lists: alphabetic by title;
1956 — 6th LP; Capitol/10th

**#960   South — To a Warmer
Place**
Publication Date: 1980
Music: Alec Wilder
Words: Loonis R. McGlohon
Recorded: 7/21/81-b
Arranger: Gordon Jenkins
Conductor/Band: G. Jenkins/studio
orchestra
Key Release: **She Shot Me Down**
see Album Lists: alphabetic by title;
1981 — 1st LP; Reprise/55th

#961   Speak Low
Publication Date: 1943
Music: Kurt Weill
Words: Ogden Nash
Recorded: 1943 radio — "Songs by
Sinatra"
Arranger: Axel Stordahl
Conductor/Band: A. Stordahl/radio
orchestra
Key Release: **Frank Sinatra**
see Album Lists: alphabetic under
"radio"; early 1960s; Cameron/
4th

**#962   Spend an Afternoon with
Me**
Publication Date: 1959
Music: Jimmy Van Heusen
Words: Sammy Cahn
Recorded: 1959 television special
Arranger: Nelson Riddle
Conductor/Band: N. Riddle/televi-
sion orchestra
Key Release: **Frank Sinatra —
Through the Years: 1944–1966**
see Album Lists: alphabetic under
"television"; mid–1960s; Ajazz/
1st

#963   S'posin'   *1st recording*
Publication Date: 1929
Music: Paul Denniker
Words: Andy Razaf
Recorded: 10/24/47-c

Arranger: Tony Mottola
Conductor/Band: T. Mottola/studio
orchestra
Key Release: Frankie
see Album Lists: alphabetic by title;
1955 — 8th LP; Columbia/20th

#964   S'posin'   *2nd recording*
Publication Date: 1929
Music: Paul Denniker
Words: Andy Razaf
Recorded: 8/22/60-d
Arranger: Nelson Riddle
Conductor/Band: N. Riddle/studio
orchestra
*Key Release: Sinatra's Swingin'
Session!!!*
see Album Lists: alphabetic by title;
1961 — 1st LP; Capitol/28th

#965   Spring Is Here   *1st record-
ing*
Publication Date: 1938
Music: Richard Rodgers
Words: Lorenz Hart
Recorded: 10/31/47-b
Arranger: Axel Stordahl
Conductor/Band: A. Stordahl/studio
orchestra
Key Release: The Voice
see Album Lists: alphabetic by title;
1955 — 9th LP; Columbia/21st

#966   Spring Is Here*   *2nd re-
cording*
Publication Date: 1938
Music: Richard Rodgers
Words: Lorenz Hart
Recorded: 5/29/58-d
Arranger: Nelson Riddle
Conductor/Band: Felix Slatkin/studio
orchestra
*Key Release: Frank Sinatra Sings
for Only the Lonely*
see Album Lists: alphabetic by title;
1958 — 5th LP; Capitol/19th
*This song only appears on the

monaural version of the LP
*Frank Sinatra Sings for Only the
Lonely* (Capitol W-1053); it was
eliminated from the stereo version of that album.

#967   Star!
Publication Date: 1967
Music: Jimmy Van Heusen
Words: Sammy Cahn
Recorded: 11/11/68-b
Arranger: Nelson Riddle
Conductor/Band: N. Riddle/studio
orchestra
*Key Release: Frank Sinatra's Great-
est Hits!* (Volume 2)
see Album Lists: alphabetic by title;
1971 — 3rd LP; Reprise/43rd

#968   Star Dust   *1st recording*
Publication Date: 1929
Music: Hoagy Carmichael
Words: Mitchell Parish
Recorded: 11/11/40-b
Arranger: Paul Weston
Conductor/Band: Tommy Dorsey &
his Orchestra
*Key Release: The Dorsey/Sinatra
Sessions* (Volume 3)
see Album Lists: alphabetic by title;
1972 — 3rd LP; RCA Victor/19th

#969   Star Dust   *2nd recording;
verse only, omitting famous chorus*
Publication Date: 1929
Music: Hoagy Carmichael
Words: Mitchell Parish
Recorded: 11/20/61-b
Arranger: Don Costa
Conductor/Band: D. Costa/studio
orchestra
Key Release: Sinatra & Strings
see Album Lists: alphabetic by title;
1962 — 1st LP; Reprise/4th

#970   Star Gazer
Publication Date: 1976

Music & Words: Neil Diamond
Recorded: 6/21/76-b
Arranger: Don Costa
Conductor/Band: Bill Miller/studio
  orchestra
Key Release: **Portrait of Sinatra [40
  Songs in the Life of a Man]**
  (English release only — 2 discs)
see Album Lists: alphabetic by title;
  1979 — 1st LP; Reprise/51st

#971   Stars Fell on Alabama
Publication Date: 1934
Music: Frank Perkins & Mitchell
  Parish
Words: Mitchell Parish
Recorded: 11/15/56-c
Arranger: Nelson Riddle
Conductor/Band: N. Riddle/studio
  orchestra
Key Release: **A Swingin' Affair!**
see Album Lists: alphabetic by title;
  1957 — 2nd LP; Capitol/12th

#972   Stars in Your Eyes «Mar»
Publication Date: 1945
Music: Gabriel Ruiz — 1941
Words: Mort Green/Ricardo
  Lopez — 1941
Recorded: 5/24/45-a
Arranger: Xavier Cugat
Conductor/Band: X. Cugat/studio
  orchestra
Key Release: 78rpm single #36842
see Album List #1: 1945 Columbia
  (4) single record — listed by
  number

#973   The Stars Will Remember
(and So Will I)
Publication Date: 1947
Music & Words: Don Pelosi & Leo
  Towers
Recorded: 7/3/47-c
Arranger: Axel Stordahl
Conductor/Band: A. Stordahl/studio
  orchestra

Key Release: 78rpm single #37809
see Album List #1: 1947 Columbia
  (4) single record — listed by
  number

#974   Stay with Me
Publication Date: 1963
Music: Joe Moross
Words: Carolyn Leigh
Recorded: 12/3/63-b
Arranger: Don Costa
Conductor/Band: D. Costa/studio
  orchestra
Key Release: **Sinatra '65**
see Album Lists: alphabetic by title;
  1965 — 2nd LP; Reprise/24th

#975   Stella by Starlight   *1st recording*
Publication Date: 1946
Music: Victor Young
Words: Ned Washington
Recorded: 3/11/47-c
Arranger: Axel Stordahl
Conductor/Band: A. Stordahl/studio
  orchestra
Key Release: **Reflections**
see Album Lists: alphabetic by title;
  1961 — 4th LP; Columbia/31st

#976   Stella by Starlight   *2nd recording*
Publication Date: 1946
Music: Victor Young
Words: Ned Washington
Recorded: 3/9/77-b
Arranger: Nelson Riddle
Conductor/Band: N. Riddle/studio
  orchestra
Key Release: **Frank's Girls** (illegal;
  from Reprise masters)
see Album Lists: alphabetic under
  "bootleg"; early 1980s; bootleg
  Alb. #5

#977   Stormy Weather   *1st recording*
Publication Date: 1933

Music: Harold Arlen
Words: Ted Koehler
Recorded: 12/3/44-d
Arranger: Axel Stordahl
Conductor/Band: A. Stordahl/studio
orchestra
Key Release: **The Frank Sinatra
Story in Music** (2 discs)
see Album Lists: alphabetic by title;
1959 — 2nd LP; Columbia/27th

#978   Stormy Weather   *2nd re-
cording*
Publication Date: 1933
Music: Harold Arlen
Words: Ted Koehler
Recorded: 3/24/59-d
Arranger: Gordon Jenkins
Conductor/Band: G. Jenkins/studio
orchestra
Key Release: **No One Cares**
see Album Lists: alphabetic by title;
1959 — 5th LP; Capitol/23rd

#979   Stormy Weather*   *3rd re-
cording*
Publication Date: 1933
Music: Harold Arlen
Words: Ted Koehler
Recorded: 5/17/84-a
Arranger: Sam Nestico
Conductor/Band: Quincy Jones & a
special all-star jazz band
Key Release: **L.A. Is My Lady**
see Album Lists: alphabetic by title;
1984 — 1st LP; Qwest/1st
*Frank Sinatra's final released re-
cording, the only tune "mas-
tered" at a session in Los
Angeles, May 17, 1984. It ap-
peared on his final LP of new
recordings, **L.A. Is My Lady**
(Qwest 9/25145-1).

#980   Strange Music
Publication Date: 1944

Music: George Forrest & Robert
Wright; from E. Grieg
Words: Robert Wright & George
Forrest
Recorded: 10/22/47-b
Arranger: Axel Stordahl
Conductor/Band: A. Stordahl/studio
orchestra
Key Release: **Reflections**
see Album Lists: alphabetic by title;
1961 — 4th LP; Columbia/31st

#981   Strangers in the Night
Publication Date: 1966
Music: Bert Kaempfert
Words: Eddie Snyder & Charles
Singleton
Recorded: 4/11/66-a
Arranger: Ernie Freeman
Conductor/Band: E. Freeman/studio
orchestra
Key Release: **Strangers in the Night**
see Album Lists: alphabetic by title;
1966 — 1st LP; Reprise/27th

#982   Street of Dreams   *1st re-
cording*
Publication Date: 1932
Music: Victor Young
Words: Sam Lewis
Recorded: 5/18/42-b
Arranger: Axel Stordahl
Conductor/Band: Tommy Dorsey &
his Orchestra
Key Release: **The Dorsey/Sinatra
Sessions** (Volume 6)
see Album Lists: alphabetic by title;
1972 — 6th LP; RCA Victor/
22nd

#983   Street of Dreams   *2nd re-
cording*
Publication Date: 1932
Music: Victor Young
Words: Sam Lewis
Recorded: 2/1/66-d
Arranger: Quincy Jones

Conductor/Band: Count Basie & his
Band
Key Release: Sinatra at the Sands
(Live Recording — 2 discs)
see Album Lists: alphabetic by title;
1966 — 3rd LP; Reprise/29th

#984   Street of Dreams   *3rd re-
cording*
Publication Date: 1932
Music: Victor Young
Words: Sam Lewis
Recorded: 9/18/79-c
Arranger: Billy May
Conductor/Band: B. May/studio
orchestra
*Key Release: Trilogy: The Past
[Collectibles of the Early Years]*
see Album Lists: alphabetic by title;
1980 — 1st LP; Reprise/52nd

#985   Strictly U.S.A.   *sung with
cast ensemble*
Publication Date: 1949
Music & Words: Roger Edens
Recorded: 1949 — 1st soundtrack (il-
legally taken from film sound)
Arranger: Conrad Salinger
Conductor/Band: Adolph Deutsch/
MGM Orchestra
*Key Release: "Take Me Out to the
Ball Game"* (LP: Five Films)
see Album Lists: alphabetic under
"soundtrack"; mid–1960s; boot-
leg Mv. #12

**#986   Stromboli (On the Island
of —)**
Publication Date: 1949
Music: Ken Lane
Words: Irving Taylor
Recorded: 9/15/49-c
Arranger: Jeff Alexander
Conductor/Band: J. Alexander/
studio orchestra
*Key Release: Adventures of the
Heart*

see Album Lists: alphabetic by title;
1956 — 3rd LP; Columbia/24th

#987   Style   *sung with Bing
Crosby & Dean Martin*
Publication Date: 1964
Music: Jimmy Van Heusen
Words: Sammy Cahn
Recorded: 4/10/64-a
Arranger: Nelson Riddle
Conductor/Band: N. Riddle/studio
orchestra
*Key Release: "Robin and the 7
Hoods"* (Official Soundtrack LP)
see Album Lists: alphabetic by title;
1964 — 6th LP; Reprise/20th

#988   Suddenly It's Spring
Publication Date: 1944
Music: Jimmy Van Heusen
Words: Johnny Burke
Recorded: 1944 radio — Sinatra's
"Vimms Vitamins Show"
Arranger: Axel Stordahl
Conductor/Band: A. Stordahl/radio
orchestra
*Key Release: My Best Songs — My
Best Years* (Volume 4)
see Album Lists: alphabetic under
"radio"; early 1970s; Pentagon/
4th

#989   Sue Me   *duet with Vivian
Blaine*
Publication Date: 1950
Music & Words: Frank Loesser
Recorded: 1955 — 1st soundtrack (il-
legally taken from film sound)
Arranger: Nelson Riddle
Conductor/Band: Jay Blackton/
MGM Orchestra
Key Release: "Guys and Dolls" (LP:
Score from "Guys and Dolls")
see Album Lists: alphabetic under
"soundtrack"; mid–1960s; boot-
leg MV. #18

#990   The Summer Knows
Publication Date: 1971
Music: Michel Legrand
Words: Alan & Marilyn Bergman
Recorded: 5/7/74-c
Arranger: Gordon Jenkins
Conductor/Band: G. Jenkins/studio orchestra
Key Release: **Some Nice Things I've Missed**
see Album Lists: alphabetic by title; 1974—1st LP; Reprise/47th

#991   Summer Me, Winter Me
Publication Date: 1969
Music: Michel Legrand
Words: Alan & Marilyn Bergman
Recorded: 8/20/79-b
Arranger: Don Costa
Conductor/Band: D. Costa/studio orchestra
Key Release: **Trilogy: The Present [Some Very Good Years]**
see Album Lists: alphabetic by title; 1980—2nd LP; Reprise/53rd

#992   Summer Wind
Publication Date: 1966
Music: Henry Mayer—1965
Words: Johnny Mercer/Hans Bradtke—1965
Recorded: 5/16/66-a
Arranger: Nelson Riddle
Conductor/Band: N. Riddle/studio orchestra
Key Release: **Strangers in the Night**
see Album Lists: alphabetic by title; 1966—1st LP; Reprise/27th

#993   Sunday
Publication Date: 1926
Music & Words: Jule Styne & Chester Conn & Ned Miller & Bennie Kreuger
Recorded: 4/7/54-a
Arranger: Nelson Riddle; full-orch.

arrng. from G. Siravo band arrng.
Conductor/Band: N. Riddle/studio orchestra
Key Release: **Swing Easy!** (original 10" LP)
see Album Lists: alphabetic by title; 1954—5th LP; Capitol/4th

#994   Sunday, Monday or Always
Publication Date: 1943
Music: Jimmy Van Heusen
Words: Johnny Burke
Recorded: 6/22/43-a
Arranger: Alec Wilder
Conductor/Band: Bobby Tucker Singers only; during musicians' strike
Key Release: **Frank Sinatra's Greatest Hits: The Early Years** (Vol. 1)
see Album Lists: alphabetic by title; 1964—3rd LP; Columbia/32nd

#995   Sunflower
Publication Date: 1948
Music & Words: Mack David
Recorded: 12/16/48-a
Arranger: Axel Stordahl
Conductor/Band: A. Stordahl/studio orchestra
Key Release: **Popular Favorites, Volume 1** (10" LP)
see Album Lists: alphabetic by title; 1949—3rd LP; Columbia/3rd

#996   Sunny
Publication Date: 1965
Music & Words: Bobby Hebb
Recorded: 12/12/67-a
Arranger: Billy May
Conductor/Band: Duke Ellington & his Band
Key Release: **Francis A. & Edward K.**

see Album Lists: alphabetic by title; 1968 — 2nd LP; Reprise/33rd

#997   Sunrise in the Morning
Publication Date: 1970
Music & Words: Paul Ryan
Recorded: 10/27/70-a
Arranger: Don Costa
Conductor/Band: D. Costa/studio orchestra
Key Release: **Sinatra & Company**
see Album Lists: alphabetic by title; 1971 — 2nd LP; Reprise/42nd

#998   Sunshine Cake   *duet with Paula Kelly*
Publication Date: 1949
Music: Jimmy Van Heusen
Words: Johnny Burke
Recorded: 11/8/49-b
Arranger: Axel Stordahl
Conductor/Band: A. Stordahl/studio orchestra
Key Release: **The Essential Frank Sinatra** (Volume 3)
see Album Lists: alphabetic by title; 1967 — 4th LP; Columbia/36th

#999   The Sunshine of Your Smile
Publication Date: 1915
Music: Lillian Ray
Words: Leonard Cooke
Recorded: 9/26/41-b
Arranger: Dorsey "house" arrng: T. Dorsey, S. Oliver, F. Stulce, P. Weston
Conductor/Band: Tommy Dorsey & his Orchestra
Key Release: **The Dorsey/Sinatra Sessions** (Volume 5)
see Album Lists: alphabetic by title; 1972 — 5th LP; RCA Victor/21st

#1000   Sure Thing (We've Got a—)
Publication Date: 1949

Music: Jimmy Van Heusen
Words: Johnny Burke
Recorded: 11/8/49-c
Arranger: Axel Stordahl
Conductor/Band: A. Stordahl/studio orchestra
Key Release: **The Essential Frank Sinatra** (Volume 3)
see Album Lists: alphabetic by title; 1967 — 4th LP; Columbia/36th

#1001   Sweet Caroline
Publication Date: 1969
Music & Words: Neil Diamond
Recorded: 5/8/74-a
Arranger: Don Costa
Conductor/Band: D. Costa/studio orchestra
Key Release: **Some Nice Things I've Missed**
see Album Lists: alphabetic by title; 1974 — 1st LP; Reprise/47th

#1002   Sweet Lorraine   *1st recording*
Publication Date: 1928
Music: Cliff Burwell
Words: Mitchell Parish
Recorded: 12/15/46-e
Arranger: Sy Oliver
Conductor/Band: S. Oliver/studio orchestra
Key Release: **The Essential Frank Sinatra** (Volume 2)
see Album Lists: alphabetic by title; 1967 — 3rd LP; Columbia/35th

#1003   Sweet Lorraine   *2nd recording*
Publication Date: 1928
Music: Cliff Burwell
Words: Mitchell Parish
Recorded: 3/14/77-b
Arranger: Nelson Riddle
Conductor/Band: N. Riddle/studio orchestra

Key Release: **Frank's Girls** (illegal; from Reprise masters)
see Album Lists: alphabetic under "bootleg"; early 1980s; bootleg Alb. #5

#1004   Swingin' Down the Lane
Publication Date: 1923
Music: Isham Jones
Words: Gus Kahn
Recorded: 1/12/56-b
Arranger: Nelson Riddle
Conductor/Band: N. Riddle/studio orchestra
Key Release: **Songs for Swingin' Lovers!**
see Album Lists: alphabetic by title; 1956 — 1st LP; Capitol/7th

#1005   Swinging on a Star
Publication Date: 1944
Music: Jimmy Van Heusen
Words: Johnny Burke
Recorded: 1/27/64-c
Arranger: Nelson Riddle
Conductor/Band: N. Riddle/studio orchestra
Key Release: **Frank Sinatra Sings "Days of Wine and Roses," "Moon River," and Other Academy Award Winners**
see Album Lists: alphabetic by title; 1964 — 1st LP; Reprise/17th

#1006   Take a Chance
Publication Date: 1932
Music: Vincent Youmans
Words: B. G. (Buddy) DeSylva
Recorded: 12/8/53-a
Arranger: Nelson Riddle
Conductor/Band: N. Riddle/studio orchestra
Key Release: **The Rare Sinatra: Volume 1** (Australian release only)
see Album Lists: alphabetic by title; 1978 — 1st LP; Capitol/65th

#1007   Take Me   *1st recording*
Publication Date: 1942
Music: Rube Bloom
Words: Mack David
Recorded: 6/9/42-a
Arranger: Axel Stordahl
Conductor/Band: Tommy Dorsey & his Orchestra
Key Release: **The Dorsey/Sinatra Sessions** (Volume 6)
see Album Lists: alphabetic by title; 1972 — 6th LP; RCA Victor/22nd

#1008   Take Me   *2nd recording*
Publication Date: 1942
Music: Rube Bloom
Words: Mack David
Recorded: 5/1/61-e
Arranger: Sy Oliver
Conductor/Band: S. Oliver/studio orchestra
Key Release: **I Remember Tommy. . .**
see Album Lists: alphabetic by title; 1961 — 7th LP; Reprise/3rd

#1009   Take Me Out to the Ball Game   *duet with Gene Kelly*
Publication Date: 1908
Music: Albert Von Tilzer
Words: Jack Norworth
Recorded: 1949 — 1st soundtrack (illegally taken from film sound)
Arranger: Adolph Deutsch
Conductor/Band: A. Deutsch/MGM Orchestra
Key Release: **"Take Me Out to the Ball Game"** (LP: Five Films)
see Album Lists: alphabetic under "soundtrack"; mid–1960s; bootleg Mv. #12

#1010   Take My Love
Publication Date: 1950
Music: Jack Wolf & Joel Herron
Words: Frank Sinatra & Joel Herron

Recorded: 11/16/50-a
Arranger: Axel Stordahl
Conductor/Band: A. Stordahl/studio
orchestra
Key Release: **Adventures of the
Heart**
see Album Lists: alphabetic by title;
1956 — 3rd LP; Columbia/24th

**#1011   Taking a Chance on
Love**
Publication Date: 1940
Music: Vernon Duke & John
Latouche & Ted Fetter
Words: John Latouche & Ted
Fetter
Recorded: 4/19/54-d
Arranger: Nelson Riddle; full-orch.
arrng. from G. Siravo band
arrng.
Conductor/Band: N. Riddle/studio
orchestra
Key Release: **Swing Easy!** (original
10″ LP)
see Album Lists: alphabetic by title;
1954 — 5th LP; Capitol/4th

**#1012   Talk to Me [Talk to Me,
Talk to Me]**
Publication Date: 1956
Music & Words: Stanley Kahan &
Eddie Snyder & Rudy Vallee
Recorded: 5/14/59-b
Arranger: Nelson Riddle
Conductor/Band: N. Riddle/studio
orchestra
Key Release: **All the Way**
see Album Lists: alphabetic by title;
1961 — 2nd LP; Capitol/29th

**#1013   Talk to Me, Baby (Tell
Me Lies)**
Publication Date: 1963
Music: Robert Emmett Dolan
Words: Johnny Mercer
Recorded: 12/3/63-a
Arranger: Don Costa

Conductor/Band: D. Costa/studio
orchestra
Key Release: **Softly, As I Leave You**
see Album Lists: alphabetic by title;
1964 — 8th LP; Reprise/21st

#1014   Tangerine
Publication Date: 1942
Music: Victor Schertzinger
Words: Johnny Mercer
Recorded: 4/11/62-e
Arranger: Neal Hefti
Conductor/Band: N. Hefti/studio
orchestra
Key Release: **Sinatra and Swingin'
Brass**
see Album Lists: alphabetic by title;
1962 — 4th LP; Reprise/5th

#1015   Tea for Two   *duet with
Dinah Shore*
Publication Date: 1925
Music: Vincent Youmans
Words: Irving Caesar
Recorded: 4/25/47-a
Arranger: Axel Stordahl
Conductor/Band: A. Stordahl/studio
orchestra
Key Release: 78rpm single #37528
see Album List #1: 1947 Columbia
(4) single record — listed by
number

#1016   Teach Me Tonight
Publication Date: 1953
Music: Gene DePaul
Words: Sammy Cahn
Recorded: 4/17/84-a
Arranger: Torry Zito
Conductor/Band: Quincy Jones & a
special all-star jazz band
Key Release: **L.A. Is My Lady**
see Album Lists: alphabetic by title;
1984 — 1st LP; Qwest/1st

**#1017   Tell Her (You Love Her
Each Day)**
Publication Date: 1965

Music & Words: Gil Ward &
Charles Watkins
Recorded: 4/14/65-e
Arranger: Ernie Freeman
Conductor/Band: E. Freeman/studio
orchestra
Key Release: **Sinatra '65**
see Album Lists: alphabetic by title;
1965 — 2nd LP; Reprise/24th

#1018   Tell Her You Love Her
Publication Date: 1957
Music: Claude Denison
Words: Ross Parker & G. Halliday
Recorded: 5/20/57-c
Arranger: Nelson Riddle
Conductor/Band: N. Riddle/studio
orchestra
Key Release: **Tell Her You Love
Her**
see Album Lists: alphabetic by title;
1965 — 3rd LP; Capitol/35th

#1019   Tell Me at Midnight
Publication Date: 1940
Music: G. Anapeta — 1939/Clay
Boland
Words: Bickley Reichner/A. Bona-
gura — 1939
Recorded: 8/29/40-c
Arranger: Dorsey "house" arrng:
T. Dorsey, S. Oliver, F. Stulce,
P. Weston
Conductor/Band: Tommy Dorsey &
his Orchestra
Key Release: **The Dorsey/Sinatra
Sessions** (Volume 3)
see Album Lists: alphabetic by title;
1972 — 3rd LP; RCA Victor/19th

#1020   The Tender Trap (Love
Is—)   *1st recording*
Publication Date: 1955
Music: Jimmy Van Heusen
Words: Sammy Cahn
Recorded: 9/13/55-a
Arranger: Nelson Riddle

Conductor/Band: N. Riddle/studio
orchestra
Key Release: **This Is Sinatra!** (Volume 1)
see Album Lists: alphabetic by title;
1956 — 6th LP; Capitol/10th

#1021   The Tender Trap (Love
Is—)   *2nd recording*
Publication Date: 1955
Music: Jimmy Van Heusen
Words: Sammy Cahn
Recorded: 10/3/62-e
Arranger: Neal Hefti
Conductor/Band: Count Basie & his
Band
Key Release: **Sinatra-Basie: An His-
toric Musical First**
see Album Lists: alphabetic by title;
1963 — 1st LP; Reprise/9th

#1022   Tenderly
Publication Date: 1945
Music: Walter Gross
Words: Jack Lawrence
Recorded: 1945 radio — Sinatra's
"Max Factor Show"
Arranger: Axel Stordahl
Conductor/Band: A. Stordahl/radio
orchestra
Key Release: **The Original . . .
Frank Sinatra**
see Album Lists: alphabetic under
"radio"; early 1960s; Cameron/
2nd

#1023   Tennessee Newsboy
«The Newsboy Blues»
Publication Date: 1952
Music: Percy Faith
Words: Dick Manning
Recorded: 6/3/52-d
Arranger: Axel Stordahl
Conductor/Band: A. Stordahl/studio
orchestra
Key Release: 45rpm single #4-39787
see Album List #1: 1952 Columbia

(5) single record — listed by number

#1024 Thanks for the Memory
Publication Date: 1938
Music & Words: Ralph Rainger &
Leo Robin
Recorded: 7/20/81-a
Arranger: Gordon Jenkins
Conductor/Band: G. Jenkins/studio
orchestra
Key Release: **She Shot Me Down**
see Album Lists: alphabetic by title;
1981 — 1st LP; Reprise/55th

#1025 That Lucky Old Sun
Publication Date: 1949
Music: Beasley Smith
Words: Haven Gillespie
Recorded: 9/15/49-a
Arranger: Jeff Alexander
Conductor/Band: J. Alexander/
studio orchestra
Key Release: **That Old Feeling**
see Album Lists: alphabetic by title;
1956 — 2nd LP; Columbia/23rd

#1026 That Old Black Magic
1st recording
Publication Date: 1942
Music: Harold Arlen
Words: Johnny Mercer
Recorded: 3/10/46-b
Arranger: Axel Stordahl
Conductor/Band: A. Stordahl/studio
orchestra
Key Release: **The Voice**
see Album Lists: alphabetic by title;
1955 — 9th LP; Columbia/21st

#1027 That Old Black Magic
2nd recording
Publication Date: 1942
Music: Harold Arlen
Words: Johnny Mercer
Recorded: 3/21/61-d
Arranger: Heinie Beau

Conductor/Band: Billy May/studio
orchestra
Key Release: **Come Swing with Me!**
see Album Lists: alphabetic by title;
1961 — 5th LP; Capitol/30th

#1028 That Old Black Magic
3rd recording
Publication Date: 1942
Music: Harold Arlen
Words: Johnny Mercer
Recorded: 3/12/75-c
Arranger: Don Costa
Conductor/Band: D. Costa/studio
orchestra
Key Release: **Late Sinatra Goodies**
(illegal; from Reprise masters)
see Album Lists: alphabetic under
"bootleg"; mid–1980s; bootleg
Alb. #6

#1029 That Old Feeling *1st re-cording*
Publication Date: 1937
Music & Words: Sammy Fain &
Lew Brown
Recorded: 8/11/47-a
Arranger: Axel Stordahl
Conductor/Band: A. Stordahl/studio
orchestra
Key Release: **That Old Feeling**
see Album Lists: alphabetic by title;
1956 — 2nd LP; Columbia/23rd

#1030 That Old Feeling *2nd recording*
Publication Date: 1937
Music & Words: Sammy Fain &
Lew Brown
Recorded: 3/1/60-c
Arranger: Nelson Riddle
Conductor/Band: N. Riddle/studio
orchestra
Key Release: **Nice 'n' Easy**
see Album Lists: alphabetic by title;
1960 — 2nd LP; Capitol/25th

#1031   That's All
Publication Date: 1952
Music: Bob Haymes
Words: Alan Brandt
Recorded: 11/21/61-c
Arranger: Don Costa
Conductor/Band: D. Costa/studio
   orchestra
Key Release: **Sinatra & Strings**
see Album Lists: alphabetic by title;
   1962 — 1st LP; Reprise/4th

#1032   That's How Much I Love You
Publication Date: 1946
Music & Words: Eddy Arnold & J.
   Graydon Hall & Wally Fowler
Recorded: 12/15/46-c
Arranger: Page Cavanaugh
Conductor/Band: P. Cavanaugh/
   studio orchestra
Key Release: **Hello, Young Lovers** (2
   discs)
see Album Lists: alphabetic by title;
   1987 — 2nd LP; Columbia/52nd

#1033   That's Life
Publication Date: 1964
Music & Words: Dean Kay & Kelly
   Gordon
Recorded: 10/18/66-a
Arranger: Ernie Freeman
Conductor/Band: E. Freeman/studio
   orchestra
Key Release: **That's Life**
see Album Lists: alphabetic by title;
   1966 — 5th LP; Reprise/30th

#1034   That's What God Looks Like (to Me)
Publication Date: 1962
Music: Lois Irwin
Words: Lan O'Kun
Recorded: 8/21/79-b
Arranger: Don Costa
Conductor/Band: D. Costa/studio
   orchestra

Key Release: **Trilogy: The Present
   [Some Very Good Years]**
see Album Lists: alphabetic by title;
   1980 — 2nd LP; Reprise/53rd

#1035   Then Suddenly Love
Publication Date: 1964
Music: Paul J. Vance
Words: Roy Alfred
Recorded: 7/17/64-b
Arranger: Ernie Freeman
Conductor/Band: E. Freeman/studio
   orchestra
Key Release: **Softly, As I Leave You**
see Album Lists: alphabetic by title;
   1964 — 8th LP; Reprise/21st

#1036   There Are Such Things
1st recording
Publication Date: 1942
Music: George W. Meyer
Words: Stanley Adams & Abel
   Baer
Recorded: 7/1/42-a
Arranger: Axel Stordahl
Conductor/Band: Tommy Dorsey &
   his Orchestra
Key Release: **The Dorsey/Sinatra
   Sessions** (Volume 6)
see Album Lists: alphabetic by title;
   1972 — 6th LP; RCA Victor/
   22nd

#1037   There Are Such Things
2nd recording
Publication Date: 1942
Music: George W. Meyer
Words: Stanley Adams & Abel
   Baer
Recorded: 5/3/61-b
Arranger: Sy Oliver
Conductor/Band: S. Oliver/studio
   orchestra
Key Release: **I Remember Tommy...**
see Album Lists: alphabetic by title;
   1961 — 7th LP; Reprise/3rd

#1038   There But for You Go I
Publication Date: 1947
Music: Frederick Loewe
Words: Alan Jay Lerner
Recorded: 3/31/47-a
Arranger: Axel Stordahl
Conductor/Band: A. Stordahl/studio
    orchestra
Key Release: **The Broadway Kick**
see Album Lists: alphabetic by title;
    1960 — 4th LP; Columbia/29th

#1039   There Used to Be a Ball-park
Publication Date: 1973
Music & Words: Joe Raposo
Recorded: 6/22/73-d
Arranger: Gordon Jenkins
Conductor/Band: G. Jenkins/studio
    orchestra
Key Release: **Ol' Blue Eyes Is Back**
see Album Lists: alphabetic by title;
    1973 — 2nd LP; Reprise/45th

#1040   There Will Never Be Another You
Publication Date: 1942
Music: Harry Warren
Words: Mack Gordon
Recorded: 9/11/61-e
Arranger: Axel Stordahl
Conductor/Band: A. Stordahl/studio
    orchestra
Key Release: **Point of No Return**
see Album Lists: alphabetic by title;
    1962 — 2nd LP; Capitol/31st

#1041   There's a Flaw in My Flue   *1st recording*
Publication Date: 1942
Music: Jimmy Van Heusen
Words: Johnny Burke
Recorded: 1942 radio — a broadcast
    with the Dorsey orchestra
Arranger: Dorsey "house" arrng:
    T. Dorsey, S. Oliver, F. Stulce,
    P. Weston

Conductor/Band: Tommy Dorsey &
    his Orchestra
Key Release: **My Best Songs — My Best Years** (Volume 5)
see Album Lists: alphabetic under
    "radio"; early 1970s; Pentagon/
    5th

#1042   There's a Flaw in My Flue   *2nd recording*
Publication Date: 1942
Music: Jimmy Van Heusen
Words: Johnny Burke
Recorded: 4/5/56-c
Arranger: Nelson Riddle
Conductor/Band: N. Riddle with or-
    chestra & the Hollywood String
    Quartet
Key Release: **Close to You** (song on
    1988 Compact Disc release only)
see Album Lists: alphabetic by title;
    1957 — 1st LP; Capitol/11th

#1043   There's a Small Hotel
Publication Date: 1936
Music: Richard Rodgers
Words: Lorenz Hart
Recorded: 8/13/57-d
Arranger: Nelson Riddle
Conductor/Band: Morris Stoloff/
    studio orchestra
Key Release: **"Pal Joey"** (Official
    Soundtrack LP)
see Album Lists: alphabetic by title;
    1957 — 8th LP; Capitol/15th

#1044   There's No Business Like Show Business
Publication Date: 1944
Music & Words: Irving Berlin
Recorded: 8/22/46-c
Arranger: Axel Stordahl
Conductor/Band: A. Stordahl/studio
    orchestra
Key Release: **The Broadway Kick**
see Album Lists: alphabetic by title;
    1960 — 4th LP; Columbia/29th

#1045   There's No You   *1st recording*
Publication Date: 1944
Music: Hal Hopper
Words: Tom Adair/Bullets Durgom
Recorded: 11/13/44-a
Arranger: Axel Stordahl
Conductor/Band: A. Stordahl/studio orchestra
Key Release: **The Essential Frank Sinatra** (Volume 1)
see Album Lists: alphabetic by title; 1967 — 2nd LP; Columbia/34th

#1046   There's No You   *2nd recording*
Publication Date: 1944
Music: Hal Hopper
Words: Tom Adair/Bullets Durgom
Recorded: 4/10/57-b
Arranger: Gordon Jenkins
Conductor/Band: G. Jenkins/studio orchestra
Key Release: **Where Are You?**
see Album Lists: alphabetic by title; 1957 — 4th LP; Capitol/13th

#1047   These Foolish Things (Remind Me of You)   *1st recording*
Publication Date: 1935
Music: Jack Strachey & Harry Link
Words: Holt Marvell
Recorded: 7/30/45-c
Arranger: Axel Stordahl
Conductor/Band: A. Stordahl/studio orchestra
Key Release: **The Voice**
see Album Lists: alphabetic by title; 1955 — 9th LP; Columbia/21st

#1048   These Foolish Things (Remind Me of You)   *2nd recording*
Publication Date: 1935

Music: Jack Strachey & Harry Link
Words: Holt Marvell
Recorded: 9/12/61-c
Arranger: Axel Stordahl
Conductor/Band: A. Stordahl/studio orchestra
Key Release: **Point of No Return**
see Album Lists: alphabetic by title; 1962 — 2nd LP; Capitol/31st

#1049   They All Laughed
Publication Date: 1937
Music: George Gershwin
Words: Ira Gershwin
Recorded: 9/18/79-d
Arranger: Billy May
Conductor/Band: B. May/studio orchestra
Key Release: **Trilogy: The Past [Collectibles of the Early Years]**
see Album Lists: alphabetic by title; 1980 — 1st LP; Reprise/52nd

#1050   They Came to Cordura
Publication Date: 1958
Music: Jimmy Van Heusen
Words: Sammy Cahn
Recorded: 12/29/58-b
Arranger: Nelson Riddle
Conductor/Band: N. Riddle/studio orchestra
Key Release: **Sinatra Sings . . . of Love and Things**
see Album Lists: alphabetic by title; 1962 — 3rd LP; Capitol/32nd

#1051   They Can't Take That Away from Me   *1st recording*
Publication Date: 1937
Music: George Gershwin
Words: Ira Gershwin
Recorded: 11/5/53-c
Arranger: Nelson Riddle; full-orch. arrng. from G. Siravo band arrng.

Conductor/Band: N. Riddle/studio
orchestra
Key Release: Songs for Young Lovers
(original 10" LP)
see Album Lists: alphabetic by title;
1954 — 1st LP; Capitol/2nd

**#1052   They Can't Take That
Away from Me**   *2nd recording*
Publication Date: 1937
Music: George Gershwin
Words: Ira Gershwin
Recorded: 4/10/62-e
Arranger: Neal Hefti
Conductor/Band: N. Hefti/studio
orchestra
*Key Release: Sinatra and Swingin'
Brass*
see Album Lists: alphabetic by title;
1962 — 4th LP; Reprise/5th

#1053   They Say It's Wonderful
Publication Date: 1944
Music & Words: Irving Berlin
Recorded: 3/10/46-a
Arranger: Axel Stordahl
Conductor/Band: A. Stordahl/studio
orchestra
Key Release: The Broadway Kick
see Album Lists: alphabetic by title;
1960 — 4th LP; Columbia/29th

**#1054   The Things We Did Last
Summer**
Publication Date: 1946
Music: Jule Styne
Words: Sammy Cahn
Recorded: 7/24/46-a
Arranger: Axel Stordahl
Conductor/Band: A. Stordahl/studio
orchestra
*Key Release: Put Your Dreams
Away*
see Album Lists: alphabetic by title;
1958 — 3rd LP; Columbia/26th

#1055   This Can't Be Love
Publication Date: 1938

Music: Richard Rodgers
Words: Lorenz Hart
Recorded: 1943 radio — Lucky
Strike's "Your Hit Parade"
Arranger: Axel Stordahl
Conductor/Band: A. Stordahl/radio
orchestra
*Key Release: The First Times . . .
Frank Sinatra*
see Album Lists: alphabetic under
"radio"; early 1960s; Cameron/
1st

#1056   This Happy Madness
duet with Antonio Carlos Jobim
Publication Date: 1962
Music: Antonio Carlos Jobim
Words: Gene Lees/Vincius De
Moraes
Recorded: 2/13/69-b
Arranger: Eumir Deodato
Conductor/Band: Morris Stoloff/
studio orchestra
Key Release: Sinatra & Company
see Album Lists: alphabetic by title;
1971 — 2nd LP; Reprise/42nd

#1057   This Is All I Ask
Publication Date: 1958
Music & Words: Gordon Jenkins
Recorded: 4/22/65-c
Arranger: Gordon Jenkins
Conductor/Band: G. Jenkins/studio
orchestra
Key Release: September of My Years
see Album Lists: alphabetic by title;
1965 — 1st LP; Reprise/23rd

#1058   This Is My Song
Publication Date: 1966
Music & Words: Charlie Chaplin
Recorded: 7/24/67-c
Arranger: Ernie Freeman
Conductor/Band: E. Freeman/studio
orchestra
*Key Release: Frank Sinatra &
Frank and Nancy*

see *Album Lists:* alphabetic by title;
1967 — 5th LP; Reprise/32nd

#1059   This Is the Beginning of the End
Publication Date: 1940
Music & Words: Mack Gordon
Recorded: 3/12/40-b
Arranger: Dorsey "house" arrng: T. Dorsey, S. Oliver, F. Stulce, P. Weston
Conductor/Band: Tommy Dorsey & his Orchestra
Key Release: **The Dorsey/Sinatra Sessions** (Volume 1)
see *Album Lists:* alphabetic by title;
1972 — 1st LP; RCA Victor/17th

#1060   This Is the Night
Publication Date: 1946
Music & Words: Lewis Bellin & Redd Evans
Recorded: 7/24/46-c
Arranger: Axel Stordahl
Conductor/Band: A. Stordahl/studio orchestra
Key Release: 78rpm single #37193, side A
see *Album List #1:* 1946 Columbia (4) single record — listed by number

#1061   This Love of Mine   *1st recording*
Publication Date: 1941
Music: Sol Parker & Henry Sanicola
Words: Frank Sinatra
Recorded: 5/28/41-d
Arranger: Axel Stordahl
Conductor/Band: Tommy Dorsey & his Orchestra
Key Release: **The Dorsey/Sinatra Sessions** (Volume 4)
see *Album Lists:* alphabetic by title;
1972 — 4th LP; RCA Victor/20th

#1062   This Love of Mine   *2nd recording*
Publication Date: 1941
Music: Sol Parker & Henry Sanicola
Words: Frank Sinatra
Recorded: 2/17/55-d
Arranger: Nelson Riddle
Conductor/Band: N. Riddle/studio orchestra
Key Release: **In the Wee Small Hours** (12" LP version)
see *Album Lists:* alphabetic by title;
1955 — 7th LP; Capitol/5th

#1063   This Nearly Was Mine
Publication Date: 1949
Music: Richard Rodgers
Words: Oscar Hammerstein II
Recorded: 2/19/63-a
Arranger: Nelson Riddle
Conductor/Band: N. Riddle/studio orchestra
Key Release: **The Concert Sinatra**
see *Album Lists:* alphabetic by title;
1963 — 2nd LP; Reprise/10th

#1064   This Town
Publication Date: 1967
Music & Words: Lee Hazlewood
Recorded: 7/24/67-f
Arranger: Billy Strange
Conductor/Band: B. Strange/studio orchestra
Key Release: **Frank Sinatra & Frank and Nancy**
see *Album Lists:* alphabetic by title;
1967 — 5th LP; Reprise/32nd

#1065   This Was (Is) My Love
1st recording
Publication Date: 1958
Music & Words: Jim Harbert
Recorded: 5/14/59-a
Arranger: Nelson Riddle
Conductor/Band: N. Riddle/studio orchestra

Key Release: **All the Way**
see Album Lists: alphabetic by title;
1961 — 2nd LP; Capitol/29th

#1066   This Was (Is) My Love
2nd recording
Publication Date: 1958
Music & Words: Jim Harbert
Recorded: 7/24/67-b
Arranger: Gordon Jenkins
Conductor/Band: G. Jenkins/studio
orchestra
Key Release: **Frank Sinatra &
Frank and Nancy**
see Album Lists: alphabetic by title;
1967 — 5th LP; Reprise/32nd

**#1067   Three Coins in the
Fountain**   *1st recording*
Publication Date: 1954
Music: Jule Styne
Words: Sammy Cahn
Recorded: 3/1/54-c
Arranger: Nelson Riddle
Conductor/Band: N. Riddle/studio
orchestra
Key Release: **This Is Sinatra!** (Volume 1)
see Album Lists: alphabetic by title;
1956 — 6th LP; Capitol/10th

**#1068   Three Coins in the
Fountain**   *2nd recording*
Publication Date: 1954
Music: Jule Styne
Words: Sammy Cahn
Recorded: 1/27/64-b
Arranger: Nelson Riddle
Conductor/Band: N. Riddle/studio
orchestra
Key Release: **Frank Sinatra Sings
"Days of Wine and Roses,"
"Moon River," and Other
Academy Award Winners**
see Album Lists: alphabetic by title;
1964 — 1st LP; Reprise/17th

**#1069   Tie a Yellow Ribbon
Round the Ole Oak Tree**
Publication Date: 1973
Music & Words: Irwin Levine & L.
Russell Brown
Recorded: 5/21/74-b
Arranger: Don Costa
Conductor/Band: D. Costa/studio
orchestra
Key Release: **Some Nice Things I've
Missed**
see Album Lists: alphabetic by title;
1974 — 1st LP; Reprise/47th

#1070   Time After Time   *1st recording*
Publication Date: 1946
Music: Jule Styne
Words: Sammy Cahn
Recorded: 10/24/46-a
Arranger: Axel Stordahl
Conductor/Band: A. Stordahl/studio
orchestra
Key Release: **Frankie**
see Album Lists: alphabetic by title;
1955 — 8th LP; Columbia/20th

#1071   Time After Time   *2nd recording*
Publication Date: 1946
Music: Jule Styne
Words: Sammy Cahn
Recorded: 11/25/57-d
Arranger: Nelson Riddle
Conductor/Band: N. Riddle/studio
orchestra
Key Release: **This Is Sinatra, Volume Two**
see Album Lists: alphabetic by title;
1958 — 4th LP; Capitol/18th

#1072   Tina
Publication Date: 1960
Music: Jimmy Van Heusen
Words: Sammy Cahn
Recorded: 12/21/60-c
Arranger: Felix Slatkin

Conductor/Band: F. Slatkin/studio
orchestra
Key Release: The Voice: Volume 2
(Italian release only)
see Album Lists: alphabetic by title;
1982 — 2nd LP; Reprise/57th

#1073   To Love a Child
Publication Date: 1981
Music: Joe Raposo
Words: Hal David
Recorded: 12/3/81-a
Arranger: Don Costa
Conductor/Band: Vinnie Falcone/
studio orchestra
Key Release: 45rpm single #7-29903
see Album List #1: 1984 Reprise (5)
single record — listed by number

#1074   To Love and Be Loved
1st recording
Publication Date: 1958
Music: Jimmy Van Heusen
Words: Sammy Cahn
Recorded: 10/28/58-a
Arranger: Nelson Riddle
Conductor/Band: N. Riddle/studio
orchestra
Key Release: 45rpm single #4103
see Album List #1: 1959 Capitol (5)
single record — listed by number

#1075   To Love and Be Loved
2nd recording
Publication Date: 1958
Music: Jimmy Van Heusen
Words: Sammy Cahn
Recorded: 12/5/58-a
Arranger: Nelson Riddle
Conductor/Band: N. Riddle/studio
orchestra
Key Release: All the Way
see Album Lists: alphabetic by title;
1961 — 2nd LP; Capitol/29th

#1076   Together
Publication Date: 1928

Music: Ray Henderson
Words: B. G. (Buddy) DeSylva &
Lew Brown
Recorded: 1/16/62-b
Arranger: Gordon Jenkins
Conductor/Band: G. Jenkins/studio
orchestra
Key Release: All Alone
see Album Lists: alphabetic by title;
1962 — 7th LP; Reprise/8th

#1077   Too Close for Comfort
Publication Date: 1956
Music & Words: George Weiss &
Jerry Bock & Larry Holofcener
Recorded: 12/23/58-a
Arranger: Heinie Beau
Conductor/Band: Billy May & his
Orchestra
Key Release: Come Dance with Me!
see Album Lists: alphabetic by title;
1959 — 1st LP; Capitol/20th

**#1078   Too Marvelous for
Words**
Publication Date: 1937
Music: Richard A. Whiting
Words: Johnny Mercer
Recorded: 1/16/56-d
Arranger: Nelson Riddle
Conductor/Band: N. Riddle/studio
orchestra
*Key Release: Songs for Swingin'
Lovers!*
see Album Lists: alphabetic by title;
1956 — 1st LP; Capitol/7th

#1079   Too Romantic (I'm —)
Publication Date: 1940
Music: James V. Monaco
Words: Johnny Burke
Recorded: 2/1/40-b
Arranger: Dorsey "house" arrng:
T. Dorsey, S. Oliver, F. Stulce,
P. Weston
Conductor/Band: Tommy Dorsey &
his Orchestra

Key Release: **The Dorsey/Sinatra Sessions** (Volume 1)
see Album Lists: alphabetic by title; 1972 — 1st LP; RCA Victor/17th

#1080   Trade Winds
Publication Date: 1940
Music & Words: Cliff Friend & Charles Tobias
Recorded: 6/27/40-a
Arranger: Dorsey "house" arrng: T. Dorsey, S. Oliver, F. Stulce, P. Weston
Conductor/Band: Tommy Dorsey & his Orchestra
Key Release: **The Dorsey/Sinatra Sessions** (Volume 2)
see Album Lists: alphabetic by title; 1972 — 2nd LP; RCA Victor/18th

#1081   The Train
Publication Date: 1969
Music & Words: Bob Gaudio & Jake Holmes
Recorded: 7/14/69-b
Arranger: Joseph Scott & Bob Gaudio
Conductor/Band: Joseph Scott/studio orchestra
Key Release: **Watertown [a love story]**
see Album Lists: alphabetic by title; 1970 — 1st LP; Reprise/40th

#1082   A Tree in the Meadow
Publication Date: 1948
Music & Words: Billy Reid
Recorded: 1948 radio — Lucky Strike's "Your Hit Parade"
Arranger: Axel Stordahl
Conductor/Band: A. Stordahl/radio orchestra
Key Release: **The Original . . . Frank Sinatra**
see Album Lists: alphabetic under "radio"; early 1960s; Cameron/ 2nd

#1083   Triste
Publication Date: 1961
Music & Words: Antonio Carlos Jobim
Recorded: 2/13/69-c
Arranger: Eumir Deodato
Conductor/Band: Morris Stoloff/ studio orchestra
Key Release: **Sinatra & Company**
see Album Lists: alphabetic by title; 1971 — 2nd LP; Reprise/42nd

#1084   Try a Little Tenderness
1st recording
Publication Date: 1933
Music: Harry Woods & Jimmy Campbell & Reg Connelly
Words: Reg Connelly & Jimmy Campbell
Recorded: 12/7/45-c
Arranger: Axel Stordahl
Conductor/Band: A. Stordahl/studio orchestra
Key Release: **The Voice**
see Album Lists: alphabetic by title; 1955 — 9th LP; Columbia/21st

#1085   Try a Little Tenderness
2nd recording
Publication Date: 1933
Music: Harry Woods & Jimmy Campbell & Reg Connelly
Words: Reg Connelly & Jimmy Campbell
Recorded: 3/1/60-d
Arranger: Nelson Riddle
Conductor/Band: N. Riddle/studio orchestra
Key Release: **Nice 'n' Easy**
see Album Lists: alphabetic by title; 1960 — 2nd LP; Capitol/25th

#1086   The Twelve Days of Christmas   *sung with Nancy, Frank Jr. and Tina Sinatra*
Publication Date: 1700s

Music: traditional; England in the 1700s
Words: traditional; England — adapted by Sammy Cahn
Recorded: 8/12/68-a
Arranger: Nelson Riddle
Conductor/Band: N. Riddle/studio orchestra
Key Release: **The Sinatra Family Wish You a Merry Christmas**
see Album Lists: alphabetic by title; 1968 — 4th LP; Reprise/35th

#1087   Twin Soliloquies «Wonder How It Feels» *duet with Keely Smith*
Publication Date: 1949
Music: Richard Rodgers
Words: Oscar Hammerstein II
Recorded: 7/31/63-b
Arranger: Nelson Riddle
Conductor/Band: Morris Stoloff/ studio orchestra
Key Release: **Reprise Musical Repertory Theatre: "South Pacific"**
see Album Lists: alphabetic by title; 1963 — 6th LP; Reprise/14th

#1088   Two Hearts Are Better Than One
Publication Date: 1945
Music: Jerome Kern
Words: Leo Robin
Recorded: 2/3/46-c
Arranger: Axel Stordahl
Conductor/Band: A. Stordahl/studio orchestra
Key Release: **Sinatra Rarities — The Columbia Years** (Volume 1)
see Album Lists: alphabetic by title; 1986 — 1st LP; Columbia/50th

#1089   Two Hearts, Two Kisses (Make One Love)
Publication Date: 1954
Music & Words: Henry Stone & Otis Williams

Recorded: 3/7/55-c
Arranger: Dave Cavanaugh
Conductor/Band: Dave Cavanaugh & his Band
Key Release: **Forever Frank**
see Album Lists: alphabetic by title; 1966 — 4th LP; Capitol/36th

#1090   Two in Love
Publication Date: 1941
Music & Words: Meredith Willson
Recorded: 8/19/41-a
Arranger: Dorsey "house" arrng: T. Dorsey, S. Oliver, F. Stulce, P. Weston
Conductor/Band: Tommy Dorsey & his Orchestra
Key Release: **The Dorsey/Sinatra Sessions** (Volume 5)
see Album Lists: alphabetic by title; 1972 — 5th LP; RCA Victor/21st

#1091   Until the Real Thing Comes Along
Publication Date: 1931
Music: Alberta Nichols & Mann Holiner/Saul Chaplin
Words: Lawrence E. (Bud) Freeman & Mann Holiner/Sammy Cahn
Recorded: 4/16/84-b
Arranger: Sam Nestico
Conductor/Band: Quincy Jones & a special all-star jazz band
Key Release: **L.A. Is My Lady**
see Album Lists: alphabetic by title; 1984 — 1st LP; Qwest/1st

#1092   The Very Thought of You *1st recording*
Publication Date: 1934
Music & Words: Ray Noble
Recorded: 1943 radio — Lucky Strike's "Your Hit Parade"
Arranger: Axel Stordahl
Conductor/Band: A. Stordahl/radio orchestra

Key Release: **The Original . . .
Frank Sinatra**
see Album Lists: alphabetic under
"radio"; early 1960s; Cameron/
2nd

**#1093   The Very Thought of
You**   *2nd recording*
Publication Date: 1934
Music & Words: Ray Noble
Recorded: 6/12/62-b
Arranger: Robert Farnon
Conductor/Band: R. Farnon/studio
orchestra
Key Release: **Sinatra Sings Great
Songs from Great Britain**
(English release only)
see Album Lists: alphabetic by title;
1962 — 5th LP; Reprise/6th

#1094   Violets for Your Furs
1st recording
Publication Date: 1941
Music: Matt Dennis
Words: Tom Adair
Recorded: 9/26/41-a
Arranger: Heinie Beau
Conductor/Band: Tommy Dorsey &
his Orchestra
Key Release: **The Dorsey/Sinatra
Sessions** (Volume 5)
see Album Lists: alphabetic by title;
1972 — 5th LP; RCA Victor/21st

#1095   Violets for Your Furs
2nd recording
Publication Date: 1941
Music: Matt Dennis
Words: Tom Adair
Recorded: 11/5/53-d
Arranger: Nelson Riddle; full-orch.
arrng. from G. Siravo band
arrng.
Conductor/Band: N. Riddle/studio
orchestra
Key Release: **Songs for Young Lovers**
(original 10" LP)

see Album Lists: alphabetic by title;
1954 — 1st LP; Capitol/2nd

#1096   Wait for Me
Publication Date: 1956
Music: Nelson Riddle
Words: Dak Stanford
Recorded: 4/5/56-f
Arranger: Nelson Riddle
Conductor/Band: N. Riddle/studio
orchestra
Key Release: **This Is Sinatra, Volume Two**
see Album Lists: alphabetic by title;
1958 — 4th LP; Capitol/18th

#1097   Wait Till You See Her
Publication Date: 1942
Music: Richard Rodgers
Words: Lorenz Hart
Recorded: 4/4/56-d
Arranger: Nelson Riddle
Conductor/Band: N. Riddle with orchestra & the Hollywood String
Quartet
Key Release: **Frank Sinatra Sings
Rodgers and Hart**
see Album Lists: alphabetic by title;
1964 — 7th LP; Capitol/34th

#1098   Walk Away
Publication Date: 1967
Music: Elmer Bernstein
Words: Carolyn Leigh
Recorded: 6/22/73-b
Arranger: Gordon Jenkins
Conductor/Band: G. Jenkins/studio
orchestra
Key Release: **The Unissued Sinatra**
(illegal; from Reprise masters)
see Album Lists: alphabetic under
"bootleg"; early 1980s; bootleg
Alb. #4

#1099   Walkin' in the Sunshine
Publication Date: 1951
Music & Words: Bob Merrill

Recorded: 1/7/52-c
Arranger: Axel Stordahl
Conductor/Band: A. Stordahl/studio orchestra
Key Release: **The Essential Frank Sinatra** (Volume 3)
see Album Lists: alphabetic by title; 1967 — 4th LP; Columbia/36th

#1100   Wandering
Publication Date: 1968
Music & Words: Gayle Caldwell
Recorded: 11/14/68-b
Arranger: Don Costa
Conductor/Band: Bill Miller/studio orchestra
Key Release: **Cycles**
see Album Lists: alphabetic by title; 1968 — 6th LP; Reprise/37th

#1101   Watch What Happens
Publication Date: 1964
Music: Michel Legrand — 1960
Words: Norman Gimbel/Jacques Demy — 1960
Recorded: 2/24/69-a
Arranger: Don Costa
Conductor/Band: D. Costa/studio orchestra
Key Release: **My Way**
see Album Lists: alphabetic by title; 1969 — 1st LP; Reprise/38th

#1102   Watertown
Publication Date: 1969
Music & Words: Bob Gaudio & Jake Holmes
Recorded: 7/15/69-a
Arranger: Charles Calello
Conductor/Band: C. Calello/studio orchestra
Key Release: **Watertown [a love story]**
see Album Lists: alphabetic by title; 1970 — 1st LP; Reprise/40th

#1103   Wave
Publication Date: 1960

Music & Words: Antonio Carlos Jobim
Recorded: 2/11/69-c
Arranger: Eumir Deodato
Conductor/Band: Morris Stoloff/ studio orchestra
Key Release: **Sinatra & Company**
see Album Lists: alphabetic by title; 1971 — 2nd LP; Reprise/42nd

#1104   The Way You Look To-night   *1st recording*
Publication Date: 1936
Music: Jerome Kern
Words: Dorothy Fields
Recorded: 11/21/43-b; "Songs by Sinatra" rehearsal
Arranger: Axel Stordahl
Conductor/Band: A. Stordahl/radio orchestra
Key Release: **Frank Sinatra on V-Disc, Volume 1** (English release only; album of wartime Victory Discs)
see Album Lists: alphabetic under "v/disc"; early 1970s; Apex/1st

#1105   The Way You Look Tonight   *2nd recording*
Publication Date: 1936
Music: Jerome Kern
Words: Dorothy Fields
Recorded: 1/27/64-a
Arranger: Nelson Riddle
Conductor/Band: N. Riddle/studio orchestra
Key Release: **Frank Sinatra Sings "Days of Wine and Roses," "Moon River," and Other Academy Award Winners**
see Album Lists: alphabetic by title; 1964 — 1st LP; Reprise/17th

#1106   We Hate to Leave   *duet with Gene Kelly*
Publication Date: 1944
Music: Jule Styne

Words: Sammy Cahn
Recorded: 1945 soundtrack (illegally taken from film sound)
Arranger: Axel Stordahl
Conductor/Band: George Stoll/ MGM Orchestra
Key Release: "Anchors Aweigh" (LP: Score from "Anchors Aweigh")
see Album Lists: alphabetic under "soundtrack"; mid–1960s; bootleg Mv. #7

#1107   We Just Couldn't Say Goodbye
Publication Date: 1932
Music & Words: Harry Woods
Recorded: 10/24/47-b
Arranger: Tony Mottola
Conductor/Band: T. Mottola/studio orchestra
Key Release: Hello, Young Lovers (2 discs)
see Album Lists: alphabetic by title; 1987 – 2nd LP; Columbia/52nd

#1108   We Kiss in a Shadow
Publication Date: 1951
Music: Richard Rodgers
Words: Oscar Hammerstein II
Recorded: 3/2/51-b
Arranger: Axel Stordahl
Conductor/Band: A. Stordahl/studio orchestra
Key Release: Adventures of the Heart
see Album Lists: alphabetic by title; 1956 – 3rd LP; Columbia/24th

#1109   We Open in Venice
sung with Dean Martin & Sammy Davis Jr.
Publication Date: 1948
Music & Words: Cole Porter
Recorded: 7/10/63-a
Arranger: Billy May
Conductor/Band: Morris Stoloff/ studio orchestra

Key Release: Reprise Musical Repertory Theatre: "Kiss Me Kate"
see Album Lists: alphabetic by title; 1963 – 5th LP; Reprise/13th

#1110   We Three (My Echo, My Shadow, and Me)
Publication Date: 1940
Music & Words: Sammy Mysels & Nelson Cogane & Dick Robertson
Recorded: 8/29/40-d
Arranger: Sy Oliver
Conductor/Band: Tommy Dorsey & his Orchestra
Key Release: The Dorsey/Sinatra Sessions (Volume 3)
see Album Lists: alphabetic by title; 1972 – 3rd LP; RCA Victor/19th

#1111   We Wish You the Merriest   *duet with Bing Crosby*
Publication Date: 1944
Music: Les Brown
Words: Ben Homer
Recorded: 6/19/64-b
Arranger: Jack Halloran & Harry Betts
Conductor/Band: Jack Halloran/ studio orchestra
Key Release: Twelve Songs of Christmas
see Album Lists: alphabetic by title; 1964 – 9th LP; Reprise/22nd

#1112   The Wedding of Lili Marlene
Publication Date: 1949
Music & Words: Tommy Connor & Johnny Reine
Recorded: 7/21/49-c
Arranger: Morris Stoloff
Conductor/Band: M. Stoloff/studio orchestra
Key Release: 78rpm single #38555
see Album List #1: 1949 Columbia

(4) single record — listed by number

#1113   Weep They Will
Publication Date: 1955
Music: Carl Fischer
Words: Bill Carey
Recorded: 10/17/55-c
Arranger: Nelson Riddle
Conductor/Band: N. Riddle/studio orchestra
Key Release: **Tell Her You Love Her**
see Album Lists: alphabetic by title; 1965 — 3rd LP; Capitol/35th

#1114   We'll Be Together Again
Publication Date: 1945
Music: Carl Fischer
Words: Frankie Laine
Recorded: 1/16/56-e
Arranger: Nelson Riddle
Conductor/Band: N. Riddle/studio orchestra
Key Release: **Songs for Swingin' Lovers!**
see Album Lists: alphabetic by title; 1956 — 1st LP; Capitol/7th

#1115   Well, Did You Evah?
duet with Bing Crosby
Publication Date: 1939
Music & Words: Cole Porter
Recorded: 5/7/56-a
Arranger: Skip Martin
Conductor/Band: Johnny Green/ MGM Orchestra
Key Release: **"High Society"** (Official Soundtrack LP)
see Album Lists: alphabetic by title; 1956 — 5th LP; Capitol/9th

#1116   We'll Gather Lilacs in the Spring
Publication Date: 1945
Music & Words: Ivor Novello
Recorded: 6/14/62-c
Arranger: Robert Farnon
Conductor/Band: R. Farnon/studio orchestra
Key Release: **Sinatra Sings Great Songs from Great Britain**
(English release only)
see Album Lists: alphabetic by title; 1962 — 5th LP; Reprise/6th

#1117   We'll Meet Again
Publication Date: 1936
Music & Words: Ross Parker & Hughie Charles
Recorded: 6/14/62-a
Arranger: Robert Farnon
Conductor/Band: R. Farnon/studio orchestra
Key Release: **Sinatra Sings Great Songs from Great Britain**
(English release only)
see Album Lists: alphabetic by title; 1962 — 5th LP; Reprise/6th

#1118   What a Funny Girl (You Used to Be)
Publication Date: 1969
Music & Words: Bob Gaudio & Jake Holmes
Recorded: 7/17/69-c
Arranger: Charles Calello
Conductor/Band: C. Calello/studio orchestra
Key Release: **Watertown [a love story]**
see Album Lists: alphabetic by title; 1970 — 1st LP; Reprise/40th

#1119   What Are You Doing the Rest of Your Life?
Publication Date: 1969
Music: Michel Legrand
Words: Alan & Marilyn Bergman
Recorded: 5/21/74-a
Arranger: Don Costa
Conductor/Band: D. Costa/studio orchestra
Key Release: **Some Nice Things I've Missed**

see Album Lists: alphabetic by title;
1974 — 1st LP; Reprise/47th

#1120   What Do I Care for a Dame?   *show's finale*
Publication Date: 1940
Music: Richard Rodgers
Words: Lorenz Hart
Recorded: 9/25/57-b
Arranger: Nelson Riddle
Conductor/Band: Morris Stoloff/
studio orchestra
Key Release: **"Pal Joey"** (Official
Soundtrack LP)
see Album Lists: alphabetic by title;
1957 — 8th LP; Capitol/15th

#1121   What Is This Thing Called Love?
Publication Date: 1929
Music & Words: Cole Porter
Recorded: 2/16/55-a
Arranger: Nelson Riddle
Conductor/Band: N. Riddle/studio
orchestra
Key Release: **In the Wee Small Hours** (12" LP version)
see Album Lists: alphabetic by title;
1955 — 7th LP; Capitol/5th

#1122   What Makes the Sun Set?
Publication Date: 1944
Music: Jule Styne
Words: Sammy Cahn
Recorded: 12/1/44-c
Arranger: Axel Stordahl
Conductor/Band: A. Stordahl/studio
orchestra
Key Release: **Frank Sinatra in Hollywood, 1943–1949**
see Album Lists: alphabetic by title;
1968 — 1st LP; Columbia/38th

#1123   What Now My Love?
«Et Maintenant»
Publication Date: 1962

Music: Gilbert Becaud
Words: Carl Sigman/Pierre
Delanoe
Recorded: 11/17/66-b
Arranger: Ernie Freeman
Conductor/Band: E. Freeman/studio
orchestra
Key Release: **That's Life**
see Album Lists: alphabetic by title;
1966 — 5th LP; Reprise/30th

#1124   What Time Does the Next Miracle Leave?   *from*
"The Future" cantata
Publication Date: 1979
Music & Words: Gordon Jenkins
Recorded: 12/18/79-b
Arranger: Gordon Jenkins
Conductor/Band: G. Jenkins and the
L.A. Philharmonic Symphony
Orchestra
Key Release: **Trilogy: The Future [Reflections on the Future in 3 Tenses]**
see Album Lists: alphabetic by title;
1980 — 3rd LP; Reprise/54th

#1125   What'll I Do?   *1st recording*
Publication Date: 1924
Music & Words: Irving Berlin
Recorded: 10/29/47-a
Arranger: Axel Stordahl
Conductor/Band: A. Stordahl/studio
orchestra
Key Release: 78rpm single #38045,
side B
see Album List #1: 1947 Columbia
(4) single record — listed by
number

#1126   What'll I Do?   *2nd recording*
Publication Date: 1924
Music & Words: Irving Berlin
Recorded: 1/17/62-a
Arranger: Gordon Jenkins

Conductor/Band: G. Jenkins/studio
orchestra
*Key Release: **All Alone***
see Album Lists: alphabetic by title;
1962 — 7th LP; Reprise/8th

#1127   What's New?
Publication Date: 1939
Music: Bob Haggart — 1938, as "I'm
Free"
Words: Johnny Burke
Recorded: 6/24/58-b
Arranger: Nelson Riddle
Conductor/Band: N. Riddle/studio
orchestra
*Key Release: **Frank Sinatra Sings
for Only the Lonely***
see Album Lists: alphabetic by title;
1958 — 5th LP; Capitol/19th

#1128   What's Now Is Now
Publication Date: 1969
Music & Words: Bob Gaudio &
Jake Holmes
Recorded: 7/16/69-b
Arrangers: Bob Gaudio & Joseph
Scott
Conductor/Band: Joseph Scott/studio
orchestra
*Key Release: **Watertown [a love
story]***
see Album Lists: alphabetic by title;
1970 — 1st LP; Reprise/40th

#1129   What's Wrong with Me?
duet with Kathryn Grayson
Publication Date: 1947
Music: Nacio Herb Brown
Words: Edward Heyman
Recorded: 1948 soundtrack (illegally
taken from film sound)
Arranger: Leo Arnaud
Conductor/Band: George Stoll/
MGM Orchestra
*Key Release: **"The Kissing Bandit"***
(LP: Five Films)
see Album Lists: alphabetic under

"soundtrack"; mid–1960s; bootleg Mv. #11

#1130   When I Lost You
Publication Date: 1912
Music & Words: Irving Berlin
Recorded: 1/15/62-d
Arranger: Gordon Jenkins
Conductor/Band: G. Jenkins/studio
orchestra
*Key Release: **All Alone***
see Album Lists: alphabetic by title;
1962 — 7th LP; Reprise/8th

#1131   When I Stop Loving You
Publication Date: 1954
Music: George Cates
Words: Sanford Green & Allan
Copeland
Recorded: 8/23/54-a
Arranger: Nelson Riddle
Conductor/Band: N. Riddle/studio
orchestra
*Key Release: **Look to Your Heart***
see Album Lists: alphabetic by title;
1959 — 4th LP; Capitol/22nd

#1132   When I Take My Sugar
to Tea
Publication Date: 1931
Music: Sammy Fain & Pierre Nor-
man Connor
Words: Irving Kahal
Recorded: 12/20/60-g
Arranger: Johnny Mandel
Conductor/Band: J. Mandel/studio
orchestra
*Key Release: **Ring-a-Ding Ding!***
see Album Lists: alphabetic by title;
1961 — 3rd LP; Reprise/1st

#1133   When I'm Not Near the
Girl I Love
Publication Date: 1947
Music: Burton Lane
Words: E. Y. ("Yip") Harburg
Recorded: 7/18/63-b

Arranger: Nelson Riddle
Conductor/Band: Morris Stoloff/
studio orchestra
Key Release: **Reprise Musical Repertory Theatre: "Finian's Rainbow"**
see Album Lists: alphabetic by title;
1963 — 3rd LP; Reprise/11th

#1134   When Is Sometime?
Publication Date: 1947
Music: Jimmy Van Heusen
Words: Johnny Burke
Recorded: 12/30/47-c
Arranger: Axel Stordahl
Conductor/Band: A. Stordahl/studio
orchestra
Key Release: **Sinatra Rarities — The Columbia Years** (Volume 1)
see Album Lists: alphabetic by title;
1986 — 1st LP; Columbia/50th

#1135   When No One Cares
Publication Date: 1959
Music: Jimmy Van Heusen
Words: Sammy Cahn
Recorded: 5/14/59-c
Arranger: Gordon Jenkins
Conductor/Band: G. Jenkins/studio
orchestra
Key Release: **No One Cares**
see Album Lists: alphabetic by title;
1959 — 5th LP; Capitol/23rd

#1136   When Somebody Loves You
Publication Date: 1965
Music: Howard Greenfield
Words: Jack Keller & K. Smith
Recorded: 4/14/65-f
Arranger: Ernie Freeman
Conductor/Band: E. Freeman/studio
orchestra
Key Release: **Sinatra '65**
see Album Lists: alphabetic by title;
1965 — 2nd LP; Reprise/24th

#1137   When the Sun Goes Down
Publication Date: 1948
Music: J. Orton
Words: Walter O'Keefe
Recorded: 2/23/50-b
Arranger: Axel Stordahl
Conductor/Band: A. Stordahl/studio
orchestra
Key Release: **Come Back to Sorrento**
see Album Lists: alphabetic by title;
1960 — 5th LP; Columbia/30th

#1138   When the Wind Was Green
Publication Date: 1949
Music & Words: Don Hunt
Recorded: 4/14/65-b
Arranger: Gordon Jenkins
Conductor/Band: G. Jenkins/studio
orchestra
Key Release: **September of My Years**
see Album Lists: alphabetic by title;
1965 — 1st LP; Reprise/23rd

#1139   When the World Was Young «Ah, the Apple Trees»
Publication Date: 1950
Music: M. Philippe-Gerard
Words: Johnny Mercer
Recorded: 9/11/61-f
Arranger: Axel Stordahl
Conductor/Band: A. Stordahl/studio
orchestra
Key Release: **Point of No Return**
see Album Lists: alphabetic by title;
1962 — 2nd LP; Capitol/31st

#1140   When You Awake   *1st recording*
Publication Date: 1940
Music & Words: Henry Nemo
Recorded: 9/9/40-a
Arranger: Dorsey "house" arrng:
   T. Dorsey, S. Oliver, F. Stulce,
   P. Weston

Conductor/Band: Tommy Dorsey & his Orchestra
Key Release: **The Dorsey/Sinatra Sessions** (Volume 3)
see Album Lists: alphabetic by title; 1972 — 3rd LP; RCA Victor/19th

#1141   When You Awake   *2nd recording*
Publication Date: 1940
Music & Words: Henry Nemo
Recorded: 11/5/47-a
Arranger: Axel Stordahl
Conductor/Band: A. Stordahl/studio orchestra
Key Release: **Frankly Sentimental** (10" LP)
see Album Lists: alphabetic by title; 1949 — 4th LP; Columbia/4th

#1142   When Your Lover Has Gone   *1st recording*
Publication Date: 1931
Music & Words: E. A. Swan
Recorded: 12/19/44-b
Arranger: Axel Stordahl
Conductor/Band: A. Stordahl/studio orchestra
Key Release: **Reflections**
see Album Lists: alphabetic by title; 1961 — 4th LP; Columbia/31st

#1143   When Your Lover Has Gone   *2nd recording*
Publication Date: 1931
Music & Words: E. A. Swan
Recorded: 2/17/55-c
Arranger: Nelson Riddle
Conductor/Band: N. Riddle/studio orchestra
Key Release: **In the Wee Small Hours** (12" LP version)
see Album Lists: alphabetic by title; 1955 — 7th LP; Capitol/5th

#1144   When You're Smiling   *1st recording*
Publication Date: 1930

Music & Words: Larry Shay & Joe Goodman & Mark Fisher
Recorded: 4/24/50-a
Arranger: George Siravo
Conductor/Band: G. Siravo/studio orchestra
Key Release: **Love Is a Kick**
see Album Lists: alphabetic by title; 1960 — 3rd LP; Columbia/28th

#1145   When You're Smiling   *2nd recording*
Publication Date: 1930
Music & Words: Larry Shay & Joe Goodwin & Mark Fisher
Recorded: 8/22/60-a
Arranger: Nelson Riddle
Conductor/Band: N. Riddle/studio orchestra
Key Release: **Sinatra's Swingin' Session!!!**
see Album Lists: alphabetic by title; 1961 — 1st LP; Capitol/28th

#1146   Where Are You?
Publication Date: 1936
Music: Jimmy McHugh
Words: Harold Adamson
Recorded: 5/1/57-a
Arranger: Gordon Jenkins
Conductor/Band: G. Jenkins/studio orchestra
Key Release: **Where Are You?**
see Album Lists: alphabetic by title; 1957 — 4th LP; Capitol/13th

#1147   Where Do You Go?
Publication Date: 1958
Music & Words: Alec Wilder
Recorded: 3/26/59-b
Arranger: Gordon Jenkins
Conductor/Band: G. Jenkins/studio orchestra
Key Release: **No One Cares**
see Album Lists: alphabetic by title; 1959 — 5th LP; Capitol/23rd

#1148   Where Do You Keep Your Heart?
Publication Date: 1940
Music: Fred Ahlert
Words: Al Stillman
Recorded: 5/23/40-c
Arranger: Dorsey "house" arrng:
    T. Dorsey, S. Oliver, F. Stulce,
    P. Weston
Conductor/Band: Tommy Dorsey &
    his Orchestra
Key Release: **The Dorsey/Sinatra
    Sessions** (Volume 2)
see Album Lists: alphabetic by title;
    1972 — 2nd LP; RCA Victor/18th

#1149   Where Does Love Begin?
duet with Anne Jeffreys
Publication Date: 1944
Music: Jule Styne
Words: Sammy Cahn
Recorded: 1944 soundtrack (illegally
    taken from film sound)
Arranger: Axel Stordahl
Conductor/Band: Constantin Baka-
    leinikoff/RKO Orchestra
Key Release: **"Step Lively"** (LP:
    Complete "Step Lively" Film
    Soundtrack)
see Album Lists: alphabetic under
    "soundtrack"; mid–1960s; boot-
    leg Mv. #5

**#1150   Where Is My Bess? «Oh
Bess, Oh Where's My Bess?»**
Publication Date: 1935
Music: George Gershwin
Words: DuBois Heyward & Ira
    Gershwin
Recorded: 2/24/46-b
Arranger: Axel Stordahl
Conductor/Band: A. Stordahl/studio
    orchestra
Key Release: **The Broadway Kick**
see Album Lists: alphabetic by title;
    1960 — 4th LP; Columbia/29th

#1151   Where Is the One?   *1st
recording*
Publication Date: 1947
Music: Alec Wilder
Words: Edwin Finckel & Alec
    Wilder
Recorded: 12/30/47-b
Arranger: Axel Stordahl
Conductor/Band: A. Stordahl/studio
    orchestra
Key Release: **Sinatra Rarities — The
    Columbia Years** (Volume 1)
see Album Lists: alphabetic by title;
    1986 — 1st LP; Columbia/50th

#1152   Where Is the One?*   *2nd
recording*
Publication Date: 1947
Music: Alec Wilder
Words: Edwin Finckel & Alec
    Wilder
Recorded: 4/10/57-a
Arranger: Gordon Jenkins
Conductor/Band: G. Jenkins/studio
    orchestra
Key Release: **Where Are You?**
see Album Lists: alphabetic by title;
    1957 — 4th LP; Capitol/13th
*Sinatra's first song recorded in
    stereo at the Capitol Records
    Tower. Some stereophonic re-
    cording had been done previ-
    ously at motion picture studios.

#1153   Where or When   *1st re-
cording*
Publication Date: 1937
Music: Richard Rodgers
Words: Lorenz Hart
Recorded: 1/29/45-b
Arranger: Axel Stordahl
Conductor/Band: A. Stordahl/studio
    orchestra
Key Release: **Reflections**
see Album Lists: alphabetic by title;
    1961 — 4th LP; Columbia/31st

#1154   Where or When   *2nd recording*
Publication Date: 1937
Music: Richard Rodgers
Words: Lorenz Hart
Recorded: 9/11/58-c
Arranger: Nelson Riddle
Conductor/Band: N. Riddle/studio orchestra
Key Release: **The Rare Sinatra: Volume 1** (Australian release only)
see Album Lists: alphabetic by title; 1978 — 1st LP; Capitol/65th

#1155   Where or When   *3rd recording — medley; duet with Dinah Shore*
Publication Date: 1937
Music: Richard Rodgers
Words: Lorenz Hart
Recorded: 1962 television special
Arranger: Don Costa
Conductor/Band: D. Costa/television orchestra
Key Release: **Frank Sinatra — Through the Years: 1944–1966**
see Album Lists: alphabetic under "television"; mid–1960s; Ajazz/1st

#1156   Where or When   *4th recording*
Publication Date: 1937
Music: Richard Rodgers
Words: Lorenz Hart
Recorded: 2/1/66-o
Arranger: Quincy Jones
Conductor/Band: Count Basie & his Band
Key Release: **Sinatra at the Sands** (Live Recording — 2 discs)
see Album Lists: alphabetic by title; 1966 — 3rd LP; Reprise/29th

#1157   While the Angelus Was Ringing
Publication Date: 1945

Music: Jean Villard
Words: Dick Manning
Recorded: 12/19/48-c
Arranger: Axel Stordahl
Conductor/Band: A. Stordahl/studio orchestra
Key Release: 78rpm single #38407
see Album List #1: 1948 Columbia (4) single record — listed by number

#1158   Whispering
Publication Date: 1920
Music & Words: John Schonberger & Richard Coburn & Vincent Rose
Recorded: 6/13/40-a
Arranger: Dorsey "house" arrng: T. Dorsey, S. Oliver, F. Stulce, P. Weston
Conductor/Band: Tommy Dorsey & his Orchestra
Key Release: **The Dorsey/Sinatra Sessions** (Volume 2)
see Album Lists: alphabetic by title; 1972 — 2nd LP; RCA Victor/18th

#1159   White Christmas   *1st recording*
Publication Date: 1942
Music & Words: Irving Berlin
Recorded: 11/13/44-b
Arranger: Axel Stordahl
Conductor/Band: A. Stordahl/studio orchestra
Key Release: **Christmas Dreaming**
see Album Lists: alphabetic by title; 1957 — 3rd LP; Columbia/25th

#1160   White Christmas   *2nd recording*
Publication Date: 1942
Music & Words: Irving Berlin
Recorded: 12/28/47-c
Arranger: Axel Stordahl
Conductor/Band: A. Stordahl/studio orchestra

Key Release: 78rpm single #DO-3745 (Australian release only)
see Album List #1: 1948 Columbia (3) single record—listed by number

#1161   White Christmas   *3rd recording*
Publication Date: 1942
Music & Words: Irving Berlin
Recorded: 8/23/54-b
Arranger: Nelson Riddle
Conductor/Band: N. Riddle/studio orchestra
Key Release: 45rpm single #2954, side A
see Album List #1: 1954 Capitol (5) single record—listed by number

#1162   Who Takes Care of the Caretaker's Daughter?   *duet with Bob Hope*
Publication Date: 1924
Music & Words: Chick Endor & Paul Revere
Recorded: 1963 television special
Arranger: Don Costa
Conductor/Band: D. Costa/television orchestra
*Key Release: **Frank Sinatra— Through the Years: 1944–1966***
see Album Lists: alphabetic under "television"; mid–1960s; Ajazz/1st

#1163   Who Wants to Be a Millionaire?   *duet with Celeste Holm*
Publication Date: 1956
Music & Words: Cole Porter
Recorded: 4/20/56-b
Arranger: Conrad Salinger
Conductor/Band: Johnny Green/ MGM Orchestra
*Key Release: **"High Society"*** (Official Soundtrack LP)
see Album Lists: alphabetic by title; 1956—5th LP; Capitol/9th

#1164   Whose Baby Are You?
Publication Date: 1920
Music: Jerome Kern
Words: Anne Caldwell
Recorded: 1947 soundtrack (illegally taken from film sound)
Arranger: Axel Stordahl
Conductor/Band: Johnny Green/ MGM Orchestra
*Key Release: **"It Happened in Brooklyn"*** (LP: Score from "It Happened in Brooklyn")
see Album Lists: alphabetic under "soundtrack"; mid–1960s; bootleg Mv. #9

#1165   Why Can't You Behave?
Publication Date: 1948
Music & Words: Cole Porter
Recorded: 12/15/48-b
Arranger: Phil Moore
Conductor/Band: P. Moore/studio orchestra
*Key Release: **The Broadway Kick***
see Album Lists: alphabetic by title; 1960—4th LP; Columbia/29th

#1166   Why Should I Cry Over You?
Publication Date: 1922
Music & Words: Chester Conn & Ned Miller
Recorded: 12/8/53-c
Arranger: Nelson Riddle
Conductor/Band: N. Riddle/studio orchestra
*Key Release: **Swing Easy*** (later 12" version of LP)
see Album Lists: alphabetic by title; 1960—6th LP; Capitol/26th

#1167   Why Shouldn't I?
Publication Date: 1935
Music & Words: Cole Porter
Recorded: 12/7/45-b
Arranger: Axel Stordahl

Conductor/Band: A. Stordahl/studio
orchestra
Key Release: **The Essential Frank
Sinatra** (Volume 1)
see Album Lists: alphabetic by title;
1967 – 2nd LP; Columbia/34th

#1168   Why Shouldn't It Happen to Us?
Publication Date: 1946
Music: Alberta Nichols
Words: Mann Holiner
Recorded: 10/15/46-d
Arranger: Axel Stordahl
Conductor/Band: A. Stordahl/studio
orchestra
Key Release: **The Essential Frank
Sinatra** (Volume 2)
see Album Lists: alphabetic by title;
1967 – 3rd LP; Columbia/35th

#1169   Why Try to Change Me Now?*   *1st recording*
Publication Date: 1952
Music: Cy Coleman
Words: Joseph A. McCarthy
Recorded: 9/17/52-a
Arranger: Percy Faith
Conductor/Band: P. Faith/studio
orchestra
Key Release: **The Essential Frank
Sinatra** (Volume 3)
see Album Lists: alphabetic by title;
1967 – 4th LP; Columbia/36th
*The last song Sinatra recorded
for Columbia Records – the session took place on September
17, 1952 – and also his last released single record for that
label, coupled with *The Birth of
the Blues.* Ironically, after a succession of the novelty releases
and light '50s pop tunes which
Sinatra felt had helped to wreck
his career, this last release contained beautiful versions of two

great songs. His contract, however, was not renewed.

#1170   Why Try to Change Me Now?   *2nd recording*
Publication Date: 1952
Music: Cy Coleman
Words: Joseph A. McCarthy
Recorded: 3/24/59-b
Arranger: Gordon Jenkins
Conductor/Band: G. Jenkins/studio
orchestra
Key Release: **No One Cares**
see Album Lists: alphabetic by title;
1959 – 5th LP; Capitol/23rd

#1171   Why Was I Born?
Publication Date: 1929
Music: Jerome Kern
Words: Oscar Hammerstein II
Recorded: 12/28/47-g
Arranger: Axel Stordahl
Conductor/Band: A. Stordahl/studio
orchestra
Key Release: **The Frank Sinatra
Story in Music** (2 discs)
see Album Lists: alphabetic by title;
1959 – 2nd LP; Columbia/27th

#1172   Willow Weep for Me
Publication Date: 1932
Music & Words: Ann Ronell
Recorded: 5/29/58-h
Arranger: Nelson Riddle
Conductor/Band: Felix Slatkin/studio
orchestra
Key Release: **Frank Sinatra Sings
for Only the Lonely**
see Album Lists: alphabetic by title;
1958 – 5th LP; Capitol/19th

#1173   Winchester Cathedral
Publication Date: 1966
Music & Words: Geoff Stephens
Recorded: 11/17/66-d
Arranger: Ernie Freeman
Conductor/Band: E. Freeman/studio
orchestra

Key Release: **That's Life**
see Album Lists: alphabetic by title;
   1966 — 5th LP; Reprise/30th

#1174   Winners
Publication Date: 1973
Music & Words: Joe Raposo
Recorded: 6/21/73-a
Arranger: Don Costa
Conductor/Band: Gordon Jenkins/
   studio orchestra
Key Release: **Ol' Blue Eyes Is Back**
see Album Lists: alphabetic by title;
   1973 — 2nd LP; Reprise/45th

#1175   Witchcraft   *1st recording*
Publication Date: 1957
Music: Cy Coleman
Words: Carolyn Leigh
Recorded: 5/20/57-a
Arranger: Nelson Riddle
Conductor/Band: N. Riddle/studio
   orchestra
Key Release: **All the Way**
see Album Lists: alphabetic by title;
   1961 — 2nd LP; Capitol/29th

#1176   Witchcraft   *2nd recording*
Publication Date: 1957
Music: Cy Coleman
Words: Carolyn Leigh
Recorded: 4/30/63-a
Arranger: Nelson Riddle
Conductor/Band: N. Riddle/studio
   orchestra
Key Release: **Sinatra's Sinatra**
see Album Lists: alphabetic by title;
   1963 — 7th LP; Reprise/15th

#1177   With Every Breath I
   Take
Publication Date: 1935
Music & Words: Ralph Rainer &
   Leo Robin
Recorded: 4/5/56-d
Arranger: Nelson Riddle
Conductor/Band: N. Riddle with

orchestra & the Hollywood
   String Quartet
Key Release: **Close to You**
see Album Lists: alphabetic by title;
   1957 — 1st LP; Capitol/11th

#1178   Without a Song   *1st recording*
Publication Date: 1929
Music: Vincent Youmans
Words: Billy Rose & Edward
   Eliscu
Recorded: 1/20/41-c
Arranger: Sy Oliver
Conductor/Band: Tommy Dorsey &
   his Orchestra
Key Release: **The Dorsey/Sinatra
   Sessions** (Volume 4)
see Album Lists: alphabetic by title;
   1972 — 4th LP; RCA Victor/20th

#1179   Without a Song   *2nd recording*
Publication Date: 1929
Music: Vincent Youmans
Words: Billy Rose & Edward
   Eliscu
Recorded: 10/24/45-b; "The Frank
   Sinatra Old Gold Show" re-
   hearsal
Arranger: Axel Stordahl
Conductor/Band: Tommy Dorsey &
   his Orchestra
Key Release: **Frank Sinatra on V-
   Disc** (Japanese release only; al-
   bum of wartime Victory Discs)
see Album Lists: alphabetic under
   "v/disc"; early 1970s; Dan/1st

#1180   Without a Song   *3rd recording*
Publication Date: 1929
Music: Vincent Youmans
Words: Billy Rose & Edward
   Eliscu
Recorded: 5/2/61-a
Arranger: Sy Oliver

Conductor/Band: S. Oliver/studio orchestra
Key Release: **I Remember Tommy...**
see Album Lists: alphabetic by title; 1961 — 7th LP; Reprise/3rd

#1181   Wives and Lovers
Publication Date: 1963
Music: Burt Bacharach
Words: Hal David
Recorded: 6/12/64-c
Arranger: Quincy Jones
Conductor/Band: Count Basie & his Band
Key Release: **It Might as Well Be Swing**
see Album Lists: alphabetic by title; 1964 — 5th LP; Reprise/19th

#1182   The World Is in My Arms
Publication Date: 1940
Music: Burton Lane
Words: E. Y. ("Yip") Harburg
Recorded: 7/17/40-d
Arranger: Dorsey "house" arrng: T. Dorsey, S. Oliver, F. Stulce, P. Weston
Conductor/Band: Tommy Dorsey & his Orchestra
Key Release: **The Dorsey/Sinatra Sessions** (Volume 3)
see Album Lists: alphabetic by title; 1972 — 3rd LP; RCA Victor/19th

#1183   World War None   *from* "The Future" cantata
Publication Date: 1979
Music & Words: Gordon Jenkins
Recorded: 12/18/79-c
Arranger: Gordon Jenkins
Conductor/Band: G. Jenkins and the L.A. Philharmonic Symphony Orchestra
Key Release: **Trilogy: The Future [Reflections on the Future in 3 Tenses]**

see Album Lists: alphabetic by title; 1980 — 3rd LP; Reprise/54th

#1184   The World We Knew «Over and Over»
Publication Date: 1967
Music: Bert Kaempfert & Herbert Rehbein
Words: Carl Sigman
Recorded: 6/29/67-b
Arranger: Ernie Freeman
Conductor/Band: E. Freeman/studio orchestra
Key Release: **Frank Sinatra & Frank and Nancy**
see Album Lists: alphabetic by title; 1967 — 5th LP; Reprise/32nd

#1185   Wrap Your Troubles in Dreams
Publication Date: 1931
Music: Harry Barris
Words: Ted Koehler & Billy Moll
Recorded: 4/7/54-d
Arranger: Nelson Riddle; full-orch. arrng. from G. Siravo band arrng.
Conductor/Band: N. Riddle/studio orchestra
Key Release: **Swing Easy!** (original 10" LP)
see Album Lists: alphabetic by title; 1954 — 5th LP; Capitol/4th

#1186   Yellow Days
Publication Date: 1933
Music: A. Carrillo
Words: A. Bernstein
Recorded: 12/11/67-b
Arranger: Billy May
Conductor/Band: Duke Ellington & his Band
Key Release: **Francis A. & Edward K.**
see Album Lists: alphabetic by title; 1968 — 2nd LP; Reprise/33rd

#1187 Yes, Indeed! «A Jive Spiritual»
Publication Date: 1941
Music & Words: Sy Oliver
Recorded: 3/21/61-a
Arranger: Billy May
Conductor/Band: B. May/studio orchestra
Key Release: Come Swing with Me!
see Album Lists: alphabetic by title; 1961 — 5th LP; Capitol/30th

#1188 Yes, Indeedy *sung with Gene Kelly & Jules Munshin*
Publication Date: 1949
Music: Roger Edens
Words: Betty Comden & Adolph Green
Recorded: 1949 — 1st soundtrack (illegally taken from film sound)
Arranger: Conrad Salinger
Conductor/Band: Adolph Deutsch/ MGM Orchestra
Key Release: "Take Me Out to the Ball Game" (LP: Five Films)
see Album Lists: alphabetic under "soundtrack"; mid–1960s; bootleg Mv. #12

#1189 Yes Sir, That's My Baby
Publication Date: 1925
Music: Walter Donaldson
Words: Gus Kahn
Recorded: 5/11/66-b
Arranger: Nelson Riddle
Conductor/Band: N. Riddle/studio orchestra
Key Release: Strangers in the Night
see Album Lists: alphabetic by title; 1966 — 1st LP; Reprise/27th

#1190 Yesterday [All My Troubles Seemed So Far Away]
Publication Date: 1965
Music & Words: Paul McCartney/John Lennon
Recorded: 2/20/69-b

Arranger: Don Costa
Conductor/Band: D. Costa/studio orchestra
Key Release: My Way
see Album Lists: alphabetic by title; 1969 — 1st LP; Reprise/38th

#1191 Yesterdays [Days I Knew as Happy ... Sequester'd Days]
Publication Date: 1933
Music: Jerome Kern
Words: Otto Harbach
Recorded: 11/20/61-c
Arranger: Don Costa
Conductor/Band: D. Costa/studio orchestra
Key Release: Sinatra & Strings
see Album Lists: alphabetic by title; 1962 — 1st LP; Reprise/4th

#1192 You and I
Publication Date: 1941
Music & Words: Meredith Willson
Recorded: 6/27/41-b
Arranger: Sy Oliver
Conductor/Band: Tommy Dorsey & his Orchestra
Key Release: The Dorsey/Sinatra Sessions (Volume 5)
see Album Lists: alphabetic by title; 1972 — 5th LP; RCA Victor/21st

#1193 You and Me (We Wanted It All)
Publication Date: 1979
Music: Peter Allen
Words: Carole Bayer Sager
Recorded: 8/20/79-a
Arranger: Don Costa
Conductor/Band: D. Costa/studio orchestra
Key Release: Trilogy: The Present [Some Very Good Years]
see Album Lists: alphabetic by title; 1980 — 2nd LP; Reprise/53rd

#1194   You and the Night and the Music
Publication Date: 1934
Music: Arthur Schwartz
Words: Howard Dietz
Recorded: 12/20/60-f
Arranger: Johnny Mandel
Conductor/Band: J. Mandel/studio orchestra
Key Release: Ring-a-Ding Ding!
see Album Lists: alphabetic by title; 1961 – 3rd LP; Reprise/1st

#1195   You Are the Sunshine of My Life   *1st recording*
Publication Date: 1972
Music & Words: Stevie Wonder
Recorded: 5/24/74-a
Arranger: Don Costa
Conductor/Band: D. Costa/studio orchestra
Key Release: Some Nice Things I've Missed
see Album Lists: alphabetic by title; 1974 – 1st LP; Reprise/47th

#1196   You Are the Sunshine of My Life   *2nd recording*
Publication Date: 1972
Music & Words: Stevie Wonder
Recorded: 10/13/74-h
Arranger: Don Costa
Conductor/Band: Bill Miller/Woody Herman's Young Thundering Herd band
Key Release: Sinatra – The Main Event (Live Recording)
see Album Lists: alphabetic by title; 1974 – 2nd LP; Reprise/48th

#1197   You Are There
Publication Date: 1966
Music: Harry Sukman
Words: Paul Francis Webster
Recorded: 6/29/67-a
Arranger: Gordon Jenkins

Conductor/Band: G. Jenkins/studio orchestra
Key Release: Frank Sinatra & Frank and Nancy
see Album Lists: alphabetic by title; 1967 – 5th LP; Reprise/32nd

#1198   You Are Too Beautiful
Publication Date: 1933
Music: Richard Rodgers
Words: Lorenz Hart
Recorded: 8/22/45-d
Arranger: Axel Stordahl
Conductor/Band: A. Stordahl/studio orchestra
Key Release: The Essential Frank Sinatra (Volume 1)
see Album Lists: alphabetic by title; 1967 – 2nd LP; Columbia/34th

#1199   You Belong in a Love Song
Publication Date: 1943
Music: Jimmy McHugh
Words: Harold Adamson
Recorded: 1943 soundtrack (illegally taken from film sound)
Arranger: Axel Stordahl
Conductor/Band: Constantin Bakaleinikoff/RKO Orchestra
Key Release: "Higher and Higher" (LP: Four Sinatra Movies)
see Album Lists: alphabetic under "soundtrack"; mid–1960s; bootleg Mv. #4

#1200   You Brought a New Kind of Love to Me   *1st recording*
Publication Date: 1930
Music: Sammy Fain & Pierre Norman Connor
Words: Irving Kahal
Recorded: 10/3/45-b; "The Frank Sinatra Old Gold Show"
Arranger: Axel Stordahl

Conductor/Band: A. Stordahl/radio orchestra

Key Release: **Sinatra for the Collector: Vol. 1—The V-Disc Years** (Canadian release only; album of wartime Victory Discs)

see Album Lists: alphabetic under "v/disc"; early 1970s; My Way/ 1st

#1201   You Brought a New Kind of Love to Me   *2nd recording*

Publication Date: 1930

Music: Sammy Fain & Pierre Norman Connor

Words: Irving Kahal

Recorded: 1/9/56-a

Arranger: Nelson Riddle

Conductor/Band: N. Riddle/studio orchestra

Key Release: **Songs for Swingin' Lovers!**

see Album Lists: alphabetic by title; 1956—1st; Capitol/7th

#1202   You Brought a New Kind of Love to Me   *3rd recording*

Publication Date: 1930

Music: Sammy Fain & Pierre Norman Connor

Words: Irving Kahal

Recorded: 2/21/63-b

Arranger: Nelson Riddle

Conductor/Band: N. Riddle/studio orchestra

Key Release: **Sinatra '65**

see Album Lists: alphabetic by title; 1965—2nd LP; Reprise/24th

#1203   You Call Everybody Darling

Publication Date: 1946

Music & Words: Ben Trace & Sam Martin & Al Trace (Clem Watts)

Recorded: 1946 radio—"The Frank Sinatra Old Gold Show"

Arranger: Axel Stordahl

Conductor/Band: A. Stordahl/radio orchestra

Key Release: **My Best Songs—My Best Years** (Volume 1)

see Album Lists: alphabetic under "radio"; early 1970s; Pentagon/ 1st

#1204   You Can Take My Word for It, Baby

Publication Date: 1946

Music: Ticker Freeman

Words: Irving Taylor

Recorded: 12/15/46-d

Arranger: Page Cavanaugh

Conductor/Band: P. Cavanaugh/ studio orchestra

Key Release: **The Essential Frank Sinatra** (Volume 2)

see Album Lists: alphabetic by title; 1967—3rd LP; Columbia/35th

#1205   You Can't Be True, Dear «Du Kannst Nicht Treu Sein»

Publication Date: 1948

Music: Hans Otten—1935/Ken Griffin

Words: Hal Cotten/Gerhard Ebeler—1935

Recorded: 1948 radio—Lucky Strike's "Your Hit Parade"

Arranger: Axel Stordahl

Conductor/Band: A. Stordahl/radio orchestra

Key Release: **My Best Songs—My Best Years** (Volume 1)

see Album Lists: alphabetic under "radio"; early 1970s; Pentagon/ 1st

#1206   You Do

Publication Date: 1947

Music: Josef Myrow

Words: Mack Gordon

Recorded: 1947 radio — Lucky
Strike's "Your Hit Parade"
Arranger: Axel Stordahl
Conductor/Band: A. Stordahl/radio
orchestra
Key Release: **Frank Sinatra**
see Album Lists: alphabetic under
"radio"; early 1960s; Cameron/
4th

**#1207   You Do Something to
Me** *1st recording*
Publication Date: 1928
Music & Words: Cole Porter
Recorded: 4/14/50-b
Arranger: George Siravo
Conductor/Band: G. Siravo/studio
orchestra
Key Release: **Love Is a Kick**
see Album Lists: alphabetic by title;
1960 — 3rd LP; Columbia/28th

**#1208   You Do Something to
Me** *2nd recording*
Publication Date: 1928
Music & Words: Cole Porter
Recorded: 8/22/60-c
Arranger: Nelson Riddle
Conductor/Band: N. Riddle/studio
orchestra
Key Release: **Sinatra's Swingin'
Session!!!**
see Album Lists: alphabetic by title;
1961 — 1st LP; Capitol/28th

#1209   You Don't Remind Me
Publication Date: 1950
Music & Words: Cole Porter
Recorded: 11/16/50-c
Arranger: Axel Stordahl
Conductor/Band: A. Stordahl/studio
orchestra
Key Release: 45rpm single #4-39079
see Album List #1: 1951 Columbia
(5) single record — listed by
number

**#1210   You Forgot All the
Words**
Publication Date: 1955
Music: Bernie Wayne
Words: E. H. Jay
Recorded: 10/17/55-a
Arranger: Nelson Riddle
Conductor/Band: N. Riddle/studio
orchestra
Key Release: **This Is Sinatra, Volume 2**
see Album Lists: alphabetic by title;
1958 — 4th LP; Capitol/18th

#1211   You Go to My Head   *1st
recording*
Publication Date: 1938
Music: J. Fred Coots
Words: Haven Gillespie
Recorded: 7/30/45-b
Arranger: Axel Stordahl
Conductor/Band: A. Stordahl/studio
orchestra
Key Release: **The Frank Sinatra
Story in Music** (2 discs)
see Album Lists: alphabetic by title;
1959 — 2nd LP; Columbia/27th

#1212   You Go to My Head
2nd recording
Publication Date: 1938
Music: J. Fred Coots
Words: Haven Gillespie
Recorded: 3/1/60-a
Arranger: Nelson Riddle
Conductor/Band: N. Riddle/studio
orchestra
Key Release: **Nice 'n' Easy**
see Album Lists: alphabetic by title;
1960 — 2nd LP; Capitol/25th

#1213   You Lucky People You
Publication Date: 1941
Music: Jimmy Van Heusen
Words: Johnny Burke
Recorded: 1/15/41-a
Arranger: Sy Oliver

Conductor/Band: Tommy Dorsey & his Orchestra
Key Release: **The Dorsey/Sinatra Sessions** (Volume 4)
see Album Lists: alphabetic by title; 1972 – 4th LP; RCA Victor/20th

#1214 You Make Me Feel So Young *1st recording*
Publication Date: 1946
Music: Josef Myrow
Words: Mack Gordon
Recorded: 1/9/56-c
Arranger: Nelson Riddle
Conductor/Band: N. Riddle/studio orchestra
Key Release: **Songs for Swingin' Lovers!**
see Album Lists: alphabetic by title; 1956 – 1st LP; Capitol/7th

#1215 You Make Me Feel So Young (Old) *2nd recording – duet with Nancy Sinatra*
Publication Date: 1946
Music: Josef Myrow
Words: Mack Gordon (with additional lyrics by Sammy Cahn)
Recorded: 1960 television special
Arranger: Nelson Riddle
Conductor/Band: N. Riddle/television orchestra
Key Release: **Frank Sinatra – Through the Years: 1944–1966**
see Album Lists: alphabetic under "television"; mid–1960s; Ajazz/1st

#1216 You Make Me Feel So Young *3rd recording*
Publication Date: 1946
Music: Josef Myrow
Words: Mack Gordon
Recorded: 2/1/66-e
Arranger: Quincy Jones
Conductor/Band: Count Basie & his Band

Key Release: **Sinatra at the Sands** (Live Recording – 2 discs)
see Album Lists: alphabetic by title; 1966 – 3rd LP; Reprise/29th

#1217 You Might Have Belonged to Another
Publication Date: 1940
Music: Paul West
Words: L. Harmon
Recorded: 1/6/41-b
Arranger: Dorsey "house" arrng: T. Dorsey, S. Oliver, F. Stulce, P. Weston
Conductor/Band: Tommy Dorsey & his Orchestra
Key Release: **The Dorsey/Sinatra Sessions** (Volume 4)
see Album Lists: alphabetic by title; 1972 – 4th LP; RCA Victor/20th

#1218 You, My Love
Publication Date: 1954
Music: Jimmy Van Heusen
Words: Mack Gordon
Recorded: 9/23/54-c
Arranger: Nelson Riddle
Conductor/Band: N. Riddle/studio orchestra
Key Release: **Look to Your Heart**
see Album Lists: alphabetic by title; 1959 – 4th LP; Capitol/22nd

#1219 You Turned My World Around
Publication Date: 1973
Music: Bert Kaempfert & Herbert Rehbein
Words: Kim Carnes & David Ellingson
Recorded: 5/8/74-b
Arranger: Don Costa
Conductor/Band: D. Costa/studio orchestra
Key Release: **Some Nice Things I've Missed**

see *Album Lists:* alphabetic by title;
1974 — 1st LP; Reprise/47th

#1220   You Will Be My Music*
Publication Date: 1973
Music & Words: Joe Raposo
Recorded: 6/4/73-b
Arranger: Gordon Jenkins
Conductor/Band: G. Jenkins/studio
orchestra
Key Release: **Ol' Blue Eyes Is Back**
see *Album Lists:* alphabetic by title;
1973 — 2nd LP; Reprise/45th
*Recorded at a session on June 4,
1973, this was Sinatra's first
track after retirement that was
given release; it also appeared
on his comeback album **Ol' Blue
Eyes Is Back** (Reprise FS-2155).

#1221   You'd Be So Nice to Come Home To
Publication Date: 1942
Music: Cole Porter; from P. de
Sarasate
Words: Cole Porter
Recorded: 11/28/56-d
Arranger: Nelson Riddle
Conductor/Band: N. Riddle/studio
orchestra
Key Release: **A Swingin' Affair!**
see *Album Lists:* alphabetic by title;
1957 — 2nd LP; Capitol/12th

#1222   You'll Always Be the One I Love
Publication Date: 1947
Music: Ticker Freeman
Words: Sunny Skylar
Recorded: 12/11/57-a
Arranger: Nelson Riddle
Conductor/Band: N. Riddle/studio
orchestra
Key Release: **This Is Sinatra, Volume 2**
see *Album Lists:* alphabetic by title;
1958 — 4th LP; Capitol/18th

#1223   You'll Get Yours
Publication Date: 1955
Music: Jimmy Van Heusen
Words: Dak Stanford
Recorded: 9/13/55-b
Arranger: Nelson Riddle
Conductor/Band: N. Riddle/studio
orchestra
Key Release: **Forever Frank**
see *Album Lists:* alphabetic by title;
1966 — 4th LP; Capitol/36th

#1224   You'll Know When It Happens
Publication Date: 1946
Music & Words: John Jacob Loeb
Recorded: 7/24/46-b
Arranger: Axel Stordahl
Conductor/Band: A. Stordahl/studio
orchestra
Key Release: **MM-1** (illegal; from
Columbia masters)
see *Album Lists:* alphabetic under
"bootleg"; early 1970s; bootleg
Alb. #1

#1225   You'll Never Know
Publication Date: 1943
Music: Harry Warren
Words: Mack Gordon
Recorded: 6/7/43-c
Arranger: Axel Stordahl
Conductor/Band: Bobby Tucker
Singers only; during musicians'
strike
Key Release: **Frankie**
see *Album Lists:* alphabetic by title;
1955 — 8th LP; Columbia/20th

#1226   You'll Never Walk Alone
1st recording
Publication Date: 1945
Music: Richard Rodgers
Words: Oscar Hammerstein II
Recorded: 5/1/45-c
Arranger: Axel Stordahl

Conductor/Band: A. Stordahl/studio orchestra
Key Release: **The Frank Sinatra Story in Music** (2 discs)
see Album Lists: alphabetic by title; 1959 — 2nd LP; Columbia/27th

#1227   You'll Never Walk Alone
2nd recording
Publication Date: 1945
Music: Richard Rodgers
Words: Oscar Hammerstein II
Recorded: 2/19/63-b
Arranger: Nelson Riddle
Conductor/Band: N. Riddle/studio orchestra
Key Release: **The Concert Sinatra**
see Album Lists: alphabetic by title; 1963 — 2nd LP; Reprise/10th

#1228   Young at Heart   *1st recording*
Publication Date: 1953
Music: Johnny Richards — 1939, as "Moonbeams"
Words: Carolyn Leigh
Recorded: 12/9/53-b
Arranger: Nelson Riddle
Conductor/Band: N. Riddle/studio orchestra
Key Release: **This Is Sinatra!** (Volume 1)
see Album Lists: alphabetic by title; 1956 — 6th LP; Capitol/10th

#1229   Young at Heart   *2nd recording*
Publication Date: 1953
Music: Johnny Richards — 1939, as "Moonbeams"
Words: Carolyn Leigh
Recorded: 4/29/63-c
Arranger: Nelson Riddle
Conductor/Band: N. Riddle/studio orchestra
Key Release: **Sinatra's Sinatra**

see Album Lists: alphabetic by title; 1963 — 7th LP; Reprise/15th

#1230   Younger Than Springtime
Publication Date: 1949
Music: Richard Rodgers
Words: Oscar Hammerstein II
Recorded: 9/20/67-a
Arranger: Billy Strange
Conductor/Band: B. Strange/studio orchestra
Key Release: **The Voice: Volume 4** (Italian release only)
see Album Lists: alphabetic by title; 1982 — 4th LP; Reprise/59th

#1231   Your Love for Me
Publication Date: 1956
Music & Words: Brian Parker
Recorded: 12/3/56-a
Arranger: Nelson Riddle
Conductor/Band: N. Riddle/studio orchestra
Key Release: **Forever Frank**
see Album Lists: alphabetic by title; 1966 — 4th LP; Capitol/36th

#1232   You're a Lucky Fellow, Mr. Smith
Publication Date: 1941
Music: Saul Chaplin
Words: Sammy Cahn
Recorded: 1/2/64-a
Arranger: Jack Halloran
Conductor/Band: J. Halloran/studio orchestra
Key Release: **America, I Hear You Singing**
see Album Lists: alphabetic by title; 1964 — 2nd LP; Reprise/18th

#1233   You're a Sweetheart
Publication Date: 1937
Music: Jimmy McHugh
Words: Harold Adamson
Recorded: 1951 — 2nd soundtrack

(illegally taken from film sound)

Arranger: Joseph Gershenson

Conductor/Band: J. Gershenson/ Universal-International Orchestra

Key Release: "Meet Danny Wilson" (LP: Score from "Meet Danny Wilson")

see Album Lists: alphabetic under "soundtrack"; mid–1960s; bootleg Mv. #15

#1234   You're Awful   *duet with Betty Garrett*

Publication Date: 1949

Music: Roger Edens

Words: Betty Comden & Adolph Green

Recorded: 1949 — 2nd soundtrack (illegally taken from film sound)

Arranger: Conrad Salinger

Conductor/Band: Lenny Hayton/ MGM Orchestra

Key Release: "On the Town" (LP: "On the Town" & Others)

see Album Lists: alphabetic under "soundtrack"; mid–1960s; bootleg Mv. #13

#1235   You're Breaking My Heart All Over Again

Publication Date: 1940

Music: Arthur Altman

Words: James Cavanaugh & John Redmond

Recorded: 9/17/40-b

Arranger: Dorsey "house" arrng: T. Dorsey, S. Oliver, F. Stulce, P. Weston

Conductor/Band: Tommy Dorsey & his Orchestra

Key Release: The Dorsey/Sinatra Sessions (Volume 3)

see Album Lists: alphabetic by title; 1972 — 3rd LP; RCA Victor/19th

#1236   You're Cheatin' Yourself (If You're Cheatin' on Me)

Publication Date: 1957

Music: Al Hoffman

Words: Dick Manning

Recorded: 5/20/57-d

Arranger: Nelson Riddle

Conductor/Band: N. Riddle/studio orchestra

Key Release: This Is Sinatra, Volume 2

see Album Lists: alphabetic by title; 1958 — 4th LP; Capitol/18th

#1237   You're Driving Me Crazy!

Publication Date: 1930

Music & Words: Walter Donaldson

Recorded: 5/11/66-c

Arranger: Nelson Riddle

Conductor/Band: N. Riddle/studio orchestra

Key Release: Strangers in the Night

see Album Lists: alphabetic by title; 1966 — 1st LP; Reprise/27th

#1238   You're Getting to Be a Habit with Me

Publication Date: 1932

Music: Harry Warren

Words: Al Dubin

Recorded: 1/10/56-c

Arranger: Nelson Riddle

Conductor/Band: N. Riddle/studio orchestra

Key Release: Songs for Swingin' Lovers!

see Album Lists: alphabetic by title; 1956 — 1st LP; Capitol/7th

#1239   You're Gonna Hear from Me

Publication Date: 1965

Music: Andre Previn

Words: Dory Previn

Recorded: 11/18/66-b

Arranger: Ernie Freeman

Conductor/Band: E. Freeman/studio
  orchestra
Key Release: **That's Life**
see Album Lists: alphabetic by title;
  1966 — 5th LP; Reprise/30th

**#1240 You're Lonely and I'm
  Lonely**
Publication Date: 1939
Music & Words: Irving Berlin
Recorded: 4/23/40-a
Arranger: Dorsey "house" arrng:
  T. Dorsey, S. Oliver, F. Stulce,
  P. Weston
Conductor/Band: Tommy Dorsey &
  his Orchestra
Key Release: **The Dorsey/Sinatra
  Sessions** (Volume 2)
see Album Lists: alphabetic by title;
  1972 — 2nd LP; RCA Victor/18th

#1241 You're My Girl
Publication Date: 1947
Music: Jule Styne
Words: Sammy Cahn
Recorded: 10/19/47-b
Arranger: Axel Stordahl
Conductor/Band: A. Stordahl/studio
  orchestra
Key Release: **The Broadway Kick**
see Album Lists: alphabetic by title;
  1960 — 4th LP; Columbia/29th

**#1242 You're Nobody 'Til
  Somebody Loves You** *1st re-
  cording*
Publication Date: 1944
Music: Russ Morgan & Larry
  Stock
Words: James Cavanaugh
Recorded: 5/23/61-b
Arranger: Billy May
Conductor/Band: Billy May & his
  Orchestra
Key Release: **Sinatra Swings** (origi-
  nal title: "Swing Along with
  Me")

see Album Lists: alphabetic by title;
  1961 — 6th LP; Reprise/2nd

**#1243 You're Nobody 'Til
  Somebody Loves You** *2nd re-
  cording*
Publication Date: 1944
Music: Russ Morgan & Larry
  Stock
Words: James Cavanaugh
Recorded: 1966 television special
Arranger: Billy May
Conductor/Band: B. May/television
  orchestra
Key Release: **Frank Sinatra —
  Through the Years: 1944–1966**
see Album Lists: alphabetic under
  "television"; mid–1960s; Ajazz/
  1st

#1244 You're on Your Own
  sung with cast ensemble
Publication Date: 1943
Music: Jimmy McHugh
Words: Harold Adamson
Recorded: 1943 soundtrack (illegally
  taken from film sound)
Arranger: Axel Stordahl
Conductor/Band: Constantin Baka-
  leinikoff/RKO Orchestra
Key Release: **"Higher and Higher"**
  (LP: Four Sinatra Movies)
see Album Lists: alphabetic under
  "soundtrack"; mid–1960s; boot-
  leg Mv. #4

#1245 You're Sensational *1st
  recording*
Publication Date: 1956
Music & Words: Cole Porter
Recorded: 4/5/56-g
Arranger: Nelson Riddle
Conductor/Band: N. Riddle/studio
  orchestra
Key Release: 45rpm single #3469
see Album List #1: 1956 Capitol (5)
  single record — listed by number

#1246 You're Sensational 2nd recording
Publication Date: 1956
Music & Words: Cole Porter
Recorded: 4/20/56-a
Arranger: Nelson Riddle
Conductor/Band: Johnny Green/ MGM Orchestra
Key Release: **"High Society"** (Official Soundtrack LP)
see Album Lists: alphabetic by title; 1956 — 5th LP; Capitol/9th

#1247 You're So Right (for What's Wrong in My Life)
Publication Date: 1972
Music: Teddy Randazzo & Victoria Pike & Roger Joyce
Words: Victoria Pike & Roger Joyce
Recorded: 8/20/73-a
Arranger: Gordon Jenkins
Conductor/Band: G. Jenkins/studio orchestra
Key Release: **Ol' Blue Eyes Is Back**
see Album Lists: alphabetic by title; 1973 — 2nd LP; Reprise/45th

#1248 You're the One (for Me)
Publication Date: 1940
Music: Jimmy McHugh
Words: Johnny Mercer
Recorded: 1/16/51-b
Arranger: Axel Stordahl
Conductor/Band: A. Stordahl/studio orchestra
Key Release: **The Essential Frank Sinatra** (Volume 3)
see Album Lists: alphabetic by title; 1967 — 4th LP; Columbia/36th

#1249 You're the Top
Publication Date: 1934
Music & Words: Cole Porter
Recorded: 1944 radio — Sinatra's "Vimms Vitamins Show"
Arranger: Axel Stordahl
Conductor/Band: A. Stordahl/radio orchestra
Key Release: **My Best Songs — My Best Years** (Volume 4)
see Album Lists: alphabetic under "radio"; early 1970s; Pentagon/4th

#1250 Yours Is My Heart Alone «Dein Ist Mein Ganzes Herz»
Publication Date: 1931
Music: Franz Lehar — 1929
Words: Harry Bache Smith/Ludwig Herzer & Fritz Lohner — 1929
Recorded: 4/10/40-d
Arranger: Dorsey "house" arrng: T. Dorsey, S. Oliver, F. Stulce, P. Weston
Conductor/Band: Tommy Dorsey & his Orchestra
Key Release: **The Dorsey/Sinatra Sessions** (Volume 2)
see Album Lists: alphabetic by title; 1972 — 2nd LP; RCA Victor/18th

#1251 Zing Went the Strings of My Heart
Publication Date: 1934
Music & Words: James Hanley
Recorded: 12/20/60-e
Arranger: Johnny Mandel
Conductor/Band: J. Mandel/studio orchestra
Key Release: **Love Songs** (illegal; from Reprise masters)
see Album Lists: alphabetic under "bootleg"; early 1970s; bootleg Alb. #3

Catalog of Songs by Date Published

The final catalog in this chapter lists the songs, by date published; within each year, songs listed are in key-number order. Refer to the key number following the song title to locate full information in the Master Song List (including special notes referenced by an asterisk [*]). When a song has been recorded more than once by Sinatra, the title is followed by a sequence number: *All of Me*[1], *All of Me*[2], etc.

In the case of the earliest years (1580 — 1800) the dates are approximations based on the estimates of other researchers. From that point onward, dates are precise. When a publication date was specified, that was the date used; otherwise, they are copyright dates. In any case where sources offered contradictory dates, the earlier year was used. When the recording session took place before the formal publication date, the recording year is listed. In cases where the melody was composed before the lyric was written, the date of the lyric is the one referenced.

1580
The Bells of Christmas «Greensleeves» 78

1600
The First Noel 242

1700
The Twelve Days of Christmas 1086

1787
La Ci Darem la Mano 597

1800
Go Tell It on the Mountain 290
I've Got a Home in That Rock 571
Jesus Is a Rock (in a Weary Land) 582
Let Us Break Bread Together 619

1818
Silent Night «Stille Nacht, Heilige Nacht»[1] 916

Silent Night «Stille Nacht, Heilige Nacht»[2] 917

1841
Adeste Fidelis «O Come, All Ye Faithful»[1] 3
Adeste Fidelis «O Come, All Ye Faithful»[2] 4

1850
It Came upon a Midnight Clear[1] 526
It Came upon a Midnight Clear[2] 527

1855
Hark! The Herald Angels Sing 314

1857
Jingle Bells «In a One Horse Open Sleigh»[1] 583
Jingle Bells «In a One Horse Open Sleigh»[2] 584

1950

Accidents Will Happen 1
Adelaide 2
American Beauty Rose[1] 33
American Beauty Rose[2] 34
Autumn Leaves «Les Feuille Mortes»
60
Azure'te «Paris Blues» 62
Chattanoogie Shoe Shine Boy 120
Cherry Pies Ought to Be You 122
Don'cha Go 'way Mad 181
The End of a Love Affair 219
Faithful 235
Fugue for Tinhorns 271
God's Country 291
Goodnight, Irene 302
Guys and Dolls[1] 308
Guys and Dolls[2] 309
I Am Loved 360
If Only She'd Look My Way 458
I'm Gonna Live Till I Die 498
It's Only Money 561
I've Never Been in Love Before 580
Kisses and Tears 595
Life Is So Peculiar 627
London by Night[1] 640
London by Night[2] 641
London by Night[3] 642
Luck Be a Lady 674
The Oldest Established (Perma-
nent)... 812
One Finger Melody 822
Peach Tree Street 846
Remember Me in Your Dreams 873
Sue Me 989
Take My Love 1010
When the World Was Young 1139
You Don't Remind Me 1209

1951

Castle Rock 114
Farewell, Farewell to Love 238
Hello, Young Lovers[1] 325
Hello, Young Lovers[2] 326
I Have Dreamed 403
I Whistle a Happy Tune 433
I'm a Fool to Want You[1] 492
I'm a Fool to Want You[2] 493
In the Cool, Cool, Cool of the Eve-
ning 513
Lean Baby* 611

Mama Will Bark 681
Walking in the Sunshine 1099
We Kiss in a Shadow 1108

1952

Bim Bam Baby 85
Don't Ever Be Afraid to Go Home 187
Luna Rossa «Blushing Moon» 676
Somewhere Along the Way 946
Tennessee Newsboy «The Newsboy
Blues» 1023
That's All 1031
Why Try to Change Me Now?[1]* 1169
Why Try to Change Me Now?[2] 1170

1953

Anytime—Anywhere 43
Baubles, Bangles and Beads[1] 70
Baubles, Bangles and Beads[2] 71
C'est Magnifique 116
Don't Make a Beggar of Me 192
Ebb Tide 210
From Here to Eternity 265
Half as Lovely (Twice as True) 312
Here's That Rainy Day 329
I Can Read Between the Lines 366
I Could Have Told You 375
I Love Paris[1] 412
I Love Paris[2] 413
I'm Walking Behind You 506
It's All Right with Me[1] 548
It's All Right with Me[2] 549
It's All Right with Me[3] 550
Montmart' *ends overture* 709
My One and Only Love 747
An Old Fashioned Christmas 806
Rain (Falling from the Skies) 868
Secret Love 891
Teach Me Tonight 1016
Young at Heart[1] 1228
Young at Heart[2] 1229

1954

All of You 17
The Christmas Waltz[1] 126
The Christmas Waltz[2] 127
The Christmas Waltz[3] 128
Don't Change Your Mind About Me
184
Fly Me to the Moon «In Other
Words»[1] 247

Chapter 4: The Composers

Now we come to the people who wrote the music. Sinatra recorded songs by famous composers and by those who were soon forgotten, by prolific craftsmen and by the composers of one or two great melodies. Nearly 400 of these recorded songs were written before Sinatra began cutting records in 1939. Many were songs that he grew up hearing. They had survived for decades, a few for centuries. This music and its evolution had shaped Sinatra's ideas of melody and of the musical possibilities of singing. Once he was a recording star, he could pick and choose among the successful composers of the '40s. As regional music and rock began to push Tin Pan Alley into the past, Sinatra cultivated his own cluster of songwriters to preserve the styles and standards of earlier days in pop music. By the mid–1960s, when even these stalwarts were becoming anachronisms, the singer struggled to come to terms with contemporary composers whose work ranged from art-rock and soft-rock to soul and rhythm-and-blues. He even tried a few songwriters with country roots. Songs from modern stage and films were another source that lasted.

What these composers had in common — once Sinatra had recorded their work — was representation by a fellow artist who took their art seriously. With the exception of a few tunes pressed on Sinatra for commercial purposes, he sang the songs because he liked them, admired them, and was inspired to express something of himself through them. He favored songwriters who had a story to tell.

Out of the hundreds of composers represented in this compilation, I will profile one dozen, those who have 12 or more songs recorded by Frank Sinatra. I will also touch briefly on another 20 composers who are included because their songs were of special importance in Sinatra's career, or because their work maintained an especially high level of quality.

242

The 12 composers represented by 12 or more songs are quantitatively ranked as follows:

Rank	Name	Songs	Recordings
1	Jimmy Van Heusen	76	95
2	Richard Rodgers	44	63
3	Jule Styne	38	48
4	Cole Porter	33	49
5	Irving Berlin	24	34
6	Harold Arlen	19	30
7	Jimmy McHugh	19	23
8	Antonio Carlos Jobim	17	17
9	Jerome Kern	14	20
10	George Gershwin	13	21
11	Harry Warren	12	13
12	Gordon Jenkins	12	13
Totals		321	426

I will now profile these 12 composers, both as individuals and in relation to Sinatra's recording their work. Generally, the most space will be devoted to those with more than 20 songs recorded by Sinatra; this is without regard to their critical or popular acclaim, or to their place as an influence in musical history. Styne and Van Heusen will get somewhat less coverage, since their writing partners are dealt with extensively in Chapter 5.

James (Jimmy) Van Heusen (1913–1990)
Composer, Music Publisher, Pianist—ASCAP member: 1938

Christened as Edward Chester Babcock, this prolific composer of popular songs attended Cazenovia Seminary and then had formal training in music at Syracuse University, studying with Howard Lyman Colburn. At age 16, he was an announcer at a Syracuse radio station, later performing early compositions on his own radio program.

When he was 20, Van Heusen moved to New York City and found work as a songwriter at Harlem's famous Cotton Club, and as a piano player with various Tin Pan Alley publishing houses.

After a few years, he contracted with Remick Music as a songwriter. Early collaborators included lyricists Johnny Burke, Eddie DeLange and Johnny Mercer. Some notable songs from this period were *Deep in a Dream, All This and Heaven Too* and *I Thought About You.* He wrote scores for Broadway shows like *Swingin' the Dream* and *Nellie Bly,* as well as songs for "Billy Rose's New Aquacade," presented at the 1940 New York World's Fair. There was also some work with Johnny Burke on songs for the Tommy Dorsey band.

Van Heusen moved to Hollywood in 1940, and was signed by Paramount Studios to write film scores; during the war years, he also served as a test pilot for Lockheed Aircraft. In Hollywood, he resumed contact with Johnny Burke and began his first major partnership. The team hitched up with Bing Crosby. They worked on films like *Love Thy Neighbor, Going My Way, A Connecticut Yankee in King Arthur's Court* and *Riding High.* Top songs with Johnny Burke included *Imagination, Polka Dots and Moonbeams, It's Always You, It Could Happen to You, Swinging on a Star* (the 1944 Oscar winner), *But Beautiful* and *Here's That Rainy Day.*

In his long association with Bing Crosby in radio and movies, Van Heusen composed songs for six of the Crosby/Hope "Road" pictures. With comedian Phil Silvers, he wrote a tune commemorating the birth of Frank Sinatra's first child, *Nancy (with the Laughing Face).* Van Heusen also continued with his occasional musicals for the stage.

He and Burke formed a music publishing enterprise in the '50s, but their songwriting teamwork ended in the middle of the decade; for more on that collaboration, see the Johnny Burke profile in Chapter 5.

At the urging of his pal, Frank Sinatra, James Van Heusen began to work with Sammy Cahn — another old pro without a current partner — and the composer's second and last major collaboration began. It endured for 14 years and produced dozens of songs. As with Burke, many songs were written for use in movies, but now with the decline in film musicals, the songs were seldom full scores; instead the team provided incidental tunes and title songs like *Indiscreet, Pocketful of Miracles,* and *Come Blow Your Horn.* They also wrote full scores for Broadway shows — *Skyscraper* (1965), *Walking Happy* (1966) — and did special nightclub and television material for various singers. Chiefly, the pair wrote fine songs in the now-retrograde realm of pop music, some debuting in films and others going straight to the record store. A few examples are *All My Tomorrows, Nothing in Common, To Love and*

Be Loved, The Second Time Around, (I've Seen) The Look of Love and *Call Me Irresponsible.*

Frank Sinatra initially used their work for TV productions (*Our Town, Love and Marriage, Spend an Afternoon with Me*) and later for film songs (*The Tender Trap, All the Way, High Hopes*), including a full score for his *Robin and the 7 Hoods (Mr. Booze, My Kind of Town, Style)*. But more importantly, they wrote songs specifically to enunciate the themes of several Capitol and Reprise concept albums; noteworthy examples are *Come Fly with Me, Only the Lonely, Come Dance with Me, When No One Cares, Ring-a-Ding Ding,* and *The September of My Years.* As close friends and long-time colleagues of Sinatra, both Van Heusen and Cahn could personalize and focus these pieces, knowing the singer's greatest strengths as an artist and as an emotional being.

After his work with Sammy Cahn ended in 1969, when he was 56 years old, Jimmy Van Heusen's massive production slowed down. He worked again in 1973 with the great Johnny Mercer, one of his earliest partners in songwriting. He died at age 67.

Van Heusen was awarded many honors during his long and consistently prosperous career, from his songwriting peers and from the worlds of pop music, motion pictures and television. In addition to the collaborators mentioned above, his music had lyrics by Carl Sigman, Arthur Williams, Mack Gordon, Buddy Kaye, Dak Stanford, Lillian Small and Bobby Worth.

Notable songs never recorded by Sinatra include *It's the Dreamer in Me, So Help Me, Birds of a Feather, Road to Morocco, Going My Way, The Day After Forever, Once and for Always,* and *Where Love Has Gone.*

Richard Rodgers (1902–1979)
Composer, Lyricist, Librettist, Theater Producer — ASCAP member: 1926

One of the most versatile and productive of the great song composers, Richard Charles Rodgers' education was spread among ten formal institutions, including Columbia University, the Julliard School of Music, and the New England Conservatory of Music. But years before he entered Columbia University, Rodgers was writing songs. At age 14, he wrote music and lyrics for his first tune, *Campfire Days,* and later that same year, he composed *Auto Show Girl* with a lyric by David Dyrenforth; this was locally distributed as Rodgers' first copyrighted song. A number of tunes followed—most written for publicly presented social club revues—with Rodgers' own lyrics or with the aid of his brother's words. His father financed the publication of some of these pieces. Then two years before starting at Columbia, he was introduced to Lorenz Hart, and their collaboration began at once. Their first published piece was 1919's *Any Old Place with You,* a novel and attractive song with comical and very attention-getting lyrics.

One key to Sinatra's numerous recordings of Rodgers' songs is undoubtedly the powerful cohesion of melody and words. In the earlier days of American musical theater, composers like Victor Herbert and Sigmund Romberg far outshown the lyricists whose relatively light and pallid words accompanied their songs. With the emphasis on semioperatic vocal production, the words became little more than sounds to hang notes on, and the shows' stories required little advancement by lyrics. Later, with the work of composers like Jerome Kern and Vincent Youmans (until the mid–1920s) the lyrics were stronger, but still overshadowed by melody. Even Ira Gershwin's deft lyrics were taken for granted when wrapped in his charismatic brother's music. Something about Richard Rodgers' nature and training created a new era for lyrics in theater music. In working with Hart there was a synergy, a spirit of compromise, a subordination of each man's ego to the song's own demands, that fused the words and music into a unit seemingly created as a whole, as if by one man. This generated the first "co-billed" song team in American theater. It led to an increase in drama and story-coherence in songs and groups of songs, and eventually reformed the musical comedy revue into a unified musical play. No wonder Frank Sinatra—a singer who acted out the drama of songs—was drawn to the work of Richard Rodgers.

Rodgers and Hart wrote the score for *Fly with Me,* and had it accepted for Columbia's annual Varsity Show. Oscar Hammerstein II was a member of the Varsity Show committee and collaborated with Rodgers on one tune, an augury of things to come. Some of the songs in this production were chosen by producer Lew Fields for his new show, *Poor Little Ritz Girl,* and he commissioned 12 new songs by the pair for the same production. He later replaced some of the Rodgers and Hart numbers with songs by Sigmund Romberg. When New York critics singled out the Rodgers/Hart tunes over Romberg's, the team was truly launched.

Between 1925 and 1943, Rodgers and Hart wrote scores for 24 Broadway musicals. Among the most successful, each with over 300 performances, were *The Girl Friend, A Connecticut Yankee, Peggy-Ann, On Your Toes, I Married an Angel, Pal Joey* and *By Jupiter.* Most of the other productions were very successful by normal standards of the time, both with critics and the public. Through the years, their shows tended toward a more self-contained story with which the songs interacted. The peak in this trend was *Pal Joey,* where most of the songs directly advanced the story; when this show was revived in 1952, it won the New York Drama Critics Award, having proved to be the harbinger of a new era in musical theater. Rodgers' increasing involvement and control resulted in his acting as co-librettist for *On Your Toes* and *By Jupiter.* For the latter show, he was also co-producer.

Rodgers and Hart songs which have had a life outside their shows are numerous. A few top examples are *Mountain Greenery, My Heart Stood Still, Thou Swell, Dancing on the Ceiling, Lover, Blue Moon, Little Girl Blue, There's a Small Hotel, Where or When, My Funny Valentine, The Lady Is a Tramp, Spring Is Here, I Didn't Know What Time It Was, It Never Entered My Mind* and *Bewitched (Bothered and Bewildered).* Sinatra recorded all but two of these, as well as 14 others, most of them years after they were written.

The combination of Hart's mental, witty, sharp-edged lyrics with Rodgers' warm, beautiful melodies had a very special effect, almost the flip-side of the collaboration of the Gershwin brothers, yet by 1942 the team was almost through. Hart had always been unpredictable, given to dark moods and disappearances. Now his vanishing acts lasted weeks and became more frequent. Rodgers—who worked without Hart as co-producer on other songwriter's shows—felt his partner couldn't go on for long. He discussed joining forces with old friend Oscar Hammerstein when that time should come. When Rodgers was offered the play which would be converted into *Oklahoma,* Hart didn't want to do it and suggested another lyricist be used; he didn't feel well and found the property was too offbeat for a musical. Rodgers began work on *Oklahoma* with Hammerstein. The show was a great success in early '43. On opening night of the revised version of Rodgers and Hart's *A Connecticut Yankee* (November 17, 1943), Hart disappeared again. He was found unconscious in a hotel room and died of pneumonia on November 22 at the age of 48.

Despite this painful transition, Rodgers' pairing with Hammerstein was immediately successful. When Oscar presented him with the first completed lyric for *Oklahoma* — *Oh, What a Beautiful Mornin'* — Rodgers was inspired to a new degree of melodic story-telling. The show broke many conventions of musical theater, was the first fulsome story musical. It's huge success on Broadway (2,248 performances) crowned both the revolution and the beginning of Rodgers' second great collaboration.

Rodgers and Hammerstein's biggest triumphs after *Oklahoma* were *Carousel, South Pacific, The King and I* and *The Sound of Music.* The creative richness of the songs in these shows gave many of them independent life in nightclubs, on the radio and in recordings.

If the Rodgers/Hart team could be called sweet/sour, then the Rodgers/Hammerstein pairing would be termed sweet/sweet. What was lost in a contrast of tones was gained in a unity of purpose, and Oscar Hammerstein's technical brilliance generally undercut the dangers of too much sweetness. Often-recorded songs by these men include *People Will Say We're in Love, It Might as Well Be Spring, If I Loved You, Soliloquy, You'll Never Walk Alone, Some Enchanted Evening, A Wonderful Guy, Younger Than Springtime, Hello, Young Lovers; Love, Look Away* and *My Favorite Things.* Sinatra recorded eight of these songs, often when they were brand-new, and ten other Rodgers and Hammerstein pieces.

When Hammerstein died, at the age of 65, on August 23, 1960, Richard Rodgers was only 58. Having outlived his two great partnerships, Rodgers went on to compose and produce for the stage for another decade, reviving other writer's shows in New York and London, and creating new works such as *No Strings, Do I Hear a Waltz?* and *Two by Two.* He wrote his own lyrics for some songs and collaborated with Stephen Sondheim, Sheldon Harnick and Martin Charnin on others.

In addition to Rodgers' prodigious career in the theater, he wrote original movie musicals with both Hart and Hammerstein, produced other composer's shows like Irving Berlin's *Annie Get Your Gun,* and composed scores for original television productions. He received many high honors and positions, and served as a director of the American Society of Composers, Authors, and Publishers (ASCAP) from 1941 to 1947, and again from 1960 to 1974.

Jule Styne (born 1905)
Composer, Music Publisher, Theater Producer — ASCAP member: 1931

Born in London as Julius Kerwin Stein and moving to the United States when he was eight years old, Jule Styne was something of a musical prodigy. At age three he sang a duet on stage with Harry Lauder. His early accomplishments as a pianist were such that he was a guest soloist with the Chicago and Detroit Symphonies at age nine, and four years later he won a scholarship to the Chicago College of Music, studying piano and composition. Graduated with distinction, he continued study at Northwestern University.

Despite his classical training, Styne was intrigued by the music of Tin Pan Alley and Broadway. He worked with three professional songwriters in 1926 to complete *Sunday,* a tune that did well and has lasted for decades. That was a taste of what he loved, and Styne abandoned plans for a concert career to play piano with a dance band. In 1931, he formed his own orchestra to play hotels and nightclubs; Styne conducted, played piano, wrote arrangements, and even composed some songs for his group. It was the songwriting that came to mean most to the young man. He disbanded the orchestra and moved to Hollywood, having contracted with Twentieth Century–Fox as both a composer and vocal coach.

Success came with writing for the movies. Jule Styne's first personal hit song, with lyrics by Frank Loesser, was *I Don't Want to Walk Without You* from the 1942 film *Sweater Girl.* That same year he teamed up with Sammy Cahn; they remained collaborators for more than a decade. One of their early efforts was *I've Heard That Song Before,* which was used in the film *Youth on Parade,* sung by the hot new vocalist Frank Sinatra. Sinatra was a pal of Sammy Cahn from their days together with the Dorsey organization. When Sinatra signed to make *Step Lively* for RKO, he supported the Styne/Cahn duo as writers of the 1943 score, which included *As Long as There's Music* and the beautifully unusual *Some Other Time.* A year later, when MGM was planning their big-budget *Anchors Aweigh,* they naturally wanted to use top-name songwriters. Sinatra pushed for Styne and Cahn; his clout prevailed and the team got their first major credit, along with critical praise for songs like *What Makes the Sun Set?* and the Oscar-nominated *I Fall in Love Too Easily.*

Styne liked the good life and money in Hollywood, but longed for the greater creative control and respect of Broadway. He and Cahn got their first chance on a stage musical with *Glad to See You*. Despite fine songs, including *Guess I'll Hang My Tears Out to Dry*, the show folded after a Boston tryout.

Back in Hollywood, the team prospered, writing direct pop hits like *Saturday Night (Is the Loneliest Night of the Week)* and scoring more films; one hit movie was 1947's *It Happened in Brooklyn*, with Sinatra, Durante, and Kathryn Grayson.

That same year, another chance on Broadway came with *High Button Shoes*. This time Styne and Cahn achieved a long-running show, but Sammy Cahn found that he preferred Hollywood. From that point onward, Styne collaborated with other lyricists for stage shows, while continuing with Cahn on pop and film work until the mid–1950s; for more on this partnership, see the Sammy Cahn profile in Chapter 5.

Jule Styne alternated between stage and screen writing for many years, but progressively tipped more toward the stage. While his screen credits became less notable, his stage work spiraled upward, with shows like *Gentlemen Prefer Blondes* (lyrics: Leo Robin), *Bells Are Ringing, Do Re Mi, Fade Out — Fade In* and *Lorelei* (all with lyrics by Betty Comden and Adolph Green), *Gypsy* (a score — with lyrics by Stephen Sondheim — which some consider Styne's masterpiece), and 1964's *Funny Girl* (lyrics: Bob Merrill).

In addition to composing for films and theater, Styne worked as a producer of stage dramas and musicals such as *Will Success Spoil Rock Hunter?* and *Mr. Wonderful*. He composed songs and music for children's television specials. Styne also has music publishing interests.

Some of Jule Styne's most famous songs are *Let It Snow (Let It Snow, Let It Snow)*, *Five Minutes More*, *It's the Same Old Dream*, *Time After Time*, *Diamonds Are a Girl's Best Friend*, *Three Coins in the Fountain* (the 1954 Oscar winner), *Just in Time*, *The Party's Over*, *Small World*, *Everything's Coming Up Roses*, *Together*, *Make Someone Happy*, *People* and *Don't Rain on My Parade*. Collaborators not previously mentioned include Bob Hilliard, Walter Bishop, and his son Stanley.

Although Frank Sinatra recorded none of the show tunes Jule Styne composed during the '60s and '70s, he did record two of Styne's 1980 songs written with Susan Birkenhead, *It's Sunday* and *Hey Look, No Crying;* these fine performances were among the last Sinatra committed to record.

Cole Porter (1891–1964)
Composer, Lyricist — ASCAP member: 1931

Cole Albert Porter was born in the American midwest, on the 750-acre Indiana farm of his affluent parents. Despite their bucolic locale, his family had sophistication as well as money. In this cultured family, young Cole's musical interest was encouraged, and by the time he was ten, he had written two songs, one of which — *The Bobolink Waltz* — his mother had published by a Chicago firm. That was all very well for childish fun, but the boy had a rich maternal grandfather who wanted his namesake and future heir to be a lawyer. Rich grandfather J. O. Cole was the family financial fountain, so everyone agreed the young man would be a lawyer. He was sent to Worcester Academy in Massachusetts. That preparation was followed by undergraduate work at Yale and then Harvard Law School. Surely these environments would get Cole's mind off a frivolity like music.

Not so. At 17, Remick Music published the song *Bridget* without parental subsidy. At Yale, Porter wrote the *Yale Bulldog Song* and *Bingo Eli Yale,* which remain in use today. By the time he had spent some months at Harvard Law School, it was evident to everyone that his heart and application of ability weren't in the law. Even his financially supportive grandfather accepted his transfer to the Harvard School of Music. He later furthered his studies with Vincent d'Indy in Paris.

At Harvard, Porter collaborated with a student writer and lyricist named T. Lawrason Riggs to create *See America First.* They found production backing for the show within moneyed circles and it opened in New York in March of 1916. It lasted only 15 performances.

Discouraged and seeking adventure, the 27-year-old Porter joined the French Foreign Legion. He continued writing songs, entertaining Legion troops in North Africa. When the U.S. entered the First World War, Porter was transferred to a French artillery school. To his love of music was added the love of travel, in general, and particularly a love of Paris.

He had an allowance from his grandfather, so there was no need to work when his military time ended. He supplemented his allowance by writing both music and words to songs for New York musical revues, including his first hit, *An Old-Fashioned Garden.* Porter returned to Paris, married, and enjoyed a life of relative leisure and the continued study of harmony and counterpoint.

In 1923, old Mr. Cole died and Porter was a millionaire. From that point until the end of the '20s, Porter's life was a mixture of international society, travel, parties and — always — songwriting. Back in the U.S. after 1928, he became more intent on his musical career. Having previously worked with lyrics by Irving Caesar and Murray Anderson, now Porter wrote show after show of totally Porter songs: *Fifty Million Frenchmen, Gay Divorcee, Anything Goes, Jubilee; Red, Hot and Blue; Du Barry Was a Lady* and four other productions established his reputation in the 1930s. Lush melodies and witty lyrics, both infused with sophisticated craft, were Porter's developing hallmark. He was an original, celebrating his own view of America and the world. Songs of this period which became "standards" included *Let's Do It, You Do Something to Me, What Is This Thing Called Love?, Love for Sale, Night and Day, I Get a Kick Out of You, You're the Top, Anything Goes, Begin the Beguine, Just One of Those Things, Ridin' High, Easy to Love, I've Got You Under My Skin, In the Still of the Night, At Long Last Love* (with rare lyrical assistance by Robert Katscher) and *My Heart Belongs to Daddy.*

Cole Porter songs had also been used in movies, some written directly for the screen, many lifted from stage productions. His first movie involvement had been the early sound musical, 1929's *Battle of Paris* from Paramount. During his hot period in the '30s, Porter songs appeared in a trio of well-received MGM pictures: *Born to Dance, Rosalie,* and one of a series of "Broadway Melody" films, this one starring Fred Astaire.

During the 1940s and '50s, Porter's career had its ups and downs. Some attributed his popular and critical difficulties to his songs being locked into the spirit of the 1920s. Others decided his problem was constant pain; Porter had been in a grave accident in 1937, both his legs and nervous system being shattered in a horse-riding accident. Certainly a life of multiple operations (31, with one leg finally amputated in 1958) and continuing pain would have its effect. And Porter's style did remain fairly constant from the '20s. But perhaps he was mostly a victim of cycles in taste and fashion. His first four Broadway shows of the '40s had runs between 400 and 500 performances, excellent by earlier standards, but not so great compared to the new standard of longevity set by Rodgers and Hammerstein. The more dramatic libretto's of the new musicals also contrasted with the revue-like nature of Porter's shows, and in the mid–1940s he had two relative flops in a row. In 1940s movies, Porter worked with three productions starring the likes of Fred Astaire and Gene Kelly, and including such fine new songs as *Since I Kissed My Baby Goodbye* and *You'd Be So Nice to Come Home To.*

When Irving Berlin did *Annie Get Your Gun* — a new-style integrated musical — at the age of 57, Cole Porter was inspired to write the score which was his own Broadway masterpiece, *Kiss Me Kate.* This 1948 production met the new standards and even surpassed them in some areas of craft, achieving a run of over a thousand performances. Its songs comprised contemporary moods like *Why Can't You Behave?*, *So in Love, Too Darn Hot,* and a number of songs with tones derived from Shakespeare.

His three final Broadway shows, written in the 1950s, maintained his reputation. *Out of This World, Can-Can* and *Silk Stockings* contained such tunes as *I Am Loved, From This Moment On* (which was dropped before opening), *It's All Right with Me, I Love Paris* and *All of You.* Porter also wrote largely original scores for two successful MGM films of the '50s, *High Society* (with Crosby, Sinatra, and Louis Armstrong) and *Les Girls* (with Gene Kelly).

In addition to all this work over the years, Porter had done one original TV musical, *Aladdin,* and the ballet *Within the Quota.* He was 73 when he died in California in 1964.

Considering Frank Sinatra's concentration on storytelling and drama in songs, it's no surprise that he greatly admired the work of Cole Porter, with it's unity of style and sophisticated point of view. The fusion of intent when one man writes both music and words was fully evident in Porter's classic creations. Toward the end of his life, Porter objected to some of the changes Sinatra made in performing his songs over and over, bringing them from the '20s spirit into the '60s, but even these tonal changes merely underscored the songs' durability.

Irving Berlin (1888-1989)
Composer, Lyricist, Publisher, Singer — ASCAP Charter Member: 1914

He was born in a Russian village at a time of growing anti-semitism and danger, an eighth child, named Israel Baline by his devout mother and cantor father. When he was only four, the family fled cossack terror and managed to reach the United States, where they settled into one of the impoverished immigrant communities of the

Lower East Side of Manhattan. His father died when the boy was eight. He stopped attending school and left home at 14, to ease his mother's financial strain. The year was 1902, and young Israel Baline was on his own.

Irving Berlin's career as a writer of songs was so long and diverse that it is hard now to keep its elements in perspective. Viewed by some today as a relic of a pop mainstream, Berlin was in fact a pioneer, an *avant-garde* innovator. Praised for his "native simplicity," he was the author of many subtle, complex, and experimental works. Unable to read or write music, he was instrumental in laying the foundations of American popular music, turning common expressions into truthful poetry, and straightforward melodies into profound statements. He wrote songs for over three-fourths of his 101 years. Through all that time, Irving Berlin managed to fuse a deep insecurity — born of rough-hewn beginnings and a lack of formal education — with the confident action of genius. That fusion produced songs that struck sympathetic chords with the masses at the same time they stimulated the musical elite. He did this as a writer of popular music, as a theater composer, and as a songwriter for the movies. These three careers overlapped, running parallel for many years, and Berlin was immensely successful in all three modes.

His earliest musical career was singing and writing songs for the mass audience. After he left home at 14, the boy made his meager living by singing popular ballads in Bowery saloons. He had been trained in the music of the Jewish faith by his late father. Now his secular singing naturally carried the mournful emotions of current ballads. He received enough pennies to live.

In one of these saloons was a serviceable upright piano. Berlin taught himself to play a little; self-teaching was to be his sole mode of education in music from then on. Experience and inspiration were his masters. He toured briefly in the chorus of a musical show, then got a job as a song-plugger/theater-shill for songwriter Harry Von Tilzer's publishing business. Next he was a singing waiter at a Chinatown cafe. It was here that his course was set. Two waiters at a rival establishment had just published a song. Berlin's competitive employer wanted to match that, so he had his piano player, Nick Nicholson, write a tune. When Berlin sang, he had often improvised comic words to popular ditties, so he was asked to set words to Nicholson's melody. The result was Berlin's first published song, *Marie from Sunny Italy,* for which he earned 37 cents royalties. It was for publication credit on this song that Israel Baline first adopted the name of Irving Berlin.

Berlin began writing songs alone, experimenting with his own melodies. One lyric, *Dorando,* was commissioned by a vaudeville performer who never came for the work. Not wanting the lyric to go to waste, Berlin took it to composer/publisher Ted Snyder, who offered $25 for the lyric and it's nonexistent melody. Berlin improvised a melody — by voice — while Snyder's arranger wrote it down. The song sold, even had some success, and Irving Berlin was on his way.

Soon Snyder hired him. He was now a salaried staff lyricist in Tin Pan Alley. Berlin worked like a demon, producing both words and music all day and night. He had enough hits so that Snyder made him a partner.

By 1911, he had published more than 50 songs. His advent into theater came then, but his "pop" career continued, flooding the world with sheet music, nightclub exposure, radio performances, phonograph records and — later — use of his songs on live and filmed television. Berlin's songs from Tin Pan Alley are well represented by *Everybody's Doin' It, That International Rag, When I Lost You* (Berlin's first ballad, inspired by his young bride's death six months after their wedding), *You'd Be Surprised, All Alone, What'll I Do?, Always, Remember, Blue Skies, The Song Is Ended, Marie* and *How Deep Is the Ocean?*

More than a third of Sinatra's recordings of Berlin songs (13 of 34) come from his "pop" work, most of them written in the '20s.

The second of Berlin's careers was writing songs for the stage. In 1911 — already a successful songwriter and publisher — Berlin was to appear as a performer in the Friars Club's first annual musical revue. Also appearing was George M. Cohan. Berlin idolized Cohan, and therefore wanted to produce something very special for the show. He combined a modified lyric from an earlier song with an instrumental piece he'd done, and he created *Alexander's Ragtime Band.* It was enthusiastically received at the Friars' revue, then rejected by a New York vaudeville house, then played in a burlesque show. Later, in Chicago, the song became a vaudeville success whose popularity spread until *Alexander's Ragtime Band* became Berlin's first big national hit and his stage career was under way. Also in 1911, he contributed songs to the Ziegeld Follies, and other material began to appear in various musical comedies and revues.

In 1914, Berlin was commissioned to compose his first full theater score, *Watch Your Step,* starring Vernon and Irene Castle. This show was a success by the standards of the time, and during the next decade Irving Berlin had a production on Broadway every year, including three more Ziegfeld Follies, four Music Box Revues, a Marx Brothers' vehicle, *The Cocoanuts,* and the military musical *Yip, Yip, Yaphank,* for which Berlin wrote *God Bless America.* (Berlin removed this song from the score before opening, deciding it was too heavy for a light revue; it remained unpublished for 20 years.) These productions benefited from performers like Fannie Brice, Leon Errol, Eddie Cantor, W. C. Fields, Robert Benchley, and Ruth Etting. Berlin wrote all the songs for the majority of these shows. In some cases, songs by others such as Victor Herbert and George M. Cohan were also used. The principal Berlin songs from these 14 shows included *Woodman, Woodman, Spare That Tree; Play a Simple Melody, The Girl on the Magazine Cover, I Love a Piano; Oh, How I Hate to Get Up in the Morning; A Pretty Girl Is Like a Melody, Say It with Music* and *Shaking the Blues Away.*

After 1927, Berlin's movie work reduced the volume of his stage output, but he still produced the scores for eight more musicals, chief among which were 1946's *Annie Get Your Gun* and 1950's *Call Me Madame,* both starring Ethel Merman, an ideal voice and energy for Berlin. Songs from these later musicals include *Let's Have Another Cup of Coffee, Easter Parade* (a new lyric for an earlier tune, *Smile and Show Your Dimple), Heat Wave, Supper Time, You're Lonely and I'm Lonely, Let's Take an Old-Fashioned Walk, The Hostess with the Mostes' on the Ball, It's a Lovely Day Today/You're Just in Love* and, from Berlin's masterpiece about Annie Oakley, *Doin' What Comes Natur'lly, The Girl That I Marry, There's No Business Like Show Business, They Say It's Wonderful, I Got the Sun in the Morning* and *Anything You Can Do.*

Berlin's stage writing was often less appropriate for Frank Sinatra's attitude and technique. Only seven of Sinatra's 34 Berlin recordings are from his theater productions.

The latest to start of Berlin's three careers was composing for the movies. Obviously, this was because the first true sound films — with synchronized music and effects — didn't begin until 1926. By 1928, the famous songwriter had begun his involvement with the medium, his music being used in the now-obscure *The Awakening.* The following year, MGM brought the Marx Brothers to the screen in *The Cocoanuts,* along with Berlin songs from the stage version, including *When My Dreams Come True.* In 1929, MGM commissioned Berlin's first new song expressly written for a film; this was *Waiting at the End of the Road,* the only new song among the blues and spirituals sung in King Vidor's all-black *Hallelujah.*

For the next 20 years, Irving Berlin devoted more time to film music than to either theater or direct "pop" songs. The 15 movies using his songs in this period were all original productions, except for adaptations of his stage shows *Louisiana Purchase* and *This Is the Army.* The songs were a mixture of Berlin standards and new material. Prominent among these films were *Mammy, Top Hat, Follow the Fleet, On the Avenue, Holiday Inn, Blue Skies* and *Easter Parade.* Stars of the 15 films included Harry Richman, Al Jolson, Bing Crosby, Eddie Cantor, Ethel Merman, Rudy Vallee, Bob Hope, Fred Astaire and Ginger Rogers. Among the new tunes written for movies, the most famous are *Let Me Sing and I'm Happy, Cheek to Cheek; Top Hat, White Tie and Tails; Let's Face the Music and Dance, I've Got My Love to Keep Me Warm, Change Partners, White Christmas; Be Careful, It's My Heart; It Only Happens When I Dance with You, Steppin' Out with My Baby* and two versions of the great *Puttin' on the Ritz,* one with Harlem-oriented lyrics for the 1930 film of the same name, the second version with lyrics written for Fred Astaire in 1946's *Blue Skies.*

During the 1950s, Berlin was involved with five more films. His late stage successes, *Annie Get Your Gun* and *Call Me Madame,* were brought to the screen. Two other film productions celebrated Berlin's earlier songs and added a few new ones like *Count Your Blessings Instead of Sheep.* Finally, Berlin wrote the theme song for 1957's *Sayonara.*

Sinatra recorded more of Berlin's original movie songs than the other two categories (14 out of 34 recordings); most of these were initially sung by Fred Astaire, and Sinatra's records are fascinating to compare with Astaire's delicate renderings.

Irving Berlin wrote more than 1,500 songs. As a mosaic, they demonstrate the man's root-toughness, his blend of simplicity and innovating creation, his unique weave of humor, irony, rhythm, honor and love. A man of modest public demeanor, Berlin clearly yearned to be taken seriously, and would respond to such treatment in kind. In 1962, Sinatra recorded an album of classic songs about lost love. Named for a succinct Berlin ballad, the album was titled *All Alone.* Half of the songs are by Irving Berlin, and the treatment by Gordon Jenkins and Sinatra is deeply respectful. Responding to the album,

Berlin said he was delighted with the wonderful way Sinatra did the old songs, that he hadn't heard them sung as well in many years.

Harold Arlen (1905–1986)
Composer, Lyricist, Pianist, Arranger, Singer —
ASCAP member: 1930

There are points of comparison between the careers of Harold Arlen and Irving Berlin. Both had fathers who were cantors, learned their earliest music in singing the songs of their faith, and had success writing songs for the pop world, the theater and the movies. Also, both were influenced by the regional musics abounding in the United States.

There are also contrasts separating the two men. Arlen had formal training in music with Arnold Cornelissen and Simon Bucharoff. He was an accomplished pianist, playing professionally by age 15. Berlin's start in grinding poverty led to a predilection for ragtime and an ebullient sound. Arlen's more comfortable youth left him with a taste for the blues.

Born Chaim Arluk, which was shifted to Hyman Arluck and later fully anglicized, Harold Arlen went from solo piano jobs to forming The Snappy Trio, later called the Southbound Shufflers. They played in nightclubs and anywhere else they could. Next came stints as a singer, pianist and arranger with various dance bands.

By the late 1920s, Arlen was playing in a pit orchestra on Broadway and touring Loew's vaudeville circuit. He wanted to be a singer. Instead, his affiliation with stage musical revues led to his teaming with lyricist Ted Koehler to write songs. Their first published effort was 1930's *Get Happy,* introduced by Ruth Etting in the *9:15 Revue.* They contributed songs to the 1930 edition of the *Earl Carroll Vanities* which had success. These accomplishments confirmed the collaboration, and Arlen and Koehler worked together on and off for several years.

The other songwriting team for the '30s Vanities had been composer Jay Gorney and lyricist E. Y. ("Yip") Harburg. After Arlen wrote his first full Broadway score, *You Said It,* with Jack Yellen in 1931, he teamed with Harburg and Ira Gershwin for his second, *Life Begins at 8:40.* Arlen's collaboration with Harburg would continue for decades, producing songs both for theater and movies.

Arlen's film work began in 1934 with *Let's Fall in Love.* From that point onward, he alternated stage, film, and pop writing, working variously with other fine lyricists such as Billy Rose, Leo Robin, Ralph Blane, Lew Brown, Dorothy Fields, and Dory Previn. Arlen wrote one stage show with Truman Capote and worked several times — stage and screen — with the great Johnny Mercer.

His most prominent stage scores were for *Bloomer Girl, St. Louis Woman* and *Jamaica*. Film work included *The Wizard of Oz, Blues in the Night, Cabin in the Sky, Kismet,* and the Judy Garland version of *A Star Is Born.* Harold Arlen also composed a blues opera, *Free and Easy,* and instrumental works like *Americanegro Suite* and *Mood in Six Minutes;* these latter, like many of his songs, drew deeply from southern black and blues cultures. Representing the cream of Arlen's more than 500 songs are *Between the Devil and the Deep Blue Sea, I've Got the World on a String, Stormy Weather, Ill Wind, Last Night When We Were Young, Over the Rainbow, Blues in the Night, That Old Black Magic, My Shining Hour, One for My Baby, Ac-Cen-Tchu-Ate the Positive, Any Place I Hang My Hat Is Home, Come Rain or Come Shine, Ain't It the Truth, The Man (Gal) That Got Away* and *A Sleepin' Bee.*

Sinatra's affinity for Arlen songs is demonstrated by the fact that he has recorded several of them two and three times over the decades. The rich, bluesy melodies and pulsing rhythms — always accompanied by wonderful, storytelling lyrics — have provided a springboard for Sinatra's own gifts, from his days as a romantic crooner all the way through to his last recording in 1984, a third version of *Stormy Weather.*

Jimmy McHugh (1894–1969)
Composer, Pianist, Music Publisher — ASCAP member: 1922

Born in Boston, McHugh went to college on both coasts and remained a bicoastal professional in music throughout his career. He served early days as a rehearsal pianist for the Boston Opera House and worked for a New York music publisher. Once he began to write songs, Jimmy McHugh concentrated on introduction of his work in musical revues — like those at Harlem's Cotton Club — and by dance bands, at first in live performance and soon via radio. He supplemented this "pop" work with theater (East Coast) and movies (West Coast), but nightclub and band singers and then recording artists were the main purveyors of his work.

Collaborating with Gene Austin and Irving Mills, McHugh produced his first hit in 1924 with *When My Sugar Walks Down the Street*. A few songs and years later came *I Can't Believe That You're in Love with Me*, lyrics by Clarence Gaskill, introduced in the 1927 "Gay Paree" revue. By the 1930s, McHugh was scoring for Broadway, and in 1935 he wrote songs for his first movie, *Hooray for Love*. His most important collaborators were lyricists Dorothy Fields and—later—Harold Adamson. Intermittently, he also wrote with such notables as Johnny Mercer, Ned Washington, Frank Loesser and Buddy Kaye.

Jimmy McHugh's Broadway shows were *International Revue; Hello, Daddy; Streets of Paris, Keep Off the Grass* and *As the Girls Go*. Some of his films were *Let's Sing Again, Buck Benny Rides Again, Higher and Higher, Happy Go Lucky* and *Doll Face*. Late in McHugh's career, he worked on the instrumental score for the film *Jack the Ripper*, a remarkably frightening work full of screaming brass.

Frank Sinatra made his starring debut in films—playing himself—in the screen adaptation of the Rodgers and Hart stage musical *Higher and Higher*. Little of the stage production was used, most of the songs being replaced by new work from Jimmy McHugh and Harold Adamson, including Sinatra's principal numbers in the film, *I Couldn't Sleep a Wink Last Night, A Lovely Way to Spend an Evening* and *The Music Stopped*. Sinatra also sang McHugh tunes on the radio (*Exactly Like You, I'm in the Mood for Love*) and many years later reached back to record such '30s and '40s McHugh songs as *On the Sunny Side of the Street, Where Are You?, Say It (Over and Over Again)* and *Hush-a-Bye Island*.

McHugh formed his own music publishing company in the 1950s, and founded the polio fund which evolved into the Jimmy McHugh Charities. During the last decade of his life he served as a director of ASCAP. Among his finest songs not recorded by Sinatra are *I Can't Give You Anything But Love, Baby; Lovely to Look At* and *It's a Most Unusual Day*.

Antonio Carlos Jobim (born 1927)
Composer, Lyricist, Musician, Producer—Argentine professional societies

During the mid-to-late 1950s, when rock music was taking over the pop charts in the United States and elsewhere, an Argentine composer in his late twenties was becoming a key figure in the introduction of a new dance music and beat in his own country. Antonio Carlos Jobim — functioning as composer, songwriter, singer and producer — succeeded in spreading this new beat and sound, this *bossa nova*, from his native Rio de Janiero to popular music circles around the world. Its heyday in the United States was during the 1960s, via collaborations with a variety of lyricists, translative lyricists, singers, solo musicians and bands.

Although Sinatra generally picked up on new post–1960 musical trends well after they had become established, in the case of Jobim's sound, he was attracted while it was still in recent flower. Recording for three consecutive days in early 1967, then three more in early 1969, Sinatra committed a total of 21 songs to tape in the *bossa nova* beat. Seventeen of these were composed by Jobim, who played and sometimes sang along with Sinatra.

With much of his most popular output written from the late 50s to the late 60s, Jobim's songs were very much of a time and place, but their appeal may be expected to last well beyond that era, with their lovely melodies and thoughtful, humane words. Jobim sometimes wrote his own lyrics, other times collaborating with national colleagues such as Newton Mendonca and Vincius De Moraes, or international lyricists like Jon Hendricks, Gene Lees, and Norman Gimbel, who either translated from Portuguese or wrote original English words.

The Jobim songs recorded by Sinatra were a fine sample of the composer's work; they included *Desafinado, One Note Samba, Wave, Triste, Quiet Nights of Quiet Stars, Aqua de Beber, How Insensitive, The Girl from Ipanema, Meditation, Don't Ever Go Away, Once I Loved* and *If You Never Come to Me.*

In addition to his independent songs, Jobim composed for films like *Black Orpheus, The Adventurers, Gabriela, Moments of Play* and *Fonte Da Sandate* (Deep Illusion). Along with his composition and touring, Jobim served as music director with Odeon Records.

Jerome Kern (1885–1945)
Composer — ASCAP Charter Member: 1914

Sinatra primarily recorded songs from the latter part of Kern's long and prolific career, largely eschewing his work from 1900 through the mid–1920s. As a result, Sinatra recorded only 14 Kern songs. Since the profiles in this volume are weighted to those composers most recorded by Sinatra, the relative brevity of this piece in no way reflects the pivotal role played by Jerome David Kern in the history of American popular song.

Kern was the central figure in the conversion of European opera and operetta into the native American musical play. He wrote songs for movies, as well, but was most emphatically a composer for the theater, an early source of inspiration for teenage hopefuls like George Gershwin and Richard Rodgers, and the first composer to consciously push for the evolution of the "integrated" musical, where the characters sang words consistent with their personalities and the songs furthered and heightened the play's storyline.

Intended by his father to join the family merchandising business, Kern composed songs for his high school plays (publishing one of them) and longed for a career in music. For awhile the father insisted on a proper business for his son, but gave in when the boy was 17 and allowed him to attend the New York College of Music, then to study music theory and composition in Europe. In London, Kern got a job writing incidental songs for the theater. At age 19, he returned to the United States and got jobs — in quick succession — as a song plugger, music salesman, stage rehearsal pianist, then as a songwriter contributing to various publications. From 1904 onward, Kern never looked back.

In 1905 he experienced his first hit song, *How'd You Like to Spoon with Me,* with a lyric by Edward Laska. Kern was soon in demand for adding spritely "American" tunes to the imported European shows which were to dominate Broadway for the next decade. After contributing songs and partial scores for several years, Kern teamed with lyricist Paul West to write his first complete score, for a 1912 production, *The Red Petticoat.* A few years later, Kern worked with librettist Guy Bolton and lyricist P. G. Wodehouse on a series of musicals — including the highly successful *Oh, Boy!* — that developed the true native musical theater and advanced the concept of integrating music and drama. These five notable collaborations were interspersed with many others through 1924.

At the quarter-century mark, Jerome Kern's rapid pace began to slow a little, but with a deepening of control and increased daring. Standing out as his masterpiece was 1927's *Show Boat,* with libretto and lyrics by Oscar Hammerstein II. Following *Show Boat,* Kern wrote five more Broadway productions, the last in 1939. He began writing for the movies in 1934, and did eight films during this latter career. His most famous stage productions after 1930 were *The Cat and the Fiddle, Music in the Air* and *Roberta.* His films included *Swing Time; High, Wide and Handsome; Cover Girl* and *Centennial Summer.*

He rarely wrote his own words, collaborating with a distinguished roster of stage lyricists, chief among them M. E. Rourke (beginning in 1907), Harry B. Smith (1912), P. G. Wodehouse (1917), Anne Caldwell (1919), Clifford Grey (1920), Oscar Hammerstein II (1925), and Otto Harbach (1925). For movies, Kern worked with such lyricists as Johnny Mercer, E. Y. ("Yip") Harburg, Dorothy Fields and Ira Gershwin. He had less prominent stage and screen collaborations with Howard Dietz, Harry Ruby, Bert Kalmar and more than a dozen others.

Standing out among Jerome Kern's immortal songs are *They Didn't Believe Me, Till the Clouds Roll By, Look for the Silver Lining, Make Believe, Ol' Man River, Can't Help Lovin' Dat Man, Why Was I Born?, The Song Is You, Smoke Gets in Your Eyes, Yesterdays, I Won't Dance, The Way You Look Tonight, A Fine Romance, All the Things You Are* and *Long Ago (and Far Away).*

Sinatra sang *Ol' Man River* in a film tribute to Jerome Kern, *Till the Clouds Roll By,* and recorded the song in 1944 and again in 1963. Of the 12 other Kern songs Sinatra recorded, perhaps the most outstanding interpretations were *Yesterdays, A Fine Romance* and his 1964 version of *The Way You Look Tonight.*

Kern served as a director of ASCAP from 1924 to 1929 and 1932 to 1942.

George Gershwin (1898–1937)
Composer—ASCAP member: 1920

As with Kern, the limited number of Gershwin songs recorded by Sinatra (13) fails to indicate the composer's place in music. The several forces that influenced the singer's choice of material happened to pass over many appropriate Gershwin tunes, but Sinatra liked those selected so much he recorded nearly all of them more than once. His renderings gave these great songs the creative treatment they deserved.

Gershwin was the second of four children born to Rose and Morris Gershovitz, emigrees from St. Petersburg in Russia, who wanted their Brooklyn-born offspring to bear "American" names; mistakenly

registered at birth as Jacob Gershwine, the family used the intended
name, George Gershwin. His elder brother was called Ira.

Having demonstrated a remarkable native gift for the piano,
Gershwin started down the road to becoming a concert pianist and
composer, beginning his serious studies with Charles Hambitzer. But
he soon was drawn by the combined spells of Broadway, Tin Pan
Alley, and the money to be made there. He greatly admired the songs
of Irving Berlin and Jerome Kern; wishing to emulate these men,
Gershwin left his high school at age 15 and became the youngest piano
player/song plugger to work for the prominent Joseph H. Remick
Music Publishing Company.

He composed his first two songs while working for Remick, but
couldn't get them published. A third song, *When You Want 'Em, You
Can't Have 'Em — When You Have 'Em, You Don't Want 'Em,* with lyrics by
Murray Roth, was sold for $5 to Harry Von Tilzer's publishing com-
pany in 1914. During the next five years, Gershwin followed a time-
honored course to a songwriting career, but did it at an accelerated
pace and then soared well beyond the usual limits of that realm.

Seeing Remick's as a dead end, Gershwin became a piano accom-
panist in vaudeville, then quit to accept a temporary job as a rehearsal
pianist for a show with songs by the burgeoning Jerome Kern and the
august Victor Herbert. This led to playing piano at the Century
Theatre and the introduction of some of his own songs, which — in
turn — resulted in a job with Max Dreyfus as a staff composer. From
there he achieved the status of contributor to musical revues. By 1918,
George Gershwin began his collaboration with brother Ira. In the next
six years, Ira would develop a lighthearted style of lyric-writing to
match the spirit of George's music.

Then, in 1919, Gershwin's intense rush to success reached its first
real plateau in the complete scoring of a Broadway musical comedy,
La La Lucille, with lyrics by Buddy DeSylva and Arthur Jackson. That
same year, he and Irving Caesar wrote *Swanee,* which Al Jolson spotted
playing in a revue and incorporated into the score of his hit show *Sin-
bad.* Jolson put *Swanee* over sufficiently to make it the biggest hit song
in the country, accelerating Gershwin's progress ever further.

A series of scores for the annual George White's Scandals produced great songs and confirmed the young marvel's reputation. In the
1922 version of the Scandals, Gershwin included a short black-jazz
opera, *Blue Monday,* which put off most critics and patrons, but caused

Paul Whiteman to commission a native concert work from Gershwin.

That work — *Rhapsody in Blue* — was premiered in 1924 to general good reaction. In the same eventful year, George and Ira did the songs for *Lady, Be Good,* Gershwin's first major story-show, starring Fred and Adele Astaire. More big productions and concert work ensued, including the full opera *Porgy and Bess.* The Gershwin brothers began composing scores for the movies with 1931's *Delicious.*

It was fortunate for the world that all this came about so rapidly. In 1937, at the age of 38, George Gershwin died of a brain tumor. His legacy of concert work included *An American in Paris, The Second Rhapsody, The Cuban Overture* and his masterpiece, *Piano Concerto in F.* Some major stage musicals with songs by Gershwin were *Tip-Toes; Oh, Kay!; Funny Face, Rosalie, Strike Up the Band, Girl Crazy* and *Of Thee I Sing.* Gershwin film scores included *Shall We Dance?* and *A Damsel in Distress* (both with Fred Astaire), and *The Goldwyn Follies.*

While he collaborated often with his brother after 1924, Gershwin also worked with major lyricists like Otto Harbach, Oscar Hammerstein II, Gus Kahn, B. G. (Buddy) DeSylva, and P. G. Wodehouse. The unforgettable songs produced by these collaborations can be represented by *Somebody Loves Me, Fascinating Rhythm; Oh, Lady Be Good; The Man I Love, Someone to Watch Over Me, S'Wonderful, I've Got a Crush on You, Embraceable You, I Got Rhythm, But Not for Me, They All Laughed, They Can't Take That Away from Me, A Foggy Day, Nice Work If You Can Get It, Love Is Here to Stay,* the major arias from *Porgy and Bess,* and the great, posthumously published *Love Walked In.*

Of all the composers profiled in this chapter, Gershwin is the most prodigious in terms of accomplishment in different musical forms, and the only one to fully make it from the basic pop world to the concert stage.

Harry Warren (1893–1981)
Composer, Pianist — ASCAP member: 1924

Warren's career followed a progression which reflects the changing world of the craftsman songwriter from the 1920s to the 1960s. Born in Brooklyn and named Salvatore Guaragna, his musical education was self-taught. He first made money as a rehearsal pianist in silent movie production, setting the mood for action and emotional expression on the set. Next he worked as a song plugger for '20s Tin Pan Alley publishers including Remick Music, developing his own melodies full time, writing for Broadway shows like *Sweet and Low* and *The Laugh Parade*. By 1932, he moved to the West Coast, where the "action" was writing songs for the thriving sound motion picture industry, signing with Warner Bros. for seven years. In 1940, he contracted to Twentieth Century–Fox, in 1944 to MGM, and finally wrote for Paramount between 1952 and 1961. For the last part of his working life, Harry Warren was free-lance.

As a composer nearly always working under contract, Warren was generally writing less from inspiration than assignment, but his talent led to good assignments and fine collaborators. The lyricists with whom he was most prominently teamed were Al Dubin, the ubiquitous Johnny Mercer and then Mack Gordon, but in Warren's lengthy career, he also wrote with such wordsmiths as Mort Dixon, Edgar Leslie, Ted Koehler, Arthur Freed, Johnny Burke, Ralph Blane, Ira Gershwin, Leo Robin, Jack Brooks, Sammy Cahn, Harold Adamson and Richard O. Kramer.

With Warren, the plays and films he worked on are generally less remembered than fine individual songs. Sinatra cut a few Harry Warren songs in his boy-singer days — examples are *Devil May Care, I'll String Along with You* and *You'll Never Know* — but he recorded most of his Warren selections during the years at Capitol Records and his own label, Reprise, bringing his more "knowing" mature style to such beauties as *You're Getting to Be a Habit with Me, I Only Have Eyes for You, September in the Rain, Jeepers Creepers, I Had the Craziest Dream, Serenade in Blue* and *There Will Never Be Another You.*

Also deserving mention are important songs in Warren's career that were never recorded by Sinatra; among these are *You're My Everything, 42nd Street, About a Quarter to Nine, The Lullaby of Broadway, You Must Have Been a Beautiful Baby, Chattanooga Choo-Choo, I Found a Million Dollar Baby; On the Atcheson, Topeka and the Santa Fe; That's Amore, I've Got a Gal in Kalamazoo* and, as a television studio assignment in his later career, *The Legend of Wyatt Earp.*

Gordon Jenkins (1910–1984)
Composer, Arranger, Lyricist, Pianist — ASCAP member: 1935

Gordon Hill Jenkins' eminent work as an arranger and conductor is covered in Chapter 6, along with some general biography. Considering his work as a songwriter alone is an interesting story.

Jenkins' several careers carried him through the worlds of big dance bands on the road, Broadway theater, radio, movies, concerts, television production, nightclubs and the recording studio. In the course of all these associations, Gordon Jenkins found the time and inspiration to write better than two dozen principal songs. Examples of those unsung by Sinatra are *Married I Can Always Get, The Letter, You Have Taken My Heart* and *Blue Evening.* Occasional lyricist partners included Tom Adair and Johnny Mercer, but Jenkins usually wrote his own words and — in a few cases — supplied lyrics for the melodies of others.

During their long relationship, Sinatra recorded an even dozen Jenkins songs, including *P.S. I Love You, Goodbye; Homesick, That's All; This Is All I Ask, How Old Am I?* and *I Loved Her.*

Instrumental works complemented Jenkins' output of songs; he penned *Manhattan Tower Suite,* plus a concerto for clarinet and the film score for *Bwana Devil.* Combining songs with the symphonic in 1979, Jenkins wrote a cantata about Frank Sinatra's life, titled *The Future (Reflections on the Future in Three Tenses),* which was arranged and conducted by its composer, and performed by Sinatra and chorus with the Los Angeles Philharmonic Symphony Orchestra. The recording of this work comprised the final section of a three-part album, **Trilogy: Past, Present, Future.**

Finally, let me touch on the composers less dominant in Sinatra's choice of songs, but nevertheless important in his career. They are listed in alphabetical order by last name:

Fred Ahlert. Sinatra sang Ahlert's tunes a good deal on the radio (*I'll Get By, Mean to Me,* and *I Don't Know Why*), and they were otherwise prominent in his early career. His three recordings of *The Moon Was Yellow,* in the 1940s, '50s, and '60s, provide a fine example of his evolution in style and voice.

Leonard Bernstein. The theater score for *On the Town* was mostly carried over into one of Sinatra's best screen musicals, but it was a song left out of the movie version — *Lonely Town* — which stands as one of Sinatra's greatest recorded performances.

Rube Bloom. Bloom's fine *Don't Worry 'Bout Me* became one of Sinatra's "signature" tunes. He made definitive records of *Fools Rush In*, first on RCA Victor with Tommy Dorsey, then with Stordahl at Columbia, and finally at Capitol with Nelson Riddle. Two versions of *Take Me*, from 1942 and 1961, show how far Sinatra took the Dorsey sound.

Jacques Brel. Only two of this distinctive French composer's songs were recorded by Sinatra *(If You Go Away* and *I'm Not Afraid,* both with English lyrics by Rod McKuen), but they were two of his finest performances.

Hoagy Carmichael. This unique composer was more widely recorded by other singers, but Sinatra's versions of *Star Dust, The Nearness of You,* and *I Get Along Without You Very Well* should withstand the ravages of time.

J. Fred Coots. Coots is listed because he wrote the melody for *You Go to My Head*. Recorded in 1945 and 1960, both versions speak to the essence of Sinatra's greatness as a singer of love ballads.

Matt Dennis. Dennis and Sinatra met while they were both working for Tommy Dorsey. Dennis was not prolific, but Sinatra made 14 recordings using only seven of his songs. Five titles cover 40 years of recorded memories: *Everything Happens to Me, Let's Get Away from It All, Violets for Your Furs, The Night We Called It a Day* and *Angel Eyes.*

Vernon Duke. Sinatra recorded four songs by composer Vernon Duke; each made for a career highlight. They were *April in Paris, Autumn in New York, I Can't Get Started,* and *Taking a Chance on Love.* Great songs.

Duke Ellington. As with Vernon Duke, Sinatra only recorded four songs from Edward Kennedy Ellington's output, but the results were powerful, especially with *Mood Indigo* in 1955 and *I'm Beginning to See the Light* in 1962.

Sammy Fain. Fain composed songs over four decades, but it was his tunes of the 1930s such as *That Old Feeling, I'll Be Seeing You,* and *You Brought a New Kind of Love to Me,* that figured large in Sinatra's career.

Bob Gaudio and Jake Holmes. This pair wrote the score for *Watertown,* a "theme album" in the deepest sense. It was a cycle of ten songs which told a story of disruption and dissolution within a man/ woman relationship and family. It was created especially for Sinatra and originally intended to accompany an animated film. Though the film never happened, a great LP remains.

Bob Haggart. Sinatra only recorded one song with a Haggart melody, but that was one of his all-time classic recordings, *What's New?*, with lyrics by Johnny Burke and arrangement by Nelson Riddle.

Isham Jones. This great musician, bandleader and composer provided Sinatra with one of his most-sung and recorded vehicles, *The One I Love (Belongs to Somebody Else)* and one of his greatest songs, *It Had to Be You.*

Michel Legrand. During the 1960s, '70s and '80s, Sinatra recorded a number of Legrand compositions. These were among his most successful later efforts to deal with songs contemporary to the era of their recording. Especially fine were *Summer Me, Winter Me; What Are You Doing the Rest of Your Life?*, and *How Do You Keep the Music Playing?*

Joe Raposo. Just before his intended retirement in late 1970, Sinatra recorded Raposo's child-directed commentary on racial prejudice, *Bein' Green.* It was a fine match-up of talents. When Sinatra began to record again in 1973, Raposo wrote the words and music to five new songs for Sinatra, four of which were used in his comeback LP. These songs provided mixed attitudes of youthfulness, optimism and nostalgia that were wonderful for Sinatra's return to singing.

Jacques Revaux. Having written the melody for *Comme d'habitude*, which Paul Anka made over into *My Way*, Revaux had to be included in this section. The song became Sinatra's latter-day anthem.

Stephen Sondheim. A professed admirer of Sondheim's songs, Sinatra would have recorded many more had he not reached the closing days of his career. As it was, *Send in the Clowns* and *Good Thing Going* made for some wonderful, original moments in his post–1973 albums.

Alec Wilder. Wilder and Sinatra viewed each other with great admiration. Sinatra conducted a number of Wilder's orchestral pieces. Wilder's distinctive compositions highlighted Sinatra recording sessions from 1943 to 1981. Among the most impressive songs were *I'll Be Around*, *Where Do You Go?* and *A Long Night.*

Jack Wolf and Joel Herron. This pair worked with a lyric-writing Sinatra on the creation of a few songs in the early '50s. Most notable was the devastatingly personal ballad of love lost, *I'm a Fool to Want You.*

Victor Young. Out of Young's impressive catalog of compositions, Sinatra recorded eight songs. *A Ghost of a Chance* and *Stella by Starlight* were each recorded twice, always outstandingly. Two other songs were done at both the beginning and end of Sinatra's career as recording artist; *One Hundred Years from Today* (1943 & 1984) and *Street of Dreams* (1942 & 1979).

Index to Composers

Most of the hundreds of songwriters listed in the following Index to Composers did excellent work. Those I have discussed are distinguished by the fact that Frank Sinatra favored their work in his recordings, or they exhibited some special professional or personal quality that influenced him. Only the smallest minority of the composers listed wrote songs that were foisted on a resistant Sinatra, either through commercial pressure or the desire to keep up with the musical times.

Composers are listed alphabetically, by their last name. The key numbers after each name may be cross-referenced to the Master Song List (Chapter 3) for further data.

Chapter 5: The Lyricists

As a storyteller and actor in his singing, Sinatra put great emphasis on the drama present in a song, and therefore on the lyrics. Whereas many vocalists — even great ones — use the words of a tune as distinctive sounds to hang notes on, Frank Sinatra always concentrated on the words' literal and connotative meaning, and on their poetic feeling. Many singers bend a word through six or more notes to get an effect, sometimes even going to the extreme of taking a breath between syllables. With such stylists, meaning may not be lost, but it is often misplaced. Sinatra did not completely eschew such jazz and soul effects — especially from 1960 onward — but never sacrificed a song's message in the process. The cause of articulate pronunciation and communicated meaning came first; feeling and drama arose from the same focus of attention.

Whether songs by famous lyricists or those now largely forgotten, whether by prolific craftsmen or those who wrote little, Frank Sinatra performed them in a manner that took the words seriously. With the exception of a few tunes pressed on him for commercial purposes, he sang the songs because he liked them and had something of himself to express through them.

Out of the hundreds of lyricsts represented in this compilation, I will profile one dozen, those who have 12 or more songs recorded by Sinatra, disregarding those two lyric-writing gentlemen, Irving Berlin and Cole Porter, who are already dealt with in the preceding chapter as prime composers.

I will also touch briefly on another 20 lyricists who are included because their songwriting was generally wonderful, or because their work was of special importance in Sinatra's career.

The 12 lyricsts represented by 12 or more songs are quantitatively ranked as follows:

278

Rank	Name	Songs	Recordings
1	Sammy Cahn	88	112
2	Johnny Burke	32	37
3	Johnny Mercer	31	44
4	Lorenz Hart	26	39
5	Oscar Hammerstein II	24	36
6	Ira Gershwin	16	25
7	Harold Adamson	14	17
8	Frank Loesser	14	15
9	Mack Gordon	13	16
10	Rod McKuen	13	14
11	Comden & Green	13	13
12	Ted Koehler	12	15
Totals		296	383

Now to profile these artist/craftsmen in some detail. The 12 lyricists will receive a varied degree of coverage, depending on the complexity of their careers.

Sammy Cahn (born 1913)
Lyricist, Composer, Publisher, Violinist, Singer — ASCAP member: 1936

The long and versatile career of lyricist Sammy Cahn began shortly after his graduation from a New York high school. He started as a violinist in a vaudeville orchestra. Then he met Saul Chaplin and they organized a dance band. Soon the young men turned to songwriting. Sammy Cahn turned 20 years old and had found his calling.

The best way to follow Cahn's career is decade by decade. It doesn't fall into isolated ten-year lumps, but there are clear phases involved.

His first songs were published in the 1930s. Initially, Cahn and Chaplin teamed up on lyrics for melodies by other men, including the great bandleader Jimmie Lunceford. Next they tended toward writing both words and music together, sometimes with other collaborators joining the team. As time passed, Cahn did more with the words, Chaplin did more with the music. Their work was performed by dance bands like Andy Kirk and his Clouds of Joy, Tommy Dorsey's orchestra, and the Lunceford orchestra.

The partners also scored for New York nightclub black revues such as *Connie's Hot Chocolates of 1936* (Louis Armstrong sang their *Shoe Shine Boy*), 1937's *The New Grand Terrace Revue*, with Fletcher Henderson's orchestra, and the *Cotton Club Parade* of 1939.

Writing to music by Sholom Secunda, they created songs for the Yiddish musical *I Would If I Could,* including *Bei Mir Bist Du Schon,* which later became a number one hit record for the Andrews Sisters. Other good songs of this '30s period were *Rhythm Is Our Business, Until the Real Thing Comes Along, Dedicated to You, If It's the Last Thing I Do* and *Please Be Kind.* In the '50s and '60s, Frank Sinatra finally recorded the last two of these tunes.

Jule Styne was Cahn's main collaborator in the 1940s. Whether the songs were done for the stage, the movies, or for dance bands, all but a few had Styne melodies and Cahn lyrics.

Among the exceptions, most notable were *Day by Day* and *I Should Care,* for which Sammy Cahn wrote words to melodies by the team of Axel Stordahl and Paul Weston. Both songs were presented in 1945 by the Tommy Dorsey orchestra.

The Styne/Cahn team had an auspicious year in 1944. Cahn had known Frank Sinatra from his early '40s dealings with the Dorsey band; he and Styne had written *I've Heard That Song Before* for an early Sinatra film appearance. Now the two men gave Sinatra a solo hit with *Saturday Night (Is the Loneliest Night of the Week).* That same year they wrote full song scores for the Sinatra movies *Step Lively* and *Anchors Aweigh.* They also saw their first Broadway score presented, albeit unsuccessfully.

For the rest of the decade, Cahn and Styne turned out hit songs and shows. They did "pop" work for dance bands like Harry James's and Charlie Spivak's. Redemption on Broadway came with a 727-performance hit show, *High Button Shoes.* Their biggest success was in the movies, with full scores for nine films and individual songs for a dozen more. Their movies included *It Happened in Brooklyn* (again with Sinatra), *Romance on the High Seas, Sweetheart of Sigma Chi* and *Follow the Boys.*

Among the songs from this period are *It's Been a Long, Long Time; Let It Snow (Let It Snow, Let It Snow); You're My Girl; Papa, Won't You Dance with Me?; It's You or No One, Put It in a Box (Tie It with a Ribbon and Throw It in the Deep Blue Sea)* and *Five Minutes More.* They received Oscar nominations for *I Fall in Love Too Easily, Anywhere, It's Magic, It's a Great Feeling* and *I'll Walk Alone.*

Sinatra recorded better than two dozen Styne/Cahn tunes. For more on their film work together, see the Jule Styne profile in Chapter 4.

The 1950s brought a new era for Sammy Cahn. While his partner of the '40s — Jule Styne — became more and more involved with Broadway musicals, Cahn chose to continue with movie and pop work. After the pair did two movie scores together in 1950, they largely went their separate ways. Cahn wrote pop songs for Sinatra *(Same Old Saturday Night, Hey! Jealous Lover)* and other singers, working with composers like Frank Reardon, Lew Spence, Phil Tuminello, Gene DePaul, Fred Spielman, Kay Twomey and Bee Walker. He did individual film songs with Ray Heindorf, Paul Weston and Elmer Bernstein, sometimes helping with the melody. But his mainstay was still movie song scores.

Cahn wrote full scores for seven musical films with composer Nicholas Brodszky, three starring Mario Lanza. Putting romantic words to Brodszky's semiclassical melodies was a novel experience for Cahn, and songs like *Be My Love* and *Because You're Mine* showed a new side to Cahn's talent. He also did film scores with Sammy Fain, Arthur Schwartz, Vernon Duke (they also did *Two's Company* on Broadway), Sylvia Fine, George Stoll and Johnny Green.

His separation from Jule Styne wasn't complete in the '50s. There were songs for Disney's *Peter Pan*. They published *The Christmas Waltz* in 1954, and wrote the Oscar-winning title song for *Three Coins in the Fountain* that same year.

Movie title songs became a steady line for Sammy Cahn. Musical films were decreasing in number, but title tunes were a steady market. Cahn wrote them with Alfred Newman, Victor Young, Alex North, Bronislau Kaper, Ray Heindorf and Cyril Mockridge for the films *Woman's World, Forever Darling, Pete Kelly's Blues* (sung by Ella Fitzgerald), *Written on the Wind, Somebody Up There Likes Me, The Long Hot Summer* and *The Best of Everything*.

The latter part of the '50s brought the start of Cahn's last major collaboration. Frank Sinatra brought him together with Jimmy Van Heusen to score the 1955 TV musical drama *Our Town*. They followed up with pop songs like *Closer Than a Kiss* for Vic Damone, and movie songs like *To Love and Be Loved, Nothing in Common* and *Indiscreet*. For Frank Sinatra films, the new Cahn/Van Heusen team wrote *The Tender Trap* and two Oscar winners, *All the Way* and *High Hopes*.

Beginning in '57, the two men wrote special Sinatra concept-album songs; for more on that, see the Van Heusen profile in Chapter 4.

The 1960s were a high time for Cahn. The partnership with Jimmy Van Heusen would continue successfully for much of the decade. Apart from their close work with Sinatra, they did pop songs (*Love Is a Bore* was popularized by Barbra Streisand), Broadway shows (*Skyscraper, Walking Happy*), songs for the marionette show *Les Poupees de Paris,* and the title songs for films like *Say One for Me, Let's Make Love, Road to Hong Kong, The Boys Night Out, Thoroughly Modern Millie* and *Star!*. Two of their most-recorded film songs were *The Second Time Around* and the Oscar-winning *Call Me Irresponsible.*

Sinatra commissioned the pair to score his *Robin and the 7 Hoods* movie musical, and he sang their title songs for *Come Blow Your Horn* and *Pocketful of Miracles.*

Toward the end of the '60s, Sammy Cahn ended his work with Van Heusen. He did some writing with other composers, but his pace had slowed dramatically.

In the 1970s, a whole new career opened up for Sammy Cahn. He starred in a 1974 show at the Golden Theater, *Words and Music,* singing his own songs. It was a hit. Cahn also starred as a performer in two TV specials that featured his tunes. There was some new lyric writing, too, including *Let Me Try Again* for Sinatra; an English lyric for a French melody, done with Paul Anka. Cahn's main collaborator of the period was composer George Barrie. They wrote songs like *A Touch of Class, Now That We're in Love* and the Oscar-nominee, *All that Love Went to Waste.*

During the 1980s, Cahn continued to do some writing. The last Cahn lyric recorded by Sinatra was *Say Hello,* melody by Richard Evan Behrke.

Sammy Cahn has been a music publisher since 1955. He has been elected president of the Songwriter's Hall of Fame and served on the ASCAP board of directors. Over the decades, he became famous for writing special musical and comedy material for performers like Bob Hope, Bing Crosby, Doris Day, Vic Damone, Perry Como, Dean Martin, Barbra Streisand, Paul Anka and—of course—his longtime friend, Sinatra.

Johnny Burke (1908–1964)
Lyricist, Composer, Music Publisher — ASCAP member: 1932

One of the major keys to Johnny Burke's approach was humor. It pervades his lyrics, revealed in titles, general word choice and attitude. Even his deeply romantic ballads are tinged with humor and irony.

After graduating from the University of Wisconsin, Burke served as a staff member with music publishers in Chicago and New York City. Through most of the 1930s he wrote lyrics for pop songs and numbers used by dance bands. His most frequent composer during the period was Harold Spina. Together, they produced tunes like *The Beat of My Heart, It's Dark on Observatory Hill* and *My Very Good Friend, the Milkman.* Their reputations were enhanced when men such as Fred Waring, Paul Whiteman, Ozzie Nelson and Bob Crosby used their songs.

Burke headed for the West Coast in the mid–1930s, and teamed with composer Arthur Johnston for movie scores at Columbia and Paramount. Both films starred Bing Crosby. *Pennies from Heaven* (1936), which also starred Louis Armstrong, featured the immortal title song, plus *One, Two, Button Your Shoe* and *Skeleton in the Closet. Double or Nothing* (1937) had Crosby crooning *It's the Natural Thing to Do* and *The Moon Got in My Eyes.* Burke's track record was growing.

Between 1938 and mid–1940, he did scores for seven films, all starring Bing Crosby, all composed with James V. Monaco. These songs with Monaco further established Burke's repute as a craftsman who delivered; they included *Don't Let That Moon Get Away, Laugh and Call It Love, An Apple for the Teacher, April Played the Fiddle* and *I Haven't Time to Be a Millionaire.* One of these seven movies was *Road to Singapore,* the first of a famous series with Bing Crosby, Bob Hope and Dorothy Lamour. Monaco and Burke's *Too Romantic* came from that score. *Rhythm on the River* (1940) contained the Oscar-nominated *Only Forever.*

In the midst of his Hollywood successes, the year 1939 was a key one for Johnny Burke. He took the melody to Bob Haggart's instrumental, *I'm Free* — written the previous year — and lyrically transformed it into his first great song, *What's New?* He also wrote the Frankie Masters band theme song, *Scatterbrain,* collaborating on both words and music with Masters, Keene Kahn and Carl Bean. And perhaps most importantly, he wrote his first song with Jimmy Van Heusen. Their *Oh, You Crazy Moon* was played by the Tommy Dorsey orchestra, live and on radio. A team of highly successful songwriters had started to fly.

The next year brought more Burke/Van Heusen hits with Dorsey, namely *Polka Dots and Moonbeams* and *Imagination*. Then Burke headed back to the West Coast, with his new collaborator, for more than a decade of movie songwriting. Later on, Burke and Van Heusen formed a music publishing company, to take fullest advantage of their burgeoning success.

They worked primarily for Paramount, doing complete scores for better than 20 movies and individual songs for several others. Bing Crosby starred in at least 14 of these pictures, continuing his previous association with Johnny Burke's lyrics. Among the more solid of the 30-plus films were *My Favorite Spy*, 1943's *And the Angels Sing* (with the classic ballad, *It Could Happen to You*), the smash hit, *Going My Way*, its first sequel, *The Bells of St. Mary's*, and 1953's *Carnival in Flanders*. Burke and Van Heusen also did the songs for five Hope/Crosby "Road" pictures between 1941 and 1952, the most successful being *Road to Zanzibar* and *Road to Morocco*. Exemplar songs from these productions are *Humpty Dumpty Heart, It's Always You, Moonlight Becomes You, If You Please; Sunday, Monday, or Always; The Day After Forever, Swinging on a Star* (the 1944 Oscar winner), *Aren't You Glad You're You?* (Oscar nominee), *Like Someone in Love, Sleigh Ride in July* (Oscar nominee), *Harmony, If You Stub Your Toe on the Moon, When Is Sometime?, Life Is So Peculiar,* and a true masterpiece, *Here's That Rainy Day.*

Burke's sense of humor got full play writing joke ballads with Van Heusen for Crosby's "Flop Parade" radio feature of the '40s, with tunes like *Bluebirds in My Belfrey; Yah-Ta-Ta, Yah-Ta-Ta (Talk, Talk, Talk)* and *There's a Flaw in My Flue.*

After his work with Jimmy Van Heusen ended in the mid–1950s, Johnny Burke continued his writing, but at a slower pace. Prominent among his later efforts were the Perry Como hit, *Wild Horses,* for which Burke wrote the music, and his famous collaboration with Erroll Garner, 1955's *Misty.*

Frank Sinatra's had first encountered Burke and Van Heusen when he joined the Tommy Dorsey organization in 1940. The singer had hits with their songs recorded by Dorsey, and went on as a soloist to record 23 other Burke pieces. Outstanding among his post–Dorsey recordings of songs by Johnny Burke are *But Beautiful* and *What's New?*

Johnny Mercer (1909–1976)
Lyricist, Music Publisher, Composer, Singer —
ASCAP member: 1933

John H. Mercer shares the distinction with Irving Berlin of being among the most prolific and gifted songwriters in history. Like Berlin, he experienced parallel and equally great careers with pop music, movie songs and stage scores. Mercer, too, was capable of great sophistication and great simplicity. Unlike Berlin, he possessed a confidence and humor about himself and his work that made him more secure.

He was born in Savannah, Georgia. During and after his school days, Mercer was a performer in little theater groups. He also liked to sing, and as he passed his twentieth birthday, Mercer began to try his wings as a songwriter, both words and music. Throughout his career he occasionally wrote music, but words became the magic tool of his life; smart words, simple words, funny words, lovely words. Johnny Mercer produced over 1,000 songs, every one at least interesting, and many of them great.

The songs which came first were for the pop worlds of 1930's radio and dance bands. A wiseguy tone and clever melodies marked such early pieces as *Out of Breath, Wouldja for a Big Red Apple?, Whistling for a Kiss* and *Satan's Li'l Lamb.* In 1933, he and Hoagy Carmichael wrote *Lazy Bones,* which was popularized by the great Mildred Bailey. The song gave Mercer's reputation a welcome boost. Gradually, he could pick the bands and singers that he wanted to play his songs.

Through the '30s and '40s, he wrote pieces introduced by bandleaders like Paul Whiteman, Guy Lombardo, Kay Kyser, Bob Crosby, Glenn Miller, Tommy Dorsey, Woody Herman and — especially — Benny Goodman. The composers he worked with were a diverse group of talents. In addition to kindred spirit Hoagy Carmichael, Mercer wrote pop songs with Gordon Jenkins, Matty Malneck, Bernie Hanighen, Walter Donaldson, Rube Bloom, Jimmy Van Heusen, Jerome Kern and many others. Sometimes he did both words and music by himself.

In 1938 and 1939, Mercer appeared as both singer and MC with the Whiteman and Goodman orchestras. He loved to perform live and on radio.

Great pop songs of Mercer's early phase are represented by *Moon Country, P.S. I Love You, Fare-Thee-Well to Harlem, Goody Goody, Could Be, I Thought About You, Day In — Day Out, Fools Rush In, Skylark, Dream, Two Hearts Are Better Than One* and *Midnight Sun*.

From the '50s into the '70s, Mercer varied his pop work. The big bands were all but gone by the early 1950s, so he began directing his efforts toward the record audience. A great finale to his band days was a lyric for Ellington and Strayhorn's *Satin Doll*, played by Duke Ellington's jazz band and sung by the great Ella Fitzgerald. He wrote *Here's to My Lady* with Rube Bloom, and Nat "King" Cole sang it. Tony Bennett had a hit record with *I Wanna Be Around*, a tune on which Mercer collaborated with a nonprofessional named Sadie Vimmerstedt.

Mercer bent his language gifts to the translation and adaptation of international songs in the '50s and '60s. Fine early instances of this were *Autumn Leaves* (French composer Joseph Kosma) and *When the World Was Young* (M. Philippe-Gerard; also French). Other fine examples are his brilliant *Song of India* (Rimsky-Korsakov; Russian), *Glow Worm* (Paul Lincke; German) and a Sinatra hit, *Summer Wind* (Henry Mayer; French).

Finally, there were late tunes with Johnny Mandel, Doris Tauber and Jimmy Van Heusen. One fine Mercer/Van Heusen song, *Empty Tables*, was published in 1976, the year of Mercer's death.

Nearly half of the Mercer songs recorded by Frank Sinatra came from his "pop" and dance band work.

The second of Johnny Mercer's careers was songwriting for movies; that began in 1935, when he collaborated with Matty Malneck on both words and music for the score of *To Beat the Band*. In that film, Mercer also acted and sang *Eeny, Meeny, Miney, Mo* and *I Saw Her at Eight O'Clock*. He worked steadily after that fun beginning.

Over the next 23 years, Mercer did scores for 23 films, He wrote four with Richard A. Whiting, six with Harry Warren, five with Harold Arlen, two with Gene DePaul, and single pictures with Jimmy McHugh, Arthur Schwartz, Victor Schertzinger (who also directed that film, *The Fleet's In*), Jerome Kern and Saul Chaplin. Mercer wrote songs on his own for the 1955 Fred Astaire film, *Daddy Long Legs*, including *Sluefoot* and the Oscar-nominated *Something's Gotta Give*. The wide range of these collaborations is staggering.

Certain studios and performers sought out Mercer. Warner Bros. was his main employer in the '30s, Paramount in the '40s and MGM in the '50s. Dick Powell starred in six of the movies, while four had the great Fred Astaire and three featured Betty Hutton.

The best-remembered movies with Mercer scores include *Hollywood Hotel* (1937), *Garden of the Moon* (a 1938 film directed by Busby Berkeley; Mercer and Al Dubin combined on lyrics for Harry Warren's melodies), *The Sky's the Limit* (1943), *The Harvey Girls* (1946; with Judy Garland), *Seven Brides for Seven Brothers* (1954), and the film with Mercer's last movie score, *Merry Andrew* (1958; with Danny Kaye).

During the same period, and continuing into the 1970s, Mercer did individual songs and title tunes for movies as diverse as *Rhythm on the Range, The Birth of the Blues, To Have and Have Not, Laura, I'll Cry Tomorrow, Breakfast at Tiffany's, Days of Wine and Roses, Darling Lili* and *Kotch.* Many of his film songs in later years were written with Henry Mancini.

The variety of Johnny Mercer's film songs is truly impressive. There are comic pieces, brilliant psychological studies, light romances, saloon blues, dreams of youth and reflections of old age. In every mood, Mercer's standards of art remained high. Top examples of his movie tunes are *I'm an Old Cow Hand (from the Rio Grande), Too Marvelous for Words, Hooray for Hollywood, You Must Have Been a Beautiful Baby, Jeepers Creepers, I'd Know You Anywhere, Blues in the Night, Tangerine, I'm Old-Fashioned, Dearly Beloved, That Old Black Magic, One for My Baby, My Shining Hour, Ac-Cen-Tchu-Ate the Positive* (which won the 1944 Best Song Oscar), *Laura; On the Atcheson, Topeka and the Santa Fe* (1946 Oscar), *In the Cool, Cool, Cool of the Evening* (1951 Oscar), *Moon River* (1961 Oscar), *Days of Wine and Roses* (1962 Oscar), *Charade* and — from 1971 — *Life Is What You Make It,* one of Johnny Mercer's last songs, written with Marvin Hamlisch. In addition to the five Oscar-winners among these examples, there are also seven in the list that were Best Song nominees.

Fifteen of the 31 Mercer songs recorded by Frank Sinatra came from the lyricist's movie assignments.

The third and latest of Johnny Mercer's careers was writing scores for Broadway shows. His first stage work was 1940's *Walk with Music,* music by Hoagy Carmichael.

Six years later, Mercer and Harold Arlen had *St. Louis Woman* on Broadway, with Pearl Bailey in an all-black cast, and great songs like

Come Rain or Come Shine, Legalize My Name, Any Place I Hang My Hat Is Home and *Leavin' Time*. With Harold Arlen, Mercer also did the stage musical *Saratoga* and a blues-opera expansion of their *St. Louis Woman* called *Free and Easy*.

In 1949, Mercer joined composer Robert Emmett Dolan for *Texas, Li'l Darling*. They collaborated for the stage again in 1963 with *Foxy*.

The Phil Silvers musical, *Top Banana* (1952), had songs written entirely by Johnny Mercer.

His biggest Broadway hit was clearly 1956's *Li'l Abner*, written with Gene DePaul. The lively, good-natured songs from that score included *If I Had My Druthers, Jubilation T. Cornpone* and *Namely You*.

While only two of Mercer's stage songs were recorded by Frank Sinatra — *Talk to Me, Baby (Tell Me Lies)* and *Come Rain or Come Shine* — they both got very loving treatment.

Johnny Mercer was a director of ASCAP in 1940 and 1941. During the mid–1950s, he served as president of the TV Academy. Mercer cut many records himself as a singer, and was a founder of Capitol Records.

Lorenz Hart (1895–1943)
Lyricist, Librettist — ASCAP member: 1926

Lorenz Milton Hart had a uniquely homogenous career as a lyricist, compared with the others in this chapter. He basically developed along one aesthetic line and had one significant collaborator. Born to a literary family, Hart saw his first play at age 7 and fell in love with the theater. His lifelong absorption with classical literature and drama were reflected in the style and attitude of his lyrics.

Hart went to Columbia University and wrote sketches and lyrics for their annual Varsity Shows. His first professional work was translating German plays for the Schubert brothers. While he was still at Columbia, a mutual friend with theatrical connections introduced Hart to a youngster he felt would make the ambitious Hart a fine collaborator, the 16-year-old Richard Rodgers. Though Hart was 23, the two hit it off, and a partnership ensued very quickly. That mutual friend, Philip Leavitt, brought the new team's work to producer/entertainer Lew Fields, who took one of their songs for his current show.

When Rodgers entered Columbia in 1919, the pair wrote a score that was accepted for the Varsity Show. Lew Fields took songs from that college musical for his planned *Poor Little Ritz Girl* production, and urged Rodgers and Hart to write other material for the show. After another Varsity Show score with Hart, Rodgers left Columbia for more intensive musical study, but the pair continued writing songs for musical revues, often with Lew Fields' son, Herbert. Lorenz Hart's thrust during this time was to expand song lyrics beyond the simple-minded subjects and monosyllabic rhyme cliches which prevailed in popular theater. He wanted to be fresher, funnier, and more complex than the competition. Hart placed rhymes at the start of lines, as well as at the end. He varied his couplets with multisyllabic tags such as the hypothetical example: "see a cottage RISING IN MAINE/. . . blessedly SURPRISING REFRAIN."

Lorenz Hart continued to develop. Within a few years, he and Rodgers began a successful series of Broadway musicals, with Herbert Fields writing the librettos. Once Hart's career was established, he expanded into writing librettos himself, and working on movie scores. He and Rodgers progressed steadily throughout their joint career until ennui, illness and death overtook Hart at the age of 48. His literary intelligence motivated Hart to always increase the sophistication and novelty of his lyrics, often highlighting the work with surprising rhymes and comic innuendo. His subtlety and wit allowed him to deal with touchy subjects in an acceptable way. The coupling of Hart's sharpness and irony with the freshness and beauty of Rodger's music created songs that helped to change the direction and style of musical theater in America.

Some early songs which particularly showcase Hart's words are *Mountain Greenery, This Funny World, Thou Swell, With a Song in My Heart* and *Ten Cents a Dance*. For exemplar titles of Hart's stage and screen work, see the profile of Richard Rodgers in Chapter 4.

With Sinatra's delight in sophisticated storytelling, it is no wonder he interpreted Lorenz Hart's lyrics with so much relish, whether the treatment was slow and feelingly expressed or up-tempo and witty. The singer made multiple recordings of *Lover, The Most Beautiful Girl in the World, The Lady Is a Tramp, Where or When, Falling in Love with Love, Have You Met Miss Jones?, Spring Is Here, Bewitched (Bothered and Bewildered), I Could Write a Book* and, from late in Hart's career, that classic of cultured simplicity, *It Never Entered My Mind*.

Oscar Hammerstein (1895–1960)
Lyricist, Librettist, Producer, Music Publisher —
ASCAP member: 1923

He was christened Oscar Greeley Clendenning Hammerstein, the name Oscar given after his prominent grandfather, the producer of operas and operettas. To unburden himself of his middle names, the young Oscar designated himself Oscar Hammerstein II. He wanted to make a name for himself in the theater. This he certainly did.

Growing up in a theatrical family, Hammerstein was urged to break tradition and take up the legal profession. He attended Columbia with that career in mind, but soon became involved in the university's noted Varsity Shows, writing an added scene for the 1916 show and appearing as a performer, along with Lorenz Hart. He entered the Columbia Law School, but quit after a short while to take a job from his Uncle Arthur as stage manager for three Rudolf Friml musicals.

Despite the fact that he'd left school, Hammerstein remained deeply involved with the Columbia Varsity Shows. He directed one show, writing libretto and lyrics for that show and others. Along the way he met a teenage Richard Rodgers, and in 1920 contributed one lyric to an otherwise all Rodgers and Hart university show. That first Rodgers and Hammerstein song was *Room for One More;* it would be more than 20 years before they would write another.

In 1919, Hammerstein had his first professional opportunity as a writer for the theater, a drama titled *The Light.* It failed. The next year he did the libretto and collaborated with Herbert Stothart on the songs for his first musical, *Always You.* That show made it to Broadway, but only for 66 performances. As producer of both these weak efforts, Hammerstein's Uncle Arthur urged him to share book and lyric duties with the gifted Otto Harbach, a veteran of Friml operettas. Writing again to Stothart's music, the new collaboration created the successful *Tickle Me.*

During the next eight years, this Hammerstein/Harbach writing team (joined at intervals by various other librettists and lyricists) produced a goodly number of successful shows. Some of the music was again by Herbert Stothart, but the stronger productions had music by major composers like Vincent Youmans, Rudolf Friml, Jerome Kern,

George Gershwin, and Sigmund Romberg. Some key titles of this period were *Rose-Marie, Sunny* and *The Desert Song.*

Feeling he had learned and grown since his failed solo writing at the start of the decade, Hammerstein interrupted his writing with Otto Harbach to do a production with libretto and lyrics all his own. His composer for the project was the great Jerome Kern, and the result was 1927's *Show Boat,* a powerful early attempt to integrate the elements of musical theater and to tackle subjects of weight and controversy.

After one more production with Otto Harbach, Oscar Hammerstein permanently struck off on his own as a lyricist — creating most often for melodies by either Romberg and Kern — with successful shows like *Sweet Adeline* and *Music in the Air.*

In 1934, Hammerstein joined with Sigmund Romberg to do his first movie songs, the MGM production of *The Night Is Young.* He would do songs for a handful of other films, writing a few straight screenplays, and the book and lyrics for one original TV musical. He also engaged in music publishing after 1945. Other than this activity, it was all musical theater for Hammerstein.

His greatest popular success began in 1942. Earlier, he had failed to interest Jerome Kern in a musical version of *Green Grow the Lilacs.* Now the project was offered to Richard Rodgers, who also failed to engage Lorenz Hart's attention with the material. Rodgers and Hammerstein — friends since college days — combined to turn this rural drama into the history-making *Oklahoma!,* which opened on Broadway in '43 and ran for a record-breaking 2,248 performances.

Except for writing a new English libretto and lyrics to Bizet's opera *Carmen* (December 1943's *Carmen Jones*), the rest of Oscar Hammerstein's life was devoted to his great partnership with Rodgers. Their biggest hit shows, between 1945 and Hammerstein's death in 1960, were *Carousel, South Pacific, The King and I, Flower Drum Song* and *The Sound of Music.* Film versions of these scores also met with great success.

Considering Richard Rodgers' two famous lyricists, it is interesting to note that while Hart was concerned with overt sophistication in the form of irony and polysyllabic rhymes, Hammerstein worked for the more hidden sophistication of natural dialect and monosyllabic stacked and internal rhymes. An example of such a rhyme-scheme would be:

```
TRITE ...... GAY
DAIsy ....... MAY
cliCHE ..... TRUE
......... BRIGHT
.......... NIGHT
LIGHT ..... DEW
```

Examples of Hammerstein lyrics — from work with a variety of composers, displaying his special skill with dialect, his optimistic attitude, and his flowing sense of rhyme — include *Indian Love Call, Who, Make Believe, Ol' Man River, Can't Help Lovin' Dat Man, Wanting You, I'll Take Romance, All the Things You Are* and, with Richard Rodgers, *Oh, What a Beautiful Mornin', The Surrey with the Fringe on Top, People Will Say We're in Love, It Might as Well Be Spring, Soliloquy, You'll Never Walk Alone, Some Enchanted Evening, A Wonderful Guy, This Nearly Was Mine, We Kiss in a Shadow; Love, Look Away* and *My Favorite Things.*

Sinatra found in the lyrics of Oscar Hammerstein a source of drama, an opportunity for the theatrical presentation he sometimes desired to make; strong examples of this are his recordings of *Ol' Man River, Soliloquy, This Nearly Was Mine* and *Hello, Young Lovers.* Only six songs have been recorded four times by Sinatra, and Hammerstein wrote the words for two of them, *The Song is You* (with Kern) and *Some Enchanted Evening* (with Rodgers). One of the singer's most famous recordings is his November 21, 1961, rendition of *It Might as Well Be Spring,* during which Sinatra weaves Hammerstein's lyric into a hypnotic web of sound and meaning.

Ira Gershwin (1896–1983)
Lyricist, Author — ASCAP member: 1920

Ira Gershwin started out writing for newspapers and touring with carnival shows. His first stage lyrics were written for a failed show with his brother George, *A Dangerous Maid,* and for 1921's *Two Little Girls in Blue* (under the pen-name Arthur Francis), which was composer Vincent Youmans' first Broadway show, with additional melodies by Paul Lannin. He developed his skill as a lyricist in order to resume work with his genius brother. His own gift was such that he learned to blend with the high energy and novel sounds of his brother's music, to create words that flowed with those tunes as if they were created by the same mind. Had George not died so young, it is likely the brothers' fine collaboration would have continued for many years. As it was, that partnership represents the largest part of Ira's work. But with George's death in 1937, Ira found the need and the ability to go on, to write with other talented composers in theater and films. For the details of the years with George, see the Gershwin profile in Chapter 4.

Gershwin songs which best display Ira's words — both the elegant feeling and playful energy — are exemplified by *I'll Build a Stairway to Paradise, Fascinating Rhythm, The Man I Love, Someone to Watch Over Me, Funny Face, How Long Has This Been Going On?, But Not for Me, Lorelei, Let's Call the Whole Thing Off, Love Is Here to Stay, Love Walked In* and virtually the whole of Ira's contribution to *Porgy and Bess*.

After his brother's premature death, Ira let a few years go by before really getting back to work. Barring odd exceptions (teaming to write lyrics with "Yip" Harburg for Harold Arlen's 1934 stage musical *Life Begins at 8:40,* and creating songs with Vernon Duke for the 1936 *Ziegfeld Follies* and *The Goldwyn Follies,* their final film project with George), Ira had been dedicated to working with his brother. Their pace together had been as urgent as his brother's drive. When Ira started to write again, he kept the pace leisurely and thoughtful, choosing the collaborators and projects which would allow him to stretch, experiment.

This was especially true with his stage work, which he reinstituted with the 1941 production of *Lady in the Dark.* The composer was Kurt Weill; in line with Weill's career, this musical pushed the bounds of the form, advancing integration among characterization, story and song.

In 1944, Ira resumed his movie work, joining with a 59-year-old Jerome Kern to write the songs for *Cover Girl.*

Back on Broadway the next year — again with Kurt Weill — Ira did the lyrics for *The Firebrand of Florence.* His final stage effort was *Park Avenue* (1946), which represented a return to stage productions by composer Arthur Schwartz.

Ira's last original film songs were written for *The Barkleys of Broadway* in 1949 with Harry Warren, and for two movies collaborating with Harold Arlen, the 1954 version of *A Star Is Born* with Judy Garland, and *The Country Girl* with Bing Crosby, also in 1954.

Examples of Ira's lyrics for composers other than George include *Oh Me! Oh My!, Who's Who with You?, I Can't Get Started (with You), You're a Builder-Upper, Spring Again, One Life to Live, My Ship, Long Ago (and*

Far Away), The Man That Got Away, Someone at Last and *All the Livelong Day.*

In addition to the career projects listed above, Ira Gershwin also published the book *Lyrics on Several Occasions,* and wrote music with Burton Lane and Aaron Copeland.

Sinatra recorded warm, innovative versions of 13 classic songs by George and Ira Gershwin. Of Ira's work with other composers, the singer only selected three numbers: with Vernon Duke, *I Can't Get Started (with You);* with Jerome Kern, *Long Ago (and Far Away);* and, with Harold Arlen, *The Gal (Man) That Got Away.*

Harold Adamson (1906–1980)
Lyricist — ASCAP member: 1932

While attending Harvard, young Harold Campbell Adamson wrote lyrics for the university's Hasty Pudding shows. He knew then he wanted to be a professional lyricist and proceeded directly to it. By the time he was 24, Adamson had his first crack at Broadway, working with other lyricists on Vincent Youmans' score for *Smiles.* The next year, 1931, he collaborated with Burton Lane on songs for that year's *Earl Carroll Vanities.*

In 1933, Adamson moved to Hollywood. He worked on songs for two films directed by Robert Z. Leonard, *Dancing Lady* (1933) and *The Great Ziegfeld* (1936). In the following decade, he wrote movie scores in partnership with Jimmy McHugh; their work together included *Banjo on My Knee, You're a Sweetheart, That Certain Age, A Date with Judy* and *Higher and Higher,* the latter film containing a young Frank Sinatra's first starring role.

Adamson returned to Broadway in 1941 for the Eddie Cantor musical *Banjo Eyes,* collaborating on the score with lyricist John Latouche and composer Vernon Duke. A bit more stage work followed, but Adamson's primary endeavor was writing songs for movies and the pop world, continuing strongly through the 1950s. Some of his better known '50s films were *Gentlemen Prefer Blondes, An Affair to Remember* and *Around the World in Eighty Days.*

During his theater days (12 Broadway shows), film work (45 movies) and pop song years, Adamson had many collaborators besides those already mentioned. Some of these were Louis Alter, Mack Gordon, Hoagy Carmichael, Peter DeRose, Walter Donaldson, Duke

Ellington, Jan Savitt and Johnny Watson. His most prominent later film work was done with Victor Young and Sammy Fain.

Examples of notable Adamson lyrics from stage and screen are *Time on My Hands, Everything I Have Is Yours, It's Been So Long, Where Are You?, Moonlight Mood, The Music Stopped, A Lovely Way to Spend an Evening, It's a Most Unusual Day, Around the World* and — working with Harry Warren and Leo McCarey — the Oscar-nominated movie title song, *An Affair to Remember.*

Much of what Sinatra recorded of Harold Adamson's work came from his movie collaborations with Jimmy McHugh (see the McHugh profile in Chapter 4). The most widely known of these songs was *I Couldn't Sleep a Wink Last Night,* recorded in 1943 with an Axel Stordahl arrangement, and in 1956 with charts by Nelson Riddle. Outside of songs with melodies by McHugh, Sinatra had a great time with the Adamson lyric which bounced along to a Savitt/Watson melody for *It's a Wonderful World,* and Sinatra twice recorded *Daybreak,* which Adamson made into a song by writing words for the *Mardi Gras* theme from Ferde Grofe's 1926 work, *Mississippi Suite.*

Frank Loesser (1910–1969)
Composer, Lyricist, Librettist, Publisher, Producer — ASCAP member: 1934

In the earlier part of his career, Frank Henry Loesser wrote lyrics to the melodies of several composers; it wasn't until the later 1940s that he began to work exclusively with his own melodies. It is for this reason that Loesser is represented more often in Sinatra's recording work as a lyricist than as a composer.

Loesser was born into a musical family. His father was a teacher of piano. His brother, Arthur, performed as a concert pianist. The classics were revered in the family, but popular music was disdained. Loesser wrote his first song, *The May Party,* at six years of age, but since he wasn't inclined toward classic training, his father wrote off his music, and he was left to teach himself the piano and composition as a teenager.

His college work was indifferent, though he enjoyed working on songs for school productions. Dropping out of college, Loesser worked at a variety of jobs, among them writing news for a local paper. On one newspaper assignment, he found himself writing couplets about members of the local Lion's Club. These were well received and gave him the idea to channel his musical interests into writing lyrics. Earning his way at odd jobs during the Depression, Loesser did lyrics and sketches for vaudeville and radio.

He published his first song, *In Love with a Memory*, in 1931; the music was by William Schuman. A few years later, he teamed with a composer named Irving Actman, and Loesser performed some of their songs himself at a 52nd Street nightclub where he played piano and sang. Five of those songs were selected for *The Illustrator's Show* in 1936, including *If You Didn't Love Me*. That showcase led to Actman and Loesser signing a songwriting contract with Universal Pictures.

Moving to Hollywood, Loesser followed a very unusual route by making a name in movies and later establishing himself in the theater. His first hit song—written with Alfred Newman—was *The Moon of Manakoora* from *The Hurricane*. Between 1937 and 1942, he contributed to many films, writing songs or full scores. Composers with whom he collaborated included Burton Lane, Frederick Holland, Hoagy Carmichael, Joseph J. Lilley, Jimmy McHugh, Victor Schertzinger, Jule Styne, and Arthur Schwartz. Some of the best-received of his films from this period were *Destry Rides Again* (in which Marlene Dietrich sang *See What the Boys in the Back Room Will Have*), *Buck Benny Rides Again,* and *Thank Your Lucky Stars* (Eddie Cantor's rendition of *They're Either Too Young or Too Old* received an Oscar nomination).

Then came the war years and the Army for Loesser. It was in the Army that he wrote his first full song—music and lyrics—since childhood. A number of collaborators had urged him to try writing his own music, since his lyrics had a rhythm that virtually forced the phrasing of melodies, as well as establishing meter. His 1942 military first effort was *Praise the Lord and Pass the Ammunition*. It was a big success, and he did other material for Army shows.

When Loesser returned to civilian life and Hollywood in 1946, he resumed his movie career, now writing both music and words. There were two films with Loesser songs released in 1947, *The Perils of Pauline* and *Variety Girl*. From the former came the Oscar-nominated tune, *I Wish I Didn't Love You So.*

Some of Frank Loesser's colleagues in the movie world were preparing to produce Broadway musicals. They asked Loesser to join them, and the first result was 1948's *Where's Charley?*, starring Ray Bolger. The show ran for 792 performances on Broadway. Loesser's score was a major factor in the play's success, with songs like *Once in Love with Amy, Make a Miracle* and *My Darling, My Darling.* This major hit show signaled the end of Loesser's Hollywood period. He did a few individual songs for movies and full scores for two films, one with Fred Astaire (*Let's Dance* — 1950) and one with Danny Kaye (*Hans Christian Andersen* — 1952), but the rest of his career was devoted to the theater as songwriter, librettist, publisher and producer.

In the year 1950, Loesser opened a show with his finest score to date. *Guys and Dolls* had a unity of attitude, theme and musical structure that gave it some of the qualities of opera, yet achieved the huge popular success of 1,200 performances. These songs expressed character and advanced the plot, mixing classical elements with Broadway tradition. This tendency was advanced further in 1956's *The Most Happy Fella,* in its structure and tone a species of folk opera; writing the entire libretto and massive score himself, the venture took Loesser better than four years to complete. Then came the low-key *Greenwillow.* He capped his career in 1961 with *How to Succeed in Business Without Really Trying,* which won Pulitzer, New York Drama Critics and Grammy awards.

During the '50s and '60s, Frank Loesser was also instrumental in advancing other talented songwriters, as both producer and publisher.

Prominent songs written with other composers include *Heart and Soul, Two Sleepy People, Say It (Over and Over Again), I Don't Want to Walk Without You, I'll Never Let a Day Pass By* and *Jingle, Jangle, Jingle.* Working alone, Loesser produced such fine songs as *Spring Will Be a Little Late This Year, On a Slow Boat to China; Baby, It's Cold Outside; I'll Know, If I Were a Bell, I've Never Been in Love Before, Thumbelina, Inchworm; Joey, Joey, Joey; Standing on the Corner, My Heart Is So Full of You; Summertime Love, Never Will I Marry* and *I Believe in You.*

Guys and Dolls was one of Sinatra's favorite Broadway shows. He was cast as Nathan Detroit in the film version, singing *Adelaide, Sue Me,* and *The Oldest Established.* He performed other tunes from the score on his own. *Luck Be a Lady* became one of his standards. Years earlier, Sinatra had recorded Loesser lyrics with the Dorsey band, on radio, and for Columbia Records. The last Loesser song he recorded was one highly appropriate to the singer, *I Believe in You.*

Mack Gordon (1904–1959)
Lyricist, Composer, Singer — ASCAP member: 1933

Gordon was primarily a movie lyricist. He had an extraordinarily tidy career for a man in that field. Apart from a few studio loan-outs, he worked under contract for Paramount, then Twentieth Century-Fox. Though he occasionally wrote or collaborated on his own melodies and did a few songs with lyricist partners, by far the majority of his career was in writing lyrics alone to music by single composers, first Harry Revel, then Harry Warren, then James V. Monaco, and — finally — with Josef Myrow.

Songs were produced-to-order by Gordon and his partners, and they frequently worked on three or four films a year. They did some individual songs, but most often produced whole scores to fit a wide range of musicals. Some of these movie musicals were noteworthy, but the songs have generally outlasted the films.

Mack Gordon was born Morris Gittelson in Warsaw, Poland, but moved to the United States at an early age. In the midst of a grade school education, he began to sing as a boy soprano in minstrel shows. When his public schooling was over, Gordon made a living as a singer and comic in vaudeville. This naturally led to his hanging out with songwriters, where he caught the idea of writing words for songs himself.

His first significant achievement was *Time on My Hands*, for which he shared lyric credit with Harold Adamson; the song's melody was by Vincent Youmans, written for his 1930 show, *Smiles*. Gordon was 26.

In the course of his associations, Gordon had met composer Harry Revel. Between 1930 and 1932, these men established themselves as songwriters, contributing to a couple of Broadway shows and writing pop songs to be performed by nightclub bands. Ruth Etting introduced their *Cigarettes, Cigars* in the 1931 *Ziegfeld Follies*, and a 1932 swing number, *Underneath the Harlem Moon*, got play from several bands.

The net effect of their efforts was relocation to Hollywood, a Paramount contract, and an assignment to produce the song score for a movie about two songwriters striking it rich, 1933's *Sitting Pretty*. The film starred Ginger Rogers and had appearances by Gordon and Revel.

Between '33 and '39, the pair wrote for better than two dozen films. Through 1935, all but two were for Paramount Pictures; in 1936, the team switched to Twentieth Century–Fox. Among the best received of these films were *The Gay Divorcee, We're Not Dressing, Stowaway, Poor Little Rich Girl, Ali Baba Goes to Town* and *Rose of Washington Square*. Several were yarns about singers and or songwriters. Fred Astaire, Ethel Merman, Eddie Cantor and Al Jolson were among the stars. One film had a rare appearance by the ill-fated early singing idol, Russ Columbo. Repeat performers in these films included Bing Crosby, Burns and Allen, Alice Faye, Tony Martin and Shirley Temple. Of the many lyrics and songs Mack Gordon wrote with Harry Revel, among the most engaging are *Did You Ever See a Dream Walking?, With My Eyes Wide Open I'm Dreaming, Stay as Sweet as You Are* and *There's a Lull in My Life*.

In 1940, Gordon wrote *This Is the Beginning of the End* by himself, for the picture *Johnny Apollo*. That same year, still working for Fox, he began his second major partnership. From 1940 to 1944, Mack Gordon wrote lyrics to the music of Harry Warren. The pair did complete scores or songs for more than a dozen Fox musicals, nearly all of them with a geographic theme, and therefore exploiting many different styles of music. The first collaboration was *Down Argentine Way,* with Carmen Miranda singing the Oscar-nominated title song. This film was followed by such musical exotics as *Sun Valley Serenade, Weekend in Havana, That Night in Rio, Song of the Islands, Iceland, Springtime in the Rockies* and *Hello, Frisco, Hello*. These musicals contained top Gordon/ Warren tunes like *Chattanooga Choo-Choo, I Yi Yi Yi Yi I Like You Very Much, There Will Never Be Another You, I Had the Craziest Dream, My Heart Tells Me, The More I See You* and the 1943 Oscar-winner, *You'll Never Know*. Alice Faye continued to be a repeating star in Gordon's films, along with Carmen Miranda, Hilo Hattie, Dick Haymes, and often Betty Grable. Glenn Miller and his Orchestra were featured in several of the movies, and in 1942's highly successful *Orchestra Wives,* they presented Gordon and Warren's *I've Got a Gal in Kalamazoo, At Last* and *Serenade in Blue*.

In the 1944–45 period, Gordon wrote songs for three Fox musicals with composer James V. Monaco. They starred Betty Grable and featured bands like Charlie Spivak's and Benny Goodman's. Pinup girls and music were the point of these movies, with songs like *I'm Making Believe* and *I Can't Begin to Tell You*.

Gordon joined composer Edmund Goulding to write *Mam'selle* for the soundtrack of 1946's *The Razor's Edge.* Then he began the last of his major collaborations, this time with Josef Myrow. Their first film together was one Gordon produced himself, *Three Little Girls in Blue.* It contained some of Gordon's best mature writing, with songs like *On the Boardwalk at Atlantic City, You Make Me Feel So Young* and *Somewhere in the Night.* This team worked on pictures for Fox, MGM and RKO until the end of Gordon's career. Betty Grable, Dan Dailey, Judy Garland, Gene Kelly, Donald O'Connor and Dennis Day were among the stars in movies like *Mother Wore Tights* and *When My Baby Smiles at Me.* The Gordon/Myrow songs from this later period are represented by *You Do* (1947 Oscar nominee), *Kokomo, Indiana; It Happens Every Spring* and *Wilhelmina* (1950 Oscar nominee). Gordon ended his work with Myrow after the 1956 film *Bundle of Joy.*

Mack Gordon had another song nominated for the Academy Award when he worked with a longtime associate — musical director Alfred Newman — on the soundtrack song, *Through a Long and Sleepless Night.* One of his last pieces was 1954's *You, My Love;* written with Jimmy Van Heusen. The acclaimed film *Tom Jones* used a Gordon lyric posthumously for a love song with a John Addison melody.

Sinatra recorded Gordon lyrics all through his career, selecting tunes from most of the writer's various periods. In the early '50s, the singer gave 1946's *You Make Me Feel So Young* a fresh new life, making the song his own and recording it three times. His 1980 release of *I Had the Craziest Dream* is one of the finest of Sinatra's latter-day recordings.

Rod McKuen (born 1933)
Composer, Lyricist, Poet, Singer — ASCAP member: 1957

While most widely known as a poet, Rod Marvin McKuen has devoted much of his education and career to music, both as writer and singer. He taught himself music theory, harmony and orchestration, then attended the West Lake School of Music in Los Angeles.

During the early '50s, he worked as a singer at San Francisco clubs like The Purple Onion, performing some of his own music and providing songs to local groups, including a fledgling Kingston Trio.

McKuen went to Hollywood in 1955. He furthered his musical studies with Arthur Greenslade and Henry Mancini, and he wrote songs for movies and television. He also had the opportunity to orchestrate music with composer Igor Stravinsky in Hollywood.

Though he did both melodies and lyrics for songs, McKuen worked with many collaborators, sometimes writing lyrics for composers, other times composing melodies for lyricists. Some of these collaborators were Henry Mancini, John Williams, Anita Kerr, Lee Holdridge, Francis Lai, Bruce Johnston and Petula Clark. He also did English lyrics for European songs by men like Jacques Brel and Gilbert Becaud. Among his songs, written alone and in collaboration, are *Doesn't Anybody Know My Name?*, *Toward the Unknown*, *Jean* (an Oscar nominee for 1969's *The Prime of Miss Jean Brodie*), *The World I Used to Know*, *I'll Catch the Sun*, *Listen to the Warm*, *A Cat Named Sloopy*, *Children One and All*, *The Wind of Change*, *Seasons in the Sun* and *That Golden Summer by the Sea*.

A number of McKuen's songs were based on his verse writing, which had found a large popular audience unusual for poetry in its era. Along the way, he also composed instrumental works, including four symphonies, seven concertos and scores for ballets and operas; his *The City* received a Pulitzer Prize nomination.

A longtime admirer of the art of Frank Sinatra, McKuen had tried for years to get material to the singer's attention. Finally, in 1968, they got together and discussed some possible songs. Sinatra had liked what McKuen had done for the film *Joanna*. He agreed to do a whole album of McKuen pieces written expressly for him. The album, *A Man Alone,* was recorded in 1969. It consisted of four orchestrated verse recitations interspersed among seven songs, including the fine title song and *The Beautiful Strangers, Love's Been Good to Me, Empty Is* and *I've Been to Town.* This album's themes of loneliness, contemplation and love were well suited to both the songwriter and the singer. In addition to their album together, Sinatra recorded two of McKuen's extraordinary songs via French songwriter Jacques Brel, *If You Go Away* and *I'm Not Afraid.*

Working in all his different modes, McKuen has received many honors during the '60s and '70s, among them a Royal Philharmonic Orchestra commendation, an Emmy, and the 1978 Carl Sandburg Poetry Award. He was named Los Angeles Entertainer of the Year in 1975.

Betty Comden (born 1915) and Adolph Green (born 1915)
Lyricists, Librettists, Writers, Singers — ASCAP members: 1944 and 1945

They were born just seven months apart, Betty Comden in Brooklyn, Adolph Green in the Bronx. They met in their late teens and shortly afterward combined with fellow unknowns Judy Holliday, John Frank and Alvin Hammer to form a club act called "The Revuers." The group collectively wrote and performed satiric musical sketches, many concerning the arts. Their first venue was a drafty basement in Greenwich Village called the Village Vanguard. Between 1939 and 1943, the group established themselves in New York, playing at the RCA Building's Rainbow Room and at the Blue Angel, performing witty pieces like *The Reader's Digest, Baroness Bazooka* (a satire on fulsome Broadway operettas) and *Movie Ads*. Their reputation got them to the Trocadero nightclub in Hollywood, which led to roles in a Fox film titled *Greenwich Village*. By the time the movie was released, Comden and Greene's modest roles had been edited down to almost nothing. Discouraged, they returned to New York to make a career assault on the theater.

Luck was with them. A young Leonard Bernstein had just established himself as a conductor and had composed the music for a ballet, *Fancy Free*, about three sailors on a spree in New York City. The ballet's popularity spawned the notion to recreate it as a Broadway musical. Bernstein had known Adolph Green as a singer, actor, writer and friend since 1937. He had spent many evenings enjoying "The Revuers" in the Village. Now he convinced his producers to hire Comden and Green as librettists and lyricists for this new show idea, which would become 1944's *On the Town*.

From that point onward, Comden and Green were a highly successful partnership. After the mid–1960s, they occasionally wrote separately, but this profile will confine itself to the work they did together, work that mixed their gift for satire with a love of stage and film musicals.

These two writers loved to perform, so they wrote themselves good parts for *On the Town*. But when the show was a hit, they were in demand as writers, not as performers. The musical's "book" was praised, as were the lyrics for songs like *New York, New York (a*

Wonderful Town); I Can Cook, Too; Come Up to My Place, I Get Carried Away, Lonely Town, Ya Got Me, Lucky to Be Me and *Little Bit in Love.*

Leonard Bernstein was primarily occupied by the concert world, so Comden and Green had to go forward without the creative composer. They wrote book and lyrics for 1946's *Billion Dollar Baby* to music by Morton Gould, then headed back to Hollywood.

Between 1947 and 1949, Comden and Green had one of their most intense creative periods. Working for lyricist and film-musical producer Arthur Freed at MGM, they wrote stories, screenplays and lyrics for three movies and the story/script for one more, *The Barkleys of Broadway* (1949), with Fred Astaire and Ginger Rogers, and a score by Harry Warren and George and Ira Gershwin. *Good News* (1947) had music by Roger Edens, and Comden and Green worked with Edens again on their two biggest films of the period, *Take Me Out to the Ball Game* and the movie version of *On the Town*. Both these 1949 releases starred Gene Kelly and Frank Sinatra, and new songs made up the bulk of the scores, including pieces like *Yes, Indeedy; O'Brien to Ryan to Goldberg; It's Fate, Baby, It's Fate; The Hat My Father Wore, The Right Girl for Me, Count on Me, On the Town, Prehistoric Man* and *You're Awful.*

Back on Broadway in 1951, Comden and Green did most of the sketches and lyrics for *Two on the Aisle,* with the songs *Hold Me, Hold Me, Hold Me; There Never Was a Baby Like My Baby, Catch Our Act at the Met; If You Hadn't but You Did* and *How Will He Know?* It was their first work with composer Jule Styne, who would prove to be their major theatrical collaborator over the years.

Their next two assignments—by producer Arthur Freed at MGM—were for story and screenplay only, the song scores to be created by others. They were the huge hits *Singin' in the Rain* and *The Band Wagon*. The latter gained the team an Oscar nomination.

Comden and Green had a second and final opportunity to work with Leonard Bernstein, writing the lyrics for 1953's *Wonderful Town,* starring Rosalind Russell. The ingenious score contained songs like *Conversation Piece, Christopher Street, Ohio, One Hundred Easy Ways, What a Waste, A Quiet Girl, Conga!, Swing!, It's Love* and *Wrong Note Rag,* and the show won a New York Drama Critics Circle Award and a Tony.

The majority of Comden and Green's work from 1954 on was written with Jule Styne for the Broadway stage, but there were notable exceptions to this. They did lyrics, some music, and the Oscar-nominated screenplay for MGM's 1955 Gene Kelly film, *It's Always*

Fair Weather, working with Andre Previn. Their association with Rosalind Russell got them the screenplay credit for 1958's *Auntie Mame.* Back on stage as performers in 1958, Comden and Green did *A Party,* reviving their previous hits. The pair also won a Tony award for their 1970 play *Applause.*

But the collaboration with Styne was their mainstay. The trio contributed about half the songs for Mary Martin's *Peter Pan.* Then they soared into a string of hits, with Comden and Green writing lyrics and most often the scripts for *Bells Are Ringing* (1956), *Say, Darling* (1958), *Do Re Mi* (1960), *Subways Are for Sleeping* (1961), *What a Way to Go* (Film — 1963), *Fade Out — Fade In* (1964) and *Lorelei* (1974). Both the Jule Styne melodies and the Comden/Green lyrics grew in richness and craft as they progressed from show to show. Representative songs include *Wendy, Distant Melody, Never-Never Land, It's a Perfect Relationship, It's a Simple Little System, Just in Time, Long Before I Knew You, The Party's Over, It's the Second Time You Meet That Matters; Say, Darling; Dance Only with Me, Something's Always Happening on the River, Make Someone Happy, I Know About Love, Fireworks, Cry Like the Wind, Asking for You, What Is This Feeling in the Air?, Ride Through the Night, I'm Just Taking My Time, How Can You Describe a Face?, Girls Like Me, What a Way to Go, Fade Out — Fade In, Close Harmony* and *Looking Back.*

One of the highlights of their later work — and the source of another Tony award — is *On the Twentieth Century,* for which the partners wrote book and lyrics in 1978. Cy Coleman wrote most of the music for this production, although Jule Styne also contributed.

Because of the nature of many of Comden and Green's lyrics, Sinatra didn't choose to record many of their songs outside of his two film soundtracks with pal Gene Kelly, *Take Me Out to the Ball Game* and *On the Town.* Alone, in duets and with groups, Sinatra sang 11 of the Comden/Green lyrics in those two scores. Apart from these soundtracks (never released in "official" versions but available in other editions), Sinatra recorded three songs by the pair. While on the Columbia label, he recorded an Axel Stordahl arrangement of *The Right Girl for Me,* and later, at Capitol, did a peppy Billy May version of *Just in Time.* Sinatra's most extraordinary interpretation of their words was *Lonely Town,* a Leonard Bernstein/Comden and Green song from the stage version of *On the Town.* It had been dropped from the film score. Sinatra reached back to revive the song from that fine 1944 stage production, and poured his heart into a great recording, surrounded by an arrangement that Gordon Jenkins called some of his best writing. This song clearly reveals the human feeling which informed the satire of Comden and Green.

Ted Koehler (1894–1973)
Lyricist, Pianist — ASCAP member: 1926

Koehler used his youthful skills as a piano player to break away from work as a photo engraver. He played in silent movie theaters and became a pioneer in the exploitation of hit songs at major film palaces. This led to Koehler writing material for vaudeville and nightclub revues; he also produced floor shows for the clubs. During the '20s, he began to write words for songs full-time. An early hit was 1923's *When Lights Are Low,* written with Gus Kahn and bandleader Ted Fiorito.

In 1930, Koehler was introduced to an unknown Harold Arlen by their mutual friend, composer Harry Warren. Arlen had a musical theme he was being urged to turn into his first published song, and Warren believed that Koehler was the man for the job. The result, *Get Happy,* was a substantial hit—admired by the likes of George Gershwin—and Koehler began a nonexclusive collaboration with Arlen that lasted almost 20 years. Throughout the 1930s, the pair contributed songs to musical revues, both on and off Broadway, including the 1931 *Rhythmania* revue and several editions of the Earl Carroll Vanities and the Cotton Club Parade. They also did some movie work together and wrote pop tunes for bands; for details, see the Harold Arlen profile in Chapter 4. Among the top Koehler/Arlen songs are *Between the Devil and the Deep Blue Sea, I Love a Parade, I Gotta Right to Sing the Blues, I've Got the World on a String, Stormy Weather, Let's Fall in Love, Ill Wind* and the 1944 Oscar-nominee, *Now I Know,* from Danny Kaye's first movie, *Up in Arms.*

Interspersed with his lyrics for Arlen melodies, Koehler did stage, film and pop songwriting with notable composers like Harry Barris, Duke Ellington, Rube Bloom, Sammy Fain, Jay Gorney, Ray Henderson, Burton Lane, Jimmy McHugh, James V. Monaco, Sam Stept and Harry Warren. He occasionally co-wrote with other lyricists like Billy Moll, Irving Caesar and Edward Heyman. Films that Koehler did without Harold Arlen include *Rainbow Round My Shoulder* with Bing Crosby, *King of Burlesque* with Fats Waller, *Hollywood Canteen* with Eddie Cantor, and two Shirley Temple movies, *Curly Top* and

Dimples. Some representative Koehler lyrics from these collaborations are *Wrap Your Troubles in Dreams, Animal Crackers in My Soup, I've Got My Fingers Crossed, I'm Shooting High, Picture Me Without You* and *Stop, You're Breaking My Heart.*

After the late 1940s, Ted Koehler's work decreased radically, though he produced a few songs even into the 1960s.

Most of the Koehler words sung by Frank Sinatra were set to the blues-based melodies of Harold Arlen. *I've Got the World on a String* was a big record for the singer and a staple of his live performances. He recorded *Stormy Weather* three times between 1944 and 1984. Sinatra also recorded three of Koehler's songs with Rube Bloom, the most important being *Don't Worry 'Bout Me,* first introduced in the 1939 edition of *Cotton Club Parade* by Cab Calloway.

The following brief references to lyric writers cover those who had important but not major roles in Sinatra's recording career; they are listed alphabetically by last name:

Tom Adair. All the Adair lyrics recorded by Sinatra were published between 1941 and 1944. They are beautiful love-verse, ranging from the humorously ironic *(Everything Happens to Me),* to the mournful *(The Night We Called It a Day).* These songs were important in establishing Sinatra's range in the early days of his career.

Alan Bergman and Marilyn Keith Bergman. Sinatra sang their lyrics from two different phases. Working as partners in the late '50s and early '60s, they wrote light ballad lyrics like *Sleep Warm* and *Nice 'n' Easy* for Lew Spence melodies. As a married couple in the '70s and '80s, they asked complex questions to the music of Michel Legrand. Among these were *What Are You Doing the Rest of Your Life?* and *How Do You Keep the Music Playing?*

Earl K. Brent. Brent's words to *Angel Eyes* clearly had special meaning for Sinatra. One of the greatest of saloon songs, it graced many live performances, including the end of a special preretirement performance in 1971. The definitive version was recorded in 1958 for the *...Only the Lonely* album.

Carroll Coates. Only two Coates lyrics were recorded by Sinatra, but they were tops: *No One Ever Tells You* (co-written with Hub Atwood) and *London by Night.*

Buddy DeSylva. Working with such composers as George Gershwin and Ray Henderson in the 1920s — often collaborating with

Lew Brown—B. G. (Buddy) De Sylva produced fine lyrics. Most important to Sinatra was *It All Depends on You*.

Howard Dietz. He wrote simply great words which flowed with the music of Arthur Schwartz: *I Guess I'll Have to Change My Plan, Dancing in the Dark, You and the Night and the Music*.

Ervin Drake. Drake wrote the words and music for *It Was a Very Good Year*, one of those songs that defined an era in Sinatra's work.

Al Dubin. In 1945, Sinatra recorded *I Only Have Eyes for You* as a dreamy ballad. In 1962, he did the 1934 song as a swinger with Count Basie. Other Al Dubin lyrics have served with equal versatility, including the artful piece, *September in the Rain*.

Fred Ebb. The theme from the movie *New York, New York* provided Sinatra with his last big single hit (May 1980). Ebb wrote to John Kander's music.

Dorothy Fields. Creating lyrics for such greats as Jerome Kern and Jimmy McHugh, she gave Sinatra wonderful things to say in recordings over 20 years: *On the Sunny Side of the Street, The Way You Look Tonight, I'm in the Mood for Love, A Fine Romance*.

Haven Gillespie. Although Sinatra recorded several Gillespie lyrics, the one that clearly resonates through his career is *You Go to My Head*.

Yip Harburg. A highly gifted and versatile wordsmith, E. Y. ("Yip") Harburg wrote such classics as *April in Paris* (with Vernon Duke), *It's Only a Paper Moon, Last Night When We Were Young* and *Over the Rainbow* (with Harold Arlen), and *Old Devil Moon* (with Burton Lane).

Edward Heyman. Of the Heyman lyrics among Sinatra's records, a very special example is set to music by Oscar Levant and is titled *Blame It on My Youth*.

Irving Kahal. Two songs with Kahal words were each recorded three times. One was *I'll Be Seeing You*, between 1940 and 1961, the other *You Brought a New Kind of Love to Me*, between 1945 and 1963.

Gus Kahn. Kahn worked with many fine composers. Songs like *It Had to Be You, The One I Love (Belongs to Somebody Else)*, and *None But the Lonely Heart* have inspired Sinatra to some of his richest interpretations.

Carolyn Leigh. Songs with words by this gifted lady have included two of Sinatra's biggest single hits, *Young at Heart* and *Witchcraft*.

Ruth Lowe. Only two Lowe songs were handled by Sinatra. They were both classic "signature tunes" for him. *I'll Never Smile Again* was his first big hit, recorded in 1940, 1945, 1959 and 1965. *Put Your Dreams Away* ended many a live Sinatra radio program and was recorded in 1945, 1957 and 1963.

Mitchell Parish. Often named as one of the greatest of American lyricists, Parish is only represented among Sinatra records by six songs, *Star Dust* and *Moonlight Serenade* among them.

Billy Rose. Most of the time, showman Billy Rose did lyrics in collaboration; with Edward Eliscu, he wrote the words to *Without a Song* (which Sinatra recorded three times) and the Gershwin-esque *More Than You Know*. Alone, he wrote *It Happened in Monterey* to Mabel Wayne's melody.

Ned Washington. Washington's sassy lyric to *One Hundred Years from Today* was first recorded by Sinatra during a 1943 radio broadcast. It showed up more than 40 years later on his last new album, **L.A. Is My Lady;** the words of the song still worked, after all that time. Other timeless lyrics include his collaboration with Bing Crosby: *(I Don't Stand) a Ghost of a Chance (with You),* and his own *The Nearness of You* and *Stella by Starlight.* He also penned a lyric with special echoes for Sinatra — *I'm Getting Sentimental Over You* — because it was Tommy Dorsey's theme song.

Index to Lyricists

There are hundreds of names listed in the following Index to Lyricists. Those discussed in this chapter are distinguished by the fact that Sinatra favored their work in his recordings, or they exhibited some professional or personal quality that influenced him.

Lyric writers are listed alphabetically, by their last name. The key numbers after each name may be cross-referenced to the Master Song List (Chapter 3) for further data.

Chapter 6: The Arrangers

When it comes to the recording of a song, the arranger is almost the equivalent of the director in moviemaking. The arranger composes the interlocking parts for each instrument, frequently rehearses the musicians and conducts the orchestra at the recording session, and occasionally acts as the producer. Frank Sinatra's respect for musicians and arrangers has allowed him to evolve through his association with them, in many ways functioning almost as an instrumental soloist fronting the orchestra, a heritage from his days with Tommy Dorsey.

Song choice often fell initially to the arranger for Sinatra sessions. Composition of the band was also determined by the arranger — apart from favorite sidemen the singer demanded — within the budgetary limits of each session. His best arrangers mounted Sinatra as a jewel in the setting of their orchestration.

The recording of these songs involved 68 different arrangers. Some, in the early days, wrote instrumental scorings which were only variations on familiar arrangements for particular songs, but the great majority provided original backing for Sinatra. Out of the 68 arrangers, five extraordinarily talented men served as fundamental forces in Sinatra's recording career. In addition, the Tommy Dorsey Orchestra "house" arrangements were very important. These six sources of orchestration will be discussed in detail, since they cover the bulk of recordings included in this volume, specifically 952 out of 1,251 entries. The Dorsey House Arrangements cover 52 of the entries; Axel Stordahl — 325 entries; Nelson Riddle — 315; Gordon Jenkins — 90; Billy May — 72; and Don Costa — 98.

Tommy Dorsey House Arrangements

These "house" arrangements were sometimes written by Dorsey himself, while in other cases they involved creation or collaboration by

316

Dorsey, Paul Weston, Sy Oliver, and Fred Stulce. Dorsey's dominating personality and musical style had an influence on all of them. These arrangements were highly successful with the public in their day, but are considered here for their influence on Sinatra's popularity and rapidly developing vocal technique.

The first thing to remember is that these were primarily dance-band arrangements. The folks out on the dance floor needed secure support, not surprises. Tempos were neither very fast nor very slow, but somewhere in a narrow middle range; usually a swinging beat, but swinging gently. Once a tempo was set, it didn't vary within a tune. By the same token, the dramatic quality of a number started out moderate and stayed level.

The Tommy Dorsey Orchestra was almost seven years old by the time Sinatra first recorded with them. They had begun with a strong dixieland jazz flavor, but by 1942 had shifted to a relatively sweet-sounding variety of big band swing. One distinctive feature of the orchestra's arrangements was the emphasis placed on the "vocal refrain" for each tune, showcasing the band's solo and group singers.

Personnel changed through time in the Dorsey band, but instrumental composition remained fairly constant; trumpets, trombones, saxophones, clarinets, plus piano, guitar, bass fiddle, and drums. By the time Sinatra came along, the house arrangements using these instruments had developed a basic pattern and some variations on that design. It was a pattern similar to that of competing bands, but the sound of Dorsey's trombone and the more extensive use of vocalists made their records distinctive.

The arrangement pattern would begin with a few bars of ensemble playing, then a trombone (usually Dorsey, playing either open or with a mute) would take the melody line. Rhythm from drums, bass, or piano would be unobtrusive. Two choruses and either a breakstrain or "release" would be carried by the solo trombone. Sometimes other soloists or pairs would take part of this melody. After the release strain and a brief introductory fanfare, the song would start over — with one or more singers — for two choruses and the release, while the band played simply and softly. This vocal portion did not dominate the record, but rather served as another species of instrumental solo or ensemble. Then the band would quickly finish the tune with a flourish, jazzy trumpets and saxes heating up over stronger drumming. A drum, cymbal, or piano would make a definite stop for the number, often with a single thump, clang, or plunk. The dancers would definitely know the tune had ended.

Influenced by Dorsey, Sinatra sang more and more like a trombone, and thus blended well with the arrangements. Though many solo band vocalists resisted singing with groups, Sinatra worked just as hard to blend with The Pied Pipers as he did to coordinate with the band, though he generally performed the most solos within the vocal group's work. Sometimes the pattern was reversed, with the singer taking the first two choruses and the release, followed by a center-of-the-arrangement Dorsey solo — enlivened by the noodling of other instruments — and with the singer or vocal group doing the final chorus.

And there were several variations to the basic pattern. The first release would be taken from the trombone by a solo clarinet and pairs of trumpets or saxes. In the final choruses, there was often increased improvisation on the melody by both trombone and other soloists, including Bunny Berigan or Ziggy Elman on trumpet. Sometimes trumpets or clarinets would play jazzy riffs around the opening melody and then band members (or The Pied Pipers) would do similar vocal riffs around Sinatra's lyric expression. A hot and sweet variation would have brilliant brass and woodwind passages moving in and out of the gentle trombone melody, saxes playing in very close harmony or identical-note duets, trumpet and clarinet soloists dueling in a jazz-like interplay. Such variations kept the basic pattern fresh.

During the period from 1940 to 1942, there was increasing use of arrangements by Axel Stordahl, Sy Oliver, Fred Stulce and others. These broke the "house" pattern in various ways, including slower or faster tempos, comic novelty songs, and the singer-dominated tunes which provided some of the band's biggest hits. In that same period, however, the Dorsey House Arrangements remained generally stable. Along with Tommy Dorsey's relaxed, intimate *legato* playing, they provided a dependable base for the development of Sinatra's trombone-like phasing.

Axel Stordahl (born 8/8/13, New York; died 8/30/63) Trumpeter, Singer, Composer, Conductor, Live-Radio Conductor

Career Summary. Early career as sideman/arranger with Bert Bloch, 1934–35. Joined the Tommy Dorsey organization in early 1936;

played trumpet, sang in vocal trio, and was an important arranger with Dorsey until 1943. When Sinatra left Dorsey, Stordahl went with him. He was Sinatra's principal arranger and conductor during his initial solo career at Columbia Records, from 1943 to 1952, also handling all of Sinatra's work on radio, many of his movie songs, his first TV show, and the Victory Disc recording sessions for the wartime military. Separating from Sinatra during the 1950s, Axel Stordahl worked as an arranger/conductor for such artists as Eddie Fisher, Gisele MacKenzie, Nannette Fabray, Dinah Shore, Dean Martin and Bing Crosby. Stordahl was also the composer of several popular songs. Less than two years before his death, he conducted and did arrangements for Sinatra's last-recorded Capitol Records album, ***Point of No Return.***

WORK WITH SINATRA — begun when Stordahl was age 27 and Sinatra 25.

Axel Stordahl wrote the arrangement for the very first record Sinatra cut with the Dorsey Band *(The Sky Fell Down)* on February 1, 1940. When the singer was allowed his first true solo work in recording — two years later — Axel Stordahl was the man who arranged and conducted. A personal friend of Frank's, he oversaw his work on radio and Victory Disc recording. When Sinatra's departure from Dorsey had been negotiated, Stordahl went with him to Columbia Records; 221 of the 280 Columbia tracks in this volume were arranged by Stordahl. He also scored for Sinatra's early film work.

This partnership lasted from 1940 to 1953, with the first session at Capitol Records. Then Voyle Gilmore, Sinatra's new producer at Capitol, wanted to "capitalize" on the new nightclub sound Sinatra had been developing, and Stordahl was assigned to other singers.

The lush, string-laden, tender arrangements of Axel Stordahl were an ideal setting for the romantic, frail-sounding vocalist of the mid-1940s. Whereas Sinatra had sung tender love ballads for Dorsey's swing band without the benefit of a string section, at Columbia Records these ballads were set in full-orchestral Tchaikovskian splendor.

Some of the songs recorded with Stordahl arrangements were up-tempo, hot/sweet, ragtime, novelty, or humorous show songs. For such tunes, Stordahl provided punchy, brassy charts. Many of these were done for radio shows. Other up-tempo sounds such as *Saturday Night (Is the Loneliest Night of the Week)* from the November 14, 1944, session, were hit recordings. But these were not the mainstream of Stordahl's work with Sinatra, and other arrangers were often used.

For the most part, in those Columbia recordings (1943–1952), Sinatra sang the melody and lyrics as written, concentrating on the emotional and dramatic expression of the song. While the singer rode on the melody, Stordahl's orchestrations would weave a spell behind and around that melody. The string section would stay closer to the melodic line, other instruments straying farther from it. Very often the violin section would provide the main support, sometimes with straightforward harmony, other times plucking little stairsteps of sound, then shimmering like the wind through trees. Playing around the violins and cellos were a tinkling piano, a xylophone or a celesta. Vocal groups were occasionally used — a strong carry-over from the Dorsey days — singing in close harmony with Sinatra on the choruses, or producing "ooohs, aaaaahs, and tooo, dooo, mmmeeeeee, waaaahs." When horns came into the arrangements, more often than not they were oboes, clarinets, and flutes rather than the sharper personality of saxophones or brass instruments. Brass, when used, were frequently played with mutes. Instead of drums to keep the beat, bass fiddles predominated. Stordahl would often turn to his harpist or his much-used oboe player when he wanted a climax, rather than the more conventional trumpet runs or clarinet trills.

Tempos were slow to medium, in order to showcase the story of a song thoughtfully and feelingly. As Sinatra's baritone grew deeper between 1945 and 1950, some tempos slowed even further to accommodate long-held deep notes, changes in vocal texture, and dramatic pauses.

Overall, these arrangements were subtle and supportive, rather than showy and driving. The volume was low, allowing Sinatra to sing very intimately into the microphone, not covering up the increasing delicacy and nuance of his style. At times an arrangement would bring all the instruments to silence for several measures, in order to place special emphasis on the words being sung. If the tune were a rumba, samba, or had a Caribbean flavor, most often the beat and tone would be established with a guitar and woodwinds rather than the traditional drums and brass. Guitar solos and lead-ins were used for especially quiet numbers.

In the early 1950s, as comic tunes and a burgeoning rock and roll began to infiltrate the Top–30, Axel Stordahl traveled with an unhappy Frank Sinatra into the realm of novelty, soul-shout, and the contemporary pop songs demanded by Columbia's management, as opposed to their own choice of 1920-to-1945–vintage songs. Neither man seemed comfortable with this. Then Sinatra's contract was not renewed. Their collaborative era soon ended.

After nearly a decade's hiatus, their last work together was the reminiscent album *Point of No Return.* That assignment was a fine gesture on Sinatra's part — not long before Stordahl's death — but it was more than that; even though some tracks seem too slow and lush, the best of them are marvelous, bringing a mature Sinatra sensibility and voice back to the music of a man who played such a potent role in his life's work.

Nelson Riddle (born 6/1/21, New Jersey; died 10/6/85) Trombonist, Composer, Conductor, Movie/TV Scores

Career Summary. Early career as trombonist with Charley Spivak, starting in 1941, then as trombonist/arranger with Jerry Wall and Tommy Dorsey. After his WWII military service, Riddle worked with Bob Crosby on the West Coast. In 1947, he went back to arranging for Tommy Dorsey, then served as a staff arranger for NBC radio. In the 1950s, he came into special prominence as a free-lance arranger for recording sessions at Capitol Records, where the young label had acquired Frank Sinatra at a low point in his career. The company wanted a new sound for Sinatra and they got it from Riddle. He continued recording with Sinatra until the late '70s, although his contract with Capitol kept them apart from September '60 to November '61.

Riddle showed a rare gift for "setting" vocalists. At Capitol, Verve, and various other labels, he worked with many recording artists, including such greats as Bing Crosby, Judy Garland, Nat "King" Cole, Peggy Lee, Ella Fitzgerald and Johnny Mathis.

He was active composing, arranging, and conducting for movies in the '50s and '60s. The wide range of Riddle's film scores is represented by *Pal Joey, Li'l Abner, Lolita, Robin and the 7 Hoods* and *Camelot.*

Riddle was musical director for Sinatra's second TV series. He wrote the background music for "The Untouchables" and, in the '60s and '70s, worked on many TV specials and series like "The Smothers Brothers Comedy Hour" and "Rowan and Martin's Laugh-In." Two years before his death in 1985, he prepared classic Riddle arrangements for Linda Ronstadt's successful revival of torch-song ballad recording.

WORK WITH SINATRA — begun when Riddle was age 31 and Sinatra 37.

From the beginning, Nelson Riddle brought a special intensity to his work with Frank Sinatra. The first two songs mastered during their first session together were the classic records *I've Got the World on a String* and *Don't Worry 'Bout Me* (April 30, 1953). These two arrangements demarcate the range of moods covered by the pair over the years. The joyful triumph expressed by Sinatra in *I've Got the World on a String* is present from the first notes of the arrangement, with shrilling trumpets stair-stepping down into a trough of woodwinds. Blue saxophones back up the reflective loneliness of *Don't Worry 'Bout Me.*

Later, the duo would push the extremes of this range, from the painful isolation of "saloon" songs to the bubbling happiness of light swing love ballads, and every shade and style in between. In fact, variety and change are the keynotes of the Riddle/Sinatra collaboration.

Among all the singer's arrangers, none showed as much continuing inventiveness, depth and width of range as Nelson Riddle. They did all kinds of work together. Records meant for singles release were often more danceable, always more blatant in their approach, than the album work. But both singles and albums ran the gamut of styles; brand-new pop tunes, movie title songs, standard love ballads, Christmas songs, hot jazz numbers, Broadway showtunes, concert moods with a string quartet, bluesy saloon songs, TV production pieces, light swing tunes, film scores, and much more. Every different mode received a different Riddle treatment, and even when they repeated a type of music, there was a difference in arrangement from the last time they had tackled that mode.

In terms of this discussion, all that variety and versatility makes Riddle's work with Sinatra harder to pin down — to analyze — than any of the other arrangers covered in this chapter. While each album had an integration of mood and style, there was still a great variety of orchestration within each LP. And there were so many albums. Riddle was the sole or principal arranger for 29 of the albums covered by this book. The permutations of style represented by this amount of work are nearly endless.

There are some traits, however, that characterize many of Riddle's charts. Perhaps the best approach is to summarize these traits, dividing them into rough categories, rather than dealing with specific albums or separate recordings, as can be done with later arrangers. (For specific information on the nature of the Riddle-arranged LPs, see their entries in Chapter 8.)

The characteristic traits found in many Riddle charts fall into three basic groupings: those that apply to all styles of LP; those that pertain mostly to the happy LPs; and those that show up mainly in the sad LPs. Here are some of the most frequently observed features of Riddle's charts:

General Traits Grouping

Expression of Theme: Despite the diversity among all of Riddle's arrangements, each theme album has a unity of feeling and sound. It's as if the LP is a play, while each song is a scene within that play. Song selection is an important part of this, but so are the particular selection of session musicians and a dominance of certain tempos and instrumental auras. The up-tempo LPs range from light and cool to hot and heavy. The down-tempo LPs range from loving ballads to reflective sadness to agonized loneliness. But each stakes out a certain territory and holds it.

Understatement: Whether swinging or brooding, Riddle's charts most often tend toward understatement, the belief in less is more. Certainly he wrote some fulsome arrangements, especially for movie songs, the singles market and for showtune production numbers. But the majority of his work is subtle, inferential, slightly withholding. There are charts which give the effect of simple jazz combos. A saloon song might be accompanied by a piano, one hand keeping the beat, the other hand playing blues countermelodies, while a few strings and horns highlight certain moments. In extreme cases, the arrangement is almost nonexistent, with no melodic passages or countermelodies, just a rhythmic pulse of music behind the singer.

Unique Sounds: In the danceband era from which Riddle graduated, certain instruments were used for their distinct sounds and personalities. In his writing after 1950, he worked against that tradition in several ways. Unlikely combinations of instruments would play together, both in unison and in counterpoint; low trumpets and high trombones were common, as were strings with brass, while less frequent combinations included guitar and piano, flutes and strings, violin and bass, trombones and violins, bassoon and flute, and unison vibraphone and guitar. While most arrangers write a musical phrase for a consistent group of instruments, not shifting until the next phrase, Riddle's charts were full of musical phrases not completed by one sound, but rather passed around from one group to another, all within a few bars. This was often done so smoothly that the effect was like one instrument or section continuously playing the phrase, but changing its sound as it went along. Another unique area was the way Riddle had his musicians switch roles in a passage. Strings playing sustained notes behind a horn melody line would be suddenly transformed into horns sustaining notes behind melodic strings. With such effects, it's often hard to identify which instruments are playing.

Integration: Sinatra singing with Riddle music has a feeling of inevitability, of organic unity. It was a fusing, intuitive exchange, in which Riddle's great variety encouraged a similar versatility in the singer. After they had collaborated for awhile, Riddle began to write with Sinatra's old and new strengths in mind, and Sinatra sang in reaction to the arrangements and the way certain musicians played. With previous arrangers, Sinatra had been singing over and in front of the music; with Riddle, he was inside the arrangement, interacting with it and sharing solo leads with various horns and strings. Former trombonist Riddle sometimes wrote so that Sinatra took the place of a lead trombone part. All these things combined with other techniques to produce a great integration of singer/musician/orchestra. In a seeming contradiction, Riddle's arrangements were strongly present but never obtrusive; they could stand alone as instrumental pieces — especially if some horn were to take the whole melody — but the charts were always collaborative with a singer, not competitive.

Originality vs. Cliche: Riddle was generally original, not sounding like anyone else. In fact, the Sinatra/Riddle swinging sound was highly imitated in its day, and has left its mark on such arrangements ever since. His slow ballad work, too, stood apart from other arranger's, with its highly varied use of trombones and jazz inflections. But Nelson Riddle declared his independence in another way. He reserved the freedom to use a cliche or an obvious idea if that's what worked the best. For *Ebb Tide,* woodwinds and strings create a rhythmic surging of tide and blowing of wind. A sentimental *With Every Breath I Take* is filled with the traditional sweet playing of strings. The lyric for *Mam'selle* speaks of violins several times, so the violin is featured in the chart. Riddle also liked to take a page from Billy

May's book now and then, with screaming brass and musical catch phrases, but Riddle's use of jazz piano and varying instrumental textures would make the arrangement his own, as would high strings playing in the background of a jazzy chart.

Endings: One of the most vivid traits of Riddle's writing was the way he played with the end of a chart. Unexpected instruments would play for the first time. Music would stop abruptly to underscore a sustained closing note by Sinatra. Many endings incorporated a series of playful instruments, each performing a different little riff; just when you thought it was over, there would be another little ding or plunk or boom, or a clarinet trill. Some of these stacked endings included changes of tempo.

Happy/Up-Tempo Grouping

Tempo: In the first decade of Riddle's work with Sinatra, most of the swinging records were arranged and conducted to a beat that matched the tempo of a heart's beat during a brisk walk. This heartbeat meter gave the songs a natural, sexy rhythm that stimulated the unconscious awareness of musicians, singer and listener. This rhythm was sometimes emphasized by staccato playing, single horn notes coming right on the beat. Within the framework of this tempo, Riddle maintained the feeling of sensuality with other effects; he knew how to use a bass clarinet or trombone to kick off a rhythmic phrase, how to slowly build tension, holding off on his climactic explosion of brass. In early days, this tempo of the heart was used in lightly swinging arrangements. A few years later, the same beat was maintained with a hotter jazz sound. During the final years of his work with Sinatra, Riddle began to use tempos that were either much faster or much slower.

Textures: There were four phases in Riddle's up-tempo charts, as far as instrumental texture was concerned. In the first swinging LPs, he used lots of runs with muted trumpets, clarinets, trombones and other solo horns. A plucked bass usually kept the beat, not drums. There might be a solo jazz fiddle now and then, but otherwise strings were reserved for special seasoning, sometimes used as another arranger would use brass. Repeat phrases were engaged to begin charts (the same figure played first by woodwinds, then strings, then brass) and then to answer vocal phrases within the song, with Sinatra tending to imitate these horn sounds with his voice. And there was always novelty — surprise — like the sparing use of saxophones or loud brass, or a xylophone alternating with jazzy woodwinds. The same textures were still present in Phase Two, but with the addition of more violins, brass instruments and drums, for a balance of sweet and spicy. Tempo changes were more dramatic. Sinatra deviated from written lyrics and melody with greater frequency, and this creative play was accentuated when horns would get right in unison with the singer for awhile and then break away. For Phase Three, the new thing was charts featuring a solo swing piano and a jazz combo sound. The final phase additions included electric organ in many cuts, plus faster or slower than usual swing tempos, and more use of drums.

Song Structure: There were several ways that Riddle played off standard '40s song structure in his charts. In the early days, he would often skip the verse, swing lightly through the first two choruses, then swing harder in the final chorus. Another variation was for a certain instrument to open the arrangement, then the same horn would take a semi-improvised solo in the middle breakstrain, and finally that same musician would come in at the end. Some charts followed the song structure as written, but with lightly swinging choruses divided by a hot, brassy instrumental centerpiece. Sinatra would often stick to the melody and lyric as written for the early sections, then make changes in both for the last chorus. Riddle would occasionally exaggerate the quality of balance in older song structures by beginning and ending the piece with the same music; in between, he wrote two sets of the same two choruses, the first set light, the second hot. After the mid-1960s, when Riddle was arranging newer songs, he responded to their different structures with charts that remained more consistent within themselves, and with faster or slower swinging tempos than before.

Sad/Down-Tempo Grouping

Transition from Stordahl: In the first of Riddle's lonely albums, there are clear echoes of Axel Stordahl; soft strings, moody wood-winds, xylophone and faint brass. Even so, Riddle has a distinctive voice. He puts greater emphasis on melodic recapitulation in break-strains, spices things with original woodwind licks, plucked violins, jazzy piano elements. Blue saxes and muted trumpets play in a jazz obligato and riff mode, replacing Stordahl's oboe and string solos. With both Dorsey and Stordahl, Sinatra had utilized a legato line and extended phrasings. Riddle wrote charts designed to emphasize and underwrite those effects. In contrast to Stordahl's rich harmonies, Riddle often did very spare charts (simple musical figures passed from instrument to instrument), which provided a real jolt when the full orchestra came crashing in at key moments. String sections were used far less by Riddle, so their sweetness held special power for the emotional climax of some arrangements.

Lonely Moods: Sometimes horns would take over for part of a vocal passage, as if the singer couldn't go on. Trumpets, trombones and French horns played in unison for a highly mournful brass sound. In the midst of some intimate singing, there might come a wave of surprisingly hot instrumental work, forcing the singer to project his pain over that hot and blue sound. Riddle's "saloon" charts contained many semi-improvisational solos such as a sax playing with a melody while trombones kept the beat.

Unique Variations: There were some sad arrangements by Nelson Riddle that were especially distinctive. One set of charts had Sinatra singing with the Hollywood String Quartet—composed of Felix Slatkin and Paul Shure (violins), Alvin Dunkin (viola) and Eleanor Slatkin (cello)—and soft background work by a trumpet, French horn, clarinet, flute, oboe, piano, bass guitar, harp and drums. Sinatra functions almost as a lead cello, his past study of master string soloists demonstrated in the way he "bows" his voice seamlessly from note to note and phrase to phrase, almost singing *a cappella* at times. Another LP involves very slow tempos and lengthy arrangements: introductions might be played by oboe or blue trombone or classical piano; there's a steady bass beat throughout; breakstrains can have a tenor-trombone playing the melody and a bass-trombone doing riffs around that melody; and endings include a bassoon and oboe sounding like the weary tread of a man walking down some last lonely road.

All these Nelson Riddle techniques—plus many others not mentioned—ebbed and flowed to produce unique LPs through the years; the happy albums *(Songs for Swinging Lovers!, A Swinging Affair!, Sinatra's Swingin' Sessions!!!)*, the sad albums *(In the Wee Small Hours, Close to You, Frank Sinatra Sings for Only the Lonely)*, and the mature expressions of the Riddle/Sinatra alliance, with love ballads revisited in *Nice 'n' Easy*, famous movie songs savored in *Frank Sinatra Sings "Days of Wine and Roses," "Moon River," and Other*

Academy Award Winners, and modern songs included in *Strangers in the Night.*

Creating music in partnership with Nelson Riddle both broadened and deepened the singing of Frank Sinatra. He entered the collaboration with all his early skills intact, grew simultaneous with Riddle, and took what he had learned into every musical partnership that came later.

Gordon Jenkins (born 5/12/10, Missouri; died 5/1/84) Musician — Piano and Banjo, Singer, Composer/ Lyricist, Conductor

Career Summary. Early work as banjoist in Saint Louis, Missouri, dance band, then staff pianist on a local radio station. Noted as songwriter in 1930s: *P.S. I Love You* (with Johnny Mercer), *Blue Prelude* and *Goodbye.* Pianist/arranger in '30s with the great Isham Jones Band; Jenkins' arrangements were considered a major contribution to the band's quality. Later in the 1930s, arranged for Paul Whiteman, Benny Goodman, Vincent Lopez and Andre Kostelanetz. Arranger on Broadway, and musical director for NBC's West Coast radio, also scoring for movies and nightclubs. He bridged the worlds of concert music and popular composition with his 1945 piece, *Manhattan Tower Suite.* In the late 1940s, he conducted on Dick Haymes' radio show and did arrangements for Decca recording sessions with artists like Louis Armstrong, Ella Fitzgerald and Artie Shaw. Collaborated with lyricist Tom Adair on 1949's Broadway show *Along 5th Avenue.* At Capitol Records, Jenkins arranged and conducted for Nat "King" Cole and Peggy Lee, and he began his important association with Frank Sinatra. Arranger for Sinatra sessions from 1957 to 1981. Conductor/arranger for Sinatra's 1973 comeback television special, *Ol' Blue Eyes Is Back.* More songwriting in that period, including *This Is All I ask, How Old Am I?* and *I Loved Her.* Also wrote the music, lyrics, choral parts and orchestration for *The Future,* a biographical cantata written about Sinatra.

WORK WITH SINATRA — begun when Jenkins was age 45 and Sinatra 41.

Among his new arrangers at Capitol Records in the 1950s, Nelson Riddle was Sinatra's inspiration to reach new depths, Billy May was his jolly energizer, and Gordon Jenkins was his link to more than a decade of emotional ballad singing.

Jenkins' arrangements varied remarkably little in their basic "feel" during the more than twenty years he wrote for Sinatra. Most of the dominant features were present in their first album, ***Where Are You?*** His charts hearkened back to Sinatra's work with Axel Stordahl in several ways. Jenkins' arrangements were supportive, showcasing and setting Sinatra's voice, rather than competing like Billy May's, or even commingling like Nelson Riddle's. The charts were a delicate cloud floating under the singer's voice, lifting it, building to climaxes coincident with the drama presented by the voice, accentuating more than accompanying. Stringed instruments dominated, horns most often played softly. Bright accents would be achieved with the xylophone, celesta or chimes. These were all aspects that recalled Axel Stordahl, but were even more emphasized with Jenkins than with Stordahl. Overall, this glowing supportiveness allowed Sinatra to sing with more nuance than ever before. And unlike Stordahl, Jenkins wrote with consciously symphonic elements, less dance band influence, and with a mournful black-blues underpinning brought from his days with Isham Jones's group.

Compared to many other Sinatra arrangers, Jenkins wrote longer introductions to set a mood and longer closes to bring the listener out of that mood. Tempos were often slow, the rhythms unobtrusive. And always supportive. These charts encouraged Sinatra to reach for his maximum emotional expressiveness, in songs of loving warmth and tender sentiment as well as in songs of loneliness, nostalgia and painful reflection.

Arrangements would usually open with a musical phrase drawn from some part of the song's melody, whether verse, release or chorus. This phrase sometimes adhered closely to the composer's writing and, other times, was so altered that the source was nearly unrecognizable. This restructured melodic piece would often serve as a background phrase within the arrangement, appear in the breakstrain, or resurface at the end of an arrangement. Wherever Jenkins used these melodic restatements — and whether obvious or subtle — they served to give the arrangement unity and "organic" relationship to the song they were setting.

The openings were frequently played by one of Jenkins' favored group of instruments. A classic example would be a solo oboe, followed

by a solo flute, followed by a section of violins. Another common opening was by French horn, or perhaps strings, then French horn, then
woodwinds.

After opening, the charts were often dominated by strings, with
solo French horn and soft trombones taking on the brass parts. Woodwind sections usually played without saxophones, but rather with a
solo clarinet, flute, oboe or bassoon. String passages might begin with
one or two violins, then quickly add more violins, then all the strings
(violas, cellos, sometimes a bowed bass fiddle), and build to great
volume and richness, a crescendo made not by louder playing, but by
more musicians.

There was a general absence of drums; instead, bass and or guitar
kept the beat. This lack of percussion was frequently offset by pizzicato
playing of strings, plucked violins and harp, with piano, chimes, and
even flutes emulating the effect of a run of plucked notes.

More often than not, Jenkins used his instrumental breakstrains
to restate the main chorus melody of the song, sometimes infusing it
with a countermelody of his own.

There was often less orchestration in the release portion of a song
than elsewhere. This was also where Jenkins might use a light effect
like staccato horns and or plucked string runs behind long violin
phrases. To end a piece, Jenkins turned again to his restructured portion of the song's melody, but he sometimes finished with a special
sound such as the slow unison plucking of violin and harp to recall a
church bell.

The majority of these elements was present in *Where Are You?*,
that first work with Sinatra, an LP of soft, sighing strings and the delicate playing of woodwinds and French horn. Sinatra sang lots of sustained, melancholy tones. More than any Sinatra/Jenkins collaboration except for 1980's *Trilogy: The Future,* this album shows the influence of the concert hall. *Laura* has an extended introduction — with
strings, French horn and woodwinds — that develops into a tone poem
for the body of the song. *Lonely Town* brings a feeling of self-contained
musical drama, the result of composer Leonard Bernstein's serious
background and a disposition to operatic expression on the part of
Sinatra and Jenkins. The treatment of *I Think of You,* based on a
Rachmaninoff theme, respects its concert roots.

From that first album onward, the only big departure from this
basic Jenkins style was in *Trilogy;* all the other LPs are variations.

The main variation for *A Jolly Christmas from Frank Sinatra* is the extensive use of a large male/female choir; they introduce pieces, sometimes take over the second chorus from Sinatra (especially in the traditional carols), and often sing behind him in wordless harmony.

No One Cares adds to the mix more of the blues sensibility Jenkins brought from his '30s arrangements for Isham Jones. In this LP — often called one of the singer's greatest — it becomes very evident that Jenkins' charts inspired Sinatra to sing in the manner of a cello or a violin, as opposed resembling a trombone with Nelson Riddle or singing more like a trumpet with Billy May. It is also one of Sinatra's "downest" albums, perhaps even more so than the renowned . . . *Only the Lonely.* There is a use of minor chords and painful silences. *Stormy Weather*'s lyric hangs in the air over weeping strings, while bass and guitar pluck out a heartbeat and an oboe probes at open wounds.

There are several variations from Jenkins' mainstream in *All Alone.* This album has very slow tempos, heavy use of the breakstrain for a full recapitulation of melody, and many instances of a guitar used to replace drums. *The Girl Next Door* opens in classic Jenkins style, with a solo oboe, then piano and plucked violins, then a French horn introducing a section of sweetly bowed violins. Throughout the LP, slow tempos and extended breakstrains make for long cuts, and encouraged Sinatra to emphasize his predilection for long-held notes and carry-overs tying phrases together.

September of My Years came eight years after Jenkins' first collaboration with Sinatra, and it is remarkable how similar the arrangements are to that first effort. The main difference is that this album evokes less of a concert sound and more the feeling of pop songs. The album's most widely heard arrangement, *It Was a Very Good Year,* is written in four sections, each played bigger and fuller than the one before, to reflect the maturing-of-a-man theme. The first section opens with a single oboe in a classic Jenkins melody variant; a soft accompaniment follows. The second section opens with clarinets and is louder. The third opens with violins, and the whole section is played vividly. The fourth starts with many high-pitched strings and builds to a dramatic peak, and the chart closes with a repeat of the introductory oboe.

Gordon Jenkins arranged two-thirds of the songs used in Sinatra's back-from-retirement album, *Ol' Blue Eyes Is Back.* Here the chief variation from Jenkins' basic approach is the extensive use of drums, which he generally avoids. Jenkins also conducted the orchestra for the arrangements written by Don Costa; these Costa arrangements might account for the presence of drums in the session group. There is also the novel use of a mixed chorus.

The Future [Reflections on the Future in Three Tenses] is the LP which stands apart from all Jenkins' other work with the singer (it's one of three discs for *Trilogy*). The whole album is devoted to Jenkins' own cantata on the subject of Sinatra's life and career, played by the Los Angeles Philharmonic Symphony Orchestra and sung by Sinatra and a large chorale. This work's difference is evident from the start; the cantata opens with the sounds of an orchestra tuning up, then procedes into a semioperatic structure of recitative and aria vocal passages lasting for ten minutes or more, interspersed with orchestral sections. There are far more brass parts than usual, especially for the trumpets which are so rare in Jenkins' arrangements. There is the big timpani sound, plus other drums and even cymbals for the operatic climaxes. The chorale is heavily used, singing alone, or with Sinatra, or in the background; they also accompany the orchestra with nonverbal musical sounds. The work has a wide range of moods and tempos, at times imitating "sound effects" or the music of Beethoven, Puccini and other Sinatra favorites. There are also echoes of past Sinatra charts, for songs like *It Was a Very Good Year, One for My Baby* and *My Way*. A unique piece for both Sinatra and Jenkins.

For his final work with Sinatra—*She Shot Me Down*—Jenkins returns to his basic style, this time with the minor chords and blues tonality of the earlier masterpiece, *No One Cares*. In comparison to that album, however, the strings are less evident and solo or group woodwinds are used more. The maintenance of beat by guitar and or bass is especially notable. *A Long Night* has a novel passage with clarinets and trombones playing in unison, in the manner of strings. As to Jenkins' penchant for reworked melody phrases, there's a remarkable example during the breakstrain of *Monday Morning Quarterback*, with French horn and oboe soloists playing off one another for a beautiful effect.

On reflection, it is remarkable how many variations Gordon Jenkins was able to work from a limited number of basic elements, and how appropriately his arrangements serve a wide variety of songs.

Billy May (born 11/10/16, Pennsylvania)
Musician — Trumpet and Trombone, Bandleader, Conductor

Career Summary. E. William May began his career as a sideman with various bands. As a youngster, he had learned to write instrumental arrangements, beginning with trumpet parts. Held an early job with Baron Elliot on CBS radio. Began arranging and playing trumpet for Charly Barnet in 1938. With Glenn Miller from the end of 1940 through 1942, prominent arrangements including *Take the A Train* and — with Bill Finnegan — *At Last* and *Serenade in Blue.* Played trombone with Les Brown, then Woody Herman, and wrote charts for the Alvino Ray Orchestra. Based on the West Coast, Billy May got active in the recording studios; also on radio with performers such as Ozzie and Harriet, Red Skelton and Bing Crosby. In late 1940s, became free-lance arranger for bands backing singers. Rose to fame in early 1950s as the leader of a Jimmy Lunceford–style band given to original voicings and phrasings, with a glissing unison saxophone style which became absorbed into mainstream music. Gained reputation as a brilliant arranger in any style. Arranged and conducted for several top vocalists including Bing Crosby, Ella Fitzgerald, Nat "King" Cole, Peggy Lee and Anita O'Day. He presided over important Sinatra sessions during a span of 22 years. May also composed for TV and films.

WORK WITH SINATRA — begun when May was age 40 and Sinatra 41.

The body of May's work with Sinatra resides in six theme LPs done between 1957 and 1979, three for Capitol and three for Sinatra's own Reprise label. Though each of these albums is distinctive, there are common bonds among them. Those bonds have to do with the "Billy May sound," which was well-developed before the two ever worked together.

Capitol Records had wanted to unite their two contract artists earlier, but it wasn't until October of 1957 that May and Sinatra first collaborated. The result — containing musical qualities new to both of them — was the travel theme album *Come Fly with Me.* That album certainly contained elements of the "May sound," but was dominated by other moods.

Up to that time, May was most noted for his swinging, flamboyant, lightheartedly joyful arrangements. The features of this style were brought to high fruition while working with Sinatra. These features included less use of strings, heavy use of brass and percussion, emphatic drumming; lots of staccato notes for woodwinds, brass and violins; unison playing by brass sections and saxophones, the saxes often glissing together on riffs and syncopated phrases. A singer's phrases would be lightly accompanied, then each vocal phrase would be capped with an instrumental-response phrase; sax, trumpet and trombone sections would take turns trading riffs, bouncing back and forth; a passage of brass and woodwinds playing together would end with a much-exaggerated vibrato. Also included in this style was the humorous use of "foreign" musical color, surprise contrasts in tone, and the alternation of subtlety with blatancy; brief "signature" phrases repeated throughout an arrangement; sudden finishes. These features and more — combined with a lively spirit and a happy, disrespectful sense of humor — produced the "Billy May sound."

On that first May/Sinatra collaboration, **Come Fly with Me,** six of the 12 cuts departed from the expected May arrangement in many ways. Four of these were recorded in one session (October 3, 1957) and were a musical set: *Autumn in New York, London by Night, April in Paris* and *Moonlight in Vermont.* Here the arrangements used many strings — in some cases practically excluding brass and woodwinds — and displayed a lush, romantic attitude, sometimes taking an almost Gordon Jenkins approach, with shimmering strings and mellow French horns laying back to support a vocal that clearly dominated the instruments. At times in these medium-to-slow-tempo charts, May would accentuate Sinatra's long, breathless carry-overs between major phrases by silencing all instruments after the singer's phrase-linking note began, then restarting his accompaniment before that note was finished, thus underscoring the lack of breathing. The *April in Paris* chart begins with the song's release portion, procedes to the chorus, then repeats the release and finishes the song; this was a highly novel approach at the time. *London by Night* ends with harp and piano work that sounds like a science fiction movie effect.

Even with the other six arrangements on the LP, the "May sound" is often given a lighter, more lilting feel that usual, though still pushing Sinatra into new stylistic channels. *Brazil* is more typical of May's mainstream work, noodling along during the singer's phrases, then responding to each phrase; the middle of the chart has an instrumental reiteration of the melody, with "response phrases" still coming after each bit of melody. *It's Nice to Go Trav'ling* mixes the album's two modes, with lots of strings and gliding passages on the one hand, bits of brassy phrase/response, phrase/response on the other; during the breakstrain, May really lets go with his brilliant, sassy brass, well beyond the degree employed by Nelson Riddle.

Because of its huge commercial success, it was their second album — *Come Dance with Me!* — that established the idea of how May and Sinatra sounded together. Here the work is more in the May tradition and Sinatra's approach is more altered; he responded to the charts with a great deal of high-energy singing, more high notes and bigger finishes. There is extensive use of special "signature" sounds or phrases by May; opening songs, repeated throughout, ending songs, or all three in one arrangement. The effect was sometimes deliberately comic, with things like "come with me (beep-de-boop) to the sea (beep-de-boop) where the light and love are all free (beep-de-boop, boop-duh-beep!) Eight of the ten cuts in the album are fast and furious pieces, with May using his "sound" to great effect. *Something's Gotta Give* almost jumps off the record. Even the two slightly more easy-tempo charts, for *Just in Time* and *Dancing in the Dark,* are played and sung with a throbbing pulse. Most of these classic May arrangements end suddenly, with emphatic drums, and none of the ingenious little extensions made famous by Nelson Riddle in his Sinatra charts.

The final Capitol album for the two men was *Come Swing with Me!* It had many of the same features as its predecessor, but with tempos a bit slower and the effects pushed further. The heart of these arrangements is an experiment with stereophonic recording, by then a major force in the marketplace. Each of the horn sections was split in two, positioned apart from each other in the studio, and recorded by separate mikes. When the saxes and brass traded riffs now, the effect was hyped into stereo ping-pong for systems with split speakers. Unison section play was doubled and quadrupled. It was an obvious experiment, given Billy May's style, but one that was not repeated with Sinatra.

The first May/Sinatra album for Reprise — *Sinatra Swings* — was released almost simultaneously with *Come Swing with Me!* It has the same general type of arrangements, but like most of the early Reprise LPs, the tone is hotter, jazzier, with fuller backing throughout sung phrases. At the same time, the beat is less driving, more lightly swinging than the **Come Dance with Me!** charts, and there is more use of strings and gentle solo instruments like the vibraphone. Because of this less rowdy approach, it is easier to hear the influence of Billy May's time arranging for Glenn Miller, especially in the use of trombones and saxes. There are nice examples of May's satiric use of international music archetypes in *Moonlight on the Ganges* and *Granada*.

May's arrangements for **Francis A. & Edward K.**, the Sinatra album with Duke Ellington, are in some ways his most extraordinary work. The basic style is still there, but with dramatic changes. The biggest difference is the long, long breakstrains — which allow recapitulation of the song in a form of symphonic jazz — as opposed to 20 seconds of breakstrain in the standard three minute pop song format. A second factor is that May did arrangements which accommodated the various instrumental sections and principal soloists of the Ellington orchestra. He wrote horn passages with room for jazz improvisation within the arrangement framework, and created orchestral tones which properly set the raspy trumpet and trombone effects and scat saxophone work. The Billy May sound is still there, but broadened, slowed down and made more subtle. *Yellow Days* has a wonderful example of his humorous but jazzy orchestration; trombones play a series of loud staccato notes, after each of which the trumpets play a softer equivalent, stepping immediately on the trombone notes before they die out and creating the effect of echoes off a distant wall.

Bill May's last work with Sinatra was for one of three sections in the Past-Present-Future **Trilogy** album. May arranged and conducted for **The Past [Collectibles of the Early Years]**, which echoes many styles of the '30s and '40s; nightclub torch songs, burlesque, dance band, and radio ballads. Under all this, the basic May sound is present, but these are very sophisticated charts which create the illusion of being simple. There are many special touches. *But Not for Me* has a single trombone evoking Tommy Dorsey; it also uses the song's opening verse, but places it after the release. A sweet trumpet solo opens and weaves through *I Had the Craziest Dream,* which has a gentle, swing band sound (but with strings) and a Pied-Pipers type chorus. Two numbers contain musical wisecracks at their finish; *They All Laughed* had band members and Sinatra guffawing, and there is a burst of Mexican trumpets in *Let's Face the Music and Dance.* The full verse of *It Had to Be You* is used, and then the melody of that verse is orchestrated as a leit motif throughout the chorus of the song. Finally, the *Street of Dreams* chart sounds like a burlesque show pit band (heavy drums and crude brass sounds, but really using the full orchestra), in amusing contrast to the theme of the lyrics.

Don Costa (born 6/10/25, Massachusetts; died 1/19/83) Composer, Conductor, Producer

Career Summary. He was the youngest of five kids in a musical family. A self-taught musician with no formal training, Costa started as arranger in radio, working on Vaughn Monroe's program in the 1940s. Arranged and produced over 200 hit records during a 30-year career, working in nearly all types of pop, country and western, rhythm and blues, rock, jazz, and disco. Within the realm of '40s and '50s pop, Costa arranged for top vocalists like Vic Damone, Sarah Vaughan, Steve Lawrence and Edie Gorme. In the late 1950s, he was A & R director for ABC/Paramount, known for discovering untapped talent such as 16-year-old Paul Anka. His own label, DCP (Don Costa Productions) Records, had hits in the mid–1960s with groups including Little Anthony and the Imperials. He produced records of his own such as *I Walk the Line* and movie themes from *The Unforgiven* and *Never on Sunday.* Having moved to California in the 1960s, Costa became active as a composer in films and television, very conscious of soft-rock influences; also a conductor of theater music. He wrote arrangements for Perry Como, Barbra Streisand, Johnny Mathis, Dean Martin, Frankie Avalon and Sammy Davis, Jr. His first arrangements for Sinatra came in 1961, and he later produced such Sinatra albums of contemporary songs as *My Way* and *Cycles.* Costa's original film scores include *Rough Night in Jericho* and *Madigan.* With his 10-year-old daughter, Nikki, Costa produced an LP which sold millions of copies, titled *Out Here on My Own.* He died of heart failure at the age of 57.

WORK WITH SINATRA — begun when Costa was age 36 and Sinatra 45.

Sinatra's key arrangers have tended to be around his own age; Axel Stordahl was two years older, Gordon Jenkins four years older, Billy May less than a year younger. Interestingly, the two arrangers who presided over recontemporizations of Sinatra's career were both younger men. Riddle was six years younger than the singer and Don Costa was nine years his junior. Riddle updated Sinatra's "sound" more than he did his material. Costa changed both. While Gordon

Jenkins and Billy May each tended to do one type of album with Sinatra, Don Costa and Nelson Riddle both arranged a wide variety of LPs.

To get the general picture of this collaboration, you have to skip over their great 1961 recordings for the *Sinatra & Strings* album (which I will discuss later), plus a little bit of TV and singles work in 1962–1964. The mainstream Costa/Sinatra recording began in November 1968, seven years after the unique *Sinatra & Strings* sessions. Their goal was to make commercially viable albums of new songs. Sinatra had finished work with arranger Ernie Freeman in July 1967 — after three years of successfully recapturing a part of the teen singles market — and he felt that Costa, with his soft-rock background, was the man to update his LP repertoire.

They did two albums in quick succession, *Cycles* and *My Way;* in these LPs, the basic Costa/Sinatra arrangement style was established. Like Riddle in the 1950s, Don Costa was highly versatile — bringing a new Sinatra sound to several styles of music — but there is a distinctive core to most of this work, with Costa often producing and conducting as well as writing the charts. The core sound begins with the frequent use of an emphatic, "busy" rhythm line. This heavy beat is a link to the world of rock music. Two or more instruments carry the beat and the rhythmic figures around it. Piano and guitar are the ones most often employed, others being snare drum, bass fiddle, vibraphone, bongos, chimes, full drum set, mandolin, or a musical synthesizer played like an organ, harpsichord or banjo. Occasionally there is a novel rhythmic pairing such as a Herb Alpert–style trumpet combined with chimes. When the frequent piano beat is used, it is often percussive, but sometimes tinkles with an abundance of grace notes; the equally common guitar is usually strummed, sometimes picked like a banjo. Whichever combination of instruments is used for this beat element, it is generally played loud, carrying steadily throughout the arrangement.

Costa doesn't use introductory and closing passages very often. Once the beat is established, he proceeds with an arrangement in a medium range of tempo, slower than Billy May, faster than Gordon Jenkins, and without the pulsing rhythms of Nelson Riddle.

There is a heavy use of strings, especially the violin section. Horns are there for both bright and dark accents. The strings and horns ride over the beat but seldom cover it. Unlike Gordon Jenkins, when Costa applies lots of strings and French horn, the effect is romantic, not melancholy, and the songs are about love found rather than love lost. Costa's strings often surge and crash like waves behind Sinatra, so unlike Stordahl's and Jenkins' use of them to play delicately around the singer.

The charts are written fully, continuously present behind Sinatra's vocals. Costa uses instrumental breakstrains infrequently, so the singing is also continuous. Though the recording was done "live," there is a layered feeling to this work, almost like the heavily produced sound of rock singers and musicians.

On the other hand, the playing is seldom very loud in Costa's work for Sinatra, and neither is the singing. There is a light, easy, reflective, conversational quality to the vocals in many of these pieces. An exception to this comes in songs which have a whole series of verses, each finishing with a dramatic tag. Here Sinatra sings in a declamatory, triumphant fashion that is unique to his work with Costa, who often accompanied these melodramatic phrase endings with horn fanfares, surging strings and pounding drums.

When a song's tempo is faster than medium, Costa writes in a style that echoes Billy May's trumpets, saxes and drums, but the charts retain a soft-rock beat and are less humorous and driving, more like a Las Vegas lounge version of Billy May. With tempos slower than medium, Costa brings in more strings and soft woodwinds and brass, reducing the beat.

Sinatra's main repertoire of songs from the '30s and '40s generally followed the structure of verse-chorus-chorus-release-chorus. Many of the songs he recorded with Costa—from the '60s and '70s—broke away from that structure. Some followed a kind of verse-chorus-verse-chorus pattern. In other cases, choruses were replaced by sections that had the shape of verses, but without the "recitative" tradition from opera; the songs would simply be verse-verse-verse-verse, with a repeating "tag" at the end of each verse. The shapes of these songs were a big factor in the way Don Costa arranged for Sinatra. This extended to the occasional use of volume fade-outs at the end of records, which the singer had previously rejected as "nonlive." Vocal backing groups were also used in the contemporary manner, singing nonverbally as part of the arrangement.

With a few exceptions, the Costa/Sinatra LPs did not follow themes. Their concept was newly written love songs that reflect on the changes in life. Most of the charts followed the mainstream I've described. Here and there, Costa did a unique arrangement, standing apart from all Sinatra's other work. When a great new song was discovered, Costa would revert to an approximation of his *Sinatra & Strings* sound, a fine fusion of big, sweet, dramatic strings with jazzy drums and bluesy horn accents.

Sinatra's new LP releases from 1968 through 1981 were dominated by the arrangements and production of Don Costa. The 1968 album *Cycles* was the singer's first album made up entirely of modern songs. He had done current material for singles throughout his recording career, but albums had been drawn largely from compositions that had aged like fine wine. *Softly, As I Leave You* (1964) and 1966's *That's Life* had been mostly new songs, but many were tunes written in the styles of the past. *Cycles* was brand-new and it sounded brand-new. Costa's arrangements epitomize the mainstream of his work with Sinatra. *Little Green Apples* stood apart with an unusual pattern of soft violins for the verses and harp-like guitar arpeggios for the choruses.

My Way came right after *Cycles*. Again, these were contemporary songs, but some of the arrangements are more swinging, with touches of May and Riddle. *A Day in the Life of a Fool* is atypical, because of its bossa nova beat and the violin breakstrain which restates the melody. One of Costa's unique charts supports a great Sinatra performance of *If You Go Away;* there is a soft bass beat, followed each time by a throb of strings — violin or viola or cello — with a synthesized harpsichord background and a minirelease played by oboe and harp. The LP's title song, *My Way,* has a chart that builds with each of the tune's five sections, starting with a piano and bass and growing into heavy brass fanfares and loud drums, then finishing with a high horn bridge followed by a soft vocal coda.

Sinatra's next release was *A Man Alone.* It was his only true theme album arranged by Costa; the album title states the theme. Composed exclusively for Sinatra by Rod McKuen, one-third of the lyrics are recited to music, the other two-thirds sung, but the whole of the LP is intimately conversational. Costa's charts follow his medium-tempo mainstream of busy rhythm, piano, guitar, violins and wall-to-wall musical presence behind soft and reflective vocals. One piece that stands out is *I've Been to Town,* with an improvising blues saxophone over violins, a drum/bass beat and noodling piano. *Lonesome Cities* has honky-tonk piano and drums.

After a break from Costa for **Watertown,** the two men were back together for one side of Sinatra's final LP release before his intended retirement, **Sinatra & Company.** These seven cuts follow most of the trends they had established for recording contemporary songs, with the addition of a few novel instruments. A special track is *Bein' Green,* with an introduction by celesta and guitar, then a piano/guitar beat and the buildup to subtle horns and strings.

When Sinatra abandoned his retirement after a couple of years, Don Costa wrote three charts for the first new album, **Ol' Blue Eyes Is Back.** Again, these were new songs, medium tempo. The arrangements were like those that had preceded the retirement, only more dramatically charged, with bigger drum runs — including timpani — and the strings high and surging; brass sections were used less, except for French horns, and the beat was heavy with percussive piano. Sinatra often built up to big dramatic climaxes amidst harp flourishes. This singing was less an emotional communication than a shout of triumph.

Costa did eight of ten songs in **Some Nice Things I've Missed,** the next postretirement LP. As the album title implies, these were songs written just prior to and during Sinatra's time off. The two medium tempo love songs follow Costa's main pattern. Four up-tempo numbers all sound like Billy May, but with a tendency to an ongoing busy beat. A great song like *What Are You Doing the Rest of Your Life?* once again receives special treatment, harkening back to **Sinatra & Strings.** In another of Costa's occasional surprise charts, *Satisfy Me One More Time* is done like a jazz combo, with a plucked bass and vibraphone rhythm, jazzy piano and brass accents, and finishing up like a full jazz orchestra.

Costa's final album with Sinatra was recorded two years later. It was **The Present [Some Very Good Years],** the middle disc of the three part **Trilogy** album. This time — because of thematic context — a collection of contemporary songs was truly part of a concept, and was one of the best sets Costa and Sinatra did of this kind. All the familiar elements are there, the medium tempo pieces with soft-rock charts, the up-tempo Billy May sounds, the loving arrangement of a great Legrand/Bergman song. There are also some novel tracks. *For the Good Times,* a country/western song, includes a duet with soprano Eileen Farrell. One of Costa's unique arrangements enlivens the movie theme *New York, New York,* written with a kind of honky-tonk burlesque show flavor and a simple five-note repeating figure (plink-plink, dum-de-dunk) that's hard to get out of your head; there's piano, brass, heavy drums and cymbals, varied tempos, lots of tonal variety, and finally a use of the whole orchestra. This piece was recorded a month after the others arranged by Costa, and was conducted by Vinnie Falcone, who also conducted the one non–Costa work on the LP; the Beatles song *Something*, which had the last great new Nelson Riddle arrangement recorded by Sinatra.

Before leaving the subject of Don Costa, it's important to return to late 1961 and the sessions which produced ***Sinatra & Strings***. There are a few correspondences here to their later work—such as the rhythmic use of piano and guitar and the omnipresence of arrangement—but for the most part this LP stands alone. The songs are not contemporary to the recording dates, instead ranging from the 1920s to the 1950s, and mostly from the 1930s and 1940s. Since the album was part of the early period at Sinatra's own label, Reprise, there is a large jazz influence. The many symphonic strings of the LP's title are given a unique flavor by the way they are fused with jazz/blues sounds from woodwinds (with little use of saxophone), full and muted brass (especially French horns and trumpets), and the light beat of drums and cymbals played with both brushes and sticks. Often brass and string sections play in unison for an extraordinary sweet yet blue sound. When sections of the orchestra are playing different notes, the contrast is increased by high-low effects; violins and French horns play high, cellos and trombones play low, and the combinations are varied through high-low to high-high to low-low. The overall result is like some remarkable combination of Jenkins' romantic charts, Riddle's darker jazzed-based moments, and a declamatory drama that was all Costa's own. Generally, there are no instrumental breakstrains in these arrangements, and the album is an extreme case of Sinatra functioning as an instrumental soloist fronting an orchestra, singing alternately in the manner of horns and strings. These charts represent a fusion of moods and a variety of tempos. In response to them, Sinatra sang with a combination of sweetness and irony, plus more changes in the melody line than was usual for him at the time. Everything about this album is special. Sinatra never did another like it. Each arrangement stands on its own, yet all are united in spirit. Costa said, years later, that his arrangement for *Come Rain or Come Shine* was the best he ever wrote.

Sessions in July 1968 — nearly seven years after *Sinatra & Strings* was recorded — began the main body of Costa's work with the maturing singer, a decade of exploring new ways to deal with new songs. After the arranger's contributions to *Trilogy* in 1979, they did three more singles in 1981. Any further possibilities were ended by Costa's untimely death in 1983, one year prior to Sinatra's final retirement from regular, commercially released recording.

Now that I've covered the six most influential sources of Sinatra's instrumentation, I would like to make brief reference to several other arrangers in the upcoming catalog. These gentlemen worked with Sinatra far less, and had less influence in consequence, but each of them presided over some special sessions. They are presented in the order they first worked with Frank Sinatra.

Andy Gibson deserves to be singled out — if for no other reason — because he wrote the orchestrations for Sinatra's ten earliest recordings including *All or Nothing at All* and *Ciribiribin.* These arrangements, written for the fledgling Harry James band, were not specifically tailored to Sinatra, but he took good advantage of them.

Sy Oliver wrote several of the arrangements Sinatra recorded with the Tommy Dorsey orchestra, and some of them were special; however, in terms of this book's interests, Oliver's crowning achievement came two decades later, when he wrote and conducted all the charts for Sinatra's classic album *I Remember Tommy...*, which restated the Dorsey/Sinatra sound in modern terms, providing — at the same time — a beautiful tribute to the musical personality of the early 1940s.

Alec Wilder — a talented songwriter/composer/arranger — wrote some special vocal-group-only backing for Sinatra recordings during a long musician's strike in 1943–44. These records kept Sinatra on the charts at a crucial stage of his career.

George Siravo had done a small number of arrangements for Sinatra's late recordings at Columbia Records. His main contribution was in writing a quantity of small-combo arrangements, lightly swinging in tempo, which Sinatra took on the road to nightclubs when his career was faltering in the early 1950s. These arrangements began to bring out the deeper-voiced, more knowing, jazzy sound that helped attract new attention when things were crumbling for the singer. At the beginning of his key years at Capitol Records, many of these arrangements were rewritten by Nelson Riddle and adapted for a larger orchestra. These arrangements comprised the content of the first two Capitol 10" LPs, *Songs for Young Lovers* and *Swing Easy!*

Heinie Beau had written arrangements for two major early records: *Violets for Your Furs* with Dorsey, and *The Birth of the Blues* at Columbia. In the late '50s and early '60s, Beau wrote some wondrous (uncredited) arrangements for Billy May on *Come Dance with Me* (three songs) and *Come Swing with Me!* (six songs), plus two extraordinary arrangements for Axel Stordahl on *Point of No Return: I'll Remember April* and *It's a Blue World.*

Johnny Mandel only recorded with Sinatra for two sessions in late 1960, but those 14 tracks are amazing. Sinatra wanted to push farther into jazz-oriented experimentation for his own record label, Reprise Records. Mandel arranged and conducted a jazzy band for the first Reprise album, *Ring-a-Ding Ding!* These tracks set the tone for much of Sinatra's work in the 1960s, a punching, driving, crisp approach, with extended jazz obligatos and more interpretation of melody and lyric. Twelve of Mandel's arrangements comprise that first Reprise album, the other two appearing on the bootleg LP *Love Songs.* It seems a shame that Johnny Mandel never arranged for Sinatra recordings again.

Neal Hefti furthered the trend towards jazz elements in Sinatra's work, first in *Sinatra and Swingin' Brass,* and then as arranger for the first album with Count Basie's band, *Sinatra/Basie: An Historic Musical First.* His chart for Porter's *I Get a Kick Out of You,* for the former album, became Sinatra's definitive concert arrangement.

Quincy Jones served to bring Sinatra some arrangements from the emerging world of "new jazz/pop," first with the Basie band in *It Might as Well Be Swing,* then for the live Las Vegas performances captured in *Sinatra at the Sands* and, finally, as producer and conductor of an all-star jazz band for Sinatra's final recording sessions and his last album, 1984's *L.A. Is My Lady.*

Ernie Freeman's beat-heavy, repetitious arrangements are not to my personal taste, but in the '70s he brought Sinatra back to Top–10 single record popularity with his charts for tunes like *Strangers in the Night* and *That's Life.* Along the way, Freeman did some admirable arrangements, including a novel approach to *The World We Knew (Over and Over),* and a delicate, supportive orchestration for *The Impossible Dream.*

Finally, both **Claus Ogerman** and **Emuir Deodato** wrote arrangements for lovely, soft bossa nova sessions, with Sinatra singing the music of Antonio Carlos Jobim. Here are showcased many of the finest nuances of expression which Sinatra had evolved by the late 1960s.

In listening to more than 45 years of recordings by Frank Sinatra, one can't help but gain a strong appreciation for the contributions of all these talented and giving arrangers.

Catalog of Arrangers

The catalog for this chapter organizes each Arranger's credits alphabetically by their last name. Within an arranger's section, the songs are listed in key-number order, which is also alphabetical. Only four of the arranger-name entries require explanation:

House Arrangement refers to a Tommy Dorsey Orchestra "house" arrangement, written by some combination of Tommy Dorsey, Sy Oliver, Fred Stulce and Paul Weston.

Jones & company refers to a single arrangement co-written by Quincy Jones, Dave Matthews, Jerry Hey and Torry Zito.

Riddle, N. @May–style refers to a pair of charts which Nelson Riddle did in the style of Billy May — with May's blessing.

Riddle, N. @Siravo arng refers to a group of arrangements which Riddle adapted from original small-band arrangements by George Siravo.

If a song was recorded more than once by Sinatra, that is shown with a sequence number such as *Night and Day*[1], *Night and Day*[2], etc.

Refer to the key number following the song title to locate full information in the Master Song List in Chapter 3 (including special notes referenced by an asterisk [*]).

Alexander, J.: Mad About You 679; Nature Boy 759; Stromboli (On the Island Of–) 986; That Lucky Old Sun 1025

Arnaud, L.: Siesta 915; What's Wrong with Me? 1129

Ayres, M.: Once in Love with Amy 820

Barnum, H.: Some Enchanted Evening[4] 932

Beau, H.: American Beauty Rose[2] 34; The Birth of the Blues 86; Don't Take Your Love from Me[1] 194; I'll Remember April[2] 487; It's a Blue World 544; The Last Dance[1] 605; Lean Baby* 611; Lover[2] 671; On the Sunny Side of the Street 817; Saturday Night (Is the Loneliest Night...)[2] 886; Sentimental Journey 896; That Old Black Magic[2] 1027; Too Close for Comfort 1077; Violets for Your Furs[1] 1094

Beck, J.: All or Nothing at All[4] 21; Night and Day[4] 775

Betts, H.: We Wish You the Merriest 1111

Byers, B.: The Lady Is a Tramp[2] 602

Calello, C.: Elizabeth 211; Everybody Ought to Be in Love 227; For a While 255; Lady Day[1] 598; Michael and Peter 696; Watertown 1102; What a Funny Girl (You Used to Be) 1118

Capps, A.: I Believe I'm Gonna Love You 364

Cavanaugh, D.: From the Bottom to

Most Beautiful Girl in The World[2] 728; My Shining Hour[2] 751; Nothing in Common 789; The Oldest Established (Permanent) 812; On the Road to Mandalay 816; Paper Doll 843; Pass Me By 845; Please Don't Talk About Me When I'm Gone 853; Poor Butterfly 859; Same Old Song and Dance 881; Something's Gotta Give 944; The Song Is You[3] 953; The Song Is You[4] 954; Street of Dreams[3] 984; Sunny 996; They All Laughed 1049; We Open in Venice 1109; Yellow Days 1186; Yes, Indeed! «A Jive Spiritual» 1187; You're Nobody 'Til Somebody Loves You[1] 1242; You're Nobody 'Til Somebody Loves You[2] 1243

Miller, M.: American Beauty Rose[1] 33; Dear Little Boy of Mine 170; Goodnight, Irene 302

Moore, P.: Bop! Goes My Heart 96; If You Stub Your Toe on the Moon 466; Why Can't You Behave? 1165

Mottola, T.: It's Sunday 563; My Cousin Louella 736; S'posin'[1] 963; We Just Couldn't Say Goodbye 1107

Nestico, S.: If I Should Lose You 455; It's All Right with Me[3] 550; One Hundred Years from Today[2] 827; Stormy Weather[3]* 979; Until the Real Thing Comes Along 1091

Ogerman, C.: Baubles, Bangles and Beads[2] 71; Change Partners 117, Dindi 177; Drinking Again 203; The Girl from Ipanema «Garota de Ipanema» 284; How Insensitive «Insensatez» 352; I Concentrate on You[3] 373; If You Never Come to Me 464; Like a Sad Song (Sometimes I Feel—) 629; Meditation «Meditacao» 691; Once I Loved 819; Quiet Nights of Quiet Stars «Corcovado» 867

Oliver, S.: Daybreak[2] 167; Dolores 180; East of the Sun (and West of the Moon)[1] 207; East of the Sun (and West of the Moon)[2] 208; I'll Be Seeing You[2] 471; I'll Take Tallulah 490; I'm Getting Senti-

mental Over You[1] 495; I'm Getting Sentimental Over You[2] 496; Imagination[2] 508; In the Blue of Evening[2] 512; It Started All Over Again[2] 540; It's Always You[2] 554; Let's Get Away from It All[1] 624; Oh! Look at Me Now![1] 797; The One I Love (Belongs to Somebody Else)[1] 828; The One I Love (Belongs to Somebody Else)[3] 830; Polka Dots and Moonbeams[2] 858; Snooty Little Cutie (You're a—) 922; Somewhere a Voice Is Calling 945; Sweet Lorraine)[1] 1002; Take Me[2] 1008; There Are Such Things[2] 1037; We Three (My Echo, My Shadow, and Me) 1110; Without a Song[1] 1178; Without a Song[3] 1180; You and I 1192; You Lucky People You 1213

Paich, M.: Here's to the Losers 331; Love Isn't Just for the Young 661

Parnello, J. The Best of Everything 81; Here's to the Band 330; How Do You Keep the Music Playing? 351

Reynolds, D.: I'm Gonna Live Till I Die 498; The Little Drummer Boy 635; Melody of Love «Melody d'Amour» 693

Riddle, N.: Adelaide 2; All My Tomorrows[1] 11; All or Nothing at All[3] 20; All the Way[1] 23; All the Way[2] 24; Always[2] 30; America the Beautiful[2] 32; Angel Eyes[1] 37; Angel Eyes[3] 39; Anything Goes 41; Anytime—Anywhere 43; At Long Last Love[1] 54; At Sundown 56; Barbara 69; The Bells of Christmas «Greensleeves» 78; Bewitched (Bothered and Bewildered)[1] 83; Bewitched (Bothered and Bewildered)[2] 84; Blame It on My Youth 88; Blue Moon 90; Blues in the Night 93; California 106; Call Me 107; Call Me Irresponsible 108; Can I Steal a Little Love? 110; Can't We Be Friends?[1] 111; Can't We Be Friends?[2] 112; C'est Magnifique 116; Chicago (That Toddling Town) 123; The Christmas Waltz[1] 126; The Christmas Waltz[3] 128; Close to You

Chapter 7: The Sessions

For the majority of Frank Sinatra's career, recording was a special nighttime affair. A love affair.

In the beginning, it was more like a flirtation from afar. The singer's early bandleaders, Harry James and Tommy Dorsey, scheduled recording sessions based on a combination of record company dictates, their orchestras' collective schedule, and the cost of studio time and technicians. Sinatra was there — when ordered — to do his work.

This began to change after he contracted with Columbia Records in 1943. Sinatra was a hot item by then, and he exercised his clout by having some say in the nature of studio sessions. His good friend and arranger, Axel Stordahl, was usually there to oversee the musicians and conduct his own orchestration. When possible, recording was done in the evening. The mastering of four songs became the optimal goal for a session. Since the centers of recording were in New York City and Hollywood, Sinatra's radio and movie work could be coordinated with studio time on either coast. Twelve to 24 days a year were devoted to making records.

As his career fell on hard times in the early '50s, Sinatra's recording was restricting in many ways. Unwanted songs, duets, arrangements and sessions were forced on him. The amount of studio time diminished. In 1951, he only spent six days in the studio.

The glory days of recording began for Sinatra when he moved to the young and adventurous Capitol Records in 1953. He had some lively single hits, some hot albums in the new 12" long-playing format, plus fresh awards and honors for both singing and acting. His clout was back. Using that clout, he worked to shape his ideal world for cutting records.

Sinatra's recording comeback was accomplished with a maturing voice and sensibility, a new image that was more sexy and swinging, less romantic and tender. To match this new persona, there were the cool/hot arrangements of Nelson Riddle, who presided over the instrumental side of those early Capitol sessions with an unflappable control.

By the singer's preference, recording was consistently set up for nighttime, usually at 8 P.M. or later. Since Capitol recorded exclusively in the Los Angeles area—at its own studios in the Capitol Tower—the conditions, climate and facilities became very familiar for Sinatra. He was treated like the hottest of a whole roster of hot artists (Peggy Lee, Nat "King" Cole, The Four Freshmen, etc.), and accorded a respect and courtesy that caused him to thrive. The concentration shifted from singles (where rock, novelty and regional music were beginning to take over the youngster's "dance" market) to albums on the new high fidelity LPs; Sinatra dramatized the nature of LPs with unifying themes accenting many of his albums.

As for the critically important musical arrangements, there was Nelson Riddle to do the "deep" down moods and the lightly swinging concepts. A few years later, Gordon Jenkins came on board to provide the lushness of strings and French horns when Sinatra did albums of slow love ballads with theatrical drama. Shortly after that, Billy May joined the Sinatra team for a fresh richness in romantic songs, a lighter-hearted attitude and a brassier swinging. These three great arranger/conductors alternated during Sinatra's Capitol years.

Working with his producers and arrangers, the singer would agree to a set of tunes. An orchestra would be scheduled for a session, with Sinatra's selected sidemen included. When the night came, an intimate audience of colleagues, entertainment-world peers and friends would assemble. The musicians were already rehearsed and ready. Coming down from an active day, yet rested and in pampered voice, Sinatra would arrive. He would do run-throughs with the band, then record the night's group of songs until he was satisfied with a "master" recording of each. Most commonly, four songs were finished in a session (by this era, that represented one-third of an LP), though the number completed during the Capitol sessions varied from three to six, with as many as eight done on a few special nights.

These sessions were live concerts in the most important sense. The singer and musicians all performed together in real time, before a reacting audience of knowledgeable "fans." Because of this, the interactive energy of live performance was present for the singer and on the tapes.

Much of this '50s recording was done in the earlier part of the year and then again during the latter part—around ten to 12 days each year—though a smaller number of sessions was scheduled for May, June and August dates, and a Christmas album was recorded in July to accommodate its seasonal release. This coordinated with Sinatra's intense schedule of TV and movie commitments and his numerous nightclub and theater appearances.

At the start of the 1960s, Sinatra gained even more control over his recording by forming his own label, Reprise. Now the choice of arrangers, songs, album themes, production cost allocation, bands and sidemen were under his full reign. Though Los Angeles and Hollywood remained his primary recording bases, now sessions could again be arranged in New York City when desirable, as well as in London and Las Vegas on special occasions. Though Nelson Riddle was bound to Capitol until 1963, Billy May and Gordon Jenkins were immediately free to record with Sinatra. A wealth of other arranger/conductors was brought into the fold: Johnny Mandel, Sy Oliver (from the Dorsey days), Don Costa, Neal Hefti and many more. Instead of available musicians collected for a studio session, standing orchestras could be used on occasion such as the Count Basie band, Woody Herman's Young Thundering Herd, the Los Angeles Philharmonic Symphony Orchestra, and the Duke Ellington band. Album production budgets could be stretched for certain projects, to utilize a special recording facility or a giant orchestra. Most important, perhaps, was the freedom to produce intensely varied albums, many of them moving deeper into jazz territory, others reaching back into the '20s, '30s, and '40s for their material, in a time when the Beatles and the rock explosion were dominating album releases as well as singles. As for Sinatra's own single releases, he could experiment with contemporary arrangements—and with rock and country sounds—which allowed him to again become a viable seller of single records in an age when many of his contemporaries were hardly recording at all.

The style of the sessions remained fairly constant. New microphones of higher resolution and multitrack recording equipment were used, but the everybody-plays-at-one-time *live* approach was retained. Four songs per session remained a general goal, but there were several sessions where six or more were completed. And nighttime was still the right time to make music with friends and for friends. Sinatra felt his voice was looser, richer, the throat more open and relaxed at night.

This continued in full swing through the decade. In 1969, Sinatra recorded on 16 days, averaging three songs "mastered" per session. Then came the 1970s. Frank Sinatra was on the trail that runs between 45 and 50 years of age. First he slowed down, then he stopped.

The retirement lasted a couple of years, and then in 1973 he was back in the studio. But with a difference. Sessions were fewer and shorter. Increasingly, finished recordings were withheld from release. Great records were still produced, but not so many. During the 1980s — even as his concert appearances increased — his recording time diminished further. There had been 16 recording days in 1969 alone. Now, only 16 sessions took place in the whole period from 1980 to 1984; out of the 34 tracks mastered, only 25 were released, and five of those only as singles. In the middle of the '80s (the sixth decade in which he made records), Frank Sinatra wrapped it up with some glorious sessions backed by Quincy Jones's specially assembled all-star jazz band. A handful of sessions were to follow, but no commercial releases.

Sinatra's session producers over the years served in many capacities. For the singles work at RCA and Columbia, the producers were in charge in the traditional sense, following company policy and enforcing song choice, supervising the technology of the session, overseeing the logistics, watching the budget. Starting with Voyle Gilmore at Capitol, Sinatra still relied on his producers to set the stage and watch the technical details, but he took perfectionist charge of the aesthetics and environment of his sessions, working closely with his arrangers and deciding for himself when each song was done right. The producer had to fit sessions into Sinatra's travel lifestyle including movies and Vegas and radio and TV and international concert activity. When he started his own label, the producers were often musicians themselves, people like Felix Slatkin, Neal Hefti and Don Costa. His most frequent Reprise producers were Sonny Burke for albums and Jimmy Bowen for singles. Quincy Jones acted as producer for Sinatra's final album.

The singer had always learned from the musicians around him. He was inspired by them during rehearsals and recording. With the

Dorsey band, he had learned the value of simple melodic beauty from Bunny Berigan, learned how to diversify musical textures from Ziggy Elman; drummer Buddy Rich was his school for rhythm and "time," and of course there was always Tommy Dorsey's own flowing legato line. With such a background, it's no wonder that Sinatra always wanted special, familiar sidemen playing his sessions. Here are a few of his favorites over the years. *Trumpet:* Chris Griffin, Bobby Hackett, Billy Butterfield, Harry Edison; *Trombone:* Will Bradley, Si Zentner, Buddy Morrow; *Saxophone:* Herbie Haymer, Babe Russin, Sam Butera; *Piano:* Stan Freeman, Bill Miller; *Guitar:* Dave Barbour, Tony Mottola.

This chapter's first catalog organizes 1,251 entries in terms of recording session date; within each session, the songs are listed in the order they were recorded. The recording session date is printed in year, month/day order. The single letter following the date indicates the sequence of recording within that session; a = 1st, b = 2nd, etc. This volume disregards which "take" of a song was released. In the case of recordings made from radio broadcasts, movie soundtracks and television broadcasts, the session date is replaced by different formats, as shown in the following examples:

"43RADIOdL" — 1943 is year of inception, source is radio broadcast, "d" for 4th month of that year, "L" is one of six codes for name of radio show. The codes are as follows: D = radio broadcast with the Tommy Dorsey orchestra; G = "The Frank Sinatra Old Gold Show"; L = Lucky Strike's "Your Hit Parade"; S = "Songs by Sinatra"; M = "Max Factor Show — Starring Frank Sinatra"; V = "Vimms Vitamins Show," starring Sinatra

"48bSndTrk" — 1948 is year of film's initial release, "b" representing the year's 2nd Sinatra film listed, for which the source is a bootleg recording from a movie soundtrack.

"59aTELEVS" — 1959 is year of inception, "a" for 1st TV special listed, source is television broadcast.

If a song was recorded more than once by Sinatra, that title is followed with a sequence number, as in *All of Me*[1], *All of Me*[2], etc.

Refer to the key number following the song title to locate full information in the Master Song List in Chapter 3 (including special notes referenced by an asterisk [*]).

The 2nd catalog is a date-listing of the various cities where Sinatra was recording during the different periods of his career, plus an explanation of significant breaks in recording.

Catalog of Recording Sessions

55,10/17a: You Forgot All the Words 1210

55,10/17b: Love Is Here to Stay[1] 658

55,10/17c: Weep They Will 1113

55aSndTrk: Adelaide 2

55aSndTrk: Sue Me 989

55bSndTrk: The Man with the Golden Arm* 687

56,1/9a: You Brought a New Kind of Love to Me[2] 1201

56,1/9b: I Thought About You 428

56,1/9c: You Make Me Feel So Young[1] 1214

56,1/9d: Memories of You[1] 694

56,1/10a: Pennies from Heaven[1] 847

56,1/10b: How About You?[2] 344

56,1/10c: You're Getting to Be a Habit with Me 1238

56,1/12a: It Happened in Monterey 531

56,1/12b: Swingin' Down the Lane 1004

56,1/12c: Flowers Mean Forgiveness 246

56,1/12d: I've Got You Under My Skin[1] 574

56,1/16a: Makin' Whoopee 680

56,1/16b: Old Devil Moon[1] 804

56,1/16c: Anything Goes 41

56,1/16d: Too Marvelous for Words 1078

56,1/16e: We'll Be Together Again 1114

56,3/8a: Don't Like Goodbyes 191

56,3/8b: P.S. I Love You 841

56,3/8c: Love Locked Out 663

56,3/8d: If It's the Last Thing I Do 457

56,4/4a: I've Had My Moments 578

56,4/4b: Blame It on My Youth 88

56,4/4c: Everything Happens to Me[2] 230

56,4/4d: Wait Till You See Her 1097

56,4/5a: The End of a Love Affair 219

56,4/5b: It Could Happen to You 528

56,4/5c: There's a Flaw in My Flue[2] 1042

56,4/5d: With Every Breath I Take 1177

56,4/5e: How Little We Know[1] 353

56,4/5f: Wait for Me 1096

56,4/5g: You're Sensational[1] 1245

56,4/9b: Five Hundred Guys 243

56,4/9c: Hey! Jealous Lover 332

56,4/9d: No One Ever Tells You 780

56,4/20a: You're Sensational[2] 1246

56,4/20b: Who Wants to Be a Millionaire? 1163

56,4/20c: Mind If I Make Love to You? 700

56,5/7a: Well, Did You Evah? 1115

56,10/1a: I Couldn't Sleep a Wink Last Night[2] 381

56,10/1b: It's Easy to Remember 555

56,10/1c: Close to You [I Will Always Stay][2] 132

56,11/15a: I Got Plenty o' Nuttin' 395

56,11/15b: I Won't Dance[1] 441

56,11/15c: Stars Fell on Alabama 971

56,11/20a: At Long Last Love[1] 54

56,11/20b: I Guess I'll Have to Change My Plan 397

56,11/20c: I Wish I Were in Love Again 437

56,11/20d: Nice Work If You Can Get It[1] 768

56,11/26a: The Lady Is a Tramp[1] 601

56,11/26b: Night and Day[2] 773

56,11/26c: The Lonesome Road 646

56,11/26d: If I Had You[2] 451

56,11/28a: I Got It Bad (and That Ain't Good) 394

56,11/28b: From This Moment On 270

56,11/28c: Oh! Look at Me Now![2] 798

56,11/28d: You'd Be So Nice to Come Home To 1221

56,12/3a: Your Love for Me 1231

56,12/3b: Can I Steal a Little Love? 110

57,3/14a: So Long, My Love 925

57,3/14b: Crazy Love 156

57,4/10a: Where Is the One?* 1152

57,4/10b: There's No You[2] 1046

57,4/10c: The Night We Called It a Day[2] 778

57,4/10d: Autumn Leaves «Les Feuille Mortes» 60

57,4/29a: I Cover the Waterfront* 382

57,4/29b: Lonely Town 643

57,4/29c: Laura[2] 610

57,4/29d: Baby, Won't You Please Come Home? 63

61,9/12d: As Time Goes By 52
61,9/12e: It's a Blue World 544
61,9/12f: I'll Remember April[2] 487
61,11/20a: As You Desire Me 53
61,11/20b: Star Dust[2] 969
61,11/20c: Yesterdays [Days I Knew As Happy . . . Days] 1191
61,11/20d: I Hadn't Anyone Till You 401
61,11/21a: It Might as Well Be Spring[1] 533
61,11/21b: Prisoner of Love 863
61,11/21c: That's All 1031
61,11/21d: Don't Take Your Love from Me[2] 195
61,11/21e: Misty 704
61,11/22a: Come Rain or Come Shine[2] 145
61,11/22b: Night and Day[3] 774
61,11/22c: All or Nothing at All[2] 19
61,11/22d: Pocketful of Miracles* 854
62,1/15a: The Song Is Ended 950
62,1/15b: All Alone 9
62,1/15c: Charmaine 119
62,1/15d: When I Lost You 1130
62,1/16a: Remember[1] 871
62,1/16b: Together 1076
62,1/16c: The Girl (Boy) Next Door[2] 286
62,1/16d: Indiscreet 518
62,1/17a: What'll I Do?[2] 1126
62,1/17b: Oh, How I Miss You To-night 796
62,1/17c: Are You Lonesome Tonight? 48
62,1/17d: Come Waltz with Me 147
62,2/27a: Everybody's Twistin' 228
62,2/27b: Nothing but the Best 788
62,3/6a: I Gotta Right to Sing the Blues* 396
62,4/10a: I'm Beginning to See the Light 494
62,4/10b: I Get a Kick Out of You[2] 390
62,4/10c: Ain't She Sweet? 7
62,4/10d: I Love You [Hums the April Breeze] 414
62,4/10e: They Can't Take That Away from Me[2] 1052

62,4/10f: Love Is Just Around the Corner 660
62,4/11a: At Long Last Love[2] 55
62,4/11b: Serenade in Blue 903
62,4/11c: Goody Goody 303
62,4/11d: Don'cha Go 'Way Mad 181
62,4/11e: Tangerine 1014
62,4/11f: Pick Yourself Up 850
62,6/12a: If I Had You[3] 452
62,6/12b: The Very Thought of You[2] 1093
62,6/12c: I'll Follow My Secret Heart[2] 476
62,6/12d: A Garden in the Rain 278
62,6/13a: London by Night[3] 642
62,6/13b: The Gypsy 310
62,6/13c: Roses of Picardy 878
62,6/13d: A Nightingale Sang in Berkeley Square 779
62,6/14a: We'll Meet Again 1117
62,6/14b: Now Is the Hour «Maori's Haere Ra»[2] 791
62,6/14c: We'll Gather Lilacs in the Spring 1116
62,8/27a: The Look of Love [I've Seen—] 649
62,8/27b: I Left My Heart in San Francisco 408
62,10/2a: Nice Work If You Can Get It[2] 769
62,10/2b: Please Be Kind 852
62,10/2c: I Won't Dance[2] 442
62,10/2d: Learnin' the Blues[2] 613
62,10/3a: I'm Gonna Sit Right Down and Write. . .[2] 501
62,10/3b: I Only Have Eyes for You[2] 420
62,10/3c: My Kind of Girl 741
62,10/3d: Pennies from Heaven[2] 848
62,10/3e: The Tender Trap (Love Is—)[2] 1021
62,10/3f: Looking at the World Thru Rose-Colored Glasses 651
62,10/22a: Me and My Shadow 689
62aTELEVS: Where or When[3] 1155
63,1/21a: Come Blow Your Horn 138
63,1/21b: Call Me Irresponsible 108
63,2/18a: Lost in the Stars[2] 654
63,2/18b: My Heart Stood Still 739
63,2/18c: Ol' Man River[2] 810

63,2/19a: This Nearly Was Mine 1063
63,2/19b: You'll Never Walk Alone[2] 1227
63,2/19c: I Have Dreamed 403
63,2/20a: California 106
63,2/20b: Bewitched (Bothered and Bewildered)[2] 84
63,2/20c: America the Beautiful[2] 32
63,2/21a: Soliloquy[2] 928
63,2/21b: You Brought a New Kind of Love to Me[3] 1202
63,4/29a: In the Wee Small Hours of the Morning[2] 516
63,4/29b: Nancy (with the Laughing Face)[2] 757
63,4/29c: Young at Heart[2] 1229
63,4/29d: The Second Time Around[2] 890
63,4/29e: All the Way[2] 24
63,4/30a: Witchcraft[2] 1176
63,4/30b: How Little We Know[2] 354
63,4/30c: Put Your Dreams Away[3] 866
63,4/30d: I've Got You Under My Skin[2] 575
63,4/30e: Oh, What It Seemed to Be[3] 802
63,7/10a: We Open in Venice 1109
63,7/10b: Guys and Dolls[1] 308
63,7/18a: Old Devil Moon[2] 805
63,7/18b: When I'm Not Near the Girl I Love 1133
63,7/18c: I've Never Been in Love Before 580
63,7/24a: So in Love 924
63,7/24b: Some Enchanted Evening[3] 931
63,7/24c: Luck Be a Lady 674
63,7/24d: Guys and Dolls[2] 309
63,7/29a: Fugue for Tinhorns 271
63,7/29b: The Oldest Established (Permanent...) 812
63,7/31a: Some Enchanted Evening[2] 930
63,7/31b: Twin Soliloquies «Wonder How It Feels» 1087
63,7/31c: Here's to the Losers 331
63,7/31d: Love Isn't Just for the Young 661
63,10/13a: Have Yourself a Merry Little Christmas[3] 321

63,12/3a: Talk to Me, Baby (Tell Me Lies) 1013
63,12/3b: Stay with Me 974
63aTELEVS: Who Takes Care of the Caretaker's Daughter? 1162
64,1/2a: You're a Lucky Fellow, Mr. Smith 1232
64,1/2b: The House I Live In (That's America...)[2] 341
64,1/27a: The Way You Look Tonight[2] 1105
64,1/27b: Three Coins in the Fountain[2] 1068
64,1/27c: Swinging on a Star 1005
64,1/27d: In the Cool, Cool, Cool of the Evening 513
64,1/27e: The Continental[2] 151
64,1/28a: It Might as Well Be Spring[2] 534
64,1/28b: Secret Love 891
64,1/28c: Moon River 714
64,1/28d: Days of Wine and Roses 168
64,1/28e: Love Is a Many-Splendored Thing 657
64,2/4a: Let Us Break Bread Together 619
64,4/8a: My Kind of Town [Chicago Is—][1] 742
64,4/8b: I Like to Lead When I Dance 410
64,4/8c: I Can't Believe I'm Losing You 367
64,4/10a: Style 987
64,4/10b: Mr. Booze 701
64,4/10c: Don't Be a Do-Badder 182
64,6/9a: The Best Is Yet to Come 80
64,6/9b: I Wanna Be Around 430
64,6/9c: I Believe in You 365
64,6/9d: Fly Me to the Moon «In Other Words»[1] 247
64,6/10a: Hello, Dolly! 324
64,6/10b: The Good Life 296
64,6/10c: I Wish You Love «Que Reste-il de Nos Amours» 438
64,6/12a: I Can't Stop Loving You 370
64,6/12b: More 725
64,6/12c: Wives and Lovers 1181
64,6/16a: An Old Fashioned Christmas 806

84,4/17a: Teach Me Tonight 1016
84,4/17b: It's All Right with Me[3] 550
84,4/17c: After You've Gone 6

84,4/17d: Mack the Knife «Moritat»
 678
84,5/17a: Stormy Weather[3]* 979

Sessions Supplement

In the Introduction to this book, I stated that Frank Sinatra was unlikely to record again after 1984. While this has remained largely true in the case of commercial recordings, there have been several post–1984 records attempted, a few released in special circumstances. These are as follows:

On October 30, 1986, Sinatra recorded three tracks in a Hollywood studio. Quincy Jones conducted a 41-piece orchestra: 1) a new vocal track for *Mack the Knife* was sung over the 4/16/84 orchestral track of Frank Foster's arrangement (this vocal track was used instead of the 1984 original on the Japanese CD version of the *L.A. Is My Lady* album, and this version was also used in a big multi–CD package Reprise issued for Sinatra's 75th birthday commemoration); 2) a full new recording of *The Girls I've Never Kissed,* arranged by Billy May (not released); 3) a full new recording of *One to a Customer,* arranged by Billy May (not released).

On June 6, 1988, the singer made one complete recording — and three other orchestra-only tracks were done — in a Hollywood session conducted by Frank Sinatra Jr. The complete work was *My Foolish Heart,* arranged by Billy May; it was not released.

On August 27, 1991, Sinatra did a special recording of *Silent Night* for a charity album being produced by Judy Garland's daughter, Lorna Luft.

This late recording takes place in the context of a revival of classic American songs being recorded by several young singers. Sinatra himself continues to appear live before enthusiastic audiences. These live shows, and the current CD releases of his music, ranked Sinatra 25th of the 40 highest earning entertainers in a 1990-91 *Forbes* magazine listing.

The Cities
for the Sessions

2/3/39 thru 8/31/39: New York City
10/13/39 thru 10/13/39: Chicago
11/8/39 thru 11/8/39: Hollywood
2/1/40 thru 2/1/40: Chicago
2/26/40 thru 9/17/40: New York City
10/16/40 thru 11/11/40: Hollywood
1/6/41 thru 9/26/41: New York City
12/22/41 thru 3/9/42: Hollywood
3/18/42 thru 7/2/42: New York City

*Left Tommy Dorsey — significant break in
recording: 7/3/42 thru 6/6/43*

6/7/43 thru 11/10/43: New York City

*A.O.N.A.A. strike — significant break in
recording: 11/11/43 thru 11/12/44*

11/13/44 thru 12/3/44: New York City
12/19/44 thru 5/16/45: Hollywood
5/24/45 thru 5/24/45: New York City
7/30/45 thru 8/27/45: Hollywood
11/15/45 thru 12/7/45: New York City
2/3/46 thru 3/10/46: Hollywood
4/7/46 thru 4/7/46: New York City
5/28/46 thru 11/7/46: Hollywood
12/15/46 thru 12/15/46: New York City
1/9/47 thru 9/23/47: Hollywood
10/19/47 thru 12/8/47: New York City
12/26/47 thru 4/10/48: Hollywood
12/15/48 thru 12/15/48 A.M.: New York
City
12/15/48 thru 12/15/48 P.M.: Hollywood
12/16/48 thru 5/6/49: Hollywood
7/10/49 thru 7/15/49: New York City
7/21/49 thru 2/23/50: Hollywood
3/10/50 thru 5/10/51: New York City
7/9/51 thru 6/3/52: Hollywood
9/17/52 thru 9/17/52: New York City

*Left Columbia label — significant break in
recording: 9/18/52 thru 4/1/53*

4/2/53 thru 5/23/61: Los Angeles
11/20/61 thru 11/22/61: Hollywood

1/15/62 thru 2/27/62: Los Angeles
4/10/62 thru 4/11/62: Hollywood
6/12/62 thru 6/14/62: London
8/27/62 thru 1/21/63: Los Angeles
2/18/63 thru 2/21/63: Hollywood
4/29/63 thru 11/11/64: Los Angeles
4/13/65 thru 4/22/65: Hollywood
5/6/65 thru 5/6/65: Los Angeles
5/27/65 thru 11/30/65: Hollywood
1/26/66 thru 2/1/66: Concert, Las
Vegas
4/11/66 thru 2/1/67: Hollywood
6/29/67 thru 6/29/67: New York City
7/24/67 thru 12/12/67: Hollywood
7/24/68 thru 7/24/68: New York City
8/12/68 thru 3/21/69: Hollywood
7/14/69 thru 7/17/69: New York City
8/18/69 thru 8/18/69: Hollywood
10/13/69 thru 10/13/69: New York City
11/7/69 thru 11/7/69: Hollywood

*Preretirement — significant break in record-
ing: 11/8/69 thru 10/25/70*

10/26/70 thru 11/2/70: Hollywood

*Full retirement — significant break in record-
ing: 11/3/70 thru 4/28/73*

4/29/73 thru 9/24/74: Hollywood
10/2/74 thru 10/13/74: East Coast tour
(Massachusetts, New York,
Pennsylvania)
2/20/75 thru 3/12/75: Hollywood
8/18/75 thru 8/18/75: New York City
10/24/75 thru 6/21/76: Hollywood
9/27/76 thru 9/27/76: New York City
11/12/76 thru 1/19/77: Hollywood
2/16/77 thru 2/16/77: New York City
3/9/77 thru 3/14/77: Hollywood

*Dislikes results — significant break in record-
ing: 3/15/77 thru 7/16/78*

7/17/78 thru 7/17/78: Hollywood

Dislikes results — significant break in recording: 7/18/78 thru 7/15/79

7/16/79 thru 7/18/79: Los Angeles
8/20/79 thru 8/22/79: New York City
9/17/79 thru 12/18 79: Los Angeles

Semiretirement — significant break in recording: 12/19/79 thru 4/7/81

4/8/81 thru 4/8/81: Hollywood
7/20/81 thru 9/10/81: New York City

12/3/81 thru 12/3/81: Los Angeles
8/17/82 thru 1/25/83: New York City
2/28/83 thru 3/16/83: Los Angeles

Semiretirement — significant break in recording: 3/17/83 thru 4/12/84

4/13/84 thru 4/17/84: New York City
5/17/84 thru 5/17/84: Los Angeles

Recording career ends May 18th, 1984, but live shows continue.

Chapter 8: The Albums

A detailed analysis of Sinatra's albums is beyond the scope of this book, but a summary of the LPs referenced in the Master Song List can be useful to fans, collectors and students. This chapter will touch lightly on all the albums in which these 1,251 recordings have been collected: theme albums, compilations, collections, re-packages, commemoratives, bootlegs, et cetera. I will deal more heavily with the lesser number of LPs which were landmarks in Sinatra's long career.

These albums contain all the recordings in this book except for 72 available only as singles, where no album release could be identified; these singles are included in Album List #1 at the end of this chapter.

The "specials" referenced include the one demonstration disc cut by Sinatra in 1939 (not available for purchase, but included for historical purposes), and the various legally released albums of radio and television broadcast tapes and wartime Victory discs, plus "bootleg" albums of film soundtracks and studio recordings that were never officially issued.

Albums will be discussed in the order in which they were initially released—decade by decade—irrespective of date recorded or company label. Those albums which are fundamental to a good Sinatra collection are preceded by an asterisk (*).

The '40s

The advent of micro-groove recording on plastic made it possible to release collections of songs on a single disc; one that was light and hard-to-break. This was a great advantage over the literal "albums" of four to six heavy, easily cracked 78 rpm discs. But when Columbia Records commercially developed the technology, in June of 1948, few music lovers were inspired to buy the new phonographs needed for these long-playing (LP) records, despite the fact that their sound quality was a great improvement as well. Times were a little tough in the post-war years and 78 rpm single phonographs had become an institution at home, in juke boxes, and over the radio. It wasn't until the early '50s that economic and technological momentum brought microgroove records (33.3 rpm LPs and 45 rpm singles) into popular favor.

Nevertheless, some people did buy the new record players right away and some LPs were released in the late '40s. Frank Sinatra was the very first artist released on one of these 10", eight-song LPs, and therefore had the first number one–selling LP — Columbia's *The Voice of Frank Sinatra.* This was followed up, in December, with *Christmas Songs by Sinatra.*

Since this book only references the best current LP source for each recording, only a handful of these early Columbia 10-inchers are included: only those which represent the sole LP placement of a particular track. Here are the two referenced LPs of the 1940s:

Popular Favorites, Volume 1
1949 / 3rd LP from Columbia / 10" / 8 songs

Like all the early LPs, a collection of previously released singles, in this case by eight different singers. This LP contains the only legal album appearance of Sinatra's December 16, 1948, recording of *Sunflower.*

Frankly Sentimental
1949 / 4th LP from Columbia / 10" / 8 songs

A Sinatra singles collection, with the only legal album appearance of the November 5, 1947, recording of *When You Awake.*

Other albums of the '40s containing Sinatra tracks — not otherwise referenced in this volume — include the compendium *Columbo, Crosby, Sinatra* (1948 — RCA Victor), *Getting Sentimental with Tommy Dorsey* (1948 — RCA Victor), and *Tommy Dorsey All Time Hits* (1949 — RCA Victor). The Sinatra recordings in such unreferenced LPs are generally duplicated in the LPs that are referenced, except for cases where Sinatra only conducted the orchestra rather than singing.

The '50s

As this decade began, vinyl LPs were still unusual, but that changed quickly. First, 45 rpm microgroove plastic singles began to pick up in sales with respect to the old 78s, and relatively inexpensive little 45 players with improved sound quality accelerated that trend. Then came the expanding purchase of high fidelity phonographs to play both the 7" 45s and the 10" and 12" 33.3 rpm LPs.

By 1953, rock and roll was selling a serious volume of 45s. The family record player could handle all formats and speeds. LPs started to move. That was the year Sinatra began his contract with the young Capitol Records label, in an attempt to revive his ailing career. After recording eleven sides for singles release (which had some commercial success), Sinatra got together with Nelson Riddle for their first album sessions. The concept of the unified theme album was instigated with their first project, and quickly grew into the huge commercial/artistic success of the Capitol LPs of that decade. This continued into the 1960s to such an extent that Sinatra holds the record for the most number one LPs during the rock 'n' roll era.

Stereophonic recording consolidated the new medium in the mid-'50s. Many of the albums listed here as monaural were later re-released in a synthesized stereo; Capitol's promotional people called this process "Duophonic," and I will use that term for all variations on the process.

Simultaneous with the Capitol album releases, Columbia Records began to repackage Sinatra's many single recordings for release on the 12", 12-song LP format. RCA Victor also began repackaging the older Dorsey/Sinatra songs for release in this thriving new product line. Here are the referenced LPs of the 1950s, in order of release:

Songs by Sinatra, Volume 1
1950 / 5th LP from Columbia / 10" / 8 songs
A singles collection, with the only legal album appearance of the October 24, 1946, recording of *I'm Sorry I Made You Cry*.

** Songs for Young Lovers*
1954 / 2nd LP from Capitol / 10" / 8 songs
An historic Capitol LP and their first all–Sinatra album. Here began Sinatra's true era of theme LPs, the tunes selected, arranged,

played and sung to provide a sequence of individual dramatic statements that collectively form a kind of overdrama. Working with producer Voyle Gilmore, Nelson Riddle rewrote some romantic and swinging George Siravo "small combo" arrangements for the full studio orchestra. Sinatra's maturing voice bloomed in this garden. Five of the eight numbers were straight romantic ballads, the other three were lightly swinging. Later, in 1960, four related tunes (recorded with Riddle during the same period) were added to make a 12" LP version.

Swing Easy!
1954 / 4th LP from Capitol / 10" / 8 songs

More of the George Siravo arrangements—which Sinatra had been using in nightclubs during his comeback attempt—were redone by Riddle for full orchestra. These were all lightly swinging. The powerful Sinatra/Riddle teamwork was building fast. As with the preceding LP, four more cuts were added to make a 12" version in 1960. The two original eight-song versions were combined into one 16-song LP in 1955, using the two album titles jointly; this latter version became the most widely sold format for these recordings, since 10" LPs were fast fading commercially.

Boys & Girls Together
1955 / 16th LP from Columbia / 10" / 6 songs; final ref. 10" LP

The earliest non–Christmas theme LP involving Sinatra. Columbia packaged six duets by six pairs of noted singers; one of the pairs was Frank Sinatra and Jane Russell warbling *Kisses and Tears*.

In the Wee Small Hours
1955 / Capitol / 12" / 16 songs

This was the first "masterwork" album. It was also the first time Nelson Riddle wrote original orchestration for a collection of songs performed to a central theme, and is classified by some historians as the first true "concept" album in popular music. Many of Sinatra's favorite songwriters were represented. As a lonely experience—though not as painful as later albums of its kind—this creation influenced fans and singers for years to come. Initially released as two 10" LPs of eight songs each, the big popular impact came when the two were combined into this one-disc giant collection. Capitol suffered the expense of many song royalties to pay on one product.

Frankie
1955 / Columbia / 12" / 12 songs

This was the first of many Columbia Records 12" LP compilations of singles releases. Later, there would be an attempt to assemble tunes so as to copy the Capitol "theme albums" approach, but during this period they just selected a variety of love songs. There were many fine 1943–1952 recordings from which to choose.

The Voice
1955 / Columbia

Another good singles compilation, this time mostly slow ballads.

*Songs for Swingin' Lovers!
1956 / Capitol

After the late-night loneliness and dejection of **In the Wee Small Hours,** Sinatra and Riddle turned joyous and bouncy for a set of 15 great tunes. This LP really consolidated Sinatra's popular revival. Riddle's arrangements were never happier. One of them came from a last-minute decision. While initially intending to scale their 12" LPs down to 12 tunes, Capitol management decided this LP wasn't the place to do it. On the evening before recording, Sinatra was told they wanted to add three songs. Sinatra phoned Riddle that night, instructing him to produce the three new arrangements by the next morning; one of them was his classic chart for Cole Porter's *I've Got You Under My Skin.*

That Old Feeling
1956 / Columbia

A mixture of up-tempo love songs and slow ballads recorded in the latter half of the 1940s.

Adventures of the Heart
1956 / Columbia

Another fine singles collection; most tunes recorded in the early '50s.

"High Society"
1956 / Capitol soundtrack

Johnny Green conducted the MGM studio orchestra, using the work of several different arrangers, to capture this Cole Porter score.

Sinatra does four tunes, aiming two love ballads at Grace Kelly, harmonizing with Celeste Holme on another, and rollicking through a drunken duet with Bing Crosby in a screen "first."

This Is Sinatra!
1956 / Capitol
In the beginning of Sinatra's time at Capitol, he recorded a series of singles with Riddle. Several of these— *Young at Heart, Love and Marriage, From Here to Eternity, Learnin' the Blues, Three Coins in the Fountain, The Tender Trap,* etc. —were the big radio hits which got the singer going again commercially. These and six other fine singles make up this LP; at Capitol, they weren't titled as "greatest hits" albums.

Close to You
1957 / Capitol
Not wanting to be stereotyped as swingers, Sinatra and Riddle next produced an album of slow-tempo love ballads including members of the L.A. Philharmonic in the studio orchestra and using arrangements which were dominated by violinist Felix Slatkin and the other musicians of the Hollywood String Quartet. For this beautiful, serious album, Sinatra and Riddle conceived a joke on the Capitol executives. They recorded *There's a Flaw in My Flue,* a comic ballad written for Bing Crosby's "Flop Parade" radio feature. The company executives approved that number along with everything else, putting the joke back on Sinatra. The song was cut from the original LP, but restored in the 1980s for the compact disc release.

A Swingin' Affair!
1957 / Capitol
The next album with Nelson Riddle was back to swinging, this time a hotter and jazzier swinging than ever. There was great variety in the song selection and the style of arrangement. Less danceable than the cuts in **Songs for Swingin' Lovers!,** the album still got heavy radio play and climaxed the first phase of the Riddle period.

Christmas Dreaming
1957 / Columbia
Past compilations of Christmas singles were reshuffled into this set of five Christmas carols and five seasonal pop tunes. All ten tracks were arranged by Axel Stordahl.

*Where Are You?
1957 / Capitol / 1st stereo

Having just signed with Capitol, Gordon Jenkins began his long history of recording with Sinatra. The songs spoke of loneliness and love lost — as with *In the Wee Small Hours* — but more symphonically and mournfully with Jenkins's orchestration conceived for stereophonic sound. Six of Sinatra's classics (including *Laura* and *I'm a Fool to Want You*) were recorded for the second time, in each case surpassing the original versions. Many people did not have stereo phonographs in 1957, so the album was released in both monaural and stereophonic editions. Because early stereo tracks required more disc space, and only about 22 minutes would fit on a side, one of the 12 tracks was cut from the stereo edition.

A Jolly Christmas from Frank Sinatra
1957 / Capitol

There were a number of past Christmas recordings by Sinatra, and Columbia Records had been repackaging them as new albums. Capitol wanted to compete, so for three days — during the hot California July of 1957 — the singer performed many of the same songs and classic carols. Gordon Jenkins arranged and conducted. Choral work was provided by the Ralph Brewster Singers. The album remained popular during holiday seasons for the next decade.

We Three
1957 / RCA Victor

This was another repackaging of recordings with the Dorsey orchestra. The special thing here is the inclusion of Sinatra's first four solo records, made with Axel Stordahl and a studio orchestra during a break that Dorsey permitted; the four were released on the Bluebird label.

"Pal Joey"
1957 / Capitol soundtrack

Morris Stoloff conducted Riddle arrangements of the Rodgers and Hart songs which Sinatra sang in the movie. *The Lady Is a Tramp* became one of his concert standards.

Come Fly with Me
1958 / Capitol / 2nd stereo

Finally the third of Capitol's major arrangers — Billy May — recorded with Sinatra. It was also the first time Jimmy Van Heusen and Sammy Cahn wrote new songs to frame the theme of an album. Many of the charts were atypical for Billy May, and this collaboration also inspired the singer to break new ground. It was Sinatra's first number one *Billboard* album of the '50s. Both creatively and commercially, things were building toward the peak of Sinatra's Capitol career. Again, stereo and mono LP editions differed.

Put Your Dreams Away
1958 / Columbia

This Columbia singles compilation works to emulate the Capitol theme albums. There are a dozen songs arranged by Axel Stordahl, beginning with *I Dream of You* and ending with *Put Your Dreams Away*. The songs in between are all dreamy ballads.

This Is Sinatra, Volume Two
1958 / Capitol

The second singles compilation for Capitol. The recordings were not all big hits, but they were very fine examples of the different styles which Sinatra adopted for singles.

Frank Sinatra Sings for Only the Lonely
1958 / Capitol / 3rd stereo

Many writers, fans, and historians — as well as Sinatra himself — have called this his greatest album. Certainly it's his most excruciating collection of late-night songs of anguish: his "saloon songs." Since Voyle Gilmore had retired, this was Dave Cavanaugh's debut as producer for Sinatra. Originally, Gordon Jenkins was scheduled to write the charts, as he had with the previous "saloon" set, *Where Are You?* When schedule conflicts interposed themselves, Nelson Riddle was brought in to orchestrate the work, and since Riddle was touring with Nat "King" Cole when the first session was scheduled in late May 1958, Felix Slatkin conducted Riddle's arrangements. Nelson Riddle conducted his own work during the final two album sessions in late June. Despite these changes, shifts and divisions of labor, the monaural version of the album is seamless and brilliant. The stereo version (with two less songs because of track-width requirements) has slightly more tape hiss, but is still beautiful in its dimensional richness. Stereo technology was maturing and taking over the industry. This was the last Sinatra album recorded simultaneously in stereo and mono on separate tapes, the last LP with two distinct editions. The album hit number one and spent nearly two and a half years on the *Billboard* sales charts.

*Come Dance with Me!
1959 / Capitol / new recordings from here on are all stereo

This follow-up to Sinatra's immensely successful *. . Only the Lonely* album was an even bigger hit commercially, holding for 140 weeks on the album charts and winning the Grammy for Album of the Year. Billy May wrote most of the brassy arrangements and conducted his own band for this up-tempo extravaganza; Heinie Beau ghost-wrote three of the arrangements in May's style. Again, the Van Heusen/Cahn team created special opening and closing numbers. A fun album!

The Frank Sinatra Story in Music
1959 / Columbia / 2 discs / mono

To take advantage of their former star's new surge, Columbia Records assembled a review of Sinatra's earlier solo career, ranging from the 1939 Harry James version of *All or Nothing at All* to the 1952 recording of *The Birth of the Blues*. Such was Sinatra's drawing power that even this older material reached *Billboard*'s number 12 album spot.

Look to Your Heart
1959 / Capitol / mono

On August 5, 1955, Sinatra went into the studio with Nelson Riddle to record four songs by James Van Heusen and Sammy Cahn. These were to be used in the TV musical production of Thornton Wilder's *Our Town,* in which Sinatra played the narrator/stage manager. One of these songs, *Love and Marriage,* was released the next year in the first Capitol singles compilation, **This Is Sinatra!** The other three songs — *Our Town, The Impatient Years* and *Look to Your Heart* — form the nexus of this album, establishing its theme and feeling, even though the balance of the 12 tunes are all singles from Sinatra's early days at Capitol Records.

*No One Cares
1959 / Capitol

This is the album that Gordon Jenkins arranged after missing the intended assignment which became *Frank Sinatra Sings for Only the Lonely*. As a classic saloon song LP, this one stands tall beside its more famous predecessor. Opening with a theme piece, *When No One Cares*, by Cahn and Van Heusen, this album contains definitive renditions of song masterpieces like *A Cottage for Sale, Here's That Rainy Day* and *I Can't Get Started*, along with neglected art songs like *Where Do You Go?* and *None But the Lonely Heart*. Arguably the pinnacle of Jenkins's career, and one peak reached by Sinatra.

"Can-Can"
1959 / Capitol soundtrack

Nelson Riddle was musical director for this film, arranging and conducting for all performers. Sinatra does fine Cole Porter solos, plus duets with Maurice Chevalier and Shirley MacLaine. The film put a very satisfactory finish to the singer's triumphant decade.

Sinatra albums not referenced from the '50s are again those with contents duplicated on more prominent and available releases, and those for which the singer only conducted. In several cases, the LPs are only part–Sinatra. The principal examples of such albums are *Harry James Greatest Hits* (10" 1950 — Columbia), *Dedicated to You* (10" 1950 — Columbia), *This Is Tommy Dorsey!* (10" 1950 — RCA Victor), *Popular Favorites, Vol. 2* (10" 1950 — Columbia), *Sing and Dance with Frank Sinatra* (10" 1951 — Columbia), *Popular Favorites, Vol. 3* (10" 1951 — Columbia), *Fabulous Frankie* (10" 1951 — RCA Victor), *This Is My Best* (10" 1952 — Columbia, *Honor Roll of Hits: 1940–1941* (10" 1952 — RCA Victor), *Requested by You* (10" 1953 — Columbia), *Today's Top Hits* (10" 1953 — Capitol — first for label), *Honor Roll of Hits: 1942–1943* (10" 1953 — RCA Victor), *Top Hits of '54, Vol. 1* (10" 1954 — Capitol), *Honor Roll of Hits: 1944–1945* (10" 1954 — RCA Victor), *In the Wee Small Hours, Parts 1 & 2* (two 10" LPs 1954 — Capitol), *I've Got a Crush on You* (10" 1954 — Columbia #CL-6290), *Young at Heart* (10" 1955 — Columbia — with Doris Day), *Get Happy!* (10" 1955 — Columbia), *The Metronome All-Stars* (10" 1955 — Columbia), *I've Got a Crush on You* (10" 1955 — Columbia #CL-2539 House Party), *Christmas with Sinatra* (10" 1955 — Columbia), *Hall of Fame* (10" 1955 —

Columbia), *The RCA Victor Encyclopedia of Recorded Jazz* (10" 1955 —
RCA Victor), *Frank Sinatra Conducts the Music of Alec Wilder* (new
12" 1955 — Columbia), *Frankie and Tommy* (12" 1957 — RCA Victor),
Tone Poems of Color (12" 1957 — Capitol), *The Man I Love* (12" 1958 —
Capitol — conducts for Peggy Lee), *Sinatra Plus* (12" 1958 — Fontana —
2 disc), *Sleep Warm* (12" 1959 — Capitol — conducts for Dean Martin)
and, lastly, the hard-to-find *Sinatra Souvenir* (12" 1959 — Fontana).

The '60s

The release years of 1960 and 1961 were huge ones for Sinatra,
with 17 albums issued legally. The rest of the decade followed suit:
RCA Victor continued to reissue Dorsey/Sinatra material; Columbia
finished packaging new albums of old singles; Capitol used up their
main body of unreleased tracks by the mid–1960s and began to repackage; Cameron Records released Sinatra radio tracks; a number
of bootleg movie soundtracks appeared; and all this was on top of
many brand-new records from the singer's own label, Reprise. It made
for a huge glut of Sinatra, but somehow it didn't serve to repress the
market; that's how big Frank Sinatra was at the time.

There were numerous experiments conducted by Sinatra now
that he was on his own label. Choice of arrangers, producers and songs
had the most visible impact, but the changing cast of musicians playing at his studio sessions was also important. During the '40s and '50s,
Sinatra had hand-picked certain players (some of these are listed in
Chapter 7). Now with more control over budgets and industry dealings, he spiced many of his sessions with great jazz and soul men like
Don Fagerquist (trumpet), Emil Richards (vibes), Bud Shank (flute),
Leon Russell (piano), Chuck Berghofer (bass) and Tommy Tedesco
(guitar). Now add experiments with album concepts and overall attitude and you have the '60s Sinatra. Here are the referenced LPs of the
1960s, in release-order:

*Nice 'n' Easy
1960 / Capitol

For their first concept album since . . . *Only the Lonely,* Sinatra
and Nelson Riddle decided to rework 12 of the great love ballads which
had been among the singer's favorite recordings of the Columbia era,

tunes like *You Go to My Head, That Old Feeling* and *Try a Little Tenderness*. With the new stereo recording technology, the inspiration of Riddle charts, and a Sinatra voice and style at its mature peak, these would be classic recordings of great songs. The project was a complete success. Just before release, however, Sinatra had a hit with the contemporary song *Nice 'n' Easy*. For sales purposes, this was made the leadoff song of the LP, replacing *The Nearness of You*, which was later released on the 1962 album **Sinatra Sings . . . of Love and Things.**

Love Is a Kick
1960 / Columbia / mono
A singles compilation focused on the title theme of up-tempo love songs with a "kick." This is a more recent group of recordings, nine of the 12 coming from sessions held in the 1950s.

The Broadway Kick
1960 / Columbia / mono
A collection of show tune singles recorded during the central portion of Sinatra's time at Columbia. All but Gershwin's 1935 *Where Is My Bess?* were recorded when the Broadway shows and songs were new.

*Come Back to Sorrento
1960 / Columbia / mono
This singles compilation — all songs arranged by Axel Stordahl — consists of rich, slow-paced ballads, several with the flavors of opera, operetta and the concert hall.

Swing Easy
1960 / Capitol / 12" version / Duophonic stereo
Four "singles" recordings from the beginning of Sinatra's time at Capitol were added to the 10" LP of the same title, originally released in 1954. These four tracks don't really fit the sound and theme of the album, but at least it made them available in LP form.

Songs for Young Lovers
1960 / Capitol / 12" version / Duophonic stereo
As with the preceding LP, four tracks were added to the original 10" album. Three of the four 1953–54 Sinatra/Riddle recordings had

not been released on LP before. They fit the original LP better than was the case with the revised *Swing Easy* disc.

The First Times ... Frank Sinatra
early 1960s / Cameron radio tracks / mono

The huge Sinatra popularity and sales of the '60s resulted in lots of reissues of studio recordings. The Cameron label released several collections of recordings from 1940s radio shows featuring the young Sinatra; this LP was the first. These recordings were taken primarily from Lucky Strike's "Your Hit Parade." Axel Stordahl was Sinatra's arranger and musical director for these shows. The collections are valuable because many of these songs were never recorded in the studio. The sound quality is mediocre. Some tracks contain the audience reactions, including bobby-soxer shrieking.

The Original ... Frank Sinatra
early 1960s / Cameron radio tracks / mono

The second Cameron radio track collection, most from "Your Hit Parade." One highlight is a feeling version of *Tenderly*.

Frank Sinatra
early 1960s / Cameron radio tracks / mono

The fourth Cameron radio album drawn from "Your Hit Parade." It is interesting to hear Sinatra do songs contemporary to the radio show which are unlike those selected for his Columbia records: *Ballerina,* for example.

Sinatra's Swingin' Session!!!
1961 / Capitol

This was the last all-new Sinatra/Riddle work for Capitol, and their first "swinging" album since 1957's *A Swingin' Affair!* It was made up mostly of songs Sinatra had recorded as ballads for Columbia. With a big hot session band (up to 34 musicians) and new ideas filling Riddle's charts, these renditions really cook. Some writers feel the singer was anxious to finish his Capitol commitments and just tossed this album off in short sessions. It is definitely brisk. For me, it works.

All the Way
1961 / Capitol / part Duophonic, part true stereo

This was Sinatra's fourth Capitol singles collection including the title song and big hits like *Witchcraft* and *French Foreign Legion.*

Ring-a-Ding Ding!
1961 / Reprise

This was the first LP released by Sinatra's own label. It signaled the experimental period to come. As arranged and conducted by former Basie trombonist Johnny Mandel and with many jazz-based sidemen playing, this album has a unique sound. It straddles the line between swinging and ballads. The taste of the tunes is both delicate and spicy. Apart from the new Van Heusen/Cahn title song, the contents were all written decades before, nine of them in the 1930s and two in the '40s. A great LP.

Reflections
1961 / Columbia / mono

This was the last of the Columbia compilations packaged to compete directly with the Capitol albums and the even more contemporary tone of Sinatra's own Reprise label. From this point on, Columbia reissues were packaged more for the collector and nostalgia markets. *Reflections* contains 12 widely varying songs written between 1868 and 1950. It is an excellent sampler of work by Sinatra in his first decade of recording.

Come Swing with Me!
1961 / Capitol

Billy May again, going after that *Come Dance with Me!* market, this time playing with the possibilities of separated-speaker stereo systems. May forsook his own band this time, assembling a group with eight trumpets, four French horns, one tuba, six tenor trombones, two bass trombones, plus rhythm, percussion and a harp. He split these musicians into two camps (four trumpets in one camp, four in the other, etc.) and had each camp microphoned separately. His arrangements were written so that the musical phrases bounced back and forth from one camp to the other, from one stereo speaker to the other. It was an interesting effect, but somewhat limiting as well.

Sinatra Swings
1961 / Reprise

Originally titled *Swing Along with Me,* the initial release of this album was contested by Capitol Records who were competing head-to-head with their *Come Swing with Me!* album by the singer. They forced Sinatra to withdraw the LP and change the title for rerelease. As with the competing Capitol album, this was arranged by Billy May, who conducted his own orchestra in the fresh, lively charts. Most of the songs were being recorded by Sinatra for the first time; one of these was *The Curse of an Aching Heart,* which he had first performed with the Hoboken Four in 1935.

*I Remember Tommy. . .
1961 / Reprise
Conceived as a tribute to his old boss and mentor, this is one of Sinatra's most remarkable works. Sy Oliver was brought in to help plan the project, write the arrangements and conduct a studio orchestra capable of bringing a Tommy Dorsey feel to the music; Oliver had been one of Dorsey's solo arrangers, as well as a contributor to the numerous "house" arrangements. The album is opened and closed with the Dorsey theme, *I'm Getting Sentimental Over You,* sung very much as Tommy played it on his trombone. The rest of the songs were all recorded by Dorsey and sung by Sinatra in the '40s. To compare the earlier renditions with these new tracks is a vivid demonstration of the singer's growth. Important aspects of Sinatra's style had been formed by a study of Tommy Dorsey's technique. This album is consciously given over to singing the way Dorsey played. The singer considered this some of his best work.

*Sinatra & Strings
1962 / Reprise
Don Costa wore many hats in the music business, had worked with musicians and singers from many realms of rock and pop, both as producer and arranger. This album was his first experience with Sinatra; the idea was to drench the songs with strings, yet retain the jazzy tension that informed many of the singer's Reprise recordings. Fifty musicians were assembled to play arrangements that proved to be some of the most impressive in Costa's career, redefining classic songs like *Yesterdays* and *I Hadn't Anyone Till You.* Sinatra was also at the top of his form. He did amazing things with *It Might as Well Be Spring* and fused two decades together in a reprise of *All or Nothing at All.* There is a version of *Star Dust* that uses the neglected verse and drops the famous chorus. Don Costa, in later years, expressed the opinion that *Come Rain or Come Shine* was his best chart ever. A must for

every Sinatra fan. Two unused cuts were restored in a Japanese-release version in 1972.

Point of No Return
1962 / Capitol

This was the last Capitol theme album. An aging and ailing Axel Stordahl rejoined Sinatra for this blue and dreamy set. Stordahl did all the orchestrations except for two arrangements by Heinie Beau. Some of the pieces seem a little weary, but most of them are wonderful, especially *I'll Remember April* and *Memories of You*. A fitting tribute to Stordahl and his massive contribution to Sinatra's career.

Sinatra Sings . . . of Love and Things
1962 / Capitol / last of Capitol's "new" releases

This is mostly a singles collection, plus the sole product of Sinatra's last Capitol session, arranged by Skip Martin: *I've Gotta Right to Sing the Blues*. It contains the first LP release of the 1957 single *Chicago* plus other singles and left-over album material. Felix Slatkin arranged one of these past works, Nelson Riddle the balance of them.

*Sinatra and Swingin' Brass
1962 / Reprise

As a follow-up to **Sinatra & Strings,** this LP more than fills the bill. Neal Hefti arranged a Sinatra session for the first time, conducting a session-band loaded with jazz players; the group included four rhythm men and five-each trumpets, trombones and saxophones. The songs range from hot-tempo joyrides to jazzy ballads, but an ingenious use of countermelody throughout gives the album an homogenous feel. Sinatra had just finished weeks of filming *The Manchurian Candidate,* and his well-rested vocal equipment was in great shape. Hefti's chart for *I Get a Kick Out of You* became a concert standard for the singer. Sinatra's treatment of Cole Porter's 1944 ballad, *I Love You,* shows how a mediocre song can become great, while the album's version of *I'm Beginning to See the Light* shows how a great song can be made greater.

Sinatra Sings Great Songs from Great Britain
1962 / Reprise / English release only

Recorded in London at the end of a world tour, this LP was arranged by Robert Farnon. The songs are all associated with England.

Sinatra sounds a little tired, but it's an interesting collection. Never released in the United States. One unused cut was restored in the 1972 Japanese release.

*All Alone
1962 / Reprise
After several albums with arrangers new to him, Sinatra worked with Gordon Jenkins for the first time since leaving Capitol. The result was one of their most distinctive collaborations. Although an album dealing with loneliness and lost love, the nature of the music keeps it from being a saloon song LP. Nine of 11 tunes were written in the 1920s or before, five of them by Irving Berlin. The elegant simplicity of Berlin's lyrics set the tone for the collection, a tone of grief and remembrance more than one of bluesy dejection. Sinatra exercises impressive technical control with precise phrasing and slow tempos. His longing performance of *When I Lost You* — a song Berlin wrote on the early death of his young bride — was aided by Sinatra's own grief for friend Ernie Kovaks, for whom he would serve as pall bearer the same day he recorded the song. One unused cut was restored to the 1972 Japanese release of the LP.

Tommy Dorsey & His Orchestra, featuring Frank Sinatra
1962 / Coronet radio tracks / mono
Here is an unusual collection which includes band numbers without vocals, plus three early Sinatra radio tracks, all with the Dorsey orchestra. He was never recorded singing any of these songs again; the songs themselves are obscure. Sound quality is adequate.

*Sinatra-Basie: An Historic Musical First
1963 / Reprise
Considering how long these two New Jersey guys had been mutual admirers, it's surprising that Sinatra and Basie hadn't recorded together before. Neal Hefti was a stimulus in making this happen, and he did the arrangements. It's a swingin' album, with Basie on piano, fronting his band of five trumpets, three trombones, five men on saxes (doubling on other woodwinds), plus bass, drums and guitar. Sinatra reworks melodies to a greater extent than usual, plays with lyrics, and echoes sounds coming from the band. Songs range from 1926 to 1961 vintage.

The Concert Sinatra
1963 / Reprise

This album marked Nelson Riddle's freedom from his Capitol contract and his return to Sinatra. Their teamwork was never as complete as it had been at Capitol, but the pair produced some great tunes on and off through the next six years. This album consists of eight Broadway songs arranged and sung in semiclassical style. Riddle wrote for a full concert orchestra of 73 musicians, playing on sound stages at the Goldwyn studio—mostly Stage 7, famous for its natural reverberation in recording—and utilizing state-of-the-art microphones, high output recording film, Westrex recorders and an 8-track mixer console. All this resulted in a beautiful high fidelity stereo album. Standing out among the eight songs are the ultimate versions of two of Sinatra's favorite "production pieces," *Ol' Man River* from *Show Boat* and *Soliloquy* from *Carousel.*

Reprise Musical Repertory Theatre
1963 / Reprise / 4 discs: *"Finian's Rainbow," "Guys and Dolls," "Kiss Me Kate," "South Pacific"*

This set of four LPs was originally offered by mail-order subscription as a boxed set. The idea was to take four of Sinatra's favorite Broadway shows and replicate them with overtures and key songs. Which character sang what song in the play was ignored. Instead, appropriate singers (all signed with Sinatra's label) performed alone and in combination on the various songs. These included Bing Crosby, Rosemary Clooney, The Hi-Lo's, Dean Martin, Sammy Davis Jr., The McGuire Sisters, Jo Stafford, Keely Smith, Dinah Shore and—of course—Sinatra. A number of different arrangers contributed, with Morris Stoloff conducting.

Sinatra's Sinatra
1963 / Reprise

This was planned as an LP showcasing key songs associated with the singer, in the spirit of the art book *Picasso's Picasso*. Nelson Riddle used his arrangements of new Sinatra film hits (*The Second Time Around, Pocketful of Miracles, Call Me Irresponsible*), reworked some of his own classics (*I've Got You Under My Skin, In the Wee Small Hours of the Morning, Young at Heart*, etc.), and wrote fresh charts for some early notables (*Nancy, How Little We Know; Oh, What It Seemed to Be*, etc.); a nice summary of past and present hits, it gave Sinatra versions of these tunes on his own label. The first Sinatra LP using 4-track recording.

Have Yourself a Merry Little Christmas
1963 / Reprise

All the holiday numbers in this album were by other singers, except for the title song; Sinatra's third recording of the Martin/Blane classic.

Frank Sinatra Sings "Days of Wine and Roses," "Moon River" & Other Academy Award Winners
1964 / Reprise

Ten selected Oscar-winners for Best Song—ranging from 1934's *The Continental* to the 1962 winner, *Days of Wine and Roses*—make up this album. Nelson Riddle did the novel arrangements for the LP; he had done the original movie orchestration for Sinatra in the case of two winners presented, *Three Coins in the Fountain* (1954) and *All the Way* (1957). The way singer and arranger merge on the 1936 Oscar-winner *The Way You Look Tonight* clearly exemplifies how great they were together.

America, I Hear You Singing
1964 / Reprise

Sinatra teamed up with Bing Crosby and Fred Waring's Pennsylvanians to present an album of patriotic and American-philosophic songs. This was a labor of love more than of commerce or even art.

Frank Sinatra's Greatest Hits: The Early Years
1964 / Columbia / mono

A wide-ranging selection of hits from the Columbia era. Several different arrangers are represented. Since this LP was compiled in 1964, the selection of tunes is hind-sightfully different than it would have been if produced in the late 1940s.

Frank Sinatra's Greatest Hits: The Early Years, Volume 2
1964 / Columbia / mono

A second collection of late-'40s hits. One of the most interesting cuts is *People Will Say We're in Love*, recorded with vocal accompaniment only in an Alec Wilder arrangement. The song was new then. Sinatra wanted to record it despite the musician's strike that was going on at the time.

It Might as Well Be Swing
1964 / Reprise

A second album with Count Basie and his band, this time arranged by Quincy Jones. Less consistently tight than the *Sinatra-Basie* album, this one is still very worthwhile. The song selection is novel, including three Tony Bennett hits (Bennett is one of Sinatra's favorite singers), two foreign songs in English versions, and a country and western tune. One track from this LP caused Sinatra to be heard from space; astronauts on Apollo XI liked his *Fly Me to the Moon* so they took it up with them on July 16, 1969, and played it for Mission Control broadcast.

"Robin and the 7 Hoods"
1964 / Reprise soundtrack

A Chicago gangster musical; Jimmy Van Heusen and Sammy Cahn tailored the score for Sinatra, Crosby, Sammy Davis Jr. and other pals. Both the film and its score were successful, with *My Kind of Town* becoming a perennial for Sinatra, one of his great "city songs."

Frank Sinatra Sings Rodgers and Hart
1964 / Capitol / Duophonic stereo

Although this collection was a repackaging job by Capitol, drawing from several earlier LPs, it did have one track never before released. This was the lovely *Wait Till You See Her,* recorded in April 1956, with Nelson Riddle and the Hollywood String Quartet during the sessions that produced the *Close to You* album.

Softly, As I Leave You
1964 / Reprise

This album represents the first solid instance of Sinatra searching for a new audience, throwing out feelers. All the tunes were written in the 1960s. The title song and two others were recorded in July 1964 with arranger/conductor Ernie Freeman, who had helped Dean Martin reach the youth market. The rest of the LP sounds unrelated to the three Freeman cuts. Sinatra's solo LPs — when not singles collections or newly packaged reissues — have avoided the patchwork approach so common with most recording artists. Though containing many fine tracks, this album has that production/assembly feel. There are two July '63 single releases arranged by Martin Paich, two separate single releases with Don Costa, the 1963 movie-title recording from *Come Blow Your Horn,* a 1962 Riddle/Hefti single, and three October '64 recordings with Riddle and May to fill in the set of 12 cuts. An augury of things to come.

Twelve Songs of Christmas
1964 / Reprise

A second and final package with Crosby and Fred Waring. Several of the songs are unusual for a Christmas set. A very feeling album.

**September of My Years*
1965 / Reprise

When Sinatra worked next with arranger/conductor Gordon Jenkins, it was for a brand-new purpose, an album of songs about growing old. The singer was only working on his fiftieth year of life, but he had begun to consider mortality. For the first (and last) time since *Ring-a-Ding Ding!* Cahn and Van Heusen were commissioned to write title and theme songs for a concept album. Jenkins contributed another. The rest, old and new, were songs of age reflecting on youth and the flight of time. *It Was a Very Good Year* became the biggest hit from this award-winning LP. All the performances were memorable, especially *When the Wind Was Green.*

Sinatra '65
1965 / Reprise

Another case of album-as-product. Six of the songs are from single releases, five of them contemporary tunes, four of these arranged by Ernie Freeman in a simple, heavy-beat style. The other five tracks were lifted from recent Reprise LPs. Three of these are understandable, coming from the 1963 Musical Repertory Theatre mail-order set. The other two reissues — apparently just filling out the LP — came from the previous year's *"Robin and the 7 Hoods"* official soundtrack LP. A couple of the singles were actual Top–50 singles hits; this album seemed to have been assembled to keep after that new audience.

Tell Her You Love Her
1965/ Capitol / part Duophonic, part true stereo

An LP of reissues with two mid–'50s Capitol singles not previously available in album form, namely the title song and *Weep They Will.*

My Kind of Broadway
1965 / Reprise

Songs from musical theater scores. Another album that is mostly reissues, despite the fact that new work was being done. With so much Sinatra material on the market, why was this necessary? There are three brand-new Broadway tunes freshly recorded for the album. The songs were orchestrated by a variety of arrangers.

Frank Sinatra: A Man and His Music
1965 / Reprise / 2 discs

The Man's career synopsized with 31 songs, a bit of film soundtrack and a Vegas comedy sketch. One nice feature is Sinatra's narrative statements between tracks. But again, most of the material is reissue. There are only three new recordings; these were made because the songs were important to his career, yet not available in Reprise versions. The original arrangements were used for these new cuts.

Frank Sinatra — Through the Years: 1944–1966
mid–1960's / Ajazz television tracks

This is an unusual LP, mostly drawn from five TV specials broadcast between 1959 and 1966. Earlier broadcast years are covered by radio tracks. Sound quality is mediocre. The chief value is a chance to hear duets with folks like Ella Fitzgerald, Bob Hope and Dinah Shore.

Four Sinatra Movies
mid–1960s / bootleg / 4 soundtrack sources

This album contains Sinatra's earliest commercial film performances, from *Las Vegas Nights* (1941), *Ship Ahoy* (1942), *Reville with Beverly* (1943), and *Higher and Higher* (1943). Outstanding on this particular disc are the McHugh/Adamson songs from *Higher and Higher;* the record quality is pretty good for this type of product. A number of bootleg LPs were drawn from Sinatra's films through the years, especially those not released as official soundtrack albums. Some sound as if they were recorded off a TV showing. Others have an echoing quality as if recorded in a movie theater. The bootleg LPs included in this book are illegally distributed and not easy to find new, but they are not so unusual in secondhand record stores.

Complete "Step Lively" Film Soundtrack
mid–1960s / bootleg / 1 soundtrack source

The Styne/Cahn score for this 1944 film is very original. Sinatra does justice to its special qualities, especially with *As Long as There's Music* and *Some Other Time.*

Score from "Anchors Aweigh"
mid–1960s / bootleg / 1 soundtrack source

Sinatra's fourth starring role, his second in a film with a novel and tuneful Jule Styne/Sammy Cahn score. *I Fall in Love Too Easily* and *What Makes the Sun Set?* are among the highlights of the 1945 hit movie.

Score from "It Happened in Brooklyn"
mid–1960s / bootleg / 1 soundtrack source

The third and final major Styne/Cahn film score for Sinatra, who sings *Time After Time* and *It's the Same Old Dream,* among other tunes from the 1947 film, and also performs duets with Jimmy Durante and Kathryn Grayson. This score is also available in a legal release on the Hollywood Soundstage label, their album #HS-5006, *"It Happened in Brooklyn."*

Five Films
mid–1960s / bootleg / 5 soundtrack sources

This LP collects Sinatra bits and pieces out of the scores from the short film *The House I Live In* (1945), and from four feature-length movies, *Till the Clouds Roll By* (1946), *The Miracle of the Bells* (1948), *The Kissing Bandit* (1948), and *Take Me Out to the Ball Game* (1949). The title song from *The House I Live In* is a plea for racial and religious tolerance. He sings *Ol' Man River* in the 1946 pseudobiography of Jerome Kern. There is a delicate version of *Ever Homeward* from *The Miracle of the Bells,* sung without accompaniment by either instruments or chorus.

"On the Town" & Others
mid–1960s / bootleg / 5 soundtrack sources

This bootleg release features the full score from the film version of *On the Town* (1949), plus two songs from *Double Dynamite* (1951), the title tracks from *Young at Heart* (1955) and *The Tender Trap* (1955), as well as a Van Heusen/Cahn title song for *The Man with the Golden Arm* (1955) which was deleted from the finished film.

Score from "Meet Danny Wilson"
mid–1960s / bootleg / 1 soundtrack source
In this 1951 film, Sinatra plays a nightclub singer and performs nine solid standards including *She's Funny That Way, That Old Black Magic, I've Got a Crush on You* and *How Deep Is the Ocean?* Despite the fine singing in this picture, Sinatra's career was failing at the time, and there was no official soundtrack album released.

Score from "Guys and Dolls"
mid–1960s / bootleg / 1 soundtrack source
There are many legitimate sources for the songs from this famous Frank Loesser score—including several cuts by Sinatra—but this is the only full movie soundtrack I could locate. Cast members other than Sinatra get most of the best songs.

Score from "The Joker Is Wild"
mid–1960s / bootleg / 1 soundtrack source
Sinatra's career was taking a nose dive when the fine score for *Meet Danny Wilson* was not released on an LP, but it's harder to understand why this film was not given an official soundtrack album during the Sinatra boom in 1957, especially considering that *All the Way* took that year's best song Oscar and *Chicago* was a big hit in live shows. Most likely it was because he only did four numbers in the film, and Walter Scharf's instrumental score did not lend itself to fill-in tracks. Playing Joe E. Lewis, Sinatra croaked out song parodies.

Strangers in the Night
1966 / Reprise
With this fresh album, Sinatra's label stopped its two-year period of marketing reissues and packaged product. Nelson Riddle arranged and conducted the album sessions, interestingly mixing new songs with ones written in the '20s and '30s; a nice balance is struck between targeting younger and older fans. This balance is best exemplified by a great recording of 1965's *Summer Wind* and an up-tempo rendition of 1939's *All or Nothing at All*. To help sell the LP, they added Sinatra's current smash single *Strangers in the Night* arranged by Ernie Freeman. Though Sinatra didn't care for the song himself, it won Grammys as Best Solo Vocal and Record of the Year.

Moonlight Sinatra
1966 / Reprise

Again working with Nelson Riddle on a concept album (for the last time in official release, as it turned out), Sinatra reached back into earlier days and sang about love and the moon. All ten songs deal with that nighttime presence, nine having been published in the '30s, one in the early '40s. This was a controversial album, perhaps because it was so unexpected at the time.

**Sinatra at the Sands*
1966 / Reprise / 2 discs (live)

Sinatra sings live, responding to the energy of a Vegas crowd and the Count Basie band. Quincy Jones did the new and reworked charts. These are the special elements of this album. The 20 tracks on two discs include two monologues, three Basie instrumentals and many of the songs Sinatra favored in concerts of the period, some of them older classics (*I've Got You Under My Skin, Don't Worry 'Bout Me, One for My Baby, Angel Eyes*) and others recent hits (*Fly Me to the Moon, It Was a Very Good Year, My Kind of Town*). Loose and lively.

Forever Frank
1966 / Capitol / Duophonic stereo

An invaluable LP for the really serious collector, all but one of the 12 cuts had never been released in an album before. Recorded between April '53 and March '58, with various arrangers, these songs were done only once in Sinatra's career; included are his two early attempts at rock and several other pop styles of mid–1950s songwriting.

That's Life
1966 / Reprise

This is the only album entirely arranged and conducted by Ernie Freeman, the man responsible for many of Sinatra's hit singles during the 1960s. After an October '66 session produced the *Billboard* number four title song, the balance of the album was done over two days in November '66. Many longtime fans consider this LP a career low for the singer, but there are some pieces that depart from Freeman's often beat-heavy, repetitive approach, including *Sand and Sea,* a delicate *The Impossible Dream* and a lively rendition of *You're Gonna Hear from Me.*

Francis Albert Sinatra & Antonio Carlos Jobim
1967 / Reprise

A delicate, soft-sung, swaying album of bossa nova music. There are seven Jobim tunes, plus Latin rebirths for Berlin's *Change Partners,* Porter's *I Concentrate on You* and Forrest and Wright's *Baubles, Bangles and Beads.* Jobim worked directly with Sinatra and co-producers Ray Gilbert and Sonny Burke on the shape of the project. Claus Ogerman wrote the hypnotic arrangements. A specially configured session band was augmented by Jobim's personal drummer, and Jobim did some vocal backing on four of the selections. Among the great tracks are *Quiet Nights of Quiet Stars* and *If You Never Come to Me.*

The Essential Frank Sinatra, Volumes 1–3
1967 / Columbia / 3 discs / Duophonic stereo

This three-disc Columbia release is important for several reasons. It samples the full scope of Sinatra's 1939 to 1952 work. A variety of his early arrangers are represented. More than 30 of the 48 recordings were not released in the initial wave of Columbia's Sinatra LPs. All in all, an essential part of a good Sinatra collection.

Frank Sinatra & Frank and Nancy
1967 / Reprise

This was conceived as two separate albums, and initially given two product release numbers, but the ten cuts were finally assembled into this one-disc release, sometimes referred to as **The World We Knew,** after one of the more interesting songs, one which begins the LP. The second tune is *Something Stupid,* Sinatra's million-selling duet with daughter Nancy. The rest of the album consists of a wide range of contemporary songs (except for one from '58), arranged by four different men, including Nancy's youthful associate, Billy Strange, who charted the hit duet and a fine Lee Hazlewood tune, *This Town.*

Frank Sinatra in Hollywood, 1943–1949
1968 / Columbia / Duophonic stereo

For the purposes of this volume, I have referenced this album in favor of many other sources for the same songs. It is a chronological display of Sinatra's movie hits, but in studio recordings rather than soundtracks; the performances are excellent, the sound quality high. A majority of the tunes were written by either Jule Styne and Sammy

Cahn or by Jimmy McHugh and Harold Adamson: *I Couldn't Sleep a Wink Last Night, What Makes the Sun Set?* and *I Fall in Love Too Easily* are among the most memorable pieces.

Francis A. & Edward K.
1968 / Reprise

Duke Ellington — long a towering figure in American music — was near the end of his main productivity when he and his band got together with Sinatra for this album. The classic band was still largely intact, including Johnny Hodges and Cootie Williams. Billy May wrote arrangements that took full advantage of the musicians, long jazz charts with extended instrumental passages. None of the eight songs had ever been recorded by the singer, and Sinatra savors them like eight vintage wines.

Frank Sinatra's Greatest Hits!
1968 / Reprise

Contains many of Sinatra's hit singles of the '60s. One of these, *Forget Domani*, had not appeared before on an album.

The Sinatra Family Wish You a Merry Christmas
1968 / Reprise

Sinatra got together with his son and two daughters to produce this novel set of Christmas tunes with arrangements by Nelson Riddle. This turned out to be the last time an album was legally released with a full set of Riddle arrangements. Frank sang on five of the selections. The kids performed without him on the other cuts, including the Vietnam-directed antiwar song, *It's Such a Lonely Time of Year*.

Cycles
1968 / Reprise

One of arranger/producer Don Costa's projects to bring Sinatra closer to the current musical scene. The songs are all recorded for the first (and only) time, all written in the '60s. Composers include Teddy Randazzo, Joni Mitchell, Gayle Caldwell, Jimmy Webb and John Hartford. Most pieces were conducted by Sinatra's longtime pianist, Bill Miller.

My Way
1969 / Reprise

Again, with Don Costa arrangements, the singer works through relatively current styles of music. The title song was one of his biggest hits ever, almost a personal anthem. There are works written by the Beatles, Michel Legrand, Ray Charles and Paul Simon. Outstanding are two songs of European origin, the Bonfa/Sigman *A Day in the Life of a Fool* and *If You Go Away,* by Jacques Brel, with English lyrics by Rod McKuen.

*A Man Alone
1969 / Reprise

One of only two times in Sinatra's career where all the songs of an album were written exclusively for him and for the project. Rod McKuen did these, some full songs, others recitations to a melodic musical background. Don Costa arranged and conducted. The LP is an organic progression of reveries on the title theme. Sinatra was in fine voice, and clearly empathetic with McKuen's words.

There was just one album with Sinatra as conductor-only in the 1960s: this was **Frank Sinatra Conducts Music from Pictures and Plays** (1962 — Reprise). Among the albums of repeat material, there were a few interesting releases such as **Memory #427** (a Canadian bootleg with all of the Harry James period recordings), **That Sentimental Gentleman** (a two-disc RCA set of Dorsey air-checks, including the singer's farewell to the band), and **My Favorite Hits — Mickey Mantle** (a novel compilation of the Yankee player's choice in "hit" records, with Sinatra singing *I'll Never Smile Again*). The other albums, however, were nearly all just reshufflings of old material, some structured for artificial themes. Too numerous to list in full are Capitol titles like **Sinatra Sings the Select Johnny Mercer** (or **Harold Arlen** or **Cole Porter**), and LPs named after key songs like **The Night We Called It a Day, The Nearness of You,** etc. Columbia Records added their share to the load with many albums named after famous songs — such as **Someone to Watch Over Me** — and nostalgia packages like **In the Beginning, Frank Sinatra** (two discs). Along with the new market for cassette-tape versions came a proliferation of foreign license deals to repackage old Sinatra tracks, thus adding to the confusion.

The '70s

This is the decade where — for the first time — Sinatra collector LPs, career summations, and nostalgia packages significantly outnumbered new releases. Part of this was because he retired for two and a half years in November 1970. Part was because his postretirement recording output was never as large as before.

The 1970s was also the time of the first widely distributed bootleg albums made from illegally acquired studio "masters."

Here are the referenced LPs of the 1970s, in order of release:

* Watertown (a love story)
1970 / Reprise
The 1960s had closed with a unique LP, and the '70s began with one. *Watertown* was originally conceived as the musical score for a television special about the breakup of a marriage. When the show never came to fruition, the score was released as a self-sufficient album. The LP met with controversy among Sinatra fans, some loving it, others not understanding it; in any event, the album sold poorly. The project was produced by Bob Gaudio, a writer of hits for the Four Seasons pop/rock group. Gaudio shared arranging chores with Charles Callelo and Joe Scott, and he created all the songs with Jake Holmes. Written exclusively for Sinatra, this unfolding story of a painful family dissolution provided the singer with a subtle and original opportunity for emotional expression. Three of the songs were released on singles and got some air play.

Sinatra & Company
1971 / Reprise
This was to be the final LP of new releases — then retirement. The "Company" of the title referred to songwriter Antonio Carlos Jobim and arranger Eumir Deodato (for Side One, recorded back in 1969), and to producer/arranger Don Costa (for Side Two, fresh recordings of some new music). Side One was seven of Jobim's fine bossa nova tunes, including *Wave, Triste* and *Don't Ever Go Away.* Side Two was seven mixed styles, among them two John Denver songs, Joe Raposo's *Bein' Green,* two odd tunes by Paul Ryan, and *Lady Day,* a Bob Gaudio/Jake Holmes tribute to one of Sinatra's idols and teachers, the late Billie Holiday.

Frank Sinatra on V-Disc, Volume 1
1970s / Apex / English label / mono

During the Second World War, Frank Sinatra — like many top artists — contributed to the U.S. government's Overseas Victory Disc Program, which ran from 1943 to 1949. These records were distributed to troops in the field. Sinatra's contribution consisted of some special, exclusive recording sessions, the capturing of dress rehearsals for his radio shows, songs lifted from live radio broadcasts and the use of Columbia studio material, sometimes with spoken introductions. Many of these V-Disc releases were collected into albums abroad. They were all worthwhile (with some overlaps), but if you had to select just one for collection, this would be it. The sound is good and the songs are varied, well suited to the young Sinatra and representative of the time. Most arrangements were by Axel Stordahl.

Sinatra for the Collector: The V-Disc Years, Vols. 1 & 2
1970s / My Way / Canadian label / 2 discs / mono

An extensive assembly of wartime Victory Disc releases, all with Axel Stordahl arrangements; it's the only source for *Aren't You Glad You're You?*

Frank Sinatra on V-Disc
1970s / Dan / Japanese label / mono

More Victory Disc releases, including a rare early performance of *Come Rain or Come Shine* and two radio pieces with Tommy Dorsey and his orchestra, two years after Sinatra had left the group.

My Best Songs — My Best Years, Volumes 1–5
early 1970s / Pentagon radio tracks / 5 discs / mono

Operating under license, a Germany company released several sets of Sinatra reissues, distributing LPs and cassettes worldwide, including the United States. Among them were these five volumes on their Pentagon label, collections of recordings from 1940s radios shows featuring Sinatra. While a handful were taken from his prominent appearances on Lucky Strike's "Your Hit Parade," most came from other Sinatra shows such as "The Vimms Vitamins Show," "The Frank Sinatra Old Gold Show," "Songs by Sinatra," "The Max Factor Show — Starring Frank Sinatra" and "Light-Up Time." Axel Stordahl was Sinatra's arranger and musical director for all these programs.

Volumes 2 and 3 duplicate some Cameron albums of the early 1960s, but Volumes 1, 4 and 5 contain many songs not available elsewhere.

MM-1
early 1970s / bootleg / from Columbia "masters"

Somehow, unreleased studio master recordings got smuggled out and reproduced. The result is sub-rosa distribution of "bootleg" albums. This one has been around for two decades, and is still prized by Sinatra collectors. Copies can be found in big-city used record stores. Some of these recordings were released abroad, but most were never released officially. Many songs involved in bootlegs were never recorded again.

Rare Songs of Sinatra
early 1970s / bootleg / from Columbia "masters"

This is the only source for *Help Yourself to My Heart,* cut December 28, 1947.

Love Songs
early 1970s / bootleg / from Reprise "masters"

While there is a dearth of bootlegs made from Capitol Records masters (perhaps because they issued every scrap in their vaults after Sinatra left the label), the same was not true for his own label, Reprise Records, where more material than ever before was left unreleased, especially in the singer's later years. This earliest of Reprise-source bootlegs has some wonderful cuts, including two from the **Ring-a-Ding Ding!** sessions with arranger Johnny Mandel, and one from the **I Remember Tommy. . .** work with Sy Oliver. There was even an attempt to simulate a theme album with this bootleg, and the sound quality is nearly professional.

Frank Sinatra's Greatest Hits! Volume 2
1971 / Reprise

A collection of singles from the mid–1960s to the early 1970s. Many were genuine hits and all of the tracks are excellent, representing several arrangers. Four of these recordings did not appear on any other album, including the unique style of *I'm Not Afraid,* arranged by Lenny Hayton, and one of the last big Sinatra/Riddle productions, *Star!*

The Dorsey/Sinatra Sessions, Volumes 1–6
1972 / RCA Victor / 6 discs / mono

The ultimate in quality retrospective packaging, this six-record release has every studio recording Sinatra made with the Tommy Dorsey Orchestra, from February 1, 1940, to July 2, 1942, all 83 songs presented in the order they were cut. Excellent jacket-liner notes and discography come with each LP. The sound quality is great. A decade later, RCA distributed an edition in the United States with three 2-disc volumes. There was also a separate RCA album (*The Dorsey/ Sinatra Radio Years, 1940–42*) with radio tracks, and the singer's four initial solo recordings with Axel Stordahl first released on the Bluebird label.

Ol' Blue Eyes Is Back
1973 / Reprise / comeback album

This excellent album — timed to take advantage of his November '73 back-from-retirement TV special of the same name — has a special flavor, predominantly optimistic. Part of this is because several of the brand-new songs were written for Sinatra by Joe Raposo of "Sesame Street" renown. The rest of the optimism comes from a singer — now a true baritone — who is fired up, refreshed, and clearly glad to be back singing. He sails through *You Will Be My Music* and *Let Me Try Again.* Even the album's two "down" songs, Kris Kristofferson's *Nobody Wins* and Stephen Sondheim's *Send in the Clowns,* convey this joy of singing. Gordon Jenkins conducted, also writing six arrangements; Don Costa charted the other three songs. The recording has the famous acoustic quality of the Goldwyn studio's Stage 7.

Some Nice Things I've Missed
1974 / Reprise

Having come out of retirement, Sinatra used this album to catch up with songs of the 1970s, the work of such composer/lyricists as Neil Diamond, Floyd Huddleston, David Gates, Stevie Wonder and Jim Croce. Among the album's highlights are two songs by Michel Legrand and Alan and Marilyn Bergman, *What Are You Doing the Rest of Your Life?* and *The Summer Knows.* Don Costa, the album's main producer, arranged eight of the songs; Gordon Jenkins did the other two. Sinatra was in good voice.

Sinatra — The Main Event
1974 / Reprise / Live

The second and last live performance album. Tapes were selected from several concert appearances recorded at northeastern cities in October 1974. Better than half the tracks were from the televised Madison Square Garden performance of October 13. Sinatra sings most of his concert favorites of the period, plus some of his classics, using a variety of favorite arrangements. His voice is a bit ragged from extensive touring just eight weeks short of his 60th birthday, but the energy of live singer/audience contact is evident in the recordings. Bill Miller conducted Woody Herman's Young Thundering Herd.

The Rare Sinatra, Volume 1
1978 / Capitol / Australian release only

This fine album, distributed throughout the British Commonwealth, contains many of the unreleased Capitol recordings that might otherwise have been sought by bootleggers. Capitol arrangers Riddle, May and Jenkins are all represented. Most of the songs were recorded other times, but 1958's *I Couldn't Care Less,* by Van Heusen and Cahn, and *Take a Chance,* written in 1932 by Youmans and DeSylva, were only recorded once.

Portrait of Sinatra (40 Songs in the Life of a Man)
1979 / Reprise / 2 discs

Among the various Reprise repackagings, this set is distinguished by five recordings not available on any other LP including two Jobim songs arranged by Eumir Deodato and not used on 1971's **Sinatra & Company.**

As to other 1970's releases, by this period the glut of reissues was overwhelming. There were some special products sold during Sinatra's temporary retirement, like the Dorsey-period set called **This Love of Mine** (1972 — RCA Victor) and the massive release, **Sinatra — The Works** (1972 — Capitol — a ten-disc mail-order boxed set). Later in the decade came the first latter-day retrospective, **Frank Sinatra — The Reprise Years** (1977 — Reprise — four discs).

The '80s

The final decade in which Sinatra recorded regularly. Digital recording was coming on strong, the LP was dying. Neo-rock trends had produced a cluster of recording phenomena, including megatrends from Michael Jackson and Madonna, the growth of rap music and the comebacks of several '60s rockers. It would seem that a Frank Sinatra would be quite out of things. Still, he managed to finish with multiple triumphs. There were also special releases by the Italian Reprise Records, plus more bootleg LPs and Columbia Records retrospective sets. Here are the referenced LPs of the 1980s, in order of release:

* Trilogy
1980 / Reprise / 3 discs: *The Past (Collectibles of the Early Years) The Present (Some Very Good Years), The Future (Reflections on the Future in Three Tenses)*

An album package that recapitulates Sinatra's whole career, and at the same time, exemplifies it. Each record was a separate project.

The Past was recorded in professional studio facilities on Sunset Boulevard, with a 12-voice choir and a 55-piece orchestra. Billy May wrote the arrangements and conducted. All but one of the ten songs was written before 1944. The composers are practically an honor roll: Jerome Kern, George Gershwin, Irving Berlin, Isham Jones, Vincent Youmans, Harry Warren, Victor Young, Harold Arlen and Cole Porter. An imaginative Billy May, plus an inspired Sinatra, combined with the orchestra and chorus to evoke an enchanted memory of the big band and grand Broadway eras. Sinatra rarely sang better.

The Present was produced in a vault-ceilinged CBS studio on East 30th in New York City, with 50 musicians and 16 singers. Don Costa was the arranger/producer. All but one of ten songs were written in the '60s and '70s, all but one being recorded by Sinatra for the first and only time. The songwriters were proven talents like Billy Joel, George Harrison, Jim Webb, Michel Legrand, Neil Diamond and Kris Kristofferson. There were tips of the hat to Sinatra's teen-idol successors Elvis and the Beatles, and the LP produced his last Top–40 hit, the *New York, New York* movie theme.

The Future was recorded on two successive days in December 1979 at the Los Angeles Shrine Auditorium, utilizing a chorus and 154 musicians of the Los Angeles Philharmonic Symphony Orchestra.

The music was a cantata dealing with the life and career of Frank Sinatra, reflecting off ideas of the future. This work was composed, orchestrated and conducted by Gordon Jenkins. The various sections are contemplative, humorous, hopeful and grandiose; they are interspersed with orchestral passages. To hear Sinatra singing about his life, friends, family, fears, goals and sources of inspiration is a unique experience.

Those who praised *Trilogy* spoke of past greatness, present growth and future dreams. Those who were critical pointed to each disc proving the sequence of the singer's life: true genius, followed by compromise, followed by self-aggrandizement. Most agreed it was a remarkable album.

She Shot Me Down
1981 / Reprise

At the time the album was recorded, many things suggested this would be Sinatra's last new LP. It would be a saloon song album. Gordon Jenkins, who had arranged most of Sinatra's famous albums of this kind, did eight of the ten charts, conducting the orchestra. It had been nearly 16 months since Sinatra had last been in the studio when they began on April 8, 1981, in Hollywood. Jenkins presided over the unlikely title song. Then Vinnie Falcone (who had worked with Sinatra in concert) conducted some reworked Nelson Riddle arrangements from the 1950s. One was not used in the LP, but the other piece — a wonderful fusion of *The Gal That Got Away* and *It Never Entered My Mind* closed the album and highlighted it; Sinatra was in good voice. Then during two nights in New York — three and a half months later — Jenkins and Sinatra laid down four more tracks, with the singer effective but a little hoarse. One month after that, Don Costa conducted his arrangement of a Stephen Sondheim song Sinatra loved, *Good Thing Going;* unhappily, the voice was hardly there that night. Still in New York in September, Jenkins handled the last two songs for the LP, and Sinatra was in excellent shape for this session. The work had been something of a struggle and the result did not sell well, despite some great pieces. It was two and a half years before Sinatra recorded his true final album.

The Unissued Sinatra
early 1980s / bootleg / from Reprise "masters"

A lot of the recordings Sinatra made in the late 1970s and the early 1980s didn't completely satisfy him and were not issued on singles or

LPs. A number of bootleggers took advantage of this, and the resulting albums are often more of interest to the collector than the fan. This album has several tracks not available elsewhere, including a Joe Beck–arranged disco version of *All or Nothing at All* and a *Desafinado* done with Antonio Carlos Jobim and arranger Eurmir Deodato.

Frank's Girls
early 1980s / bootleg / from Reprise "masters"

A very special bootleg. In March of 1977, Sinatra and Nelson Riddle got together for what proved to be their final full collaboration, an album of songs about girls. They completed six tracks — *Nancy (with the Laughing Face), Stella by Starlight, Emily, Linda, Sweet Lorraine, Barbara* — which were "mastered" but not released. The project was abandoned. This bootleg LP is based on those recordings, with four more girl-tunes added from the storehouse of released Sinatra material. It's worth having.

The Voice, Volumes 1–4
1982 / Reprise / Italian release only

Through their Italian branch, Reprise Records issued a quantity of material not available on their domestic albums. Some had been released on U.S. singles. Among the points of interest in these four LPs are a song that Van Heusen and Cahn wrote about the singer's youngest child, *Tina,* and a rendition of *I Left My Heart in San Francisco* which was released briefly on a single and then pulled from distribution.

I Sing the Songs
1982 / Reprise / Italian release only

Six of the 12 cuts on this LP make their only album appearance here. This includes one of Sinatra's rare country/western efforts, a Don Costa arrangement of *The Only Couple on the Floor.*

The Singles
1982 / Reprise / Italian release only

These recordings were issued in the States, but only as singles. Of special interest are the Joe Beck disco arrangement of Porter's *Night and Day,* and a version of Sondheim's *Send in the Clowns* with solo piano accompaniment and a spoken introduction.

*L.A. Is My Lady
1984 / Qwest / final LP of new material

After a more than two-year layoff from album recording, Sinatra came back to do his last new legal album. The voice — after a rest — had been exercised and conditioned and was ready for a great finale. A special all-star jazz band had been assembled by Quincy Jones. The arrangements were by Sam Nestico, Frank Foster, Torry Zito, Joe Parnello, Dave Matthews, Jerry Hey and Quincy Jones. Jones was producer and conductor. The 40-piece band boasted such notables as Frank Wess, Randy and Michael Brecker, Ralph MacDonald, Jon Faddis, Frank Foster, George Benson, Tony Mottola, Lionel Hampton, Bob James, Jerome Richardson, Lee Ritenour, Ray Brown, Steve Gadd, Joe Newman, Urbie Green and Major "Mule" Holley. A new label subsidiary, Qwest Records, had been formed to accommodate all the contract players. The 11 songs ranged from very old to brand-new. Everything was played with tremendous energy, the hot arrangements complex and modern. Frank Sinatra pulled out all the stops for the last time on record.

Late Sinatra Goodies
mid–1980s / bootleg / from Reprise "masters"

The most recent bootleg LP referenced, this album contains an assortment of '70s and '80s recordings left out of other official LPs and bootlegs. The performance quality varies widely.

Sinatra Rarities — The Columbia Years, Volume 1
1986 / Columbia / mono

An album that lives up to its title. The songs were released on singles back in the late '40s and early '50s, but this is the first album issuance for ten out of the 15 tracks.

*The Voice, 1943–1952
1987 / Columbia / 6 discs / Duophonic stereo

All except three of the 70 recordings in this retrospective are available on other LPs. The value of this package lies in its sound quality, size and organization. Songs are grouped by virtue of their source for Sinatra: stage, screen, dance band, nightclub, Tin Pan Alley. The majority were arranged by Axel Stordahl. The three tracks unique to this album are *All Through the Day* (February 3, 1946), *If I Had You*

(August 11, 1947) and *Oh, What a Beautiful Morning* (August 5, 1943), the latter a voice-only chart by Alec Wilder.

Hello, Young Lovers
1987 / Columbia / 2 discs / Duophonic stereo

Such nostalgic repackagings may soon only be issued on digitally rerecorded compact discs. This large collection of love ballads includes three songs recorded only once and not found on any other LP: *We Just Couldn't Say Goodbye* (Tony Mottola arrangement), *I Fall in Love with You Every Day* (Axel Stordahl arrangement) and the Eddie Arnold hit, *That's How Much I Love You,* arranged by Page Cavanaugh.

There was one new album with Sinatra as conductor during the 1980s. This was *Sinatra and Syms* (1983 — Reprise), which the singer conducted for Sylvia Syms, utilizing the last arrangements written by Don Costa. Sinatra also served as producer for the album, taking over from Costa after his heart attack.

During the final years of Sinatra's recording career, the 45 rpm single was fading, the LP album was rapidly losing ground, and even magnetic tape cassettes were being somewhat supplanted by digitally recorded compact discs. There were still many licensed cassette repackagings of Capitol material, as well as foreign editions of all-era Sinatra. But as the '80s advanced, the compact disc releases by RCA, Columbia, Capitol and Reprise were the predominant thing. In the future, these CDs — and whatever may come after them — will be the chief source for collections of Frank Sinatra's music. For now they are an evolving medium, and are not the province of this book. Hopefully, CDs will maintain the aesthetic integrity of the concept albums.

Introduction to the Three Album Lists

This chapter has three valuable catalog listings.

The first list provides the contents of each album (listed alphabetically by title), with songs displayed in the order they appeared on the initial release of the LP. When sequence numbers are missing, it means that track was nonvocal, or sung by someone other than Sinatra, or duplicated on another LP, or — in a very few instances — key information about the track was missing.

After the main group of album titles, a series of special entries are listed by the lowercase prefixes "bootleg," "demonstration disc," "radio," "single," "soundtrack," "television" and "v/disc." In these cases, the prefix is followed by the special LP's title, alphabetic within each prefix set. An exception to this rule comes with "singles," where the prefix is followed by record company label and release numbers, listed numerically within label and playing-speed (45 rpm, 78 rpm) grouping.

An asterisk (*) following a song title indicates a special note found in the Master Song List at the end of that particular song's entry.

If a song has been recorded more than once by Sinatra, which version resides in an LP is shown by a sequence number such as *What'll I Do*[1], *What'll I Do*[2], etc.

Key numbers are included for each track of each album (or single), so that items can be cross-referenced to the Master Song List in Chapter 3.

Finally, label and release-date entries allow cross-reference to the other two album lists in this chapter. In the case of the 72 single records listed, the label entry includes a code number to distinguish among special categories of singles.

These label codes for singles (e.g., Capitol-5) are defined as

1 = Brunswick 78 rpm singles cut with Harry James's band
2 = Columbia 78 rpm singles cut with Harry James's band
3 = 78 rpm singles for foreign-release only
4 = 78 rpm singles (post–1943) for domestic release
5 = 45 rpm singles for domestic release
6 = 45 rpm extended play singles for domestic release

Sinatra's studio recordings are the prime focus of this volume; the best LP source for these is given, except for the few only available on a single. To this is added some radio and v-disc recordings, mostly of songs not recorded otherwise. There are a small sampling of television performances. Bootleg versions of unreleased studio "masters" have been included to complete the picture of studio work. And in cases where no official soundtrack LP was issued, movie recordings are included in bootleg versions; when a movie song was available in a studio recording, that song is not referenced in the bootleg soundtrack album. No bootleg tapes of Sinatra's many nightclub and concert appearances are referenced.

The second list presents the album titles in release date order, irrespective of company label or when the contents were recorded. In the case of casual distribution by small labels, approximate dates are used such as "early 1960s." Otherwise, dates are precise and represent the time of an LP's initial release. Special notes give information about many of the albums. A label-and-sequence entry is also given for each title; together with the release-entry, this allows cross-reference to the other two album lists in this chapter, as well as reference from the Master Song List.

The third list presents the album titles organized by record company label, in order of release. Following the main alphabetic listing is a short section of "bootleg album" and "bootleg movie" entries. Each album's producer (or production team) is named, except for some LPs that are singles collections, bootlegs and compilations. A release-date and sequence entry is given for each title; together with the label-entry, this allows cross-reference to the other two album lists in this chapter and reference from the Master Song List.

Album List #1
Contents; Alphabetical by LP Title

Adventures of the Heart (Columbia-24, 1956 — 3rd LP): 1) I Guess I'll Have to Dream the Rest[2] 399; 2) If Only She'd Look My Way 458; 3) Love Me 665; 4) Nevertheless (I'm in Love with You)[1] 763; 5) We Kiss in a Shadow 1108; 6) I Am Loved 360; 7) Take My Love 1010; 8) I Could Write a Book[1] 377; 9) Mad About You 679; 10) Sorry 958; 11) Stromboli (On the Island of—) 986; 12) It's Only a Paper Moon[1] 559

All Alone (Reprise-8, 1962 — 7th LP): 1) All Alone 9; 2) The Girl (Boy) Next Door[2] 286; 3) Are You Lonesome Tonight? 48; 4) Charmaine 119; 5) What'll I Do?[2] 1126; 6) When I Lost You 1130; 7) Oh, How I Miss You Tonight 796; 8) Indiscreet 518; 9) Remember[1] 871; 10) Together 1076; 11) The Song Is Ended 950; 12) *(Japan 1972 version only)* Come Waltz with Me 147

All the Way (Capitol-29, 1961 — 2nd LP): 1) All the Way[1] 23; 2) High Hopes 335; 3) Talk to Me [Talk to Me, Talk to Me] 1012; 4) French Foreign Legion 262; 5) To Love and Be Loved[2] 1075; 6) River Stay 'Way from My Door 877; 7) Witchcraft[1] 1175; 8) It's Over, It's Over, It's Over 562; 9) Ol' MacDonald[1] 807; 10) This Was (Is) My Love[1] 1065; 11) All My Tomorrows[1] 11; 12) Sleep Warm 921

America, I Hear You Singing (Reprise-18, 1964 — 2nd LP): 3) The House I Live In (That's America...)[2] 341; 7) Let Us Break Bread Together 619; 11) You're a Lucky Fellow, Mr. Smith 1232

Boys & Girls Together (10″ LP) (Columbia-16, 1955 — 5th LP): 2) Kisses and Tears 595

The Broadway Kick (Columbia-29, 1960 — 4th LP): 1) There's No Business Like Show Business 1044; 2) They Say It's Wonderful 1053; 3) Some Enchanted Evening[1] 929; 4) You're My Girl 1241; 6) Why Can't You Behave? 1165; 7) I Whistle a Happy Tune 433; 9) Can't You Just See Yourself? 113; 10) There But for You Go I 1038; 11) Bali Ha'i 66) 12) Where Is My Bess? «Oh, Bess, Oh Where's...» 1150

"Can-Can" (soundtrack LP) (Capitol-24, 1960 — 1st LP): 2) It's All Right with Me[2] 549; 6) Let's Do It (Let's Fall in Love) 620; 7) Montmart' 709; 8) C'est Magnifique 116; 11) I Love Paris[1] 412

Christmas Dreaming (Columbia-25, 1957 — 3rd LP): 1) Adeste Fidelis «O Come, All Ye Faithful»[1] 3; 2) White Christmas[1] 1159; 3) Have Yourself a Merry Little Christmas[1] 319; 4) Let It Snow (Let It Snow, Let It Snow) 615; 5) Silent Night «Stille Nacht, Heilige Nacht»[1] 916; 6) Christmas Dreaming (a Little Late...) 124; 7) Jingle Bells «In a One Horse Open Sleigh»[1] 583; 8) It Came Upon a Midnight Clear[1] 526; 9) Santa Claus Is Comin' to Town 883; 10) O Little Town of Bethlehem[1] 792

Close to You (Capitol-11, 1957 — 1st LP): 1) Close to You [I Will Always Stay][2] 132; 2) P.S. I Love You 841; 3) Love Locked Out 663; 4) Everything Happens to Me[2] 230; 5) It's Easy to Remember 555; 6) Don't Like Goodbyes 191; 7) With Every Breath I Take 1177; 8) Blame It on My Youth 88; 9) It Could Happen to You 528; 10) I've Had My Moments 578; 11) I Couldn't Sleep a Wink Last Night[2] 381; 12) The End of a Love Affair 219; 13) *(1988 compact disc version only)* There's a Flaw in My Flue[2] 1042

Come Back to Sorrento (Columbia-30, 1960 — 5th LP): 1) When the Sun Goes Down 1137; 2) None But the Lonely Heart[1] 784; 3) Luna Rossa «Blushing Moon»

676; 4) My Melancholy Baby «Melancholy» 746; 5) Embraceable You[1] 212; 6) Day by Day[1] 161; 7) Come Back to Sorrento 137; 8) I Hear a Rhapsody 405; 9) Someone to Watch Over Me[1] 937; 10) September Song[1] 900; 11) Among My Souvenirs 35; 12) Always[1] 29

Come Dance with Me! (Capitol-20, 1959 — 1st LP): 1) Come Dance with Me 139; 2) Something's Gotta Give 944; 3) Just in Time 590; 4) Dancing in the Dark 159; 5) Too Close for Comfort 1077; 6) I Could Have Danced All Night 374; 7) Saturday Night (Is the Loneliest Night...)[2] 886; 8) Day In — Day Out[2] 164; 9) Cheek to Cheek 121; 10) Baubles, Bangles and Beads[1] 70; 11) The Song Is You[3] 953; 12) The Last Dance[1] 605

Come Fly with Me (Capitol-17, 1958 — 2nd LP): 1) Come Fly with Me[1] 140; 2) Around the World 50; 3) Isle of Capri* 519; 4) Moonlight in Vermont[1] 720; 5) Autumn in New York[2] 58; 6) On the Road to Mandalay 816; 7) Let's Get Away from It All[2] 625; 8) April in Paris[2] 46; 9) London by Night[2] 641; 10) Brazil «Aquarela do Brasil» 99; 11) Blue Hawaii 89; 12) It's Nice to Go Trav'ling 558

Come Swing with Me! (Capitol-30, 1961 — 5th LP): 1) Day by Day[2] 162; 2) Sentimental Journey 896; 3) Almost Like Being in Love[2] 28; 4) Five Minutes More[2] 245; 5) American Beauty Rose[2] 34; 6) Yes, Indeed! «A Jive Spiritual» 1187; 7) On the Sunny Side of the Street 817; 8) Don't Take Your Love from Me[1] 194; 9) That Old Black Magic[2] 1027; 10) Lover[2] 671; 11) Paper Doll 843; 12) I've Heard That Song Before 579

The Concert Sinatra (Reprise-10, 1963 — 2nd LP): 1) I Have Dreamed 403; 2) My Heart Stood Still 739; 3) Lost in the Stars[2] 654; 4) Ol' Man River[2] 810; 5) You'll Never Walk Alone[2] 1227; 6) Bewitched (Bothered and Bewildered)[2] 84; 7) This Nearly Was Mine 1063; 8) Soliloquy[2] 928

Cycles (Reprise-37, 1968 — 6th LP): 1) Rain in My Heart 869; 2) From Both Sides, Now «Clouds» 264; 3) Little Green Apples 637; 4) Pretty Colors 862; 5) Cycles 158; 6) Wandering 1100; 7) By the Time I Get to Phoenix 104; 8) Moody River [More Deadly Than ... Knife] 711; 9) My Way of Life 755; 10) Gentle on My Mind 279

The Dorsey/Sinatra Sessions (Vol. 1) (RCA Victor-17, 1972 — 1st LP): 1) The Sky Fell Down 920; 2) Too Romantic (I'm —) 1079; 3) Shake Down the Stars 907; 4) Moments in the Moonlight 706; 5) I'll Be Seeing You[1] 470; 6) Say It (Over and Over Again) 888; 7) Polka Dots and Moonbeams[1] 857; 8) The Fable of the Rose 233; 9) This Is the Beginning of the End 1059; 10) Hear My Song, Violetta «Hor Mein Lied, V...» 323; 11) Fools Rush In (Where Angels Fear to Tread)[1] 252; 12) Devil May Care 174; 13) April Played the Fiddle 47; 14) I Haven't Time to Be a Millionaire 404

The Dorsey/Sinatra Sessions (Vol. 2) (RCA Victor-18, 1972 — 2nd LP): 1) Imagination[1] 507; 2) Yours Is My Heart Alone 1250; 3) You're Lonely and I'm Lonely 1240; 4) East of the Sun (and West of the Moon)[1] 207; 5) Head on My Pillow 322; 6) It's a Lovely Day Tomorrow 546; 7) I'll Never Smile Again[1] 481; 8) All This and Heaven Too 25; 9) Where Do You Keep Your Heart? 1148; 10) Whispering 1158; 11) Trade Winds 1080; 12) The One I Love (Belongs to Somebody Else)[1] 828; 13) The Call of the Canyon 109; 14) Love Lies 662

The Dorsey/Sinatra Sessions (Vol. 3) (RCA Victor-19, 1972 — 3rd LP): 1) I Could Make You Care 376; 2) The World Is in My Arms 1182; 3) Our Love Affair 836; 4) Looking for Yesterday 652; 5) Tell Me at Midnight 1019; 6) We Three (My Echo, My Shadow, and Me) 1110; 7) When You Awake[1] 1140; 8) Anything 40; 9) Shadows on the Sand 906; 10) You're Breaking My Heart All Over Again 1235; 11) I'd Know You Anywhere 444; 12) Do You Know Why? 179; 13) Not So Long Ago 787; 14) Star Dust[1] 968

The Dorsey/Sinatra Sessions (Vol. 4) (RCA Victor–20, 1972 – 4th LP): 1) Oh! Look at Me Now![1] 797; 2) You Might Have Belonged to Another 1217; 3) You Lucky People You 1213; 4) It's Always You[1] 553; 5) I Tried 429; 6) Dolores 180; 7) Without a Song[1] 1178; 8) Do I Worry? 178; 9) Everything Happens to Me[1] 229; 10) Let's Get Away from It All[1] 624; 11) I'll Never Let a Day Pass By 480; 12) Love Me As I Am 666; 13) This Love of Mine[1] 1061

The Dorsey/Sinatra Sessions (Vol. 5) (RCA Victor–21, 1972 – 5th LP): 1) I Guess I'll Have to Dream the Rest[1] 398; 2) You and I 1192; 3) Neiani 762; 4) Free for All 261; 5) Blue Skies[1] 91; 6) Two in Love 1090; 7) Pale Moon 842; 8) I Think of You[1] 426; 9) How Do You Do Without Me? 350; 10) A Sinner Kissed an Angel 919; 11) Violets for Your Furs[1] 1094; 12) The Sunshine of Your Smile 999; 13) How About You?[1] 343; Snooty Little Cutie (You're a–) 922

The Dorsey/Sinatra Sessions (Vol. 6) (RCA Victor–22, 1972 – 6th LP): 1) Poor You 860; 2) I'll Take Tallulah 490; 3) The Last Call for Love «from 1863's "Taps"» 604; 4) Somewhere a Voice Is Calling 945; 5) Just As Though You Were Here[1] 586; 6) Street of Dreams[1] 982; 7) Take Me[1] 1007; 8) Be Careful, It's My Heart[1] 72; 9) In the Blue of Evening[1] 511; 10) Dig Down Deep 176; 11) There Are Such Things[1] 1036; 12) Daybreak[1] 166; 13) It Started All Over Again[1] 539; 14) Light a Candle in the Chapel 628

The Essential Frank Sinatra (Vol. 1) (Columbia-34, 1967 – 2nd LP): 3) My Buddy 735; 4) Here Comes the Night «These Are the Things . . .» 328; 5) Close to You [I Will Always Stay][1] 131; 6) There's No You[1] 1045; 9) I Should Care 424; 10) A Friend of Yours 263; 11) My Shawl 749; 13) You Are Too Beautiful 1198; 14) Why Shouldn't I? 1167; 15) One Love 831; 16) Something Old, Something New 941

The Essential Frank Sinatra (Vol. 2) (Columbia-35; 1967 – 3rd LP): 2) Guess I'll Hang My Tears Out to Dry[1] 306; 3) Why Shouldn't It Happen to Us? 1168; 4) It's the Same Old Dream[1] 564; 5) You Can Take My Word for It, Baby 1204; 6) Sweet Lorraine[1] 1002; 7) My Romance 748; 9) It All Came True[2] 522; 12) I Went Down to Virginia 432; 13) If I Only Had a Match 454; 14) Everybody Loves Somebody[1] 225; 15) Comme Ci, Comme Ca «Clopin-Clopant» 149; 16) If You Stub Your Toe on the Moon 466

The Essential Frank Sinatra (Vol. 3) (Columbia-36, 1967 – 4th LP): 2) The Huckle-Buck 357; 3) If I Ever Love Again 447; 5) Sunshine Cake 998; 6) Sure Thing (We've Got a–) 1000; 10) You're the One (for Me) 1248; 12) I'm a Fool to Want You[1] 492; 14) Walkin' in the Sunshine 1099; 15) Azure'te «Paris Blues» 62; 16) Why Try to Change Me Now?[1]* 1169

Forever Frank (Capitol-36, 1966 – 4th LP): 2) Melody of Love «Melody d'Amour» 693; 3) Can I Steal a Little Love? 110; 4) Five Hundred Guys 243; 5) From the Bottom to the Top 268; 6) Two Hearts, Two Kisses (Make One Love) 1089; 7) You'll Get Yours 1223; 8) Same Old Song and Dance 881; 9) Flowers Mean Forgiveness 246; 10) Your Love for Me 1231; 11) If It's the Last Thing I Do 457; 12) Don't Make a Beggar of Me 192

Francis A. & Edward K. (Reprise-33, 1968 – 2nd LP): 1) Follow Me 251; 2) Sunny 996; 3) All I Need Is the Girl 10; 4) Indian Summer 517; 5) I Like the Sunrise 409; 6) Yellow Days 1186; 7) Poor Butterfly 859; 8) Come Back to Me 136

Francis Albert Sinatra–Antonio Carlos Jobim (Reprise-31, 1967 – 1st LP): 1) The Girl from Ipanema «Garota de Ipanema» 284; 2) Dindi 177; 3) Change Partners 117; 4) Quiet Nights of Quiet Stars «Corcovado» 867; 5) Meditation «Meditacao» 691; 6) If You Never Come to Me 464; 7) How Insensitive «Insensatez» 352; 8) I Concentrate on You[3] 373; 9) Baubles, Bangles and Beads[2] 71; 10) Once I Loved 819

Frank Sinatra: A Man and His Music (2 discs) (Reprise-26, 1965 — 5th LP): 3) I'll Never Smile Again[4] 484; 14) Come Fly with Me[2] 141; 21) Love and Marriage[2] 656

Frank Sinatra & Frank and Nancy (Reprise-32, 1967 — 5th LP): 1) The World We Knew «Over and Over» 1184; 2) Something Stupid 942; 3) This Was (Is) My Love[2] 1066; 4) Born Free 97; 5) Don't Sleep in the Subway 193; 6) This Town 1064; 7) This Is My Song 1058; 8) You Are There 1197; 9) Drinking Again 203; 10) Some Enchanted Evening[4] 932

Frank Sinatra in Hollywood, 1943/1949 (Columbia-38, 1968 — 1st LP): 1) I Couldn't Sleep a Wink Last Night[1] 380; 2) The Music Stopped[1] 730; 3) A Lovely Way to Spend an Evening 669; 4) I Begged Her 361; 5) What Makes the Sun Set? 1122; 6) I FAll in Love Too Easily 387; 7) The Charm of You 118; 11) The Brooklyn Bridge 100; 12) I Believe [in Wishing Wells][1] 362; 13) Senorita (I Offer You the Moon —) 894; 14) If I Steal a Kiss 456; 15) Ever Homeward 220; 16) The Right Girl for Me (She's —) 874

Frank Sinatra Sings "Days of Wine and Roses," "Moon River" and Other Academy Award Winners (Reprise-17, 1964 — 1st LP): 1) Days of Wine and Roses 168; 2) Moon River 714; 3) The Way You Look Tonight[2] 1105; 4) Three Coins in the Fountain[2] 1068; 5) In the Cool, Cool, Cool of the Evening 513; 6) Secret Love 891; 7) Swinging on a Star 1005; 8) It Might as Well Be Spring[2] 534; 9) The Continental[2] 151; 10) Love Is a Many-Splendored Thing 657

Frank Sinatra Sings for Only the Lonely (Capitol-19, 1958 — 5th LP): 1) Only the Lonely 834; 2) Angel Eyes[1] 37; 3) What's New? 1127; 4) It's a Lonesome Old Town* 545; 5) Willow Weep for Me 1172; 6) Goodbye [You Take the High Road] 301; 7) Blues in the Night 93; 8) Guess I'll Hang My Tears Out to Dry[2] 307; 9) Ebb Tide 210; 10) Spring Is Here[2]* 966; 11) "Gone with the Wind" 295; 12) One for My Baby (and One More for the Road)[2] 824

Frank Sinatra Sings Rodgers and Hart (Capitol-34, 1964 — 7th LP): 5) Wait Till You See Her 1097

The Frank Sinatra Story in Music (2 discs) (Columbia-27, 1959 — 2nd LP): 1) Ciribiribin (They're So in Love) 129; 2) All or Nothing at All[1] 18; 4) If You Are But a Dream[1] 459; 6) You Go to My Head[1] 1211; 7) Stormy Weather[1] 977; 8) The House I Live In (That's America . . .)[1] 340; 9) If I Loved You 453; 10) Soliloquy[1] 927; 11) How Deep Is the Ocean?[1] 348; 12) Ol' Man River[1] 809; 13) You'll Never Walk Alone[1] 1226; 14) I Concentrate on You[1] 371; 15) Castle Rock 114; 16) Why Was I Born? 1171; 17) I've Got a Crush on You[1] 568; 18) Begin the Beguine 76; 19) The Birth of the Blues 86; 20) April in Paris[1] 45; 21) I'm Glad There Is You 497; 23) One for My Baby (and One More for the Road)[1] 823

Frank Sinatra's Greatest Hits! (Vol. 1) (Reprise-34, 1968 — 3rd LP): 4) Forget Domani 259

Frank Sinatra's Greatest Hits! (Vol. 2) (Reprise-43, 1971 — 3rd LP): 3) Something[1] 939; 9) I'm Not Afraid 504; 10) Goin' Out of My Head 292; 11) Star! 967

Frank Sinatra's Greatest Hits: The Early Years (Vol. 1) (Columbia-32, 1964 — 3rd LP): 9) The Coffee Song[1] 134; 10) Sunday, Monday or Always 994

Frank Sinatra's Greatest Hits: The Early Years (Vol. 2) (Columbia-33, 1964 — 4th LP): 3) The Moon Was Yellow[1] 716; 10) People Will Say We're in Love 849

Frankie (Columbia-20, 1955 — 8th LP): 1) Hello, Young Lovers[1] 325; 2) I Only Have Eyes for You[1] 419; 3) Falling in Love with Love[1] 236; 4) You'll Never Know 1225; 5) It All Depends on You[1] 523; 6) S'posin'[1] 963; 7) All of Me[3] 15; 8) Time After Time[1] 1070; 9) How Cute Can You Be? 347; 10) Almost Like Being in Love[1] 27; 11) Nancy (with the Laughing Face)[1] 756; 12) Oh, What It Seemed to Be[2] 801

Frankly Sentimental (10″ LP) (Columbia-4, 1949 — 4th LP): 7) When You Awake[2] 1141

Have Yourself a Merry Little Christmas (Reprise-16, 1963 — 8th LP): 1) Have Yourself a Merry Little Christmas[3] 321

Hello, Young Lovers (2 discs) (Columbia-52, 1987 — 2nd LP): 8) We Just Couldn't Say Goodbye 1107; 20) I Fall in Love with You Ev'ry Day 388; 24) That's How Much I Love You 1032

"High Society" (soundtrack LP) (Capitol-9, 1956 — 5th LP): 4) Who Wants to Be a Millionaire? 1163; 6) You're Sensational[2] 1246; 9) Well, Did You Evah? 1115; 10) Mind If I Make Love to You? 700

I Remember Tommy (Reprise-3, 1961 — 7th LP): 1) I'm Getting Sentimental Over You[1] 495; 2) Imagination[2] 508; 3) There Are Such Things[2] 1037; 4) East of the Sun (and West of the Moon)[2] 208; 5) Daybreak[2] 167; 6) Without a Song[3] 1180; 7) I'll Be Seeing You[2] 471; 8) Take Me[2] 1008; 9) It's Always You[2] 554; 10) Polka Dots and Moonbeams[2] 858; 11) It Started All Over Again[2] 540; 12) The One I Love (Belongs to Somebody Else)[3] 830; 13) I'm Getting Sentimental Over You[2] (reprised) 496

I Sing the Songs (Italy release only) (Reprise-60, 1982 — 5th LP): 3) The Hurt Doesn't Go Away 358; 4) Empty Tables[1] 217; 6) Anytime (I'll Be There —) 42; 7) The Only Couple on the Floor 833; 9) Saddest Thing of All 879; 12) I Sing (Write) the Songs 425

In the Wee Small Hours (Capitol-5, 1955 — 7th LP): 1) In the Wee Small Hours of the Morning[1] 515; 2) Mood Indigo 710; 3) Glad to Be Unhappy 289; 4) I Get Along Without You Very Well 392; 5) Deep in a Dream 171; 6) I See Your Face Before Me 423; 7) Can't We Be Friends?[1] 111; 8) When Your Lover Has Gone[2] 1143; 9) What Is This Thing Called Love? 1121; 10) Last Night When We Were Young[1] 607; 11) I'll Be Around[2] 468; 12) Ill Wind 491; 13) It Never Entered My Mind[2] 536; 14) Dancing on the Ceiling 160; 15) I'll Never Be the Same 479; 16) This Love of Mine[2] 1062

It Might as Well Be Swing (Reprise-19, 1964 — 5th LP): 1) Fly Me to the Moon «In Other Words»[1] 247; 2) I Wish You Love «Que Reste-il de Nos Amours» 438; 3) I Believe in You 365; 4) More 725; 5) I Can't Stop Loving You 370; 6) Hello, Dolly! 324; 7) I Wanna Be Around 430; 8) The Best Is Yet to Come 80; 9) The Good Life 296; 10) Wives and Lovers 1181

A Jolly Christmas from Frank Sinatra (Capitol-14, 1957 — 6th LP): 1) Jingle Bells «In a One Horse Open Sleigh»[2] 584; 2) The Christmas Song 125; 3) Mistletoe and Holly 703; 4) I'll Be Home for Christmas 469; 5) The Christmas Waltz[2] 127; 6) Have Yourself a Merry Little Christmas[2] 320; 7) The First Noel 242; 8) Hark! The Herald Angels Sing 314; 9) O Little Town of Bethlehem[2] 793; 10) Adeste Fidelis «O Come, All Ye Faithful»[2] 4; 11) It Came Upon a Midnight Clear[2] 527; 12) Silent Night «Stille Nacht, Heilige Nacht»[2] 917

L.A. Is My Lady (Qwest-1, 1984 — 1st LP): 1) L.A. Is My Lady 596; 2) The Best of Everything 81; 3) How Do You Keep the Music Playing? 351; 4) Teach Me Tonight 1016; 5) It's All Right with Me[3] 550; 6) Mack the Knife «Moritat» 678; 7) Until the Real Thing Comes Along 1091; 8) Stormy Weather[3]* 979; 9) If I Should Lose You 455; 10) One Hundred Years from Today[2] 827; 11) After You've Gone 6

Look to Your Heart (Capitol-22; 1959 — 4th LP): 1) Look to Your Heart 650; 2) Anytime — Anywhere 43; 3) Not As a Stranger 786; 4) Our Town 837; 5) You, My Love 1218; 6) Same Old Saturday Night 880; 7) Fairy Tale 234; 8) The Impatient Years 509; 9) I Could Have Told You 375; 10) When I Stop Loving You 1131; 11) If I Had Three Wishes 449; 12) I'm Gonna Live Till I Die 498

Love Is a Kick (Columbia-28, 1960 — 3rd LP): 1) You Do Something to Me[1]

1207; 2) Bim Bam Baby 85; 3) My Blue Heaven [1] 733; 4) When You're Smiling[1] 1144; 5) Saturday Night (Is the Loneliest Night . . .)[1] 885; 6) Bye Bye Baby 105; 7) The Continental[1] 150; 8) Deep Night 172; 9) Should I?[2] 913; 10) American Beauty Rose[1] 33; 11) Five Minutes More[1] 244; 12) Farewell, Farewell to Love 238

A Man Alone (Reprise-39, 1969 — 3rd LP): 1) A Man Alone[1] 684; 2) Night 770; 3) I've Been to Town 566; 4) From Promise to Promise 266; 5) The Single Man 918; 6) The Beautiful Strangers 74; 7) Lonesome Cities 644; 8) Love's Been Good to Me 673; 9) Empty Is 216; 10) Out Beyond the Window 838; 11) Some Traveling Music 934; 12) A Man Alone[2] (reprised) 685

Moonlight Sinatra (Reprise-28, 1966 — 2nd LP): 1) Moonlight Becomes You 719; 2) Moon Song (That Wasn't Meant for Me) 715; 3) Moonlight Serenade 724; 4) Reaching for the Moon 870; 5) I Wished on the Moon 439; 6) Oh, You Crazy Moon 803; 7) The Moon Got in My Eyes 712; 8) Moonlight Mood 722; 9) Moon Love 713; 10) The Moon Was Yellow[3] 718

My Kind of Broadway (Reprise-25, 1965 — 4th LP): 1) Everybody Has the Right to Be Wrong 224; 2) Golden Moment 294; 6) I'll Only Miss Her When I Think of Her 485

My Way (Reprise-38, 1969 — 1st LP): 1) Watch What Happens 1101; 2) Didn't We? 175; 3) Hallelujah, I Love Her So 313; 4) Yesterday [All My Troubles Seemed So Far Away] 1190; 5) All My Tomorrows[2] 12; 6) My Way «Comme d'habitude»[1] 753; 7) A Day in the Life of a Fool 165; 8) For Once in My Life 257; 9) If You Go Away «Ne Me Quitte Pas» 462; 10) Mrs. Robinson 729

Nice 'n' Easy (Capitol-25, 1960 — 2nd LP): 1) Nice 'n' Easy 767; 2) That Old Feeling[2] 1030; 3) How Deep Is the Ocean?[2] 349; 4) I've Got a Crush on You[2] 569; 5) You Go to My Head[2] 1212; 6) Fools Rush In (Where Angels Fear to Tread)[3] 254; 7) Nevertheless (I'm in Love with You)[2] 764; 8) She's Funny That Way[2] 911; 9) Try a Little Tenderness[2] 1085; 10) Embraceable You[2] 213; 11) Mam'selle[2] 683; 12) Dream[2] 201

No One Cares (Capitol-23, 1959 — 5th LP): 1) When No One Cares 1135; 2) A Cottage for Sale 152; 3) Stormy Weather[2] 978; 4) Where Do You Go? 1147; 5) A Ghost of a Chance (I Don't Stand —)[2] 283; 6) Here's That Rainy Day 329; 7) I Can't Get Started (with You) 369; 8) Why Try to Change Me Now?[2] 1170; 9) Just Friends 589; 10) I'll Never Smile Again[3] 483; 11) None But the Lonely Heart[2] 785

Ol' Blue Eyes Is Back (Reprise-45, 1973 — 2nd LP): 1) You Will Be My Music* 1220; 2) You're So Right (for What's Wrong in My Life) 1247; 3) Winners 1174; 4) Nobody Wins 783; 5) Send in the Clowns[1] 892; 6) Dream Away 202; 7) Let Me Try Again «Laisse Moi le Temps»[1] 617; 8) There Used to Be a Ballpark 1039; 9) Noah 782

"Pal Joey" (soundtrack LP) (Capitol-15, 1957 — 8th LP): 3) I Didn't Know What Time It Was 384; 6) There's a Small Hotel 1043; 8) I Could Write a Book[2] 378; 10) The Lady Is a Tramp[1] 601; 14) Bewitched (Bothered and Bewildered)[1] 83; 16) What Do I Care for a Dame? 1120

Point of No Return (Capitol-31, 1962 — 2nd LP): 1) When the World Was Young 1139; 2) I'll Remember April[2] 487; 3) September Song[2] 901; 4) A Million Dreams Ago 698; 5) I'll See You Again 488; 6) There Will Never Be Another You 1040; 7) Somewhere Along the Way 946; 8) It's a Blue World 544; 9) These Foolish Things (Remind Me of You)[2] 1048; 10) As Time Goes By 52; 11) I'll Be Seeing You[3] 472; 12) Memories of You[2] 695

Popular Favorites, Volume 1 (10" LP) (Columbia-3, 1949 — 3rd LP): 4) Sunflower 995

Portrait of Sinatra (England only: 2 discs) (Reprise-51, 1979 — 1st LP): 8) Bonita

95; 23) Song of the Sabia 955; 25) Empty Tables[2] 218; 26) I Believe I'm Gonna Love You 364; 27) Star Gazer 970

Put Your Dreams Away (Columbia-26, 1958 – 3rd LP): 1) I Dream of You (More Than You Dream I Do) 386; 2) Dream[1] 200; 3) I Have But One Heart «O Marenariello» 402; 4) The Girl That I Marry 287; 5) The Things We Did Last Summer 1054; 6) Lost in the Stars[1] 653; 7) If I Forget You 448; 8) Mam'selle[1] 682; 9) The Song Is You[2] 952; 10) It Never Entered My Mind[1] 535; 11) Ain'tcha Ever Comin' Back? 8; 12) Put Your Dreams Away[1] 864

The Rare Sinatra: Vol. 1 (Australia only) (Capitol-65, 1978 – 1st LP): 3) Day In – Day Out[1] 163; 4) Memories of You[1] 694; 6) I Couldn't Care Less 379; 7) Take a Chance 1006; 10) Where or When[2] 1154; 11) It All Depends On You[2] 524; 12) The One I Love (Belongs to Somebody Else)[2] 829

Reflections (Columbia-31, 1961 – 4th LP): 1) Stella by Starlight[1] 975; 2) But Beautiful 101; 3) Body and Soul 94; 4) Where or When[1] 1153; 5) When Your Lover Has Gone[1] 1142; 6) Strange Music 980; 7) Goodnight, Irene 302; 8) Dear Little Boy of Mine 170; 9) Mighty Lak' a Rose 697; 10) The Cradle Song «Lullaby» 155; 11) Nature Boy 759; 12) All the Things You Are 22

Reprise Musical Repertory Theatre: "Finian's Rainbow" (Reprise-11, 1963 – 3rd LP): 7) Old Devil Moon[2] 805; 9) When I'm Not Near the Girl I Love 1133

Reprise Musical Repertory Theatre: "Guys and Dolls" (Reprise-12, 1963 – 4th LP): 2) Fuge for Tinhorns 271; 4) The Oldest Established (Permanent ...) 812; 6) Guys and Dolls[1] 308; 8) I've Never Been in Love Before 580; 12) Luck Be a Lady 674; 15) Guys and Dolls[2] (reprised) 309

Reprise Musical Repertory Theatre: "Kiss Me Kate" (Reprise-13, 1963 – 5th LP) 4) We Open in Venice 1109; 13) So in Love 924

Reprise Musical Repertory Theatre: "South Pacific" (Reprise-14, 1963 – 6th LP): 4) Twin Soliloquies «Wonder How It Feels» 1087; 5) Some Enchanted Evening[2] 930; 17) Some Enchanted Evening[3] (reprised) 931

Ring-a-Ding Ding! (Reprise-1, 1961 – 3rd LP): 1) Ring-a-Ding Ding 876; 2) Let's Fall in Love [Why Shouldn't We?] 623; 3) Be Careful, It's My Heart[2] 73; 4) A Foggy Day[2] 250; 5) A Fine Romance 241; 6) In the Still of the Night 514; 7) The Coffee Song[2] 135; 8) When I Take My Sugar to Tea 1132; 9) Let's Face the Music and Dance[1] 621; 10) Easy to Love (You'd Be So –) 209; 11) You and the Night and the Music 1194; 12) I've Got My Love to Keep Me Warm 572

"Robin and the 7 Hoods" (soundtrack LP) (Reprise-20, 1964 – 6th LP): 2) My Kind of Town [Chicago Is –][1] 742; 6) Style 987; 7) Mr. Booze 701; 8) I Like to Lead When I Dance 410) 12) Don't Be a Do-Badder 182

September of My Years (Reprise-23, 1965 – 1st LP): 1) The September of My Years[1] 898; 2) How Old Am I? 355; 3) Don't Wait Too Long 196; 4) It Gets Lonely Early 529; 5) This Is All I Ask 1057; 6) Last Night When We Were Young[2] 608; 7) The Man in the Looking Glass 686; 8) It Was a Very Good Year[1] 541; 9) When the Wind Was Green 1138; 10) Hello, Young Lovers[2] 326; 11) I See It Now 422; 12) Once Upon a Time 821; 13) September Song[3] 902

She Shot Me Down (Reprise-55, 1981 – 1st LP): 1) Good Thing Going (Going, Gone) 299; 2) Hey Look, No Crying* 333; 3) Thanks for the Memory 1024; 4) A Long Night 648; 5) Bang Bang (My Baby Shot Me Down) 68; 6) Monday Morning Quarterback 707; 7) South – To a Warmer Place 960; 8) I Loved Her 417; 9) The Gal (Man) That Got Away[2]/It Never Entered My Mind[3] 277

Sinatra '65 (Reprise-24, 1965 – 2nd LP): 1) Tell Her (You Love Her Each Day) 1017; 2) Anytime at All 44; 3) Stay with Me 974; 5) You Brought a New Kind of

Love to Me³ 1202; (7) When Somebody Loves You 1136; (8) Somewhere in Your Heart 948

Sinatra & Company (Reprise-42, 1971 — 2nd LP): 1) Drinking Water «Aqua de Beber» 204; 2) Someone to Light Up My Life 936; 3) Triste 1083; 4) Don't Ever Go Away «Por Causa de Voce» 188; 5) This Happy Madness 1056; 6) Wave 1103; 7) One Note Samba 832; 8) I Will Drink the Wine 434; 9) Close to You (They Long to Be—) 133; 10) Sunrise in the Morning 997; 11) Bein' Green 77; 12) My Sweet Lady 752; 13) Leaving on a Jet Plane 614; 14) Lady Day² 599

Sinatra & Strings (Reprise-4, 1962 — 1st LP): 1) I Hadn't Anyone Till You 401; 2) Night and Day³ 774; 3) Misty 704; 4) Star Dust² 969; 5) Come Rain or Come Shine² 145; 6) It Might as Well Be Spring¹ 533; 7) Prisoner of Love 863; 8) That's All 1031; 9) All or Nothing at All² 19; 10) Yesterdays [Days I Knew As Happy . . . Days] 1191; 11) *(Japan 1972 version only)* As You Desire Me 53; 12) *(Japan 1972 version only)* Don't Take Your Love from Me² 195

Sinatra and Swingin' Brass (Reprise-5, 1962 — 4th LP): 1) Goody Goody 303; 2) They Can't Take That Away from Me² 1052; 3) At Long Last Love² 55; 4) I'm Beginning to See the Light 494; 5) Don'cha Go 'Way Mad 181; 6) I Get a Kick Out of You² 390; 7) Tangerine 1014; 8) Love Is Just Around the Corner 660; 9) Ain't She Sweet? 7; 10) Serenade in Blue 903; 11) I Love You [Hums the April Breeze] 414; 12) Pick Yourself Up 850

Sinatra at the Sands (2 discs — live) (Reprise-29, 1966 — 3rd LP): 1) Come Fly with Me³ 142; 2) I've Got a Crush on You³ 570; 3) I've Got You Under My Skin³ 576; 4) The Shadow of Your Smile 905; 5) Street of Dreams² 983; 6) One for My Baby (and One More for the Road)³ 825; 7) Fly Me to the Moon «In Other Words»² 248; 10) You Make Me Feel So Young³ 1216; 12) The September of My Years² 899; 13) Get Me to the Church On Time 281 14) It Was a Very Good Year² 542; 15) Don't Worry 'Bout Me² 198; 17) Where or When⁴ 1156; 18) Angel Eyes² 38; 19) My Kind of Town [Chicago Is—]² 743

Sinatra-Basie: An Historic Musical First (Reprise-9, 1963 — 1st LP): 1) Pennies from Heaven² 848; 2) Please Be Kind 852; 3) The Tender Trap (Love Is—)² 1021; 4) Looking at the World Thru Rose-Colored. . . 651; 5) My Kind of Girl 741; 6) I Only Have Eyes for You² 420; 7) Nice Work If You Can Get It² 769; 8) Learnin' the Blues² 613; 9) I'm Gonna Sit Right Down and Write . . .² 501; 10) I Won't Dance² 442

The Sinatra Family Wish You a Merry Christmas (Reprise-35, 1968 — 4th LP): 1) The Twelve Days of Christmas 1086; 6) The Christmas Waltz³ 128; 8) The Bells of Christmas «Greensleeves» 78

Sinatra Rarities — The Columbia Years (Vol. 1) (Columbia-50, 1986 — 1st LP): 2) Two Hearts Are Better Than One 1088; 4) Could'ja 153; 7) So Far 923; 8) It Only Happens When I Dance with You² 538; 9) When Is Sometime? 1134; 10) Where Is the One?¹ 1151; 12) Bop! Goes My Heart 96; 13) It Happens Every Spring 532; 14) Accidents Will Happen 1; 15) London by Night¹ 640

Sinatra Sings Great Songs from Great Britain (English LP) (Reprise-6, 1962 — 5th LP): 1) The Very Thought of You² 1093; 2) We'll Gather Lilacs in the Spring 1116; 3) If I Had You³ 452; 4) Now Is the Hour «Maori's Haere Ra»² 791; 5) The Gypsy 310; 6) A Nightingale Sang in Berkeley Square 779; 7) A Garden in the Rain 278; 8) London by Night³ 642; 9) We'll Meet Again 1117; 10) I'll Follow My Secret Heart² 476; 11) *(Japanese version only)* Roses of Picardy 878

Sinatra Sings . . . of Love and Things (Capitol-32, 1962 — 3rd LP): 1) The Nearness of You² 761; 2) Hidden Persuasion 334; 3) The Moon Was Yellow² 717; 4) I Love Paris² 413; 5) Monique 708; 6) Chicago (That Toddling Town) 123; 7) Love

Looks So Well on You 664; 8) Sentimental Baby 895; 9) Mr. Success 702; 10) They Came to Cordura 1050; 11) I Gotta Right to Sing the Blues* 396

Sinatra Swings (originally "Swing Along with Me") (Reprise-2, 1961 — 6th LP): 1) Falling in Love with Love[2] 237; 2) The Curse of an Aching Heart 157; 3) Don't Cry Joe (Let Her Go, Let Her . . .)[2] 186; 4) Please Don't Talk About Me When I'm Gone 853; 5) Love Walked In 668; 6) Granada* 304; 7) I Never Knew 418; 8) Don't Be That Way 183; 9) Moonlight on the Ganges 723; 10) It's a Wonderful World 547; 11) Have You Met Miss Jones?[2] 318; 12) You're Nobody 'Til Somebody Loves You[1] 1242

Sinatra — The Main Event (live) (Reprise-48, 1974 — 2nd LP): 2) The Lady Is a Tramp[2] 602; 3) I Get a Kick Out of You[3] 391; 4) Let Me Try Again «Laisse Moi le Temps»[2] 618; 5) Autumn in New York[3] 59; 6) I've Got You Under My Skin[4] 577; 7) Bad, Bad Leroy Brown[2] 65; 8) Angel Eyes[3] 39; 9) You Are the Sunshine of My Life[2] 1196; 10) The House I Live In (That's America . . .)[3] 342; 11) My Kind of Town [Chicago Is —][3] 744; 12) My Way «Comme d'habitude»[2] 754

Sinatra's Sinatra (Reprise-15, 1963 — 7th LP): 1) I've Got You Under My Skin[2] 575; 2) In the Wee Small Hours of the Morning[2] 516; 3) The Second Time Around[2] 890; 4) Nancy (with the Laughing Face)[2] 757; 5) Witchcraft[2] 1176; 6) Young at Heart[2] 1229; 7) All the Way[2] 24; 8) How Little We Know[2] 354; 9) Pocketful of Miracles* 854; 10) Oh, What It Seemed to Be[3] 802; 11) Call Me Irresponsible 108; 12) Put Your Dreams Away[3] 866

Sinatra's Swingin' Session!!! (Capitol-28, 1961 — 1st LP): 1) When You're Smiling[2] 1145; 2) Blue Moon 90 3) S'posin'[2] 964; 4) It All Depends on You[3] 525; 5) It's Only a Paper Moon[2] 560; 6) My Blue Heaven[2] 734; 7) Should I?[3] 914; 8) September in the Rain 897; 9) Always[2] 30; 10) I Can't Believe That You're in Love with Me 368; 11) I Concentrate on You[2] 372; 12) You Do Something to Me[2] 1208

The Singles (Italy release only) (Reprise-61, 1982 — 6th LP): 2) Send in the Clowns[2] 893; 4) The Best I Ever Had 79; 6) Dry Your Eyes 205; 7) Like a Sad Song (Sometimes I Feel —) 629; 8) I Love My Wife 411; 10) Night and Day[4] 775; 11) Everybody Ought to Be in Love 227

Softly, As I Leave You (Reprise-21, 1964 — 8th LP): 1) Emily[1] 214; 2) Here's to the Losers 331; 3) Dear Heart 169; 4) Come Blow Your Horn 138; 5) Love Isn't Just for the Young 661; 6) I Can't Believe I'm Losing You 367; 7) Pass Me By 845; 8) Softly, As I Leave You «Piano» 926; 9) Then Suddenly Love 1035; 10) Available 61; 11) Talk to Me, Baby (Tell Me Lies) 1013; 12) The Look of Love [I've Seen —] 649

Some Nice Things I've Missed (Reprise-47, 1974 — 1st LP): 1) You Turned My World Around 1219; 2) Sweet Caroline 1001; 3) The Summer Knows 990; 4) I'm Gonna Make It All the Way 499; 5) Tie a Yellow Ribbon Round the Ole Oak Tree 1069; 6) Satisfy Me One More Time 884; 7) If 445; 8) You Are the Sunshine of My Life[1] 1195; 9) What Are You Doing the Rest of Your Life? 1119; 10) Bad, Bad Leroy Brown[1] 64

Songs by Sinatra, Volume 1 (10″ LP) (Columbia-5, 1950 — 1st LP): 1) I'm Sorry I Made You Cry 505

Songs for Swingin' Lovers! (Capitol-7, 1956 — 1st LP): 1) You Make Me Feel So Young[1] 1214; 2) It Happened in Monterey 531; 3) You're Getting to Be a Habit with Me 1238; 4) You Brought a New Kind of Love to Me[2] 1201; 5) Too Marvelous for Words 1078; 6) Old Devil Moon[1] 804; 7) Pennies from Heaven[1] 847; 8) Love Is Here to Stay[1] 658; 9) I've Got You Under My Skin[1] 574; 10) I Thought About You 428; 11) We'll Be Together Again 1114; 12) Makin' Whoopee 680; 13) Swingin' Down the Lane 1004; 14) Anything Goes 41; 15) How About You?[2] 344

Songs for Young Lovers (Capitol-2, 1954 — 1st LP) (*original 10″ LP):* 1) My Funny

Valentine 737; 2) The Girl (Boy) Next Door[1] 285; 3) A Foggy Day[1] 249; 4) Like Someone in Love 630; 5) I Get a Kick Out of You[1] 389; 6) Little Girl Blue 636; 7) They Can't Take That Away from Me[1] 1051; 8) Violets for Your Furs[2] 1095; *(later 12" LP* — Capitol-27, 1960 — 7th LP): 9) Someone to Watch Over Me[2] 938; 11) It Worries Me 543; 12) I Can Read Between the Lines 366

Strangers in the Night (Reprise-27; 1966 — 1st LP): 1) Strangers in the Night 981; 2) Summer Wind 992; 3) All or Nothing at All[3] 20; 4) Call Me 107; 5) You're Driving Me Crazy! 1237; 6) On a Clear Day (You Can See Forever) 813; 7) My Baby Just Cares for Me 732; 8) Downtown 199; 9) Yes Sir, That's My Baby 1189; 10) The Most Beautiful Girl in the World[1] 727

Swing Easy! (Capitol-4, 1954 — 5th LP) *(original 10" LP):* 1) Just One of Those Things 591; 2) I'm Gonna Sit Right Down and Write . . .[1] 500; 3) Sunday 993; 4) Wrap Your Troubles in Dreams 1185; 5) Taking a Chance on Love 1011; 6) Jeepers Creepers 581; 7) Get Happy 280; 8) All of Me[4] 16; *(later 12" LP* — Capitol-26, 1960 — 6th LP): 9) Lean Baby* 611; 10) I Love You [Three Words] 416; 11) How Could You Do a Thing Like That to Me? 346; 12) Why Should I Cry Over You? 1166

A Swingin' Affair! (Capitol-12, 1957 — 2nd LP): 1) Night and Day[2] 773; 2) I Wish I Were in Love Again 437; 3) I Got Plenty o' Nuttin' 395; 4) I Guess I'll Have to Change My Plan 397; 5) Nice Work If You Can Get It[1] 768; 6) Stars Fell on Alabama 971; 7) No One Ever Tells You 780; 8) I Won't Dance[1] 441; 9) The Lonesome Road 646; 10) At Long Last Love[1] 54; 11) You'd Be So Nice to Come Home To 1221; 12) I Got It Bad (and That Ain't Good) 394; 13) From This Moment On 270; 14) If I Had You[2] 451; 15) Oh! Look at Me Now![2] 798

Tell Her You Love Her (Capitol-35, 1965 — 3rd LP): 1) Tell Her You Love Her 1018; 8) Weep They Will 1113

That Old Feeling (Columbia-23, 1956 — 2nd LP): 1) That Old Feeling[1] 1029; 2) Blue Skies[2] 92; 3) Autumn in New York[1] 57; 4) Don't Cry Joe (Let Her Go, Let Her . . .)[1] 185; 5) The Nearness of You[1] 760; 6) That Lucky Old Sun 1025; 7) Full Moon and Empty Arms 272; 8) Once in Love with Amy 820; 9) A Fellow Needs a Girl 240; 10) Poinciana «Song of the Tree»[2] 856; 11) For Every Man There's a Woman 256; 12) Mean to Me 690

That's Life (Reprise-30, 1966 — 5th LP): 1) That's Life 1033; 2) I Will Wait for You 435; 3) Somewhere My Love? «Lara's Theme» 949; 4) Sand and Sea 882; 5) What Now My Love? «Et Maintenant» 1123; 6) Winchester Cathedral 1173; 7) Give Her Love 288; 9) The Impossible Dream «The Quest» 510; 10) You're Gonna Hear from Me 1239

This Is Sinatra! (Vol. 1) (Capitol-10, 1956 — 6th LP): 1) I've Got the World on a String 573; 2) Three Coins in the Fountain[1] 1067; 3) Love and Marriage[1] 655; 4) From Here to Eternity 265; 5) South of the Border 959; 6) Rain (Falling from the Skies) 868; 7) The Gal (Man) That Got Away[1] 276; 8) Young at Heart[1] 1228; 9) Learnin' the Blues[1] 612; 10) My One and Only Love 747; 11) The Tender Trap (Love Is—)[1] 1020; 12) Don't Worry 'Bout Me[1] 197

This Is Sinatra! (Vol. 2) (Capitol-18, 1958 — 4th LP): 1) Hey! Jealous Lover 332; 2) Everybody Loves Somebody[2] 226; 3) Something Wonderful Happens in Summer 943; 4) Half as Lovely (Twice as True) 312; 5) You're Cheatin' Yourself 1236; 6) You'll Always Be the One I Love 1222; 7) You Forgot All the Words 1210; 8) How Little We Know[1] 353; 9) Time After Time[2] 1071; 10) Crazy Love 156; 11) Wait for Me 1096; 12) If You Are But a Dream[2] 460; 13) So Long, My Love 925; 14) It's the Same Old Dream[2] 565; 15) I Believe [in Wishing Wells][2] 363; 16) Put Your Dreams Away[2] 865

Trilogy: The Past [Collectibles of the Early Years] (Reprise-52, 1980 — 1st

LP): 1) The Song Is You[4] 954; 2) But Not for Me 103; 3) I Had the Craziest Dream 400; 4) It Had to Be You 530; 5) Let's Face the Music and Dance[2] 622; 6) Street of Dreams[3] 984; 7) My Shining Hour[2] 751; 8) All of You 17; 9) More Than You Know 726; 10) They All Laughed 1049

Trilogy: The Present [Some Very Good Years] (Reprise-53, 1980 — 2nd LP): 1) You and Me (We Wanted It All) 1193; 2) Just the Way You Are 593; 3) Something[2] 940; 4) MacArthur Park 677; 5) New York, New York 766; 6) Summer Me, Winter Me 991; 7) Song Sung Blue 956; 8) For the Good Times 258; 9) Love Me Tender «from "Aura Lee"» 667; 10) That's What God Looks Like (to Me) 1034

Trilogy: The Future [Reflections on the Future in 3 Tenses] (Reprise-54, 1980 — 3rd LP): 1) What Time Does the Next Miracle Leave? 1124; 2) World War None 1183; 3) The Future: Future 273; 4) The Future: I've Been There 274; 5) The Future: Song Without Words 275; 6) Before the Music Ends 75

Twelve Songs of Christmas (Reprise-22, 1964 — 9th LP): 1) Go Tell It on the Mountain 290; 3) I Heard the Bells on Christmas Day 406; 6) The Little Drummer Boy 635; 8) An Old Fashioned Christmas 806; 11) We Wish You the Merriest 1111

The Voice (Columbia-21, 1955 — 9th LP): 1) I Don't Know Why (I Just Do) 385; 2) Try a Little Tenderness[1] 1084; 3) A Ghost of a Chance (I Don't Stand —)[1] 282; 4) Paradise 844; 5) These Foolish Things (Remind Me of You)[1] 1047; 6) Laura[1] 609; 7) She's Funny That Way[1] 910; 8) Fools Rush In (Where Angels Fear to Tread)[2] 253; 9) Over the Rainbow 840; 10) That Old Black Magic[1] 1026; 11) Spring Is Here[1] 965; 12) Lover[1] 670

The Voice: 1943/1952 (6 discs) (Columbia-51, 1987 — 1st LP): 29) All Through the Day 26; 36) If I Had You[1] 450; 62) Oh, What a Beautiful Morning 799

The Voice: Vol. 1 (Italy release only) (Reprise-56, 1982 — 1st LP): 1) The Second Time Around[1] 889; 6) Everybody's Twistin' 228; 7) Nothing But the Best 788; 8) I Left My Heart in San Francisco 408; 9) Me and My Shadow 689; 12) Moment to Moment 705

The Voice: Vol. 2 (Italy release only) (Reprise-57, 1982 — 2nd LP): 1) Tina 1072

The Voice: Vol. 3 (Italy release only) (Reprise-58, 1982 — 3rd LP): 3) Forget to Remember 260

The Voice: Vol. 4 (Italy release only) (Reprise-59, 1982 — 4th LP): 3) Younger Than Springtime 1230

Watertown [a love story] (Reprise-40, 1970 — 1st LP): 1) Watertown 1102; 2) Goodbye (She Quietly Says —) 300; 3) For a While 255; 4) Michael and Peter 696; 5) I Would Be in Love (Anyway) 443; 6) Elizabeth 211; 7) What a Funny Girl (You Used to Be) 1118; 8) What's Now Is Now 1128; 9) She Says 908; 10) The Train 1081

We Three (songs from Bluebird 78rpm single) (RCA Victor-12, 1957 — 7th LP): 4) The Night We Called It a Day[1] 777; 5) The Lamplighter's Serenade 603; 7) The Song Is You[1] 951; 9) Night and Day[1] 772

Where Are You? (Capitol-13, 1957 — 4th LP): 1) Where Are You? 1146; 2) The Night We Called It a Day[2] 778; 3) I Cover the Waterfront* 382; 4) Maybe You'll Be There 688; 5) Laura[2] 610; 6) Lonely Town 643; 7) Autumn Leaves «Les Feuille Mortes» 60; 8) I'm a Fool to Want You[2] 493; 9) I Think of You[2] 427; 10) Where Is the One?[2]* 1152; 11) There's No You[2] 1046; 12) Baby, Won't You Please Come Home? 63

bootleg — Frank's Girls (from Reprise masters) (bootleg Alb5, early 1980s): 1) Nancy (with the Laughing Face)[3] 758; 2) Sweet Lorraine[2] 1003; 3) Linda 634; 5) Stella by Starlight[2] 976; 8) Emily[2] 215; 10) Barbara 69

bootleg — **Late Sinatra Goodies** (from Reprise masters) (bootleg Alb6, mid–1980s): 1) Lady Day[1] 598; 3) If You Could Read My Mind 461; 4) Just as Though You Were Here[2] 587; 5) Grass 305; 6) Oh, Babe, What Would You Say? 795; 7) That Old Black Magic[3] 1028; 8) Evergreen 221; 10) Remember[2] 872; 11) Isn't She Lovely? 520; 12) Everything Happens to Me[3] 231

bootleg — **Love Songs** (from Reprise masters) (bootleg Alb3, early 1970s): 1) Have You Met Miss Jones?[1] 317; 5) In the Blue of Evening[2] 512; 6) Zing Went the Strings of My Heart 1251; 12) The Last Dance[2] 606

bootleg — **MM1** (from Columbia masters) (bootleg Alb1, early 1970s): 1) If You Please 465; 3) Home on the Range 336; 4) You'll Know When It Happens 1224; 6) My Love for You 745; 7) Catana 115; 10) A Good Man Is Hard to Find[2] 298

bootleg — **Rare Songs of Sinatra** (from Columbia masters) (bootleg Alb2, early 1970s): 2) Help Yourself to My Heart 327

bootleg — **The Unissued Sinatra** (from Reprise masters) (bootleg Alb4, early 1980s): 5) Desafinado «Off Key» 173; 7) Walk Away 1098; 10) All or Nothing at All[4] 21

demonstration disc (no label, 1939 demo): Our Love* 835

radio — **The First Times . . . Frank Sinatra** (Cameron-1, early 1960s): 1) This Can't Be Love 1055; 2) My Happiness 738; 3) I'll Get By (as Long as I Have You) 477; 4) Lilli Bolero (Laroo, Laroo —) 631; 5) Hair of Gold, Eyes of Blue 311; 6) I Wish I Didn't Love You So 436; 7) I Wonder Who's Kissing Her Now 440; 8) One Hundred Years from Today[1] 826; 9) Let Me Love You Tonight «No Te Importe . . .» 616; 10) Long Ago (and Far Away) 647

radio — **Frank Sinatra** (Cameron-4, early 1960s): 1) Speak Low 961; 2) Between the Devil and the Deep Blue Sea 82; 3) After I Say I'm Sorry 5; 4) Now Is the Hour «Maori's Haere Ra»[1] 790; 5) It Only Happens When I Dance with You[1] 537; 6) Ballerina (Dance — . . . . Dance) 67; 7) You Do 1206; 8) Serenade of the Bells 904; 9) My Heart Tells Me 740; 10) Mimi 699

radio — **My Best Songs — My Best Years (Vol. 1)** (Pentagon-1, early 1970s): 1) Golden Earrings 293; 2) You Call Everybody Darling 1203; 3) Pistol Packing Mama 851; 4) I've Found a New Baby 567; 5) You Can't Be True, Dear «Du Kannst . . .» 1205; 6) I'm in the Mood for Love[1] 502; 7) A Lover Is Blue 672; 8) I'll Dance at Your Wedding 474

radio — **My Best Songs — My Best Years (Vol. 4)** (Pentagon-4, early 1970s): 1) Suddenly It's Spring 988; 2) A Good Man Is Hard to Find[1] 297; 3) You're the Top 1249; 4) Lily Belle[1] 632; 5) Don't Forget Tonight, Tomorrow[2] 190; 8) The Right Kind of Love 875; 9) It's All Up to You[1] 551; 10) Comin' In on a Wing and a Prayer 148

radio — **My Best Songs — My Best Years (Vol. 5)** (Pentagon-5, early 1970s): 1) Lulu's Back in Town 675; 3) There's a Flaw in My Flue[1] 1041; 6) Somebody Loves Me 935; 7) Oh, What It Seemed to Be[1] 800; 10) Homesick, That's All[2] 338

radio — **The Original. . . Frank Sinatra** (Cameron-2, early 1960s): 1) Tenderly 1022; 2) Little White Lies 639; 3) Haunted Heart 316; 4) The Lady from 29 Palms 600; 5) I Heard You Cried Last Night 407; 6) I'll String Along with You 489; 7) A Tree in the Meadow 1082; 8) How Soon? (Will I Be Seeing You) 356; 9) Civilization «Bongo, Bongo, Bongo» 130; 10) The Very Thought of You[1] 1092

radio — **Tommy Dorsey & His Orchestra, Featuring Frank Sinatra** (Coronet-1, 1962 — 8th LP): 1) I'll Buy That Dream 473

single — Brunswick-1 (1939), 78rpm, #8443, side A: From the Bottom of My Heart 267; side B: Melancholy Mood 692

single — Capitol-5 (1953), 45rpm, #2450/F: I'm Walking Behind You 506 *single* — Capitol-5 (1954), 45rpm, #2954, side A: White Christmas³ 1161; side B: The Christmas Waltz¹ 126

single — Capitol-5 (1954), 45rpm, #3050: Don't Change Your Mind About Me 184

single — Capitol-5 (1956), 45rpm, #3469: You're Sensational¹ 1245

single — Capitol-5 (1958), 45rpm, #3952/E, side A: Nothing in Common 789; side B: How Are Ya Fixed for Love? 345

single — Capitol-5 (1959), 45rpm, #4103: To Love and Be Loved¹ 1074

single — Columbia-5 (1950), 45rpm, #4-39014: One Finger Melody 822

single — Columbia-5 (1950), 45rpm, #4-39069: Remember Me in Your Dreams 873

single — Columbia-5 (1951), 45rpm, #4-39079: You Don't Remind Me 1209

single — Columbia-5 (1951), 45rpm, #4-39141: Cherry Pies Ought to Be You 122

single — Columbia-5 (1951), 45rpm, #4-39213: Faithful 235

single — Columbia-5 (1951), 45rpm, #4-39425: Mama Will Bark 681

single — Columbia-5 (1952), 45rpm, #4-39687: Don't Ever Be Afraid to Go Home 187

single — Columbia-5 (1952), 45rpm, #4-39787: Tennessee Newsboy «The Newsboy Blues» 1023

single — Columbia-5 (1952), 45rpm, #4-40565: Sheila 909

single — Columbia-6 (1948), 45rpm — extended play, #B2542: A Little Learnin' Is a Dang'rous Thing 638

single — Columbia-2 (1943), 78rpm, #35209: It's Funny to Everyone But Me 557

single — Columbia-2 (1943), 78rpm, #35261: On a Little Street in Singapore 814

single — Columbia-2 (1943), 78rpm, #35531: Every Day of My Life 222

single — Columbia-4 (1945), 78rpm, #36820: Homesick, That's All¹ 337

single — Columbia-4 (1945), 78rpm, #36842: Stars in Your Eyes «Mar» 972

single — Columbia-4 (1945), 78rpm, #36854, side A: Lily Belle² 633; side B: Don't Forget Tonight, Tomorrow¹ 189

single — Columbia-4 (1945), 78rpm, #36886: America the Beautiful¹ 31

single — Columbia-4 (1946), 78rpm, #36987: From This Day Forward 269

single — Columbia-4 (1946), 78rpm, #37054: Somewhere in the Night 947

single — Columbia-4 (1946), 78rpm, #37193, side A: This Is the Night 1060; side B: Hush-a-Bye Island 359

single — Columbia-4 (1946), 78rpm, #37231: I Got a Gal I Love (in N. & S. Dakota) 393

single — Columbia-4 (1947), 78rpm, #37251: I Want to Thank Your Folks 431

single — Columbia-4 (1947), 78rpm, #37528: Tea for Two 1015

single — Columbia-4 (1947), 78rpm, #37809: The Stars Will Remember (and So Will I) 973

single — Columbia-4 (1947), 78rpm, #37853, side A: I've Got a Home in That Rock 571; side B: Jesus Is a Rock (in a Weary Land) 582

single — Columbia-4 (1947), 78rpm, #37966: The Dum Dot Song (. . . Penny in the Gum Slot) 206

single — Columbia-4 (1947), 78rpm, #38045, side A: My Cousin Louella 736; side B: What'll I Do?¹ 1125

single — Columbia-4 (1947), 78rpm, #38089: I'll Make Up for Everything 478

single — Columbia-4 (1948), 78rpm, #38129: But None Like You 102

single — Columbia-4 (1948), 78rpm, #38192: A Fella with an Umbrella 239

single — Columbia-4 (1948), 78rpm, #38225: Just for Now 588 *single* — Columbia-4 (1948), 78rpm, #38287: Kiss Me Again 594

single — Columbia-4 (1948), 78rpm, #38393: No Orchids for My Lady 781

single — Columbia-4 (1948), 78rpm, #38407: While the Angelus Was Ringing 1157

single — Columbia-4 (1949), 78rpm, #38456: Night After Night 771

single — Columbia-4 (1949), 78rpm, #38513, side A: Let's Take an Old-Fashioned Walk 626; side B: Just One Way to Say I Love You 592

single — Columbia-4 (1949), 78rpm, #38555: The Wedding of Lili Marlene 1112

single — Columbia-4 (1949), 78rpm, #38556: Just a Kiss Apart 585

single — Columbia-4 (1949), 78rpm, #38572: Every Man Should Marry 223

single — Columbia-4 (1949), 78rpm, #38650: The Old Master Painter 811

single — Columbia-4 (1949), 78rpm, #38683: The Music Stopped[2] 731

single — Columbia-4 (1949), 78rpm, #38684: I Love You «Ich Liebe Dich» 415

single — Columbia-4 (1950), 78rpm, #38708, side A: God's Country 291; side B: Chattanoogie Shoe Shine Boy 120

single — Columbia-4 (1950), 78rpm, #38853: Peach Tree Street 846

single — Columbia-4 (1950), 78rpm, #38960: Life Is So Peculiar 627

single — Columbia-3 (1947), 78rpm, #DB2330 (England only): All of Me[2] 14

single — Columbia-3 (1947), 78rpm, #DB2357 (England only): Poinciana «Song of the Tree»[1] 855

single — Columbia-3 (1947), 78rpm, #DB2381 (England only): It All Came True[1] 521

single — Columbia-3 (1948), 78rpm, #DO3104 (Australia only): It's All Up to You[2] 552

single — Columbia-3 (1948), 78rpm, #DO3745 (Australia only): White Christmas[2] 1160

single — Reprise-5 (1983), 45rpm, #7-29677, side A: Here's to the Band 330; side B: It's Sunday 563

single — Reprise-5 (1984), 45rpm, #7-29903: To Love a Child 1073

single — Reprise-5 (1966), 45rpm, #P20,157, side A: California 106; side B: America the Beautiful[2] 32

single — Reprise-5 (1981), 45rpm, #RPS49827: Say Hello 887

soundtrack — **"Anchors Away"** (bootleg Mv7, mid-1960s): 2) We Hate to Leave 1106; 5) If You Knew Susie 463

soundtrack — **"Double Dynamite"** (bootleg Mv14, mid-1960s): 10) It's Only Money 561

soundtrack — **"Guys and Dolls"** (bootleg Mv18, mid-1960s): 6) Adelaide 2; 11) Sue Me 989

soundtrack — **"Higher and Higher"** (bootleg Mv4, mid-1960s): 4) You Belong in a Love Song 1199; 7) I Saw You First 421; 10) You're On Your Own 1244

soundtrack — **"It Happened in Brooklyn"** (bootleg Mv9, mid-1960s): 2) Whose Baby Are You? 1164; 7) The Song's Gotta Come from the Heart 957; 8) Black Eyes «from "Otchi Tchorniya"» 87; 9) La Ci Darem La Mano 597

soundtrack — **"The Joker Is Wild"** (bootleg Mv21, mid-1960s): 1) At Sundown 56; 2) I Cried for You (Now It's Your Turn...) 383; 3) If I Could Be with You (One Hour Tonight) 446; 6) Out of Nowhere 839

soundtrack — **"The Kissing Bandit"** (bootleg Mv11, mid-1960s): 1) What's Wrong with Me? 1129; 3) Siesta 915

soundtrack — **"The Man with the Golden Arm"** (bootleg Mv19, mid-1960s): 12) The Man with the Golden Arm 687 *soundtrack* — **"Meet Danny Wilson"** (bootleg Mv15, mid–1960s): 1) You're a Sweetheart 1233; 2) Lonesome Man Blues 645

soundtrack — **"On the Town"** (bootleg Mv13, mid–1960s): 1) New York, New York [A Wonderful Town] 765; 2) Prehistoric Man 861; 3) Come Up to My Place 146; 5) You're Awful 1234; 8) On the Town 818; 9) Count on Me (You Can —) 154

soundtrack — **"Ship Ahoy"** (bootleg Mv2, mid–1960s): 3) On Moonlight Bay 815

soundtrack — **"Step Lively"** (bootleg Mv5, mid–1960s): 5) As Long as There's Music 51; 9) Where Does Love Begin? 1149

soundtrack — **"Take Me Out to the Ball Game"** (bootleg Mv12, mid–1960s): 5) The Hat My Father Wore 315; 6) Take Me Out to the Ball Game 1009; 7) Yes, Indeedy 1188; 8) O'Brien to Ryan to Goldberg 794; 9) Boys and Girls Like You and Me* 98; 10) It's Fate, Baby, It's Fate 556; 11) Strictly U.S.A. 985

television — **Frank Sinatra** — **Through the Years** (Ajazz-1, mid–1960s): 1) Exactly Like You 232; 2) I'll Remember April[1] 486; 3) I'm in the Mood for Love[2] 503; 5) Spend an Afternoon with Me 962; 6) It's All Right with Me[1] 548; 7) Can't We Be Friends?[2] 112; 8) Love Is Here to Stay[2] 659; 9) You Make Me Feel So Young[2] 1215; 10) Ol' MacDonald[2] 808; 11) Where or When[3] 1155; 12) Who Takes Care of the Caretaker's Daughter? 1162; 13) The Most Beautiful Girl in the World[2] 728; 14) Moonlight in Vermont[2] 721; 15) You're Nobody 'Til Somebody Loves You[2] 1243

v/disc — **Frank Sinatra on V-Disc** (Japan) (Dan-1, early 1970s): 5) I'll Never Smile Again[2] 482; 6) Without a Song[2] 1179; 7) Should I?[1] 912; 12) Come Rain or Come Shine[1] 144

v/disc — **Frank Sinatra on V-Disc, Vol. 1** (England) (Apex-1, early 1970s): 3) A Hot Time in the Town of Berlin 339; 6) The Way You Look Tonight[1] 1104; 7) I'll Be Around[1] 467; 13) My Shining Hour[1] 750; 15) Some Other Time 933; 16) Come Out, Come Out, Wherever You Are 143

v/disc — **Sinatra for the Collector: Vol. 1** (Canada) (My Way-1, early 1970s): 9) Aren't You Glad You're You? 49; 11) You Brought a New Kind of Love to Me[1] 1200

v/disc — **Sinatra for the Collector: Vol. 2** (Canada) (My Way-2, early 1970s): 5) I'll Follow My Secret Heart[1] 475; 9) The Night Is Young and You're So Beautiful 776; 10) All of Me[1] 13; 15) And Then You Kissed Me 36

Album List #2
Titles by Release Date; with Notes

1949—3rd LP: **Popular Favorites, Volume 1** (10" LP). Columbia/3rd: CL-6057. Singles collection.

1949—4th LP: **Frankly Sentimental** (10" LP). Columbia/4th: CL-6059. Singles collection.

1950—1st LP: **Songs by Sinatra, Volume 1** (10" LP). Columbia/5th: CL-6087. Singles collection.

1954—1st LP: **Songs for Young Lovers** (original 10" LP). Capitol/2nd: H-488. 8 songs.

1954—5th LP: **Swing Easy!** (original 10" LP). Capitol/4th: H-528. 8 songs.

1955—5th LP: **Boys & Girls Together** (10" LP). Columbia/16th: CL-2530. Singles collection.

1955—7th LP: **In the Wee Small Hours** (12" LP). Capitol/5th: W-581. 16 songs (combining two 10" LPs of same title).

1955—8th LP: **Frankie.** Columbia/20th: CL-606. Singles collection.

1955—9th LP: **The Voice.** Columbia/21st: CL-743. Singles collection.

1956—1st LP: **Songs for Swingin' Lovers!** Capitol/7th: W-653.

1956—2nd LP: **That Old Feeling.** Columbia/23rd: CL-902. Singles collection.

1956—3rd LP: **Adventures of the Heart.** Columbia/24th: CL-953. Singles collection.

1956—5th LP: **"High Society"** official soundtrack LP. Capitol/9th: W-750.

1956—6th LP: **This Is Sinatra!** Capitol/10th: T-768. Singles collection.

1957—1st LP: **Close to You.** Capitol/11th: W-789.

1957—2nd LP: **A Swingin' Affair!** Capitol/12th: W-803.

1957—3rd LP: **Christmas Dreaming.** Columbia/25th: CL-1032. Singles collection.

1957—4th LP: **Where Are You?** (1st stereo LP). Capitol/13th: SW-855. 11 songs on stereo LP; 12 on monaural.

1957—6th LP: **A Jolly Christmas from Frank Sinatra.** Capitol/14th: W-894.

1957—7th LP: **We Three** (includes 1st four solo singles: Bluebird label). RCA Victor/12th: LPM-1632. Singles collection.

1957—8th LP: **"Pal Joey"** official soundtrack LP. Capitol/15th: W-912.

1958—2nd LP: **Come Fly with Me.** Capitol/17th: W-920.

1958—3rd LP: **Put Your Dreams Away.** Columbia/26th: CL-1136. Singles collection.

1958—4th LP: **This Is Sinatra, Volume Two.** Capitol/18th: W-982. Singles collection.

1958—5th LP: **Frank Sinatra Sings for Only the Lonely.** Capitol/19th: SW-1053. 10 songs on stereo LP; 12 on monaural.

1959—1st LP: **Come Dance with Me!** Capitol/20th: SW-1069.

1959—2nd LP: **The Frank Sinatra Story in Music.** Columbia/27th: C2L-6. 2-record singles collection.

1959—4th LP: **Look to Your Heart.** Capitol/22nd: W-1164. Partially a singles collection.

1959 — 5th LP: **No One Cares.** Capitol/23rd: SW-1221.

1960 — 1st LP: **"Can-Can"** official soundtrack LP. Capitol/24th: SW-1301.

1960 — 2nd LP: **Nice 'n' Easy.** Capitol/25th: SW-1417.

1960 — 3rd LP: **Love Is a Kick.** Columbia/28th: CL-1241. Singles collection.

1960 — 4th LP: **The Broadway Kick.** Columbia/29th: CL-1297. Singles collection.

1960 — 5th LP: **Come Back to Sorrento.** Columbia/30th: CL-1359. Singles collection.

1960 — 6th LP: **Swing Easy** (later 12″ version of LP). Capitol/26th: SW-1429. 12 songs
(4 added to original).

1960 — 7th LP: **Songs for Young Lovers** (later 12″ version of LP). Capitol/27th:
SW-1432. 12 songs (4 added to original).

Early 1960s: **The First Times ... Frank Sinatra.** Cameron/1st: CLP-5001. Radio
broadcast source.

Early 1960s: **The Original... Frank Sinatra.** Cameron/2nd: CLP-5002. Radio
broadcast source.

Early 1960s: **Frank Sinatra.** Cameron/4th: CLP-5004. Radio broadcast source.

1961 — 1st LP: **Sinatra's Swingin' Session!!!** Capitol/28th: SW-1491.

1961 — 2nd LP: **All the Way.** Capitol/29th: SW-1538. Singles collection.

1961 — 3rd LP: **Ring-a-Ding Ding!** Reprise/1st: FS-1001.

1961 — 4th LP: **Reflections.** Columbia/31st: CL-1448. Singles collection.

1961 — 5th LP: **Come Swing with Me!** Columbia/30th: SW-1594.

1961 — 6th LP: **Sinatra Swings** (original title: "Swing Along with Me"). Reprise/2nd:
FS-1002. Title change forced by Capitol suit.

1961 — 7th LP: **I Remember Tommy...** Reprise/3rd: FS-1003.

1962 — 1st LP: **Sinatra & Strings.** Reprise/4th: FS-1004. 10 songs; '72 Japanese version has 12.

1962 — 2nd LP: **Point of No Return.** Capitol/31st: SW-1676.

1962 — 3rd LP: **Sinatra Sings ... of Love and Things.** Capitol/32nd: SW-1729. Partially a singles collection.

1962 — 4th LP: **Sinatra and Swingin' Brass.** Reprise/5th: FS-1005.

1962 — 5th LP: **Sinatra Sings Great Songs from Great Britain.** Reprise/6th: FS-
1006. 10 songs on English LP; Japanese version has 12 songs.

1962 — 7th LP: **All Alone.** Reprise/8th: FS-1007. 11 songs; '72 Japanese version has
12.

1962 — 8th LP: **Tommy Dorsey and His Orchestra, Featuring Frank Sinatra.**
Coronet/1st: CX-186. Radio broadcast source.

1963 — 1st LP: **Sinatra-Basie: An Historic Musical First.** Reprise/9th: FS-1008.

1963 — 2nd LP: **The Concert Sinatra.** Reprise/10th: FS-1009.

1963 — 3rd LP: **Reprise Musical Repertory Theatre: "Finian's Rainbow."** Reprise/
11th: FS-2015. From boxed set #4FS-2019.

1963 — 4th LP: **Reprise Musical Repertory Theatre: "Guys and Dolls."** Reprise/
12th: FS-2016. From boxed set #4FS-2019.

1963 — 5th LP: **Reprise Musical Repertory Theatre: "Kiss Me Kate."** Reprise/13th:
FS-2017. From boxed set #4FS-2019.

1963 — 6th LP: **Reprise Musical Repertory Theatre: "South Pacific."** Reprise/14th:
FS-2018. From boxed set #4FS-2019.

1963 — 7th LP: **Sinatra's Sinatra.** Reprise/15th: FS-1010.

1963 — 8th LP: **Have Yourself a Merry Little Christmas.** Reprise/16th: RS-243.

1964 — 1st LP: **Frank Sinatra Sings "Days of Wine and Roses," "Moon River" and
Other Academy Award Winners.** Reprise/17th: FS-1011.

1964 — 2nd LP: **America, I Hear You Singing.** Reprise/18th: FS-2020.

1964 — 3rd LP: **Frank Sinatra's Greatest Hits: The Early Years.** Columbia/32nd: CL-2474. Singles collection.

1964 — 4th LP: **Frank Sinatra's Greatest Hits: The Early Years, Vol. 2.** Columbia/ 33rd: CL-2572. Singles collection.

1964 — 5th LP: **It Might as Well Be Swing.** Reprise/19th: FS-1012.

1964 — 6th LP: **"Robin and the 7 Hoods"** official soundtrack LP. Reprise/20th: FS-2021.

1964 — 7th LP. **Frank Sinatra Sings Rodgers and Hart.** Capitol/34th: W-1825. Reissues, except for 1 song.

1964 — 8th LP: **Softly, As I Leave You.** Reprise/21st: FS-1013.

1964 — 9th LP: **Twelve Songs of Christmas.** Reprise/22nd: FS-2022.

1965 — 1st LP: **September of My Tears.** Reprise/23rd: FS-1014.

1965 — 2nd LP: **Sinatra '65.** Reprise/24th: FS-6167. Partially a singles collection.

1965 — 3rd LP: **Tell Her You Love Her.** Capitol/35th: T-1919. Reissues, except for 2 songs.

1965 — 4th LP: **My Kind of Broadway.** Reprise/25th: FS-1015. Partially reissues.

1965 — 5th LP: **Frank Sinatra: A Man and His Music.** Reprise/26th: 2FS-1016. 2-record set; mostly reissues.

Mid-1960s: **Frank Sinatra — Through the Years: 1944–1966.** Ajazz/1st: #506. 11 songs are TV broadcast source, 3 are from radio.

Mid-1960s: **Four Sinatra Movies.** Bootleg movie #2 and #4 soundtrack. Includes *Ship Ahoy* and *Higher and Higher.*

Mid-1960s: **Complete "Step Lively" Film Soundtrack.** Bootleg movie #5 soundtrack. Bootleg from soundtrack source.

Mid-1960s: **Score from "Anchors Aweigh."** Bootleg movie #7 soundtrack. Bootleg from soundtrack source.

Mid-1960s: **Score from "It Happened in Brooklyn."** Bootleg movie #9 soundtrack. Bootleg from soundtrack source.

Mid-1960s: **Five Films.** Bootleg movie #11 and #12 soundtrack. Includes *The Kissing Bandit* and *Take Me Out to the Ball Game.*

Mid-1960s: **"On the Town" & Others.** Bootleg movie #13, #14, #19 soundtrack. Includes *On the Town, Double Dynamite* and *The Man with the Golden Arm.*

Mid-1960s: **Score from "Meet Danny Wilson."** Bootleg movie #15 soundtrack. Bootleg from soundtrack source.

Mid-1960s: **Score from "Guys and Dolls."** Bootleg movie #18 soundtrack. Bootleg from soundtrack source.

Mid-1960s: **Score from "The Joker Is Wild."** Bootleg movie #21 soundtrack. Bootleg from soundtrack source.

1966 — 1st LP: **Strangers in the Night.** Reprise/27th: FS-1017.

1966 — 2nd LP: **Moonlight Sinatra.** Reprise/28th: FS-1018.

1966 — 3rd LP: **Sinatra at the Sands.** Reprise/29th: 2FS-1019. Live recording; 2-record set.

1966 — 4th LP: **Forever Frank.** Capitol/36th: T-2602. Singles collection.

1966 — 5th LP: **That's Life.** Reprise/30th: FS-1020.

1967 — 1st LP: **Francis Albert Sinatra & Antonio Carlos Jobim.** Reprise/31st: FS-1021.

1967 — 2nd LP: **The Essential Frank Sinatra — Volume 1.** Columbia/34th: CL-2739. Singles collection.

1967 — 3rd LP: **The Essential Frank Sinatra — Volume 2.** Columbia/35th: CL-2740. Singles collection.

1967 — 4th LP: **The Essential Frank Sinatra — Volume 3.** Columbia/36th: CL-2741. Singles collection.

1967 — 5th LP: **Frank Sinatra & Frank and Nancy.** Reprise/32nd: FS-1022/FS-1023. Two LP concepts combined.

1968 — 1st LP: **Frank Sinatra in Hollywood, 1943–1949.** Columbia/38th: CL-2913. Singles collection.

1968 — 2nd LP: **Francis A. & Edward K.** Reprise/33rd: FS-1024.

1968 — 3rd LP: **Frank Sinatra's Greatest Hits!** Reprise/34th: FS-1025. Singles collection.

1968 — 4th LP: **The Sinatra Family Wish You a Merry Christmas.** Reprise/35th: FS-1026.

1968 — 6th LP: **Cycles.** Reprise/37th: FS-1027.

1969 — 1st LP: **My Way.** Reprise/38th: FS-1029.

1969 — 3rd LP: **A Man Alone.** Reprise/39th: FS-1030.

1970 — 1st LP: **Watertown [a love story].** Reprise/40th: FS-1031.

Early 1970s: **Frank Sinatra on V-Disc, Volume 1.** Apex/1st: AX-1. English LP (Victory Disc set).

Early 1970s: **Sinatra for the Collector: Vol. 1 — The V-Disc Years.** My Way/1st: MW-1001. Canadian LP (Victory Disc set).

Early 1970s: **Sinatra for the Collector: Vol. 2 — The V-Disc Years.** My Way/2nd: MW-1002. Canadian LP (Victory Disc set).

Early 1970s: **Frank Sinatra on V-Disc.** Dan Records/1st: VC-5019. Japanese LP (Victory Disc set).

Early 1970s: **My Best Songs — My Best Years, Vol. 1.** Pentagon/1st: MB-990061. Radio broadcast source; cassette.

Early 1970s: **My Best Songs — My Best Years, Vol. 4.** Pentagon/4th: MB-990064. Radio broadcast source; cassette.

Early 1970s: **My Best Songs — My Best Years, Vol. 5.** Pentagon/5th: MB-990065. Radio broadcast source; cassette.

Early 1970s: **MM-1.** Bootleg album #1: #MM-1. Bootleg from Columbia masters.

Early 1970s: **Rare Songs of Sinatra.** Bootleg album #2: no number. Bootleg from Columbia masters.

Early 1970s: **Love Songs.** Bootleg album #3: no number. Bootleg from Reprise masters.

1971 — 2nd LP: **Sinatra & Company*.** Reprise/42nd: FS-1033. * = A. Jobim, E. Deodato and D. Costa.

1971 — 3rd LP: **Frank Sinatra's Greatest Hits!, Vol. 2.** Reprise/43rd: FS-1034. Singles collection.

1972 — 1st LP: **The Dorsey/Sinatra Sessions — Volume 1.** RCA Victor/17th: SD-1000/1. Sessions: 2/1/40 thru 4/10/40.

1972 — 2nd LP: **The Dorsey/Sinatra Sessions — Volume 2.** RCA Victor/18th: SD-1000/2. Sessions: 4/10/40 thru 7/17/40.

1972 — 3rd LP: **The Dorsey/Sinatra Sessions — Volume 3.** RCA Victor/19th: SD-1000/3. Sessions: 7/17/40 thru 11/11/40.

1972 — 4th LP: **The Dorsey/Sinatra Sessions — Volume 4.** RCA Victor/20th: SD-1000/4. Sessions: 1/6/41 thru 5/28/41.

1972 — 5th LP: **The Dorsey/Sinatra Sessions — Volume 5.** RCA Victor/21st: SD-1000/5. Sessions: 6/27/41 thru 2/19/42.

1972 — 6th LP: **The Dorsey/Sinatra Sessions — Volume 6.** RCA Victor/22nd: SD-1000/6. Sessions: 2/19/42 thru 7/2/42.

1973 — 2nd LP: **Ol' Blue Eyes Is Back.** Reprise/45th: FS-2155. Return-from-retirement album.

1974 — 1st LP: **Some Nice Things I've Missed.** Reprise/47th: FS-2195.

1974 — 2nd LP: **Sinatra — The Main Event.** Reprise/48th: FS-2207. Live recording.

1978 — 1st LP: **The Rare Sinatra — Volume 1.** Capitol/65th: ST-24311. Australian LP.

1979 — 1st LP: **Portrait of Sinatra [40 Songs in the Life of a Man].** Reprise/51st: FS-51306. English 2-record set; most reissue.

1980 — 1st LP: **Trilogy: The Past [Collectibles of the Early Years].** Reprise/52nd: 3FS2300/1.

1980 — 2nd LP: **Trilogy: The Present [Some Very Good Years].** Reprise/53rd: 3FS2300/2.

1980 — 3rd LP: **Trilogy: The Future [Reflections on the Future in 3 Tenses].** Reprise/54th: 3FS2300/3.

Early 1980s: **The Unissued Sinatra.** Bootleg album #4: Tyrecords #100. Bootleg from Reprise masters.

Early 1980s: **Frank's Girls.** Bootleg album #5: no number. Bootleg from Reprise masters.

1981 — 1st LP: **She Shot Me Down.** Reprise/55th: FS-2305.

1982 — 1st LP: **The Voice — Volume 1.** Reprise/56th: FS-5238. Italian LP; many reissues.

1982 — 2nd LP: **The Voice — Volume 2.** Reprise/57th: FS-5239. Italian LP; many reissues.

1982 — 3rd LP: **The Voice — Volume 3.** Reprise/58th: FS-5240. Italian LP; many reissues.

1982 — 4th LP: **The Voice — Volume 4.** Reprise/59th: FS-5250. Italian LP; many reissues.

1982 — 5th LP: **I Sing the Songs.** Reprise/60th: FS-54093. Italian LP; many reissues.

1982 — 6th LP: **The Singles.** Reprise/61st: FS-54101. Italian LP; mostly reissues.

1984 — 1st LP: **L.A. Is My Lady.** Qwest/1st: #9/25145-1. Sinatra's final new album release.

Mid-1980s: **Late Sinatra Goodies.** Bootleg album #6: no number. Bootleg from Reprise masters.

1986 — 1st LP: **Sinatra Rarities — The Columbia Years, Vol. 1.** Columbia/50th: FC-44236. Singles collection.

1987 — 1st LP: **The Voice: 1943–1952.** Columbia/51st: CXT-40343. 6-record set (70 songs).

1987 — 2nd LP: **Hello, Young Lovers.** Columbia/52nd: C2X-40897. 2-record singles collection.

Album List #3
Titles by Label; with Producers

Ajazz/1st: #506 (11 songs from TV and 3 songs from radio). **Frank Sinatra — Through the Years: 1944–1966** (mid-1960s). Producer not credited.

Apex/1st: AX-1 England LP. **Frank Sinatra on V-Disc, Volume 1** (early 1970s). Singles produced individually.

Cameron/1st: CLP-5001. **The First Times . . . Frank Sinatra** (radio tracks — early 1960s). Axel Stordahl, musical director.

Cameron/2nd: CLP-5002. **The Original. . . Frank Sinatra** (radio tracks — early 1960s). Axel Stordahl, musical director.

Cameron/4th: CLP-5004. **Frank Sinatra** (radio tracks — early 1960s). Axel Stordahl, musical director.

Capitol/2nd: H-488. **Songs for Young Lovers** (original 10″ LP; 8 songs; 1954 — 1st LP). Voyle Gilmore, producer.

Capitol/4th: H-528. **Swing Easy!** (original 10″ LP; 8 songs; 1954 — 5th LP). Voyle Gilmore, producer.

Capitol/5th: W-581. **In the Wee Small Hours** (16 songs; 12″ LP; combines two 10″ LPs; 1955 — 7th LP). Voyle Gilmore, producer.

Capitol/7th: W-653. **Songs for Swingin' Lovers!** (1956 — 1st LP). Voyle Gilmore, producer.

Capitol/9th: W-750. **"High Society"** official soundtrack LP (1956 — 5th LP). J. Green & S. Chaplin supervised.

Capitol/10th: T-768. **This Is Sinatra!** (1956 — 6th LP). Voyle Gilmore, producer.

Capitol/11th: W-789. **Close to You** (1957 — 1st LP). Voyle Gilmore, producer.

Capitol/12th: W-803. **A Swingin' Affair!** (1957 — 2nd LP). Voyle Gilmore, producer.

Capitol/13th: SW-855. **Where Are You?** (1st stereo LP; 1957 — 4th LP). Voyle Gilmore and David Cavanaugh, producers.

Capitol/14th: W-894. **A Jolly Christmas from Frank Sinatra** (1957 — 6th LP). Voyle Gilmore, producer.

Capitol/15th: W-912. **"Pal Joey"** official soundtrack LP (1957 — 8th LP). Morris Stoloff supervised.

Capitol/17th: SW-920. **Come Fly with Me** (1958 — 2nd LP). Voyle Gilmore, producer.

Capitol/18th: W-982. **This Is Sinatra, Volume Two** (1958 — 4th LP). Singles produced individually.

Capitol/19th: SW-1053. **Frank Sinatra Sings for Only the Lonely** (1958 — 5th LP). Dave Cavanaugh, producer.

Capitol/20th: SW-1069. **Come Dance with Me!** (1959 — 1st LP). Dave Cavanaugh, producer.

Capitol/22nd: W-1164. **Look to Your Heart** (1959 — 4th LP). Voyle Gilmore, Lee Gillette, D. Dexter, producers.

Capitol/23rd: SW-1221. **No One Cares** (1959 — 5th LP). Dave Cavanaugh, producer.

Capitol/24th: SW-1301. **"Can-Can"** official soundtrack LP (1960 — 1st LP). Nelson Riddle supervised.

Capitol/25th: SW-1417. **Nice 'n' Easy** (1960 — 2nd LP). Dave Cavanaugh, producer.

Capitol/26th: SW-1429. **Swing Easy** (later 12" version; 12 songs; 1960 — 6th LP). Voyle Gilmore, producer.

Capitol/27th: SW-1432. **Songs for Young Lovers** (later 12" version; 12 songs; 1960 — 7th LP). Voyle Gilmore, producer.

Capitol/28th: SW-1491. **Sinatra's Swingin' Session!!!** (1961 — 1st LP). Dave Cavanaugh, producer.

Capitol/29th: SW-1538. **All the Way** (1961 — 2nd LP). Dave Cavanaugh and Voyle Gilmore, producers.

Capitol/30th: SW-1594. **Come Swing with Me!** (1961 — 5th LP). Dave Cavanaugh, producer.

Capitol/31st: SW-1676. **Point of No Return** (1962 — 2nd LP). Dave Cavanaugh, producer.

Capitol/32nd: SW-1729. **Sinatra Sings . . . of Love and Things** (1962 — 3rd LP). Dave Cavanaugh and Bill Miller, producers.

Capitol/34th: W-1825. **Frank Sinatra Sings Rodgers and Hart** (1964 — 7th LP). Dave Cavanaugh and Voyle Gilmore, producers.

Capitol/35th: T-1919. **Tell Her You Love Her** (1965 — 3rd LP). Voyle Gilmore and Dave Cavanaugh, producers.

Capitol/36th: T-2602. **Forever Frank** (1966 — 4th LP). Voyle Gilmore and Dave Cavanaugh, producers.

Capitol/65th: ST-24311 (Australia LP). **The Rare Sinatra — Volume 1** (1978 — 1st LP). Singles produced individually.

Columbia/3rd: CL-6057. **Popular Favorites, Volume 1** (10" LP; 1949 — 3rd LP). Singles produced individually.

Columbia/4th: CL-6059. **Frankly Sentimental** (10" LP; 1949 — 4th LP). Singles produced individually.

Columbia/5th: CL-6087. **Songs by Sinatra, Volume 1** (10" LP; 1950 — 1st LP). Singles produced individually.

Columbia/16th: CL-2530. **Boys and Girls Together** (10" LP; 1955 — 5th LP). Singles produced individually.

Columbia/20th: CL-606. **Frankie** (1955 — 8th LP). Singles produced individually.

Columbia/21st: CL-743. **The Voice** (1955 — 9th LP). Singles produced individually.

Columbia/23rd: CL-902. **That Old Feeling** (1956 — 2nd LP). Singles produced individually.

Columbia/24th: CL-953. **Adventures of the Heart** (1956 — 3rd LP). Singles produced individually.

Columbia/25th: CL-1032. **Christmas Dreaming** (1957 — 3rd LP). Singles produced individually.

Columbia/26th: CL-1136. **Put Your Dreams Away** (1958 — 3rd LP). Singles produced individually.

Columbia/27th: C2L-6. **The Frank Sinatra Story in Music** (1959 — 2nd LP). Singles produced individually.

Columbia/28th: CL-1241. **Love Is a Kick** (1960 — 3rd LP). Singles produced individually.

Columbia/29th: CL-1297. **The Broadway Kick** (1960 — 4th LP). Singles produced individually.

Columbia/30th: CL-1359. **Come Back to Sorrento** (1960 — 5th LP). Singles produced individually.

Columbia/31st: CL-1448. **Reflections** (1961 — 4th LP). Singles produced individually.

Columbia/32nd: CL-2474. **Frank Sinatra's Greatest Hits: The Early Years** (1964 — 3rd LP). Singles produced individually.

Columbia/33rd: CL-2572. **Frank Sinatra's Greatest Hits: The Early Years, Volume 2** (1964 — 4th LP). Singles produced individually.

Columbia/34th: CL-2739. **The Essential Frank Sinatra — Volume 1** (1967 — 2nd LP). Singles produced individually.

Columbia/35th: CL-2740. **The Essential Frank Sinatra — Volume 2** (1967 — 3rd LP). Singles produced individually.

Columbia/36th: CL-2741. **The Essential Frank Sinatra — Volume 3** (1967 — 4th LP). Singles produced individually.

Columbia/38th: CL-2913. **Frank Sinatra in Hollywood, 1943–1949** (1968 — 1st LP). Singles produced individually.

Columbia/50th: FC-44236. **Sinatra Rarities — The Columbia Years, Volume 1** (1986 — 1st LP). Singles produced individually.

Columbia/51st: CXT-40343. **The Voice: 1943–1952** (6-record set; 70 songs) (1987 — 1st LP). Singles produced individually.

Columbia/52nd: C2X-40897. **Hello, Young Lovers** (1987 — 2nd LP). Singles produced individually.

Coronet/1st: CX-186 (radio tracks). **Tommy Dorsey and His Orchestra, Featuring Frank Sinatra** (1962 — 8th LP). Producer not credited.

Dan Records/1st: VC-5019. **Frank Sinatra on V-Disc** (Japan LP; early 1970s). Singles produced individually.

My Way/1st: MW-1001. **Sinatra for the Collector: Volume 1 — The V-Disc Years** (Canada LP; early 1970s). Singles produced individually.

My Way/2nd: MW-1002. **Sinatra for the Collector: Volume 2 — The V-Disc Years** (Canada LP; early 1970s). Singles produced individually.

Pentagon/1st: MB-990061. **My Best Songs — My Best Years, Volume 1** (radio tracks; cassette; early 1970s). Axel Stordahl, musical director.

Pentagon/4th: MB-990064. **My Best Songs — My Best Years, Volume 4** (radio tracks; cassette; early 1970s). Axel Stordahl, musical director.

Pentagon/5th: MB-990065. **My Best Songs — My Best Years, Volume 5** (radio tracks; cassette; early 1970s). Axel Stordahl, musical director.

Qwest/1st: #9/25145-1. **L.A. Is My Lady** (1984 — 1st LP). Quincy Jones, producer.

RCA Victor/12th: LPM-1632. **We Three** (including 1st four solo singles: Bluebird label; 1957 — 7th LP). Singles produced individually.

RCA Victor/17th: SD-1000/1. **The Dorsey/Sinatra Sessions, Volume 1** (1972 — 1st LP). E. Gabriel and D. Wardell, executive producers.

RCA Victor/18th: SD-1000/2. **The Dorsey/Sinatra Sessions, Volume 2** (1972 — 2nd LP). E. Gabriel and D. Wardell, executive producers.

RCA Victor/19th: SD-1000/3. **The Dorsey/Sinatra Sessions, Volume 3** (1972 — 3rd LP). E. Gabriel and D. Wardell, executive producers.

RCA Victor/20th: SD-1000/4. **The Dorsey/Sinatra Sessions, Volume 4** (1972 — 4th LP). E. Gabriel and D. Wardell, executive producers.

RCA Victor/21st: SD-1000/5. **The Dorsey/Sinatra Sessions, Volume 5** (1972 — 5th LP). E. Gabriel and D. Wardell, executive producers.

RCA Victor/22nd: SD-1000/6. **The Dorsey/Sinatra Sessions, Volume 6** (1972 — 6th LP). E. Gabriel and D. Wardell, executive producers.

Reprise/1st: FS-1001. **Ring-a-Ding Ding!** (1961 — 3rd LP). Felix Slatkin, producer.

Reprise/2nd: FS-1002. **Sinatra Swings** (original title: "Swing Along with Me") (1961 — 6th LP). Neal Hefti, producer.

Reprise/3rd: FS-1003. **I Remember Tommy** . . . (1961 – 7th LP). Neal Hefti, producer.

Reprise/4th: FS-1004. **Sinatra & Strings** (1962 – 1st LP). Neal Hefti and Skip Martin, producers.

Reprise/5th: FS-1005. **Sinatra and Swingin' Brass** (1962 – 4th LP). Chuck Sagle, producer.

Reprise/6th: FS-1006. **Sinatra Sings Great Songs from Great Britain** (England LP; 1962 – 5th LP). Alan Freeman, producer; in England.

Reprise/8th: FS-1007. **All Alone** (1962 – 7th LP). Neal Hefti, producer.

Reprise/9th: FS-1008. **Sinatra-Basie: An Historic Musical First** (1963 – 1st LP). Neal Hefti, producer.

Reprise/10th: FS-1009. **The Concert Sinatra** (1963 – 2nd LP). Chuck Sagle, producer.

Reprise/11th: FS-2015. **Reprise Musical Repertory Theatre: "Finian's Rainbow"** (1963 – 3rd LP). Sonny Burke, producer.

Reprise/12th: FS-2016. **Reprise Musical Repertory Theatre: "Guys and Dolls"** (1963 – 4th LP). Sonny Burke, producer.

Reprise/13th: FS-2017. **Reprise Musical Repertory Theatre: "Kiss Me Kate"** (1963 – 5th LP). Sonny Burke, producer.

Reprise/14th: FS-2018. **Reprise Musical Repertory Theatre: "South Pacific"** (1963 – 6th LP). Sonny Burke, producer.

Reprise/15th: FS-1010. **Sinatra's Sinatra** (1963 – 7th LP). Sonny Burke, producer.

Reprise/16th: RS-243. **Have Yourself a Merry Little Christmas** (1963 – 8th LP). Sonny Burke, producer.

Reprise/17th: FS-1011. **Frank Sinatra Sings "Days of Wine and Roses," "Moon River" and Other Academy Award Winners** (1964 – 1st LP). Sonny Burke, producer.

Reprise/18th: FS-2020. **America, I Hear You Singing** (1964 – 2nd LP). Sonny Burke, producer.

Reprise/19th: FS-1012. **It Might as Well Be Swing** (1964 – 5th LP). Sonny Burke, producer.

Reprise/20th: FS-2021. **"Robin and the 7 Hoods"** (official soundtrack LP; 1964 – 6th LP). Sonny Burke, producer.

Reprise/21st: FS-1013. **Softly, As I Leave You** (1964 – 8th LP). Sonny Burke and Jimmy Bowen, producers.

Reprise/22nd: FS-2022. **Twelve Songs of Christmas** (1964 – 9th LP). Sonny Burke, producer.

Reprise/23rd: FS-1014. **September of My Years** (1965 – 1st LP). Sonny Burke, producer.

Reprise/24th: FS-6167. **Sinatra '65** (1965 – 2nd LP). Sonny Burke and Jimmy Bowen, producers.

Reprise/25th: FS-1015. **My Kind of Broadway** (1965 – 4th LP). Sonny Burke, producer.

Reprise/26th: 2FS-1016. **Frank Sinatra: A Man and His Music** (1965 – 5th LP). Sonny Burke, producer.

Reprise/27th: FS-1017. **Strangers in the Night** (1966 – 1st LP). Sonny Burke, producer.

Reprise/28th: FS-1018. **Moonlight Sinatra** (1966 – 2nd LP). Sonny Burke, producer.

Reprise/29th: 2FS-1019. **Sinatra at the Sands** (live recording; 1966 – 3rd LP). Sonny Burke, producer.

Reprise/30th: FS-1020. **That's Life** (1966 – 5th LP). Jimmy Bowen, producer.

Reprise/31st: FS-1021. **Francis Albert Sinatra and Antonio Carlos Jobim** (1967 – 1st LP). Sonny Burke, producer.

Reprise/32nd: FS-1022/FS-1023. **Frank Sinatra & Frank and Nancy** (1967 – 5th LP). Jimmy Bowen, producer.

Reprise/33rd: FS-1024. **Francis A. and Edward K.** (1968 – 2nd LP). Sonny Burke, producer.

Reprise/34th: FS-1025. **Frank Sinatra's Greatest Hits!** (1968 – 3rd LP). Sonny Burke and Jimmy Bowen, producers.

Reprise/35th: FS-1026. **The Sinatra Family Wish You a Merry Christmas** (1968 – 4th LP). Sonny Burke.

Reprise/37th: FS-1027. **Cycles** (1968 – 6th LP). Don Costa, producer.

Reprise/38th: FS-1029. **My Way** (1969 – 1st LP). Don Costa and Sonny Burke, producers.

Reprise/39th: FS-1030. **A Man Alone** (1969 – 3rd LP). Sonny Burke, producer.

Reprise/40th: FS-1031. **Watertown [a love story]** (1970 – 1st LP). Charles Calello, producer.

Reprise/42nd: FS-1033. **Sinatra & Company*** (1971 – 2nd LP). Sonny Burke and Don Costa, producers.

Reprise/43rd: FS-1034. **Frank Sinatra's Greatest Hits!, Volume 2** (1971 – 3rd LP). Sonny Burke and Jimmy Bowen, producers.

Reprise/45th: FS-2155. **Ol' Blue Eyes Is Back** (1973 – 2nd LP). Don Costa, producer.

Reprise/47th: FS-2195. **Some Nice Things I've Missed** (1974 – 1st LP). D. Costa, J. Bowen, and S. Burke, producers.

Reprise/48th: FS-2207. **Sinatra – The Main Event** (live recording; 1974 – 2nd LP). Don Costa, producer.

Reprise/51st: FS-51306. **Portrait of Sinatra [40 Songs in the Life of a Man]** (England LP; 1979 – 1st LP). Various producers.

Reprise/52nd: 3FS2300/1. **Trilogy: The Past [Collectibles of the Early Years]** (1980 – 1st LP). Sonny Burke concept and production.

Reprise/53rd: 3FS2300/2. **Trilogy: The Present [Some Very Good Years]** (1980 – 2nd LP). Sonny Burke concept and production.

Reprise/54th: 3FS2300/3. **Trilogy: The Future [Reflections on the Future in 3 Tenses]** (1980 – 3rd LP). Sonny Burke concept and production.

Reprise/55th: FS-2305. **She Shot Me Down** (1981 – 1st LP). Don Costa, producer.

Reprise/56th: FS-5238. **The Voice – Volume 1** (Italy LP; 1982 – 1st LP). Various producers.

Reprise/57th: FS-5239. **The Voice – Volume 2** (Italy LP; 1982 – 2nd LP). Various producers.

Reprise/58th: FS-5240. **The Voice – Volume 3** (Italy LP; 1982 – 3rd LP). Various producers.

Reprise/59th: FS-5250. **The Voice – Volume 4** (Italy LP; 1982 – 4th LP). Various producers.

Reprise/60th: FS-54093. **I Sing the Songs** (Italy LP; 1982 – 5th LP). Various producers.

Reprise/61st: FS-54101. **The Singles** (Italy LP; 1982 – 6th LP). Various producers.

Bootleg album #1: MM-1. **MM-1** (from Columbia masters; early 1970s). Illegal production.

Bootleg album #2: no number. **Rare Songs of Sinatra** (from Columbia masters; early 1970s). Illegal production.

Bootleg album #3: no number. **Love Songs** (from Reprise masters; early 1970s). Illegal production.

Bootleg album #4: Tyrecords (TY-100). **The Unissued Sinatra** (from Reprise masters; early 1980s). Illegal production.

Bootleg album #5: no number. **Frank's Girls** (from Reprise masters; early 1980s). Illegal production.

Bootleg album #6: no number. **Late Sinatra Goodies** (from Reprise masters; mid-1980s. Illegal production.

Bootleg movie #2 and #4 soundtracks. **Four Sinatra Movies** (including *Ship Ahoy, Higher and Higher;* mid-1960s). Illegal production.

Bootleg movie #5 soundtrack. **Complete "Step Lively" Film Soundtrack** (mid-1960s). Illegal production.

Bootleg movie #7 soundtrack. **Score from "Anchors Aweigh"** (mid-1960s). Illegal production.

Bootleg movie #9 soundtrack. **Score from "It Happened in Brooklyn"** (mid-1960s). Illegal production.

Bootleg movie #11 and #12 soundtracks. **Five Films** (including *Kissing Bandit* and *Take Me Out to the Ball Game;* mid-1960s). Illegal production.

Bootleg movie #13, #14, #19 soundtracks. **"On the Town" and Others** (also including *Double Dynamite* and *Man with the Golden Arm;* mid-1960s). Illegal production.

Bootleg movie #15 soundtrack. **Score from "Meet Danny Wilson"** (mid-1960s). Illegal production.

Bootleg movie #18 soundtrack. **Score from "Guys and Dolls"** (mid-1960s). Illegal production.

Bootleg movie #21 soundtrack. **Score from "The Joker Is Wild"** (mid-1960s). Illegal production.

Index to Text

This index refers to items by page number found in the general text portions of the book. It does not include the Master Song List, or the other lists, catalogs and indexes which are cross-referenced to that Master Song List by key numbers.